The European Arrest Warrant and EU Citizenship

Joske Graat

The European Arrest Warrant and EU Citizenship

EU Citizenship in Relation to Foreseeability Problems in the Surrender Procedure

Springer

Joske Graat
Law
Utrecht University
Utrecht, The Netherlands

This work was supported by Utrecht University (Utrecht Centre for Regulation and Enforcement in Europe).

ISBN 978-3-031-07589-6 ISBN 978-3-031-07590-2 (eBook)
https://doi.org/10.1007/978-3-031-07590-2

This Springer imprint is published by the registered company Springer Nature Switzerland AG
The registered company address is: Gewerbestrasse 11, 6330 Cham, Switzerland

Contents

Chapter 1
Introduction

1.1 The Research Topic

1.1.1 Promises Made to the EU Citizen in the EU Criminal Justice Setting

The Treaty of Maastricht was the first treaty to explicitly and formally recognise EU citizenship and criminal justice as inherent aspects of the European Union (EU).[1] Since the introduction of these aspects, both have been further developed, gaining a more central position in the EU legal order. The Court of Justice of the European Union (CJEU) refers in its case law to EU citizenship as 'destined to become the fundamental status of nationals of the Member States'.[2] In particular, the years after the entering into force of the Treaty of Lisbon show an increasing significance of the EU citizen and his or her multifold interests, following first of all from Articles 3(2) Treaty establishing the European Union (TEU) and 67(1) Treaty on the Functioning of the European Union (TFEU). These provisions set the obligation for the EU to offer its citizens an Area of Freedom, Security and Justice (AFSJ) in which free movement and safety are guaranteed while fundamental rights are respected. EU citizens are thus explicitly designated as the main beneficiaries of the AFSJ, and their interests are not limited to security but also include free movement and fundamental rights protection. The post-Lisbon five-year programmes of the European Council (EUCO) affirm the central position of EU citizens. The programmes also recognise and accentuate the multifold interests of EU citizens, though not to the same degree. For instance, the 2009 Stockholm Programme states that EU citizenship requires an

---

[1] Treaty establishing the European Community (TEC) [1992] (Treaty of Maastricht) OJ C191/01, art 8.

[2] Case C-184/99 *Grzelczyk* [2001] ECLI:EU:C:2001:458, para 31.

J. Graat, *The European Arrest Warrant and EU Citizenship*,
https://doi.org/10.1007/978-3-031-07590-2_1

appropriate balance between fundamental rights protection and security measures,[3] whereas the most recently adopted Strategic Agenda 2019–2024 almost exclusively focuses on security and the prevention of cross-border criminality.[4] Increased attention for EU citizenship is not limited to these five-year programmes, but also follows from political guidelines, action plans, etc.[5] As former European Commission (hereafter Commission) President José Manuel Barroso stated in his political guidelines: 'The principles of free movement and equal treatment for EU citizens must become a reality in people's everyday lives.'[6] The political guidelines of the current President of the European Commission, Ursula von der Leyen, emphasise security, as she says, 'We can leave no stone unturned when it comes to protecting our citizens. We must improve cross-border cooperation to tackle gaps in the fight against serious crime and terrorism in Europe.'[7] Hence, on paper at least, many promises have been made to EU citizens concerning their position in the AFSJ and the facilitation and realisation of their EU citizenship rights.

1.1.2 Establishing a Safe AFSJ for EU Citizens

With regard to the fulfilment of these promises, important progress has been made over the years in attaining the objective of providing EU citizens with a safe AFSJ in which cross-border criminality is adequately combatted. The Treaty of Maastricht laid down the basis for such progress by providing legal bases for the adoption of measures regulating both police and judicial cooperation.[8] The Treaty of Amsterdam then transformed criminal justice into a functional competence of the EU by linking actions in the area of criminal justice to the establishment of a Common Area of Freedom, Security and Justice in Article 2, fourth indent, Treaty on the European Union (TEU old).[9] The legislative powers provided by the treaties have been used

---

[3]European Council, 'The Stockholm Programme – An Open and Secure Europe Serving and Protecting Citizens' [2009] OJ C115/1, p. 4.

[4]European Council, *A new strategic agenda for the EU 2019-2024* <https://www.consilium.europa.eu/en/eu-strategic-agenda-2019-2024/> accessed 20 September 2021.

[5]See eg European Commission, 'Delivering an area of freedom, security and justice for Europe's citizens – Action Plan Implementing the Stockholm Programme' (Communication) COM (2010) 171 final.

[6]José Manuel Barosso, *Political guidelines for the next Commission 2009-2014* <ec.europa.eu/archives/commission_2010-2014/president/about/political/> accessed 20 September 2021, p. 3.

[7]Ursula von der Leyen, *A Union that strives for more – My agenda for Europe* (Political Guidelines 2019 – 2024) <https://ec.europa.eu/info/sites/info/files/political-guidelines-next-commission_en_0.pdf> accessed 20 September 2021, p. 13.

[8]Treaty on the European Union [2002] (Consolidated Version) (Treaty of Maastricht) OJ C325/1, art 31.

[9]This provision stated 'The Union shall set itself the following objectives: to maintain and develop the Union as an area of freedom, security and justice, in which the free movement of persons is assured in conjunction with appropriate measures with respect to external border controls, asylum,

for the adoption of new measures for judicial cooperation on the basis of the principle of mutual recognition to combat the increased risk of cross-border criminality resulting from the slow elimination of internal borders between the EU Member States.[10] Mutual recognition in its most absolute form means that the competent authority of a state should promptly and automatically (or at least with a minimum of formality) recognise and execute a request for cooperation.[11] The first example of a mutual recognition instrument is the Framework Decision on the European Arrest Warrant (FDEAW) which aims to replace the slow extradition system with a quick and efficient surrender procedure for the purpose of prosecution or the execution of a sanction.[12] The EAW is a security measure aiming to combat abuse of free movement rights and the exploitation of differences between the national judicial systems for the purpose of committing criminal offences. It contributes to the realisation of the goal set in Article 3(2) TEU to offer EU citizens a safe AFSJ, meaning one in which they can travel and reside freely without fear for crime. After the EAW, numerous other mutual recognition instruments have been adopted for the purpose of judicial cooperation during the pre-sentencing procedure and for the purpose of the enforcement of final decisions.[13] Besides these mutual recognition instruments, of which most have a strong security rationale,[14] the post-Lisbon era also shows the adoption of several EU directives on procedural safeguards, such as the right to an attorney and the presumption of innocence.[15] These

immigration and the prevention and combating of crime.' Treaty of Amsterdam amending the Treaty on European Union, the Treaties establishing the European Communities and certain related acts [1997] OJ C340/1.

[10]However, it was not until the Treaty of Lisbon that judicial cooperation on the basis of mutual recognition received an explicit legal basis in the treaties. European Council, Presidency Conclusions 1999 (Tampere Programme) <https://www.europarl.europa.eu/summits/tam_en.htm> accessed 20 September 2021, paras 2,5,6; Mitsilegas (2016), p. 125; Luchtman (2013), p. 12.

[11]Mitsilegas (2016), pp. 126–127.

[12]Council Framework Decision 2002/584/JHA of 13 June 2002 on the European arrest warrant and the surrender procedures between Member States [2002] OJ L190/1, art 1(1).

[13]See e.g. Council Framework Decision 2005/214/JHA of 24 February 2005 on the application of the principle of mutual recognition to financial penalties [2005] OJ L76/16; Directive 2014/41/EU of the European Parliament and of the Council of 3 April 2014 regarding the European Investigation Order in criminal matters [2014] OJ L130/1; Regulation (EU) 2018/1805 of the European Parliament and of the Council of 14 November 2018 on the mutual recognition of freezing orders and confiscation orders [2018] OJ L303/1.

[14]Some instruments also strongly refer to other interests, such as reintegration, the protection of the right to liberty and equal treatment. See Council Framework Decision 2009/829/JHA of 23 October 2009 on the application, between Member States of the European Union, of the principle of mutual recognition to decisions on supervision measures as an alternative to provisional detention [2009] OJ L294/20, recitals 3–5; Council Framework Decision 2008/909/JHA of 27 November 2008 on the application of the principle of mutual recognition to judgments in criminal matters imposing custodial sentences or measures involving deprivation of liberty for the purpose of their enforcement in the European Union [2008] OJ L327/27, art 3(1).

[15]See eg Directive 2013/48/EU of the European Parliament and of the Council of 22 October 2013 on the right of access to a lawyer in criminal proceedings and in European arrest warrant

instruments harmonise the minimum level of fundamental rights protection that must be offered in each Member State.

1.1.3 Possible Complications for the EU Citizen and the Role of the EAW Therein

What has been largely overlooked in the process of developing the AFSJ is that the new security measures for judicial cooperation could also cause or contribute to a series of complications—potentially fundamental rights complications—for EU citizens who exercise their free movement rights or who are confronted with others who have exercised their free movement rights. Currently, a car accident in Germany caused by a Dutch national and leading to the death of a French citizen could trigger the application of three national criminal codes and the jurisdiction to adjudicate of three states. This situation reveals foreseeability difficulties, for instance that, at the time of the offence, the Dutch national was most likely unaware of the nationality of the victim (and therefore of the application of French criminal law). Knowing which national criminal laws apply in a certain case is of importance to EU citizens, since the national criminal laws of the EU Member States still differ to a large extent. As a result, the three competent national legal orders in this hypothetical scenario may classify the car accident differently—for instance, as manslaughter with a maximum prison sentence of 20 years, or as a traffic offence with lethal consequences with a maximum sentence of 10 years. In addition, the decision whether only one of the three states should prosecute the case—and, if so, which—remains largely within the discretion of the national competent authorities. As this forum decision in fact also determines the applicable substantive and procedural criminal law(s) in the case, the broad discretion granted to the national competent authorities could be inconvenient to the suspect, to say the least.

Possible complications such as these raise questions in light of the right to an accessible and foreseeable law for criminal offences and sanctions in Article 49 of the Charter of Fundamental Rights of the European Union (CFR) and the right to a tribunal established by law, also referred to as the 'procedural counterpart of the legality principle',[16] in Article 47 CFR. In relation to Article 49 CFR, the question rises whether criminal offences and sanctions are sufficiently accessible and foreseeable when it is difficult or impossible to determine at the time of the offence which particular national criminal codes apply. The right to a tribunal established by

proceedings, and on the right to have a third party informed upon deprivation of liberty and to communicate with third persons and with consular authorities while deprived of liberty [2013] OJ L294/1; Directive (EU) 2016/343 of the European Parliament and of the Council of 9 March 2016 on the strengthening of certain aspects of the presumption of innocence and of the right to be present at the trial in criminal proceedings [2016] OJ L65/1.

[16] Swart (1983), p. 7; Luchtman (2020), p. 30. See also Böse (2014), p. 124ff.

law in the second sentence of Article 47 CFR (hereafter referred to as 47(2) CFR) sets the main rule that the elements of a state's judicial organisation are regulated by a law emanating from Parliament. Any discretion allocated to the executive or judicial power in this regard should be sufficiently limited by law to avoid arbitrary decisions.[17] The correlating question is whether the lack of an EU system for forum choices solving conflicts of jurisdictions by appointing one state as the competent one, as a result of which national competent authorities have broad discretion to make forum decisions, violates the right to a tribunal established by law.

Within the context of the above example, the EAW could potentially ensure the surrender of EU citizens to states while the applicability of their substantive criminal laws was not foreseeable at the time of the offences and while these states were not appointed as the best states for prosecution on the basis of a transparent system for forum choices. This possible effect of the EAW is a result of the fact that the surrender procedure is not complemented by a set of EU rules harmonising jurisdiction rules or regulating forum choices by appointing the competent forum in case of conflicts of jurisdiction. Had the EU legislator adopted such EU rules which regulate which national legal order is competent and, therefore, which national substantive criminal law applies, the EAW could be a mechanism enforcing these forum decisions by ensuring the surrender of the suspect to the appointed state. However, in the absence of such complementing EU rules on jurisdiction and/or forum choices, any competent state can in principle issue an EAW, which the executing judicial authority is obliged to execute unless a refusal ground applies.[18] Thus, the question arises whether the EAW in the current AFSJ contributes to prosecution and sanctioning by a state, while the validity of the jurisdiction claim of this state, which is also the issuing state, is questionable in light of Article 49(1) and Article 47 CFR.

These fundamental rights questions do not arise within a particular Member State, but rather cover situations at the interface of national legal orders. Consequently, these questions are neither answered nor resolved by the harmonisation directives for procedural safeguards, which ensure a minimum level of fundamental rights protection within the borders of each Member State. Furthermore, these possible complications and questions are not unique for the EU. The same ones can equally arise in the outer-EU setting, which also lacks a general mechanism preventing or solving conflicts of jurisdiction while intergovernmental extradition procedures could ensure the transfer of a suspect to a state whose jurisdiction claim was not foreseeable at the time of the offence. In this broader international setting, such complications and the role of extradition procedures therein have not occupied an important role or resulted in solutions. The question is whether this should not be different in the context of judicial cooperation in the AFSJ, which contrary to the outer-EU setting has an interrelated EU citizenship and free movement dimension. Whereas in the outer-EU

[17] EcHR 12 October 1978, 7360/76 (*Leo Zand/Austria*) para 69; EcHR 18 December 1980, 8603/79, 8722/79, 8723/79 & 8729/79 (*Crociani and others/Italy*) para 219; Harris et al. (2014), p. 458.

[18] See also Walsh (2020).

setting, states hold the central position and citizens are still primarily the objects of extradition procedures, even though they have received more protection over time,[19] the EAW operates in an AFSJ consisting of states and EU citizens, who are provided with free movement rights and encouraged to use them. It is also precisely the exercise of these free movement rights by EU citizens which could cause the materialisation of the complications discussed and the issuing of EAWs. In this light, the current scope of fundamental rights protection granted to EU citizens when facing such complications, as well as the influence which EU citizenship could have on the interpretation of some of criminal law's founding principles (such as the substantive and procedural legality principle), are important topics to examine.

1.2 Research Questions

In light of the previous section, the following central research question and subquestions can be formulated:

What are the foreseeability problems of jurisdiction claims and forum choices that citizens may be faced with in the context of the EAW, and to what extent could EU citizenship help to address these problems?

1. To what extent are jurisdiction claims and forum choices captured by the legality principle in Articles 47 and 49 CFR and in national law?
2. To what extent do the foreseeability of jurisdiction claims and forum decisions play a role in the FDEAW and national implementation acts?
3. What perspectives exist on the role of citizenship in judicial cooperation in criminal matters in the EU and to what extent do these perspectives play a role in addressing the foreseeability problems?
4. How could EU citizenship be a vehicle towards a solution for the foreseeability problems in the context of EAW procedure?
5. What recommendations for the EU or national level can be derived from the ways in which EU citizenship could be a vehicle for addressing the foreseeability problems?

The first part of the main research question aims to map out the current state of the position of EU citizens in mutual recognition procedures, more specifically the European Arrest Warrant. Its purpose is to establish a better understanding of the problems with which EU citizens subjected to an EAW can be confronted and how these potential problems are currently approached on the EU and national level. The second part of the main research question aims to establish how the potential problems should be approached in light of the normative setting of the AFSJ, in particular its EU citizenship dimension.

[19] Glerum (2013), p. 12; João Costa (2019), pp. 300–301.

1.3 Scientific and Societal Relevance

So far, the triangular link between EU citizenship, judicial cooperation in criminal matters on the basis of the principle of mutual recognition (most importantly the European Arrest Warrant) and fundamental rights protection in the AFSJ has been left largely unexplored in the legal literature. This is because the studies on EU citizenship mainly discuss its relation to social welfare and free movement rights, its political dimension and its relationship with fundamental rights.[20] In addition, the principle of mutual recognition has in the context of the criminal justice angle of the AFSJ primarily been studied in relation to the protection of fundamental rights and not necessarily in relation to specific ideas on how to shape EU citizenship in a common criminal justice area. The legal literature, for instance, includes a strong and ongoing debate about the need for a fair balance between effective cooperation on the basis of mutual recognition and fundamental rights protection.[21]

The societal value of this book is demonstrated by its twofold objective, which clearly designates the EU citizen as its main stakeholder. Firstly, this research aims to gain a better understanding of the problems EU citizens are confronted with in mutual recognition procedures. Secondly, it aims to discover whether EU citizenship can function as a bridge between the current EU context in which judicial cooperation takes place on the basis of mutual recognition and the need for a solution for the role which these mutual recognition instruments play in relation to complications with which EU citizens can be confronted. Thus, besides mapping out the different problems which EU citizens may face, this book also provides recommendations for a concrete solution and more importantly the role which EU citizenship itself can play in securing such a solution and stronger fundamental rights protection. Moreover, the personal interests of the EU citizen are closely linked to the legitimacy of the AFSJ as a whole. As clearly follows from Article 3(2) TEU, EU citizens are the main beneficiaries of the AFSJ and therefore have a central position in its establishment. To prevent such a central role from remaining mere theory, it needs to be translated into real and concrete legal effects.

---

[20] See eg Shaw (2007a, b); Bruzelius B, Chase E and Seeleib-Kaiser M, *Social Rights of EU Migrant Citizens: A Comparative Perspective* (2015) < https://www.uu.nl/en/research/beucitizen-european-citizenship-research/publications> accessed 20 September 2021; *A Legal Analysis of the Possibilities and Impediments for Citizens Seeking to Enforce their Social Rights* (2016) <https://www.uu.nl/en/research/beucitizen-european-citizenship-research/publications> accessed 20 September 2021(BEUcitizenship project, D6.4). In relation to fundamental rights, the relatively sparse but now upcoming discussion has focused on, for instance, fundamental rights violations as a barrier to free movement and the restricted scope of application of the Charter of Fundamental Rights. See eg Van Eijken et al. (2015), pp. 249–297.

[21] See e.g. Marin (2008); Rijken (2010); Marguery (2016). In addition, mutual recognition is nowadays still the starting point in the case law of the CJEU on the EAW, but fundamental rights have in the course of time emerged as a correction mechanism. See eg Joined Cases C-404/15 & C-659/15 *Aranyosi & Căldăraru* [2016] ECLI:EU:C:2016:198; Case C-216/18 *LM* [2018] ECLI:EU:C:2018:586.

1.4 Methodology

Answering the first part of the main research question requires a two-tiered study covering both the EU and the national level. The EU constitutes a legal order in which national and EU authorities co-exist and cooperate. The national authorities rely on the EU and its institutions to achieve goals they cannot achieve by themselves, and the European authorities need the national level to function properly.[22] This is also exemplified by the FDEAW which is not directly applicable and does not have any direct effect. Its effectiveness depends to a large extent on the implementation of this instrument by national legislators and its application by competent national judicial authorities. A two-tiered study covering the EU and national level is therefore essential to draft a more complete picture of the extent to which the complications arising in an AFSJ, in which the operation of the EAW is not complemented with fully harmonised jurisdiction rules and/or a suitable EU mechanism for forum choices, are recognised as legal (or even legality) problems, as well as the status quo of the protection offered against these potential complications.

In light of the above, both the legality principle and the protection offered by the EAW itself is studied on the EU and the national level. The content and scope of Articles 49 and 47 CFR will be examined on the basis of the the explanatory memorandum of the CFR which is 'the reference text and starting point for the court', the case law of the CJEU and legal literature.[23] Considering the link between Articles 49 and 47 CFR and their equivalents in Articles 7 and 6 of the European Convention of Human Rights (ECHR), the case law of the European Court on Human Rights (ECtHR) also plays an important role.[24] The protection offered against the complications by the FDEAW will be explored on the basis of its preparatory work as well as the case law of the CJEU on the EAW and legal literature. For the national level, the content and scope of the national legality principle will be analysed on the basis of the texts of the legal provisions, the parliamentary documentation on these legal provisions, national case law and the legal literature. The protection offered in the surrender procedure is examined on the basis of the legal provisions in the transposition acts and relevant complementary legal provisions, such as the rules on jurisdiction, parliamentary documentation, national case law and legal literature.

The second part of the research introduces two perspectives on the EAW and sets out to what extent these perspectives are adhered to on the EU and the national level,

[22] In the literature, the concept of the EU as a shared legal order has been further specified. Pernice, for instance, refers to a multi-level legal order while Besselink speaks of a composite legal order. Pernice (2002), p. 516; Besselink (2007), pp. 6, 8–9.

[23] Charter of Fundamental Rights of the European Union (CFR) [2016] OJ C202/02, art 52(7). See also Joint communication from President Costa en Skouris, (24 January 2011) <https://www.echr.coe.int/Documents/UE_Communication_Costa_Skouris_ENG.pdf> accessed 20 September 2021.

[24] CFR, art 52(3); Explanations relating to the Charter of Fundamental Rights [2007] OJ C303/17, art 52.

in particular by legislators and courts. It also discusses their potential consequences for fundamental rights, in particular the legality principle, the EAW, the need for action on the EU and/or national level and the potential role of the EU citizen in fundamental rights protection. The description of these perspectives and their analyses will be based upon the examination and conclusions of the first part of the research. Furthermore, additional research will be conducted into the development of judicial cooperation on the basis of the EAW and EU citizenship in relevant EU legislation, policy documents, case law of the CJEU and legal literature. Lastly, the recommendations for changes to the EAW are primarily based on existing proposals regulating jurisdiction and forum choices in the academic literature.

1.5 The Selected National Jurisdictions

The three national jurisdictions which will be discussed for the purpose of answering the first part of the research question are Germany, the United Kingdom (more specifically England and Wales) and the Netherlands. Besides the fact that this selection includes both civil and common law systems, each jurisdiction has a different perspective on the triangular relationship between judicial cooperation in criminal matters, fundamental rights and citizenship.

In light of its history, the German legal order shows strong ties between the German national and the German state and therefore a strong tendency to protect German nationals in cooperation procedures. Article 16(2) of the German Constitution states, 'No German may be extradited to a foreign country. The law may provide otherwise for extraditions to a Member State of the European Union or to an international court, provided that the rule of law is observed.' The FDEAW is an accepted exception to the constitutional protection against extradition, but as is further explained in Chap. 6, the protection of the German national still has an important role in the surrender procedure. The *Bundesverfassungsgericht* (German Constitutional Court, hereafter BVerfG) in fact declared the first implementation act of the FDEAW unconstitutional, because—to put it simply—the German legislator had not used all the discretion offered by the FDEAW to protect the German national against surrender.[25] Furthermore, the provisions of the second implementation act allocate an important role to the German nationality of the requested person. The mandatory refusal ground in Section 80 of the *Gesetz über die Internationale Rechtshilfe in Strafsachen* (Act on International Assistance in Criminal Matters) lays down the conditions for refusing the surrender of a German national while several other refusal grounds provide a safety net in case the conditions in Section 80 are not met.

With regard to the United Kingdom, this book focuses exclusively on the jurisdiction 'England and Wales', which together constitute one of the three legal

[25] BVerfG 18 July 2005, 2 BvR 2236/04 (*Darkazanli*).

jurisdictions in the United Kingdom.[26] As one jurisdiction, England and Wales have the same court system, which applies the Extradition Act 2003 in which the FDEAW was implemented. Compared to Germany, they also represent the other end of the spectrum, since no strong ties exist between the British national and the state.[27] This follows, for instance, from the fact that Articles 4(6) and 5(3) FDEAW, allowing states to protect their own nationals in surrender procedures, were not implemented in the UK Extradition Act 2003. British nationality or residency was in itself not a bar to surrender.[28] In fact, England and Wales depart from a different point of view, giving preference to the territoriality principle and a trial of citizens by their peers. Their starting point is that all crime is local.[29] The criminality of certain conduct should be judged according to the substantive criminal law of the place where it was committed, and it is for this state to decide whether or not to try the case. An examination of the English perspective on the research questions remains relevant despite the UK's decision to leave the EU.[30] The purpose of the chapters on the national legal orders is to illustrate how the two complications and the role of the EAW therein are perceived on the national level, which is an integral part of the EU legal order. England has a long history of applying the EAW, which remained in force until the beginning of 2021.[31] Its position towards the two complications, therefore, remains important, especially since, during its EU membership, it was one of the few Member States with a common law system.

In comparison to Germany and the UK, the Netherlands takes a more intermediate position in relation to the protection of the ties between the Dutch citizen and the state in the surrender procedure. As is further explained in Chap. 5, the guiding principle in the Dutch legal order is that an individual is prosecuted in the state in which the crime was committed. However, the provisions of the *Overleveringswet* (Surrender Act, hereafter SA) implementing Articles 4(6) and 5(3) FDEAW install a certain level of protection for Dutch nationals against the execution of an EAW.

---

[26] The other two legal jurisdictions are Scotland and Northern Ireland, neither of which will be discussed in this book.

[27] *Report of the Royal commission on Extradition* (Cmd 2039, 1878).

[28] Nationality and residency are factors taken into consideration in the context of other bars to surrender, such as the human rights clause in Section 21A(1)(a) Extradition Act 2003. *R (on the application of Bermingham) v Director of the Serious Fraud Office* [2006] EWHC Admin 200, [2007] QB 727 [120]–[121].

[29] *Macleod v AG for New South Wales* [1891] UKPC 31, [1891] AC 455, 458.

[30] For the current surrender procedure between the UK and the EU see the EU-UK Trade and Cooperation Agreement [2020] OJ L444/14, arts 76–112.

[31] Until the end of the transition period, the EAW continued to apply, but the EU Member States were allowed to issue a notification stating that they refused to surrender their own nationals to the UK. Agreement on the withdrawal of the United Kingdom of Great Britain and Northern Ireland from the European Union and the European Atomic Energy Community [2019] OJ C384 I/1, arts 62(1)(b) and 185.

1.6 Looking Ahead

This introductory chapter has briefly described the research topic and defined the research questions, scientific and societal relevance of the research and methodology. The purpose of the next chapter is to further elaborate on the research topic and clearly set the scene within which the research questions should be understood. This explanation also allows for a comprehensible and elaborate overview of the structure of this book at the end of Chap. 2. Its last section explains which topic or question is covered in each chapter and describes the specific structure of the chapters examining the status quo of fundamental rights protection on the EU level and in the national legal orders.

References

Besselink L (2007) Een samengestelde Europese Constitutie. Europa Law Publishing

Böse M (2014) Fundamental freedoms of the Union. In: Böse M, Meyer F, Schneider A (eds) Conflicts of Jurisdiction in criminal matters in the European Union. Volume II: rights, principles and model rules. Nomos

Glerum V (2013) De weigeringsgronden bij uitlevering en overlevering – Een vergelijking en kritische evaluatie in het licht van het beginsel van wederzijdse erkenning. Wolf Legal Publishers

Harris D et al. (2014) Law of the European Convention on Human Rights. Oxford University Press

João Costa M (2019) Extradition law. Reviewing grounds for refusal from the classig paradigm to mutual recognition and beyond. Maastricht University. https://doi.org/10.26481/dis.20190215mj

Luchtman M (2013) Choice of forum and the prosecution of cross-border crime in the European Union – what role for the legality principle? In: Luchtman M (ed) Choice of forum in cooperation against EU financial crime. Freedom, security and justice and the protection of specific EU-interests. Eleven International Publishing

Luchtman M (2020) Transnational law enforcement cooperation – fundamental rights in European cooperation in criminal matters. Eur J Crime Crim Law Crim Just 28:14

Marguery T (2016) Rebuttal of mutual trust and mutual recognition in criminal matters: is "exceptional" enough? Eur Pap 1:943

Marin T (2008) The European arrest warrant and domestic legal orders: tensions between mutual recognition and fundamental rights: the Italian case. Maastricht J Eur Comp law 15:473

Mitsilegas V (2016) EU criminal law after lisbon: rights, trust and the transformation of justice in Europe. Hart

Pernice I (2002) Multilevel constitutionalism in the European Union. Eur Law Rev 27:511

Rijken C (2010) Re-balancing security and justice: protection of fundamental rights in police and judicial cooperation in criminal matters. Common Mark Law Rev 47:1455

Shaw J (2007a) EU citizenship and political rights in an evolving union. Fordham Law Rev 75:2549

Shaw J (2007b) The transformation of citizenship in the European Union – electoral rights and the restructuring of political space. Cambridge University Press
Swart B (1983) Goede Rechtsbedeling en Internationale Rechtshulp in Strafzaken. Kluwer
Van Eijken H et al (2015) The European citizen as bearer of fundamental rights in a multi-layered legal order. In: van den Brink T, Luchtman M, Scholten M (eds) Sovereignty in the shared legal order of the EU: core values of regulation and enforcement. Intersentia
Walsh D (2020) The European arrest warrant in the prosecution of extraterritorial offences: the strange case of the Irish murder, the French victim and the English suspect. Eur Law Rev 45:48

Chapter 2
Setting the Scene

2.1 Introduction

This chapter sets the scene within which the central research question should be understood. It starts in Sect. 2.2 with a description of the development of EU citizenship both in and outside the specific context of the AFSJ. This section shows that EU citizenship has gained a more prominent position over time and that its development is closely connected to the protection and facilitation of the right to free movement. More specifically, in the context of the AFSJ, the EU legislator has primarily focused on providing EU citizens with a safe and secure AFSJ to exercise their free movement right. This has resulted in new methods for judicial cooperation on the basis of the principle of mutual recognition, of which the EAW is the first example. Both the principle of mutual recognition and the EAW, in particular its security dimension, are briefly introduced in Sects. 2.3 and 2.4.

Sections 2.5 and 2.6 then elaborate on the other side of the coin by portraying the influence which the EAW could have on the materialisation of two possible complications in practice with which EU citizens can be confronted when travelling in the EU. These two complications relate to the lack of foreseeability of the application of a particular national criminal code at the time of the offence and the lack of a clear EU system for forum choices, which have been criticised in light of the substantive legality principle in Article 49 CFR and the right to a tribunal established by law in Article 47 CFR. Sections 2.5 and 2.6 will describe the two complications as well as the fundamental rights questions which they raise. These sections also explain that the EAW does not cause the two problems, but it does influence them.

As was already briefly explained in Chap. 1, the two complications and the role of the EAW therein arise at the interface of national legal orders and are currently not fully solved on the EU or national level. They are also not unique for the EU, as they can also occur in the outer-EU setting. Still, the outer-EU setting does not have an EU citizenship dimension or right to free movement, the exercise of which can cause the two complications. This raises the question whether the two complications in the

J. Graat, *The European Arrest Warrant and EU Citizenship*,
https://doi.org/10.1007/978-3-031-07590-2_2

AFSJ and the role of the EAW therein could in fact be classified as strange or surprising. My opinion is that the answer to this question depends on how one views the EAW. In this light, Sect. 2.7 introduces on the basis of the existing legal literature two opposing perspectives on the surrender procedure and the normative context of the AFSJ in which it operates: the intergovernmental perspective and the transnational perspective. The decision for a certain perspective could in turn affect one's view on whether the two complications should be viewed as fundamental rights problems, the role of the EAW therein, the need for action on the national and/or EU level and the potential of EU citizenship for increased fundamental rights protection. Section 2.7 also briefly explains these possible corollaries of each perspective. Section 2.8 provides a bridge to the next chapters and serves as a reading guide by setting out the structure of this book.

2.2 The Development of EU Citizenship: A Bird's-Eye View

2.2.1 The General Development of EU Citizenship

2.2.1.1 Pre-Maastricht: The First Contours of EU Citizenship

EU citizenship was official introduced by the Treaty of Maastricht, but its contours were already being developed long before that time. The Court of Justice hinted at a status of EU citizenship in early jurisprudence, including in its landmark case *Van Gend & Loos*. In this ruling, the CJEU recognised that the EU—then the European Econcomic Community—was a community comprising both states and its nationals. The nationals of the Member States were legal subjects upon whom community law imposed obligations as well as conferred rights on which the nationals could—under the heading of the principle of direct effect—rely before their national courts.[1]

The first signs of EU citizenship also appeared in the former treaties, such as the 1957 Treaty of Rome referring to the 'European peoples' in the preamble, and on the EU policy and legislative levels. In the aftermath of the Paris Summit of 1974, the European Parliament, for instance, adopted a resolution advising the Commission to adopt legislation providing special rights to community citizens, including voting rights, civil and political rights, the right of residence and the rights mentioned in the so-called Tindemans report.[2] In this report, the former Belgium Minister Leo Tindemans devoted a chapter to 'A citizen's Europe', proposing several actions relating to the protection of fundamental rights and external signs

[1] Case C-26/62 *Van Gend & Loos* [1963] ECLI:EU:C:1963:1, pp. 12–13.

[2] Resolution on the granting of special rights to the citizens of the European Community in implementation of the decision of the Paris Summit of December 1974 (point 11 of the final communiqué).

of solidarity, such as the gradual abolishment of border controls between Member States.[3] These proposals intended to bring the EU closer to the citizen, which was deemed necessary for the legitimate construction of Europe as a community going beyond the formal cooperation between states.[4] However, despite these early signs of EU citizenship, the concept remained absent in the 1987 Single European Act, which was the first major treaty amendment after the adoption of the Treaty of Rome, and was followed up by the Treaty of Maastricht of 1992.[5]

2.2.1.2 Post-Maastricht: A Strong 'Free Movement' EU Citizen and the Careful Development of a Static EU Citizen

The Treaty of Maastricht formally introduced EU citizenship as the status of all nationals of the Member States in Article 17 TEC (old).[6] EU citizenship is, however, not intended as a replacement of national citizenship, but rather as an additional status.[7] The Treaty of Lisbon reallocated the definition of EU citizenship to what is now Article 20(1) TFEU. Art 20(2) TFEU enumerates the rights which are linked to the status of EU citizenship which are further elaborated on in Articles 21–24 TFEU and Chapter V on Citizens' Rights in the Charter of Fundamental Rights.[8] These include the right to free movement and residence,[9] electoral rights in municipality elections[10] and elections to the European Parliament,[11] protection of diplomatic and

---

[3] Leo Tindemans, 'Report on European Council' (1976) Bulletin of the European Communities, Supplement 1/76 <http://aei.pitt.edu/942/1/political_tindemans_report.pdf> accessed 20 September 2021 (Tindemans report) pp. 26–27.

[4] Tindemans report 1976, pp. 26–28.

[5] The Single European Act also did not extend the scope of the right to free movement, which was at the time exclusively granted to economically active nationals of the Member States. It did, however, provide the power to extend the right to free movement beyond economic actors in Article 235 Treaty establishing the European Economic Community (TEEC). Just before the adoption of the Treaty of Maastricht this competence was used to adopt three Directives on the free movement for students, for pensioners and for persons with sufficient means and comprehensive healthcare insurance. Single European Act [1987] OJ L169/1; Council Directive 90/366/ECC of 28 June 1990 on the right of residence for students [1990] OJ L180/30; Council Directive 90/365/EEC of 28 June 1990 on the right of residence for employees and self-employed persons who have ceased their occupational activity [1990] OJ L180/28; Council Directive 90/364/EEC of 28 June 1990 on the right of residence [1990] OJ L180/26. These Directives are no longer in force.

[6] It also codified the complementary rights, which came with the status of EU citizenship, in Articles 8a–8d Treaty establishing the European Community (Treaty of Maastricht) [1992] OJ C191/01.

[7] TFEU, art 20(1).

[8] The Charter of Fundamental Rights contains two additional rights, which are the right to good administration (art 41) and the right to access of documents (art 42).

[9] TFEU, art 21.

[10] TFEU, art 22(1).

[11] TFEU, art 22(2).

consular authorities in third countries[12] and the right to petition the European Parliament and complain to the European Ombudsman.[13]

Besides the formal recognition of EU citizenship, the Treaty of Maastricht also extended the right to free movement to non-economically active EU citizens.[14] In addition, the post-Maastricht case law of the CJEU shows a more humane approach towards the exercise of economic free movement rights.[15] The CJEU, for instance, extended the personal scope of free movement of services to tourists[16] and patients receiving medical care in another Member State.[17] The court therefore stretched the boundaries of the economic free movement rights, which indicates that the nationals of the Member States are not merely and exclusively factors of production.[18]

Furthermore, according to some legal scholars, the protection of the general right to free movement, meaning both for economically active and non-economically active EU citizens, has been extended as well. Van Eijken and others argue, for example, that whereas in the early case law the CJEU predominantly connected the right to free movement to the prohibition of discrimination on the basis of nationality,[19] it is now moving towards a general prohibition of unjustified national rules interfering with the free movement of EU citizens.[20] One of the examples mentioned is the case *Tas-Hagen* in which one of the conditions to receive a civilian war victim's benefit was residence within the Netherlands at the time of the application. The CJEU decided that this rule was an impediment to Article 18(1) TEC (old) since it is liable to dissuade Dutch nationals from exercising their right to move and reside in another Member State.[21] These impediments to free movement, which do not

[12]TFEU, art 23.

[13]TFEU, art 24.

[14]This right is further regulated in Directive 2004/38/EC of the European Parliament and of the Council of 29 April 2004 on the right of citizens of the Union and their family members to move and reside freely within the territory of the Member States [2004] OJ L158/77.

[15]See eg Nic Shuibhne (2010), p. 1610; O'Leary (2011), pp. 505–506; Van Eijken and De Vries (2011), p. 707.

[16]Joined Cases C-286/82 & C-26/83 *Luisi and Carbone* [1984] ECLI:EU:C:1984:35, para 16; Case C-186/87 *Cowan* [1989] ECLI:EU:C:1989:47, para 15.

[17]Joined Cases C-286/82 & C-26/83 *Luisi and Carbone* [1984] ECLI:EU:C:1984:35, para 16; Case C-372/04 *Watts* [2006] ECLI:EU:C:2006:325, para 87.

[18]Nic Shuibhne (2010), p. 1610; O'Leary (2011), pp. 505–506; Van Eijken and De Vries (2011), p. 707.

[19]Case C-85/96 *Maria Martinez Sala* [1998] ECLI:EU:C:1998:217, paras 62–64; Case C-184/99 *Grzelczyk* [2001] ECLI:EU:C:2001:458, paras 30-34. It follows from these cases that the prohibition of discrimination on grounds of nationality applies once an EU citizen has moved to another Member State and lawfully resides there.

[20]See Van Eijken et al. (2015), p. 259; Two-speed European Citizenship? Can the Lisbon Treaty help close the gap? (2008), p. 1.

[21]Case C-192/05 *Tas-Hagen* [2006] ECLI:EU:C:2006:676, paras 17-32. See also Joined Cases C-11/06 & C-12/06 *Morgan and Bucher* [2007] ECLI:EU:C:2007:626, paras 18–31.

directly discriminate on the basis of nationality, are in principle also prohibited under EU law.[22]

The above shows the development of the EU citizen as a free movement citizen, but the post-Maastricht case law also points to the development of a concept of EU citizenship that is more separate from or less dependent on the right to free movement. This follows from the case law in which the CJEU adopted a more liberal approach to the rule that internal situations fall outside the scope of Union law.[23] In principle, for a case to fall within the scope of EU law and for EU citizens to be protected by EU safeguards, such as the prohibition of discrimination on the basis of nationality, the case requires a cross-border element. However, the CJEU has decided on occasion that such a cross-border link was present without actual physical movement by the EU citizen. An often-cited example is the *Rottman* case concerning Austrian measures, which could have resulted in the loss of Mr. Rottman's Austrian nationality. As a result thereof he could have potentially lost his EU citizenship status with the rights attached thereto. In light of the nature and the consequences of the measure, the CJEU decided that the situation fell within the scope of Union law.[24] So, the fact that the measures threatened the exercise of the right to free movement in the future seemed to have brought the situation within the scope of Union law.[25]

In the 2010 *Zambrano* judgement, the CJEU took it one step further and for the first time declared that a purely internal situation could fall within the scope of EU law.[26] The case concerned a third-country national with two children who both had Belgian nationality and resided in Belgium. Mr. Zambrano's application for a residence permit and a work permit were refused by the Belgian competent authorities, but no real action was taken to deport him and his family. During the legal proceedings, the Employment Tribunal in Brussels in essence asked the CJEU whether the refusal to grant Mr. Zambrano a right of residence and a work permit in fact violated the provisions on EU citizenship and the Charter, as his minor children, who are EU citizens, were dependent on him. Regardless of the lack of a cross-border element in this case—the children had always resided in their state of

[22] See Van Eijken et al. (2015), p. 259.

[23] See eg Case C-175/78 *Saunders* [1979] ECLI:EU:C:1979:88, para 11.

[24] Case C-135/08 *Rottmann* [2010] ECLI:EU:C:2010:104. Two other examples are the case *Garcia-Avello* and *Chen*. In the former, the Belgium authorities refused to register two children with both the Spanish and Belgium nationality with a double surname. Even though the children resided in Belgium and had not travelled to Spain, their Spanish nationality constituted a sufficient cross-border element for the case to fall within the scope of EU law. However, it remains unclear whether the Court of Justice actually found a cross-border link in the previous migration of the parents to Belgium. In the *Chen* case, the fact that the daughter of Catherine Chen held the Irish nationality gave her the right to reside in the UK, even though her daughter had never left the territory of the UK. Case C-148/02 *Garcia Avello* [2003] ECLI:EU:C:2003:539; Case C-200/02 *Chen* [2004] ECLI:EU:C:2004:639. See also Case C-403/03 *Schempp* [2005] ECLI:EU:C:2005:446.

[25] Van Eijken and De Vries (2011).

[26] Case C-34/09 *Ruiz Zambrano* [2011] ECLI:EU:C:2011:124.

nationality and had never used their right to free movement—the CJEU did not dismiss it with the conclusion that it concerned a purely internal situation and therefore fell outside the scope of Union law. In light of the fact that the children were EU citizens, which was supposed to become the fundamental status of nationals in the Member States, the Court determined that 'Article 20 TFEU precludes national measures which have the effect of depriving citizens of the Union of the genuine enjoyment of the substance of the rights conferred by virtue of their status as citizens of the Union.'[27]

This interpretation of Article 20 TFEU opened the door to a more inclusive concept of EU citizenship. In the literature, it was argued by some that the 'substance of rights' could include fundamental rights as well, which would allow for a more direct connection between EU citizenship and the protection of fundamental rights.[28] National measures which would deprive citizens of the genuine enjoyment of their fundamental rights could fall under the scope of Union law and the Charter without the need for a cross-border dimension. However, in subsequent case law, the CJEU tampered such big expectations and ideas. In *Dereci*, the CJEU adopted a very limited interpretation to the 'denial of the genuine enjoyment of the substance of EU citizen rights' criterion. For a situation without a cross-border element to fall within the scope of Union law, the national measure in question needs to force the EU citizen to leave the territory of the EU altogether.[29] The *Zambrano* and *Dereci* criteria have been further defined and elaborated on in subsequent case law.[30] In my view, this string of case law still closely links the protection of 'static' EU citizens to free movement, but it does take a slightly different perspective.[31] It concerns the protection of the potential future exercise of free movement rights in situations in which these rights have not been exercised yet and therefore appear 'purely internal'.[32] Thus, the CJEU case law recognises that 'static EU citizens' not having used their free movement rights also could derive 'self-standing' rights from Article 20 TFEU, simply because they are EU citizens.

[27] Case C-34/09 *Ruiz Zambrano* [2011] ECLI:EU:C:2011:124, para 42.

[28] Van Eijken and De Vries (2011), p. 718.

[29] Case C-256/11 *Dereci* [2011] ECLI:EU:C:2011:734, para 66.

[30] For instance, in *Chavez-Vilchez* the post-Zambrano line of case law took an interesting turn. The CJEU determined that the right to family life in Article 7 CFR can play a role when determining whether in a concrete situation the *Dereci* criterion is fulfilled. Case C-133/15 *Chavez-Vilchez* [2017] ECLI:EU:C:2017:354.

[31] Case C-40/11 *Lida* [2012] ECLI:EU:C:2012:691, para 72; Case C-87/12 *Ymeraga* [2013] ECLI:EU:C:2013:291, para 37.

[32] See also Neuvonen (2017), p. 1220. Neuvonen states that 'the "substance" of EU citizenship rights still comes down to cross-border movement, although we now speak of "forced" movement away from the EU, as opposed to "free" movement within the EU'.

2.2.2 *The Development of the Position of the EU Citizen Within the Specific Context of the AFSJ*

Despite the common characteristics of citizenship and the AFSJ—in the sense that both are concerned with the position of the individual in a polity in which public power is exercised over individuals and both have their origin in the free movement of persons—they were not linked by the Treaties of Maastricht, Amsterdam and Nice. In the literature, one of the reasons suggested for this long-term official separation in the treaties is the implicit threat of political ambitions underlying the concept of citizenship. The initial presentation of EU citizenship in the first pillar by the Treaty of Maastricht as the codification of already acquired rights in relation to the internal market and its separation from other sensitive areas, such as criminal justice, as well as fundamental rights, made the official introduction of EU citizenship acceptable to the Member States.[33] However, even though an explicit connection between EU citizenship and the AFSJ was lacking in the treaties, an implicit one was occasionally made. The Hague Programme, for instance, states, 'The European Council reaffirms the priority it attaches to the development of an area of freedom, security and justice, responding to a central concern of the peoples of the States brought together in the Union.'[34]

In the pre-Lisbon period, the main emphasis was on providing EU citizens with an area of security.[35] In this light, EU citizen's free movement rights actually had a twofold dimension. On the one hand, they triggered the need for judicial cooperation with a higher level of automaticity, as free movement rights also increase the risk of cross-border crime, especially in the absence of a unified criminal law system.[36] On the other hand, as such new judicial cooperation mechanisms would contribute to security, they would in turn also facilitate free movement in the AFSJ.[37] The method chosen to ensure this higher level of automaticity was the principle of mutual recognition, which is further explained later on.

It follows from the above that, for a time, EU citizenship and free movement were primarily used as arguments for the promotion and adoption of new EU crime-fighting measures, including new and more efficient forms of judicial cooperation.[38] As explained in Chap. 1, the Treaty of Lisbon seemed to herald new times by designating the EU citizen as the main beneficiary of the AFSJ providing security, free movement and respect for fundamental rights.[39] To some extent, the important

[33]Coutts (2014), pp. 94–96; Anderson et al. (1994), pp. 108–109.

[34]European Council, The Hague Programme: strengthening freedom, security and justice in the European Union (The Hague Programme) [2005] OJ C53/1.

[35]The Hague Programme 2005, p. 1; Tampere Programme 1999, paras 5–6; Mitsilegas (2016), p. 125; Luchtman (2013), p. 12.

[36]Mitsilegas (2016), p. 125.

[37]See eg Tampere Programme 1999, para 2.

[38]Van Eijken and Marguery (2017), pp. 565–566.

[39]TEU, art 3(2) and TFEU, art 67(1).

position of EU citizenship was also reflected in practice, for instance, by the introduction of the ordinary legislative procedure for most criminal justice measures, which strengthened the role of the European Parliament.[40] In this legislative procedure, the EU citizen is directly represented by the European Parliament and indirectly by the Council, which both have an equal say.

Furthermore, the 2009 Stockholm program emphasised the need for fundamental rights protection and included the Roadmap on Procedural Safeguards.[41] This Roadmap was adopted only moments before the Treaty of Lisbon entered into force and stated that facilitating free movement of EU citizens required a minimum level of procedural safeguards in the Member States.[42] Even though six directives on procedural safeguards have been adopted since then, their preambles hardly refer to the facilitation of free movement of EU citizens as their core objective. Instead, the focus is on increasing mutual trust to improve efficient cooperation for security purposes.[43] In addition, the post-Stockholm programmes and strategic guidelines of the European Council paid less attention to the link between free movement and fundamental rights.[44] So, whereas EU citizenship is granted an important position by Article 3(2) TEU, the post-Lisbon five-year programmes and legislative actions do not reflect a strong role for EU citizenship, which goes beyond the need for the establishment of a safe AFSJ.

However, in the CJEU case law, the protection of EU citizens' right to free movement has gained an important position. In several cases, the court prohibited national criminal justice measures on the basis of the non-discrimination provision in Article 18 TFEU to protect the free movement of EU citizens. The cases concern nationals of Member States who have used one of their free movement rights and encounter unequal treatment in the host state when they become accused of or are victims of crimes.[45] For instance, in *Bickel and Franz*, the CJEU ruled that the refusal of the Italian authorities to conduct the criminal proceedings of two German nationals in German while this right was granted to Italian nationals violated the prohibition of discrimination. Such unequal treatment is liable to hamper the exercise of free movement rights, according to the court.[46] These cases show that the

[40] TFEU, art 294. Exceptions are, for instance, Article 86(1) TFEU, which prescribes the special legislative procedure for the establishment of a European Public Prosecutors Office.

[41] European Council, 'The Stockholm Programme – An Open and Secure Europe Serving and Protecting Citizens' [2009] OJ C115/1, pp. 4, 10.

[42] Resolution of the Council of 30 November 2009 on a Roadmap for strengthening procedural rights of suspected or accused persons in criminal proceedings [2009] OJ C295/1, paras 3–5, 10.

[43] See eg Directive 2010/64/EU of the European Parliament and of the Council of 20 October 2010 on the right to interpretation and translation in criminal proceedings [2010] OJ L280/1, recitals 1-9; Directive 2012/13/EU of the European Parliament and of the Council of 22 May 2012 on the right to information in criminal proceedings [2012] OJ L142/1, recitals 2-10.

[44] European Council, 'Strategic guidelines for the legislative and operational planning in the Area of Freedom, Security and Justice' (Strategic Guidelines) EUCO (2014) 79/14.

[45] With regard to victims see Case C-186/87 *Cowan* [1989] ECLI:EU:C:1989:47.

[46] Case C-274/96 *Bickel and Franz* [1998] ECLI:EU:C:1998:563, paras 16–19.

CJEU has developed the right to free movement into a so-called *Abwehrrecht*, prohibiting national measures and actions which hamper free movement.[47]

2.2.3 *Interim Conclusion*

It follows from the above that since its introduction in the Treaty of Maastricht, EU citizenship has gained a more prominent position. The previous sections show the development of a narrative of what I would call free-movement-based (FMB) EU citizenship both in and outside the specific context of the AFSJ.[48] Firstly, the development of this narrative follows from the extension of the right to free movement to all EU citizens by the Treaty of Maastricht. Secondly, it can be derived from the case law of the CJEU on the scope of the economic free movement rights and the prohibition of national measures, which could hamper the free movement of all EU citizens in the AFSJ or the EU in general. Besides the development of this narrative of EU citizenship, EU citizenship has also progressed in a different manner. This follows from the post-Maastricht jurisprudence which shows the slow and cautious advancement of granting rights to static or stay-at-home EU citizens, albeit on a more *ad hoc* basis and under certain specific conditions. In addition, the Treaty of Lisbon introduced the ordinary legislative procedure for most criminal justice measures. In this procedure EU citizens are directly represented by the European Parliament and indirectly by the Council. These developments, in particular the latter, constitute the basis of the narrative of EU citizenship as a cornerstone of the EU's representative democracy, which I refer to as representative-democracy-based (RDB) EU citizenship.[49] These two narratives on EU citizenship and the role which they can have in bringing about changes in the AFSJ are further discussed in Chap. 12.

On the EU legislative and policy level, bold words have often been spoken concerning the importance of EU citizens and the facilitation and protection of their rights, but in the context of the AFSJ the fulfilment of these promises is predominantly realised in the area of security. Besides the harmonisation directives for procedural safeguards, which in the end were often not explicitly connected to free movement, the focus of the EU legislator has been on providing EU citizens with an AFSJ in which they can travel without fear of crime. In this light, the right to free movement required and justified the adoption of new mutual recognition instruments, allowing quicker and more efficient judicial cooperation than was at the time possible on the basis of bilateral or multilateral treaties and agreements. The next two sections further elaborate on the principle of mutual recognition and the

[47] See also Van Eijken and Marguery (2017), pp. 573–582.

[48] See also Sect. 12.2.

[49] See also Sect. 12.2.

security dimension of the EAW as well as the role of the EAW in complications which can arise for EU citizens moving in the AFSJ.

2.3 The Principle of Mutual Recognition

The principle of mutual recognition did not originate in the AFSJ. It was first introduced by the CJEU in relation to the free movement of goods. In that context, it entails that a Member State may not prohibit goods from entering its territory when these have been lawfully produced and marketed in another Member State in accordance with the rules of that Member State.[50] Later mutual recognition played a role in the context of the other economic fundamental freedoms, such as the freedom of services and establishment.[51] It served as an alternative to detailed harmonisation measures at the EU level.[52] In 1999 the European Council 'borrowed' mutual recognition from the internal market and presented it as the future cornerstone of judicial cooperation in criminal matters in its Tampere Conclusions.[53] Even though this has resulted in the adoption of many mutual recognition instruments for the purpose of judicial cooperation, it was not until the Treaty of Lisbon that an explicit legal basis for such measures was included in the treaties.[54]

The adoption of the principle of mutual recognition in the AFSJ offered a solution to the at the time slow development of judicial cooperation in criminal matters in the context of the third pillar of the Treaty of Maastricht and the scepticism towards harmonisation of national criminal laws.[55] In the criminal justice context, mutual

[50] Case C-120/78 *Rewe-Zentral AG tegen Bundesmonopolverwaltung für Branntwein (Cassis de Dijon)* [1979] ECLI:EU:C:1979:42.

[51] See eg Directive 2005/36/EC of the European Parliament and of the Council of 7 September 2005 on the recognition of professional qualifications [2005] OJ L255/22. This Directive has been amended on several occasions, including by Directive 2013/55/EU of the European Parliament and of the Council of 20 November 2013 amending Directive 2005/36/EC on the recognition of professional qualifications and Regulation (EU) No 1024/2012 on administrative cooperation through the Internal Market Information System ('the IMI Regulation') [2013] OJ L354/132. See also Glerum (2013), p. 125.

[52] Glerum (2013), p. 125.

[53] Tampere Programme 1999, para 33. The 1998 Cardiff Conclusions already referred to a broader use of mutual recognition for court decisions. At that time, the principle of mutual recognition already underpinned the recognition and enforcement of judgments in civil and commercial matters. See European Council, Presidency Conclusions 1998 (Cardiff Programme) <https://www.consilium.europa.eu/media/21103/54315.pdf> accessed 20 September 2021, p. 39. See also Council Regulation (EC) No 44/2001 of 22 December 2000 on jurisdiction and the recognition and enforcement of judgments in civil and commercial matters [2001] OJ L12/1, in particular recitals 16–17. This Regulation was repealed by Regulation (EU) No 1215/2012 of the European Parliament and of the Council of 12 December 2012 on jurisdiction and the recognition and enforcement of judgments in civil and commercial matters [2012] OJ L351/1.

[54] TFEU, art 82.

[55] Mitsilegas (2006), pp. 1278, 1280.

recognition means that a judicial decision with extranational implications, taken by a competent national authority of a Member State, needs to be automatically recognised and enforced throughout the territory of the Union—by the national authorities of other Member States—and have the same or similar effects there, even if other Member States do not have a comparable national authority, or if their national comparable authorities would not have taken the same decision or are not competent to take such a decision.[56] In other words, it entails that a judicial decision, such as a judgement imposing a sentence or arrest warrant, is recognised and executed by another Member State without further ado or national conversion proceedings. Hence, as mutual recognition is based on the acceptance and recognition of differences between national legal systems, it can facilitate the establishment of a common AFSJ with free movement of judicial decisions while preserving the national characteristics and particularities of the national criminal law systems.[57]

Judicial cooperation in criminal matters on the basis of mutual recognition is strongly linked to the principle of mutual trust.[58] Both have been recognised as fundamental principles of EU law as they are essential to the establishment of an AFSJ.[59] However, contrary to mutual recognition, the Treaty of Lisbon has not provided a normative legal basis for mutual trust, which therefore still finds its normative basis in secondary legislation.[60] The relationship between mutual recognition and mutual trust is also not uniformly defined,[61] but the latter is often classified as a prerequisite for cooperation on the basis of mutual recognition.[62] The argument is that without a high level of trust, Member States may not want to increase the automaticity of cooperation procedures and recognise foreign judicial decisions without conversion procedures. In this light, the principle of mutual trust implies that each Member State believes in the adequacy of the legal rules of other Member States, including their compliance with EU law and fundamental rights.[63] Mutual trust also entails a prohibition to make the willingness to cooperate

---

[56] European Commission, 'Mutual Recognition of Final Decisions in Criminal Matters' (Communication) COM (2000) 495 final, pp. 2, 4; Mitsilegas (2016), p. 125.

[57] Erbežnik (2012), pp. 3–4.

[58] Opinion 2/13 [2014] ECLI:EU:C:2014:2454, para 168; Case C-216/18 *LM* [2018] ECLI:EU:C:2018:586, para 36.

[59] Opinion 2/13 [2014] ECLI:EU:C:2014:2454, para 191; Joined Cases C-404/15 & C-659/15 *Aranyosi and Căldăraru* [2016] ECLI:EU:C:2016:198, paras 77-78; Case C-241/16 *Bob-Dogi* [2016] ECLI:EU:C:2016:385, para 33.

[60] Ostropolski (2015), p. 167.

[61] See Ostropolski (2015), p. 167.

[62] Joined Cases C-404/15 & C-659/15 *Aranyosi and Căldăraru* [2016] ECLI:EU:C:2016:198, paras 77–78; Case C-477/16 *Kovalkovas* [2016] ECLI:EU:C:2016:861, para 27; Case C-216/18 *LM* [2018] ECLI:EU:C:2018:586, para 36.

[63] European Commission, 'Mutual Recognition of Final Decisions in Criminal Matters' (Communication) COM (2000) 495 final, p. 4; Joined Cases C-404/15 & C-659/15 *Aranyosi and Căldăraru* [2016] ECLI:EU:C:2016:198, paras 77-78; Case C-477/16 *Kovalkovas* [2016] ECLI:EU:C:2016:861, para 27.

dependent on a higher level of fundamental rights protection than the level required by EU law and obliges states to refrain, save in exceptional circumstances, from reviewing in concrete cases whether the other Member State observes the standard of fundamental rights protection set by EU law.[64]

2.4 The European Arrest Warrant: The First Mutual Recognition Instrument in the AFSJ

In the wake of 9/11, the establishment of a more efficient system for the surrender of suspects and convicted persons became a top priority for the EU. Whereas the period before the terrorist attacks shows failed attempts to simplify the extradition procedures between the EU Member States, afterwards the Member States managed to agree on the adoption of the Framework Decision on the European Arrest Warrant within a matter of months.[65] The EAW was approved by the Council on 13 June 2002 in the context of the Third Pillar of the Treaty of Maastricht on Police and Judicial Cooperation in Criminal Matters.[66] It was the first mutual recognition instrument adopted after the Tampere Conclusions and had to be implemented by the Member States by 31 December 2003.[67] The FDEAW replaces the often time-consuming and complicated extradition procedures between the EU Member States with an expedient and direct system of surrender between national judicial authorities for the purpose of prosecuting the requested person or the execution of a sanction imposed upon the requested person.[68] Thus, the EAW can be issued for two reasons only: for the purpose of prosecution in the issuing state—a prosecution EAW—and for the purpose of the execution of a sanction—an execution EAW. The FDEAW contains some terminology which differs from the standard terminology used in extradition treaties. Besides the fact that the FDEAW establishes a system of 'surrender' and not of 'extradition', it, for instance, also refers to the issuing and executing judicial authority instead of the requesting and requested state.

In the context of the FDEAW, mutual recognition specifically means that an EAW is recognised and enforced throughout the territory of the Union, which implies the recognition of the underlying national judicial decision, which can, for instance, be a verdict or a national arrest warrant.[69] The FDEAW is, however, not an example of an absolute or pure form of mutual recognition, since it contains several

[64] Opinion 2/13 [2014] ECLI:EU:C:2014:2454, para 192.

[65] On the other attempts and the process towards the adoption of the EAW see Plachta and Van Ballegooij (2005), pp. 13–38; Klimek (2014), pp. 11–27.

[66] Council Framework Decision 2002/584/JHA of 13 June 2002 on the European arrest warrant and the surrender procedures between Member States [2002] OJ L190/1.

[67] FDEAW, art 34(1).

[68] FDEAW, recital 5.

[69] Glerum (2013), p. 127.

mandatory and optional refusal grounds.[70] Its mutual recognition foundation is, for instance, reflected in the decision to exclude classical extradition refusal grounds, such as those based on political and fiscal offences and the partial abolition of the double criminality requirement in Article 2(2) FDEAW. Other changes made in light of mutual recognition are the replacement of a system of cooperation between governments or states, which in extradition procedures often results in lengthy proceedings, with a system of direct cooperation between national judicial authorities. This entails that a governmental organ, such as the Minister of Justice, may not be the sole executing or issuing judicial authority.[71] These and other differences between the extradition and surrender procedure are further discussed in Chap. 10.

As explained above, the EAW constitutes a security measure. It is a response to the concerns of increased cross-border crime as a result of the opening of internal borders and the free movement of persons in the AFSJ. It also contributes to free movement by limiting safe harbours for criminals. In light of its security dimension, the EAW should, however, not be viewed in a vacuum, but in combination with another development. As a result of the continuing process of globalisation and European integration characterised by migration flows and a growing significance of the internet, Member States have made extensive use of their jurisdiction to prescribe. This concept comprises the state's power to decide to which 'activities, relations or status of persons, or the interests of persons in things' its national substantive criminal law is applicable.[72] States have used this power—sometimes on their own initiative and sometimes to meet an obligation imposed by international or EU instruments—to established broad extraterritorial jurisdiction.[73] This means that their national criminal codes apply both to acts committed on their territory and to acts committed abroad.

The jurisdiction to prescribe is closely linked to the jurisdiction to adjudicate, meaning the power to apply established jurisdiction in a particular case or procedure

[70] FDEAW, arts 1(2), 3-4A.

[71] In the case law, the CJEU has also stated that the issuing judicial authority does not have to be a court or tribunal *sensu stricto*. Instead, the Member States may appoint the public prosecutor as the issuing judicial authority when the public prosecutor is part of the administration of justice and can perform his or her tasks objectively and independently from the executive. Case C-477/16 *Kovalkovas* [2016] ECLI:EU:C:2016:861, paras 41–42; Joined Cases C-508/18 & C-82/19 *OG & PI* [2019] ECLI:EU:C:2019:456, para 68.

[72] Restatement (Third) of US Foreign Relations Law, para 401(a); Böse (2013), p. 76.

[73] Certain international treaties and EU harmonization instruments which impose obligations regarding the criminalization of certain conduct also contain jurisdiction obligations. In relation to the EU the legal basis for these harmonisation measures is laid down in Article 83(1) TFEU. See eg Convention on Action against Trafficking in Human Beings [2005] CETS no 197, art 31(1); Directive 2011/36/EU of the European Parliament and of the Council of 5 April 2011 on preventing and combating trafficking in human beings and protecting its victims [2011] OJ L101/1, art 10(1)(b). See also Peers (2011), pp. 824–827; Kaiafa-Gbandi (2020), p. 209.

as well as jurisdiction to set up a court or tribunal for criminal cases.[74] National courts may not try a case—exercise jurisdiction to adjudicate—unless their national substantive criminal law was applicable to the conduct in question at the time of the offence.[75] Extending the jurisdiction to prescribe, therefore, often automatically means extending the jurisdiction to adjudicate.

The broad jurisdiction to prescribe has the effect of casting a tight net of competing applicable criminal laws in the AFSJ, which limits the chance that certain conduct is not punishable in any of the Member States.[76] In the German literature, this is referred to as the *Netzgedanke*.[77] This *Netzgedanke* also increases the chance of positive conflicts of jurisdiction which are situations in which a criminal case can be brought before the national courts of more than one Member State.[78] These two phenomena limit the chances of impunity by ensuring that certain conduct falls under the national criminal law and jurisdiction to adjudicate of one of the Member States.[79]

Within this picture, the EAW is capable of compensating for the lack of extra-territorial jurisdiction to enforce under public international law. This concerns the jurisdiction to take certain (coercive) measures to react to (alleged) violations of criminal norms.[80] This form of jurisdiction is closely connected to the jurisdiction to adjudicate, since courts enforce the law by imposing penalties on those who violate it.[81] For the purpose of this book, I view investigatory and prosecutorial actions as falling under the jurisdiction to enforce and the competence of a court or judge to try a case as falling under the jurisdiction to adjudicate. With regard to extraterritorial jurisdiction to enforce, national authorities are in principle prohibited from entering the territory of another state to conduct criminal investigations and to exercise investigatory powers, such as an arrest. In this light, when its conditions are met and no refusal grounds apply the EAW facilitates the territorial and extraterritorial

[74] Restatement (Third) of US Foreign Relations Law, para 401(b); European Committee on Crime Problems (Council of Europe), *Extraterritorial criminal jurisdiction* (Strasbourg 1990), p. 18; Böse (2013), p. 76.

[75] European Committee on Crime Problems (Council of Europe), *Extraterritorial criminal jurisdiction* (Strasbourg 1990) p. 20; Böse (2013), p. 75.

[76] Hecker (2011), p. 86; Meyer and Böse (2011), p. 337.

[77] Lagodny (2001), p. 101; Hecker (2011), p. 86; Meyer and Böse (2011), p. 337; Eser and Burchard (2006), p. 517. See also Petrig (2013), p. 35.

[78] Kaiafa-Gbandi (2020), p. 209; *Draft Legislative Proposals for the prevention and resolution of conflicts of jurisdiction in criminal matters in the European Union* (2017) <https://www.europeanlawinstitute.eu/projects-publications/publications/> accessed 20 September 2021, p. 6. A distinction is made between negative and positive conflicts of jurisdiction, but this book only focuses on the latter. Negative conflicts of jurisdiction cover the situation in which more than one state has jurisdiction, but no state is willing to exercise it. See Thorhauer (2015), p. 81.

[79] Hecker (2011), p. 86; Meyer and Böse (2011), p. 337.

[80] Restatement (Third) of US Foreign Relations Law, para 401(c); European Committee on Crime Problems (Council of Europe), *Extraterritorial criminal jurisdiction* (Strasbourg 1990), p. 18. See also Böse (2013), p. 76.

[81] Böse (2013), p. 76.

application of national criminal laws by providing states with the opportunity to bring the suspect to their territory for the purpose of prosecution or the execution of a sanction. This means that in a situation in which a French dealer travels to the Netherlands in order to buy drugs, since the criminal sanctions under Dutch law are less severe than under French law, the extraterritorial application of the French and Dutch law and the EAW together limit the risk of impunity of the French dealer. By extension, they also strengthen the safety of other EU citizens. So, in its contribution to the establishment of a safe AFSJ, the EAW is best described as an extended enforcement arm of the national prosecution authorities.[82]

It can be concluded that the package deal of mutual recognition instruments, like the quasi-automatic EAW and broad national extraterritorial jurisdiction contributes to the establishment of a secure AFSJ in which impunity is avoided and an EU citizen can safely exercise his or her free movement rights. At the same time, however, the combination of the two also increases the risk of a series of complications for EU citizens, in particular for those who have used their free movement rights or are confronted with someone who has. The next section describes two possible downsides of the combination of broad extraterritorial jurisdiction and the EAW for EU citizens and raises questions from the perspective of the substantive and procedural legality principle in Articles 49 and 47(2) CFR. Section 2.5 explains the complication which raises questions in light of Article 49 CFR and the role of the EAW in that context. Section 2.6 conducts the same exercise in relation to the second issue which raises questions in light of Article 47 CFR.

2.5 The EAW and the Foreseeability of Criminal Offences and Sanctions

Legal scholars have argued that the difficulty for EU citizens to foresee whose national criminal laws to obey constitutes an important downside of the *Netzgedanke* and resulting positive conflicts of jurisdiction.[83] EU citizens are provided with the right to free movement, but those who exercise this right, or who are confronted with someone who has, face the risk of not being exclusively subjected to the law of the host state, meaning the state to which they decide to move. Due to the extraterritorial scope of many national criminal laws, they can be confronted with the application of several national criminal codes at the same time while their application may have been difficult to predict at the time of the offence. This is because the law of the host state usually does not warn the individual of the applicability of other national criminal laws.[84]

[82] Meyer and Böse (2011), p. 336; Mitsilegas (2012), pp. 321–322.
[83] See eg Eser and Burchard (2006), p. 519; Schönberger (2015), p. 298.
[84] Petrig (2013), p. 35.

A jurisdiction ground which clearly reflects this problem is the passive nationality principle, since at the time of the offence the alleged perpetrator is usually unaware of the nationality of the victim.[85] The suspect is therefore confronted with a national criminal law, including its criminal offences and sanctions, that was not foreseeable to him at the time of the offence.[86] Another example is the effects doctrine, which is part of the territoriality principle, since the results of a crime could accidentally or unintentionally occur in a particular state.[87] For instance, a French national who is shot in Germany near the Dutch border may die in a Dutch hospital. As the consequences of the criminal act—the death of the person—occurred in the Netherlands, Dutch law is applicable as well.[88] However, for the French national the applicability of Dutch law was difficult or even impossible to foresee at the time of the offence. These examples illustrate that the *Netzgedanke* and positive conflicts of jurisdiction can confront the EU citizen in the AFSJ with an intangible network of overlapping jurisdictions. In the legal literature, this situation has been described as a theoretical obligation for EU citizens travelling in the EU to know and abide by the law of all the Member States, since it is difficult to tell which particular criminal laws are applicable at a certain place and time.[89]

The difficulties in foreseeing which particular national criminal laws to obey can be problematic, since offences and sanctions in the national criminal laws of the Member States still differ to a large extent. Criminal law is closely connected to state sovereignty and national identity as a result of which states still hold different views as to whether certain conduct should be criminalised, how the conduct should be classified—as a minor or serious offence—and what sort of sanctions—type and severity—can be imposed.[90] Deviating opinions in relation to controversial and moral issues such as, euthanasia, abortion and drugs are also reflected in national substantive criminal laws.[91] In light of the fact that states can classify the same conduct as different criminal offences and national criminal laws can prescribe different sanctions for the same conduct, EU citizens will want to know whose particular national criminal law to obey at any given time.

This complication with which EU citizens can be confronted raises questions in light of the accessibility and foreseeability requirement correlating from the substantive legality principle as codified in Article 49 CFR and Article 7 ECHR, in particular regarding the link between jurisdiction and criminal offences and sanctions. The accessibility requirement entails that the law must provide an adequate indication of the applicable legal rules in a given case,[92] whereas the foreseeability

[85] Strijards (1985), pp. 200. See also Van der Beken (1999), p. 110.

[86] Böse (2014a), p. 88.

[87] Schönberger (2015), p. 507.

[88] Dutch Criminal Code (DCC) art 2.

[89] Eser and Burchard (2006), p. 519; Schönberger (2015), p. 298.

[90] Gleß (2004), p. 361; Schönberger (2015), p. 298.

[91] Thorhauer (2015), p. 82.

[92] ECtHR 26 April 1979, 6538/74 (*Sunday Times/UK*) para 49.

requirement demands that the law is sufficiently clear and precise with regard to the criminal conduct and penalties that can be imposed.[93] With regard to the risk of overlapping applicable national criminal codes which still differ to a large extent, the question arises whether criminal offences and sanctions are indeed foreseeable and accessible?[94] More specifically, are citizens provided with an adequate indication as to the applicable rules, and are they able to understand, on the basis of the law, what constitutes a criminal act and what sanction can be imposed when they could not have known at the time of the offence which national criminal codes to obey?

It follows from the above that the *Netzgedanke* has resulted in questions concerning the compatibility of the law codifying criminal offences and sanctions with the accessibility and foreseeability requirement. The EAW adds another dimension to this discussion. It does not of itself create the possibility of prosecution by a state while the applicability of its national criminal law was not foreseeable at the time of the offence. This risk exists without the EAW as well, but in the absence of the EAW—or extradition procedures outside the context of the EU—citizens would be (relatively) safe from such prosecutions as long as they do not enter the territory of the state exercising jurisdiction.[95] As a mutual recognition instrument with only a limited set of refusal grounds, the question arises whether the EAW increases the risk of having to face an actual prosecution and trial in a state while criminal liability and sanctions according to the law of that state were difficult to foresee? In addition, could the current legal framework for surrender force the executing judicial authority to surrender the requested person while the validity of the jurisdiction claim of the issuing state raises concerns in light of Article 49 CFR?

2.6 The EAW and the Right to a Tribunal Established by Law

The second possible complication which EU citizens—especially those using free movement rights—could encounter follows from the fact that the EAW is not complemented by an EU system preventing or solving conflicts of jurisdiction by appointing the best forum for prosecution and trial for a particular case. As explained before, as a result of the extensive use of the jurisdiction to prescribe by the Member States, the range of states in which a person can be prosecuted and tried is extended, which may result in positive conflicts of jurisdiction.[96] The *ne bis in idem* principle is

[93] Case C-42/17 *M.A.S and M.B* [2017] ECLI:EU:C:2017:936 (*Taricco II*), para 56; Case C-72/15 *Rosneft* [2017] ECLI:EU:C:2017:236, para 162; Case C-303/05 *Advocaten voor de Wereld* [2007] ECLI:EU:C:2007:261, paras 49-50; ECtHR 11 November 1996, 17,862/91 (*Cantoni/France*) para 29; ECtHR 19 March 2006, 67,335/01 (*Achour/France*) para 41.

[94] See also Kaiafa-Gbandi (2020), p. 210.

[95] Gleß (2004), p. 361.

[96] Spencer (2013), p. 72.

currently the most well-known forum rule to solve positive conflicts of jurisdiction, since it prohibits consecutive prosecutions and sanctioning after a final decision has been reached in a Member State.[97] However, the *ne bis in idem* principle does not prohibit or solve such conflicts of jurisdiction *before* a final decision has been made in one of the Member States. This has been criticised by, for instance, Advocate General (AG) Sharpston, who stated that the *ne bis in idem* principle is 'not a satisfactory substitute for action to resolve such conflicts [of jurisdiction] according to an agreed set of criteria.'[98]

In the past EU institutions have stated that the yardstick of the fair administration of justice or the most appropriate forum for the concrete case should be used to establish a binding system for forum choices.[99] However, the attempts made either failed like the proposal for a Framework Decision on the Transfer of Criminal Proceedings,[100] were not of a general nature like the rules on forum choices in specific EU instruments, such as the EPPO Regulation,[101] or were downgraded like the Framework Decision 2009/948 on conflicts of jurisdiction. The latter aims to facilitate efficient prosecutions and to improve the proper administration of justice.[102] For this purpose, Member States are obliged to contact each other if they have reasonable grounds to believe that parallel proceedings are being conducted and to try to allocate the case among them. However, this Framework Decision does not prescribe a concrete procedure or a set of criteria guiding such coordination actions.[103] In addition, the Framework Decision does not go as far as to oblige Member States to concentrate the criminal proceedings in the most appropriate state for prosecution, prohibiting other states from starting criminal proceedings.

The absence of an overarching system for forum choices entails that citizens can try to influence the forum decision by choosing to commit the crime in a particular

[97] CFR, art 50; Convention implementing the Schengen Agreement of 14 June 1985 between the Governments of the States of the Benelux Economic Union, the Federal Republic of Germany and the French Republic on the gradual abolition of checks at their common borders (CISA) [2000] OJ L239/19, art 54.

[98] Case C-398/12 *M* [2014] ECLI:EU:C:2014:65, Opinion of Advocate General (AG) Sharpston, para 51.

[99] See eg The Hague Programme 2005, p. 1; European Commission, 'Green paper on Conflicts of Jurisdiction and the Principle of *ne bis in idem* in Criminal Proceedings' COM (2005) 696 final, p. 3; Council Framework Decision 2009/948/JHA of 30 November 2009 on prevention and settlement of conflicts of exercise of jurisdiction in criminal proceedings (FD on conflicts of jurisdiction) [2009] OJ L328/42, art 1 and recital 2.

[100] The proposal for a Framework Decision on the transfer of criminal proceedings established the proper administration of justice as one of the guiding principles in determining whether the criminal proceedings should be transferred from one state to another. It also established a set of criteria, which had to be taken into consideration when making this decision. Draft Council Framework Decision on the transfer of proceedings in criminal matters [2009] OJ C219/7, arts 1 and 7, recital 9.

[101] Council Regulation (EU) 2017/1939 of 12 October 2017 implementing enhanced cooperation on the establishment of the European Public Prosecutor's Office [2017] OJ L283/1, arts 26(4) 36(3).

[102] FD on conflicts of jurisdiction [2009] OJ L328/42, art 1 and recital 2.

[103] Kaiafa-Gbandi (2020), p. 209.

state.[104] At the same time it means that national authorities in the Member States are provided with broad discretion with regard to the decision to prosecute. Consequently, EU citizens who have used their free movement rights or are confronted with someone who has could be confronted with uncoordinated or coordinated forum decisions.[105] In the first situation, the eventual forum for prosecution and trial is decided on the basis of the 'first-come, first-served' rule correlating from the *ne bis in idem* principle. As this principle only prohibits iterative procedures after a final decision has been made in a Member State, the possibility exists that states end up racing each other towards this final decision. Another scenario is that a competent state only becomes aware of the criminal offence after another state has already reached a final decision.[106] For the citizen, such a forum decision—which is in fact based on chance—could be advantageous, as it can result in prosecution by the state with the most lenient sanctioning regime. However, the opposite can also be true, since citizens could by chance be prosecuted in the state whose national procedural law offers him the least protection and/or on the basis of the national criminal law allowing the strictest sanction.

Another possibility is that national competent authorities, such as public prosecutors, decide amongst each other who will prosecute the case.[107] The lack of rules regulating the discretion to make this decision means that it is made in a so-called 'black box' without the (obligatory) input of other actors, such as the accused whose legal position can be affected by the decisions made.[108] By the time the accused becomes aware of such a coordination decision—if he or she becomes aware of it—it could be too late to challenge it before a judge, if this is even possible at all. It has been argued in the legal literature that the black box comes with the risk that national prosecution authorities exploit the differences between the national criminal laws in case of cross-border crimes.[109] In other words, the absence of an overarching system for forum choices ensuring case allocations in light of the proper administration of justice brings about the risk of abuse of power and forum shopping to the detriment of the suspect.[110]

The lack of an appropriate overarching EU system for forum choices based on the proper administration of justice also raises questions in light of the right to a tribunal

---

[104] Kaiafa-Gbandi (2020), p. 210; Eicker (2005), p. 631.

[105] Biehler et al. (2003), p. 12; Van der Beken et al. (2002), pp. 624–625; Eicker (2005), p. 631; Schönberger (2015), p. 349.

[106] European Commission, 'Green paper on Conflicts of Jurisdiction and the Principle of *ne bis in idem* in Criminal Proceedings' COM (2005) 696 final, p. 3.

[107] Moreover, not only public prosecutors, but also policemen are in a position to influence the choice of forum as they can (secretly) agree amongst each other to refrain from arresting the accused until he or she enters the territory of the preferred state. Lagodny (2001), p. 67.

[108] Luchtman (2020), p. 30; Luchtman (2013), p. 9; Meyer (2013), p. 185; Schönberger (2015), p. 349.

[109] Eicker (2005), p. 631; Eser and Burchard (2006), pp. 517–518.

[110] Kaiafa-Gbandi (2020), p. 210; Meyer (2014), p. 206; Van der Beken et al. (2002), p. 624; Franken (2013), p. 111.

established by law as codified in Articles 47(2) CFR and 6 ECHR. This right demands that the organisation of the judicial system of a state is not made dependent on the discretion of the executive power, but is 'regulated by law emanating from Parliament'.[111] The ratio of this right is to protect individuals against arbitrary actions by the executive and the judiciary in the context of a state's judicial organisation in which jurisdiction to adjudicate is exercised.[112] The questions which follow are whether conflicts of jurisdiction in case of cross-border crimes should be prevented or solved by law and whether any discretion offered to the executive and judicial power in this regard should be restricted to avoid arbitrary decisions. In other words, is a national court or tribunal 'established by law' when the national jurisdiction of which this court or tribunal is part has not been appointed on the basis of a clear and transparent set of rules as the best jurisdiction for prosecution in light of the proper administration of justice?

Additionally, as a result of the absence of a clear system for forum choices preventing or solving conflicts of jurisdiction on the basis of the proper administration of justice, the operation of the EAW is also not guided by this yardstick. Currently, the EAW is not a means to an end in the sense that it facilitates the prosecution of EU citizens by the forum which is appointed on the basis of a clear set of rules in light of the proper administration of justice.[113] Similar to the first complication on the relation between jurisdiction and the foreseeability of criminal offences and sanctions, the EAW also does not cause the potential problems following from the lack of an overarching EU system for forum choices in light of the proper administration of justice. These problems with which EU citizens can be confronted also exist without the EAW. However, the main question is whether the EAW could—so to say—worsen these problems or contribute to their materialisation in practice by transferring citizens to a state while concerns exist with regard to the compatibility of its jurisdiction claim with Article 47 CFR?

[111] EcHR 12 October 1978, 7360/76 (*Leo Zand/Austria*) para 69; ECtHR 22 June 2000, 32492/96, 32547/96, 32548/96, 33209/96, 33210/96 (*Coëme and others/Belgium*) para 98. See also Joined Cases C-542/18 RX-II and C-543/18 RX-II *Simpson v Council of the European Union and HG v European Commission* [2020] ECLI:EU:C:2020:232, para 73.

[112] Böse (2014b), p. 125; Panzavolta (2013), p. 154.

[113] See also Walsh (2020).

2.7 Two Perspectives on the EAW: An Intergovernmental and a Transnational One

2.7.1 Introduction

The previous sections discussed two types of complications which EU citizens exercising their free movement rights may encounter,[114] the role of the EAW therein and the fundamental rights questions which they raise. Whether these complications actually entail legality problems and whether the EAW can therefore indeed be classified as an enforcement mechanism for jurisdiction claims which violate Article 49 and/or 47 CFR, in my opinion, depends on how one views the EAW and the AFSJ as the normative context within which it operates. The academic debate shows two main perspectives on the surrender procedure: an intergovernmental and a transnational one. A decision for either one could also influence the answer to the question whether the two complications discussed can and should be classified as legality problems, the view on the role of the EAW in these complications, the need for action on the EU and/or national level to solve these complications and the potential meaning and role of EU citizenship with regard to fundamental rights protection in the future. Both perspectives and their potential consequences are briefly set out in the next sections. They are discussed in more detail in Chaps. 9 and 10.

2.7.2 The Intergovernmental Perspective

The intergovernmental perspective is primarily reflected in the older literature. The legal scholars who take this view consider judicial cooperation on the basis of mutual recognition in the AFSJ as not fundamentally different from interstate cooperation in the outer-EU context.[115] More specifically, the surrender procedure is viewed as a (modern) extradition procedure and, therefore, as classical intergovernmental cooperation. In this light, Keijzer has, for instance, referred to the FDEAW as an extradition treaty *sui generis* and according to Plachta surrender is a different name for extradition.[116] Satzger has argued that mutual recognition can be found in the traditional systems of judicial cooperation as well and that it also exists in cooperation procedures between non-EU Member States. Thus, the EU is not the inventor of the principle of mutual recognition and the intensity with which this

---

[114] As well as EU citizens who are confronted with someone who has exercised his or her free movement right.

[115] Conway (2005), p. 255; Van Sliedregt (2009), p. 67. See also Deen-Racsmany (2007), p. 171.

[116] Keijzer (2005), p. 139; Plachta (2003), p. 191.

principle is applied is not extreme.[117] As further explained in Chap. 9, these points of view are often based on the remaining similarities between the FDEAW and the extradition procedure. One of the arguments that is often brought forward is that the inclusion of many of the traditional extradition refusal grounds in the FDEAW illustrates that the surrender procedure is not a definite farewell to extradition.[118]

When the EAW is viewed from the intergovernmental perspective, the complications which the package deal of overlapping national criminal jurisdictions and the EAW may cause for EU citizens, along with the fundamental rights questions which they raise, will most likely not trigger discussion or action, and this is for several reasons. Firstly, in an intergovernmental setting, states are the primary and central actors, while citizens are still predominantly viewed as the objects of the extradition procedure. The protection of citizens is also considered to be primarily the obligation of the state of nationality.[119] Secondly, the intergovernmental setting has what I would call a predominant 'state-focused' interpretation of fundamental rights standards. This entails that each Member State is obliged to uphold fundamental rights for those who find themselves within its territorial borders.[120] As explained before, the two complications, however, occur at the interface of national legal orders and not within a particular Member State. Thus the intergovernmental perspective goes hand in hand with the protection of the state as the central actor, the protection of citizens by their state of nationality instead of chosen domicile, as well as a state-focused interpretation of fundamental rights.

Those who adhere to this perspective may not be directly puzzled by the two complications and, in that light, demand action on the EU or national level to solve them and the role of the EAW therein. In light of the 'state-focused' interpretation of fundamental rights, adherents of this perspective may be of the opinion that no legality problems exist as the complications do not occur within the borders of a particular state. Furthermore, since the state is the dominant actor in the intergovernmental context and nationality is more important than citizenship defined by free movement, there may be no need to exchange the 'state-focused' interpretation of fundamental rights for one in light of Article 3(2) TEU. In addition, the important role of the state and focus on the national citizen could also narrow the possibility to see EU citizenship as something more than nationality of a Member State and its potential as a vehicle for more fundamental rights protection.[121]

---

[117] However, in relation to the EAW, he is of the opinion that the direct communication between the judicial authorities, the formalization of the procedure and increase in efficiency is a noticeable evolution of the traditional forms of cooperation. Satzger (2019), pp. 51–52.

[118] Van Sliedregt (2007), pp. 245, 251–252. See also Case C-241/15 *Bob-Dogi* [2016] ECLI:EU:C:2016:131, Opinion of AG Bot, paras 47–48.

[119] Luchtman (2013), p. 12; Eser et al. (2002), p. 697ff.

[120] Luchtman (2017) p. 9; Meyer (2014), p. 206.

[121] See also Eser and Burchard (2006), p. 519.

2.7.3 *The Transnational Perspective*

A Brief Introduction

The legal literature shows another perspective in which legal scholars move away from the view that the surrender procedure based on the principle of mutual recognition is an intergovernmental procedure. They argue that the EAW should not be perceived as a modern form of extradition, but as a new and different mechanism for cooperation.[122] Luchtman has classified the EAW as a form of transnational cooperation, since contrary to the extradition procedure cooperation occurs *directly* between national judicial authorities.[123] These authorities can be prosecution bodies as well as judges and courts.[124] In addition, the EAW does not operate in an intergovernmental community consisting of states, but in a shared legal order consisting of states and EU citizens.[125] Within this shared legal order, the EU citizen is provided with unique free movement rights, as well as a voice in the EU legislative process for criminal justice measures exercised via the European Parliament and indirectly via the Council of Ministers. The meaning of EU citizenship is therefore not limited to simply being a national of a Member State, even though nationality of one of the Member States is a prerequisite for EU citizenship.[126] Instead, as mentioned before, EU citizenship reveals the narratives of FMB EU citizenship and RDB EU citizenship.[127] These narratives are further elaborated on in Chap. 12.

This perspective is founded on the differences between the surrender procedure and the extradition procedure. These can roughly be divided into two categories, which are discussed in detail in Chap. 9. The first category of arguments focuses on the differences in the procedures themselves. For example, the fact that the EAW uses a different terminology than classical extradition treaties, the limited amount of refusal grounds, the partial abolition of the double criminality requirement, the restricted political dimension of the surrender procedure etc. The second group of arguments focuses on the differences between the normative contexts within which the extradition and surrender procedure operate.[128] For instance, contrary to the outer-EU

---

[122] Case C-303/05 *Advocaten voor de Wereld* [2006] ECLI:EU:C:2006:552, Opinion of AG Ruiz-Jarabo Colomer, paras 40–41, 46; Case C-551/18 *IK* [2018] ECLI:EU:C:2018:890, Opinion of AG Sharpston, para 39; Luchtman (2017), p. 19; Klip (2007), para 24. See also Spencer (2013), p. 63; Kraniotis (2016), pp. 254–257.

[123] In addition, as the surrender procedure aims to avoid that national authorities have to cross borders for law enforcement purposes, the term cross-border cooperation is less suitable to characterize the EAW. Luchtman (2017), p. 19. See also Spencer (2013), p. 63.

[124] FDEAW, recital 5. See also Case C-477/16 *Kovalkovas* [2016] ECLI:EU:C:2016:861, para 42.

[125] See Schönberger (2015), p. 620.

[126] TEU, art 3(2); Schönberger (2015), p. 620.

[127] TEU, art 10(1-2).

[128] See eg Schönberger (2015), p. 302; Thorhauer (2019), pp. 574–575. See also the Michel Barnier, *Speech at the European Union Agency for Fundamental Rights* [2018] https://ec.europa.eu/commission/presscorner/detail/en/SPEECH_18_4213> accessed 20 September 2021.

context, the EU is explicitly founded on the rule of law and has an EU citizenship and interrelated free movement dimension.[129] Furthermore, cooperation in the intergovernmental setting exists, because separate Member States have similar individual interests, whereas the EU has the ambition to establish common areas, such as an internal market and AFSJ, for the purpose of which judicial cooperation measures are adopted.[130]

The Position of Fundamental Rights and the Role of EU Citizenship

The transnational approach also opens the door to a different view on the current scope and position of fundamental rights in the AFSJ. As stated before, in an intergovernmental context in which state borders and nationality occupy a central position, questions regarding the 'state-focused' interpretation of fundamental rights may not necessarily arise. However, those who adhere to the transnational approach may question the 'state-focused' interpretation in light of the differences between the AFSJ and intergovernmental setting, in particular EU citizenship and free movement, and may require a fundamental rights interpretation which reflects these differences. Such an interpretation in fact surfaces in the *ne bis in idem* jurisprudence. The CJEU has adjusted the *ne bis in idem* principle in light of the two objectives of the AFSJ—security and free movement—in Article 3(2) TEU.[131] Should the legality principle in Articles 49 and 47 CFR also be interpreted in light of the normative transnational context of the AFSJ as laid down in Article 3(2) TEU?

An important interrelated question to this one is what effect a non-state-focused or transnational interpretation of the legality principle could have on the operation of the EAW? Could such a transnational interpretation turn the EAW into an enforcement mechanism for jurisdiction claims violating the legality principle? If so, does the FDEAW currently have the tools to prevent surrender in such situations without severely hampering its effectiveness, or is legislative or judicial action necessary?

Lastly, the role of the EU citizen in realising any required changes may differ from the role which the EU citizen may have in strengthening or adapting fundamental rights under the intergovernmental perspective. Whereas the intergovernmental context focuses on national citizenship, the transnational perspective views the EU citizen as an integral part of a shared legal order. This EU citizen is not just a national of a Member State, but a free movement citizen and a citizen who is directly and indirectly represented in the EU legislative process. Hence, EU citizenship may therefore be in a position or even imply a responsibility to contribute to any necessary changes in the fundamental rights area. This is further examined in Chap. 12.

---

[129] TEU, arts 2 and 3(2).

[130] TEU, art 3(2-3); Opinion 2/13 [2014] ECLI:EU:C:2014:2454, para 172; Case C-303/05 *Advocaten voor de Wereld* [2006] ECLI:EU:C:2006:552, Opinion of AG Ruiz-Jarabo Colomer, paras 42–45.

[131] See Sects. 10.4.2.3 and 10.5.3.4.

2.8 Concluding Remarks and the Structure of the Book

This chapter has explained two difficulties EU citizens could encounter in the AFSJ, the role of the EAW therein and the questions which they trigger in light of Articles 49 and 47 CFR. It has subsequently linked the question whether these complications should be classified as legality issues and what that would mean for the EAW to two perspectives on how the EAW can be viewed. Furthermore, it has set out what the possible consequences of both the intergovernmental or transnational perspective could be for one's view on the required fundamental rights framework in the AFSJ, the need for national or EU action to solve the complications and the role of the EAW therein, and the potential of EU citizenship as a vehicle towards more fundamental rights protection.

To answer the main research question, the next chapters examine to what extent both perspectives are currently reflected in legal practice on the EU and national level, meaning in legislation, policy and case law. In addition, they will elaborate further on the content and scope of the possible consequences of each perspective for fundamental rights, the EAW, the need for action on the EU and/or national level and the position of the EU citizen. For this purpose, Chaps. 3–8 will explore to what extent the EU and national level recognise the two complications discussed in Sects. 2.5 and 2.6, as legality problems and the EAW as a possible mechanism for enforcing jurisdiction claims violating the legality principle. Thus, these chapters provide the answer to the first part of the research question concerning the existence and recognition of foreseeability problems of jurisdiction claims and forum choices citizens may be faced with in the context of the EAW. Chapter 3 explains to what extent the two complications could fall within the scope of the *nullum crimen sine lege* principle in Article 49(1) CFR, in particular the requirement of an accessible and foreseeable law for criminal offences and sanctions, and the right to a tribunal established by law in Article 47 CFR. Chapter 4 then examines to what extent the FDEAW and complementary CJEU case law have installed protection mechanisms in case the two underlying complications occur and to what extent this protection is based on legality concerns. Chapters 5–7 comprise the studies of the national legal orders of which Chap. 5 discusses the Dutch legal system, Chap. 6 the German legal system and Chap. 7 the English legal system. Each chapter examines to what extent the two complications are recognised as legality issues in light of the applicable national legality principle. In addition, they will explore whether the complications have influenced the exercise of discretion granted to the national legislators and the competent issuing and executing authorities in the surrender procedure. The available discretion follows, for instance, from the optional nature of the refusal grounds in Article 4 FDEAW whose implementation into national law is, therefore, up to the national legislator.[132] In addition, the issuing judicial authority can be provided with

[132] However, in the implementation process the parameters set by primary EU law, such as the non-discrimination clause in Article 18 TFEU have to be obeyed. Case C-42/11 *Da Silva Jorge* [2012] ECLI:EU:C:2012:517.

discretion, since some national laws hardly regulate the issuing of an EAW.[133] The rationale behind the use of the discretion offered to the national legislators and competent authorities in the surrender procedure as well as the role of the two problems therein are examined. Does it reflect a consideration of the two complications which EU citizens may face, more specifically from a legality perspective? Chapter 8 constitutes the synthesis. On the basis of the information collected in Chaps. 3–7 it will determine to what extent the two issues are currently recognised as legality issues and the EAW as a mechanism which could enforce jurisdiction claims which violate the legality principle.

Chapter 9 provides an explanation for the conclusions drawn in Chap. 8 on the basis of the intergovernmental perspective. Chapter 10 sets out the arguments against the intergovernmental perspective on the EAW and presents the transnational perspective. The consequences which the transnational perspective can have for the legality principle and the functioning of the EAW are described in Chap. 11. Chapter 12 discusses the role EU citizenship can play with regard to fundamental rights protection and in realising the necessary legislative action on the EU level to solve the problems at hand and the role of the EAW therein. Chapter 13 answers the central research question, and it also provides specific recommendations on how the need for EU legislative action that follows from the previous chapters could best be met.

References

Anderson M, Den Boer M. Miller G (1994) European citizenship and cooperation in justice and home affairs. In: Duff A, Pinder J, Pryce R (eds) Maastricht and beyond. Building a European Union. Routledge

Biehler A et al. (eds) (2003) Freiburg proposal on concurrent jurisdictions and the prohibition of multiple prosecutions in the European Union. Max Planck Institute for Foreign and International Criminal Law

Böse M (2013) Choice of forum and jurisdiction. In: Luchtman M (ed) Choice of forum in cooperation against EU financial crime. Freedom, security and justice and the protection of specific EU-interests. Eleven International Publishing

Böse M (2014a) Fundamental freedoms of the union. In: Böse M, Meyer F, Schneider A (eds) Conflicts of jurisdiction in criminal matters in the European Union. Volume II: rights, principles and model rules. Nomos

Böse M (2014b) Fundamental rights of the EU-charter. In: Böse M, Meyer F, Schneider A (eds) Conflicts of jurisdiction in criminal matters in the European Union. Volume II: rights, principles and model rules. Nomos

Conway G (2005) Judicial interpretation and the third pillar: Ireland's acceptance of the European arrest warrant and the Gözütok and Brügge case. Eur J Crime Crim Law Crim Just 13:255

Coutts S (2014) Citizenship of the European Union. In: Arcarazo DA, Murphy C (eds) EU security and justice law: after Lisbon and Stockholm. Hart

[133] For instance, the Dutch Surrender Act hardly regulates the procedure for the issuing of an EAW. See Chap. 5.

Deen-Racsmany Z (2007) Lessons of the European arrest warrant for domestic implementation of the obligation to surrender nationals to the international criminal court. Leiden J Int Law 20:167

Editorial Comment (2008) Two-speed European citizenship? Can the Lisbon treaty help close the gap? Common Mark Law Rev 45:1

Eicker A (2005) Zur Vermeidung simultaner Strafverfahren im zwischenstaatlichen Kontext: Modell einer (über)individuell-konkreten Kriterien Gewichtung. StV 631

Erbežnik A (2012) The Prinicple of mutual recognition as a utilitarian solution, and the way forward. Eur Crim Law Rev 2:3

Eser A, Burchard C (2006) Interlokales "*ne bis in idem*" in Europa? Von "westfälischem" Souveränitätspathos zu europäischem Gemeinschaftsdenken. In: Hans-Jürgen (ed) Freiheit, Sicherheit und Recht: Festschrift für Jürgen Meyer zum 70. Geburtstag. Nomos

Eser A, Blakesly C, Lagodny O (eds) (2002) The individual as subject of international cooperation in criminal matters – a comparative study. Nomos

European Committee on Crime Problems (1990) Extraterritorial criminal jurisdiction. Strasbourg

Franken S (2013) The perspective of the defence lawyer. In: Luchtman M (ed) Choice of forum in cooperation against EU financial crime. Freedom, security and justice and the protection of specific EU-interests. Eleven International Publishing

Glerum V (2013) De weigeringsgronden bij uitlevering en overlevering – Een vergelijking en kritische evaluatie in het licht van het beginsel van wederzijdse erkenning. Wolf Legal Publishers

Gleß S (2004) Zum Prinzip der gegenseitigen Anerkennung. ZStW 116:353

Hecker B (2011) Statement: Jurisdiktionskonflikte in der EU. ZIS 6:60

Kaiafa-Gbandi M (2020) Addressing the problems of jurisdictional conflicts in criminal matters within the EU. EUcrim 209

Keijzer N (2005) The double criminality requirement. In: Blekxtoon R, van Ballegooij W (eds) Handbook on the European arrest warrant. Asser

Klimek L (2014) European arrest warrant. Springer

Klip A (2007) Case note HR 28 November 2006. NJ 489

Kraniotis T (2016) Het vertrouwensbeginsel bij de interstatelijke samenwerking in strafzaken. Kluwer

Lagodny O (2001) Empfiehlt es sich, eine europäische Gerichtskompetenz für Strafgewaltskonflikte vorzusehen? Gutachten im Auftrag des Bundesministeriums der Justiz

Luchtman M (2013) Choice of forum and the prosecution of cross-border crime in the European Union – what role for the legality principle? In: Luchtman M (ed) Choice of forum in cooperation against EU financial crime. Freedom, security and justice and the protection of specific EU-interests. Eleven International Publishing

Luchtman M (2017) Transnationale rechtshandhaving: Over fundamentele rechten in de Europese strafrechtelijke samenwerking. Boom

Luchtman M (2020) Transnational law enforcement cooperation – fundamental rights in European cooperation in criminal matters. Eur J Crime Crim Law Crim Just 28:14

Meyer F (2013) Country report Germany. In: Böse M, Meyer F, Schneider A (eds) Conflicts of jurisdiction in criminal matters in the European Union. Volume I: National Reports and comparative analysis. Nomos

Meyer F (2014) An area of freedom, security and justice. In: Böse M, Meyer F, Schneider A (eds) Conflicts of jurisdiction in criminal matters in the European Union. Volume II: rights, principles and model rules. Nomos

Meyer F, Böse M (2011) Die Beschränkung nationaler Strafgewalten als Möglichkeit zur Vermeidung von Jurisdiktionskonflikten in der Europäischen Union. ZIS 6:336

Mitsilegas V (2006) The constitutional implications of mutual recognition in criminal matters in the EU. Common Mark Law Rev 43:1277

Mitsilegas V (2012) The limits of mutual trust in Europe's area of freedom, security and justice: from automatic inter-state cooperation to the slow emergence of the individual. Yearb Eur Law 31:319

Mitsilegas V (2016) EU criminal law after Lisbon: rights, trust and the transformation of justice in Europe. Hart Publishing
Neuvonen P (2017) EU citizenship and its "very specific" essence: Rendón Marin and CS. Common Mark Law Rev 54:1201
Nic Shuibhne N (2010) The resilience of EU market citizenship. Common Mark Law Rev 47:1597
O'Leary S (2011) Free movement of persons and services. In: Craig P, de Búrca G (eds) The evolution of EU law. Oxford University Press
Ostropolski T (2015) The CJEU as a defender of mutual trust. New J Eur Crim Law 6:166
Panzavolta M (2013) Choice of forum and the lawful judge concept. In: Luchtman M (ed) Choice of forum in cooperation against EU financial crime. Freedom, security and justice and the protection of specific EU-interests. Eleven International Publishing
Peers S (2011) EU justice and home affairs law. Oxford University Press
Petrig A (2013) The expansion of Swiss criminal jurisdiction in light of international law. Utrecht Law Rev 9:34
Plachta M (2003) European arrest warrant: revolution in extradition. Eur J Crime Crim Law Crim Just 11:178
Plachta M, Van Ballegooij W (2005) The framework decision on the European arrest warrant and surrender procedures between member states of the European Union. In: Blekxtoon R, van Ballegooij W (eds) Handbook on the European arrest warrant. Asser
Satzger H (2019) Is mutual recognition a viable general path for cooperation? New J Eur Crim Law 10:44
Schönberger C (2015) Positive transnationale Jurisdiktionskonflikte – Causae, rechtliche Lösungsnotwendigkeit und -konzepte. Schulthess Verlag
Sliedregt V (2009) The dual criminality requirement. In: Keijzer N, van Sliedregt E (eds) The European arrest warrant in practice. Asser
Spencer J (2013) Mutual recognition and choice of forum. In: Luchtman M (ed) Choice of forum in cooperation against EU financial crime. Freedom, security and justice and the protection of specific EU-interests. Eleven International Publishing
Strijards G (1985) Het passief personaliteitsbeginsel. DD 15:189
Thorhauer N (2015) Conflicts of jurisdiction in cross-border criminal cases in the area of freedom, security, and justice. Risks and opportunities from an individual rights-oriented perspective. New J Eur Crim Law 6:78
Thorhauer N (2019) Jurisdiktionskonflikte im Rahmen transnationaler Kriminalität. Zur Koordination der Strafgewalten über natürliche Personen und Unternehmen in der Europäischen Union. Dike Verlag and Nomos
Van der Beken T (1999) Forumkeuze in het internationaal strafrecht. Maklu
Van der Beken T, Lagodny O, Vermeulen G (2002) Kriterien für die jeweils Strafgewalt in Europa – Zur Lösung von Strafgewaltskonflikten jenseits eines transnationalen Ne-bis-in-idem. NStZ 624
Van Eijken H, De Vries S (2011) A new route into the promised land? Being a European citizen after Ruiz Zambrano. Eur Law Rev 36:704
Van Eijken H, Marguery T (2017) the federal entrenchment of citizens in the European Union member states' criminal laws: or how EU citizenship is shaping criminal law. In: Kochenov D (ed) EU citizenship and federalism. Cambridge University Press
Van Eijken H et al (2015) The European citizen as bearer of fundamental rights in a multi-layered legal order. In: van den Brink T, Luchtman M, Scholten M (eds) Sovereignty in the shared legal order of the EU: Core values of regulation and enforcement, Intersentia
Van Sliedregt E (2007) The European arrest warrant: between trust, democracy and the rule of law: introduction. The European arrest warrant: extradition in transition. Eur Const Law Rev 3:244
Walsh D (2020) The European arrest warrant in the prosecution of extraterritorial offences: the strange case of the Irish murder, the French victim and the English suspect. Eur Law Rev 45:4

Chapter 3
The Legality Principle: Its Link to the EAW, Jurisdiction and Forum Choices

3.1 Introduction

Chapters 1 and 2 show that EU citizens travelling in the AFSJ may be confronted with certain complications, which raise questions in light of the legality principle. The EAW adds another dimension to these questions, since the actual classification of the two complications as legality issues could affect its functioning. This classification could turn the surrender procedure into an enforcement mechanism for legality violations, unless the EAW contains criteria or refusal grounds which prevent surrender in these situations. The goal of this chapter is to determine whether the two complications discussed in paragraphs 2.5 and 2.6 have been recognised as legality problems in light of the current scope of Articles 49 and 47 CFR. Chapter 4 subsequently examines to what extent the FDEAW offers safeguards against surrender in situations in which the two underlying problems occur and to what extent these safeguards were installed, because of legality concerns. As Article 52(3) CFR states that the scope and meaning of the fundamental rights and principles in the Charter follow the scope and meaning of their equivalents in the ECHR, this chapter also discusses the ECtHR case law on Articles 7(1) and 6(1) ECHR.[1] These provisions constitute the counterparts of respectively the *nullum crimen sine lege* principle in Article 49(1) CFR and the right to a tribunal established by law in Article 47(2) CFR.[2]

The discussion of the matter to what extent unforeseeable jurisdiction claims and forum choices are currently recognised as legality problems in light of Articles 49 and 47 CFR, needs to be preceded by the preliminary question to what extent

[1] Case C-72/15 *Rosneft* [2017] ECLI:EU:C:2017:236, para 165.

[2] Explanations relating to the Charter of Fundamental Rights [2007] OJ C303/17, p. 34. The wording of Article 49 CFR, matches the wording of Article 7(1) ECHR, except for the last sentence, which codifies the *lex mitior* principle. Article 47(2) CFR and 6(1) ECHR show a small difference as well, since the former states that the tribunal should be 'previously' established by law.

J. Graat, *The European Arrest Warrant and EU Citizenship*,
https://doi.org/10.1007/978-3-031-07590-2_3

these problems or situations fall within the scope of application of the CFR. According to Article 51(1) CFR, the Charter solely addresses the Member States when they implement EU law, which is definitely the case when the national rules implementing the FDEAW are applied.[3] However, since this research focuses on the role of the surrender procedure in relation to two problems which exist independent of the EAW, it is no certainty that the EAW can bring the national jurisdiction rules or other national measures that constitute the foundation of these problems within the scope of the Charter of Fundamental Rights. In other words, the question is whether the two underlying problems can be brought within the scope of the CFR via the surrender procedure or the underlying national criminal procedure dealing with the merits of the case in the issuing state. In this light, Sect. 3.2 first explores whether the EAW can bring the two problems within the scope of application of the CFR and, therefore, whether the existence of a link between these problems and Articles 47 and 49 CFR can be assessed in the context of the surrender procedure itself. Afterwards, it examines whether in the context of the national criminal case in the issuing state EU law offers possibilities for bringing the national rules on jurisdiction or the decision to prosecute that constitute the foundation of the two underlying problems within the scope of application of the CFR.

In case the CFR is applicable in either the surrender procedure or the national criminal case, the question can be posed to what extent unforeseeable jurisdiction claims and forum choices are problematic for EU citizens in light of the legality principle in Articles 47 and 49 CFR, more specifically the right to foreseeable criminal offences, sanctions and tribunals. This question is addressed in Sects. 3.3 and 3.4. Section 3.3 discusses the substantive or material legality principle, also referred to as the *nullum crimen, nulla poena sine lege* principle, in Article 49(1) CFR. It focuses in particular on the requirement that criminal offences and sanctions are based on an accessible and foreseeable law. First, the section explains that the CJEU and ECtHR do not recognise a direct link between the substantive legality principle and the EAW. In other words, the surrender procedure does not fall within the scope of this principle. The section then examines to what extent the right to a foreseeable and accessible law for criminal offences and sanctions is influenced by the foreseeability of the application of national criminal laws at the time of the offence.

Section 3.4 conducts a similar examination in relation to the right to a tribunal previously established by law. It explores to what extent forum decisions in cross-border cases made by national authorities, such as public prosecutors fall within the scope of Article 47(2) CFR. To put it differently, it answers the question whether Article 47 CFR demands that forum decisions in the AFSJ are regulated by law and, if so, to what extent discretion may then be granted to the executive or judicial branches of the Member States? As stated before, an affirmative answer to this question and the one regarding Article 49 CFR could have consequences for the EAW, potentially classifying it as an enforcement mechanism for jurisdiction claims

[3] Case C-414/20 *MM* [2021] ECLI:EU:C:2021:4, para 71.

that are incompatible with fundamental right standards. Section 3.5 provides the conclusion.

3.2 The Scope of Application of the Charter

3.2.1 Four Categories of National Rules and Measures

The EU Charter of Fundamental Rights became a binding instrument and part of primary EU law when the Treaty of Lisbon entered into force. The outer boundaries of the scope of this instrument are set by Article 6(1) TEU and Article 51(2) CFR, from which it follows that the provisions of the Charter may not extend the current competences of the Union provided by the treaties or establish new ones. The CFR applies to acts of EU institutions, bodies, offices and agencies and addresses the Member States when they are implementing Union law.[4] In relation to the latter, the CJEU has decided that the Charter addresses the Member States when they act within the scope of Union law.[5]

The legal literature describes four categories of national measures and situations which fall within the scope of the CFR of which the first two are the most important ones in relation to the situations discussed in this book.[6] The first category covers national measures that implement specific EU obligations and in that light, the Member States act as agents of the EU.[7] This category will hereafter be referred to as 'the legislation route'. The second category covers national measures which impede upon free movement rights and in relation to which the Member States rely on a justification ground provided by EU law.[8] The third category covers enforcement measures of which the case *Åkerberg Fransson* constitutes an example.[9] In this case the CJEU decided that the national measures on which a tax penalty and criminal proceedings for tax evasion were founded fell within the scope of Union law, even though they were not adopted to transpose Directive 2006/112 on the common system of value added tax. The CJEU concluded that the purpose of these national measures was to penalise violations of that Directive and, therefore,

---

[4] The CFR has the same scope of application as the general principles of Union law. CFR, art 51(1). Explanations relating to the Charter of Fundamental Rights [2007] OJ C303/17, p. 32; Case C-5/88 *Wachauf* [1989] ECLI:EU:C:1989:321; Case C-260/89 *ERT* [1991] ECLI: EU:C:1991:254. See also Case C-198/13 *Hernández* [2014] ECLI:EU:C:2014:2055, para 33.

[5] Case C-617/10 *Åklagaren v Åkerberg Fransson* [2013] ECLI:EU:C:2013:105, paras 19–20. See also Case C-483/12 *Pelckmans* [2014] ECLI:EU:C:2014:304, para 18.

[6] Hanneke van Eijken et al. (2015), pp. 256–257. For a similar categorization see Hancox (2013), pp. 1418–1421.

[7] Hanneke van Eijken et al. (2015), p. 257.

[8] Hanneke van Eijken et al. (2015), pp. 257–260.

[9] Case C-617/10 *Åklagaren v Åkerberg Fransson* [2013] ECLI:EU:C:2013:105, paras 19–20; Hanneke van Eijken et al. (2015), pp. 263–265.

they aimed to implement the enforcement obligations imposed on the Member States by Article 325 TFEU.[10] The fourth and most recently developed category is the one in which EU citizens have not exercised their free movement rights, but national measures threaten to deny them 'the genuine enjoyment of the substance of the rights conferred by virtue of their status as citizens of the Union'.[11] In the case *Dereci*, the CJEU has adopted a very limited interpretation of this category, since the national measure in question needs to force the EU citizen to leave the territory of the European Union altogether.[12] Only when this *Dereci* criterion is fulfilled does the situation fall under the scope of EU law and, by extension, the Charter.[13]

The next sections discuss to what extent the first two categories can bring national rules establishing the scope of application of national substantive criminal laws and national rules on the decision to prosecute, which constitute the foundation of the two problems discussed, within the scope of application of the CFR.[14] In relation to the first route, the examination includes the possibilities offered by EU rules covering the surrender procedure and EU rules on jurisdiction and forum choices, which affect the national criminal procedure in the issuing state.

3.2.2 *The Legislation Route*

3.2.2.1 Introduction

As stated above, the first category covers national measures or actions implementing obligations imposed by EU law. This includes the implementation of Treaty obligations like the competition rules in Articles 101 and 102 TFEU and national measures implementing or transposing framework decisions and directives, as well as their subsequent application.[15] It also follows from the CJEU case law that national legislation or national measures only fall within the scope of Union law if they have a sufficiently strong link with EU law, meaning that there needs to exist 'a certain degree of connection above and beyond the matters covered being closely related or one of these matters having indirect impact on the other'.[16] Whether this is the case depends on several factors among them 'whether that legislation is intended

[10] Case C-617/10 *Åklagaren v Åkerberg Fransson* [2013] ECLI:EU:C:2013:105, paras 27–28.

[11] Case C-34/09 *Ruiz Zambrano* [2011] ECLI:EU:C:2011:124, para 42. See Sect. 2.2.

[12] Case C-256/11 *Dereci* [2011] ECLI:EU:C:2011:734, para 66.

[13] In *Chavez-Vilchez* the post-*Zambrano* line of case law took an interesting turn. The CJEU determined that the right to family life in Article 7 of the Charter can play a role when determining whether in a concrete situation the *Dereci* criterion is fulfilled. Case C-133/15 *Chavez-Vilchez* [2017] ECLI:EU:C:2017:354.

[14] The third and fourth category are not relevant. The fourth category is currently also limited to national measures which remove the EU citizen from the territory of the EU.

[15] Hanneke van Eijken et al. (2015), p. 257.

[16] Case C-206/13 *Siragusa* [2014] ECLI:EU:C:2014:126, para 24.

to implement a provision of EU law; the nature of that legislation and whether it pursues objectives other than those covered by EU law, even if it is capable of indirectly affecting EU law; and also whether there are specific rules of EU law on the matter or capable of affecting it'.[17] In its case law, the CJEU often considers the similarity between the purpose of the national rule and the EU provision, and the question whether EU law—either the treaties or secondary law—imposes an obligation on the Member States in the situation at hand.[18] In addition, in the case *TSN* the CJEU stated that 'Where the provisions of EU law in the area concerned do not govern an aspect of a given situation and do not impose any specific obligation on the Member States with regard thereto, the national rule enacted by a Member State as regards that aspect falls outside the scope of the Charter and the situation concerned cannot be assessed in light of the provisions of the Charter.'[19]

3.2.2.2 The FDEAW

Section 3.1 already mentioned that the answer to the question whether the EAW can bring problems regarding national rules on criminal jurisdiction and forum decisions within the scope of application of the CFR is not clear-cut, since the EAW is in fact 'merely' an additional dimension to the problem of unforeseeable jurisdiction claims and forum choices without a transparent legal basis in case of conflicts of jurisdiction. This is best illustrated with an example. Imagine a situation in which Erica, a Dutch national, is accused of assaulting a Bulgarian national during his holiday in Rotterdam. Bulgaria subsequently issues an EAW for Erica to the Netherlands. In this scenario, the two complications can occur, since Erica may be surprised by the application of Bulgarian criminal law and Bulgaria has not been appointed on the basis of a clear set of rules as the most appropriate forum in light of the proper

[17] Case C-206/13 *Siragusa* [2014] ECLI:EU:C:2014:126, para 25. See also Case C-87/12 *Ymeraga* [2013] ECLI:EU:C:2013:291, para 41.

[18] It is not sufficient that the situation simply falls within the competences of the EU. Case C-206/13 *Siragusa* [2014] ECLI:EU:C:2014:126, paras 26–28; Case C-144/95 *Jean-Louis Maurin* [1996] ECLI:EU:C:1996:235, paras 11–13; Case C-198/13 *Hernandez* [2014] ECLI:EU:C:2014:2055, paras 35–36, 41.

[19] Joined Cases C-609/17 & C-610/17 *TSN* [2019] ECLI:EU:C:2019:981, para 53. See also Case C-198/13 *Hernández* [2014] ECLI:EU:C:2014:2055, para 35; Case C-333/13 *Dano* [2014] ECLI:EU:C:2014:2358, paras 35–44, 85, 89–91. The case *Dano* concerned a Romanian national whose application for certain benefits, classified as special non-contributory cash benefits, was refused by the German authorities. The referring German court asked whether Articles 1, 20 and 51 CFR require that the Member States set certain conditions concerning the grant of such benefits or whether they may decide to limit the grant of the fund for the purpose of return to the home state. The special non-contributory benefits in question have been the subject of EU legislation, including Regulation 883/2004, but this instrument and all other secondary EU legislation for that matter lack specific rules concerning the conditions creating the right to the benefit. Consequently, the CJEU stated that it did not have jurisdiction to answer the question, since the situation did not fall within the scope of the Charter. In other words, the Member States 'are not implementing EU law' when they adopt and apply conditions concerning the grant of the benefits.

administration of justice. The reason for the doubts as to whether the rules of the surrender procedure—either the Dutch rules on the execution of the EAW or the Bulgarian law on the issuing of the EAW—bring this situation (including the two complications) within the scope of the Charter, is based on the decision of the CJEU in the *TSN* case.[20] As explained before, the CJEU has stated in this case that when the provisions of EU law do not govern certain aspects of a particular situation, the national rules covering this aspect fall outside the scope of the Charter and 'the situation concerned cannot be assessed in light of the provisions of the Charter'.[21]

With regard to the matter of unforeseeable jurisdiction claims, the Bulgarian rules on jurisdiction are the cause of the difficulty to foresee the applicability of Bulgarian criminal law at the time of the offence and not the FDEAW itself or the national measures implementing it. In fact, the FDEAW does not address the Member States jurisdiction to prescribe and therefore neither do the national implementation laws. Consequently, in light of the *TSN* ruling, the conclusion in Erica's case could be that the FDEAW does not govern an important aspect of the situation, which is the matter of jurisdiction, as a result of which the case falls outside the scope of the CFR.

With regard to the fact that Bulgaria exercises jurisdiction, even though it is not appointed as the most appropriate forum for prosecution on the basis of a clear set of rules which ensures forum choices in light of the proper administration of justice, a similar conclusion can be drawn, since the FDEAW is not an instrument for forum choices. Some of its provisions indirectly touch upon the matter of forum choices, but none of the rules and conditions directly address the Member States' jurisdiction to adjudicate or forum choices in cross-border cases. The indirect influence which some of the conditions in the FDEAW can have on forum choices is, for instance, illustrated by Article 4(2) FDEAW, which allows the executing judicial authority to refuse the EAW in case of domestic criminal proceedings for the same offence.[22] This refusal ground lacks a direct link to forum decisions, because its application does not force the issuing state to cease its criminal proceedings. However, in practice this is the influence which Article 4(2) FDEAW could have in a concrete case, because the absence of the suspect on the territory of the issuing state can complicate its criminal proceedings.[23] Hence, the application of this refusal grounds could *de facto* settle a conflict of jurisdiction by hindering the prosecution in the issuing state. More examples of conditions for the issuing and execution of an EAW which can indirectly influence forum decisions are further discussed in Sect. 4.2.1. In light of the *TSN* case, it can be argued that it is unlikely that these conditions can bring the problems relating to forum decisions within the scope of the Charter. The

[20] See also the discussion on the limits of the CJEU's competences to protect the rule of law and the role of the preliminary procedure therein. Van Elsuwege and Gremmelprez (2020).

[21] Joined Cases C-609/17 & C-610/17 *TSN* [2019] ECLI:EU:C:2019:981, para 53. See also Case C-198/13 *Hernández* [2014] ECLI:EU:C:2014:2055, para 35; Case C-333/13 *Dano* [2014] ECLI:EU:C:2014:2358, paras 35–44, 85, 89–91.

[22] See Sect. 4.2.1.

[23] Herrnfeld (2013), p. 191.

national rules on the exercise of jurisdiction to prosecute a case do not show a degree of connection to the FDEAW that goes beyond anindirect one, as required by the CJEU case law.

However, in the case *AB* the CJEU considered, what is in my opinion, an indirect link between the EAW procedure and national criminal procedural rules sufficient for the case to fall within the scope of the CFR.[24] The case *AB* concerned a situation in which criminal prosecutions against certain suspects were resumed after an amendment to the Slovakian Constitution had resulted in a resolution revoking the amnesty covering their offences. The referring court intended to issue a European arrest warrant, but decided to first ask the CJEU whether issuing an EAW in this situation would be in compliance with the *ne bis in idem* principle in Article 50 CFR. The first part of the ruling addresses the jurisdiction of the CJEU. The Slovak Government argued that the CJEU did not have jurisdiction, since EU law does not govern adoptions and revocations of amnesties. Hence, the case did not fall within the scope of application of the CFR.

Contrary to the Slovak government, the CJEU decided that the case did fall within the scope of the CFR, since the preliminary question did not cover the interpretation of the national offenses or rules on amnesty as such. Instead, the preliminary question covered the interpretation of article 50 CFR 'in the context of the procedure for issuing a European arrest warrant'. The CJEU concluded that the answer to the question on the interpretation of article 50 CFR in relation to the national rules and decisions on amnesty affected the procedure for issuing an EAW. Hence, since the referring court asked the preliminary question in the specific context of the decision to issue an EAW, the CJEU decided that the CFR was applicable. The CJEU also dismissed the argument that the issuing judicial authority was not (yet) implementing EU law, since no EAW had been issued yet. The CJEU stated that the referring court posed the preliminary question to ensure that any decision to issue an EAW would comply with the obligations following from the FDEAW, such as the protection of the right to effective judicial protection.[25]

In my view this preliminary ruling shows a more lenient interpretation of the conditions for brining a case within the scope of application of the CFR. No direct link exists between the conditions for issuing an EAW and the national rules on amnesty. The provisions of the FDEAW regarding the issuing procedure do not touch upon the adoption and revocation of amnesties. However, the fact that the decision to issue an EAW is influenced by the preliminary question concerning rules on amnesty is sufficient to bring this case within the scope of the CFR. Hence, in my opinion, the preliminary ruling implicitly connects the decision to issue an EAW to national rules which define and limit the power to prosecute a case. On a more general level, the preliminary ruling seems to suggest that a serious intention to issue an EAW is sufficient to bring questions on the compliance of different aspects of the decision to prosecute with fundamental rights within the scope of the Charter. This

[24] Case C-203/20 *AB and others* [2021] ECLI:EU:C:2021:1016.

[25] Case C-203/20 *AB and others* [2021] ECLI:EU:C:2021:1016, paras 40–42, 52.

would mean that since the decision to issue an EAW is also inherently connected to the issuing state's jurisdiction to prosecute and adjudicate, the compliance of the jurisdictionclaim with the legality principe in article 49 and 47 CFR could also be viewed as a question posed 'in the context of the issuing procedure'.

It follows from the above that on the one hand the case *AB* seems to open the door for the issuing procedure to bring questions concerning the legality of national jurisdiction claims within the scope of the CFR. On the other hand, the case *AB* exclusively focuses on the triangular link between article 50 CFR, national rules on amnesty and the issuing procedure. In addition, the CJEU case law has consistently stated that cases fall within the scope of application of the CFR when there is a sufficiently strong link with EU law, meaning a link which goes beyond the direct impact of one matter on the other.[26] In light of this general rule, it is uncertain whether the EAW would be sufficient to bring the question of the EAW as a possible enforcement mechanism of unforeseeable jurisdiction claims and forum decisions within the scope of application of the CFR. As stated before, the provisions of the FDEAW do not directly address jurisdiction and forum decisions. Hence, the FDEAW may not show a sufficiently strong connection to national rules on jurisdiction and the decision to prosecute to bring the foreseeability problems within the scope of the Charter.

So, it remains uncertain to what extent the EAW can bring the national jurisdiction rules and other national measures that constitute the foundation of the foreseeability problems within the scope of the Charter of Fundamental Rights. In this light, the next section examines the possibility to bring the two underlying problems relating to criminal jurisdiction and forum decisions within the scope of the CFR via the national criminal procedure in the issuing state in which different EU rules could apply which directly address the matters of jurisdiction and forum decisions.

3.2.2.3 EU Rules on Jurisdiction and Forum Choices

This section discusses the secondary EU legislative measures which directly address the Member States' jurisdiction to prescribe and adjudicate as well as situations of conflicts of jurisdiction. The argument can be made that in the national criminal procedure dealing with the merits of the case, the problems regarding the foreseeability of the jurisdiction claim of the issuing state and forum choices could fall within the scope of the CFR, because the applicable national jurisdiction rules and rules addressing conflicts of jurisdiction have a direct link to EU legislative measures specifically regulating these matters.

With regard to the matter of unforeseeable jurisdiction claims, this can be illustrated by the hypothetical situation in which Germany receives an EAW from the Netherlands for the purpose of prosecuting a Dutch national for acts of terrorism committed in Germany. This case concerns a criminal act which is subject to EU

[26] Case C-206/13 *Siragusa* [2014] ECLI:EU:C:2014:126, paras 24–25.

legislation, namely Directive 2017/541 on combatting terrorism.[27] Article 19(1)(c) of this Directive obliges each Member State to establish jurisdiction to prosecute its own nationals for acts committed abroad. Hence, in this case, the extension of the scope of application of the Dutch criminal law, more specifically the crime of terrorism, to Dutch nationals who commit this crime abroad is directly linked to EU minimum harmonisation measures for criminal offences and sanctions, which could bring the case within the scope of the CFR. Still, this route to bring unforeseeable jurisdiction claims within the scope of the Charter is limited, because the Member States jurisdiction to prescribe is not addressed in a general EU instrument. Instead, the EU harmonisation measures adopted on the basis of, for instance, Article 83 TFEU only set out the jurisdiction rules for a specific criminal offence, such as terrorism or category of criminal offences.

Important examples of EU secondary measures which address forum choices are Framework Decision 2009/948 on conflicts of jurisdiction, which is an instrument that generally addresses positive conflicts of jurisdiction, and Articles 26(4) and 36(3) of the EPPO Regulation.[28] When the EPPO becomes operational the main rule is that a case will be handled by the European delegated prosecutor from the Member State where the focus of the criminal activities is or the Member State where the bulk of the offences has been committed. Exceptions to this rule are possible when they are duly justified and based on the hierarchical list of criteria in Article 26(4). Besides these two main examples, some EU instruments harmonising criminal offences, such as the previously mentioned Directive 2017/541 on combatting terrorism include provisions on the exercise of jurisdiction in case of positive conflicts of jurisdiction.[29] This particular Directive encourages Member States to centralise the case in one state and provides criteria which should guide the forum decision. Consequently, the national rules implementing these specific provisions of the terrorism Directive as well as Framework Decision 2009 on conflicts of jurisdiction are most likely applicable in the hypothetical scenario in which the Netherlands receives a German EAW for a Dutch national, who is accused of committing acts of terrorism in Germany. These national implementation rules can, therefore, pull the aspect of forum decisions in this case within the scope of application of the Charter.

[27] Directive (EU) 2017/541 of the European Parliament and of the Council of 15 March 2017 on combating terrorism and replacing Council Framework Decision 2002/475/JHA and amending Council Decision 2005/671/JHA [2017] OJ L88/6.

[28] Council Regulation (EU) 2017/1939 of 12 October 2017 implementing enhanced cooperation on the establishment of the European Public Prosecutor's Office [2017] OJ L283/1.

[29] Directive (EU) 2017/541 of the European Parliament and of the Council of 15 March 2017 on combating terrorism and replacing Council Framework Decision 2002/475/JHA and amending Council Decision 2005/671/JHA [2017] OJ L88/6, art 19(3).

3.2.3 *The Free Movement Route*

3.2.3.1 National Derogation Measures and Their Justification

The second category of national measures that can fall within the scope of EU law and, therefore, within the scope of the CFR are those which derogate from free movement rights of EU citizens.[30] It follows from the CJEU case law that fundamental rights are applicable in the process of justifying a national measure considered incompatible with one of the free movement rights. This is illustrated by the case *ERT* concerning a Greek law that restricted broadcasting and established a television monopoly, which clashed with the free movement of services.[31] The CJEU ruled that the justification grounds for such national measures provided by the treaties—public policy, public security and public health—have to be interpreted in conformity with fundamental rights as general principle of EU law.[32]

Another example is the case *Carpenter* which concerned the deportation order of a third-country national, Mrs. Carpenter, the spouse of an EU citizen, from the UK.[33] The court ruled that this national measure interfered with Mr. Carpenter's right to provide services in other states and that the possibility for the UK to rely on reasons of public interest to justify the deportation order was dependent on its compliance with fundamental rights.[34] After deciding that the deportation order in fact constituted a violation of the right to family life, the CJEU assessed the existence of a fair balance between respect for this fundamental right and the maintenance of UK immigration laws for the purpose of public security and public order in light of the proportionality principle. It concluded that considering the specific circumstances of the case the UK deportation measure was a disproportionate infringement of the right to family life. Consequently, it was precluded on the basis of the right to free movement of services as read in light of the right to family life.[35]

Hence, it follows from the CJEU case law that when a Member State relies on a justification ground provided by the treaty or the rule of reason[36] to justify national measures interfering with free movement, the justification must be interpreted in conformity with the general principles of EU law and the fundamental rights guaranteed by the Charter. This entails that in the context of the EU requirements for the justification of a national measure obstructing the right to free movement, the

---

[30] Van Eijken et al. (2015), pp. 258–260; Prechal et al. (2011), p. 217; Case C-390/12 *Pfleger* [2013] ECLI:EU:C:2013:747, Opinion of AG Sharpston, para 46.

[31] Case C-260/89 *ERT* [1991] ECLI: EU:C:1991:254.

[32] Case C-260/89 *ERT* [1991] ECLI: EU:C:1991:254, paras 43–45.

[33] Case C-60/00 *Carpenter* [2002] ECLI:EU:C:2002:434.

[34] Case C-60/00 *Carpenter* [2002] ECLI:EU:C:2002:434, paras 39–40.

[35] Case C-60/00 *Carpenter* [2002] ECLI:EU:C:2002:434, paras 41–46.

[36] The CJEU has determined that national rules interfering with free movement can also be justified on the basis of overriding reasons in the public or general interests as long as they are independent of the nationality of the persons concerned. Joined Cases C-11/06 & C-12/06 *Morgan* [2007] ECLI: EU:C:2007:626, para 33; Case C-220/12 *Meneses* [2013] ECLI:EU:C:2013:683, para 29.

national measure needs to comply with EU fundamental rights.[37] In the case *Pfleger*, the CJEU explicitly connected this obligation to the scope of application of the Charter. More specifically, it stated that Member States implement Union law in the sense of Article 51(1) CFR when they rely on an exception provided by the treaties or the rule of reason to justify a national measure interfering with one of the free movement rights.[38]

It follows from the above that the free movement route can bring the difficulties for EU citizens to foresee the applicable national criminal laws at the time of the offence and the risk of arbitrary forum decisions due to the absence of a clear overarching system appointing the most suitable national jurisdiction for prosecution and trial within the scope of application of the Charter. This is the case when the national measures and actions that are at the foundation of these problems constitute an impediment to one of the free movement rights and the Member States need to rely on a justification ground provided by EU law. Such national measures or rules are most likely jurisdiction rules determining the scope of applicability of a particular national substantive criminal law and national rules on the prosecution of specific cases. More concretely, in the situation in which Bulgaria prosecutes a Dutch national accused of assaulting a Bulgarian national in France, the Bulgarian rule establishing the extraterritorial scope of Bulgarian criminal law on the basis of the passive nationality principle and the Bulgarian rules regarding the jurisdiction to adjudicate need to constitute obstructions to free movement to bring them within the scope of the Charter.

So far, the CJEU has not yet had the opportunity to rule on the question whether unforeseeable jurisdiction claims and forum choices in the absence of a clear system of case allocations restrict free movement rights. In that light, the next paragraphs first describe the conditions set out in the CJEU case law for determining whether a national measure or action constitutes an obstruction or interference with one of the free movement rights. Afterwards, they explore to what extent national rules on jurisdiction and the decision to prosecute which can cause the difficulties for EU citizens can be classified as such in light of the existing case law on barriers to free movement.[39]

---

[37] Case C-260/89 *ERT* [1991] ECLI:EU:C:1991:254, para 43; Case C-390/12 *Pfleger* [2014] ECLI:EU:C:2014:281, paras 35–36; Case C-368/95 *Familiapress* [1997] ECLI:EU:C:1997:325, paras 24–27; Joined Cases C-482/01 & C-493/01 *Orfanopoulos and Oliveri* [2004] ECLI:EU:C:2004:262, para 97.

[38] Case C-390/12 *Pfleger* [2014] ECLI:EU:C:2014:281, para 36. See also Case C-390/12 *Pfleger* [2013] ECLI:EU:C:2013:747, Opinion of AG Sharpston, para 46.

[39] Unless it is stated differently, the next section discusses the different free movement rights together. In other words, it does not discuss the economic free movement rights, such as the free movement of services and the free movement of workers and the free movement right in Article 21 TFEU separately.

3.2.3.2 The Legal Framework to Assess Possible Obstacles to Free Movement: The Disadvantage Criterion and Criterion of Serious Inconveniences

In its early case law, the CJEU primarily connected the right to free movement to the prohibition of direct and indirect discrimination on the basis of nationality in Article 18 TFEU.[40] In this context it has, for instance, ruled that national rules which exclusively protect a state's own nationals against extradition to third states can constitute impediments to free movement.[41] However, over the course of time the CJEU has moved towards a general prohibition of national rules or actions which restrict or constitute an obstacle to one of the free movement rights.[42] This general prohibition includes discriminatory and non-discriminatory rules and is addressed to both the host state and the home state of the moving EU citizen. Neither state may adopt measures which are liable to deter or dissuade EU citizens from exercising their free movement rights to pursue economic or non-economic activities in other Member States. This obstacle or restriction criterion, for instance, covers national rules which set residence requirements for the receipt of certain monetary benefits and can, therefore, dissuade nationals of that state from exercising their free movement rights. One example is the case *Tas-Hagen*, in which the CJEU decided that Dutch rules which made the receipt of a civilian war victim's benefit dependent upon residence within the Netherlands at the time of the application were liable to dissuade Dutch nationals from exercising their right to move to and reside in another Member State.[43]

The case law of the CJEU shows two different overarching criteria on the basis of which national jurisdiction rules could possibly fall under the general prohibition of national rules obstructing free movement. These are the 'disadvantage' criterion and the criterion of 'serious inconveniences'.[44] The former means that the CJEU makes a comparison between the situation of the static and the moving EU citizen and assesses whether the exercise of free movement rights places the EU citizen at a

[40] Case C-85/96 *Martinez Sala* [1998] ECLI:EU:C:1998:217, paras 62–64; Case C-184/99 *Grzelczyk* [2001] ECLI:EU:C:2001:458, paras 30–34. It follows from these cases that the prohibition of discrimination on grounds of nationality applies once an EU citizen has moved to another Member State and lawfully resides there.

[41] Case C-182/15 *Petruhhin* [2016] ECLI:EU:C:2016:630; Case C-191/16 *Pisciotti* [2018] ECLI:EU:C:2018:222.

[42] Case C-406/04 *Cuyper* [2006] ECLI:EU:C:2006:491, para 39; Case C-353/06 *Grunkin and Paul* [2008] ECLI:EU:C:2008:559, para 21; Case C-192/05 *Tas-Hagen* [2006] ECLI:EU:C:2006:676, paras 17–32. See also Joined Cases C-11/06 & C-12/06 *Morgan* [2007] ECLI:EU:C:2007:626, paras 18–31; Barnard (2016), p. 356; 'Two-speed European Citizenship? Can the Lisbon Treaty help close the gap?' (2008), p. 1; Van Eijken et al. (2015), p. 259.

[43] Case C-192/05 *Tas-Hagen* [2006] ECLI:EU:C:2006:676, para 30. See also Joined Cases C-11/06 & C-12/06 *Morgan* [2007] ECLI:EU:C:2007:626, paras 18–31.

[44] Some legal scholars also argue that some jurisdiction grounds constitute an interference with the prohibition of discrimination on the basis of nationality. See Böse (2014a).

disadvantage.[45] This disadvantage criterion is, for instance, applied in cases in which the national law of the home state of the moving EU citizen imposes residence requirements or other conditions for financial benefits which discourage the EU citizen from leaving the home state.[46]

The Disadvantage Criterion

When comparing the situation of a moving EU citizen and an EU citizen who is not moving, also referred to as a static EU citizen, national jurisdiction rules establishing the scope of applicability of a state's national criminal law and national rules regarding the decision to prosecute a particular case may not be classified as interferences with Article 21 TFEU or one of the economic free movement rights.[47] This is because both a non-moving Dutch national and a moving German national who are accused of assaulting a Bulgarian national in the Netherlands can be prosecuted by Bulgaria on the basis of the passive nationality principle and be surrendered to this state by the Amsterdam District Court. In other words, EU citizens who have never left their home state and are confronted with moving EU citizens might just as well be prosecuted by a state whose jurisdiction claim they could not foresee at the time of the offence and which is not appointed as the best national jurisdiction for prosecution and trial on the basis of a clear system for case allocations. Even though the risk of the occurrence of these problems may be higher for moving EU citizens, they are not inextricably linked to free movement. It is therefore questionable whether the national

[45] However, the case law on the free movement of workers offers a possibility to work around the 'disadvantage' criterion. In this line of case law national rules which hamper access to the employment market of another Member State have been classified as prohibited impediments to free movement, even though the rules negatively affect both static EU citizens and moving EU citizens. In *Bosman*, the CJEU decided that the obligatory payment of a transfer fee for a professional football player to the old club restricts the free movement of workers, despite the fact that this transfer fee applies in case of transfers between clubs within the same Member State and the transfer to a club in another Member State. Hence, the rule on transfer fees was equally disadvantageous to those exercising their free movement rights and those who did not, but the fact that this rule could *also* directly affect the access of football players to the employment market of another Member State was sufficient to classify it as an obstacle to free movement. This broad 'restrictions' or 'obstacles' rule has also been referred to as the 'market access' approach, as it includes national rules that block access to the employment market. To ensure that this obstacle rule does not become all-embracing and prohibit all national rules which in one way or another affect access to the employment market, the CJEU has set certain thresholds. Case C-415/93 *Bosman* [1995] ECLI:EU:C:1995:463, paras 98–100, 103. See also Case C-515/14 *European Commission v Republic of Cyprus* [2016] ECLI:EU:C:2016:30, para 47; Case C-187/15 *Pöpperl* [2016] ECLI:EU:C:2016:550, para 28; Case C-190/98 *Graf* [2000] ECLI:EU:C:2000:49; Barnard and Peers (2017), p. 396.

[46] Chalmers et al. (2014), p. 486.

[47] In this light, the Conclusion of AG Bobek in *Krah* is also interesting. In relation to free movement of workers, he states that 'although perhaps not always explicitly examined, there is still some sort of comparability and differentiation analysis going on in cases in which only restriction to the free movement of workers is being assessed. Thus, the case law of the Court does not support the proposition that the logic of obstacles to free movement is to be cut loose entirely from considerations of discrimination. There still is, in all of the cases analysed in this section, some sort of difference in treatment. But what exactly is then supposed to be analysed under the heading of obstacles?' Case C-703/17 *Krah* [2019] ECLI:EU:C:2019:450, Opinion AG Bobek, para 74.

jurisdiction rules actually place the moving EU citizen at a strong enough disadvantage in comparison to the static EU citizen to conclude that the rules are precluded on the basis of the right to free movement.

The Serious Inconveniences Criterion

The serious inconveniences criterion has been consistently applied in the case law regarding the composition of surnames and is not based on a comparison between the moving and non-moving EU citizen. The main point is that discrepancies in surnames on official documents, such as a passport and birth certificate as a result of diverging national rules on the composition of surnames, can cause doubts about the identity of EU citizens which can result in impracticalities in their daily lives.[48] The case *Grunkin Paul* is a clear example in which the criterion of serious inconveniences is applied. It concerned a German national born in Denmark who had resided there all his life. His surname on the Danish birth certificate was a combination of the last names of his parents, but Germany—his state of nationality—refused to put the composite surname on his passport, as this was not allowed under German law. The CJEU decided that this refusal constituted an impediment to free movement, since discrepancies in surnames on official documents will raise doubts about identity. In other words, this refusal on the basis of the German law was liable to cause serious inconveniences in the personal and professional life of the EU citizen when remaining in his home state—Denmark—or when moving to another EU Member State, such as his state of nationality.[49]

Different positions can be taken with regard to the question whether national rules establishing extraterritorial jurisdiction or regulating the decision to prosecute restrict the right to free movement, because they cause serious inconveniences in the professional and private life of the EU citizen. On the one hand, the CJEU has stated in its case law that the restrictive effects or impact of national measures on free movement may not be too indirect or uncertain or depend on future or hypothetical events.[50] In that light, one can be of the opinion that it is uncertain whether national rules establishing extraterritorial jurisdiction and regulating the decision to exercise extraterritorial jurisdiction in concrete cases can be classified as measures that are liable to hamper free movement. As mentioned in the discussion of the disadvantage criterion, the problems and serious inconveniences that could arise from the national rules in question are not inextricably linked to free movement, since they can also occur without the exercise of free movement as well. In addition, it can be argued that whether a moving EU citizen will actually be confronted with the negative effects of national jurisdiction rules often depends on hypothetical and future circumstances, such as who the EU citizen will meet, whether the national criminal

[48] Case C-148/02 *Garcia Avello* [2003] ECLI:EU:C:2003:539, para 36.

[49] Case C-353/06 *Grunkin and Paul* [2008] ECLI:EU:C:2008:559, paras 21–28. See also Case C-208/09 *Ilonka Sayn-Wittgenstein* [2010] ECLI:EU:C:2010:806, paras 52–71.

[50] Case C-190/98 *Graf* [2000] ECLI:EU:C:2000:49, paras 24–25; Case C-437/17 *Gemeinsamer Betriebsrat EurothermenResort Bad Schallerbach* [2019] ECLI:E:C:2019:193, para 40; Case C-483/12 *Pelckmans* [2014] ECLI:EU:C:2014:304, para 25; Case C-40/11 *Iida* [2012] ECLI:EU:C:2012:691, para 77.

law of the prosecuting state has a higher maximum sanction for the crime in question than another competent state, what the prosecution policy of states is in case of extraterritorial crimes etc. Hence, the impact of national rules regulating jurisdiction and the decision to prosecute on free movement can be viewed as quite uncertain and indirect.[51]

On the other hand, legal scholars like Böse and Meyer take different positions. The former has stated that extraterritorial jurisdiction claims can cause inconveniences that are at least equal to the inconveniences caused by diverging national rules on the composition of names. He argues that moving to the Member State with an extraterritorial jurisdiction claim will subject the EU citizen to the risk of criminal prosecution, which goes hand in hand with the risk of violations of the right to liberty and privacy, for behaviour that occurred in another state. These risks can be classified as serious inconveniences in the professional and personal life of the EU citizen.[52] Böse further solidifies his argument by referring to the *ne bis in idem* case law, which underscores the discouraging effect which criminal investigations and prosecutions may have on the exercise of free movement rights. The gist of this jurisprudence is that the exercise of free movement rights is hampered when citizens can face new prosecutions for the same act in other Member States after a case has been finally decided on.[53]

Meyer is of the opinion that unpredictable extraterritorial jurisdiction claims can have a chilling effect on free movement rights. He refers to the human rights doctrine which shows signs of a careful recognition of the problems arising from the uncertain application of national rules. An important example is the case *Digital Rights Ireland*, in which the Advocate General stated that the rules on data retention could create a vague feeling of surveillance, which could influence the decision of citizens to exercise their freedom of expression.[54] One of the leading arguments of the CJEU for ruling that Directive 2006/24 constitutes an interference with Articles 7 and 8 CFR was that the exercise of the freedom of expression is hampered 'by the fact that data are retained and subsequently used without the subscriber or registered user being informed [which] is likely to generate in the minds of the persons concerned the feeling that their private lives are the subject of constant surveillance.'[55] By analogy, it could be argued that the close net of applicable substantive national criminal laws in the AFSJ and risk of unforeseeable jurisdiction claims

[51] See also Luchtman (2013), p. 14.

[52] Even though the presence of the suspect on the territory of the prosecuting state is in fact no longer required or can be ensured with the use of the EAW, the difficulties of transnational prosecutions make it more likely that suspects who exercise their free movement rights will face prosecution on the basis of extraterritorial jurisdiction claims. Böse (2014b), p. 74.

[53] Böse (2014b), pp. 74–75.

[54] Case C-293/12 *Digital Rights Ireland* [2013] ECLI:EU:C:2013:845, Opinion of AG Cruz Villalón, para 52.

[55] Joined Cases C-293/12 & C-594/12 *Digital Rights Ireland* [2014] ECLI:EU:C:2014:238, para 37.

could also create a feeling of constant exposure for EU citizens, which dissuades them from exercising their free movement rights.[56]

Meyer does not link his reasoning directly to the serous inconveniences criterion, but I would argue that the uncertainty resulting from the possible exposure to different national substantive criminal laws can cause serious inconveniences in the private and professional lives of EU citizens. The inconveniences which unforeseeable jurisdiction claims can cause have been elaborated on in Chap. 2. They include the possible unexpected criminality of certain conduct, in particular when the conduct does not constitute a criminal offence in the state where it occurred, being prosecuted for a serious offence instead of a minor one and facing a higher maximum sanction than the one that could be imposed in the *locus delicti*.[57] In addition, the absence of a clear overarching system for forum choices in light of the good administration of justice which guides national decisions to prosecute could also cause serious inconveniences for the EU citizen and, therefore, restrict the right to free movement. As explained in Chap. 2, the lack of a transparent set of rules for forum choices could force EU citizens to defend themselves in more than one state at a time or subject them to prosecution by a state chosen for its strict sentencing and pre-trial detention regime.[58]

3.2.4 Interim Conclusion

It follows from the above that it is uncertain whether the surrender procedure provides a clear possibility to bring the questions on the compliance of national jurisdiction rules and forum decisions with article 49 and 47 CFR within the scope of the CFR. In addition, within the context of the national criminal procedure conducted in the issuing state, these problems could fall within the scope of the CFR via the legislation route or free movement route. However, neither one unambiguously brings national rules establishing the scope of application of national substantive criminal laws and national rules regarding the exercise of jurisdiction in a particular case within the scope of application of the CFR. With regard to the legislation route, the matter of unforeseeable jurisdiction claims and forum decisions will most likely fall within the scope of the CFR, when the applicable jurisdiction rule is linked to EU measures harmonising a particular criminal offence and when EU rules on the prevention and solving of conflicts of national jurisdictions influence the decision to prosecute on the national level. With regard to the free movement route, I am of the opinion that the criterion of serious inconveniences can bring national jurisdiction rules and the decision to prosecute within the scope of the CFR. Still, the CJEU has not yet ruled on this specific matter and it could go in a different

[56] Meyer (2014), pp. 181–182.

[57] Section 2.5.

[58] Section 2.6.

direction in light of its case law on indirect and uncertain restrictive effects of national measures on free movement.

In cases in which the Charter is indeed applicable as a result of one of these routes, it is possible to assess whether unforeseeable jurisdiction claims and forum decisions without a transparent legal framework are linked to the requirement of foreseeable offences, sanctions and tribunals correlating from Articles 49 and 47 CFR. This question is addressed in the next sections.

3.3 Article 49 CFR: The *Nullum Crimen Sine Lege, Nulla Poena Sine Lege* Principle

3.3.1 An Introduction

The substantive legality principle is codified in Article 49 CFR:

> No one shall be held guilty of any criminal offence on account of any act or omission which did not constitute a criminal offence under national law or international law at the time when it was committed. Nor shall a heavier penalty be imposed than the one that was applicable at the time the criminal offence was committed. If, subsequent to the commission of a criminal offence, the law provides for a lighter penalty, that penalty shall be applicable.

The legality principle correlates from the principle of legal certainty, which is a fundamental principle of EU law.[59] The latter requires that laws are sufficiently clear and precise so that they unambiguously inform individuals about their rights and obligations and enable them to adapt their conduct in conformity with the rules.[60] Hence, legal provisions need to be sufficiently 'clear, precise and predictable as regards their effects, in particular where they may have unfavourable consequences, such as criminal sanctions, for individuals and undertakings'.[61]

The specific rationale of the legality principle in Article 49 CFR is to prevent the arbitrary prosecution, conviction and punishment of individuals.[62] It comprises the same sub-principles and requirements as Article 7 ECHR.[63] The first one discussed in detail in the next paragraph is the requirement that criminal offences and sanctions

---

[59] Case C-72/15 *Rosneft* [2017] ECLI:EU:C:2017:236, paras 161–162; Case T-279/02 *Degussa* [2006] ECLI:EU:T:2006:103, para 66; Case C-2/19 *AP* [2020] ECLI:EU:C:2020:80, Opinion of AG Bobek, para 95.

[60] Case C-72/15 *Rosneft* [2017] ECLI:EU:C:2017:236, para 161; Case T-279/02 *Degussa* [2006] ECLI:EU:T:2006:103, para 66.

[61] Joined Cases C-72/10 & C-77/10 *Costa and Cifone* [2012] ECLI:EU:C:2012:80, para 74. See also Case T-279/02 *Degussa* [2006] ECLI:EU:T:2006:103, para 66; Case C-318/10 *SIAT* [2012] ECLI:EU:C:2012:415, para 58; Case C-282/12 *Itelcar* [2013] ECLI:EU:C:2013:629, para 44.

[62] See eg ECtHR 22 January 2013, 42931/10 (*Camilleri/Malta*) para 34.

[63] CFR, art 52(3). See also Case C-42/17 *M.A.S., M.B* [2017] ECLI:EU:C:2017:936 (*Taricco II*), paras 51, 54.

are laid down in accessible and foreseeable laws. The second one is the prohibition of a retroactive application of the law, which entails that criminal offences and sanctions need to have had a proper legal basis at the time of the offence.[64] The third sub-principle, commonly known as the *lex mitior* principle, constitutes an exception to the prohibition of a retroactive application of the law. It entails that a more lenient penalty may be applied even when the law establishing this penalty entered into force after the criminal act was committed.[65] The fourth one constitutes the prohibition of a too extensive interpretation of criminal offences and sanctions, such as an interpretation by analogy to the detriment of the accused.[66]

3.3.2 An Accessible and Foreseeable Law: The Requirement Explained

The requirement of a law for criminal offences and sanctions is interpreted from a substantive perspective instead of a formal one. Consequently, the law concept does not merely comprise formally enacted statutes, but delegated legislation and case law as well.[67] This definition has been criticised in light of the principle of democratic legitimisation, since it could result in the imposition of penalties for acts or omissions which have not been classified as criminal offences by national parliaments, but by, for instance, the judiciary.[68] However, the formal interpretation of the law concept in both Articles 7 ECHR and 49 CFR accommodates the common law Member States of the Council of Europe and the European Union. In addition, the formal interpretation is compensated with two quality requirements, which are the requirements of accessibility and foreseeability.[69]

---

[64] Case C-42/17 *M.A.S., M.B* [2017] ECLI:EU:C:2017:936 (*Taricco II*), para 57; Case C-7/11 *Caronna* [2012] ECLI:EU:C:2012:396, paras 52, 55. In relation to directives, this means that the provisions of a directive cannot independently of a national transposition law have the effect of determining or aggravating criminal liability. Case C-60/02 *X* [2004] ECLI:EU:C:2004:10, para 61.

[65] CFR, art 49(1); Joined Cases C-387/02, C-391/02 and C-403/02 *Berlusconi* [2005] ECLI:EU:C:2005:270, paras 66–69.

[66] Joined Cases C-74/95 & C-129/95 *X* [1996] ECLI:EU:C:1996:491, para 25; ECtHR 25 May 1993, 14307/88 (*Kokkinakis/Greece*) para 52.

[67] Joined Cases C-189/02, C-202/02, C-205/02 to C-208/02 and C-213/02 *Dansk Rørindustri* [2005] ECLI:EU:C:2005:408, para 216; ECtHR 12 February 2008, 21906/04 (*Kafkaris/Cyprus*) para 139; Tocildo (2012), p. 318.

[68] Tocildo (2012), pp. 318–320.

[69] Case C-42/17 *M.A.S., M.B* [2017] ECLI:EU:C:2017:936 (*Taricco II*), paras 54–55; ECtHR 12 February 2008, 21906/04 (*Kafkaris/Cyprus*) para 140.

These two quality conditions apply to laws defining criminal offences and penalties.[70] The accessibility requirement entails that an individual must be provided with an adequate indication of the applicable legal rules in a given case.[71] The foreseeability requirement demands that the individual is able to understand from the wording of the legal provision, and if necessary with the assistance of the court's interpretation of the legal provision, for what kind of conduct, including acts and omissions, he or she can be held criminally liable and what penalties can be imposed.[72] Hence, the foreseeability requirement demands that the law defining criminal offences and sanctions is sufficiently clear and precise. Whether a particular legal provision satisfies the foreseeability requirement needs to be decided on the basis of the relevant domestic law as a whole and the way it was applied at the material time.[73] In its case law, the CJEU refers to the general factors developed by the ECtHR which demarcate the foreseeability assessment. These include the 'content of the text in issue, the field it is designed to cover and the number and status of those to whom it is addressed'. In addition, the foreseeability requirement can still be met when individuals need to ask, to a degree reasonable in light of the circumstances, for legal advice on the content of the law.[74]

The requirement of an accessible and foreseeable law has two dimensions. On the one hand, it contributes to the legitimacy of coercive action by the authorities, including the imposition of sanctions.[75] Such actions are possible, since the law informs citizens on how to avoid criminal liability and warns them of the possible consequences of criminal actions. On the other hand, accessible and clear laws provide legal certainty and protect individuals by restricting the actions of the public prosecutor and judiciary.[76] In other words, they serve as a safeguard against arbitrary interferences.[77] However, even though a strict interpretation of the foreseeability requirement would increase legal certainty and avoid arbitrary prosecutions and sanctions, it can also result in excessive rigidity and therefore limit the possibility

---

[70] Cases C-634/18 *JI* [2020] ECLI:EU:C:2020:455, para 47; Joined Cases C-74/95 & C-129/95 *X* [1996] ECLI:EU:C:1996:491 paras 22, 25; ECtHR 19 March 2006, 67335/01 (*Achour/France*) para 41; ECtHR 12 February 2008, 21906/04 (*Kafkaris/Cyprus*) para 140; Tocildo (2012), p. 318.

[71] ECtHR 26 April 1979, 6538/74 (*Sunday Times/UK*) para 49.

[72] Case C-42/17 *M.A.S., M.B* [2017] ECLI:EU:C:2017:936 (*Taricco II*), para 56; Case C-72/15 *Rosneft* [2017] ECLI:EU:C:2017:236, para 162; Case C-303/05 *Advocaten voor de Wereld* [2007] ECLI:EU:C:2007:261, paras 49–50; ECtHR 11 November 1996, 17862/91 (*Cantoni v France*) para 29; ECtHR 19 March 2006, 67335/01 (*Achour/France*) para 41.

[73] ECtHR 12 February 2008, 21906/04 (*Kafkaris/Cyprus*) para 145.

[74] Joined Cases C-189/02, C-202/02, C-205/02 to C-208/02 and C-213/02 *Dansk Rørindustri* [2005] ECLI:EU:C:2005:408, para 219; ECtHR 11 November 1996, 17862/91 (*Cantoni v France*) para 35.

[75] Tineke Cleiren in Tekst en Commentaar Strafrecht, art 1 Sr, para 3 (February 1, 2021).

[76] Groenhuijsen and Kristen (2001), p. 332; Pompe (1959), p. 49.

[77] ECtHR 4 October 2016, 37462/09 (*Žaja/Croatia*) para 93; Pompe (1959), p. 49.

to develop the law in conformity with changing circumstances.[78] Hence, some degree of vagueness, which grants the national courts discretion in interpreting the law, should be allowed to make the law future-proof.[79] The role of the national courts in clarifying the law and adapting legal provisions to changing circumstances is in turn restricted by the conditions that the results of the interpretation must be in conformity with the essence of the offence and must have been reasonably foreseeable for the individual in question.[80]

3.3.3 The EAW: Outside the Scope of the Substantive Legality Principle?

The case law of the ECtHR is very clear with regard to the relationship between the substantive legality principle and the EAW. The Strasbourg court has consistently decided that both the extradition procedure and the EAW do not fall under the scope of Article 7 ECHR, because these cooperation procedures do not define criminal offences nor do they constitute penalties.[81] A decision on an EAW or extradition request is not a decision on the merits of the case, but one on assistance and cooperation for the purpose of prosecution and the execution of sanctions.[82]

In principle, the fundamental rights in the EU Charter of Fundamental Rights have the same meaning and scope as their equivalents in the ECHR, but Article 52(3) CFR does allow for a higher level of protection. So far, this possibility has not (yet) resulted in an extension of the scope of Article 49 CFR to the surrender

---

[78] Another drawback of a strict interpretation of the foreseeability requirement is that it clashes with the premise that legislation has a general application. Case C-72/15 *Rosneft* [2017] ECLI:EU:C:2017:236, para 164. The CJEU refers to ECtHR 11 November 1996, 17862/91 (*Cantoni/France*) paras 31–32.

[79] Joined Cases C-189/02, C-202/02, C-205/02 to C-208/02 and C-213/02 *Dansk Rørindustri* [2005] ECLI:EU:C:2005:408, para 217; ECtHR 11 November 1996, 17862/91 (*Cantoni/France*) para 31; ECtHR 17 September 2009, 10249/03 (*Scoppola/Italy No.2)* para 100. See also *Baskaya and Okcuoglu* in which the ECtHR prohibited 'over-broad discretion' for courts. ECtHR 8 July 1999, 23536/94 and 24408/94 *(Baskaya and Okcuoglu/Turkey)* para 39.

[80] Case C-72/15 *Rosneft* [2017] ECLI:EU:C:2017:236, para 167; Joined Cases C-189/02, C-202/02, C-205/02 to C-208/02 and C-213/02 *Dansk Rørindustri* [2005] ECLI:EU:C:2005:408, para 218; ECtHR 17 September 2009, 10249/03 (*Scoppola/Italy No 2)* para 101.

[81] EcHR 6 July 1976, 7512/76 (*X/The Netherlands*) paras 185–186; ECtHR 7 October 2008, 41138/05 (*Monedero Angora/Spain*); ECtHR 23 October 2012, 1997/11 (*Giza/Poland*) paras 30–31.

[82] Case C-303/05 *Advocaten voor de Wereld* [2006] ECLI:EU:C:2006:552, Opinion of AG Ruiz-Jarabo Colomer, paras 102–105; Borgers (2007), para 4; Glerum (2013), pp. 335–336. The ECtHR has reached the same conclusion in relation to other cooperation procedures. See eg ECtHR 27 June 2006, 22318/02 (*Csoszanszki/Sweden*); ECtHR 27 June 2006, 28578/03 (*Szabo/Sweden*); ECtHR 6 September 2011, 48058/09 (*Muller/Czech Republic*); ECtHR 23 October 2012, 498/10 (*Ciok/Poland*) paras 32–35. See also *Saccoccia* in which the ECtHR ruled that the enforcement of a forfeiture order does not concern the penalty itself but its execution. ECtHR 5 July 2007, 69917/01 (*Saccoccia/Austria).*

procedure.[83] In this light, the CJEU has issued two rulings on the EAW which to a certain extent discuss the foreseeability requirement as it follows from the legality principle or the overarching principle of legal certainty, but in these rulings it does not explicitly bring the EAW under the scope of Article 49 CFR.

The first case is *Advocaten voor de Wereld*, in which the CJEU decided that the abolishment of the double criminality requirement for certain categories of offences without clearly defining the meaning of these offences does not violate the substantive legality requirement. The court based this decision on the argument that Article 2(2) FDEAW, which partially abolishes the double criminality requirement, does not aim to harmonise the categories of offences listed.[84] Whether the legality principle is met depends on the national law of the issuing state which needs to satisfy its requirements, including the requirements of foreseeability and accessibility.[85] In other words, the CJEU linked the application of the substantive legality principle to the criminal law of the issuing state and not directly to the EAW.[86]

This conclusion was confirmed in the case *X*, which concerned another requirement for the partial abolishment of the double criminality requirement, namely the condition that the offence in question is punishable with a custodial sentence of at least 3 years in the issuing state. The referring court asked the CJEU which version of the law of the issuing state it had to take into account when determining whether the three-year requirement was met: the version of the law applicable at the time of the facts of the case or the version in force at the time of the issuance of the EAW.[87] The CJEU decided on the former, since the latter would clash with the foreseeability requirement correlating from the principle of legal certainty.[88] Hence, the CJEU confirmed that the law of the issuing state needs to satisfy the requirements of the substantive legality principle.

It can be concluded that, at the moment, Article 49 CFR does not cover the issuing and execution of an EAW. More concretely, this means that the interpretation of Article 49 CFR does not allow for the conclusion that the EAW should also meet the requirement of foreseeability or the conclusion that it does not meet the foreseeability requirement when the jurisdiction claim of the issuing state was not foreseeable at the time of the offence. In that light, the next section discusses to what extent the underlying difficulty of foreseeing the national applicable laws at the time of the offence falls under the scope of the substantive legality principle and had been linked to the accessibility and foreseeability of criminal offences and sanctions in the CJEU and ECtHR case law. In relation to the EAW, the outcome of this examination

[83] See also Case C-717/18 *X* [2019] ECLI:EU:C:2019:1011, Opinion of AG Bobek, paras 92–100.

[84] Case C-303/05 *Advocaten voor de Wereld* [2007] ECLI:EU:C:2007:261, paras 49–54.

[85] Case C-303/05 *Advocaten voor de Wereld* [2007] ECLI:EU:C:2007:261, para 53.

[86] See also Case C-717/18 *X* [2019] ECLI:EU:C:2019:1011, Opinion of AG Bobek, paras 99, 104; Case C-303/05 *Advocaten voor de Wereld* [2006] ECLI:EU:C:2006:552, Opinion of AG Ruiz-Jarabo Colomer, paras 102–104.

[87] Case C-717/18 *X* [2020] ECLI:EU:C:2020:142, para 16.

[88] Case C-717/18 *X* [2020] ECLI:EU:C:2020:142, para 38.

affects the answer to the question whether the EAW could potentially be classified as a mechanism capable of enforcement jurisdiction claims which are incompatible with Article 49 CFR.

3.3.4 Jurisdiction and the Right to an Accessible and Foreseeable Law

3.3.4.1 The Case Law of the CJEU

The CJEU has not (yet) specifically decided on the existence of a connection between the foreseeability of a particular jurisdiction claim and the accessibility and foreseeability of criminal offences and sanctions. A case on a similar matter is *Taricco I* in which the CJEU ruled on the link between the prohibition of the retroactive application of criminal offences and sanctions and statutory rules of limitation.[89] The latter determine the time frame within which criminal offences in a national substantive criminal law may be applied to a certain set of facts. In this case the Italian rules on limitation in criminal proceedings could bar the application of effective and deterrent sanctions for certain crimes affecting the EU's financial interests. The CJEU concluded in light of Article 49 CFR that the decision not to apply the Italian rules, which broadened the chance of an effective prosecution, would not result in a conviction for conduct which was not criminalised at the time of the offence or the imposition of a penalty which was not laid down by national law at the time of the offence.[90] Hence, disapplying the national rules on limitation would not constitute a violation of the substantive legality principle.[91]

[89] Case C-105/14 *Taricco I* [2015] ECLI:EU:C:2015:555.

[90] Case C-105/14 *Taricco I* [2015] ECLI:EU:C:2015:555, paras 46–48, 55–56; Case C-42/17 *M.A.S and M.B* [2017] ECLI:EU:C:2017:936 (*Taricco II*), paras 42,44, 58–61. In *Tarico II* the CJEU does not seem to go back on this point. It does, however, add that in the absence of EU legislation on rules on limitation at the material time it was in fact for the competent Italian court to decide whether the national legality principle blocked the duty to disapply national rules which hamper the effective enforcement of EU law. This part of the case is further elaborated on in Chap. 12. For a discussion of the *Taricco II* case, see Staffler (2019), pp. 59–80; Luchtman (2018), p. 2688.

[91] The CJEU also referred to the case law of the ECtHR. According to the Strasbourg jurisprudence, which has been further developed since *Taricco I* and *II*, Article 7 ECHR has some influence over statutory rules of limitation, even though they are not criminal offenses and sanctions. In principle, statutes of limitation may be amended and immediately applied to the disadvantage of the suspect, unless the old statute of limitations had already lapsed at the time of the amendments. According to the ECtHR, the conduct in question is no longer punishable when the statute of limitations has run out and this possibility may not be revived by the retroactive application of the new rules. Case C-105/14 *Taricco I* [2015] ECLI:EU:C:2015:555, para 57; Case C-42/17 *M.A.S and M.B* [2017] ECLI:EU:C:2017:936 (*Taricco II*), para 42; ECtHR 22 June 2000, 32492/96, 32547/96, 32548/96, 33209/96, 33210/96 (*Coëme and others/Belgium*) para 149. See also ECtHR 12 November 2019, 57849/12 (*Smoković/Croatia*) para 52; ECtHR 18 June 2020, 7523/10 (*Antia and Khupenia/Georgia*) para 42; Billis (2016), p. 33.

In principle, the same reasoning could be applied in case the CJEU is confronted with the question whether a change in jurisdiction rules falls under the scope of Article 49 CFR, in particular the prohibition of the retroactive application of the criminal law. The CJEU could argue that extending the possibility of prosecution by retroactively expanding the scope of applicability of a national criminal law does not affect the fact that the offences and sanctions were clearly laid down by law at the time of the act. In other words, it is not the criminality of the act which is established with retroactive force, but the possibility of prosecuting and sanctioning these criminal acts. However, this is mere speculation, meaning that the CJEU could take a different direction when it has to rule on the link between jurisdiction and the prohibition of retroactive application. In addition, an answer to this question would still leave the main one unanswered, which is whether the CJEU considers the difficulties in foreseeing the applicable national criminal law at the time of the offence problematic for the accessibility and foreseeability of criminal offences and sanctions.

3.3.4.2 The Case Law of the ECtHR

An examination of the jurisprudence of the ECtHR reveals that the link between jurisdiction and the legality principle, or the accessibility and foreseeability requirements specifically, is scarcely discussed. Important examples are the cases *Isakkson*, *Camilleri/Malta* and *Seychell/Malta*.[92] In *Isakkson*, the Strasbourg court seems to apply the sub-principles of the legality principle to Swedish jurisdiction rules. In this case, the applicants were accused of creating an internet business through which they had illegally sold medicinal products outside of Sweden. According to the Swedish Penal Code, Swedish law applies and Swedish courts are competent when the criminal act is perpetrated or completed in Sweden. It has been established in the Swedish case law that when only a part of the criminal act has occurred in Sweden, the entire criminal act may be considered to have been committed in Sweden. According to the Swedish courts, they had jurisdiction in the applicants' case, since their different activities combined had to be considered as one crime and some of these activities had also occurred in Sweden. The applicants, however, argued that the acts had not been committed in Sweden, since the medicinal products had not been transferred through Sweden. The application of Swedish penal law and the exercise of jurisdiction by the Swedish courts was therefore in violation of Article 7 ECHR.[93]

[92] ECtHR 8 March 2016, 29688/09 (*Isaksson/Sweden*); ECtHR 22 January 2013, 42931/10 (*Camilleri/Malta*) para 40; ECtHR 28 August 2018, 43328/14 (*Seychell/Malta*) para 46. See also ECtHR 29 January 2019, 38161/15 (*Holmes/Malta*). This case was, however, struck out of the court's list of cases.

[93] ECtHR 8 March 2016, 29688/09 (*Isaksson/Sweden*) paras 3–16, 38.

The ECtHR decided that sufficient material existed in the case law and preparatory works, which substantiated the interpretation of the jurisdiction provisions by the Swedish courts. The fact that only part of the crime had to be committed in Sweden for jurisdiction to be established was, therefore, foreseeable for the applicants. It also added that the applicants had a duty to ask for legal advice in case they were uncertain about the potential legal consequences of their intended actions. The court decided in the end that the application of the Narcotics Penal Act criminalising some of the behaviour was sufficiently clear and foreseeable and that individuals could have foreseen their criminal liability of the basis of this act.[94]

So, in this case the ECtHR seems to apply Article 7 ECHR to the Swedish jurisdiction rules, in particular the requirement that the interpretation of open or more vague legal provisions by courts needs to be reasonably foreseeable for individuals. The fact that the meaning and scope of the applicable rules of jurisdiction were clear was at least part of the reason why Article 7 ECHR was not violated. The ECtHR does not say it with so many words, but its argumentation suggests that national jurisdiction rules themselves need to comply with Article 7 ECHR, as well.

However, such a finding would still not provide a clear answer to the question what the Strasbourg court specifically thinks about situations in which the national jurisdiction rules are perfectly in compliance with the legality principle, but the application of the national criminal law still comes as a surprise to the individual. For instance, what would the court have decided if Sweden had exercised jurisdiction on the basis of the effects doctrine, which would in itself constitute a clear and precise jurisdiction rule, and the applicants had argued that as the consequences of the actions had unexpectedly occurred in Sweden, the application of Swedish law was not foreseeable? Would the clarity of the Swedish jurisdiction rule then also have been sufficient to decide that Article 7 ECHR was not violated?[95]

In the cases *Camilleri/Malta* and *Seychell/Malta*, the ECtHR discusses the link between the foreseeability of the applicability of a certain penalty bracket and the

[94] ECtHR 8 March 2016, 29688/09 (*Isaksson/Sweden*) paras 51–52, 57.

[95] See also ECtHR 17 March 2009, 13113/03 (*Ould Dah/France*). This case concerned the situation in which a French national court exercised universal jurisdiction and convicted a Mauritanian officer for acts of torture committed in Mauritania. The question before the ECtHR was whether the application of French criminal was incompatible with Article 7 ECHR, because of a Mauritanian amnesty law which was already applicable before the criminal proceedings had started. The ECtHR decided that the Mauritanian amnesty law which intended to prevent prosecution could not block the application of French law. One of the reasons for this decision was that Articles 4 and 7 of the United Nations Convention against Torture allowed for the conclusion that French courts have both jurisdiction to prosecute and the power to apply French law. However, even though the ECtHR then discussed the accessibility and foreseeability of French law, it did not go into the question of whether the application of French law on the basis of universal jurisdiction was in fact foreseeable at the time of the offence and whether this affected the accessibility and foreseeability of the French criminal offenses and sanctions.

foreseeability of a specific forum, on the national level.[96] Both cases concern the situation in which the Maltese Advocate General had the authority to decide whether the applicant would be tried before the Criminal Court or the Court of Magistrates. This decision was also decisive for the minimum and maximum penalty which could be imposed. If the case was tried before the Court of Magistrates, the punishment could vary between 6 months and 10 years—and, if it was tried before the criminal court, between 4 years and life imprisonment.[97]

The ECtHR stated that the applicable legal provisions clearly described the actions which constitute criminal offences as well as the possible penalties which could be imposed.[98] Still, it came to the conclusion that the foreseeability requirement of Article 7 ECHR was violated, because the Maltese law did not sufficiently clarify on the basis of which criteria or factors the decision for one of the two courts (and therefore the applicable penalty bracket) had to be made.[99] The obligation to obtain legal advice did not change this conclusion, since even if the applicants had obtained such advice, they would not have been able to predict the applicable penalty bracket due to the lack of transparent rules restricting the discretion of the Advocate General to make the decision.[100]

In these two cases, the ECtHR explicitly connects the *nullum crimen, nulla poena sine lege* principle to choice of forum in situations in which this choice also determines the applicable criminal sanctions. These judgements show that the ECtHR is not against the applicability of more than one set of rules laying down criminal offences and penalties. However, even though overlapping sets of criminal rules and conflicts of jurisdiction, therefore, seem accepted, they need to be accompanied by regulations which avoid arbitrary decisions regarding the applicable set of rules in concrete cases. In other words, the discretion of the deciding authority needs to be sufficiently restricted by law to avoid arbitrary prosecutions, convictions and sanctions. The question is, however, to what extent these conclusions could be transferred to the cross-border European level, since both *Camilleri* and *Seychell* concern national situations.[101] Hence, we cannot tell yet whether the ECtHR would take the same position when confronted with the question whether the lack of rules determining which national criminal law applies in a concrete case violates the accessibility and foreseeability requirement of Article 7 ECHR and therefore creates a risk of arbitrary prosecution, conviction and sanctioning.

---

[96] ECtHR 22 January 2013, 42931/10 (*Camilleri/Malta*); ECtHR 28 August 2018, 43328/14 (*Seychell/Malta*). The difference between the two cases is that in *Camilleri* the Medical and Kindred Professions Ordinance applied and in *Seychell* the Dangerous Drugs Ordinance.

[97] ECtHR 22 January 2013, 42931/10 (*Camilleri/Malta*) para 40; ECtHR 28 August 2018, 43328/14 (*Seychell/Malta*) para 46.

[98] ECtHR 28 August 2018, 43328/14 (*Seychell/Malta*) para 46.

[99] ECtHR 22 January 2013, 42931/10 (*Camilleri/Malta*) para 40; ECtHR 28 August 2018, 43328/14 (*Seychell/Malta*) para 47.

[100] ECtHR 22 January 2013, 42931/10 (*Camilleri/Malta*) paras 41–44; ECtHR 28 August 2018, 43328/14 (*Seychell/Malta*) paras 48–52.

[101] Zimmerman (2015), p. 232.

It follows from the above that neither the CJEU nor the ECtHR has unambiguously recognised the existence of a link between jurisdiction and the accessibility and foreseeability of criminal offences and sanctions on the cross-border EU level. More specifically, these two courts have not explicitly decided whether the foreseeability of the applicability of a particular national criminal law at the time of the offence influences the accessibility and foreseeability of criminal offences and sanctions. By extension, it is difficult to say in light of the current scope of Article 49 CFR set out by the case law whether the EAW could be viewed as a mechanism which, when its criteria are met, could enforce a jurisdiction claim which is incompatible with the legality principle due to the difficulties for the requested person at the time of the offence to foresee the application of the law of the issuing state.

3.3.4.3 The Position of the EU Legislator

The EU legislator up until now seems to deny a link between the accessibility and foreseeability of criminal offences and the foreseeability of the applicability of national criminal laws. The adoption of multiple EU instruments with minimum harmonisation measures for the definition of criminal offences and sanctions points in this direction. These EU measures do not only impose the obligation to criminalise and penalise certain conduct, but also the obligation to establish territorial and extraterritorial jurisdiction.[102] These specific jurisdiction obligations contribute to the establishment of a net of applicable national criminal laws (*Netzgedanke*) which reduces the chances of impunity.[103]

In addition, some of these harmonisation instruments prohibit requirements, such as the double criminality requirement demarcating the establishment of extraterritorial jurisdiction, or they only provide the Member States with the discretion to add such additional conditions.[104] The double criminality requirement restricts the exercise of extraterritorial jurisdiction to situations in which the act is also criminal

[102] See eg Council Framework Decision 2004/757/JHA of 25 October 2004 laying down minimum provisions on the constituent elements of criminal acts and penalties in the field of illicit drug trafficking [2004] OJ L335/8, art 8; Directive (EU) 2017/1371 of the European Parliament and of the Council of 5 July 2017 on the fight against fraud to the Union's financial interests by means of criminal law [2017] OJ L198/29, art 11; Directive 2014/62/EU of the European Parliament and of the Council of 15 May 2014 on the protection of the euro and other currencies against counterfeiting by criminal law, and replacing Council Framework Decision 2000/383/JHA [2014] OJ L151/1, art 8; Directive (EU) 2017/541 of the European Parliament and of the Council of 15 March 2017 on combating terrorism and replacing Council Framework Decision 2002/475/JHA and amending Council Decision 2005/671/JHA [2017] OJ L88/6, art 19.

[103] Hecker (2012), p. 86; Meyer and Böse (2011), p. 337.

[104] See eg Directive 2014/62/EU of the European Parliament and of the Council of 15 May 2014 on the protection of the euro and other currencies against counterfeiting by criminal law, and replacing Council Framework Decision 2000/383/JHA [2014] OJ L151/1, art 8(2); Directive 2011/36/EU on preventing and combating trafficking in human beings and protecting its victims [2011] OJ L101/1, art 10(3)(a); Council Framework Decision 2008/913/JHA of 28 November 2008 on combating

de lege loci. Its application can, therefore, ensure that EU citizens are at the time of the offence at least able to know that their actions were criminal *somewhere*.[105] Furthermore, as stated before, the passive nationality principle is one of the most problematic jurisdiction principles in terms of foreseeability, since the alleged perpetrator is often not aware of the nationality of the victim at the time of the offence. However, even though Directive 2011/36/EU does not impose the obligation to establish jurisdiction on the basis of the passive nationality principle, it does seem to encourage states to do so.[106] Such an encouragement seems strange when the EU legislator would be of the opinion that the link to a particular national criminal justice system needs to be foreseeable at the time of the offence. It can therefore be concluded that the EU instruments harmonising criminal offences and sanctions suggest that the EU legislator, which adopted them at the time, was not of the opinion that Article 49 CFR requires that an individual is at the time of the offence in a position to foresee which specific national criminal is applicable.

3.3.4.4 The Legal Literature

The legal literature shows many different opinions with regard to the question whether the substantive legality principle as codified in international and European instruments and in national law is in one way or another linked to jurisdiction. These opinions can roughly be divided into two categories.[107] Firstly, several authors deny the existence of any link between jurisdiction rules and the substantive legality principle, which in some states also seems to constitute the majority opinion.[108] Some legal scholars base their position on the argument that jurisdiction concerns the demarcation of the power of a sovereign state to determine the scope of application of its national criminal law and enforce its national criminal law vis-à-vis other states in the international setting.[109] In other words, these scholars approach jurisdiction from the perspective of public international law and view it as the delimitation of states' jurisdiction to prescribe, adjudicate and enforce in their relationship with each other. This relationship is not subject to or regulated by the *nullum crimen sine lege* principle. Other scholars who reject the idea of a link between the requirement of *lex certa* and jurisdiction are of the opinion that

certain forms and expressions of racism and xenophobia by means of criminal law [2008] OJ L328/55, art 9(3).

[105] Wolswijk (1998), p. 87; Luchtman (2013), p. 24.

[106] Luchtman (2012), p. 53.

[107] Luchtman identifies three categories. Luchtman (2012). For an overview of the Dutch and German legal literature on the different positions, see Wolswijk (1998), pp. 59–66. See also Scholten (1995), p. 65ff.

[108] 't Hart (1982), pp. 332–333, 336, 338; Pompe (1959), pp. 54, 60–61, 500, 504–505; Reijntjes (2002), paras 10–11. See also Hirsch Ballin (2000), p. 488; Wolswijk (1998), p. 82.

[109] See eg Jescheck and Weigend (1996), pp. 163–167. This point is discussed in Wolswijk (1998), pp. 72–73; Luchtman (2012), p. 48.

jurisdiction is part of procedural or formal criminal law. In other words, jurisdiction rules determine and restrict the competences of the investigatory and prosecuting authorities. Consequently, the absence of jurisdiction would not change or affect the criminality of the behaviour as such, but instead demarcates the competence to investigate, prosecute and try a case.[110]

The second category of legal scholars criticises the position that jurisdiction is not affected by the *nullum crimen, nulla poena sine lege* principle at all.[111] Some authors have argued that the substantive legality principle, in particular the prohibition of a retroactive application of the law, also applies directly to rules on jurisdiction. They also question whether an act can be considered a criminal offence according to Dutch law if Dutch criminal law does not apply to the act committed abroad.[112] Hence, this point of view primarily focuses on the conformity of the jurisdiction rules themselves with the requirements correlating from the substantive legality principle.

Others have argued that the substantive legality principle, in particular the requirements of accessibility and foreseeability, is not directly applicable to rules of jurisdiction, but influences them.[113] This point of view follows, for instance, from the German legal literature in which rules on jurisdiction are often defined as *objektive Bedingungen der Strafbarkeit* (objective preconditions of criminal liability). This means that these rules are not determinative for the unlawfulness of certain conduct nor do they constitute elements of the criminal offence, but they do contribute to the decision of whether criminal liability can be established.[114] In this capacity, rules on jurisdiction have a close link to the substantive legality principle and the warning function of the accessibility and foreseeability requirement. The objective of these quality requirements is to put citizens in a position in which they can adapt their behaviour in conformity with the law to avoid criminal liability and prosecution. However, the lack of a foreseeable and accessible link to a national legal order negatively affects this warning function.[115] Without such a clear link, citizens are hardly in a position to know and be deterred by the applicable national criminal offences and sanctions.

[110] Remmelink and Hazewinkel-Suringa (1996), p. 511. Also discussed in Luchtman (2012b), p. 353; Luchtman (2012a), p. 48.

[111] Knigge (1984), pp. 241, 370; Strijards (1984), p. 43ff; European Committee on Crime Problems (Council of Europe), *Extraterritorial criminal jurisdiction* (Strasbourg 1990) 23–24; Thorhauer (2015), pp. 89–91; Böse (2014b), pp. 111–114; Meyer and Böse (2011), pp. 339–340. See also Oehler (1983), pp. 131–132.

[112] Knigge (1984), pp. 241, 370. See also Schulze-Fielitz (2008), para 23. According to this, author the German *Bestimmtheitsgebo*t (*lex certa* requirement) covers all requirements for *Strafbarkeit* (criminal liability or criminal act/offense) to which Article 103(2) GG refers, and not merely the components of the crime describing its wrongfulness.

[113] See eg Strijards (1984), p. 43.

[114] Meyer (2013), p. 170; Scholten (1995), p. 91ff; Hecker (2015), p. 28; Ambos (2018), p. 4; Jescheck and Weigend (1996), pp. 180, 555. *A contrario* see Kubiciel (2015), para 26; Böse (2010), pp. 69–72.

[115] Strijards (1984), pp. 43–47; Thorhauer (2015), pp. 90–91. See also Luchtman (2013), p. 23; Luchtman (2012), p. 51; Böse (2014b), pp. 112–114.

Among these scholars, the position that an individual should at the time of the offence foresee which particular national criminal law will apply is a minority opinion.[116] The objection against this position is that it increases the risk of forum shopping, since citizens intending to commit crimes will look for the state with the most lenient criminal system.[117] Hence, most authors are satisfied when citizens could have known at the time of the offence that their conduct was prohibited and could result in criminal liability and sanctions somewhere. In other words, a citizen should be able to foresee that his or her actions constitute a criminal offence according to the law of a single state.[118] This requirement is usually already met when states subject the exercise of extraterritorial jurisdiction to the double criminality requirement on the basis of which the conduct needs to constitute a criminal offence *de lege loci*. In other words, ignorance of the law (of another state) cannot be used as a defence if the criminality of the act was foreseeable on the basis of the law of the *locus delicti*.[119] In addition, the obviousness of the criminality of certain behaviour, such as genocide or human trafficking, could be a reason to conclude that the individual could have known at the time of the offence that the conduct was prohibited and could result in a criminal penalty.[120]

However, this position neglects the fact that the substantive legality principle does not only cover criminal offences, but penalties as well. The lack of a uniform European criminal code not only results in differences between criminal offences in the Member States; it results in differences with regard to the possible criminal penalties, as well. A simple example is the fact that only in some national laws is murder punishable with a life-long sentence. Interpreting the accessibility and foreseeability requirement in a way which requires that an individual should be able to know that his or her conduct is criminal somewhere partially meets the concerns regarding the foreseeability of criminal behaviour, but not the same concerns with regard to the applicable criminal sanctions.[121]

[116] This minority opinion is, for instance, held by Oehler. He is of the opinion that an individual should be able to know that the national criminal law of a particular state is applicable to him when states exercise jurisdiction that is based on the protection of their own – meaning state – interests. In these situations, the criminality of the conduct will strike the individual like a 'deus ex machina'. Oehler (1970), pp. 116–117. His point of view is summarized by Scholten (1995), p. 67. See also Strijards (1984), pp. 42–43; Böse (2014b), p. 114.

[117] Eser (2012), pp. 566–567.

[118] Ambos (2018), p. 11; Wolswijk (1998), p. 87. See (also for further references) Luchtman (2012a), pp. 23, 51.

[119] Wolswijk (1998), p. 87; Luchtman (2013), p. 24.

[120] Ambos (2018), p. 11; Luchtman (2012a), p. 54.

[121] Luchtman (2012a), p. 52. See also Fichera (2011), pp. 98–99.

3.3.4.5 Interim Conclusion

It can be concluded that neither the CJEU nor the ECtHR has provided a clear and unambiguous answer to the question whether the foreseeability of the applicability of a particular national criminal law affects the question whether the accessibility and foreseeability requirement for criminal offences and sanctions is satisfied, in particular in case of conflicts of jurisdiction on the EU level. Furthermore, it follows from the EU harmonisation measures for criminal offences and sanctions that the EU legislator seems primarily focused on avoiding negative conflicts of jurisdiction in which no state is competent to exercise jurisdiction. Lastly, even though the legal literature reveals a category of scholars who are of the opinion that the requirements of foreseeability and accessibility in one way or another affect the rules on jurisdiction, the requirement that the applicability of a particular national criminal law needs to be foreseeable is only a minority opinion. Hence, on the EU level, it has not (yet) been unambiguously determined whether the accessibility and foreseeability of criminal offences and sanctions is affected by the difficulties in foreseeing the applicability of a particular national criminal law. As a result of the lack of an answer to this question, it is also difficult to say, in light of the scope of Article 49 CFR as set out in the case law, whether the EAW is on the EU level viewed as a mechanism which could, if its criteria are met, enforce unforeseeable jurisdiction claims which are incompatible with Article 49 CFR.

3.4 Article 47 CFR: The Right to a Tribunal Established by Law

3.4.1 An Introduction

Article 47(2) CFR states, 'Everyone is entitled to a fair and public hearing within a reasonable time by an independent and impartial tribunal previously established by law. Everyone shall have the possibility of being advised, defended and represented.' The right to a tribunal established by law as laid down in Article 47(2) CFR has a broader scope than its equivalent in Article 6 ECHR, since it is not limited to cases concerning the determination of a criminal charge or civil rights and obligations.[122] Consequently, the EAW procedure falls within the scope of Article 47(2) CFR, but outside the scope of Article 6 ECHR as it does not concern the

[122] Explanations relating to the Charter of Fundamental Rights [2007] OJ C303/17, 34. Article 6(1) ECHR also leaves out the word 'previously', which according to Böse is not an important difference. He states that this term refers to the initiation of the proceedings and not to the commission of the crime. Furthermore, despite this difference, the Explanations to the CFR state that the meaning of Articles 6(1) and 47(2) are the same. I will therefore continue to refer to the right to a tribunal established by law in this book. See also Case C-487/19 *WZ* [2021] ECLI:EU:C:2021:798, para 123.

determination of a criminal charge.[123] With regard to the latter, the Strasbourg case law states that the surrender procedure does not entail an assessment or ruling on the merits of the underlying criminal case.[124]

The relevant question in this section is whether the lack of a clear and accessible EU system preventing or solving conflicts of jurisdiction in light of the good administration of justice constitutes a violation of the right to a tribunal established by law in Article 47 CFR.[125] As explained in Chap. 2, the EU citizen who decides to exercise his or her free movement rights runs the risk of falling under the criminal jurisdiction of more than one state. In such situations, national competent authorities, who may be public prosecutors or members of the judiciary, have broad discretion in deciding whether or not to prosecute a case in their own national legal order or to decide amongst each other in which state prosecution should occur. Consequently, EU citizens face the risk that they are by chance prosecuted in the state whose national procedural law offers the least protection, or that the national competent authorities exploit the differences between the national criminal substantive laws and procedural laws to their detriment.[126] The EAW procedure constitutes an additional dimension to such risks, since it can ensure that EU citizens are surrendered, even though they encounter such problems in their underlying criminal cases.

The right to a tribunal established by law reflects both the principle of the rule of law and the separation of powers doctrine.[127] Together with the requirement of an independent and impartial tribunal,[128] it protects the confidence which courts in a

---

[123] Glerum (2013), pp. 104–105; Peers (2011), p. 685. Some of the directives harmonizing procedural safeguards which are part of the right to a fair trial also cover the surrender procedure. See eg Directive 2013/48/EU of the European Parliament and of the Council of 22 October 2013 on the right of access to a lawyer in criminal proceedings and in European arrest warrant proceedings, and on the right to have a third party informed upon deprivation of liberty and to communicate with third persons and with consular authorities while deprived of liberty [2013] OJ L294/1.

[124] ECtHR 7 October 2008, 41138/05 (*Monedero Angora/Spain*). However, fair trial issues can arise in an extradition case in a different way. The ECtHR has acknowledged that Article 6 ECHR can prevent extradition when the extradition request comes from a state where the person in question has in the past suffered or may in the future suffer a flagrant denial of the right to a fair trial. ECtHR 4 February 2005, 46827/99 and 46951/99 (*Mamatkulov and Askarov/Turkey*) paras 90–91; ECtHR 6 July 2010, 24027/07, 11949/08 and 36742/08 *(Babar Ahmad and Others/United Kingdom)* para 132.

[125] It is, therefore, not clear what the direct application of the right to a tribunal established by law to the surrender procedure would mean. It could possibly mean that the executing judicial authority should meet this requirement as well.

[126] Eicker (2005), p. 631; Eser and Burchard (2006), pp. 517–518.

[127] Joined Cases C-542/18 RX-II & C-543/18 RX-II *Simpson v Council of the European Union and HG v European Commission* [2020] ECLI:EU:C:2020:232, para 75; ECtHR 1 December 2020, 26374/18 (*Guðmundur Andri Ástráðsson/Iceland*) paras 211, 215; ECtHR 5 October 2010, 19334/03 (*DMD Group/Slovakia*) para 58; ECtHR 22 June 2000, 32492/96, 32547/96, 32548/96, 33209/96 and 33210/96 (*Coëme and others/Belgium*) para 98.

[128] On the link between the 'tribunal established by law' and 'independence' and 'impartiality' see ECtHR 1 December 2020, 26374/18 (*Guðmundur Andri Ástráðsson/Iceland*) paras 231–234; Panzavolta (2013), p. 154.

democratic society need to inspire in the people.[129] In this light, the right to a tribunal demands that the organisation of the judicial system of a state is not made dependent on the discretion of the executive power or the judiciary in states in which the law is codified, but is 'regulated by law emanating from Parliament'.[130] Similar to Article 7 ECHR, this law should be both accessible and foreseeable. Its ratio is to protect individuals against arbitrary actions by the executive and the judiciary taken in the context of a state's judicial organisation in which jurisdiction to adjudicate is exercised. In that sense, the right to a tribunal established by law addresses the executive, judicial and legislative power.[131] The former two may not establish prerogative courts, and the latter needs to guarantee that the role and the discretion of the executive and judiciary in the organisation of the judicial system is restricted to protect citizens against arbitrary decision-making.[132]

In light of the ratio of the right to a tribunal established by law, the question arises whether forum decisions, in particular forum decisions by judicial authorities and public prosecutors on the EU level, fall within the scope of this right and what this would mean. In addition, the question can be asked as to what exactly the requirement of a foreseeable and accessible law in Article 47 CFR entails, especially in relation to forum choices. These questions are examined in the next sections on the basis of the case law of the CJEU and ECtHR.

3.4.2 *Forum Choices and the Right to an Accessible and Foreseeable Law: Case Law*

3.4.2.1 The Requirement of an Accessible and Foreseeable Law

It follows from the case law that the requirement of a tribunal established by law comprises the entire organisational set-up of the judicial organisation.[133] It includes

[129] ECtHR 23 April 2015, 29369/10 (*Morice/France*) para 78.

[130] EcHR 12 October 1978, 7360/76 (*Leo Zand/Austria*) para 69; ECtHR 22 June 2000, 32492/96, 32547/96, 32548/96, 33209/96, and 33210/96 (*Coëme and others/Belgium*) para 98; ECtHR 1 December 2020, 26374/18 (*Guðmundur Andri Ástráðsson/Iceland*) paras 214, 226; Case C-487/19 *WZ* [2021] ECLI:EU:C:2021:798, para 129.

[131] ECtHR 22 June 2000, 32492/96, 32547/96, 32548/96, 33209/96, and 33210/96 (*Coëme and others/Belgium*) para 98; Böse (2014b), p. 125; Panzavolta (2013), pp. 151, 154. See also Joined Cases C-542/18 RX-II and C-543/18 RX-II *Simpson v Council of the European Union and HG v European Commission* [2019] ECLI:EU:C:2019:977, Opinion of AG Sharpston, paras 67, 79.

[132] Luchtman (2011), p. 89.

[133] Joined Cases C-542/18 RX-II and C-543/18 RX-II *Simpson v Council of the European Union and HG v European Commission* [2020] ECLI:EU:C:2020:232, para 73; EcHR 12 October 1978, 7360/76 (*Zand/Austria*) para 68; ECtHR 20 July 2006, 29458/04 and 29465/04 (*Sokurenko and Strygun/Ukraine*) para 24.

the legal basis for the actual establishment of the tribunal,[134] the appointment of judges,[135] the competence of the judicial organs and the composition of the bench in each case, as well as the obligation to act in accordance with the national rules governing the judicial organisation.[136] In addition, the concept of law also includes legal provisions which, if violated, would exclude the participation of a judge or more judges in a certain case. These could be provisions concerning 'the independence of the members of a tribunal, the length of their term of office, impartiality, and the existence of procedural safeguards'.[137]

Additionally, in its case law, the ECtHR has clarified that it is predominantly the 'framework' of the judicial organisation which needs to be regulated by a law emanating from Parliament. The regulation of the specific details of the judicial organisation may be left to the discretion of the executive or judiciary.[138] The power to specify certain aspects of the judicial organisation may therefore be delegated if the domestic law, including the Constitution, allows for such delegations.[139] This division also means that the concept of 'law' in Article 6 ECHR has two different meanings. Elements of the general framework of the judicial organisation, such as the subject-matter jurisdiction of a court, need to be regulated by statutory law, whereas the details of this framework may be regulated by both written and unwritten laws.[140] It does not follow clearly from the case law which elements of the judicial organisation are part of the general framework.[141] However, this seems

[134] On the question of whether the establishment of the tribunal itself must be regulated by primary legislation see Leloup (2020), p. 1149; Case C-61/65 *Vaassen – Göbbels* [1966] ECLI:EU:C:1966:39

[135] ECtHR 1 December 2020, 26374/18 (*Guðmundur Andri Ástráðsson/Iceland*); ECtHR 22 July 2021, 43447/19 (*Reczkowicz/Poland*).

[136] Joined Cases C-542/18 RX-II and C-543/18 RX-II *Simpson v Council of the European Union and HG v European Commission* [2020] ECLI:EU:C:2020:232, para 73; Case C-413/18 *H v Council* [2019] ECLI:EU:C:2019:1044, paras 45–62; Case C-127/13 *Strack* [2014] ECLI:EU:C:2014:2250, paras. 48–55; EcHR 12 October 1978, 7360/76 (*Zand/Austria*) para 68; ECtHR 20 July 2006, 29458/04 and 29465/04 (*Sokurenko and Strygun/Ukraine*) para 24; ECtHR 5 October 2010, 19334/03 (*DMD Group/Slovakia*) para 59; ECtHR 4 May 2000, 31657/96 (*Buscarini/Saint-Marin*); ECtHR 4 March 2003, 63486/00 (*Posokhov/Russia*) para 39.

[137] Joined Cases C-542/18 RX-II and C-543/18 RX-II *Simpson v Council of the European Union and HG v European Commission* [2020] ECLI:EU:C:2020:232, para 73; ECtHR 5 October 2010, 19334/03 (*DMD Group, A.S./Slovakia*). See also, ECtHR 28 November 2002, 58442/2000 (*Lavents/Latvia*) para 114. See also ECtHR 22 April 2010, 40984/07 (*Fatullayev/Azerbaijan*) para 145; ECtHR 11 July 2006, 36455/02 (*Gurov/Moldova*) para 37.

[138] EcHR 12 October 1978, 7360/76 (*Zand/Austria*) para 69; EcHR 18 December 1980,8603/79, 8722/79, 8723/79 and 8729/79 (*Cociani/Italy*) para 219; ECtHR 22 June 2000, 32492/96, 32547/96, 32548/96, 33209/96 and 33210/96 (*Coëme and others/Belgium*) para 98; Harris et al. (2014), p. 458.

[139] EcHR 12 October 1978, 7360/76 (*Zand/Austria*) para 69, 71; ECtHR 28 April 2009, 17214/05, 20329/05 and 42113/04 (*Savino and others/Italy*) para 94.

[140] Kuijer (2004), pp. 185–186.

[141] Leloup (2020), p. 1150.

to include the subject-matter jurisdiction and personal jurisdiction of the courts.[142] In *Zand*, the European Commission on Human Rights (EcHR) also stated that the local jurisdiction of courts and tribunals needs to be regulated by law, which seems to imply that territorial jurisdiction also falls under the scope of 'tribunal established by law'.[143]

The requirements of accessibility and foreseeability also apply, but they are as such and in relation to forum choices rarely discussed. However, the ECtHR has unambiguously decided that the right to a tribunal established by law does not grant the defendant the right to choose his or her court or to have different proceedings joined together.[144] It follows from this conclusion that the requirements of accessibility and foreseeability do not demand that the law tells the citizen at the time of the offence which court will try his or her case.[145] In this sense, it reveals an important difference with Article 7 ECHR, which requires that the law informs citizens at the time of the offence in a sufficiently accessible and clear manner about the unlawfulness of their actions and possible sanctions.[146] Several authors have argued—or interpreted the term 'previously' in Article 47(2) CFR in such a way—that for the right to a tribunal established by law, the relevant point in time is instead the moment when the competent court is chosen.[147]

In addition, some cases on Article 6 ECHR more generally emphasise the need for the law to be clear and understandable. An example is the case *Sokurenko and Struygen* in which the Ukrainian Supreme Court upheld the decision of the Court of Appeal after quashing the resolution of the Higher Commercial Court. The ECtHR stated that no domestic legal provision existed which allowed the Supreme Court to uphold the decision of the Court of Appeal in the case before it. The provisions in the Ukrainian Constitution were too general to be a legal basis for such a very specific competence. The ECtHR, therefore, concluded that the right to a tribunal established

142 EcHR 12 October 1978, 7360/76 (*Zand/Austria*) paras 68–69; ECtHR 20 July 2006, 29458/04 and 29465/04 (*Sokurenko and Strygun/Ukraine*) paras 24–25; ECtHR 22 June 2000, 32492/96, 32547/96, 32548/96, 33209/96, and 33210/96 (*Coëme and others/Belgium*) paras 107–109. The ECtHR also explicitly states that the jurisdiction of the national courts is not a matter which falls within the ambit of Article 7 ECHR. ECtHR 12 July 2007, 74613/01 (*Jorgic/Germany*) paras 64–72; ECtHR 17 March 2009, 13113/03 (*Ould Dah/France*).

143 The ECtHR has in subsequent case law also referred to the ruling of the EcHR in *Zand*. EcHR 12 October 1978, 7360/76 (*Zand/Austria*) paras 68–69; EcHR 5 September 1990, 13272/87 (*Giuffrida/Italy*); ECtHR 20 July 2006, 29458/04 and 29465/04 (*Sokurenko and Strygun/Ukraine*) para 24; ECtHR 24 November 2020, 30836/07 (*Bahaettin Uzan/Turkey*) para 49.

144 ECtHR 12 July 2007, 74613/01 (*Jorgic/Germany*) para 65; EcHR 10 October 1990, 16875/90 (*G/Switzerland*).

145 In addition, contrary to criminal offenses and sanctions, which are rules of substantive criminal law, procedural rules like those regulating the judicial organization are subject to the maxim *tempus regit actum*. Hence, prosecution, conviction and sanctioning may occur on the basis of procedural rules which have been adopted or changed after the crime was committed. The principle of no retroactive application does not apply. ECtHR 17 September 2009, 10249/03 (*Scoppola/Italy No. 2*) para 110; Luchtman (2012b), pp. 352–353; Böse (2014b), pp. 126–127; Thorhauer (2019), p. 617.

146 Luchtman (2013), pp. 30–31; Panzavolta (2013), p. 161.

147 Böse (2014a), p. 126; Panzavolta (2013), p. 161; Thorhauer (2019), p. 617.

by law was violated in the national proceedings. This ruling shows that the competences, especially specific ones, of national courts need to be clearly defined by law. However, like in most cases, the ECtHR did not directly link this conclusion to the right to an accessible and foreseeable law.[148]

One exception in this regard is the case *Savino*, in which the applicant claimed that the bodies which handled his case, 'la Commission juridictionnelle pour le personnel' (the Commission) in first instance and 'la Section juridictionnelle du Bureau' (the Section) on appeal, were not tribunals established by law. The applicant stated that the accessibility requirement was not fulfilled, since the internal regulation (*Règlement pour la protection juridictionnelle du personnel de la Chambre des deputes*, hereafter RPJ) on the basis of which the bodies were established was not published in the official journal.[149] However, the Court stated that the criterion of accessibility demands that the law can be consulted without much difficulty by those affected by it. Considering that the RPJ concerned internal judicial procedures of la Chambre des députés, its publication in an internal bulletin sufficed.[150] In relation to the foreseeability requirement, the ECtHR stated that the applicable provisions were sufficiently precise to be able to understand the rules concerning the procedure before the Commission and the Section.[151] Hence, foreseeability would entail that the procedural rules before a court or tribunal need to be sufficiently clear.

3.4.2.2 Forum Decisions: Within the Scope of Article 47 CFR?

It follows from the above that the case law on the requirement of an accessible and foreseeable law is not strongly connected to the matter of forum choices, except for the fact that it clarifies that citizens do not have the right to choose their court. The matter of forum choices has been discussed independently of the accessibility and foreseeability requirement in other cases, in particular in jurisprudence regarding the specific composition of a court. In this case law, the ECtHR has ruled that the allocation of a case to a particular chamber or judge within a court or the composition of the bench should not be influenced by the executive. In addition, the power

[148] ECtHR 20 July 2006, 29458/04 and 29465/04 (*Sokurenko and Strygun/Ukraine*) paras 26–28. See also EcHR 7 March 1984, 9006/80, 9262/81, 9263/81, 9265/81, 9266/81, 9313/81 and 9405/8 (*Sir William Lithgow and Others/United Kingdom*) para 458. In this case, the Commission stated that the Arbitration Tribunal was established by law, since its establishment had a legal basis in the 1977 Act 'which specified in sufficient detail both its composition and the scope of its jurisdiction'. Another case is ECtHR 9 February 2021, 15227/19 (*Xhoxhaj/Albania*) paras 281–288.

[149] ECtHR 28 April 2009, 17214/05, 20329/05 and 42113/04 (*Savino and others/Italy*) paras 37, 95.

[150] ECtHR 28 April 2009, 17214/05, 20329/05 and 42113/04 (*Savino and others/Italy*) paras 98–99.

[151] ECtHR 28 April 2009, 17214/05, 20329/05 and 42113/04 (*Savino and others/Italy*) paras 98–99. The Court deviated in this regard from its ruling in *Coëme* in which it decided that a lack of sufficiently clear procedural rules violated the suspect's right to a fair trial, but not his right to a 'tribunal established by law. ECtHR 22 June 2000, 32492/96, 32547/96, 32548/96, 33209/96 and 33210/96 (*Coëme and others/Belgium*) paras 98–104. Panzavolta (2013), pp. 150–151.

granted to the judiciary in this regard should be restricted in such a way that arbitrary decision are avoided.[152] These cases, however, primarily concern the allocation of a case within a court after the decision has been made where, meaning before which court, the case should be brought. Only a few judgements touch upon or are linked to the decision before which court to bring the case and more specifically conflicts of jurisdiction. One of these cases is *G v Switzerland*, in which the applicant had to stand trial for different offences in different cantons. His request to join the cases and to let them be handled by one canton was rejected by the Federal Court of Switzerland. He then complained before the Strasbourg court that he was not tried by a tribunal established by law, because the Federal Court had too much discretion in making the decision. According to the ECtHR, the decision of the Federal Court was based on reasonable grounds.[153] This assessment of the reasonableness of the forum decision has been repeated in subsequent case law. It is based on the principle that it is in the first place for the national courts to interpret provisions of domestic law, including the rules of jurisdiction. Hence, the jurisdiction of the ECtHR is restricted to a marginal test, examining whether the decision for a particular venue is based on reasonable grounds.[154]

The case law shows that rules on case allocation or choice of venue fall within the scope of Articles 6 ECHR and 47 CFR. Articles 6 ECHR and 47 CFR require that when a state has adopted rules on forum choices, it is obliged to act in conformity with these rules and to come to a reasonable decision.[155] Hence, in light of Article 47 CFR, the allocation of some discretion to the judiciary is not prohibited, but the domestic law should ensure reasonable decisions and avoid the arbitrary exercise of this discretion.[156] The current ECtHR case law, however, focuses on forum decisions by the judiciary and does not discuss forum decisions by public prosecutors. As public prosecutors are often not part of a state's 'court organisation' or 'organisation of the judiciary' the question arises whether forum decisions by public prosecutors would also fall within the scope of the right to a tribunal established by law. With Luchtman, I believe that excluding forum choices by the public prosecutor would threaten the substance of the right to a tribunal established by law.[157] Prosecutorial authorities are often the doorkeepers to the criminal justice area and therefore to the courts. They usually decide whether or not a case will be handled

[152] ECtHR 2 May 2019, 50956/16 (*Pasquini/San Marino*) paras 103, 110–112; ECtHR 8 July 2014, 8162/13 (*Biagioli/San Marino*) paras 79–80.

[153] EcHR 10 October 1990, 16875/90 (*G/Switzerland*); ECtHR 2 December 1992, 17495/90 (*Kübli/ Switzerland*). See also EcHR 25 November 1996, 28899/95 (*Stieringer/Germany*).

[154] ECtHR 12 July 2007, 74613/01 (*Jorgic/Germany*) para 65; ECtHR 2 December 1992, 17495/90 (*Kübli/ Switzerland*); EcHR 25 November 1996, 28899/95 (*Stieringer/Germany*); ECtHR 14 January 2020, 51111/07 and 42757/07 (*Khodorkovskiy and Lebedev/Russia No 2*) para 421.

[155] Luchtman (2011), p. 88.

[156] See also ECtHR 22 June 2000, 32492/96, 32547/96, 32548/96, 33209/96, and 33210/96 (*Coëme and others/Belgium*) para 98.

[157] Luchtman (2013), p. 30.

under criminal law and, if so, before which court.[158] Hence, a certain control on the powers of the public prosecutor in relation to forum choices seems appropriate to avoid arbitrary decisions by the executive and judiciary in the context of a state's court organisation.[159]

The question remains what the observations above mean in relation to the lack of an overarching EU system for forum choices and the broad discretion granted to national authorities in that regard. In case these findings would also be applicable in relation to the decision for a national jurisdiction, this could mean the following. Article 6 ECHR and 47 CFR do not demand that the law regulates case allocations between states. However, when such a law does exist, it should sufficiently restrict the discretion of the executive or judiciary to ensure reasonable and non-arbitrary decisions. However, this is guesswork, since the current relevant case law of the ECtHR exclusively covers internal situations, meaning situations in which a choice of venue is made within the state on the basis of domestic law.[160] Both the ECtHR and CJEU have thus so far remained silent on the link between the right to a tribunal established by law and the choice of a national jurisdiction for prosecution and trial. In relation to the EAW, this means that it is difficult to determine in light of Article 47 CFR whether on the EU level the surrender procedure could be viewed as a mechanism with the potential of enforcing a violation of Article 47 CFR by surrendering a person to a state, while this national jurisdiction was not appointed as the appropriate and reasonable forum on the basis of a clear system of forum choices.

3.4.3 *The Legal Literature*

In the legal literature, different opinions exist with regard to the question whether Article 47(2) CFR demands that forum choices in cross-border cases are regulated by law and in such a way that any arbitrary decisions by national competent authorities are avoided. Some authors argue that broad discretion for public prosecutors or other authorities in cross-border cases does not violate the right to a tribunal established by law because, in principle, the national courts in each Member State are established by law. In other words, the decision for a particular national jurisdiction does not fall within the scope of the right to a tribunal established by law, because the national courts within the competent states are all established by law.[161]

---

[158] Luchtman (2011), p. 87; Luchtman (2013), p. 30. See also Schönberger (2015), pp. 303, 313.

[159] Luchtman (2011), p. 87.

[160] See also Meyer (2014), p. 206. The preliminary question posed by the Irish Supreme Court regarding the application of the *LM* test in case of possible violations of the right to a tribunal established by law in the issuing state due to its rules on the allocation of cases also concerns an 'internal' situation. See case C-480/21 *W O, J L v Minister for Justice and Equality*; Rb. Amsterdam 14 September 2021, ECLI:NL:RBAMS:2021:505 (Amsterdam District Court).

[161] Linke (1970), pp. 90–91. See also Panzavolta (2013), pp. 156–157.

The literature also shows a relatively large category of legal scholars who are of the opinion that in the current AFSJ, the lack of a clear system for forum choices appointing a national jurisdiction for prosecution and trial contradicts the right to a tribunal established by law. They argue that fundamental rights, including Article 47 CFR, should be interpreted in conformity with the normative context of the AFSJ characterised by EU citizenship, the CFR and new forms of cooperation on the basis of mutual recognition.[162] In such a context, the ratio of the right to a tribunal established by law requires that protection against arbitrary decisions by the executive and judiciary should be extended to the preliminary step of the appointment of a specific national court, which is the appointment of a national jurisdiction.[163] Another argument in favour of a link between forum choices in cross-border cases and Article 47 CFR is the continuing development of a system of vertical EU law enforcement, such as the establishment of the EPPO which reflects the creation of an integrated legal area. The removal of national boundaries in the context of crime-fighting demands that the matter of forum decisions should be brought under the scope of Article 47 CFR.[164] In addition, in EU rules and case law on jurisdiction in commercial and civil matters, both the EU legislator and the CJEU strongly emphasise the principle of legal certainty, even though they do not explicitly refer to Article 47(2) CFR.[165] In its jurisprudence, the CJEU has ruled that rules on jurisdiction in civil matters aim to enable applicants to identify the court before which their claims can be brought, such as the court of the defendant's domicile, and allow defendants to foresee to a reasonable degree before which court they may be sued.[166] Considering the fact that in the field of criminal law, fundamental rights such as the right to liberty are often in play, the possibility to foresee to a reasonable degree in which national jurisdiction the case will be brought seems even more important.[167]

3.5 Conclusion

It can be concluded that in the setting of the national criminal case, both the legislation route and the free movement route could bring the question regarding the link between jurisdiction and forum choices and the legality principle within the

[162] Schönberger (2015), pp. 302–303. See also Luchtman (2011), pp. 74–101; Thorhauer (2015), p. 95.

[163] Thorhauer (2015), p. 95; Böse (2014b), p. 153; Meyer (2014), p. 206; Luchtman (2013), pp. 28–33; Schönberger (2015), p. 303.

[164] Panzavolta (2013), p. 157.

[165] Regulation (EU) No 1215/2012 of the European Parliament and of the Council of 12 December 2012 on jurisdiction and the recognition and enforcement of judgments in civil and commercial matters [2012] OJ L351/1, recital 15.

[166] Case C-386/05 *Color Drack* [2007] ECLI:EU:C:2007:262, para 20; Case C-533/07 *Falco Privatstiftung* [2009] ECLI:EU:C:2009:257, para 22.

[167] Böse (2014b), p. 159; Panzavolta (2013), p. 161; Schönberger (2015), p. 304.

scope of the CFR. In these situations, the question could be posed whether unforeseeable jurisdiction claims and forum decisions without a transparent legal framework are problematic for EU citizens in light of their right to foreseeable criminal offences, sanctions and tribunals correlating from Articles 49 and 47 CFR. In relation to this question, it follows from Sects. 3.3 and 3.4 that we do not know (yet) whether the two complications discussed in Chap. 2 are recognised as legality issues in light of the current interpretation and scope of Articles 49 and 47 CFR set out in the case law. For the internal setting, it follows from the ECtHR and CJEU jurisprudence that Article 49 CFR does not prohibit overlapping sets of criminal rules. Article 49 CFR does require that the power of the competent authority to decide on the applicable set of offences and sanctions in a concrete case is sufficiently restricted by law to avoid arbitrariness. Article 47 covers forum choices, but does not demand that the matter is regulated by law. However, in case national rules on choice of venue exist, the competent authorities have to come to a reasonable decision. To what extent these findings are also relevant for the difficulties arising at the interface of the national legal orders remains unclear. The Strasbourg and Luxembourg case law have so far not unambiguously clarified whether the accessibility and foreseeability of criminal offences and sanctions is influenced by the foreseeability of a particular national criminal law nor whether the discretion granted to national competent authorities to decide on a national jurisdiction for prosecution and trial should be adequately restricted by law.

The legal literature does not show a unanimous answer, either. However, a group of legal scholars strongly argues in favour of some kind of link between jurisdiction and Article 49 CFR, and forum choices on the EU level and Article 47 CFR, in particular in light of the current normative context of the AFSJ characterised by EU citizenship and free movement. Some are of the opinion that an AFSJ in which EU citizens are encouraged to cross-borders—while at the same time more intense forms of judicial cooperation to combat crime are adopted—requires that the two complications with which travelling EU citizens can be confronted should be viewed as legality issues. In relation to the *nullum crimen sine lege* principle, the idea that a particular national criminal law needs to be foreseeable at the time of the offence is, however, a minority opinion. Most authors believe it to be sufficient that the citizen can foresee at the time of the offence that his actions were criminal somewhere.

On the basis of the above, it is difficult to answer the question whether, in light of the current scope of Articles 49 and 47 CFR, the EAW could on the EU level be viewed as a system which could enforce violations of the legality principle by surrendering citizens to a state whose jurisdiction claim was not foreseeable or a state which was not appointed as the appropriate one on the basis of a clear legal framework. The next chapter examines to what extent the FDEAW and complementary CJEU case law have installed protection mechanisms in case the two underlying complications occur, and to what extent this protection is based on legality concerns.

References

Ambos K (2018) Internationales Strafrecht: Strafanwendungsrecht – Völkerstrafrecht – Europäisches Strafrecht – Rechtshilfe. Beck

Barnard C (2016) The substantive law of the EU: the four freedoms. Oxford University Press

Barnard C, Peers S (eds) (2017) European Union law. Oxford University Press

Billis E (2016) European court of justice: a "quasi-consitutional court" in criminal matters? The Taricco judgment and its shortcomings. New J Eur Crim Law 7:20

Borgers M (2007) Case note HvJ EG 16 May 2007, C-303/05, ECLI:EU:C:2006:552, (*Advocaten voor de Wereld*). NJ 2007/619

Böse M (2010) Die Stellung des sog. Internationalen Strafrechts im Deliktsaufbau und ihre Konsequenzen fur den Tatbestandsirrtum. In: Bloy R, Böse M (eds) Gerechte Strafe und legitimes Strafrecht: Festschrift fur Manfred Maiwald zum 75. Geburtstag. Duncker & Humblot

Böse M (2014a) Fundamental freedoms of the union. In: Böse M, Meyer F, Schneider A (eds) Conflicts of jurisdiction in criminal matters in the European Union. Volume II: rights, principles and model rules. Nomos

Böse M (2014b) Fundamental rights of the EU-charter. In: Böse M, Meyer F, Schneider A (eds) Conflicts of jurisdiction in criminal matters in the European Union. Volume II: rights, principles and model rules. Nomos

Chalmers D, Davies G, Monti G (2014) European Union law. Cambridge University Press

Cleiren T in Tekst en Commentaar Strafrecht, art 1 Sr, para 3 (February 1, 2021)

Editorial Comment (2008) Two-speed European citizenship? Can the Lisbon treaty help close the gap? Common Mark Law Rev 45:1

Eicker A (2005) Zur Vermeidung simultaner Strafverfahren im zwischenstaatlichen Kontext: Modell einer (über)individuell-konkreten Kriterien Gewichtung. StV 631

Eser A (2012) Kritische Würdigung der Modellentwürfe eines Regelungsmechanismus zur Vermeidung von Jurisdiktionskonflikten. In: Sinn A (ed) Jurisdiktionskonflikte bei grenzüberschreitender Kriminalität. V&R Unipress, Ein Rechtsvergleich zum Internationalen Strafrecht

Eser A, Burchard C (2006) Interlokales "*ne bis in idem*" in Europa? Von "westfälischem" Souveränitätspathos zu europäischem Gemeinschaftsdenken. In: Hans-Jürgen (ed) Freiheit, Sicherheit und Recht: Festschrift für Jürgen Meyer zum 70. Geburtstag. Nomos

Fichera M (2011) The implementation of the European arrest warrant in the European Union: law, policy and practice. Intersentia

Glerum V (2013) De weigeringsgronden bij uitlevering en overlevering – Een vergelijking en kritische evaluatie in het licht van het beginsel van wederzijdse erkenning. Wolf Legal Publishers

Groenhuijsen M, Kristen F (2001) Het *Bestimmtheitsgebot* bepaald. DD 31:330

Hancox E (2013) The meaning of "implementing" EU law under Article 51(1) of the Charter: Åkerberg Fransson. Common Mark Law Rev 50:1411

Harris D et al (2014) Law of the European convention on human rights. Oxford University Press

't Hart J (1982) Het nulla-poenabeginsel. In: Koekkoek A, Konijnenbelt W (eds) Grondrechten: Commentaar op hoofdstuk 1 van de herziene grondwet. Stichting Ars Aequi

Hecker B (2012) Die rechtlichen Möglichkeiten der Europäischen Union zur Lösung von Kompetenzkonflikten. In: Sinn A (ed) Jurisdiktionskonflikte bei grenzüberschreitender Kriminalität. Ein Rechtsvergleich zum Internationalen Strafrecht. V&R Unipress

Hecker B (2015) Europäisches Strafrecht. Springer

Herrnfeld H-H (2013) Mechanisms for settling conflicts of jurisdiction. In: Luchtman M (ed) Choice of forum in cooperation against EU financial crime. Freedom, security and justice and the protection of specific EU-interests. Eleven International Publishing

Hirsch Ballin E (2000) De zaak-Pinochet: commentaar op de uitspraak van de House of Lords van 24 maart 1999. Ars Aequi 6:481

Jescheck H-H, Weigend T (1996) Lehrbuch des Strafrechts. Duncker & Humblot

Knigge G (1984) Verandering van wetgeving. Beschouwingen over de artt. 4 A.B. en 1 Sr. Arnhem Gouda Quint
Kubiciel M (2015) §3 IRG. In: Ambos K, König S, Rackow P (eds) Rechtshilferecht in Strafsachen. Nomos
Kuijer M (2004) The blindfold of Lady Justice – Judicial independence and impartiality in light of the requirements of Article 6 ECHR. E.M. Meijers Instituut
Leloup M (2020) The appointment of judges and the right to a tribunal established by law: the ECJ tightens its grip on issues of domestic judicial organization: review Simpson. Common Mark Law Rev 57:1139
Linke R (1970) Zwischenstaatliche Kompetenzkonflikte auf dem Gebiet des Strafrechts. In: Oehler D, Pötz P (eds) Beiträge zur Gestaltung des internationalen und supranationalen Strafrechts. Heinrich Grützner zum 65. Geburtstag. Decker
Luchtman M (2011) Choice of forum in an area of freedom, security and justice. Utrecht Law Rev 7:74
Luchtman M (2012a) Strafrechtelijke forumkeuze en de kenbaarheid van rechtsmacht – Over de positie van de Unieburger in de Europese rechtsruimte. In: Kool R, de Jong F (eds) Relaties van gezag en verantwoordelijkheid: strafrechtelijke ontwikkelingen. Boom
Luchtman M (2012b) Principles of European criminal law: jurisdiction, choice of forum, and the legality principle in the area of freedom, security, and justice. ERPL 20:347
Luchtman M (2013) Choice of forum and the prosecution of cross-border crime in the European Union – what role for the legality principle? In: Luchtman M (ed) Choice of forum in cooperation against EU financial crime. Freedom, security and justice and the protection of specific EU-interests. Eleven International Publishing
Luchtman M (2018) Kroniek van het Europees strafrecht. NJB 2684
Meyer F (2013) Country report Germany. In: Böse M, Meyer F, Schneider A (eds) Conflicts of jurisdiction in criminal matters in the European Union. Volume I: national reports and comparative analysis. Nomos
Meyer F (2014) An area of freedom, security and justice. In: Böse M, Meyer F, Schneider A (eds) Conflicts of jurisdiction in criminal matters in the European Union. Volume II: rights, principles and model rules. Nomos
Meyer F, Böse M (2011) Die Beschränkung nationaler Strafgewalten als Möglichkeit zur Vermeidung von Jurisdiktionskonflikten in der Europäischen Union. ZIS 6:336
Oehler D (1970) Theorie des Strafanwendungsrechts. In: Oehler D, Pötz P-G (eds) Aktuelle Probleme des Intemationalen Strafrechts. Heinrich Grützner zum 65. Geburtstag. Decker's Verlag
Oehler D (1983) Internationales Strafrecht: Geltungsbereich des Strafrechts, internationales Rechtshilferecht, Recht der Gemeinschaften, Völkerstrafrecht. Heymanns
Panzavolta M (2013) Choice of forum and the lawful judge concept. In: Luchtman M (ed) Choice of forum in cooperation against EU financial crime. Freedom, security and justice and the protection of specific EU-interests. Eleven International Publishing
Peers S (2011) EU justice and home affairs law. Oxford University Press
Pompe W (1959) Handboek van het Nederlandse Strafrecht. Tjeenk Willink
Prechal S, De Vries S, Van Eijken H (2011) The principle of attributed powers and the scope of EU law. In: Besselink L, Pennings F, Prechal S (eds) The eclipse of the legality principle in the European Union. Wolters Kluwer
Reijntjes J (2002) Case note HR 18 September 2001, ECLI:NL:HR:2001:AB1471 (*Decembermoorden*). NJ, 559
Remmelink J, Hazewinkel-Suringa D (1996) Inleiding tot de studie van het Nederlandse Strafrecht. Gouda Quint
Scholten H-J (1995) Das Erfordernis der Tatortstrafbarkeit in § 7 StGB. Ein Beitrag zur identischen Norm im transnationalen Strafrecht. Max-Planck-Institut für ausländisches und internationales Strafrecht

Schönberger C (2015) Positive transnationale Jurisdiktionskonflikte – Causae, rechtliche Lösungsnotwendigkeit und -konzepte. Schulthess Verlag
Schulze-Fielitz H (2008) Art. 103 II. In: *Dreier Grundgesetz Kommentar*. Mohr Siebeck
Staffler L (2019) Towards a new chapter of the Taricco Saga. Eur Crim Law Rev 9:59–80
Strijards G (1984) Internationaal Strafrecht strafmachtsrecht: algemeen deel. Gouda Quint BV
Thorhauer N (2015) Conflicts of jurisdiction in cross-border criminal cases in the area of freedom, security, and justice. Risks and opportunities from an individual rights-oriented perspective. New J Eur Crim Law 6:78
Thorhauer N (2019) Jurisdiktionskonflikte im Rahmen transnationaler Kriminalität. Zur Koordination der Strafgewalten über natürliche Personen und Unternehmen in der Europäischen Union. Dike Verlag and Nomos
Tocildo S (2012) The weakened concept of the European principle of criminal legality. In: Roca JG, Santolaya P (eds) Europe of rights: a compendium on the European convention of human rights. Brill/Nijhoff
Van Eijken H et al (2015) The European citizen as bearer of fundamental rights in a multi-layered legal order. In: van den Brink T, Luchtman M, Scholten M (eds) Sovereignty in the shared legal order of the EU: core values of regulation and enforcement. Intersentia
Van Elsuwege P, Gremmelprez F (2020) Protecting the rule of law in the EU legal order: a constitutional role for the court of justice. Eur Const Law Rev 16:8
Wolswijk H (1998) Locus delicti en rechtsmacht. Gouda Quint
Zimmerman F (2015) Strafgewaltkonflikte in der Europäischen Union. Ein Regelungsvorschlag zur Wahrung materieller und prozessualer strafrechtlicher Garantien sowie staatlicher Strafinteressen. Nomos

Chapter 4
The FDEAW: Safeguards Against Unforeseeable Jurisdiction Claims and the Risk of Arbitrary Forum Decisions?

4.1 Introduction

This chapter examines whether the EU legislator who adopted the FDEAW and the CJEU which has interpreted its provisions, installed safeguards to avoid surrender in case of unforeseeable jurisdiction claims or decisions to prosecute that are not based on a transparent mechanism for forum choices—and, if so, whether this protection was provided in light of Articles 49 and 47 CFR. In other words, this twofold question asks whether the conditions for the issuing and execution of an EAW contain safeguards against these two underlying problems, and whether these safeguards were installed because the two problems raised concerns in light of the legality principle. It should be noted in advance that the available preparatory work to the FDEAW is scarce and not all relevant provisions have been the subject of preliminary rulings by the CJEU. Consequently, the answer to the main question of this chapter is also based on other EU documentation, such as the European Commission Handbook on issuing an EAW as well as legal literature. In addition, it is important to mention beforehand that the conditions for the issuing and execution of an EAW can only protect citizens against surrender. In other words, if some conditions for the issuing or execution of an EAW were adopted with the two complications in mind, these do not necessarily offer protection against the underlying complications as such. The fact that protection is not necessarily offered is a result of the fact that the refusal of an EAW or the invalidity of an EAW in principle does not prohibit the issuing state from prosecuting the requested person, for instance, *in absentia*.

Section 4.2 covers the execution procedure. It will first set out which conditions in the execution procedure are relevant to examine. Afterwards, this section analyses each condition separately in order to determine to what extent it aims to protect the requested person against surrender in situations in which the jurisdiction claim of the issuing state was not foreseeable, as well as situations in which the issuing state was not appointed as the competent forum on the basis of a transparent set of rules.

J. Graat, *The European Arrest Warrant and EU Citizenship*,
https://doi.org/10.1007/978-3-031-07590-2_4

Section 4.3 conducts the same exercise for the issuing procedure. This procedure is more sparsely regulated in the FDEAW than the executing procedure, but has been elaborated on by the CJEU in several preliminary rulings. This chapter ends with a conclusion and reflections in Sect. 4.4.

4.2 Protection Offered by the FDEAW: Executing Procedure

4.2.1 The Relevant Refusal Grounds and Guarantees

Articles 3, 4 and 4A FDEAW comprise the refusal grounds in the executing procedure, while Article 5 enumerates the guarantees which the executing judicial authority may request of the issuing state in certain situations. The three mandatory refusal grounds, which as the name says oblige the executing judicial authority to refuse the surrender, are laid down in Article 3 FDEAW. These are based on the rules on amnesty in the executing state,[1] the rules on the age of criminal liability[2] and protection on the basis of the *ne bis in idem* principle.[3] Article 4 contains eight optional refusal grounds which the Member States may transpose into their national legislation. Two of these refusal grounds also relate to the *ne bis in idem* principle, complementing the refusal ground in Article 3 (2) FDEAW.[4] The others are based on the double criminality requirement,[5] ongoing criminal proceedings for the same act in the executing state,[6] statutory bars,[7] the nationality and place of residence of the requested person[8] and rules on jurisdiction.[9] Article 4A adds one more optional refusal ground covering *in absentia* judgements.[10]

Even though the CJEU has consistently stated in its case law that Articles 3–4A FDEAW exhaustively enumerate the refusal grounds in the surrender procedure, it

[1] FDEAW, art 3(1).

[2] FDEAW, art 3(3).

[3] FDEAW, art 3(2).

[4] FDEAW, arts 4(3) and 4(5).

[5] FDEAW, arts 4(1) and 2(4).

[6] FDEAW, arts 4(2).

[7] FDEAW, arts 4(4).

[8] FDEAW, art 4(6).

[9] FDEAW, art 4(7).

[10] *In absentia* convictions used to be a ground for the request of guarantees under Article 5(1) FDEAW. This guarantee was later on changed into an optional refusal ground by Council Framework Decision 2009/299/JHA of 26 February 2009 amending Framework Decisions 2002/584/JHA, 2005/214/JHA, 2006/783/JHA, 2008/909/JHA and 2008/947/JHA, thereby enhancing the procedural rights of persons and fostering the application of the principle of mutual recognition to decisions rendered in the absence of the person concerned at the trial [2009] OJ L81/24.

has also acknowledged other situations which may bar the execution of an EAW.[11] These situations are often not officially classified as refusal grounds, but they have the same effect. One example is the case *Bob-Dogi*, in which the CJEU stated that the lawfulness or validity of an EAW is impaired when it does not meet the conditions in Article 8 FDEAW, in particular the requirement that the EAW is based on a national arrest warrant or equivalent national judicial decision. The CJEU concluded that the executing judicial authority should 'refuse to give effect' to the European Arrest Warrant when it does not satisfy the requirements of lawfulness.[12] Other examples follow from the cases of *Aranyosi and Căldăraru* and *LM*. In these rulings, the CJEU decided that concerns regarding the issuing state's compliance with Article 4 CFR and the right to an independent judge in Article 47 CFR could in certain circumstances oblige the executing state to 'end' the surrender procedure or to 'refrain from giving effect to the EAW'.[13]

In addition, Article 5 FDEAW describes two situations in which the executing Member State is allowed to render the surrender of the requested person subject to certain guarantees, which the issuing state should provide. Firstly, in cases in which the issuing state may impose a life-long sentence for the offence, the executing state may request guarantees covering the rules on a review of the sentence or the possibility of clemency.[14] Secondly, the executing state may request a return guarantee when surrendering their national or resident for the purpose of prosecution.[15] The requested person is then to be returned to the executing state for the execution of the sanction in case a custodial penalty is imposed in the issuing state.

Relevant Refusal Grounds and Guarantees

In theory, each of the conditions enumerated above could, regardless of true ratio, have the (accidental) effect of protecting EU citizens against surrender when one of the two complications arises. However, the main question of this chapter is to what extent any of these conditions were introduced by the EU legislator or CJEU for the specific purpose of offering such protection. In this light, the next paragraphs will only discuss the following conditions which show a clear potential link to the two complications discussed. Firstly, important refusal grounds are the double criminality requirement in Article 4(1) FDEAW and territoriality exception in Article 4(7)(a) FDEAW, which to a certain extent complements the partial abolition of the former. These refusal grounds touch upon the question according to whose laws the conduct should be classified as a criminal offence. Secondly, the territoriality exception, the extraterritoriality exception in Article 4(7)(b) and the refusal ground in Article 4(2) FDEAW could influence forum choices. However, these refusal

[11] See e.g. Case C-123/08 *Wolzenburg* [2009] ECLI:EU:C:2009:616, para 57; Case C-396/11 *Radu* [2013] ECLI:EU:C:2013:39, para 36.

[12] Case C-241/15 *Bob-Dogi* [2016] ECLI:EU:C:2016:385, paras 63–66.

[13] Joined Cases C-404/15 & C-659/15 *Aranyosi and Căldăraru* [2016] ECLI:EU:C:2016:198, para 104; Case C-216/18 *LM* [2018] ECLI:EU:C:2018:586, para 78.

[14] FDEAW, art 5(2).

[15] FDEAW, art 5(3).

grounds do not have a direct link to forum decisions, as their application does not oblige the executing state to prosecute or continue the prosecution of the requested person – no obligation *au dedere, aut judicare*.[16] In addition, the issuing state is not obliged to refrain from prosecution or to terminate its criminal proceedings when the execution of the EAW is refused. Still, the application of these three refusal grounds could influence the decision to prosecute of the issuing state and other competent states as well, because the absence of the suspect on their territories can complicate their criminal proceedings.[17] As a result, the issuing state may decide to refrain from prosecution or to halt ongoing criminal proceedings. Hence, the application of these refusal grounds could *de facto* settle a conflict of jurisdiction by hindering the prosecution in the issuing state or any other competent state. Thirdly, because Article 16 FDEAW on multiple EAWs for the same offence and the same requested person shows a similar indirect link to forum choices, it is also examined. After all, the decision to execute a particular EAW could discourage the other issuing states from further prosecuting the case.[18] Last to be analysed is whether the fundamental rights barriers to surrender introduced in the CJEU case law include the possibility to refuse an EAW in light of a link between the two complications and Articles 49 and 47 CFR.

Excluded Refusal Grounds and Guarantees

The next paragraphs therefore exclude the refusal grounds and guarantees based on national rules on amnesty, the age of criminal liability, statutory bars to prosecution, *in absentia* judgements and life-long sentences. They do now show a similar possible link to the question whose national criminal laws to obey or forum choices. It also follows from the legal literature that the refusal grounds primarily aim to protect state sovereignty.[19] Furthermore, the refusal grounds and guarantees offering protection to nationals and residents of the executing state, as well those which are based on the *ne bis in idem* principle, are excluded, even though they clearly reflect the free movement dimension of the AFSJ and aim to protect the requested person.

As stated before, Article 5(3) FDEAW allows the executing state to subject the surrender of its nationals and residents for the purpose of prosecution to a return guarantee in case a custodial sanction is imposed in the issuing state. Article 4(6) FDEAW allows the executing state to refuse an execution EAW issued for nationals, residents and persons staying in the executing state. It follows from the case law that these provisions have 'in particular the objective of enabling the executing judicial authority to give particular weight to the possibility of increasing

[16] Herrnfeld (2013), p. 191. In contrast, see Article 4(6) FDEAW and *Poplawski I*, from which it follows that the executing state may not refuse the execution of an execution EAW when it does not guarantee that it will execute the foreign sanction itself. Case C-579/15 *Poplawski* [2017] ECLI:EU:C:2017:503.

[17] Herrnfeld (2013), p. 191.

[18] See Eurojust Guidelines for deciding on competing requests for surrender and extradition (2019), p. 10.

[19] See Glerum (2013), pp. 372, 528, 587, 603, 607.

the requested person's chances of reintegrating into society'.[20] In addition, in the case *Da Silva Jorge* the CJEU ruled that the French implementation of Article 4(6) FDEAW, which only protected French nationals, was incompatible with EU law, more specifically the prohibition of discrimination on the basis of nationality in Article 18 TFEU.[21] This equal protection of nationals, residents and persons staying in the executing state, as well as the reintegration objective, fit in an AFSJ in which EU citizens are granted the right to free movement and are also encouraged to exercise this right.[22] However, neither Article 5(3) or 4(6) FDEAW has a clear link to the foreseeability of the applicable national substantive criminal law or forum choices. In case of a prosecution EAW, the nationality or place of residence of the requested person does not serve as a refusal ground, but merely as a reason to have the sanction executed in the executing state. Hence, this provision could merely influence a forum decision concerning the place of execution of the sanction and does not show a direct or indirect link to forum choices for the purpose of prosecution. The same goes for Article 4(6) FDEAW which covers execution EAWs and therefore merely influences the place where the sanction imposed will be enforced.

The refusal grounds which are based on the *ne bis in idem* principle aim to protect citizens' legal certainty and right to free movement.[23] Once a final decision on the case has been made, the exercise of free movement should not be hampered by fear of a fresh prosecution in another Member State. Despite their obvious connection to free movement and protection of the requested person, these refusal grounds do not show a link to the foreseeability of a national criminal law or forum choices for

[20] Case C-66/08 *Kozlowski* [2008] ECLI:EU:C:208:437, para 45; Case C-123/08 *Wolzenburg* [2009] ECLI:EU:C:2009:616, para 67; Case C-306/09 *IB* [2010] ECLI:EU:C:2010:626, para 52; Case C-314/18 *SF* [2020] ECLI:EU:C:2020:191, para 48.

[21] Case C-42/11 *Da Silva Jorge* [2012] ECLI:EU:C:2012:517, para 59.

[22] The case *Kozlowski* covers the interpretation of Article 4(6) FDEAW, in particular 'staying in' the executing state. Case C-66/08 *Kozlowski* [2008] ECLI:EU:C:208:437.

[23] FDEAW, arts 3(2) and 4(5); Case C-261/09 *Gaetano Mantello* [2010] ECLI:EU:C:2010:683, para 40; Joined Cases C-187/01 & C-385/01 *Hüseyin Gözütok & Klaus Brügge* [2003] ECLI:EU:C:2003:87, paras 38, 40; Case C-261/09 *Gaetano Mantello* [2010] ECLI:EU:C:2010:501, Opinion of AG Bot, para 113; Case C-268/17 *AY* [2018] ECLI:EU:C:2018:602, para 39. In addition, Article 4(3) FDEAW does not show a connection to either of the two complications. This refusal ground seems, at least to some extent, also based on the *ne bis in idem* principle. It includes three separate refusal grounds: the judicial authorities of the executing Member State have decided not to prosecute for the same act, they have decided to halt proceedings, or a final judgment has been passed in a Member State which prevents further proceedings. Glerum has explained the first two refusal grounds in light of the protection of state sovereignty. States have an interest in enforcing their own prosecution decisions, meaning that they should not have to set these decisions aside in favour of the interests of the issuing state. The last ground in Article 4(3) FDEAW—a final judgement passed in one of the Member States for the same acts which prevents further proceedings—was most likely introduced to allow Member States to refuse the execution of an EAW when the case is already decided in out-of-court proceedings in another Member State. However, as a result of the case law of the CJEU such final judgments nowadays fall under the scope of the *ne bis in idem* principle and therefore under Article 3(2) FDEAW. Glerum (2013), pp. 527–529; Suominen (2011), p. 247; Joined Cases C-187/01 & C-385/01 *Hüseyin Gözütok & Klaus Brügge* [2003] ECLI:EU:C:2003:87. See also Case C-268/17 *AY* [2018] ECLI:EU:C:2018:602, paras 47–62.

prosecution. This is because they exclusively cover situations in which the case has *not* already been finally disposed of in one of the Member States.

4.2.2 Double Criminality: Art 4(1) FDEAW

Article 4(1) FDEAW covers the double or dual criminality principle, which requires that the act or omission on which the EAW is based constitutes a criminal offence according to the laws of the issuing and executing state. Article 2(2) FDEAW excludes its application for the enumerated categories of offences, the so-called list-offences, if these are punishable with a custodial sanction of at least 3 years according to the law of the issuing state.[24] Article 2(4) FDEAW suggests an *in abstracto* double criminality assessment as it is sufficient that the conduct in question constitutes a criminal offence under the law of the executing state, regardless of its constituent elements or its specific description. Such an assessment is also adopted for double criminality requirements in other mutual recognition instruments, including Framework Decision JHA/2008/909 on the transfer of custodial sanctions. In *Grundza*, the CJEU decided that the double criminality requirement in this instrument should be interpreted restrictively, since it constitutes an exception to the principle of mutual recognition and hampers effective cooperation. Consequently, it is sufficient that the factual elements underlying the offence in the issuing state could also result in a criminal penalty in the executing state.[25] It is not necessary for the criminal offences to have identical constituent elements nor an identical name or classification under the law. It has been argued in the legal literature that this interpretation of double criminality in the context of Framework Decision 2008/909 can be transferred to the FDEAW as well, among other reasons, because both instruments cover the execution of a custodial sanction.[26]

The double criminality requirement shows a potential link to the first problem, which focuses on the surrender of citizens, while the applicability of the substantive criminal law of the issuing state was not foreseeable at the time of the offence. On the basis of this requirement, citizens can rely on the fact that they will not be surrendered to a state exercising extraterritorial jurisdiction as long as they act in compliance with the law of the executing state. However, the main question is whether the double criminality requirement has explicitly been linked to the *nullum crimen sine*

[24] In addition, Article 4(1) FDEAW states: ‘in relation to taxes or duties, customs and exchange, execution of the European arrest warrant shall not be refused on the ground that the law of the executing Member State does not impose the same kind of tax or duty or does not contain the same type of rules as regards taxes, duties and customs and exchange regulations as the law of the issuing Member State.’

[25] Case C-289/15 *Grundza* [2017] ECLI:EU:C:2017:4, paras 34–38, 46.

[26] Falkiewicz (2017), pp. 266–268; Handbook on how to issue and execute a European arrest warrant (European Commission Notice) [2017] OJ C335/1, 30. See also Case C-488/19 *JR* [2020] ECLI:EU:2020:738, Opinion AG Kokott, para 89.

lege principle by the EU legislator or CJEU and in that light aims to avoid the surrender of requested persons in case of unforeseeable jurisdiction claims.

The preparatory work on the FDEAW does not explicitly mention the ratio of the double criminality principle. However, it can be deducted from the 2001 Commission Proposal for the EAW that, similar to extradition procedures under public international law,[27] this requirement primarily aims to protect state sovereignty. The 2001 Commission Proposal also partially abolished the double criminality requirement, which was considered incompatible with cooperation on the basis of mutual recognition. However, this proposal allowed the Member States to draw up a so-called negative list of offences for the application of the double criminality requirement would be restored.[28] Allowing such a negative list of offences was based on the view that decriminalisation of certain behaviour is the result of a state's democratic process. In that light, a state should not be forced to aid the prosecution of another state which holds a different view with regard to the criminality of certain conduct.[29] This ratio is confirmed in the previously mentioned *Grundza* ruling concerning Framework Decision 2008/909. In this case, the CJEU decided that the double criminality requirement allows Member States to refuse the recognition of a judgement and enforcement of a foreign sanction for conduct they do not find morally wrong and have therefore not classified as a criminal offence.[30]

In addition, as previously discussed in Chap. 3, the absent link between the substantive legality principle and the double criminality requirement in the executing procedure also follows from the case *Advocaten voor de Wereld*.[31] In this case, the CJEU decided that the partial abolition of the double criminality requirement is compatible with the principle of legality in Article 49 CFR. The court stated that the FDEAW does not intend to harmonise the offences on the list in Article 2(2) FDEAW. In other words, this provision does not intend to establish certain conduct as a criminal offence. Instead, the definition of the list-offences depends on the law of the issuing state, which therefore needs to comply with the substantive legality principle.[32] With this preliminary ruling, the CJEU implicitly denied the existence of an inextricable link between the double criminality requirement as applicable in the surrender procedure and *the nullum crimen sine lege* principle, more specifically the requirement of an accessible and foreseeable law.[33]

Besides the EU legislator and the CJEU, several Advocate Generals and legal scholars have adopted the position that the double criminality requirement protects

[27] Suominen (2011), p. 171; Asp et al. (2006), p. 513; Ouwerkerk (2011), p. 111.

[28] European Commission, 'Proposal for a Council Framework Decision on the European arrest warrant and the surrender procedures between the Member States' COM (2001) 522 final, p. 16, art 29.

[29] COM (2001) 522 final, p. 16.

[30] Case C-289/15 *Grundza* [2017] ECLI:EU:C:2017:4, para 45.

[31] See Sect. 3.3.3; Case C-303/05 *Advocaten voor de Wereld* [2007] ECLI:EU:C:2007:261.

[32] Case C-303/05 *Advocaten voor de Wereld* [2007] ECLI:EU:C:2007:261, paras 49–54.

[33] See also De Amicis (2012), pp. 49–50.

state interests. It should not be viewed as a corollary of the substantive legality principle or a mechanism installed in order to protect citizens against unforeseeable jurisdiction claims.[34] In his opinion for the case *X* concerning the three-year requirement in Article 2(2) FDEAW, Advocate General Bobek states that the executing state should assess this requirement in light of its national law as applicable at the time of the execution of the EAW. The issuing state should assess the criminality of the conduct according to its national law as applicable at the time the conduct occurred. The explanation for this difference is that the law of the issuing state is applicable to the case and therefore needs to satisfy the *nullum crimen sine lege* principle, which demands that the conduct in question was criminalised by law at the time of the offence. The criminal law of the executing state is instead merely a condition for recognition of the EAW and therefore does not need to comply with the prohibition of the retroactive application of the law.[35] In addition, Glerum argues, and I agree with him, that the double criminality requirement in the EAW procedure does not necessarily contribute to the foreseeability of the criminality of certain behaviour on the basis of foreign laws. For example, imagine a situation in which the Netherlands arrests a Bulgarian national who Bulgaria wishes to prosecute for an act committed in France—however, the conduct in question is not a criminal act according to French law. The foreseeability of the criminality of the conduct according to Bulgarian law at the time of the offence is in this case not improved by the double criminality requirement, which is satisfied when the act is also a criminal offence according to the law of the executing state, in this case Dutch law. In other words, the double criminality requirement in surrender procedures could merely have the effect that the act must be classified as a criminal offence according to the law of a state—in this case the Netherlands—which has no link to the criminal offence or the suspect.[36] In such situations, the double criminality requirement does not provide clear safeguards against situations in which the jurisdiction claim of the issuing state was at the time of the offence difficult to foresee.

However, some national courts and scholars have questioned the conclusion of the CJEU in *Advocaten voor de Wereld.* They emphasise that the double criminality requirement in the surrender procedure at least contributes to the protection offered by the *nullum crimen sine lege* principle. The partial abolition of the double criminality requirement is therefore considered inconsistent with this principle.[37]

---

[34] Case C-717/18 *X* [2019] ECLI:EU:C:2019:1011, Opinion of AG Bobek, para 46. See eg Suominen (2011), pp. 171, 286–287; Asp et al. (2006), p. 513; Ouwerkerk (2011), p. 111; Borgers (2007), para 5.

[35] Case C-717/18 *X* [2019] ECLI:EU:C:2019:1011, Opinion of AG Bobek, paras 45–47. The CJEU restricted its judgment to the national criminal of the issuing state. In light of the double criminality requirement, the law as applicable at the time of the criminal offense is determinative. Case C-717/18 *X* [2020] ECLI:EU:C:2020:142, para 43.

[36] Glerum (2013), pp. 336–337.

[37] See eg the judgement of the Constitutional Court of the Czech Republic of 3 May 2006, sign. Pl. Us. 66/04 and the decision of the Hungarian Court of Cassation of 08 March 2008, sign. 733/A/2007; Herlin-Karnell (2007), pp. 1154, 1156. See also Borgers (2007), paras 4–5; Glerum (2013), pp. 341–342; Falkiewicz (2017), p. 265.

This position is based on the view that the double criminality requirement could to some extent have the effect of protecting the requested person against surrender in cases in which the issuing state exercises extraterritorial jurisdiction and the criminality of the conduct was therefore not necessarily foreseeable to the requested person at the time of the offence.[38] Some legal authors are of the opinion that it is difficult for citizens to find out whether certain conduct is prohibited in other states than, for instance, the state of nationality or the state in which the citizen is present.[39] Hence, the double criminality requirement meets at least to some extent the concern that within the outer borders of the AFSJ, citizens are in theory obliged to know and obey the laws of all EU Member States, which has an impact on the actual possibility to foresee the criminality of one's actions at the time of the offence.[40]

On the basis of the above, it can be concluded that neither the preparatory work to the FDEAW nor the CJEU case law link the double criminality requirement to the substantive legality principle or the requirements of foreseeability and accessibility. Hence, it seems most likely that the primary goal of the double criminality requirement in Article 4(1) FDEAW is respect for state sovereignty. It is the prerogative of states to decide which acts and omissions should be criminalised and, by extension, whether they want to aid the prosecution of a person in another state, while the behaviour in question does not constitute a criminal offence according to its own laws. Only in the legal literature do some legal scholars defend the view that the double criminality requirement contributes to the protection offered by the *nullum crimen sine lege* principle.

4.2.3 The Territoriality Exception: Art 4(7)(a) FDEAW

4.2.3.1 Its Link to Unforeseeable Jurisdiction Claims

Article 4(7)(a) FDEAW comprises the so-called territoriality exception. It states that the executing judicial authority may refuse the surrender of the requested person when the offence has been committed in whole or in part on the territory of the executing state or in a place treated as its territory. This refusal ground was pushed for by a delegation of Member States, including the Netherlands, which considered it a compensation measure for the partial abolition of the double criminality requirement in Article 2(2) FDEAW.[41] In that light, the territoriality exception allows, for instance, the Netherlands to refuse EAWs in cases in which the issuing state aims to prosecute the requested person for abortion, which is classified as a list-offence—murder—on

[38] See eg Blekxtoon (2005), p. 228. This point is also discussed in Glerum (2013), pp. 341–342; Borgers (2007), paras 4–5.

[39] See eg Borgers (2007), para 5.

[40] Wouters and Naert (2004), p. 925.

[41] Permanent Representatives Committee, 14867/01, 3; *Kamerstukken II* 2003/04, 29042, nr. 12, p. 9; Glerum (2013), pp. 338, 573.

the EAW, but which is not a criminal offence according to Dutch law.[42] Including the territoriality exception as a refusal ground in the FDEAW reflects the fact that EU Member States still have different views on what constitutes criminal behaviour.

In my view, in its capacity as a compensation measure, the territoriality exception could very well have been based on the view that citizens should be protected against surrender when the applicability of the law of the issuing state was not foreseeable at the time of the offence. More concretely, I think it shows a link to the view on the accessibility and foreseeability requirement discussed in Chap. 3, which entails that citizens should be able to know at the time of the offence that their conduct was criminal 'somewhere' (i.e., in a state). As explained before, this accessibility and foreseeability can be achieved by subjecting extraterritorial jurisdiction grounds to the double criminality requirement which demands that the act in question constitutes a criminal offence *de lege loci*. The double criminality requirement as a demarcation of a jurisdiction ground, therefore, differs from the double criminality requirement applicable in the surrender procedure. The latter covers the law of the executing state, which is not necessarily the state where the crime or part of the crime occurred. Considering the fact that, in the context of Article 4(7)(a) FDEAW, the executing state and the state where the conduct occurred are the same, the territoriality exception could also aim to offer protection against surrender when the criminality of the act somewhere was not sufficiently foreseeable, since the act in question is not punishable *de lege loci*.

However, neither the CJEU case law nor the preparatory work to the FDEAW clearly state whose interests—those of the state or those of the citizen—the territoriality exception as a compensation measure for the double criminality requirement aims to protect. In the legal literature, this refusal ground is explained in light of the protection of state sovereignty. The argument is that the state on whose territory the act occurred should not be forced to aid a foreign prosecution when the act is not an offence according to its own national law.[43]

Still, the legal literature and national parliamentary discussions occasionally also link the territoriality exception to the legality principle and refer to the legal certainty of the requested person, but not in the manner described above. The argument is that citizens should be able to rely on the fact that when they act in compliance with the law of the executing state, on whose territory the crime at least partially occurred, its authorities will not take any coercive actions against them at the request of another state.[44] This reasoning does not so much focus on the foreseeability of the national criminal law of the issuing state as it does on the link between the criminality of one's actions according to the law of the state where the conduct occurred and the exercise of coercive procedural powers by that state. In domestic situations, a state is normally not competent to exercise coercive criminal procedural competences when

[42] *Kamerstukken II* 2003/04, 29042, nr. 12, p. 9. See also Blekxtoon (2005), p. 237.

[43] Glerum (2013), pp. 338–339; *Kamerstukken II* 2003/04, 29,451, nr. 1 p. 9; Herrnfeld (2013), p. 191; Keijzer (2009), p. 96.

[44] Glerum (2013), pp. 338–339; *Kamerstukken II* 2003/04, 29451, nr. 1, p. 9, 11.

the conduct which occurred within its borders does not constitute a criminal act according to its national law.[45] In relation to the EAW, the argument seems to be that citizens should be able to trust that acting in compliance with the law of the state in which their conduct at least partially occurs does not only protect them in domestic situations against coercive measures from that state, but also in situations in which another state requests such coercive measures on its behalf.

Additionally, the scope of Article 4(7)(a) FDEAW goes beyond situations in which the act in question is not a criminal offence according to the law of the executing state. The refusal ground in principle covers all situations in which the act was committed partially or wholly on the territory of the executing state, regardless of the question whether this act constitutes a criminal offence according to the law of the executing state. Glerum relates the territoriality exception to the lack of EU harmonisation rules on jurisdiction and the absence of an EU mechanism for binding forum choices. In this context, Member States want to protect their sovereign interests in case of conflicts of jurisdiction.[46] Furthermore, the broad scope of Article 4(7)(a) FDEAW is in the legal literature often connected to the protection of state sovereignty.[47] The state on whose territory the act was committed should not only have the possibility to refuse assistance when it holds a different view with regard to the criminality of the conduct, but also when it holds a different view as to how to respond to these actions in concrete cases.[48] In other words, the state on whose territory the act occurred should have first say in deciding whether the act constitutes a criminal offence, whether it wishes to prosecute the case, and whether the requested person should be surrendered to be prosecuted elsewhere.

It follows from the above that Article 4(7)(a) FDEAW seems primarily based on the protection of state interests. However, as a compensation mechanism for the partial abolition of the double criminality requirement, the refusal ground has in the legal literature been linked to the legality principle. Those who see this link primarily seem to focus on the fact that no coercive actions may be taken against the requested person when the conduct is not criminal *de lege loci* and not on the foreseeability of the applicability of a particular law.

4.2.3.2 The Territoriality Exception and Forum Choices

As explained in Sect. 4.2.1, the territoriality exception does not constitute a forum decision *stricto sensu*. The decision to apply this refusal ground does not force the executing state to prosecute the case itself or the issuing state to halt its prosecution.

[45] For the Netherlands see HR 24 January 1984, ECLI:NL:HR:1984:AD5669 (Supreme Court); Corstens et al. (2018), p. 198.

[46] Glerum (2013), p. 573. See also Suominen (2011), pp. 288–289.

[47] Herrnfeld (2013), p. 191; Suominen (2011), pp. 288–289. See also *Kamerstukken II* 2003/04, 29042, nr. 12, p. 9; Glerum (2013), p. 573; Keijzer (2009), p. 93.

[48] Glerum (2013), pp. 339–340; Blekxtoon (2005), p. 237.

However, the territoriality exception can have an influence on where the case is eventually prosecuted and tried. The refusal to surrender the requested person could, for instance, complicate criminal proceedings in the issuing state, as a result of which it could decide to refrain from prosecution.

Article 4(7)(a) FDEAW provides Member States with the discretion to refuse the execution of the EAW, because they are of the opinion that the suspect should not be prosecuted at all or that the executing state or even another state is the better forum.[49] This discretion is hardly restricted and is most likely granted to protect the sovereignty of the executing state, which should not be forced to prioritise the views of the issuing state, regarding the need for a prosecution and the better forum, over its own.[50] In addition, it seems unlikely that Article 4(7)(a) FDEAW aims to protect the requested person in light of Article 47 CFR against the broad discretion of the national competent authorities to make coordinated or uncoordinated forum decisions in cross-border cases. Had the territoriality exception been intended as such a safeguard, the discretion of the executing judicial authority in applying the refusal ground would most likely have been further restricted by a set of clear factors guiding the decision of the executing judicial authority. Consequently, it can be concluded that the territoriality exception does not reflect any acknowledgement of the EU legislator that citizens should be protected against surrender in light of Article 47 CFR when the decision to prosecute of the issuing state is not based on a transparent system of forum rules for cross-border cases.

4.2.4 The Extraterritoriality Exception: Art 4(7)(b) FDEAW

Article 4(7)(b) FDEAW provides Member States with the possibility to refuse the execution of an EAW when the issuing state exercises extraterritorial jurisdiction. For this refusal ground to apply the executing state needs to establish that it would itself be unable to prosecute the case if the same offences had been committed outside its own territory. Hence, this refusal ground prevents surrender when the conduct in question does not constitute a criminal offence according to the law of the executing state or, in case it does, when the executing state itself would not have had jurisdiction to prosecute in a similar situation.

Similar to the territoriality exception, the extraterritoriality exception was included in the FDEAW to compensate for the partial abolition of the double criminality requirement.[51] It aims to protect state sovereignty and the principle of reciprocity, covering the equality of states.[52] In this light, the executing state should

[49] Glerum (2013), p. 340.

[50] Herrnfeld (2013), p. 191.

[51] COM (2001) 522 final, 16; Keijzer (2009), p. 97.

[52] Case C-488/19 *JR* [2020] ECLI:EU:2020:738, Opinion of AG Kokott, para 70; Glerum (2013), pp. 340–341; Suominen (2011), p. 289. See also Keijzer (2009), p. 96; Blekxtoon (2005), p. 238.

not be forced to assist the issuing state in the enforcement of its national criminal law if it cannot request assistance in a similar case. Neither the preparatory work to the FDEAW nor the CJEU case law link this refusal ground to protection which should be offered to citizens in light of Article 47 or 49 CFR or the position that, without clear rules on forum choices, the EAW could become a mechanism for the enforcement of arbitrary forum decisions.

4.2.5 *Domestic Criminal Proceedings in the Executing State: Art 4(2) FDEAW*

Article 4(2) FDEAW allows the executing state to refuse the execution of the EAW in case of domestic proceedings against the requested person for the same acts as those on which the EAW is based.[53] Similar to Article 4(7)(a) FDEAW, this refusal ground does not constitute a forum decision *stricto sensu*, but it can influence the eventual forum decision.[54] For instance, the fact that the executing state has the suspect on its territory and has started domestic proceedings could increase its chances of reaching a final decision first. Furthermore, Article 4(2) FDEAW could cause conflicts of jurisdiction when the executing state decides to start criminal proceedings after the receipt of the EAW.[55]

The exact ratio of Article 4(2) FDEAW, as in which and whose interests it aims to protect, is not clearly explained in the preparatory work nor in the case law of the CJEU. However, it can be deduced from the legal literature that this refusal ground is not based on the legality principle, at least not primarily. Instead, it seems to be a mechanism protecting the sovereignty and national interests of the executing state.[56] In this regard, Glerum has argued that the existence of this refusal ground can be explained in light of the absence of EU rules fully harmonising jurisdiction and a

[53] It remains unclear at what point in time the requested person is in fact 'being prosecuted' in the executing state. This term has not been harmonised or explained in the preparatory work to the FDEAW or the CJEU case law while the definition of prosecution in the Member States differs. Blekxtoon (2005), pp. 559, 562; Suominen (2011), pp. 241–242.

[54] This more indirect link to forum choices also follows from the preparatory work to the FDEAW in which the European Parliament stated that the executing state had to be provided with the discretion to decide that the issuing state would be a more appropriate forum for prosecution and discontinue its domestic proceedings in light of this conclusion. European Parliament, A5-0397/2001, amendment 71.

[55] States that have adopted the principle of obligatory prosecution (legality principle) could be forced to start national criminal proceedings. See eg Chap. 6. See also Report on Eurojust's Casework in the Field of the European Arrest Warrant (2021) <https://www.eurojust.europa.eu/report-eurojusts-casework-field-european-arrest-warrant-july-2021> accessed 20 September 2021, 23, 66.

[56] Blekxtoon (2005), p. 235; Glerum (2013), p. 560 which refers back to page 556; Klimek (2014), para 7.5.2.

binding EU mechanism solving conflicts of jurisdictions.[57] In such a context Member States are provided with refusal grounds like Article 4(2) FDEAW to protect their sovereignty and national interests in case of competing jurisdiction claims.[58] Without such refusal grounds they run the risk of being forced to assist the issuing state, even though they hold a different opinion with regard to the question of which state is the better forum in light of the proper administration of justice.[59] In addition, states should not be forced to prioritise the prosecution interests of the issuing state over their own.[60]

Some legal scholars are of the opinion that Article 4(2) emphasises the avoidance and coordination of multiple prosecutions, which can also be in the interest of the citizen.[61] Still, even if this is true and Article 4(2) FDEAW has some link to the interests of the citizen, nothing suggests that this refusal ground is based on the view that the lack of a transparent EU system on forum choices, going beyond the existing Framework Decision covering conflicts of jurisdiction, constitutes a threat to the right to a tribunal established by law in Article 47 CFR. In other words, there is no clear indication that this refusal ground relates to the argument that, in light of Article 47 CFR, citizens should be protected against surrender when the decision to prosecute of the issuing state is not based on a clear EU system for forum choices in cross-border cases. This seems to be confirmed by the fact that Article 4(2) FDEAW does not restrict the discretion of the executing judicial authority in making its decision. This refusal ground does not mention any factors or criteria on the basis of which the executing judicial authority should decide whether the executing or the issuing state is the most suitable forum for prosecution and trial.

4.2.6 Fundamental Rights as a Bar to Surrender

Since its early case law on the EAW, the CJEU has consistently stated that the mandatory and optional refusal grounds are exhaustively enumerated in Articles 3, 4 and 4A FDEAW.[62] These do not include a general human rights refusal ground, which states that the execution of an EAW may or must be refused when the requested person faces a real risk of fundamental rights violations in the issuing

[57] Framework Decision 2009/948/JHA on conflicts of jurisdictions does not oblige states to reach an agreement on whom should prosecute, which means that no state can be forced to prosecute or to refrain from prosecution.

[58] Glerum (2013), pp. 149, 559.

[59] Glerum (2013), p. 560. This position is also reflected in the statement of the European Parliament. European Parliament, A5-0397/2001, amendment 71.

[60] Glerum (2013), p. 560.

[61] Suominen (2011), p. 242.

[62] Case C-123/08 *Wolzenburg* [2009] ECLI:EU:C:2009:616, para 57; Case C-396/11 *Radu* [2013] ECLI:EU:C:2013:39, para 69.

state.[63] The absence of a general human rights refusal ground can be explained in light of the principles of mutual trust and mutual recognition which constitute the basis of the EAW.[64] Mutual trust entails that states have a high level of confidence in each other's compliance with fundamental rights standards recognised by EU law.[65] Consequently, in judicial cooperation procedures like the EAW, a state may in principle not impose a higher standard of fundamental rights protection than the standard set by EU law or check in a concrete case whether the other state has observed EU fundamental rights standards. Despite the strong emphasis on the importance of this so-called presumption of mutual trust, the CJEU stated in Opinion 2/13 concerning the accession of the EU to the ECHR that this presumption can be rebutted in exceptional circumstances. In such situations, Member States are allowed to check or verify the fundamental rights situation in another state.[66] This conclusion of the CJEU opened the door to the further integration of fundamental rights protection in the context of the surrender procedure outside the scope of the official refusal grounds in the FDEAW.[67]

The possibility to rebut the presumption of mutual trust has in the context of the EAW procedure so far been used for potential violations of Article 4 CFR (the prohibition of torture and inhuman and degrading treatment) and of Article 47 CFR (the right to an independent tribunal).[68] In *Aranyosi and Căldăraru*, the CJEU established a twofold test for rebutting mutual trust in case of a possible violation of Article 4 CFR. The first step is to establish systemic or general deficiencies in the detention conditions of the issuing state on the basis of objective, reliable, specific and properly updated information.[69] The second step requires the executing judicial authority to determine specifically and precisely whether there are substantial grounds to believe that the surrender of the requested person will expose him or her to a real risk of a violation of Article 4 CFR. When both requirements are met, the execution of the EAW should be postponed. The surrender procedure may be ended all together when the existence of the concrete risk cannot be discounted within a reasonable time.[70] In

[63] However, some refusal grounds protect specific fundamental rights, such as Article 3(2) FDEAW.

[64] FDEAW, recital 10 and art 1(2); Case C-396/11 *Radu* [2013] ECLI:EU:C:2013:39, paras 33–34. See also COM (2001) 522 final 15–16; Xanthopoulou (2018), pp. 492–494.

[65] Opinion 2/13 [2014] ECLI:EU:C:2014:2454, para 191.

[66] Opinion 2/13 [2014] ECLI:EU:C:2014:2454, para 192. See also Case C-399/11 *Melloni* [2013] ECLI:EU:C:2013:107, para 63.

[67] Billing (2020), p. 190.

[68] Joined Cases C-404/15 & C-659/15 *Aranyosi and Căldăraru* [2016] ECLI:EU:C:2016:198; Case C-216/18 *LM* [2018] ECLI:EU:C:2018:586. New preliminary questions have now been posed to the CJEU with regard to the application of the *LM* test in case of a real risk of a violation to the right to a tribunal established by law in the issuing state. See case C-480/21; Rb. Amsterdam 14 September 2021, ECLI:NL:RBAMS:2021:505 (Amsterdam District Court).

[69] Joined Cases C-404/15 & C-659/15 *Aranyosi and Căldăraru* [2016] ECLI:EU:C:2016:198, para 89. On the requirement of 'systemic deficiencies', see also Von Bogdandy (2020).

[70] Joined Cases C-404/15 & C-659/15 *Aranyosi and Căldăraru* [2016] ECLI:EU:C:2016:198, paras 94, 98, 104.

LM, the CJEU applied this twofold test with some adaptions in relation to the right to an independent tribunal in Article 47 CFR.[71] In the context of the first step the executing judicial authority should decide on the basis of objective, reliable and updated information whether a real risk exists that the essence of the right to a fair trial is compromised as a result of general or systemic deficiencies concerning the judiciary of the issuing Member State relating to the guarantee that courts and tribunals are independent. The second step requires the executing judicial authority to assess specifically and precisely whether there are substantial grounds for believing that the requested person will be exposed to that risk in the concrete case. This step has two sub-steps. Firstly, the executing judicial authority needs to establish to what extent the general deficiencies regarding the independence of the courts could impact the level of courts with jurisdiction over the proceedings for which the surrender is requested. Secondly, it should determine in light of the specific concerns expressed by the requested person whether substantial grounds exist to assume that he or she will be exposed to the risk of a violation of the right to an independent court after his or her surrender. The latter determination needs to be based on the personal situation of the requested person, the nature of the offence of the underlying criminal case and the factual context which constitutes the basis of the EAW. When the information provided by the issuing judicial authority to contradict the existence of a concrete risk is insufficient, the executing judicial authority has to refrain from 'giving effect' to the EAW.[72] It follows from the above that the CJEU is very careful in the formulation of Articles 4 and 47 CFR as possible bars to surrender. It does not refer to these fundamental rights as possible refusal grounds, but states that a real risk of a violation in the issuing state could justify the 'ending' of the surrender procedure by the executing state or its decision not to 'give effect' to the EAW.

Opinion 2/13 and the subsequent case law on Articles 4 and 47 CFR show that currently the EAW procedure offers at least in theory a possibility to prevent the surrender of a citizen when concerns arise about the compatibility of the law of the issuing state with the *nullum crimen sine lege* principle and the right to a tribunal established by law. These fundamental rights could also serve as justifications for an exception to the presumption of mutual trust and the prohibition to verify another state's compliance with fundamental rights in a judicial cooperation procedure. However, exceptions to mutual trust in the EAW procedure have so far only been accepted in relation to specific fundamental rights and for specific reasons and the CJEU has not (yet) decided that possible violations of Article 49 CFR and the right to a tribunal established by law are also accepted as exceptional circumstances. Furthermore, a mere breach of fundamental rights is not sufficient for the circumstances to be classified as 'exceptional'. As explained by AG Kokott, 'not every conceivable breach of fundamental rights' in the issuing state should be viewed as an exceptional circumstance, since mutual trust in principle entails that the requested person can challenge such a breache before the national court of the

[71] On this case see Simonelli (2019), p. 335.

[72] Case C-216/18 *LM* [2018] ECLI:EU:C:2018:586, paras 60–61, 68, 74–78.

issuing state.[73] Hence, a serious and real risk of fundamental rights violations in the concrete case are required. It can, therefore, be deduced from the CJEU case law that Opinion 2/13 did not intend to establish a general human rights refusal ground in surrender proceedings which applies to any breach of fundamental rights. More concretely, this deduction follows from the fact that the exception on the basis of Article 4 CFR was made, because of its status as an absolute fundamental right, closely related to respect for human dignity.[74] With regard to Article 47 CFR the CJEU placed a lot of emphasis on the fact that judicial independence is part of the essence of the right to a fair trial. The latter is in itself is a fundamental aspect of the rule of law, which in turn is a common value of the Member States.[75] In addition, the case *TR* is an example in which the CJEU decided that a possible violation of a fundamental right, in that case the right to be present during the trial or right to a retrial as regulated in Directive 2016/343, does not fall under the scope of 'exceptional circumstances'.[76] This ruling states that the executing judicial authority cannot refuse the execution of an EAW issued for an *in absentia* judgement, because it is not completely certain that the right to a retrial will be complied with in the issuing state. This decision was based on the argument that the FDEAW itself already provides protection in case of *in absentia* judgements, which is in compliance with the right to a fair trial and specific defence rights in Articles 47 and 48 CFR.[77] Furthermore, after the surrender, requested persons can rely before the national courts on the provisions of the Directive when they meet the requirements of direct effect.[78]

It can be concluded that the fundamental rights exception currently does not provide the possibility to refuse an EAW because of legality concerns in light of Articles 49 and 47 CFR. Whether the CJEU would in the future accept possible violations of Articles 49 and 47 CFR due to unforeseeable jurisdiction claims and forum decisions without a transparent legal framework as valid reasons not to execute an EAW remains to be seen.[79]

[73] See also Case C-488/19 *JR* [2020] ECLI:EU:2020:738, Opinion of AG Kokott, paras 55–56.

[74] This argument was made in the context of Article 1(3) FDEAW which states that the EAW is not to have the effect of modifying the obligation to respect fundamental rights. Joined Cases C-404/15 & C-659/15 *Aranyosi and Căldăraru* [2016] EU:C:2016:198, paras 83–87.

[75] Case C-216/18 *LM* [2018] ECLI:EU:C:2018:586, paras 48–54.

[76] Case C-416/20 *TR* [2020] ECLI:EU:C:2020:1042. See also the opinion of AG Tanchev, who assessed whether the *Aranyosi and Căldăraru* and *LM* test should be applied in the case at hand. Case C-416/20 *TR* [2020] ECLI:EU:C:2020:1020, Opinion of AG Tanchev.

[77] Case C-416/20 *TR* [2020] ECLI:EU:C:2020:1042, paras 36–47.

[78] Case C-416/20 *TR* [2020] ECLI:EU:C:2020:1042, para 55.

[79] National courts have asked preliminary questions with regard to the application of the twofold test in relation to other fundamental rights. See Case C-699/21 and Rb. Amsterdam 14 September 2021, ECLI:NL:RBAMS:2021:5051 (Amsterdam District Court).

4.2.7 *Multiple EAWs: Art 16 FDEAW*

Article 16 FDEAW covers the situation in which the executing state receives multiple EAWs for the same person and the same criminal case. Like the refusal grounds in Articles 4(2) and 4(7) FDEAW, the application of the rules in Article 16 FDEAW could influence the eventual forum decision. This also follows from the Eurojust Guidelines on competing EAWs which state that deciding which EAW should be executed in principle means deciding which jurisdiction should prosecute.[80] This (indirect) link between forum decisions and Article 16 FDEAW designates the latter as a suitable legal provision for the preliminary question whether Article 47(2) CFR applies in the context of conflicts of national jurisdictions and by extension in the context of Article 16 FDEAW. However, this opportunity for a preliminary question has so far not been used by the national courts. In that light, the next paragraphs examine to what extent the decision of the executing judicial authority in the context of Article 16 FDEAW is guided by formal and clear factors set out by the EU legislator or rules of soft law on the basis of Article 47 CFR.

According to the European Commission Handbook on the issuing of an EAW, the main rule is that the decision is made on a case-by-case basis and that 'first-come, first-served' situations are avoided.[81] The executing judicial authority needs to fairly assess and balance the different factors and specific circumstances.[82] In cases in which the issuing states have already entered into discussions on the most appropriate forum, for instance, in the context of the obligations imposed by Framework Decision 2009/948/JHA on conflicts of jurisdiction, the executing judicial authority should take the outcome of these consultations into account.[83] In addition, the executing state should notify the issuing states of the risk of parallel proceedings, and these states should in turn inform the executing judicial authority of their progress to settle the conflict of jurisdictions.[84]

Article 16(1) FDEAW itself states that the executing judicial authority shall make the decision with due consideration for all the circumstances, but in particular the relative seriousness and place of the offences, the respective dates of the European arrest warrants and whether the warrant has been issued for the purposes of prosecution or for the execution of a custodial sentence. This constitutes a non-exhaustive list which has no strict pecking order. Such a hierarchy is also not established by

[80] Eurojust Guidelines for deciding on competing requests for surrender and extradition (2019), p. 10. See also Luchtman (2011), p. 90.

[81] FDEAW, art 16(1); Handbook on how to issue and execute a European arrest warrant (European Commission Notice) [2017] OJ C335/1, p. 53.

[82] Eurojust Guidelines for deciding on competing requests for surrender and extradition (2019), p. 7.

[83] The executing judicial authority is however not legally obliged to follow the conclusions of such coordination discussions. Handbook on how to issue and execute a European arrest warrant (European Commission Notice) [2017] OJ C335/1, p. 52.

[84] Handbook on how to issue and execute a European arrest warrant (European Commission Notice) [2017] OJ C335/1, pp. 53–54. Eurojust Guidelines for deciding on competing requests for surrender and extradition (2019) p. 8.

other instruments, such as the Eurojust Guidelines on competing EAWs. The latter only establishes a mild ranking as they, for instance, state that the relative seriousness of the offence is less important, since all EAWs are in principle issued for the same criminal act. In addition, these guidelines mention that the stage of the criminal procedure in each state should have a more important role than the date on which the EAW was issued.[85]

It follows from the above that the discretion of the executing judicial authority is only to a very limited extent restricted by Article 16 FDEAW and by non-binding EU instruments, such as the Eurojust Guidelines on competing EAWs and the Commission Handbook on the issuing of an EAW. These rules do, however, state that 'first-come, first-served decisions' should be avoided, which implies an acknowledgement of the risk that the EAW facilitates such unwanted forum choices. More generally, the preparatory work to the FDEAW and the rules of soft law do not discuss whether the broad discretion of the executing judicial authority in case of competing EAWs could contribute to the EAW as a mechanism enforcing arbitrary forum decisions. In other words, there has been no discussion of the risk that the EAW could facilitate prosecution by an arbitrary forum, nor has protection against this risk been installed by delineating the discretion of the executing judicial authority in Article 16 FDEAW. In fact, I think that the emphasis on viewing each situation as a unique one, and the obligation to take all circumstances of the case into account, suggests that flexibility in choosing which EAW should be executed—and by extension the state where prosecution should take place—is considered important. The broad discretion for the executing judicial authority, correlating from a non-exhaustive and non-hierarchical list of relevant factors in Article 16 FDEAW, could be advantageous in the sense that it expands the possibility to choose the best forum for a concrete case.

4.3 Protection Offered by the FDEAW: Issuing Procedure

4.3.1 An Introduction

The most important legal provisions in the FDEAW regulating the issuing procedure are Articles 2, 6 and 8 FDEAW. The content of these legal provisions shows that the FDEAW leaves the Member States with ample discretion to determine the issuing procedure. Before discussing them more in-depth, it is important to note beforehand that they do not require the issuing state to prove that it has jurisdiction to prescribe and adjudicate in a concrete case. Such proof is not necessary in light of the presumed trust that the issuing state does not send out an EAW unless its criminal law applies to the conduct in question and its national courts are competent to try the

[85] Eurojust Guidelines for deciding on competing requests for surrender and extradition (2019) pp. 10–11.

case.[86] However, the existing legal provisions on the issuing procedure still show a possible link to the two problems discussed, most strongly to the foreseeability of the national applicable laws. Firstly, the double criminality requirement in Article 2 FDEAW is also of importance for the issuing state, as this state needs to determine whether the offence in question is a list-offence in relation to which the double criminality requirement does not apply.[87] As explained before, the double criminality requirement touches upon the question according to whose laws the act should constitute a criminal offence. The double criminality requirement will therefore also be discussed in this section. Secondly, Article 8(1)(c) FDEAW requires that a prosecution EAW is based on an enforceable national arrest warrant or equivalent judicial order.[88] This requirement could be linked to the issuing state's jurisdiction to prescribe and adjudicate, since states may usually not exercise coercive investigative powers when their national criminal law is not applicable to the conduct in question. Thirdly, Article 6(1) FDEAW covers the appointment of the issuing judicial authority which has resulted in an important string of CJEU case law. In this case law, the CJEU interprets the requirement of an issuing judicial authority, but also sets out additional conditions for the issuing of an EAW. As the reasoning of the CJEU in this case law is strongly based on fundamental rights protection, Article 6(1) FDEAW is also discussed.

4.3.2 The Double Criminality Requirement: Art 2(4) FDEAW

As explained before, Article 2(2) FDEAW enumerates the categories of offences in relation to which the double criminality requirement is abolished. The issuing state may mark the offence as a list-offence on the EAW when it falls under one of the 32 categories and when the offence is punishable in the issuing state by a custodial sentence or detention order for a maximum period of at least 3 years. In relation to the latter requirement, the CJEU has determined in the case *X* that, for the issuing state, the criminal law in force at the time of the conduct is determinative for the

[86] Glerum (2013), p. 572. See also Rb. Amsterdam 15 October 2004, ECLI:NL:RBAMS:2004:AR4237 (Amsterdam District Court).

[87] FDEAW, art 2(2). Article 2(1) FDEAW is not relevant as it reflects a proportionality assessment. It aims to avoid that the executing state is bothered with EAWs for minor offenses and sanctions. Case C-717/18 *X* [2019] ECLI:EU:C:2019:1011, Opinion of AG Bobek, para 22; Blekxtoon (2005), p. 227.

[88] Article 8(1)(d) and (e) require a description of the nature and legal classification of the offense as well as the circumstances within which the offence was committed, covering at least the time, place and degree of participation by the requested person. The purpose of this description in the EAW is to ensure that the executing state is in a position to verify whether the conditions for surrender are met and whether refusal grounds apply. Consequently, the requirement to provide information on the offense is not linked to the right to an accessible and foreseeable law in Article 49 CFR and the right to a tribunal established by law in Article 47 CFR. Handbook on how to issue and execute a European arrest warrant (European Commission Notice) [2017] OJ C335/1, p. 68.

decision whether it is satisfied and not the version of the criminal law applicable at the time of the issuing of the EAW. The latter would clash with the foreseeability requirement correlating from the principle of legal certainty.[89] The CJEU does not further elaborate on this conclusion, nor does it explicitly refer to the *nullum crimen sine lege* principle or even Article 49 CFR. It therefore remains unclear whether it bases its ruling on the substantive legality requirement or on the more general principle of legal certainty to which AG Bobek also points in his Opinion.[90] Regardless of the answer to this question, the CJEU's decision in the case *X* is in line with its decision in *Advocaten voor de Wereld*, in which it determined that the partial abolition of the double criminality requirement does not release the issuing state of its obligation under Article 49 CFR to ensure that the criminal offences and sanctions in its national law are accessible and foreseeable. Hence, the national criminal law of the issuing state must satisfy the requirements of the *nullum crimen sine lege* principle.

So, the legality principle or legal certainty principle appears important for the interpretation of the conditions demarcating the scope of application of the double criminality requirement from the perspective of the law of the issuing state. However, the case law does not provide a clear answer to the question whether the CJEU is of the opinion that unforeseeable jurisdiction claims affect the foreseeability and accessibility of criminal offences and sanctions in light of Article 49 CFR, and whether this should in turn affect the question whether the double criminality requirement is met.

4.3.3 The Content of the EAW: Art 8(1) FDEAW

Article 8(1) FDEAW enumerates which information the EAW needs to contain. Article 8(1)(c) FDEAW demands that a prosecution EAW provides evidence of a national arrest warrant or any other enforceable judicial decision having the same effect.[91] The need for a separate national judicial decision underlying the EAW is not intended to be a mere formal requirement.[92] It is based on the argument that, within the context of the surrender procedure, the requested person should be provided with fundamental rights protection on two levels: the level at which the national arrest warrant or equivalent decision is issued, and the level at which the EAW is issued.[93]

[89] Case C-717/18 *X* [2020] ECLI:EU:C:2020:142, para 38.

[90] Case C-717/18 *X* [2019] ECLI:EU:C:2019:1011, Opinion of AG Bobek, paras 102–103. On the principle of legal certainty, see Case T-279/02 *Degussa* [2006] ECLI:EU:T:2006:103, para 66; Joined Cases C-72/10 and C-77/10 *Costa and Cifone* [2012] ECLI:EU:C:2012:80, para 74; Case C-318/10 *SIAT* [2012] ECLI:EU:C:2012:415, para 58; Case C-282/12 *Itelcar* [2013] ECLI:EU:C:2013:629, para 44.

[91] Case C-241/15 *Bob-Dogi* [2016] ECLI:EU:C:2016:385, paras 48–49.

[92] Case C-241/15 *Bob-Dogi* [2016] ECLI:EU:C:2016:131, Opinion of AG Bot, para 62.

[93] Case C-241/15 *Bob-Dogi* [2016] ECLI:EU:C:2016:385, paras 55–56. See also Case C-241/15 *Bob-Dogi* [2016] ECLI:EU:C:2016:131, Opinion of AG Bot, paras 55–56.

Hence, the requirement in Article 8(1)(c) FDEAW ensures that the requested person has enjoyed the fundamental and procedural safeguards which accompany the adoption of a national arrest warrant or equivalent judicial order on the basis of national law.[94] In *Özçelik*, the CJEU added that the national judicial decision underlying the FDEAW needs to be issued or confirmed by a national authority which participates in the administration of justice of the issuing state.[95]

Advocate General Bot views the need for a national arrest warrant in Article 8(1)(c) FDEAW as an expression of the *procedural* principle of legality. He argues that it follows from this legality principle that national authorities may only exercise coercive powers, such as arrests within the limits imposed upon them by law. As the EAW is an extension of a national arrest warrant, the latter should be issued in compliance with the applicable national criminal procedural laws.[96] However, the CJEU does not specifically and explicitly link Article 8(1)(c) FDEAW to Article 49 CFR or Article 47(2) CFR. Nothing indicates that the goal of the requirement of a national judicial decision underlying the EAW is to prevent the issuing of EAWs in light of Articles 49 and 47 CFR when the applicability of the national criminal law of the issuing state was difficult to predict or the decision to prosecute is not based on a clear overarching EU system for forum choices.

4.3.4 Issuing Judicial Authority and Other Procedural Requirements: Art 6(1) FDEAW

The requirement that the EAW is issued by a 'judicial authority' has been the subject of several preliminary rulings clarifying its meaning and purpose. It follows from this case law that Member States need to appoint a national authority which participates in the administration of justice.[97] In light of the fact that the surrender procedure aims to replace the intergovernmental extradition procedure, appointing the Minister of Justice or the police as the issuing authority is not allowed.[98] However, a public prosecutor who is competent to prosecute suspects for criminal offences and bring them before the criminal court in the domestic legal order is considered an authority participating in the administration of justice.[99] Besides this

[94] Case C-241/15 *Bob-Dogi* [2016] ECLI:EU:C:2016:385, paras 55–56.

[95] Case C-453/16 *Özçelik* [2017] ECLI:EU:C:2016:860, para 33.

[96] See also Case C-241/15 *Bob-Dogi* [2016] ECLI:EU:C:2016:131, Opinion of AG Bot, para 66. See also Case C-414/20 *MM* [2020] ECLI:EU:C:2020:1009, Opinion of AG Tour, para 78.

[97] Case C-477/16 *Kovalkovas* [2016] ECLI:EU:C:2016:861, paras 41–42. See also Case C-452/16 *Poltorak* [2016] ECLI:EU:C:2016:858, para 33; Joined Cases C-508/18 & C-82/19 *OG & PI* [2019] ECLI:EU:C:2019:456, paras 50–51.

[98] Case C-477/16 *Kovalkovas* [2016] ECLI:EU:C:2016:861, paras 41–42; Case C-452/16 *Poltorak* [2016] ECLI:EU:C:2016:858, para 35; Case C-453/16 *Özçelik* [2017] ECLI:EU:C:2016:860, para 32.

[99] Case C-509/18 *PF* [2019] ECLI:EU:C:2019:457, paras 29–39.

criterion, the issuing judicial authority needs to be objective in the sense that it takes all incriminatory and exculpatory evidence into account when making a decision. He or she also needs to be independent in the sense that the national law does not subject its decision-making powers to external directions or instructions from others, in particular members of the executive.[100] In relation to the requirement of independence, the CJEU demands that the statutory rules and institutional framework of the issuing state shows how it is beyond doubt that the decision to issue an EAW is not directly or indirectly made by the executive.[101] These demarcations of the Member States' power to appoint the issuing judicial authority are based on the argument that the EAW is capable of infringing the right to liberty in Article 6 CFR and the general need to protect fundamental rights and safeguards in the context of the surrender procedure.[102] As stated before, the FDEAW demands a dual level of procedural and fundamental rights protection of which the first level covers the national decision on which the EAW is based, and the second level the procedure for the issuing of an EAW.[103] The issuing judicial authority should be objective and independent, as it is responsible for the second level of protection, which entails that it has to review the conditions for the issuing of an EAW and whether the decision to issue an EAW is proportionate in light of the concrete circumstances of the case.[104]

The preliminary rulings on Article 6(1) FDEAW also establish other separate requirements for the issuing of an EAW, which are however not linked to the appointment of the issuing judicial authority.[105] The CJEU has, for instance, determined that the issuing judicial authority should conduct a proportionality check in each concrete case.[106] It also ruled that since the EAW could infringe upon the right to liberty and the surrender procedure is based on a twofold level of fundamental rights protection, the decision at one of these two levels needs to meet the conditions of effective judicial protection, which seems to mean a court or tribunal *stricto*

[100] Joined Cases C-508/18 & C-82/19 *OG & PI* [2019] ECLI:EU:C:2019:456, para 73; Case C-489/19 *NJ* [2019] ECLI:EU:C:2019:849, para 38.

[101] Joined Cases C-508/18 & C-82/19 *OG & PI* [2019] ECLI:EU:C:2019:456, para 74. In *JR & YC* the CJEU stated that the power of the executive to impose general instructions concerning criminal policy on the public prosecutors to ensure coherency does not affect the independence of the issuing judicial authority as long as these instructions cannot affect the discretion of the issuing judicial authority to decide in a concrete case whether the conditions for the issuing of an EAW are met. Joined Cases C-566/19 & C-626/19 *JR & YC* [2019] ECLI:EU:C:2019:1077, para 54.

[102] Joined Cases C-508/18 & C-82/19 *OG & PI* [2019] ECLI:EU:C:2019:456, paras 67–73; Case C-509/18 *PF* [2019] ECLI:EU:C:2019:457, paras 45–51.

[103] Case C-241/15 *Bob-Dogi* [2016] ECLI:EU:C:2016:385, paras 55–56.

[104] Joined Cases C-508/18 & C-82/19 *OG & PI* [2019] ECLI:EU:C:2019:456, paras 71–72; Case C-509/18 *PF* [2019] ECLI:EU:C:2019:457, paras 49–50; Case C-489/19 *NJ* [2019] ECLI:EU:C:2019:849, para 37; Case C-414/20 *MM* [2021] ECLI:EU:C:2021:4, para 64.

[105] Joined Cases C-566/19 & C-626/19 *JR & YC* [2019] ECLI:EU:C:2019:1077, paras 48–49; Case C-509/18 *PF* [2019] ECLI:EU:C:2019:457, para 56.

[106] Joined Cases C-508/18 & C-82/19 *OG & PI* [2019] ECLI:EU:C:2019:456, para 71. See also Handbook on how to issue and execute a European arrest warrant (European Commission Notice) [2017] OJ C335/1, p. 14–15.

sensu.[107] This entails that when the power to issue an EAW is allocated to the public prosecutor or another authority, which is not a court or judge, the national arrest warrant needs to meet these conditions.[108] Furthermore, with regard to prosecution EAWs when the national judicial decision meets the requirements of effective judicial protection, but the issuing judicial authority is not a court or judge, the requested person must be offered the possibility to challenge the decision to issue an EAW before a court in the issuing Member State.[109] These court proceedings in the issuing state also need to meet the requirements of effective judicial protection. Hence, in light of the right to effective judicial protection, a court or judge should be involved in the decision to issue an EAW, or the requested person should be provided with the possibility to challenge the decision to issue an EAW in the issuing state.[110] This raises the question whether the requested person should or could use this possibility of proceedings before a court or judge as a possibility to also address the foreseeability of the underlying jurisdiction claim and underlying forum decision of the issuing state. In my opinion, it is not very likely that this was the intent of the CJEU, since the case law specifically refers to the possibility to challenge the decision to issue an EAW.[111] Even though the scope of application of the issuing state's substantive criminal law and its decision to prosecute are closely related to the decision to issue an EAW, they are as such not part of the conditions to issue an EAW or regulated by the FDEAW. In addition, in the case *ZB* the CJEU decided that the right to challenge the decision to issue an EAW before the national court in the issuing state only applies in case of prosecution EAWs. In case of execution EAWs, the judgements in the criminal cases constitute the basis of the EAW and are assumed to be the result of criminal proceedings conducted in compliance with Article 47 CFR. These judgements are viewed as the equivalents of the possibility to challenge the decision to issue an EAW.[112] Hence, in light of the above, it is doubtful that the possibility of a judicial check on the decision to issue an EAW was intended as a possibility to challenge the foreseeability of the jurisdiction

[107] Joined Cases C-508/18 & C-82/19 *OG & PI* [2019] ECLI:EU:C:2019:456, para 68; Case C-509/18 *PF* [2019] ECLI:EU:C:2019:457, para 46; Case C-489/19 *NJ* [2019] ECLI:EU:C:2019:849, para 35; Joined Cases C-566/19 & C-626/19 *JR & YC* [2019] ECLI:EU:C:2019:1077, para 60. See also Bovend'Eerdt et al. (2020), p. 1124.

[108] Joined Cases C-508/18 & C-82/19 *OG & PI* [2019] ECLI:EU:C:2019:456, paras 68–70.

[109] Joined Cases C-508/18 & C-82/19 *OG & PI* [2019] ECLI:EU:C:2019:456, para 75; Joined Cases C-566/19 & C-626/19 *JR & YC* [2019] ECLI:EU:C:2019:1077, paras 62–63.

[110] Joined Cases C-566/19 & C-626/19 *JR & YC* [2019] ECLI:EU:C:2019:1077, paras 61–63.

[111] Joined Cases C-566/19 & C-626/19 *JR & YC* [2019] ECLI:EU:C:2019:1077, paras 63. See also Case C-414/20 *MM* [2021] ECLI:EU:C:2021:4. In this case the CJEU decided that the decision of a national court in the issuing state, which is both competent to review the pre-trial detention imposed on the requested person after the surrender and the validity of the EAW, that the EAW is invalid, as it is not in compliance with Article 8(1)(c) FDEAW does not affect the validity of the pre-trail detention. In other words, ruling that the EAW is invalid does not affect the decision placing the requested person in pre-trial detention after the surrender.

[112] Case C-627/19 *ZB* [2019] ECLI:EU:C:2019:1079, paras 34–39.

claim or the fairness and possible arbitrariness of the underlying forum decision which relate to the national criminal case.

On the basis of the above, it can be concluded that despite the focus on fundamental rights and the protection of the requested person, this case law does not indicate that the conditions for the appointment of the issuing judicial authority or the criterion of effective judicial protection were installed in light of Articles 49 or 47 CFR. The CJEU has not explicitly linked Article 6(1) FDEAW to the difficulties in foreseeing the applicable national criminal law or forum choices.

4.4 Conclusion and Reflections

The central question of this chapter was whether the conditions for the issuing and execution of an EAW contain any safeguards against the problems arising from unforeseeable jurisdiction claims and the lack of a transparent EU system for forum choices, and, if so, whether these safeguards were installed by the EU legislator or CJEU because the problems were viewed as legality issues. With regard to the executing procedure, we have seen that several legal scholars have linked the double criminality requirement and the territoriality exception to the requirement of an accessible and foreseeable law for criminal offences and sanctions. Some of them are of the opinion that unforeseeable jurisdiction claim are capable of impairing the accessibility and foreseeability of criminal offences and sanctions, and that protection should be offered in these situations, including in the context of the surrender procedure. Nonetheless, it follows from the preparatory work to the FDEAW, CJEU case law as well as other legal literature that the protection of state sovereignty is the primary ratio of the refusal grounds discussed. The double criminality requirement, (extra)territoriality exception and refusal ground covering domestic proceedings for the same act were included to ensure that states are not forced to assist other states in their prosecution when they hold a different view as to the criminality of the acts in question or to the proper response to a particular criminal offence. In addition, the fundamental rights exceptions in the CJEU case law were not introduced on the basis of Articles 49 and 47 CFR. Furthermore, even though decisions on the basis of Article 16 FDEAW have been viewed as forum decisions, the rules in Article 16 FDEAW have not been linked to the right to a tribunal established by law. Instead, Article 16 and the rules of soft law guiding the decision on the basis of this legal provision seem to emphasise the need for flexibility.

Similar conclusions follow from the examination of the issuing procedure. Nothing suggests that the conditions for the issuing of an EAW intend to avoid surrender in cases in which the application of the national criminal law of the issuing state was difficult to foresee at the time of the offence; or, in cases in which the issuing state's decision to prosecute does not correlate from a transparent EU system for forum choices. There are no indications that the drafters of the FDEAW or the CJEU have recognised these situations as legality problems in light of Articles

49 and 47 CFR and by extension have deemed it necessary to install suitable protection mechanisms against them in the issuing procedure.

On the basis of the above, it can therefore be concluded that no clear indications exist which suggest that the EU legislator was, at the time of the adoption of the FDEAW, of the opinion that unforeseeable jurisdiction claims and the lack of an overarching EU system for forum choices constitute legality problems in light of Articles 49 and 47 CFR, against which EU citizens should be protected in the context of the surrender procedure, as well. The case law of the CJEU on the conditions for the issuing and execution of an EAW does not point in a different direction. However, in relation to this conclusion, it should be noted that the CJEU has not yet been confronted with specific preliminary questions concerning the link between the surrender procedure and unforeseeable jurisdiction claims and forum choices in light of Articles 49 and 47 CFR. In other words, the lack of an elaborate discussion of the issues as possible legality problems and the potential consequences of such a classification for the surrender procedure in the case law can be explained on the basis of the fact that for preliminary rulings, the CJEU is dependent on the national courts. It also follows from this chapter that in fact, some provisions of the FDEAW, for instance Article 16, provide opportunities for preliminary questions addressing one of the underlying issues, but these questions have simply not been posed yet.

Besides the fact that the EU legislator and CJEU have not explicitly considered the two problems as possible legality issues in the context of the surrender procedure, Sects. 4.2 and 4.3 also show that many of the conditions in the FDEAW have quite a state-centric character. They protect important state interests, such as national sovereignty, and do not show a strong EU citizenship foundation or rationale. The same goes for the guarantees and refusal grounds which did not show a link to the current problems, but which are related to free movement and the protection of the requested person. Even though the CJEU *ne bis in idem* case law emphasises free movement, in particular the general objective of the establishment of an AFSJ in which free movement is guaranteed, the protection offered is not explicitly based on EU citizenship as defined in Article 20 TFEU.[113] In addition, the case law on Articles 5(3) and 4(6) FDEAW, such as the ruling in *Da Silva Jorge*, show that the CJEU prohibits implementation measures which discriminate on the basis of nationality and protects the chances of reintegration of the requested person. However, as is further explained in Chap. 9, these two provisions have been criticised for not clearly reflecting the concept of EU citizenship.[114] The state-centric focus of most of the refusal grounds and the limited attention for EU citizenship raise questions in light of the fact that Article 3(2) TEU explicitly designates the EU citizen as the main stakeholder of the AFSJ. This is further discussed from Chap. 8 onwards.

[113] See eg Joined Cases C-187/01 & C-385/01 *Hüseyin Gözütok & Klaus Brügge* [2003] ECLI:EU:C:2003:87, paras 36–38; Case C-436/04 *Van Esbroeck* [2006] ECLI:EU:C:2006:165, paras 33–36; Case C-486/14 *Kossowski* [2016] ECLI:EU:C:2016:483, paras 44–47.

[114] Glerum (2013), p. 402; Glerum and Rozemond (2008), pp. 823–824.

Together, Chap. 3 and this chapter have explained for the EU level that it remains unclear whether the two complications themselves fall under the scope of the legality principle in Articles 49 and 47 CFR, and that the conditions in the current legal framework for the EAW hardly aim to protect EU citizens against surrender when one of the complications occurs. Hence, in light of the current scope of Articles 49 and 47 CFR and conditions in the surrender procedure, the EAW is not unambiguously recognised as a mechanism that could potentially enforce violations of the legality principle when one of the two complications occurs. The next three chapters conduct a similar exercise to Chap. 3 and this chapter for three national legal orders. Chapter 5 covers the Dutch legal order, Chap. 6 the German legal order and Chap. 7 the UK legal order, more specifically England and Wales.

References

Asp P, Von Hirsch A, Frände D (2006) Double criminality and transnational investigative measures in EU criminal proceedings: some issues of principle. ZIS 11:512

Billing F (2020) Limiting mutual trust on fundamental rights grounds under the European arrest warrant and lessons learned from transfers under Dublin III. New J Eur Crim Law 11:184

Blekxtoon R (2005) Commentary on an article by article basis. In: Blekxtoon R, van Ballegooij W (eds) Handbook on the European arrest warrant. Asser

Borgers M. 'Case note HvJ EG 16 May 2007, C-303/05, ECLI:EU:C:2006:552, (*Advocaten voor de Wereld*)' NJ 2007/619

Bovend'Eerdt K et al (2020) Kroniek van het Europees Strafrecht. NJB 1121

Corstens G, Borgers M, Kooijmans T (eds) (2018) Het Nederlands Strafprocesrecht. Kluwer

De Amicis G (2012) Initial views of the court of justice on the European arrest warrant: towards a uniform pan-European interpretation? Eur Crim Law Rev 2:47

Falkiewicz A (2017) The double criminality requirement in the area of freedom, security and justice – reflections in light of the European court of justice judgment of 11 January 2017, C-289/15, Criminal Proceedings Against Jozef Grundza. Eur Crim Law Rev 7:258

Glerum V (2013) De weigeringsgronden bij uitlevering en overlevering – Een vergelijking en kritische evaluatie in het licht van het beginsel van wederzijdse erkenning. Wolf Legal Publishers

Glerum V, Rozemond N (2008) Overlevering van Nederlanders: Copernicaanse Revolutie of Uitlevering in Overgang? DD 816

Herlin-Karnell E (2007) In the wake of Pupino, Advocaten voor de Wereld and dell'Orto. German Law J 8:1147

Herrnfeld H-H (2013) Mechanisms for settling conflicts of jurisdiction. In: Luchtman M (ed) Choice of forum in cooperation against EU financial crime. Freedom, security and justice and the protection of specific EU-interests. Eleven International Publishing

Keijzer N (2009) *Locus delicti* exceptions. In: Keizer N, van Sliedregt E (eds) The European arrest warrant in practice. Asser

Klimek L (2014) European arrest warrant. Springer

Luchtman M (2011) Choice of forum in an area of freedom, security and justice. Utrecht Law Rev 7:74

Ouwerkerk J (2011) Case C-261/09 criminal proceedings against Gaetano Mantello, judgment of the court of justice (grand chamber) of 16 November 2010. Common Mark Law Rev 48:1687

Simonelli M (2019) "...And justice for all?" the right to an independent tribunal after the ruling of the court of justice in *LM*. New J Eur Crim Law 10:329

Suominen A (2011) The principle of mutual recognition in cooperation in criminal matters. A study of the principle in four framework decisions and in the implementation legislation in the Nordic Member States. Intersentia

Von Bogdandy A (2020) Principles of a systemic deficiencies Doctrine: how to protect checks and balances in the member states. Common Mark Law Rev 57:705

Wouters J, Naert F (2004) Of arrest warrants, terrorist offences and extradition deals: an appraisal of the EU's main criminal law measures against terrorism after "11 September". Common Mark Law Rev 41:909

Xanthopoulou E (2018) Mutual trust and rights in EU criminal and asylum law: three phases of evolution and the uncharted territory beyond blind trust 55 CMLR 489

Chapter 5
The Dutch Legal Order: The Views on the Two Complications and Their Link to the EAW

5.1 Introduction

As described in Chaps. 1 and 2, EU citizens who exercise their right to free movement may face complications arising from the difficulties in foreseeing which particular national criminal law to obey and the absence of an EU mechanism for forum choices. These complications raise questions in light of the legality principle and are influenced by the EAW. To put it differently, the EAW adds another dimension to these issues. Their actual classification as legality problems could, for instance, turn the surrender procedure into an enforcement mechanism for legality violations, unless the EAW contains criteria or refusal grounds which prevent surrender in these situations. In this light, Chaps. 3 and 4 have shown to what extent the two problems with which EU citizens can be confronted are currently recognised as legality issues on the EU level and to what extent protection against them has been linked to or integrated in the surrender procedure. The purpose of this chapter is to determine whether the surrender of a citizen is considered problematic in the Netherlands when the applicability of the substantive criminal law of the issuing state was difficult to foresee at the time of the offence and when its decision to prosecute is not based on a transparent EU system for forum choices. This chapter therefore examines to what extent the two complications discussed in Sects. 2.5 and 2.6 have been recognised as legality problems in light of the current scope of the national legality principle. In addition, it explores to what extent the surrender procedure as implemented in Dutch law and applied in practice offers safeguards against surrender in situations in which the two underlying problems occur and to what extent these safeguards were installed, because of legality concerns. Chapters 6 and 7 answer the same questions and conduct the same examination for the German and English legal order.

In light of the above, Sect. 5.2 studies the existence of a link between the EAW, jurisdiction or forum choices and the equivalents of Articles 49 and 47 CFR in the Dutch legal order, which are the substantive legality principle in Article 1 of the

J. Graat, *The European Arrest Warrant and EU Citizenship*,
https://doi.org/10.1007/978-3-031-07590-2_5

Dutch Criminal Code (DCC) and *ius de non evocando* in Article 17 of the Constitution. More specifically, it examines to what extent the influence of the EAW on the two complications is considered problematic in light of the national legality principle. For instance, is the issuing and execution of an EAW in itself viewed as a violation of the legality principle when in the underlying case the EU citizen is confronted with the two complications? Or is the EAW in itself not viewed as a violation of the legality principle, but considered a mechanism which could enforce violations of the legality principle when the two complications occur? Another option is that, similar to the EU level, the recognition of the two problems as legality issues and the link of the EAW thereto has not (or hardly) been explicitly discussed.

The question which follows the conclusions of Sect. 5.2 is to what extent any form of recognition of the two complications and the role of the EAW therein as legality problems has also been integrated in the surrender procedure itself. The FDEAW has been implemented in the *Overleveringswet* (Surrender Act, hereafter SA).[1] In 2021, the Surrender Act has been extensively amended to bring it more in compliance with the FDEAW, as explained by the case law of the CJEU.[2] Section 5.3 discusses the executing procedure and examines mostly the same guarantees, refusal grounds and other bars to surrender as discussed in Chap. 4.[3] More concretely, Sect. 5.3 examines the extent to which the different relevant conditions in the executing procedure have been installed by the Dutch legislator or interpreted by the courts for the purpose of protecting citizens against surrender in case the two problems arise. Section 5.4 conducts a similar examination for the relevant conditions in the issuing procedure. In addition, as the decision to issue an EAW and the rules on the exercise of jurisdiction are closely connected, these rules are also discussed. This chapter ends with a conclusion in Sect. 5.5.

5.2 Protection Offered by Fundamental Rights and Principles

5.2.1 The Substantive Legality Principle

The principle of *nullum crimen, nulla poena sine lege*, or the substantive legality principle, is codified in Article 1(1) of the Dutch Criminal Code and Article 16 of the Dutch Constitution. These provisions have the same scope and state that 'No offence shall be punishable unless it was an offence under the law at the time it was

[1] *Overleveringswet* (*Stb.* 2004, 195). The Surrender Act entered into force on 1 January 2004.

[2] Wet van 3 maart 2021 tot herimplementatie van onderdelen van het kaderbesluit van de Raad van de Europese Unie betreffende het Europees aanhoudingsbevel en de procedures van overlevering tussen de lidstaten van de Europese Unie (*Stb.* 2021, 125).

[3] See Sect. 4.2.1.

committed.'[4] The substantive legality principle is based on the principle of legal certainty which is in turn linked to the principle of the rule of law.[5] On the basis of these principles, citizens may not be punished for acts or omissions unless they could have known that these could result in criminal liability and certain sanctions.[6] In addition, the substantive legality principle can be divided into three sub-rights or sub-principles. The first two are the prohibition of a retroactive application of the law and the prohibition of analogous interpretation. The former means that citizens may not be held criminally liable for conduct which was not criminalised by law at the time of the offence or to be subjected to stricter sanctions[7] than the ones applicable when the conduct occurred.[8] An exception to this prohibition is allowed when the retroactive application of amendments of criminal offences and sanctions is beneficial for the suspect.[9] The prohibition of analogous interpretation precludes national courts and public prosecutors from interpreting a penal provision in such a way that it includes certain behaviour or circumstances, while the wording of the provision does not support such a broad interpretation.[10]

The third sub-right which correlates from Articles 1(1) DCC and 16 Constitution has a twofold dimension, since it covers the requirement of a legal basis for criminal offences and sanctions and the interrelated requirements of *kenbaarheid* (accessibility) and *lex certa*. The former entails that criminal offences and sanctions have to be codified in an Act of Parliament (*wet in formele zin*) which means that the law is adopted in a process of cooperation between the democratically elected Parliament and government or in legislation adopted by subordinate legislative bodies, such as a municipality (*wet in materiele zin*).[11] Subordinate legislative bodies may only adopt laws criminalising behaviour and establishing sanctions when this power is provided

[4] 't Hart (1982), pp. 335–337.

[5] Groenhuijsen (1987), p. 31; De Hullu (2012), p. 81.

[6] Kristen (2019), p. 406; Groenhuijsen (1987), p. 31.

[7] The term sanctions seems to include both punishments and orders (*maatregelen*), such as the custodial order for repeating offenders (*ISD-maatregel*). HR 29 November 2005, ECLI:NL:HR:2005:AU4799 (Dutch Supreme Court); ECtHR 12 February 2008, 21906/04 (*Kafkaris/Cyprus*), para 142; ECtHR 17 September 2009, 10249/03 (*Scoppola/Italy No. 2*), paras 96–97.

[8] Kristen (2010), pp. 233–234. Under Dutch law, an exception to the application of the prohibition of retroactive application is allowed when its application is in conflict with provisions of treaties or resolutions by international institutions that are binding on all persons. See art 94 Constitution; *Kamerstukken II* 2001/02, 28337, nr. 3, pp. 24–25; HR 18 September 2001, ECLI:NL:HR:2001:AB1471, paras 4.5–4.6 (Dutch Supreme Court); Rb. 's-Gravenhage 24 July 2007, ECLI:NL:RBSGR:2007:BB049, paras 31, 42 (The Hague District Court); Hof 's-Gravenhage 17 December 2007, ECLI:NL:GHSGR:2007:BC0287, para 12 (The Hague Court of Appeal).

[9] Art 1(2) DCC.

[10] Borgers (2011), pp. 117–118; Kristen (2010), p. 234.

[11] Art 81 Dutch Constitution; Hof Amsterdam 1 October 2008, ECLI:NL:GHAMS:2008:BH2002 (Amsterdam Court of Appeal).

to them by an Act of Parliament.[12] Contrary to Article 7 ECHR, the Dutch legality principle excludes customary law and judge-made law.[13]

The accessibility requirement entails that citizens should be able to find the applicable rules. This requirement is usually met when the criminal offences and sanctions have been published in one of the two official journals.[14] Furthermore, the legal provisions in which the criminal offences and sanctions are codified need to satisfy the *lex certa* principle, which is also referred to as the *bepaaldheidsgebod* or *Bestimmtheitsgebot*.[15] This *lex certa* principle has been referred to as the equivalent of the requirement of foreseeability correlating from Articles 49 CFR and 7 ECHR.[16] It covers the obligation for the Dutch legislator to describe criminal offences and sanctions in a sufficiently clear and concrete manner to allow citizens to adapt their behaviour in conformity with these norms.[17] This obligation has two goals. On the one hand, clear and precise criminal offences and sanctions offer citizens legal protection as they restrict the powers of the public prosecutor and judiciary and therefore avoid arbitrary interferences with fundamental rights.[18] On the other hand, the obligation contributes to crime-fighting efforts as it strengthens the legitimacy of coercive action by the authorities, including the imposition of sanctions.[19]

Whether a penal provision satisfies the *lex certa* requirement depends on the context within which it applies. In this light, the nature, content and intended scope of the legal provisions should be taken into account as well as the need for a balance between specific and general clarity and the professional capacity of the

[12] Pompe (1959), p. 49; De Hullu (2012), p. 80.

[13] De Hullu (2012), p. 81. On the role which customs do have in relation to determining the criminality of certain behavior, see Pompe (1959), p. 50.

[14] These are Staatsblad and Staatscourant. Hof Amsterdam 1 October 2008, ECLI:NL:GHAMS:2008:BH2002 (Amsterdam Court of Appeal); Hof Amsterdam 15 March 2018, ECLI:NL:GHAMS:2018:1643 (Amsterdam Court of Appeal). See also Bekendmakingswet 4 februari 1988 (*Stb*. 1988,18).

[15] HR 31 October 2000, ECLI:NL:HR:2000:AA7954, para 3.4 (Dutch Supreme Court).The Supreme Court of the Netherlands has also explicitly stated that criminal offenses and sanctions need to be formulated in Dutch. HR 24 June 1997, ECLI:NL:HR:1997:ZD0773 (Dutch Supreme Court).

[16] See the ruling of the Court of Appeal Arnhem-Leeuwarden in the ruling of the Supreme Court of 17 April 2018, ECLI:NL:HR:2018:612, para 2.2; HR 15 March 2013, ECLI:NL:PHR:2013:BZ5424 (Conclusion of AG Knigge), para 4.24. For a comparison of the *nullum crimen sine lege principle* in Article 1 DCC and 7 ECHR, see Kristen (2019), pp. 425–428.

[17] HR 31 October 2000, ECLI:NL:HR:2000:AA7954, para 3.4 (Dutch Supreme Court); HR 28 May 2002, ECLI:NL:HR:2002:AE1490, para 4.6 (Dutch Supreme Court); HR 28 March 2006, ECLI:NL:HR:2006:AV1613, para 3.6 (Dutch Supreme Court); HR 30 June 2009, ECLI:NL:HR:2009:BG4822, para 5.3 (Dutch Supreme Court); Hof Amsterdam 1 October 2008, ECLI:NL:GHAMS:2008:BH2002 (Amsterdam Court of Appeal).

[18] Groenhuijsen and Kristen (2001), p. 332; Pompe (1959), p. 49; Altena (2016), para 2.3.1.

[19] Tineke Cleiren in Tekst en Commentaar Strafrecht, art 1 Sr, para 3 (1 February 2021).

addressees.[20] In addition, the Dutch Supreme Court has determined that a certain degree of vagueness can be justified to avoid overly detailed legal provisions which threaten the general clarity of the law.[21]

5.2.2 The EAW: Outside the Scope of the Substantive Legality Principle?

The preparatory work leading to the adoption of the Surrender Act does not show a direct link between the EAW and the requirement of accessibility and *lex certa* in Article 1 DCC.[22] The preparatory work also explicitly separates the surrender procedure from a criminal procedure by stating that the decision on the execution of an EAW does not constitute a decision on the merits of the case. Instead, the surrender procedure merely focuses on the question whether prosecution or the execution of a sanction in the issuing state should be facilitated.[23] In addition, the Amsterdam District Court has stated that Article 1(2) DCC which codifies the *lex mitior* principle, another corollary of the substantive legality principle, does not apply to surrender procedures.[24]

In light of the above, it seems most likely that the EAW does not fall under the scope of the substantive legality principle in Article 1 DCC, since it has not been explicitly classified as a criminal offence or penalty. Consequently, the issuing and execution of an EAW while the jurisdiction claim of the issuing state was difficult to foresee at the time of the offence can in itself not constitute a legality issue. Section 5.2.3, therefore, focuses on the question whether Article 1 DCC links the

[20] Kristen (2019), p. 421. Professional market participants are under an obligation to ensure that they are also adequately informed about the legal limitations to their actions. See HR 31 October 2000, ECLI:NL:HR:2000:AA7954, para 3.5 (Dutch Supreme Court).

[21] HR 31 October 2000, ECLI:NL:HR:2000:AA7954, para 3.4 (Dutch Supreme Court); Groenhuijsen and Kristen (2001), p. 333.

[22] At one point in the implementation process, the Minister of Justice and Security seems to link the requirement of *lex certa* to the EAW. He argues that the surrender procedure satisfies this requirement, because the Framework Decision demands that each EAW describes the criminal act and provides a legal qualification of the act as well as a copy of the relevant legal provisions. These conditions ensure that the citizen is able to know precisely for which criminal acts his or her surrender is required. In my opinion, it is unlikely that the Minister refers to the *lex certa* principle included in Article 1 DCC, as he explains at no point why the EAW constitutes a criminal offense or sanction, which fall under the scope of the substantive legality principle. See *Kamerstukken I* 2003/04, 29042, C, p. 8.

[23] *Kamerstukken II* 2003/04, 29 042, nr. 4, p. 2; *Kamerstukken II* 2003/04, 29042, nr. 12, p. 8; Glerum (2013), p. 101. See also Rb. Amsterdam 25 October 2005, ECLI:NL:RBAMS:2005:AU4909 (Amsterdam District Court); Rb. Amsterdam 17 December 2004, ECLI:NL:RBAMS:2004:AR8294 (Amsterdam District Court).

[24] Rb. Amsterdam 18 September 2009, ECLI:NL:RBAMS:2009:BL1598 (Amsterdam District Court).

fulfilment of the requirements of accessibility and *lex certa* to the question whether the application of a particular national criminal law was foreseeable at the time of the offence. In other words, do criminal offences and sanctions satisfy the requirements of accessibility and *lex certa* when the application of the specific national criminal law in which they are codified was not clear at the time of the offence. The next section examines both the position of the Dutch legislator and judiciary in relation to the link between Article 1 DCC and jurisdiction as well as the views expressed in the legal literature. The meaning of the conclusions following this examination and their effect on the surrender procedure are further discussed in Sects. 5.2.5, 5.3 and 5.4. For instance, in case of an affirmative answer to the question, the follow-up question could be whether this would mean that the EAW is for that reason viewed as a mechanism which could enforce violations of the legality principle and by extension whether it includes safeguards against such violations? In case of a negative answer, meaning no clear link between Article 1 DCC and jurisdiction exists, the follow-up question could be whether despite the absence of such a link any of the conditions for the execution and issuing of an EAW have been installed to offer protection against the complications discussed.

5.2.3 The Substantive Legality Principle and Rules of Jurisdiction

5.2.3.1 The Legislative Level

The rules on jurisdiction are laid down in Articles 2–8c DCC. Article 2 codifies the territoriality principle which has been interpreted by the Supreme Court in light of the ubiquity theory.[25] This means that Dutch criminal law does not only apply when the criminal act occurred on Dutch territory, but also when its effects or consequences occurred in the Netherlands.[26] The grounds for extraterritorial jurisdiction are laid down in Articles 3–8c. The legislative level does not reflect a clear position on the relationship between these rules and the *nullum crimen sine lege* principle, more specifically the requirement of accessibility and *lex certa* principle.[27] On the one hand, the Minister of Justice and Security has stated on several occasions that the substantive legality principle does not apply to rules on jurisdiction, because they are

[25] The Dutch legislator has left the determination of the scope of the territoriality principle in Article 2 DCC to courts and academics. Van Elst (2015), p. 97.

[26] HR 7 May 1996, ECLI:NL:HR:1996:AB9821 (Dutch Supreme Court); Van Elst (2015), pp. 93–94 and 97–98. The Supreme Court also accepted the so-called ‘instrumental-doctrine’. This entails that the Netherlands has jurisdiction when an instrument, such as a letter, is used to commit the act, and the effects of this instrument occur in the Netherlands. HR 6 April 1915, ECLI: NL:HR:1915:BG9430 (Supreme Court).

[27] To a certain extent, this is of course understandable, as the composition of the legislator, meaning the Parliament and the government, changes after national elections.

not determinative for the criminality or unlawfulness of the conduct. They only regulate the possibility to prosecute conduct which the law has classified as criminal offences.[28] On the other hand, the 2013 review of the rules on extraterritorial jurisdiction shows some other points of view, as well.[29]

The 2014 amendments following the 2013 review broadened the extraterritorial jurisdiction of the Netherlands in several ways. They established jurisdiction on the basis of the passive nationality principle and ensured that permanent residents of the Netherlands could also be prosecuted for criminal offences committed abroad.[30] These changes were primarily justified on the basis of the increased risk of cross-border criminality and impunity in an AFSJ in which EU citizens have free movement rights.[31] At the same time, the extraterritorial jurisdiction grounds were also subjected to relatively strict criteria, such as the double criminality requirement which demands that the conduct constitutes a criminal act *de lege loci* or the requirement that under Dutch law a prison sentence of 8 years or more can be imposed for the offence in question.[32] The most important reasons for these restrictions were the priority of the territoriality principle, the sovereignty of the state on whose territory the crime was committed and the difficulties that come with investigating crimes committed abroad, especially when the conduct is not a criminal offence *de lege loci*.[33] Still, on a few occasions the Minister of Justice and Security has also stated that the double criminality requirement is important, since the prosecution of a person for conduct which is not a criminal act *de lege loci* is 'not necessarily just'.[34] In relation to the intended retroactive application of the new rules on extraterritorial jurisdiction, he was of the opinion that this should only be allowed as long as it would not result in the prosecution of citizens for crimes committed abroad which were at the time not universally recognised as criminal offences or criminal offences *de lege loci*.[35] Hence, this position of the Minister of Justice and Security reflects the opinion that citizens should at the time of the offence at least be

[28] *Kamerstukken II* 2004/05, 28484, nr. 49, p. 5 (Advice of the Council of State and response of the Minister of Justice and Security); *Kamerstukken I* 2012/13, 32840, C, pp. 5–6. However, in both documents the Minister considered that whereas the Dutch legality principle in Article 1 DCC seems to exclude jurisdiction, Article 7 ECHR does seem to provide the possibility to connect the *nullum crimen sine lege* principle to jurisdiction.

[29] Wet van 27 november 2013 tot wijziging van het Wetboek van Strafrecht in verband met de herziening van de regels over werking van de strafwet buiten Nederland (herziening regels betreffende extraterritoriale rechtsmacht in strafzaken) (*Stb.* 2013, 484).

[30] Art 5 DCC; art. 7 DCC; *Kamerstukken II* 2012/13, 33572, nr. 3, pp. 2, 7, 15; *Kamerstukken II* 2012/13, 33572, nr. 6, p. 6. See also Article 8c DCC.

[31] *Kamerstukken II* 2012/13, 33572, nr. 3, pp. 2, 15, 18; *Kamerstukken II* 2012/13, 33572, nr. 6, p. 6.

[32] Art 5(1) DCC. See also art 7(1) DCC.

[33] *Kamerstukken II* 2012/13, 33572, nr. 3, p. 5; *Kamerstukken II* 2012/13, 33572, nr. 6, pp. 13–14.

[34] *Kamerstukken II* 2012/13, 33572, nr. 3, pp. 5, 18. See also *Kamerstukken II* 2003/04, 29451, nr. 1, pp. 12–13 (*Dubbele strafbaarheid in het Nederlandse Strafrecht*).

[35] *Kamerstukken II* 2012/13, 33572, nr. 4, pp. 9–10. See also *Kamerstukken II*2003/04, 29451, nr. 1, pp. 14, 16.

in a position to know that the conduct was criminal somewhere, meaning according to the law of a state.[36]

It follows from the above that the discussions preceding the 2014 amendments to the rules on jurisdiction reflect on a few occasions the point of view that the exercise of extraterritorial jurisdiction is only allowed when the citizen could at the time of the offence have been aware of the criminality of the behaviour according to the law of *a* state. To a certain extent, this reasoning and point of view therefore seem to acknowledge the problem of unforeseeable jurisdiction claims. However, the parliamentary documentation does not reflect the point of view that citizens should be able to foresee the applicability of a *particular* national criminal law.

5.2.3.2 The Judiciary

Case law in which the relationship between legality and jurisdiction is discussed is relatively scarce, and the majority does not focus on the requirements of accessibility and *lex certa*. The Supreme Court has, for instance, decided that the prohibition of a retroactive application of the law is applicable to rules of jurisdiction, unless the Dutch legislator has explicitly stated that a jurisdiction rule should have retroactive application.[37] In addition, the Hague District Court has ruled that rules on jurisdiction and criminal offences are similarly influenced by the legality principle, since the latter are useless without the former.[38] In the same case, the Court of Appeal in The Hague acknowledged the existence of a link between jurisdiction and the legality principle on the basis of the argument that jurisdiction rules are to a certain extent comparable with penal provisions and sanctions.[39] However, these cases focus in particular on the prohibition of analogous interpretations, the requirement that rules on jurisdiction are laid down by law and that their scope may only be extended by law.[40] They do not cover the relation between jurisdiction and the right to an accessible and clear law which satisfies the *lex certa* requirement.[41]

---

[36] See also Sect. 3.3.4.4.

[37] HR 18 September 2001, ECLI:NL:HR:2001:AB1471, paras 6.1–6.4 (Dutch Supreme Court); HR 21 October 2008, ECLI:NL:HR:2008:BD6568, para 6.2 (Dutch Supreme Court). For more information on the *Decembermoorden* case and the relationship between the prohibition of a retroactive application of the law and the legality principle, see Reijntjes (2002), paras 10–11; De Hullu (2012), pp. 87–88; Buruma (2002), pp. 103–104.

[38] Rb. 's-Gravenhage 24 July 2007, ECLI:NL:RBSGR:2007:BB0494, para 39 (The Hague District Court).

[39] Hof 's-Gravenhage 17 December 2007, ECLI:NL:GHSGR:2007:BC0287, para 16 (The Hague District Court).

[40] Rb. 's-Gravenhage 24 July 2007, ECLI:NL:RBSGR:2007:BB0494, paras 39–41 (The Hague District Court); Hof 's-Gravenhage 17 December 2007, ECLI:NL:GHSGR:2007:BC0287, para 16 (The Hague Court of Appeal).

[41] The Court of Appeal refers in its verdict to the requirement of accessibility, but not in the sense that the individual needs to be able to find the applicable rules. Instead, it refers to accessibility in light of the prohibition of interpretation by analogy. Hof 's-Gravenhage 17 December 2007, ECLI:

Even if we would assume that the application of some sub-principles of Article 1 DCC to rules on jurisdiction means that all sub-principles apply, including the accessibility and *lex certa* requirement, it still remains unclear what exactly the application of these two sub-principles would entail. Would this simply mean that the jurisdiction rules themselves have to be published in an official journal and be formulated in a precise and understandable manner? Alternatively, would it mean that the requirements of accessibility and *lex certa* are satisfied when citizens could at the time of the offence have foreseen that their behaviour was criminal somewhere, for instance according to *de lege loci*? Or would it be required that the applicability of a particular law, in this case the Dutch law, was foreseeable at the time of the offence?

5.2.3.3 The Legal Literature

The Dutch legal literature reflects many different opinions on the existence and type of link between jurisdiction and Article 1 DCC. These can roughly be divided into the same two categories as set out in Chap. 3.[42] The first category denies the existence of a link between jurisdiction and the substantive legality principle, either because jurisdiction merely regulates the relationship between states or because rules on jurisdiction are viewed as rules of procedural criminal law. A substantive amount of the authoritative legal scholars falls within this category, which according to Wolswijk also represents the majority opinion in the Dutch legal literature.[43] These legal scholars, for instance, deny the existence of a link between the substantive legality principle and rules on jurisdiction, because rules on jurisdiction do not determine the criminality or unlawfulness of behaviour.[44] Even though both criminal offences and the requirements for prosecution, of which jurisdiction is one, are part of the Dutch Criminal Code, they do not seem to hold the same position, since rules on jurisdiction are not constituent elements of offences.[45] The fact that a court in State B cannot exercise jurisdiction over a criminal offence committed in State A, does not affect the criminality of the act, according to the law of State A.[46] Hence, murder remains murder, also in the absence of jurisdiction to investigate and prosecute the conduct in question.

NL:GHSGR:2007:BC0287, para 16 (The Hague Court of Appeal). See also HR 8 July 2008, ECLI: NL:PHR:2008:BD6568 (Conclusion of AG Machielse), para 7.4. *A contrario* Sliedregt states that this case 'emphasizes that accessibility and specificity are central characteristics of the Dutch rules on jurisdiction'. Van Sliedregt (2008), p. 669.

[42] Section 3.3.4.4.

[43] Klip (2016), para 11; Hirsch Ballin (2000), pp. 484 and 488; Wolswijk (1998), p. 82; Wolswijk (2013), pp. 353–354.

[44] See 't Hart (1982), pp. 332–333, 336, 338; Pompe (1959), pp. 54, 60–61, 504–505.

[45] Wolswijk (2013), p. 353.

[46] Reijntjes (2002), paras 10–11.

The second category discussed in Chap. 3, which covers the position that a connection exists between jurisdiction and the substantive legality principle, is also reflected in the Dutch legal literature. Some legal scholars disagree with the strict separation between criminal liability and jurisdiction.[47] Van Elst, for instance, disagrees with the position that jurisdiction is a matter of procedural law, because it lacks the moral element which characterises the law codifying criminal offences, on the basis of which individuals should be able to adapt their behaviour. He argues that this may be true for acts generally recognised as criminal offences, such as international crimes, but not for minor offences like the consumption of alcohol. In Van Elst's opinion, the retroactive application of a law establishing extraterritorial jurisdiction over this act has an obvious moral element.[48] On a similar note, Keijzer claims that rules on jurisdiction cannot be solely viewed as rules of procedural law. He argues that without jurisdiction to prosecute, legal provisions determining criminal liability are meaningless.[49]

Knigge takes a more careful position and states that the *ratio legis* of the *nullum crimen, nulla poena* principle does not explicitly extend the scope of this principle beyond criminal offences and sanctions, but it does not exclude or prohibit such an extension, either. After all, legal certainty, which is one of the most important foundations of the *nullum crimen, nulla poena* principle, can be affected by conditions for prosecution as well. In this light, he also questions whether an act could really be classified as a criminal offence when there is no jurisdiction to actually enforce the substantive criminal law.[50]

In addition, Wolswijk derives from the Dutch case law that Article 1(1) DCC, more specifically the prohibition of a retroactive application of the law, influences the rules of jurisdiction. The starting point seems to be that the prohibition applies, unless the legislator has explicitly decided otherwise. The reasonableness of the retroactive application of rules on jurisdiction then depends on the question whether criminal liability could have been foreseeable at the time of the offence. In this light, he poses the question whether this foreseeability of criminal offences requires that the jurisdiction of a specific state was foreseeable at the time of the offence or whether it is sufficient that the citizen could have known at the time of the offence that the conduct was criminal somewhere. He believes that the predominant position under Dutch law will be that the latter is sufficient.[51] The foreseeability requirement would then, for instance, be met when the conduct at the time of its occurrence also constituted a criminal act *de lege loci* or is universally recognised as a criminal offence.[52]

---

[47] See e.g. Nijboer (1987), p. 124; Schutte (1981), p. 451; Van Elst (2015), pp. 80–81.

[48] Van Elst (2015), pp. 80–81. See Van Elst (2002), pp. 214–215.

[49] HR 18 September 2001, ECLI:NL:PHR:2001:AB1471 (Conclusion of AG Keijzer), paras 68–69. See Nijboer (1987), pp. 124 and 162.

[50] Knigge (1984), pp. 225–226, 241, 370.

[51] Wolswijk (2013), p. 354.

[52] Wolswijk (2013), p. 354; Van Elst (2015), pp. 80–81.

The opinion that citizens should be able to foresee the law of a particular state seems to be a minority opinion, adopted by only a few legal scholars. For instance, Strijards has argued that criminal jurisdiction is influenced by Article 1 DCC. He claims that the goal of the substantive legality principle to warn citizens about criminal behaviour and its consequences cannot be achieved when citizens could not have known at the time of the conduct by which offenses and sanctions in which specific national criminal law they had to be deterred.[53] In addition, another argument in favour of the position that citizens should be able to foresee the applicability of the law of a particular state is provided by Luchtman when he criticises the opposite position that it is sufficient that citizens are able to know that their behaviour is criminal somewhere. He states that this interpretation neglects the fact that the substantive legality principle covers both criminal offences and criminal sanctions. As the type and severity of penalties in national criminal laws still substantially differ, the fact that citizens could in general have been aware of the criminality of their behaviour does not guarantee that they could have known the specific sanctions that can be imposed.[54]

5.2.4 Ius de non evocando

Articles 1–23 in the Dutch Constitution enumerate the constitutional rights. These do not include the general right to a fair trial by an impartial and independent tribunal established by law, but Article 17 states that 'No one may be prevented against his will from being heard by the courts to which he is entitled to apply under the law.'[55] This right is also referred to as *ius de non evocando* and is often considered the equivalent of the right to a tribunal established by law as laid down by Articles 47 CFR and 6 ECHR.[56] It requires that courts in the Netherlands are established by Acts of Parliament.[57]

In relation to forum choices, *ius de non evocando* has been discussed in the context of the legal framework for the transfer of criminal proceedings from and to the Netherlands. In this setting, both the Minister of Justice and Security and the Minister of Foreign Affairs explicitly stated that Article 17 Constitution does not

[53] Strijards (1984), pp. 42–45. See also Thorhauer (2015), pp. 89, 90; Van der Beken (1999), p. 23; *Handelingen I* 2003/04, nr. 26, p. 1329.

[54] Luchtman (2012), p. 52. See also Fichera (2011), pp. 98–99.

[55] Wet van 21 februari 2018 houdende verklaring dat er grond bestaat een voorstel in overweging te nemen tot verandering van de Grondwet, strekkende tot het opnemen van een bepaling over het recht op een eerlijk proces (*Stb.* 2018, 88); *Kamerstukken II*2015/16, 34517, nr. 2. Article 116 (1) and (2) of the Dutch Constitution state that the establishment, organization, composition, and powers of the courts need to be regulated by Acts of Parliament. This is, however, not a constitutional right.

[56] d'Oliveira (2016); d'Oliveira (1999); Bax (2000), p. 215.

[57] *Kamerstukken* II 1975/76, 13872, nr. 3, p. 22; *Kamerstukken*II 1980/81, 16162, nr. 8, p. 10.

demand that the law appoints the competent judge in a concrete case and, more importantly, that it does not prohibit prosecution authorities from deciding whether the case should be brought before a Dutch or a foreign court.[58] At the same time, the government officials also state that the public prosecutor needs to make reasonable decisions and that the procedure for the transfer of criminal proceedings may not become a mechanism for arbitrary forum decisions to the detriment of the suspect.[59] In other words, the public prosecutor's decision whether to transfer criminal proceedings to another state, which implies a forum decision, needs to be reasonable, but this requirement does not follow from Article 17 Constitution.

The link between Article 17 Constitution and forum choices on the EU level and national level is on occasion discussed by Advocate Generals in their conclusions for cases brought before the Supreme Court. These are, however, not binding. In relation to forum choices on the national level, AG Knigge stated in 2009 that it remains unclear whether these fall within the scope of Article 17 Constitution.[60] With regard to forum choices concerning national jurisdictions AG Paridaens concluded in 2019 that a transfer of criminal proceedings to Curaçao did not violate Article 17 Constitution, because the criminal law of Curaçao was applicable to the facts of the case.[61] This reflects the opinion that the scope of Article 17 Constitution is limited to the national level. This constitutional right is complied with as long as the suspect is brought before a national court or judge whose establishment and jurisdiction are laid down by law. These courts and judges may be situated in different Member States. In other words, there is no problem with *ius de non evocando* as long as the courts in the different competent states and their jurisdiction are established by law.[62]

Furthermore, several legal scholars have stated that the prevention of forum shopping is an important goal of *ius de non evocando*.[63] This right has also been referred to as the 'procedural counterpart of the legality principle'.[64] In that light, it requires that the legislator adopts legislation which appoints the competent tribunal or judge in a sufficiently clear and precise manner. A certain margin of discretion in deciding on the appropriate judge or court is, however, accepted as long as the law excludes the risk of arbitrariness. This means that it should not be possible to decide on a different judge in similar cases.[65]

---

[58] *Kamerstukken II* 1983/84, 15971 (R 1133) and 15972, nr. 14, pp. 5–6. The same point was made in relation to Article 116 Constitution. See *Kamerstukken II* 1981/82, 15971 (R1133) enz, nr. 10, p. 31.

[59] *Kamerstukken II* 1983/84, 15971(R 1133) and 15972, nr. 14, p. 6. See also *Kamerstukken II* 1981/82, 15971 (R1133) enz, nr. 10, p. 31.

[60] HR 8 September 2009, ECLI:NL:PHR:2009:BI3877 (Conclusion of AG Knigge), para 12.3.

[61] HR 17 December 2019, ECLI:NL:PHR:2019:1323 (Conclusion of AG Paridaens), para 63.

[62] The AG also refers to Baaijens-van Geloven (1996), p. 12.

[63] Swart (1983), pp. 8–9. Referred to by Baaijens-van Geloven (1996), p. 124. See also Corstens (1986), pp. 10–11; Luchtman (2009), p. 984.

[64] Swart (1983), p. 7.

[65] Swart (1983), pp. 8–9. Referred to by Baaijens-van Geloven (1996), p. 124.

5.2.5 Interim Conclusion

In relation to Article 1 DCC, it follows from the above that on the legislative level, different answers are provided to the question whether the requirements of accessibility and *lex certa* influence the rules on jurisdiction. On some occasions, the legislator has denied the existence of any link between the two, while on other occasions it seems to adopt the opinion that citizens should at least be able to know that the conduct was criminal somewhere. In addition, the case law has discussed the link between Article 1 DCC and jurisdiction only in a small amount of cases, and never explicitly with regard to the requirements of accessibility and *lex certa*. Furthermore, the majority opinion in the legal literature is either that no link exists between jurisdiction and Article 1(1) DCC or that it is sufficient that citizens could have known at the time of the offence that their conduct was criminal according to the law of *a* state. It can therefore be concluded that the view that citizens should be able to foresee the jurisdiction claim of a specific state is not strongly reflected on either the legislative level or in the case law and that it constitutes a minority opinion in the legal literature. As a result, the problems caused by the fact that citizens cannot foresee which specific national criminal law is applicable to them have not been explicitly recognised as legality issues in light of Article 1(1) DCC and 16 Constitution. By extension, there are no clear indications of the view that the EAW constitutes a mechanism which could enforce violations of the Dutch legality principle in cases in which these problems arise.

In relation to Article 17 Constitution, it follows from the previous sections that while some legal scholars argue that arbitrary forum decisions should be avoided in light of *ius de non evocando*, Article 17 Constitution does not seem to occupy a strong position in Dutch criminal law and practice. Its possible relationship to forum decisions in case of conflicts of national jurisdictions has hardly been discussed on the Dutch legislative level and in the case law. The scarce discussions also reveal that *ius de non evocando* currently does not demand that conflicts of national jurisdictions are prevented or solved by legislative instruments. It can therefore be concluded that the complications with which EU citizens can be confronted as a result of the absence of an EU system for forum choices are not explicitly recognised as a legality problem in light of Article 17 Constitution. By extension, there are no clear indications of the view that the EAW constitutes a mechanism which could enforce violations of Article 17 Constitution when the citizen is surrendered to the issuing state whose decision to prosecute is not based on a transparent EU system for forum choices.

So, the overall conclusion is that the difficulties arising from unforeseeable jurisdiction claims and the lack of an EU system for forum choices have not been explicitly and overwhelmingly recognised as legality issues in light of Article 1 DCC and 17 Constitution. Consequently, from the perspective of the legality principle, the Dutch legal order does not reveal a strong view that the EAW could be a mechanism for the enforcement of violations of the legality principle when these difficulties occur. If this had, however, been the case, an interesting follow-up question would have been to what extent this recognition has been integrated in the surrender procedure. The Dutch Surrender Act does not provide a refusal ground or other legal provision which directly applies in such situations. The human rights bar in Article 11 SA, which is not a refusal ground, but which does oblige the Amsterdam District Court not to give effect to the EAW in case of serious fundamental rights concerns, comes closest. However, this legal provision refers exclusively to violations of the Charter of Fundamental Rights. In addition, as explained in Chap. 3, the jurisprudence of the Luxembourg and Strasbourg court does not unambiguously answer the question whether the right to foreseeable criminal offences, sanctions and tribunals in Articles 49 and 47 CFR is influenced by the foreseeability of jurisdiction claims and forum decisions in cross-border cases. In case the jurisprudence on the EU level would in the future deny or downplay the existence of such a link, the question would arise to what extent the Netherlands would be allowed to integrate an interpretation of the national legality principle, whose scope would exceed the minimum standards imposed by Articles 49 CFR and 47 CFR, in the surrender procedure. In light of *Melloni*, the argument could be made that applying these higher national fundamental rights standards in the surrender procedure could hamper the efficiency of EU law.[66] Chapter 11 elaborates on similar questions as it discusses the ways in which a transnational interpretation of Articles 49 and 47 CFR, whose scope of protection would then cover the two problems, could be integrated in the current legal framework of the EAW.

In light of the conclusions that have been drawn, Sects. 5.3 and 5.4 examine to what extent the problems relating to jurisdiction and forum choices have influenced the surrender procedure in the Netherlands. In other words, have the Dutch legislator implementing the FDEAW and the national authorities applying it recognised the two problems at hand—perhaps even as possible legality issues—and installed safeguards to prevent surrender in these situations?

5.3 The Netherlands As the Executing State

5.3.1 An Introduction to the Executing Procedure

The FDEAW is implemented in the Surrender Act, which exclusively regulates the surrender procedure.[67] Even though the explanatory memorandum to the bill introducing the Surrender Act calls the EAW another form of international cooperation, which suggests that it is not viewed as fundamentally different from extradition, the

[66] Case C-399/11 *Melloni* [2013] ECLI:EU:C:2013:107. See Council, 'Council conclusions on mutual recognition in criminal matters. Promoting mutual recognition by enhancing mutual trust' [2018] OJ C449/6, conclusion 4; European Commission, 'Report on the implementation of Council Framework Decision of 13 June 2002 on the European arrest warrant and the surrender procedures between Member States' COM (2020) 270 final, para 3.3.2.

[67] *Overleveringswet* (*Stb.* 2004, 195).

Dutch legislator considered a simple adjustment of the Extradition Act impossible.[68] To avoid unclarities, the surrender procedure was laid down in a separate act, but was based on the model of the Dutch Extradition Act.[69] In 2021 the Surrender Act has been amended to bring it more in compliance with the FDEAW, as explained by the case law of the CJEU.[70]

The Surrender Act appoints the Amsterdam District Court as the executing judicial authority. It has the exclusive competence to decide on the execution of incoming EAWs.[71] Contrary to the extradition procedure, the Minister of Justice and Security does not have an important say in the decision on the execution of an EAW. His or her role is restricted to, for instance, decisions on competing EAWs and extradition requests.[72] However, the public prosecutors at the Amsterdam District Court also have a position in the executing procedure. They are, for instance, the first ones to consider an incoming EAW.[73] When they find that the surrender of the person is not possible—for example, because the requested person was younger than twelve when the crime was committed—the EAW will not be forwarded to the Amsterdam District Court for a decision on its execution.[74]

The following sections discuss mostly the same refusal grounds, guarantees and other conditions for the execution of an EAW as discussed in Chap. 4, since they show the same kind of potential link to unforeseeable jurisdiction claims and forum choices.[75] With regard to the problems arising from unforeseeable jurisdiction claims and their position in the surrender procedure, the next sections examine the double criminality requirement and territoriality exception in Articles 7 and 13(1)(a) SA. These touch upon the question according to whose laws the conduct should be criminalised. We will see that the territoriality exception, for instance, prohibits surrender when the conduct in question does not constitute a criminal act according to Dutch law. In addition, the extraterritoriality exception in Article 13(1)(b) SA and the refusal ground based on domestic proceedings in Article 9(1)(a) SA is examined, since they provide quite a lot of discretion to the authorities which decide on or influence their application. The main question is whether any of this discretion is provided or used to protect citizens against surrender when the jurisdiction claim of the issuing state was not foreseeable.

---

[68] *Kamerstukken II* 2002/03, 29042, nr. 3, pp. 5, 7.

[69] *Kamerstukken II* 2002/03, 29042, nr. 3, p. 7.

[70] Wet van 3 maart 2021 tot herimplementatie van onderdelen van het kaderbesluit van de Raad van de Europese Unie betreffende het Europees aanhoudingsbevel en de procedures van overlevering tussen de lidstaten van de Europese Unie (*Stb.* 2021, 125).

[71] Art 23(2) SA; *Kamerstukken II* 2002/03, 29042, nr. 3, pp. 8–9.

[72] Art 31(2) SA.

[73] Art 23(1) SA.

[74] This power of the public prosecutor is problematic in light of the case *AZ*. Art. 23(1) jo (2) SA; Glerum (2021); Case C-510/19 *AZ* [2020] ECLI:EU:C:2020:953.

[75] See Sect. 4.2.1.

Furthermore, except for the double criminality requirement, the refusal grounds mentioned above as well as the rules on concurring EAWs and extradition requests could influence forum decisions.[76] For instance, refusing an EAW because domestic proceedings in the Netherlands for the same offence are already ongoing could discourage the issuing state from continuing its prosecution, which would have to be conducted in the absence of the suspect. Lastly, in relation to both unforeseeable jurisdiction claims and forum choices, the obligation imposed on the Amsterdam District Court in Article 11 SA to refuse to give effect to an EAW in case of a real risk of a violation of the Charter of Fundamental Rights is examined, to see whether it has been used for Articles 49 or 47 CFR concerns.

The above also means that the other refusal grounds and guarantees in the Surrender Act are not examined, including those which intend to protect the requested person, such as Article 6(1) jo (3) SA. These provisions implement Article 5(3) FDEAW and state that the Amsterdam District Court has the option of making the surrender of Dutch nationals and foreigners for the purpose of prosecution dependent on a return guarantee, which allows the requested person to have a custodial sanction imposed by the issuing state executed in the Netherlands.[77] The purpose of this optional return guarantee is to increase the chances of reintegration.[78] The protection of these individuals is, therefore, not based on the idea that the Dutch state should protect its own nationals and permanent residents against surrender in case of unforeseeable jurisdiction claims or forum choices in the absence of a clear system for case allocations. We will see in Chap. 6 that the situation is different in Germany, where the German legislator has introduced a refusal ground which protects specifically German nationals against the unexpected application of foreign criminal laws. Chapter 7 will then shows the complete opposite, since British nationality can in no set of circumstances in itself never be a reason to be protected against surrender. In fact the main point of view is that surrender and extradition are blind as to nationality.

5.3.2 *The Double Criminality Requirement*

The Dutch legislator has implemented Articles 2(4) and 4(1) in Article 7 SA.[79] Hence, all acts and omissions on the EAW which do not fall under one of the categories enumerated in Article 2(2) FDEAW need to constitute criminal offences

---

[76] The rules on concurring EAWs and extradition requests are laid down in Articles 26(3) and 31(2) SA.

[77] A foreigner needs to meet additional conditions, such as a 5-year residence requirement. In addition, the Netherlands should have jurisdiction to prosecute him or her for the acts on the EAW, and there should be no expectation that he or she loses his or her right of residence in the Netherlands as a result of any criminal sanction imposed after the surrender. Art 6(3) SA.

[78] Case C-306/09 *IB* [2010] ECLI:EU:C:2010:626, para 52.

[79] Art 7(1)(a)(2°) jo (b) SA.

according to the law of the issuing state and according to the law of the Netherlands.[80] It can be derived from the legal literature and the parliamentary discussions on the use and purpose of the double criminality requirement in Dutch law that it has a dual purpose in cooperation procedures.[81] Firstly, it protects the sovereignty of the cooperating states.[82] No state should be forced to contribute to the enforcement of foreign criminal laws which contradict its own conceptions of what constitutes criminal behaviour.[83] It follows from the preparatory work to the Surrender Act that this is the main goal of the double criminality requirement in the EAW procedure.[84] Secondly, the double criminality requirement is linked to the legality principle and in that light ensures that citizens are not being subjected to repressive actions on the request of another state when they have obeyed Dutch law.[85] In other words, they should be able to trust that they will not be subjected to coercive measures on the request of another state when their conduct does not constitute a criminal act according to Dutch law.

The double criminality requirement has on occasion been linked more explicitly to the substantive legality principle and the difficulties in foreseeing which particular national criminal law is applicable at the time of the offence. In the parliamentary deliberations regarding the implementation of the FDEAW, the point was made that the failure to harmonise the categories of offences for which the application of the double criminality requirement was excluded and the vague categories on the list constitute a violation of the *lex certa* principle.[86] The lack of an additional list stating which offences fall under the different categories according to the laws of the different Member States threatens citizens' right to be able to know for which acts they can be held criminally liable. It was argued that while it might be fair to demand that a citizen knows the law of the state in which he or she resides, he or she can hardly be expected to know the laws of all EU Member States.[87] However, the Minister of Justice and Security at the time did not agree with this criticism. He stated that that the list does not intend to establish or harmonise criminal behaviour. It merely makes a distinction between cases in which the double criminality

[80] *Kamerstukken II* 2003/04, 29451, nr. 1, p. 2.

[81] *Kamerstukken II* 2003/04, 29451, nr. 1, p. 3. See also Van Sliedregt (2009), pp. 52–54; Glerum (2013), p. 293.

[82] *Kamerstukken II* 2003/04, 29451, nr. 1, p. 3; Glerum (2013), p. 353. See also *Kamerstukken II* 1964/65, 8054, nr. 3, p. 11.

[83] However, providing the requested assistance to a foreign state if the double criminality requirement is not fulfilled does not automatically mean that a state's sovereignty is violated. Providing assistance in these situations shows that the requested state respects the sovereignty of the requesting state regardless of the fact that it does not share its view with regard to the criminality of certain behavior. *Kamerstukken II* 2003/04, 29451, nr. 1, p. 8.

[84] *Handelingen I* 2004, nr. 26, p. 1345.

[85] *Kamerstukken II* 2003/04 29451, nr. 1, 3; Glerum (2013), p. 293.

[86] *Kamerstukken II* 2003/04, 29042, nr. 5, p. 16; *Kamerstukken II* 2003/04, 29042, nr. 27, p. 14; *Kamerstukken I* 2003/04, 29042, B, p. 4.

[87] *Handelingen I* 2003/04, nr. 26, p. 1329.

requirement is applicable and cases in which it is not. In addition, the exclusion of the double criminality requirement for certain offences does not affect the legal certainty of citizens, since they are always able to know which conduct is criminal in a certain state.[88] This suggests that it is sufficient that the criminal offences and sanctions in each separate national criminal law meet the legality requirements. The Minister does not seem to consider the double criminality requirement as a protection mechanism for situations in which the application of the national criminal law of the issuing state was not foreseeable.

Still, in a more general note on the application of the double criminality requirement in Dutch criminal law, the Minister of Justice and Security stated that the double criminality requirement should primarily be installed for situations in which the act occurred in the Netherlands and is not a criminal act *de lege loci*. In these cases, citizens should be able to trust that, as long as they obey Dutch law, they will not be subjected to repressive actions.[89] The Minister also argued that extending the protection of the double criminality requirement beyond these situations would be incompatible with an AFSJ based on mutual trust and in which free movement is facilitated. In other words, the double criminality requirement should not put citizens in a position in which they can escape justice when the issuing state is the *locus delicti,* but the conduct does not constitute a criminal act according to Dutch law.[90] However, in the final version of the Surrender Act, the double criminality requirement was phrased in such a way that it now blocks the execution of all EAWs when the act in question is not criminal under Dutch law.[91] Protection against surrender in situations in which the act occurred in the Netherlands but has not been criminalised under Dutch law is predominantly ensured by Article 13(1)(a) SA, which transposes Article 4(7)(a) FDEAW. This refusal ground is further discussed in the next section.

In the legal literature a certain link between the double criminality requirement and the substantive legality principle is sometimes recognised, but the former is generally not viewed as a corollary of the latter.[92] For instance, several legal scholars have argued that the executing judicial authority should assess whether the act constitutes a criminal offence according to the law of the executing state as applicable at the time of the decision on the EAW.[93] Had the double criminality requirement been considered obligatory in light of Article 1 DCC, it would in my opinion have made more sense to designate the law as applicable at the time of the offence as the correct reference point. Furthermore, according to some legal

[88] *Kamerstukken II* 2003/04, 29042, nr. 12, p. 25.

[89] *Kamerstukken II* 2003/04, 29451, nr. 1, pp. 3, 7, 9, 11.

[90] *Kamerstukken II* 2003/04, 29451, nr. 1, pp. 3, 7, 9.

[91] Unless art 7(1)(a)(1) SA applies.

[92] Glerum (2013), p. 293.

[93] Glerum (2013), p. 353; Glerum and Rozemond (2015), p. 285; Keijzer (2005), p. 146. In relation to the double criminality requirement in extradition procedures, see HR 31 August 1999, ECLI:NL:HR:1999:ZD5885 (Dutch Supreme Court); HR 16 December 2014, ECLI:NL:HR:2014:3627, para. 2.4 (Dutch Supreme Court).

scholars, the double criminality requirement in surrender proceedings is not always in a position to contribute to the foreseeability of a foreign criminal offence because it is very well possible that neither the act nor the requested person has a connection to either the executing state or the issuing state. Consequently, the fact that the behaviour in question is criminal according to the law of the executing state will not contribute to the accessibility and foreseeability of the criminal offence, since at the time of the offence, the citizen will not have been aware of the relevance of the criminal law of the executing state.[94]

It follows from the above that the need for protection against the difficulties in foreseeing the applicable national criminal laws has on occasion been linked to the double criminality requirement in the surrender procedure. However, protecting citizens against surrender when the jurisdiction claim of the issuing state—and therefore its offences and sanctions—was not foreseeable at the time of the offence does not seem to be generally recognised as the primary ratio of the double criminality requirement. Instead, the protection of state sovereignty seems to be the main goal of this requirement.

5.3.3 The Territoriality Exception

5.3.3.1 An Introduction

Article 13(1)(a) SA implements the territoriality exception in Article 4(7)(a) FDEAW. It provides the Amsterdam District Court with the discretion to refuse the execution of the EAW when the criminal act occurred partially or completely on Dutch territory. The phrasing of the territoriality exception as an optional refusal ground is the result of the 2021 amendments to the Surrender Act. Before that time, the territoriality exception was formulated as a mandatory refusal ground, but it provided the public prosecutor with the power to request the Amsterdam District Court not to apply it in a concrete case.[95] The court was obliged to grant this request unless it was unreasonable.[96] Hence, as a result of the 2021 amendments, which intend to bring Article 13 SA more in compliance with Article 4(7)(a) FDEAW, the Amsterdam District Court is now solely competent and responsible for the decision, whether it is appropriate to apply the territoriality exception.[97] The 2021 amendments grant the Amsterdam District Court broad discretion in making its decision.[98]

[94] Glerum (2013), p. 337.

[95] Art 13(2) SA (old).

[96] *Kamerstukken II* 2003/04, 29042, nr. 21, p. 3.

[97] *Kamerstukken II* 2020/2021, 35535, nr. 7, p. 19.

[98] The elimination of the role of the public prosecutor can be explained on the basis of the case *AZ* in which the CJEU criticised the designation of Dutch public prosecutors as executing judicial authorities as they can be subjected to instructions from the executive power. Case C-510/19 *AZ* [2020] ECLI:EU:C:2020:953. See Arts 127 and 128 Judicial Organization Act.

In the next sections the case law on the old and new version of Article 13(1)(a) SA will be discussed.

5.3.3.2 A Link with Unforeseeable Jurisdiction Claims?

Like the double criminality requirement, the territoriality exception has two goals. Firstly, it protects the primacy of the territoriality principle and state sovereignty. The state where the conduct occurred should be allowed to prioritise its own ideas about the criminality of conduct and the appropriate sanctions. This state should also have the first say on how a case should be handled, meaning whether it should be prosecuted—and, if so, by whom.[99] Secondly, the territoriality exception aims to safeguard the interests of the citizen, in particular in its capacity of compensation mechanism for the partial elimination of the double criminality requirement.[100] It has on the legislative level been linked to the legal certainty principle. The argument is that citizens should be able to trust that they will not be subjected to repressive actions on the request of a foreign authority for acts and omissions which occurred in the Netherlands and are not criminalised under Dutch law or are as a matter of policy not prosecuted.[101] In this context, the territoriality exception in Article 13(1)(a) SA ensures that whenever the conduct occurred in the Netherlands and is not criminal under Dutch law, the execution of the EAW can be refused even when the EAW covers a list-offence which may not be subjected to a double criminality check.[102] The preparatory work to the 2004 Surrender Act also stated that the Amsterdam District Court should classify each request on the basis of Article 13(2) SA (old) unreasonable when the non-application of the territoriality exception would hamper its functioning as a compensation mechanism.[103] However, the second ratio of the territoriality exception is not explicitly linked to the substantive legality principle or more generally the foreseeability of offences and sanctions.

Article 13(1)(a) SA also covers acts which are criminalised under Dutch law. In these situations, the public prosecutor used to have broad discretion in determining whether to make a request not to apply the territoriality exception. The text of Article 13 SA (old), its preparatory work and the case law stated that the public prosecutor needed to make the decision in light of the proper administration of justice and provide valid and substantiated reasons.[104] This criterion of the proper

[99] *Kamerstukken II* 2003/04, 29042, nr. 3, p. 17; *Kamerstukken II* 2003/04, 29042, nr. 21, p. 3; *Kamerstukken II* 2003/04, 29451, nr. 1, pp. 9, 11; Glerum (2013), p. 338.

[100] *Kamerstukken II* 2003/04, 29042, nr. 12, p. 9; HR 28 November 2006, ECLI:NL:HR:2006:AY6633, para 4.2 (Supreme Court). See also Permanent Representatives Committee, 14867/01, 3.

[101] *Kamerstukken II* 2003/04, 29451, nr. 1, pp. 9, 11; *Kamerstukken II* 2003/04, 29042, nr. 12, p. 9.

[102] *Kamerstukken II* 2003/04, 29042, nr. 3, p. 17; *Kamerstukken II* 2003/04, 29042, nr. 21, p. 3.

[103] *Kamerstukken II* 2003/04, 29042, nr. 12, pp. 9, 14; Glerum (2013), p. 350.

[104] *Kamerstukken II* 2003/04, 29042, nr. 21, p. 3. HR 28 november 2006, ECLI:NL:HR:2006:AY6631, paras 3.4.2–3.4.3 (Dutch Supreme Court).

administration of justice lacks a clear and uniform definition, but the Dutch legislator has named examples of situations in which the requirement is met.[105] This is, for instance, the case when the Dutch authorities cooperated with other Member States and decided to concentrate the prosecution against all suspects in one Member State, regardless of the question in which state or states the acts were committed.[106]

Furthermore, under the old law, the Amsterdam District Court has only to a very limited extent demarcated the power of the public prosecutor to make an assessment in light of the proper administration of justice. It has, for instance, stated that the decision not to apply Article 13 SA requires a balancing exercise between the interests of the Netherlands, which includes the interests of Dutch nationals and the issuing state.[107] With regard to the criteria that can be taken into account, it has ruled that the fact that a higher sanction could be imposed in the issuing state than in the Netherlands is not relevant.[108] Another example of factors which the case law excluded from the assessment of the proper administration of justice are humanitarian reasons, such as loss of residence due to the surrender and poor health.[109] It can therefore be concluded that neither the Dutch legislator nor the Amsterdam District Court obliged the public prosecutor to consider the problems arising from unforeseeable jurisdiction claims when making a decision.

In addition, the case law does show that public prosecutors often considered a similar variety of factors, without an obvious hierarchy, in light of the proper administration of justice. This assessment included, for instance, the place where most of the evidence was present, which legal order was most severely harmed, the place where co-offenders were prosecuted and the place where the investigation was started.[110] The foreseeability of the jurisdiction claim of the issuing state and the interlinked complications arising from the differences between criminal offences and sanctions in the Member States does not seem to have been an important consideration in the decision. This also follows from a case in which the German authorities

[105] Swart (1984), p. 117.

[106] *Kamerstukken II* 2003/04, 29042, nr. 21, p. 3. HR 28 november 2006, ECLI:NL:HR:2006:AY6631, para 3.4.2 (Supreme Court).

[107] Rb. Amsterdam 30 May 2006, ECLI:NL:RBAMS:2006:AX8631(Amsterdam District Court).

[108] Rb. Amsterdam 22 July 2009, ECLI:NL:RBAMS:2009:BK2691 (Amsterdam District Court).

[109] Rb. Amsterdam 24 November 2020, ECLI:NL:RBAMS:2020:6181 (Amsterdam District Court); Rb. Amsterdam 8 February 2011, ECLI:NL:RBAMS:2011:BQ5976 (Amsterdam District Court); Rb. Amsterdam 1 April 2005, ECLI:NL:RBAMS:2005:AT3380 (Amsterdam District Court); Glerum (2013), pp. 575–577. However, under the label of personal circumstances these humanitarian reasons may play a limited role in the decision of the public prosecutor. A lot of discussion exists about their precise role in light of the proper administration of justice. See e.g. Rb. 3 September 2010, ECLI:NL:RBAMS:2010:BO7699 (Amsterdam District Court); Rb. Amsterdam 10 December 2010, ECLI:NL:RBAMS:2010:BO8099 (Amsterdam District Court); Glerum (2013), p. 576.

[110] Rb. Amsterdam 24 November 2020, ECLI:NL:RBAMS:2020:6181 (Amsterdam District Court); Rb. Amsterdam 11 September 2020, ECLI:NL:RBAMS:2020:5863 (Amsterdam District Court); Rb. Amsterdam 12 May 2020, ECLI:NL:RBAMS:2020:2582 (Amsterdam District Court); Rb. Amsterdam 19 December 2019, ECLI:NL:RBAMS:2019:9984 (Amsterdam District Court).

had issued an EAW in order to prosecute a German national who had allegedly spread right-extremists convictions on a German webpage, arguably while residing in the Netherlands. In response to the argument that the territoriality exception should apply, because the German law could impose a higher sentence, the Dutch public prosecutor stated that citizens should simply take into account that other states with stricter sanctions can prosecute them for criminal offences with an international dimension.[111] Such a reasoning indicates that the difficulties in foreseeing which national criminal law is applicable to you at the time of the offence are not necessarily considered as problematic. It seems to be the citizen's own responsibility to not be surprised by diverging criminal laws, including offences and sanctions, in case of cross-border crimes.

Hence, it follows from the case law on Article 13 SA (new) that the Amsterdam District Court does not consider the foreseeability of jurisdiction claims a relevant factor in its decision. The court has consistently stated that the application of the territoriality exception should be an exception. In addition, the purpose of this refusal ground is to prevent cooperation in situations in which the act in question does not constitute a criminal offense according to Dutch law. Hence, the Amsterdam District Court primarily views the territoriality exception as a compensation measure for the partial abolition of the double criminality requirement. Furthermore, the case law shows that the court relies on the same factors as the public prosecutor used to when deciding against the application of the territoriality exception, including the availability of evidence, the place where co-offenders were prosecuted etc.[112]

In light of the above, it can be concluded that the territoriality exception functions to a certain extent as a safeguard for the citizen. When the conduct occurred on Dutch territory and is not criminal according to Dutch law, the requested person should on the basis of the principle of legal certainty not be subjected to repressive actions. However, this protection is not explicitly based on the general opinion that criminal offences and sanctions are not sufficiently foreseeable when a jurisdiction claim was not foreseeable.

5.3.3.3 The Territoriality Exception and Forum Choices

As explained in Chap. 4, refusal grounds like the territoriality exception do not constitute forum choices *stricto sensu,* since the refusal to execute the EAW does not oblige the Netherlands to prosecute the case and neither is the issuing state obliged to terminate its criminal proceedings in case of a refusal. However, the application of the territoriality exception may influence the decision to prosecute in the issuing state and in other competent states, since the absence of the suspect can complicate their

[111] Rb. Amsterdam 20 August 2020, ECLI:NL:RBAMS:2020:4094 (Amsterdam District Court).

[112] Rb. Amsterdam 22 December 2021, ECLI:NL:RBAMS:2021:7758 (Amsterdam District Court); Rb Amsterdam 24 November 2021 ECLI:NL:RBAMS:2021:7246 (Amsterdam District Court); Rb. Amsterdam 20 August 2021, ECLI:NL:RBAMS:2021:4360 (Amsterdam District Court).

criminal proceedings.[113] Furthermore, the decision of the Amsterdam District Court not to apply the territoriality exception could facilitate prosecution by the issuing state and discourage prosecution by other competent states. The case law on Article 13(1)(a) SA also shows that discussions regarding its application cover the question whether the case should be dealt with in the Netherlands or elsewhere.[114] Hence, the territoriality exception in Article 13(1)(a) SA could *de facto* settle a conflict of jurisdictions.

The previous section has already explained that 13(2) SA (old) provided public prosecutors with broad discretion. They had to make their decision on the application of the refusal ground in light of the proper administration of justice, but the interpretation of this criterion was hardly demarcated or influenced by the legislator and courts. In addition, the fact that the surrender procedure functions in an EU without a clear system for case allocations which ensures a reasonable forum decision has not been discussed by the Dutch legislator or Amsterdam District Court in the context of the new version of Article 13(1)(a) SA. The Dutch legislator does also not explain why it provides such broad discretion to the competent authorities. A possible explanation is that the lack of criteria defining the proper administration of justice allows flexibility in deciding whether it is best to allow the case, despite its link to the Netherlands, to be prosecuted elsewhere. In this light, the broad discretion which is now granted to the Amsterdam District Court allows the court to base its decision on the concrete circumstances of the case and to take the different interests into account.[115]

5.3.4 *The Extraterritoriality Exception*

Article 13(1)(b) SA implements Article 4(7)(b) FDEAW and is often referred to as the extraterritoriality exception. Before explaining its content it is important to note that it underwent a similar transformation as the territoriality exception. The 2021 amendments to the Surrender Act eliminated the power of the public prosecutor to request the Amsterdam District Court not to apply the refusal ground.[116] Consequently, the Amsterdam District Court now has the sole power to make this decision.

The extraterritoriality exception covers the situation in which the actions of the requested person did not partially or completely occur on Dutch territory and the issuing state exercises extraterritorial jurisdiction. In such situations, the Amsterdam District Court is allowed to refuse the execution of the EAW when the act in question could in a similar situation not be prosecuted in the Netherlands. In other words,

[113] Herrnfeld (2013), p. 191.

[114] See e.g. Rb. Amsterdam 1 October 2020, ECLI:NL:RBAMS:2020:6090 (Amsterdam District Court).

[115] Swart (1984), pp. 117–118; Van Sliedregt (2015), p. 9. See also Swart (1986), pp. 33, 217–218.

[116] Art 13(2) SA (old).

when the Netherlands would in a similar situation not have been able to exercise extraterritorial jurisdiction, it does not have to aid the prosecution in the issuing state.[117] The refusal ground applies both in the situation in which the act in question is not a criminal act according to Dutch law and in the situation in which it is considered a criminal act, but the Netherlands would lack jurisdiction.

The goal of the extraterritoriality exception is to protect the sovereignty of the executing state.[118] With regard to the role of the complications arising from the absence of an overarching EU system for forum choices and the difficulties in foreseeing the applicable national criminal laws, the same comments can be made as in relation to the territoriality exception. Under Article 13 SA (old), the discretion of the public prosecutor used to be demarcated by the criterion of the proper administration of justice, which lacks a common definition. The preparatory work to the 2004 Surrender Act and the legal literature only provide examples of factors which can be considered. The decision not to apply the refusal ground could, for instance, be justified when the issuing state and the state in which the crime was committed cooperate and decide to concentrate the criminal proceedings in the issuing state, or if prosecution by the *locus delicti* is favoured over prosecution by a state exercising extraterritorial jurisdiction.[119] The case law on Article 13(1)(b) SA (old) also shows that the public prosecutor used to consider roughly the same non-hierarchical list of factors as for the territoriality exception when making the decisions.[120] In addition, after the 2021 amendments the Amsterdam District Court has not referred to the foreseeability of the jurisdiction claim of the issuing state as a relevant factor in its decision on the applicability of the extraterritoriality exception.

It can be concluded that the foreseeability of the application of the law of the issuing state does not have an important role in relation to the decision to apply the extraterritoriality exception. With regard to the complications arising from the absence of an EU system for forum choices and correlating risk of arbitrary forum decisions, it follows from the above that these have not been criticised by the legislator or court in the context of the extraterritoriality exception. The almost unrestricted discretion granted to the public prosecutor and now the Amsterdam District Court could, however, suggest that flexibility in making the decision on its application—which can indirectly influence the forum decision—is important.

[117] Rb. Amsterdam 11 September 2009, ECLI:NL:RBAMS:2009:BK9181 (Amsterdam District Court).

[118] Glerum (2013), pp. 340–341.

[119] *Kamerstukken II* 2003/04, 29042, nr. 21, p. 3; Glerum (2013), p. 579.

[120] Rb. Amsterdam 13 February 2020, ECLI:NL:RBAMS:2020:1129 (Amsterdam District Court); Rb. Amsterdam 10 May 2016, ECLI:NL:RBAMS:2016:2765 (Amsterdam District Court); Rb. Amsterdam 14 November 2014, ECLI:NL:RBAMS:2014:9846 (Amsterdam District Court).

5.3.5 *Domestic Proceedings for the Same Offence*

Before the 2021 amendments to the Surrender Act, Article 9(1)(a) SA implementing Article 4(2) FDEAW was formulated as a mandatory refusal ground.[121] Now, it provides the Amsterdam District Court with the discretion to refuse the execution of an EAW when the requested person is already being prosecuted by the Netherlands for the conduct for which the EAW is issued.[122] Similar to the situation before the 2021 amendments, subsection 2 of Article 9 states that the refusal ground is not applicable when the Minister of Justice and Security has decided to suspend the domestic proceedings. The suspension needs to occur before the decision on the EAW has been made, and the Minister needs to ask the advice of both the public prosecutor dealing with the criminal case and the public prosecutor responsible for the EAW.[123] To sum up, Article 9(1)(a) SA provides the Amsterdam District Court with the discretion to determine whether the refusal ground should be applied, but this power is blocked when the Minister suspends the Dutch criminal proceedings before a decision on the EAW is made.

A Link with Unforeseeable Jurisdiction Claims?

Neither the preparatory legislative work on Article 9 SA nor the case law suggests that the aim of Article 9(1)(a) SA is to protect citizens against surrender when the jurisdiction claim of the issuing state was not foreseeable at the time of the offence. In the legal literature, the refusal ground is instead linked to the protection of the sovereignty of the executing state, which should be allowed to place its own national interests over those of the issuing state.[124] In addition, whereas the German provision implementing Article 4(2) FDEAW allows domestic proceedings to start after the receipt of an EAW in order to protect to some extent in particular German nationals against the unexpected application of foreign laws,[125] it has not been explicitly determined whether Article 9(1)(a) SA may be used in the same way and for the same purpose.[126]

---

[121] *Kamerstukken II* 2020/2021, 35535, 7, p. 19.

[122] The Amsterdam District Court has interpreted the meaning of 'act' in line with Article 54 CISA. Rb. Amsterdam 18 September 2009, ECLI:NL:RBAMS:2009:BK2284 (Amsterdam District Court). The rules for situations in which domestic proceedings for different acts are running against the requested person in the executing state are laid down in Article 36 SA.

[123] *Kamerstukken II* 2002/03, 29042, nr. 3, p. 23.

[124] Glerum (2013), p. 560.

[125] See Sect. 6.3.5; Von Bubnoff (2005), p. 78; BVerfG 18 July 2005, 2 BvR 2236/04 (*Darkazanli*) [95]; Böhm (2018), para 1078.

[126] The Extradition Act contains a similar refusal ground and sets the moment a decision needs to be made on the request for extradition as the reference point. Art 9(1)(a) Extradition Act; Glerum (2013), p. 554.

Forum Choices

In relation to the matter of forum choices, it follows from Article 9(1)(a) jo 9(2) SA that *de facto* the Minister of Justice and Security first decides whether prosecution in the Netherlands is preferred over prosecution in the issuing state. In case the Minister does not suspend the domestic proceedings, the Amsterdam District Court can influence the forum decision when deciding whether or not to apply the refusal ground. With regard to the use of the discretion granted to the court, the preparatory work to the 2021 amendments does not establish any limitations. In addition, it does not discuss the difficulties arising from the absence of a transparent EU system for forum choices in the context of the broad discretion granted to the Amsterdam District Court to give priority to prosecution in the Netherlands or the issuing state.

Contrary to the discretion granted to the Amsterdam District Court, the discretion granted to the Minister has to a certain extent been discussed and delineated. According to the preparatory work to the 2004 Surrender Act, the Minister needs to choose the best state for prosecution in light of the proper administration of justice and on the basis of the concrete circumstances of the case. The criterion of the proper administration of justice aims to prohibit the Minister from making the decision on the basis of political considerations, but—as explained before—this criterion lacks a clear definition.[127] However, the preparatory work does define a few situations in which surrender should be preferred over prosecution in the Netherlands in light of the good administration of justice. These situations include one in which the requested person or important witnesses reside in the issuing state.[128] Hence, the relevant considerations also cover the interests of the citizen in his or her capacity of suspect and requested person. Still, despite these examples, the preparatory work also states that it is not possible to predict on the basis of which exact criteria and considerations the Minister will eventually make the decision. Such factors are currently also not laid down in, for instance policy guidelines or the case law.[129] In addition, it should be noted that Dutch law offers limited access to judicial review of the decision of the Minister of Justice and Security. The requested person can, for instance, only challenge the decision to suspend criminal proceedings in the Netherlands by initiating preliminary relief proceedings (*kort geding*) before the civil judge, who may only assess the reasonableness of the decision.[130]

---

[127] *Kamerstukken II* 2003/04, 29042, nr. 27, p. 26.

[128] *Kamerstukken II* 2002/03, 29042, nr. 3, p. 15; Glerum (2010), para 91.20.5.

[129] That they do not follow clearly from the case law can be explained in light of the fact that the Amsterdam District Court is in principle not competent to review the decision of the Minister. The majority of the case law on art. 9(1)(a) jo (2) is concerned with the question at which point in time and under which circumstances 'criminal proceedings' are in fact in progress against the requested person. See Rb. Amsterdam 29 March 2019, ECLI:NL:RBAMS:2019:2390 (Amsterdam District Court); Rb. Amsterdam 26 May 2016, ECLI:NL:RBAMS:2016:3123 (Amsterdam District Court); Rb. Amsterdam, 11 September 2009, ECLI:NL:RBAMS:2009:BK9181 (Amsterdam District Court).

[130] Evaluation report on the fourth round of mutual evaluations 'The practical application of the European Arrest Warrant and Corresponding surrender procedures between Member States'—Report on the Netherlands, 15370/1/08 REV 1 (2008), p. 38.

On the basis of the above, it can be concluded that the discretion of the Amsterdam District Court and Minister of Justice and Security is hardly restricted by law. This broad discretion allows for flexibility and therefore facilitates a decision appointing the best forum for the specific case. The potential risk of arbitrary forum decisions which can accompany broad discretion granted to the judiciary, but in particular the executive, while the possibility of judicial review is restricted, was not discussed during the legislative process on Article 9(1)(a) SA. This could mean that it was not considered an important issue.

5.3.6 Fundamental Rights Concerns

As a result of the 2021 amendments, Article 11(1) SA prohibits the Amsterdam District Court from giving effect to an EAW when it concludes that substantial grounds exist that prove that the requested person faces a real risk of a violation of the EU Charter of Fundamental Rights in the issuing state. The 2021 amendments intended to bring Article 11 SA in compliance with EU law and to implement the *Aranyosi* and *LM* string of CJEU case law on the basis of which fundamental rights concerns can in exceptional circumstances allow for additional exceptions to the duty to execute an EAW.[131] Before these 2021 amendments, Article 11 SA was formulated as a refusal ground and stated that the execution of an EAW shall be refused in case surrender will lead to a flagrant breach of one or more of the fundamental rights in the ECHR.[132] Article 11 SA was severely criticised in its capacity of refusal ground for violating the FDEAW, which does not include a general human rights refusal ground.[133] The old version of Article 11 SA also referred to the ECHR instead of the CFR because the latter was not yet legally binding at the time the Surrender Act entered into force. However, the case law shows that over time the Amsterdam District Court started to consider fundamental rights defences referring to the rights in the CFR on the basis of Article 11 SA, as well.[134]

[131] *Kamerstukken II* 2019/20, 35535, nr. 3, p. 13.

[132] This refusal ground was an important point of discussion during the implementation process of the FDEAW. The Minister of Justice and Security opposed its inclusion in the Surrender Act, since the obligation to consider possible violations of the ECHR in the surrender procedure already follows from Article 94 Constitution. However, the Dutch Parliament had serious doubts about the actual existence of mutual trust and therefore insisted on an explicit human rights refusal ground. *Kamerstukken II* 2003/04, 29042, nr. 12, p. 22; *Kamerstukken II* 2003/04, 29042, nr. 5, pp. 12–15.

[133] Evaluation report on the fourth round of mutual evaluations 'The practical application of the European Arrest Warrant and Corresponding surrender procedures between Member States'—Report on the Netherlands, 15370/1/08 REV 1 (2008), p. 47; *Kamerstukken II* 2019/20, 35535, nr. 3, pp. 9, 13.

[134] See e.g. Rb. Amsterdam 6 October 2016, ECLI:N:RBAMS:2016:6316 (Amsterdam District Court); Rb. Amsterdam 10 January 2017, ECLI:NL:RBAMS:2017:331 (Amsterdam District Court).

It follows from the above that both the old and new version of Article 11 SA in principle offer(ed) the opportunity to refuse surrender in case of a real risk that the execution of the EAW would subject the requested person to a violation of the legality principle as laid down in Article 49 CFR and the right to a tribunal established by law in Article 47 CFR in the issuing state. In practice, however, the old version of Article 11 SA was never used for this purpose. In fact, a defence on the basis of Article 11 SA (old) has been successful in only a very few cases, none of which concerned the *nullum crimen sine lege* principle and the right to a tribunal established by law.[135] In addition, before the 2021 amendments, the *Aranyosi and Câldâraru* and *LM* case law was also applied by the Amsterdam District Court, but not in the context of Article 11 SA.[136] In these cases, the Amsterdam District Court did not take it upon itself to extend the twofold test established in the CJEU case law to fundamental rights other than Article 4 CFR and the right to an independent court in Article 47 CFR.[137] Furthermore, after the 2021 amendments, the Amsterdam District Court has not refused the execution of an EAW on the basis of Article 11 SA because of concerns with regard to Article 49 CFR or the right to a tribunal established by law in Article 47 CFR.[138]

It can be concluded on the basis of the above that neither Article 11 SA (old) nor the integration of the CJEU rulings on fundamental rights in the Dutch case law has led to refusals to execute the EAW, because this would result in a violation of Article 49 due to the unforeseeable jurisdiction claim of the issuing state or a violation of Article 47 CFR, as the issuing state's decision to prosecute was not based on a transparent system for forum choices. In my opinion, it is not likely that Article 11 SA (new) will be used for such purposes in the near future, either, and for two main reasons. Firstly, despite the fact that the scope of Article 11 SA is not limited to violations of Articles 4 CFR and 47 CFR, the legal provision is based on the *Aranyosi* and *Câldâraru* and *LM* exceptions. The CJEU has not ruled on the question whether these exceptions should in the context of the EAW be extended to Article 49 and the right to an independent court in Article 47 CFR. Consequently, the Amsterdam District Court may be hesitant to apply Article 11 SA in relation to other fundamental rights, since the interpretation of EU law is in principle the task of the

[135] Rb. Amsterdam 1 July 2005, ECLI:NL:RBAMS:2005:AT8580 (Amsterdam District Court). This case concerned a violation of Article 6 ECHR, more specifically the right to a trial within a reasonable time. However, the Amsterdam Court has changed its position since then, meaning that this right can no longer block the surrender of the requested person on the basis of Article 11 SA. The claim that this right is violated should in principle be brought before the judge in the issuing state. Rb. Amsterdam 17 October 2008, ECLI:NL:RBAMS:2008:BG6051 (Amsterdam District Court).

[136] For an explanation on the implementation of the cases *Aranyosi and Câldâraru* and *LM* in the jurisprudence of the Court of Amsterdam see Martufi and Gigengack (2020).

[137] Rb. Amsterdam 26 January 2017, ECLI:NL:RBAMS:2017:414 (Amsterdam District Court); Rb. Amsterdam 6 August 2018, ECLI:RBAMS:2018:5925 (Amsterdam District Court); Rb. Amsterdam 4 October 2018, ECLI:NL:RBAMS:2018:7032 (Amsterdam District Court).

[138] However, see Rb. Amsterdam 14 September 2021, ECLI:NL:RBAMS:2021:5051.

CJEU. Secondly, even if potential violations of Articles 49 and 47 CFR could on the basis Article 11 SA block the surrender of the requested person, it is still not clear whether these fundamental rights influence jurisdiction rules and forum choices in case of conflicts of national jurisdictions. As explained in Chap. 3 neither the EU legislator nor the CJEU has explicitly determined that unforeseeable jurisdiction claims affect the accessibility and foreseeability of criminal offences and sanctions in light of Article 49 CFR and that forum choices on the EU level fall within the scope of Article 47 CFR. Seeing that the interpretation of EU law is a task for the CJEU the Amsterdam District Court will most likely not adopt such an interpretation of the EU Charter rights itself in order to block the surrender of the requested person.

5.3.7 *Multiple EAWs and Extradition Requests for the Same Offence*

The public prosecutor decides which EAW should take priority in case multiple EAWs are issued for the same person and the same offence. Article 26(3) SA states that the decision needs to be based on the proper administration of justice and that the public prosecutor should in particular consider the enumerated factors, including the seriousness of the offence, the place where the act was committed, the dates of the EAW etc.[139] This list of factors is not limitative and does not set a pecking order. The case law shows that the public prosecutor also considers the connection of the offence to the territories of the issuing states, the place where accomplices are prosecuted, the possibility to concentrate all cases against the requested person in one state and the nationality of the victims.[140] The decision of the public prosecutor is subject to a marginal review by the Amsterdam District Court, which checks its reasonableness.[141]

The Minister of Security and Justice is competent to make the decision in case of concurring EAWs and extradition requests for the same offence.[142] This power is delineated by the *Petruhhin* and *Pisciotti* rulings of the CJEU.[143] In these cases, EU citizens had exercised their free movement rights and were in the host state subjected

[139] Subsection e and f of Article 26(3) SA contain factors which are not mentioned by the FDEAW.

[140] Rb. Amsterdam 18 July 2014, ECLI:NL:RBAMS:2014:4707 (Amsterdam District Court); Rb. Amsterdam, 13 May 2009, ECLI:NL:RBAMS:2009:BI3786 (Amsterdam District Court). The public prosecutor can also ask Eurojust for advice. See Rb. Amsterdam 14 January 2005, ECLI:NL:RBAMS:2005:AS2599 (Amsterdam District Court).

[141] Art 28(4) SA.

[142] Art 31(2) jo (3) SA.

[143] Case C-182/15 *Petruhhin* [2016] ECLI:EU:C:2016:630; Case C-191/16 *Pisciotti* [2018] ECLI:EU:C:2018:222. With regard to the case law concerning the extradition of EU citizens to third countries see also the Joint report of Eurojust and the European Judicial Network on the extradition of EU citizens to third countries (2020) <https://www.eurojust.europa.eu/joint-report-eurojust-and-ejn-extradition-eu-citizens-third-countries> accessed 20 September 2021.

to an extradition request. The CJEU decided that when the law of the host state only protects its own nationals against extradition, it should ask the EU Member State of nationality of the requested person whether it wishes to issue an EAW for the criminal offence. In case the latter decides to do so and this EAW can be executed according to the law of the host state, it should be given priority over the extradition request. Consequently, the Dutch Minister of Justice and Security is now obliged to refuse the execution of an extradition request issued for an EU citizen who has exercised the right to free movement when the Amsterdam District Court has ruled that an EAW issued for the same criminal offence by the state of nationality can be executed.[144] In all other cases the Minister of Justice and Security needs to take the factors mentioned in Article 35(1) of the Dutch Extradition Act into consideration, which are almost the same ones as enumerated in Article 26(3) SA.[145] These factors constitute guidelines and are not set out in a hierarchical order.[146]

Even though the rules discussed above could also influence the eventual forum decision in a concrete case, neither the preparatory work to the Surrender Act nor the case law include in this context an assessment of the problems arising from the lack of an EU or international system for forum choices. The increased risk of arbitrary decisions and abuse of power resulting from almost unlimited discretion in deciding which EAW or extradition request will be executed, which can by extension influence the forum decision, has not been discussed by the Dutch legislator or the courts. Again, the decision not to adopt rigid rules has not been clearly explained by the Dutch legislator, but it could be based on a preference for flexibility in making a decision in light of the proper administration of justice.

5.4 The Netherlands As the Issuing State

5.4.1 An Introduction

This section discusses first to what extent unforeseeable jurisdiction claims and the lack of a transparent EU system for forum choices are recognised as problems in the context of the issuing procedure. Afterwards, in light of the link between the decision to issue an EAW and the decision to exercise jurisdiction, the rules regulating the exercise of jurisdiction are also discussed. That part also focuses on the question to what extent unforeseeable jurisdiction claims and the absence of a transparent

[144] Art 31(2) SA jo 35(2) Extradition Act; *Kamerstukken II* 2019/20, 35535, nr. 3, pp. 18, 22. See also HR 23 February 2018, ECLI:NL:HR:2018:289, para 4.3 (Dutch Supreme Court); Rb. Den Haag 27 May 2020, ECLI:NL:RBDHA:2020:4559 (The Hague District Court); Rb. Den Haag 2 November 2017, ECLI:NL:RBDHA:2017:12708 (The Hague District Court).

[145] Art 31(3) SA jo 35 (3) Extradition Act; *Kamerstukken II* 2019/2020, 35535, nr. 3, p. 22.

[146] *Kamerstukken II* 1964/65, 8054, nr. 3, p. 15.

system for forum choices have been taken into account in the adoption and application of those rules.

5.4.2 The Issuing Procedure

The Surrender Act itself contains hardly any conditions for the issuing of an EAW. The most important criteria are laid down in Articles 44 and 2 SA.[147] The former allocates the power to issue an EAW to all investigative judges in the Netherlands.[148] This competence used to belong to all public prosecutors in the Netherlands, but after the case *OG & PI*, the Dutch legislator decided to reallocate it.[149] In this ruling, the CJEU decided that Member States may only appoint authorities which are independent of the executive as issuing judicial authorities. Consequently, the designation of Dutch public prosecutors as issuing judicial authorities was problematic, since the Dutch Minister of Justice and Security has the power to instruct them in the exercise of their powers.[150]

Article 2 SA imposes a proportionality test, since it states that prosecution EAWs may only be issued for offences punishable by a custodial sentence of 12 months or more according to Dutch criminal law. In case of an execution EAW a sanction of at least 4 months needs to have been imposed.[151] In the case *OG & PI*, the CJEU has added another proportionality test which obliges the issuing judicial authority to determine whether in the concrete case the issuing of the EAW is necessary.[152]

In addition, Article 2 SA implements Article 8(1) FDEAW and enumerates the information which the EAW needs to contain.[153] This includes the nature and legal qualification of the offences and a description of the circumstances under which the offence was committed.[154] These conditions aim to ensure that the requested person

[147] See also arts 45–45b SA on the issuing of return-guarantees, guarantees relating to the possibility of release in case of life-long sentences and *in absentia* proceedings.

[148] Wet van 10 juli 2019 tot wijziging van de Overleveringswet in verband met het arrest van het Hof van Justitie van de Europese Unie in de gevoegde zaken C-508/18 OG en C-82/19 PPU PI (*Stb.* 2019, 259).

[149] Joined Cases C-508/18 & C-82/19 *OG & PI* [2019] ECLI:EU:C:2019:456.

[150] *Kamerstukken II* 2018/2019, 35224, nr. 3. See Arts 127 and 128 Judicial Organization Act.

[151] Art 2(1) SA. In situations in which the criminal offense in question is punishable by a custodial order of 3 years or more and falls under one of the categories listed in Article 2(2) FDEAW, the issuing judicial authority may mark the offense as a list-offense on the EAW. This means that the executing judicial authority may not conduct a double criminality check when deciding on the execution of the EAW.

[152] Joined Cases C-508/18 & C-82/19 *OG & PI* [2019] ECLI:EU:C:2019:456, para 71; Case C-489/19 *NJ* [2019] ECLI:EU:C:2019:849, paras 37, 44. See also *Kamerstukken II* 2020/2021, 35535, nr. 11.

[153] Art 2(2) SA.

[154] Art 2(2)(d)(e) SA.

knows for which offence his or her surrender is requested and that the executing judicial authority is able to determine whether the conditions for the execution of an EAW are met.[155] Hence, these information requirements do not aim to enable the executing state to verify or judge the foreseeability of the jurisdiction claim of the issuing state or its decision to prosecute. Such a power would in itself also contradict the principles of mutual recognition and mutual trust.

The case law of the Amsterdam District Court also shows the integration of the *Bob-Dogi* ruling in the Dutch surrender procedure. Article 2(2)(c) SA requires that each prosecution EAW is based on a national arrest warrant or other equivalent enforceable judicial decision and that each execution EAW is based on a national enforceable judgement.[156] More concretely, prosecution EAWs require a valid underlying Dutch arrest warrant or order for police custody (*bevel tot gevangenneming*), satisfying the conditions in the Dutch Code of Criminal Procedure (DCCP).[157] It follows from the CJEU case law that the requirement of such an underlying national arrest warrant aims to ensure that the requested person receives fundamental rights protection on the national level when the national arrest warrant is issued and on the European level when the EAW is issued.[158] However, as discussed in Chap. 4, this fundamental rights protection does not specifically and explicitly cover safeguards against unforeseeable jurisdiction claims and forum choices which are not based on a transparent set of rules.[159] It can therefore be concluded that none of the conditions for the issuing of an EAW intends to protect citizens against unforeseeable jurisdiction claims and forum choices without a transparent legal basis.

5.4.3 The Rules Regulating the Power to Exercise Jurisdiction

The opportunity principle or principle of discretionary prosecution applies in Dutch criminal procedural law.[160] Contrary to the legality principle, it does not demand that

---

[155] The information also needs to ensure that the protection of the speciality principle is safeguarded. *Kamerstukken I* 2003/04, 29042, C, p. 8; *Handelingen I* 2004, 26, p. 1345; Rb. Amsterdam 3 March 2006, ECLI:NL:RBAMS:2006:AV4298 (Amsterdam District Court); Rb. Amsterdam 16 March 2017, ECLI:NL:RBAMS:2017:1699 (Amsterdam District Court); Rb. Amsterdam 30 March 2017, ECLI:NL:RBAMS:2017:2036 (Amsterdam District Court).

[156] Case C-241/15 *Bob-Dogi* [2016] ECLI:EU:C:2016:385, paras 43–44, 49, 58. See also Rb. Amsterdam 15 December 2016, ECLI:NL:RBAMS:2016:9283 (Amsterdam District Court).

[157] College van procureurs-generaal, Handboek overleveringsprocedure tussen de lidstaten van de EU op grond van een Europees Aanhoudingsbevel (1 maart 2012), p. 7.

[158] Case C-241/15 *Bob-Dogi* [2016] ECLI:EU:C:2016:385, paras 55–56. See also Case C-241/15 *Bob-Dogi* [2016] ECLI:EU:C:2016:131, Opinion of AG Bot, paras 55–56.

[159] Section 4.3.3.

[160] Art 167 jo 242 DCCP.

all cases are prosecuted when there is sufficient evidence to conduct a prosecution.[161] This means that the public prosecutor is not obliged to prosecute each case in which extraterritorial jurisdiction exists, but is provided with the discretion to refrain from prosecution for reasons of public interest. These reasons are enumerated in the 2021 Instruction on grounds of dismissal.[162] One of the accepted reasons not to prosecute a case is that it insufficiently serves national interests. In this light, the 2021 Instruction mentions several examples, such as the situation in which the suspect resides in another state and cannot be reached or prosecution by another state is preferred. These examples are not further elaborated on as a result of which it remains unclear whether preference should be given to another state when, for instance, the Dutch jurisdiction claim was not foreseeable at the time of the offence.

In case of conflicts of jurisdictions, meaning that besides the Netherlands other states have jurisdiction in a particular case, Dutch law does not prohibit the public prosecutor from prosecuting the case, save for exceptional circumstances, such as when the *ne bis in idem* principle applies.[163] The discretion of the public prosecutor to decide whether or not to prosecute the case in such a situation is hardly restricted. Neither the 2021 Instruction on the use of grounds of dismissal nor the Instruction implementing Framework Decision 2009/948/JHA on conflicts of jurisdiction provide clear criteria in this regard.[164] However, despite the lack of clear criteria in Dutch law, the matter of conflicts of jurisdictions was discussed in the legislative process leading to the amendments of the jurisdiction rules in 2014. The Dutch legislator stated that the competent Member States have to decide in light of the proper administration of justice which state should prosecute.[165] From the legislator's point of view the proper administration of justice is in most cases best served by prosecution by the *locus delicti*, even when the suspect is a Dutch national or permanently resides in the Netherlands.[166] The extraterritorial jurisdiction grounds are a safety net, in the sense that they can be used when the *locus delicti* does not prosecute a suspect or discontinues the prosecution.[167] The public prosecutor should therefore restrict the exercise of extraterritorial jurisdiction to cases in which serious crimes would otherwise not be investigated.[168] Other relevant questions to ask in order to assess the good administration of justice are where most of the investigations need to take place, a state's capacity to prosecute, and the priority which can be given to the case.[169] It can therefore be concluded that the absence of an EU

[161] The legality principle, for instance, applies in the German legal order. See art 152 StPO.

[162] Aanwijzing sepot en gebruik sepotgronden (*Stcrt.* 2020, 62570). Applicable since 1 March 2021.

[163] Art 68 DCC. The public prosecutor is not competent to prosecute.

[164] Aanwijzing rechtsmachtgeschillen bij strafprocedures (*Stcrt.* 2012, 11716).

[165] *Kamerstukken II* 2012/13, 33572, nr. 6, p. 15.

[166] *Kamerstukken II* 2012/13, 33572, nr. 3, p. 6; *Kamerstukken II* 2012/13, 33572, nr. 6, p. 15.

[167] *Kamerstukken II* 2012/13, 33572, nr. 3, p. 17; *Kamerstukken II* 2012/13, 33572, nr. 4, p. 5; *Kamerstukken II* 2012/13, 33572, nr. 6, pp. 18–20.

[168] *Kamerstukken II* 2012/13, 33572, nr. 6, pp. 2, 5.

[169] *Kamerstukken II* 2012/13, 33572, nr. 6, p. 14.

mechanism for forum choices which goes beyond the rules in Framework Decision 2009/948/JHA on conflicts of jurisdiction has not been recognised as an important problem. The Dutch legislator has acknowledged the fact that conflicts of jurisdiction may occur, but not that the absence of a clear system to solve them is problematic, let alone an issue in light of *ius de non evocando*.

In addition, in the Netherlands the decision to prosecute can only be challenged in court on the grounds that the conditions for jurisdiction are not satisfied or that the case should have been dismissed. Furthermore, Article 12 DCCP allows directly interested persons to request the competent Court of Appeal to start or continue a prosecution in the Netherlands. A suspect is often not recognised as a directly interested person, but can be when a case is already being examined in a Dutch court and a request for assistance, such as the transfer of proceedings or surrender, is received from another state.[170] The reason for these exceptions is due to one of the general principles of Dutch criminal procedural law, according to which, after the examination in court has started, the suspect has in principle a right to a continuation of the procedure until a final ruling is provided.[171] Hence, when the examination before the court has not yet started, it is unlikely that the suspect is recognised as a directly interested person.[172] In relation to EAWs, the case law shows that in such a situation, the requested person is not recognised as a directly interested person when the main reason for the request to bring the case before the Dutch judge is to avoid prosecution by the issuing state.[173] Hence, when the case is not yet in court, the suspect cannot use the Article 12 procedure to influence the forum decision.

5.5 Conclusion

This main question of this chapter was whether the surrender of a citizen is viewed as problematic in the Dutch legal order when the applicability of the substantive criminal law of the issuing state was difficult to foresee at the time of the offence or when its decision to prosecute was not based on a transparent EU system for forum choices. In this light, it has first explored the scope of the national substantive legality principle and *ius de non evocando*, more specifically their link to jurisdiction and forum choices in case of conflicts of national jurisdictions. Secondly, it has

---

[170] HR 28 February 1984, ECLI:NL:HR:1984:AC8323 (Dutch Supreme Court); Hof 's-Gravenhage 3 July 2000, ECLI:NL:GHSGR:2000:AB8486 (The Hague Court of Appeal).

[171] HR 28 February 1984, ECLI:NL:HR:1984:AC8323 (Dutch Supreme Court).

[172] In situations in which the examination in court has not yet started and the transfer of the proceedings to another state is considered, the suspect cannot rely on Article 12 DCCP, since there is the possibility of a complaint on the basis of art 5.3.1 (5) (552t old) DCCP. Hof Den Haag 3 July 2000, ECLI:NL:GHSGR:2000:AB8486 (The Hague Court of Appeal).

[173] Hof 's-Hertogenbosch 27 February 2007, ECLI:NL:GHSHE:2007:BB5053 (Court of Appeal 's-Hertogenbosch).

examined to what extent the rules in the Dutch Surrender Act intend to offer safeguards against surrender in situations in which the two problems occur.

In relation to the complications arising from unforeseeable jurisdiction claims at the time of the offence, it can be concluded that neither the courts nor the Dutch legislator have unambiguously decided on the existence of a link between jurisdiction and the *nullum crimen sine lege* principle in Dutch law. The courts have not yet ruled on the question whether compliance with the accessibility and *lex certa* requirement is influenced by the foreseeability of the application of a specific national criminal law. The Dutch legislator has both denied and acknowledged the existence of some kind of link between jurisdiction and Article 1 DCC. The acknowledgement follows from the 2013 review of the Dutch jurisdiction rules, in particular the discussions on the restriction of extraterritorial jurisdiction. In this context, the statements of the Dutch Minister of Justice and Security reflect the position that citizens should at least be able to know at the time of the offence that their actions were criminal according to the law of a state. Such foreseeability can be ensured by the double criminality requirement or the universal acknowledgement of the criminality of the conduct. In addition, in the legal literature, the majority of the legal scholars is either of the opinion that jurisdiction is in no way connected to the requirements of accessibility and *lex certa* or, like the Dutch Minister of Justice and Security, that it is sufficient that the citizen could have known at the time of the offence that the conduct was criminal somewhere.

In addition, it can be concluded that none of the conditions for the execution or issuing of an EAW were installed by the Dutch legislator or the courts for the specific purpose of protection against surrender in cases in which the applicability of the law of the issuing state was not foreseeable at the time of the offence. Only on some occasions have the problems arising from unforeseeable jurisdiction claims been discussed on the legislative level, for instance in the context of the double criminality requirement. The complaints raised in this discussion were, however, disregarded by the Minister of Justice and Security. Furthermore, the double criminality requirement and the territoriality exception also aim to protect citizens against surrender when the conduct on the EAW occurred on Dutch territory and does not constitute a criminal act according to Dutch law. However, this protection is not explicitly based on the general opinion that criminal offences and sanctions are not sufficiently foreseeable when a jurisdiction claim was not foreseeable. Hence, all in all none of the refusal grounds, conditions for the issuing of an EAW or rules on the exercise of (extra)territorial jurisdiction were intended as general safeguards against surrender when the jurisdiction claim of the issuing state was not foreseeable at the time of the offence.

The matter of a link between the right to a tribunal established by law and forum decisions without a transparent EU system for case allocations has not been a big topic of discussion, either, in the context of the surrender procedure. Article 17 Constitution allows the public prosecutor to have broad discretion in deciding in which national jurisdiction a case should be prosecuted. It follows from the examination in Sect. 5.2.4 that the need for protection against arbitrary decisions has been recognised, but that it is not derived from *ius de non evocando*. Furthermore, in the context of the executing procedure, Articles 13 and 9 SA grant broad discretion to the Amsterdam District Court—this used to be the public prosecutor and the Minister of Security and Justice. This broad discretion seem to indicate that the Dutch legislator favours flexibility when it comes to forum decisions. The same conclusion can be drawn in relation to the issuing procedure and the rules on the exercise of jurisdiction, since the investigative judge is provided with broad discretion when making the decision as to whether or not to issue an EAW, and the prosecutorial discretion of the Dutch public prosecutor is hardly restricted by law.

In light of the above, the answer to the main question of this chapter is that the two potential complications with which citizens can be confronted are hardly recognised as problems in the context of the Dutch surrender procedure, let alone as legality problems. It remains unclear to what extent these two problems fall within the scope of the legality principle and *ius de non evocando* in Articles 1 DCC and 17 Constitution. At the same time, the conditions for the execution and issuing of an EAW do not focus on protection against these issues. Consequently, there are currently no strong indications which suggest that the EAW is generally viewed as a procedure which could result in the transfer of a citizen, while the jurisdiction claim of the issuing state is not in compliance with the legality principle and *ius de non evocando* due to one of the two problems.

References

Altena J (2016) Het legaliteitsbeginsel en de doorwerking van Europees recht. Meijers-reeks

Baaijens-van Geloven Y (1996) Overdracht en overname van strafvervolging. Gouda Quint

Bax C (2000) Artikel 17. In: Koekkoek A (ed) De Grondwet: een systematische en artikelsgewijs commentaar. Tjeenk Willink

Böhm K (2018) Das Rechtshilfeverfahren. In: Ahlbrecht H et al (eds) Internationales Strafrecht. Auslieferung – Rechtshilfe – EGMR – internationale Gerichtshöfe. Müller

Borgers M (2011) De Communicatieve strafrechter. In: Voermans W, Borgers M, Sieburgh C (eds) Controverses rondom legaliteit en legitimatie. Kluwer

Buruma Y (2002) Case note HR 18 September 2001, ECLI:NL:HR:2001:AB1471. AA 51

Cleiren T in Tekst en Commentaar Strafrecht, art. 1 Sr, para 3 (February 1, 2021)

Corstens G (1986) Naar een geïnternationaliseerd strafrecht? Enkele inleidende opmerkingen. In: Corstens G et al (eds) Internationalisering van het strafrecht. Ars Aequi Libri

d'Oliveira U (1999) Rechters die afstemmen en afhouden. Vragen over de verenigbaarheid van coördinatiestrategieën met artikel 17 Grondwet en artikel 6 EVRM. NJB 377

d'Oliveira U (2016) Zaakstoedeling en het vleugellamme artikel 17 Grondwet. Een oproep tot formele regelgeving. NJB 2078

De Hullu J (2012) Materieel Strafrecht: over algemene leerstukken van strafrechtelijke aansprakelijkheid naar Nederlands recht. Kluwer

Fichera M (2011) The implementation of the European arrest warrant in the European Union: law, policy and practice. Intersentia

Glerum V (2010) Uitlevering en overlevering. In: Handboek Strafzaken, para 91.20.5, 18 August 2010

Glerum V (2013) De weigeringsgronden bij uitlevering en overlevering – Een vergelijking en kritische evaluatie in het licht van het beginsel van wederzijdse erkenning. Wolf Legal Publishers

Glerum V (2021) Tekst en Commentaar Internationaal Strafrecht, art 23 OLW, para. 2, 19 April 2021
Glerum V, Rozemond N (2015) Overlevering. In: van Elst R, van Sliedregt E (eds) Handboek Internationaal Strafrecht: Internationaal en Europees strafrecht vanuit Nederlands perspectief. Kluwer
Groenhuijsen M (1987) Straf en wet. Gouda Quint
Groenhuijsen M, Kristen F (2001) Het *Bestimmtheitsgebot* bepaald. DD 31:330
Herrnfeld H-H (2013) Mechanisms for settling conflicts of jurisdiction. In: Luchtman M (ed) Choice of forum in cooperation against EU financial crime. Freedom, security and justice and the protection of specific EU-interests. Eleven International Publishing
Hirsch Ballin E (2000) De zaak-Pinochet: commentaar op de uitspraak van de House of Lords van 24 maart 1999. Ars Aequi 6:481
Keijzer N (2005) The double criminality requirement. In: Blekxtoon R, van Ballegooij W (eds) Handbook on the European arrest warrant. Asser
Klip A (2016) Case note HR 12 May 2015, ECLI:NL:HR:2015:1230. NJ 2016:38
Knigge G (1984) Verandering van wetgeving. Beschouwingen over de artt. 4 A.B. en 1 Sr. Arnhem Gouda Quint
Kristen F (2010) Ontwikkeling van het legaliteitsbeginsel tot hoeksteen van het publiekrecht. In: Schutgens R et al (eds) Canon van het Recht. Ars Aequi Libri
Kristen F (2019) Het materieelstrafrechtelijk legaliteitsbeginsel in het bijzonder strafrecht. In: Kristen F et al (eds) Bijzonder strafrecht: Strafrechtelijke handhaving van sociaal-economisch en fiscaal recht in Nederland. Boom
Luchtman M (2009) De normering van de strafrechtelijke forumkeuze in de ruime van vrijheid, veiligheid en rechtvaardigheid. DD 39:929
Luchtman M (2012) Strafrechtelijke forumkeuze en de kenbaarheid van rechtsmacht – Over de positie van de Unieburger in de Europese rechtsruimte. In: Kool R, de Jong F (eds) Relaties van gezag en verantwoordelijkheid: strafrechtelijke ontwikkelingen. Boom
Martufi A, Gigengack D (2020) Exploring mutual trust through the lens of an executing judicial authority: the practice of the Court of Amsterdam in EAW proceedings. NJECL 11:282
Nijboer J (1987) De doolhof van de Nederlandse strafwetgeving: De systematische grondslag van het algemeen deel van het W.v.Sr. Wolters-Noordhoff
Pompe W (1959) Handboek van het Nederlandse Strafrecht. Tjeenk Willink
Reijntjes J (2002) Case note HR 18 September 2001, ECLI:NL:HR:2001:AB1471 (*Decembermoorden*). NJ 2002:559
Schutte J (1981) Enforcement measures in international criminal law. Revue Internationale de Droit Pénal 52:441
Strijards G (1984) Internationaal Strafrecht strafmachtsrecht: algemeen deel. Gouda Quint BV
Swart B (1983) Goede Rechtsbedeling en Internationale Rechtshulp in Strafzaken. Kluwer
Swart B (1984) Internationalisering van de strafrechtspleging. In: Kelk C et al (eds) Grenzen en mogelijkheden: opstellen over en rondom de strafrechtspleging. Ars Aequi Libri
Swart B (1986) Nederlands Uitleveringsrecht. W.E.J. Tjeenk Willink
't Hart J (1982) Het nulla-poenabeginsel. In: Koekkoek A, Konijnenbelt W (eds) Grondrechten: Commentaar op hoofdstuk 1 van de herziene grondwet. Stichting Ars Aequi
Thorhauer N (2015) Conflicts of jurisdiction in cross-border criminal cases in the area of freedom, security, and justice. Risks and opportunities from an individual rights-oriented perspective. NJECL 6:78
Van der Beken T (1999) Forumkeuze in het internationaal strafrecht. Maklu
Van Elst R (2002) Universele rechtsmacht over foltering: Bouterse en de Decembermoorden. NTM-NJCM Bulletin 27:208
Van Elst R (2015) Rechtsmacht. In: van Elst R, van Sliedregt E (eds) Handboek Internationaal Strafrecht – Internationaal en Europees strafrecht vanuit Nederlands perspectief. Wolters Kluwer

Van Sliedregt E (2008) Rechtsmachtgrenzen voor onbegrensde misdrijven – "Neerlands dualisme" bestendigd. DD 47:653

Van Sliedregt E (2009) The dual criminality requirement. In: Keijzer N, van Sliedregt E (eds) The European arrest warrant in practice. Asser

Van Sliedregt E (2015) Algemene inleiding. In: van Elst R, van Sliedregt E (eds) Handboek internationaal strafrecht: Internationaal en Europees strafrecht vanuit Nederlands perspectief. Kluwer

Von Bubnoff E (2005) Der Europäische Haftbefehl, Auslieferung und Neuerungen des Gemeinschaftsinstruments. Ein Leitfaden für die Praxis. Muller

Wolswijk H (1998) Locus delicti en rechtsmacht. Gouda Quint

Wolswijk H (2013) Country report the Netherlands. In: Böse M, Meyer F, Schneider A (eds) Conflicts of jurisdiction in criminal matters in the European Union. Volume I: National reports and comparative analysis. Nomos

Chapter 6
The German Legal Order: The Views on the Two Complications and Their Link to the EAW

6.1 Introduction

This chapter aims to answer the question whether the two complications with which EU citizens can be confronted in the context of surrender proceedings are recognised as legal problems or even as legality problems in the German legal order. These two complications are the fact that, in the AFSJ, an EU citizen can be surrendered for the purpose of prosecution, while the applicability of the national criminal law of the prosecuting state was not foreseeable at the time of the offence, and the fact that surrender occurs without a complementary and transparent system of forum choices in case of conflicts of national jurisdictions. Hence, similar to chapter on the Netherlands, the purpose of this chapter is to determine the *lex lata* with regard to the recognition of these issues in the context of the surrender procedure and the protection offered against them in the German legal order.

To answer the main question of this chapter, Sect. 6.2 examines to what extent the influence of the EAW on the two complications is considered problematic in light of the substantive legality principle in Article 103(2) of the German *Grundgesetz* (Constitution, hereafter GG), the right to a lawful judge in Article 101(1) GG, and the prohibition of the extradition of German nationals in Article 16(2) GG. In other words, this section explores the possible triangular link between these constitutional rights, the EAW and the problems relating to jurisdiction and forum choices. For instance, in case the two problems occur, is the issuing or execution of an EAW viewed as a violation of one of these constitutional rights, or is the surrender procedure perhaps perceived as a mechanism which can enforce violations of these constitutional rights? Another option is that the possible triangular link has not been considered at all.

Sections 6.3 and 6.4 then focus on the surrender procedure and examine to what extent the two complications play a role in the issuing and execution of EAWs. More specifically, Sect. 6.3 discusses to what extent the conditions for the execution of an EAW intend to offer protection against the two complications. Section 6.4 conducts

J. Graat, *The European Arrest Warrant and EU Citizenship*,
https://doi.org/10.1007/978-3-031-07590-2_6

the same exercise for the rules regulating the issuing procedure. In light of the link between the issuing of an EAW and the decision to prosecute a case, the German rules on the exercise of jurisdiction are also discussed. In relation to these two sections, it is important to note beforehand that the FDEAW has been implemented in Chapter 8 of the *Gesetz über die Internationale Rechtshilfe in Strafsachen* (Law on International Assistance in Criminal Matters, hereafter IRG).[1] This is a federal law applicable in all 16 *Bundesländer* (states). However, contrary to the Dutch legislator, the German legislator has not adopted most of the jargon of the FDEAW, but has instead used the terminology typical for the extradition procedure. For instance, Chapter 8 IRG refers to 'extradition' and 'requesting and requested state' instead of 'surrender' and 'issuing and executing state'.[2] To avoid confusion, any reference to the IRG and the extradition procedure in this chapter means the EAW procedure, unless the text explicitly states otherwise. This chapter furthermore ends with a conclusion in Sect. 6.5.

6.2 Protection Offered by Fundamental Rights and Principles

6.2.1 The Gesetzlichkeitsprinzip

The *Gesetzlichkeitsprinzip* or the substantive legality principle is codified in Article 103(2) GG and Article 1 *Strafgesetzbuch* (Criminal Code, hereafter StGB), which both state '*Eine Tat kann nur bestraft werden, wenn die Strafbarkeit gesetzlich bestimmt war, bevor die Tat begangen wurde.*' This principle correlates from Articles 1(1) and 2(1) GG, in which the right to human dignity and personal freedom are laid down, as well as from the personal responsibility of individuals.[3] The German substantive legality principle itself comprises four sub-principles. The first one concerns the requirement of a written legal basis for offences and penalties,[4] which mirrors the prohibition to establish criminal liability on the basis of *Gewohnheitsrecht*, meaning case law.[5] The second and third principle are the prohibition of interpretation by analogy and the prohibition of the retroactive application of the law. The former entails that criminal offences may not be applied

---

[1] Article 1(4) IRG.

[2] BT Drucksache 15/1718 [10]–[11]. See the title of Chapter 8 which is '*Auslieferungs- und Durchlieferungsverkehr mit Mitgliedstaaten der Europäischen Union*'.

[3] BVerfG 26 February 1969, 2 BvL 15/68, 23/68, NJW 1969, 1059 [1061].

[4] The BVerfG is not entirely consistent in relation to the question of whether '*Gesetz*' (law) in Article 103(2) GG exclusively means a formal law adopted by Parliament or whether material acts could also suffice. It accepts material acts in BVerfG 3 July 1962, 2 BvR 15/62, BVerfG 14, 174 [185]; BVerfG 21 September 2016, 2 BvL 1/15, NJW 2016, 3648 [3649]. *A contrario* see BVerfG 22 June 1988, 2 BvR 234/87, 1154/86, NStZ 1989, 229 [230].

[5] BVerfG 7 March 2011, 1 BvR 388/05 [21]; Remmert (2020), paras 79–80; Hecker (2015), p. 11.

analogously to conduct which in principle fall outside the scope of these offences.[6] The latter one is based on the idea that an individual should be able to know at the time of the offence that his conduct constitutes a criminal offence and which sanction could be imposed. Consequently, retroactive penalisation of behaviour or the imposition of a stricter sentence than allowed at the time of the offence is prohibited.[7] The fourth principle is the *Bestimmtheitsgebot* (*lex certa* requirement), which requires that criminal liability and the scope of the criminal actions are clearly established in legal provisions in order to stir the conduct of individuals and to warn them of the consequences which certain conduct may have.[8] Consequently, the law in question should be sufficiently concrete and precise in order to enable individuals to foresee what conduct constitutes a criminal offence and what sanctions could be imposed.[9] The goal of the *Bestimmtheitsgebod* is twofold. On the one hand, it protects the individual, as it requires that the law describes the criminal conduct as well as its consequences, meaning the sanctions which could be imposed. On the other hand, it enforces the separation of powers, ensuring that the legislator and not the judicial or executive power decides what constitutes a criminal offence and what kind of sanctions should be imposed.[10]

6.2.2 *Protection Against EAWs in Case of the Two Complications: The* Gesetzlichkeitsprinzip *and the Constitutional Prohibition to Extradite German Nationals*

The German case law states that the extradition procedure falls outside the scope of Article 103(2) GG, as the decision to extradite cannot be classified as a penalty. Instead, the extradition procedure falls under procedural law.[11] However, on occasion the German *Bundesverfassungsgericht* (German Constitutional Court, hereafter BVerfG) and other national courts have also concluded that the extradition of a German for an act which has no substantial link to a foreign state and was not

[6]BVerfG 3 July 1962, 2 BvR 15/62, BVerfGE 14, 174 [185]; BVerfG 7 December 2011, 2 BvR 2500/09, NJW 2012, 907 [907]; Remmert (2020), para 82.

[7]BVerfG 26 February 1969, 2 BvL 15/68, 23/68, BVerfGE 25, 269 [285]; Remmert (2020), para 120.

[8]BVerfG 23 October 1985, 1 BvR 1053/82, NJW 1986, 1671 [1671]; BVerfG 10 January 1995, 1 BvR 718/89, 719/89, 722/89, 723/89, NJW 1995, 1141 [1141]; BVerfG 20 March 2002, 2 BvR 794/95, NJW 2002, 1779 [1779].

[9]Remmert (2020), paras 92–97.

[10]Hecker (2015), p. 11; Remmert (2020), para 101.

[11]BVerfG 5 November 2003, 2 BvR 1243/03 [16]; OLG Stuttgart 28 January 2005, 3 Ausl. 1/05 [38]; BVerfG 18 July 2005, 2 BvR 2236/04 (*Darkazanli*) [98]; OLG Celle 16 December 2016, 1 AR (Ausl) 89/16 [16].

punishable in Germany at the time it occurred could be tantamount to a violation of the prohibition of a retroactive application of the law. Despite this conclusion, the courts have not gone as far as to state that Article 103(2) GG is generally applicable to extradition proceedings.[12]

Contrary to Article 103(2) GG, Article 16(2) GG does cover EAWs and to a certain extent aims to offer protection against extradition in case of unforeseeable jurisdiction claims. This constitutional provision states, '*Kein Deutscher darf an das Ausland ausgeliefert werden*', meaning that German nationals are protected against extradition. In relation to extradition to EU Member States or an international court, the law may make an exception, provided that the rule of law is complied with.[13] Consequently the extradition procedure as set up by the FDEAW is a justified exception to the right not to be extradited in Article 16(2) GG.

The right not to be extradited protects legal certainty and the trust which Germans may have in their own legal order to whose establishment they contributed via democratic means and whose criminal law guides their behaviour. Trust in one's own legal order is a necessary prerequisite for freedom in the sense of self-determination on how to shape your life.[14] The prohibition of extradition has therefore been classified as a 'liberty right' (*Freiheitsrechte*) which aims to protect Germans against removal—without their consent—from the legal order that they know in order to be brought before the judge of a foreign state.[15] This constitutional right functions as a shield against sometimes unexpected jurisdiction claims from other states whose substantive criminal law the German national does not need to know and whose procedural rules may differ from the German ones.[16] In other words, German nationals should—at least under certain circumstances—be protected against the difficulties of being a defendant in foreign criminal proceedings, which were difficult to foresee or estimate at the time of the offence.[17]

However, Article 16(2) GG does not aim to establish a safe haven for German nationals or exclusive jurisdiction for Germany to prosecute Germans accused of offences committed abroad.[18] In this light, it is important to note that Article 7 (2) StGB provides broad jurisdiction to prosecute German nationals on the basis of the active nationality principle in Germany. Furthermore, we will see in Sect. 6.3 on the execution of an EAW in Germany that the scope of protection of German

[12] BVerfGE 5 November 2003, 2 BvR 1243/03 [16]; BVerfG 18 July 2005, 2 BvR 2236/04 (*Darkazanli*) [98]; OLG Braunschweig 3 November 2004, Ausl. 5/04, openJur 2012, 42169 [13]; Böse (2012c), p. 10.

[13] Art. 16(2) GG.

[14] BVerfG 18 July 2005, 2 BvR 2236/04 (*Darkazanli*) [83, 85].

[15] BVerfG 13 October 1970, 1 BvR 226/70 [26]; BVerfG 18 July 2005, 2 BvR 2236/04 (*Darkazanli*) [65]; BVerfG 3 September 2009, 2 BvR 1826/09 [14–15].

[16] BVerfG 18 July 2005, 2 BvR 2236/04 (*Darkazanli*) [83]; Böse (2012b), p. 6.

[17] BVerfG 13 October 1970, 1 BvR 226/70 [27]; BVerfG 3 September 2009, 2 BvR 1826/09 [14–15]. Becker (2010), pp. 1563–1564.

[18] BVerfG 13 October 1970, 1 BvR 226/70 [27].

nationals in the extradition procedure fluctuates depending on the link which the criminal offence has to the German territory.[19]

It follows from the above that the extradition of citizens in case of unforeseeable jurisdiction claims has to a certain extent been recognised as a fundamental rights issue, but not in light of the generally applicable substantive legality principle in Article 103(2) GG. Instead, protection against extradition when these complications occur has in the German Constitution been reserved for German nationals. Consequently, the issuing and execution of an EAW while the jurisdiction claim of the issuing state was difficult to foresee at the time of the offence does in itself not constitute a violation of the substantive legality principle. The next section therefore examines to what extent compliance of criminal offences and sanctions with the *Bestimmtheitsgebot* depends on the foreseeability of the application of the specific national criminal law at the time of the offence. The consequences of the conclusions of this examination for the extradition procedure, more specifically the position of the underlying problems in the context of the extradition procedure, are discussed afterwards. For instance, in case it can be concluded that compliance with Article 103 (2) GG requires that the law of a particular state was foreseeable at the time of the offence, the follow-up question could be whether this also means that the EAW is generally viewed as a mechanism which transfers citizens to a state whose jurisdiction claim is not in compliance with Article 103(2) GG.

6.2.3 The Substantive Legality Principle and Rules of Jurisdiction

The German substantive criminal law has a broad extraterritorial scope of application as follows from the rules on jurisdiction in Articles 3–7 and 9 StGB. Articles 3 and 9 comprise the territoriality principle which is complemented by Article 4 establishing jurisdiction over crimes committed on German ships and aircrafts. The other jurisdiction grounds in Articles 5, 6 and 7 establish extraterritorial jurisdiction of which Article 7 StGB covers both the active and the passive nationality principle. The broad extraterritorial scope of the German law aims to reduce the risk of impunity in, for instance, situations in which Germans cannot be extradited, because they are protected by Article 16(2) GG.[20]

The prevailing view in the German legal order is that rules on jurisdiction are *objektive Bedingungen der Strafbarkeit* (objective preconditions of criminal liability) and not components of the crime.[21] In this light, they have been classified as

---

[19] Art. 80 IRG.

[20] BVerfGE 3 September 1009, 2 BvR 1826/09 [1]; BVerfG 18 July 2005, 2 BvR 2236/04 (*Darkazanli*) [68].

[21] Meyer (2013), p. 170; Hecker (2015), p. 28; Ambos (2018), p. 4. For a different opinion see Kubiciel (2015), p. 170.

unrechtsneutral, meaning that they do not determine or influence the wrongfulness or unlawfulness of the behaviour—murder remains murder, even if a national law is not applicable—but do contribute to determining whether criminal liability can be established.[22] Failing to meet an objective precondition prohibits the public prosecutor from starting criminal proceedings and bringing the case to trial.[23] However, despite the procedural consequences resulting from a lack of jurisdiction, Articles 3–7 and 9 StGB are part of substantive criminal law.[24] In relation to the question to what extent the substantive legality principle then also applies to the rules on jurisdiction, the German case law does not provide a clear conclusive answer. It follows from the jurisprudence that the prohibition of a retroactive application of the law, which is one of the sub-principles of Article 103(2) GG, is applicable, but whether the same is true for the *Bestimmtheitsgebot* remains unclear.[25]

Furthermore, according to Wolswijk, the general position in Germany is that the substantive legality principle also applies to rules of jurisdiction.[26] Several prominent legal scholars have argued that all sub-principles of Article 103(2) GG apply to rules of jurisdiction as they constitute part of substantive criminal law and have a decisive role in determining criminal liability.[27] For instance, Schulze-Fielitz has stated that the *Bestimmtheitsgebot* covers all requirements for *Strafbarkeit* (criminal liability or criminal act/offense) and not merely the components of the crime describing its wrongfulness.[28]

In light of this general position, the follow-up question is what exactly needs to be foreseeable according to the *Bestimmtheitsgebot*. Some legal scholars seem to be of the opinion that the applicability of the *Bestimmtheitsgebot* merely entails that the rules of jurisdiction themselves need to be sufficiently precise, enabling citizens to know what the conditions for the exercise of jurisdiction are.[29] Others have connected the link between jurisdiction and Article 103(2) GG more specifically to the difficulties in foreseeing whose national criminal law to obey. It has been argued that the applicability of a national law on the basis of the passive nationality principle or the effects principle clashes with the ratio of the *Gesetzlichkeitsprinzip*, since the (potential) perpetrator is often unaware of the nationality of the victim at the time of the offence, and consequences of a criminal act may occur in unexpected places.[30]

---

[22] Scholten (1995), pp. 91ff; Meyer (2013), p. 170.

[23] Bundesgerichtshof (BGH) 22 January 1986, 3 StR 472/8534, BGHSt 34, 1 [3].

[24] BGH 8 September1964, 1 StR 292/64 [9]; BVerfG 15 May 1995, 2 BvL 19/91 [184]; Eser (2014), para 71; Meyer (2013), p. 170; Böse (2014), pp. 110–111, 121.

[25] BVerfG 15 May 1995, 2 BvL 19/91 [182–185]; BGH 1 April 2014, 2 Ars 30/14, BeckRS 2014, 10266; Pappas (1996), p. 184.

[26] Wolswijk (1998), p. 82.

[27] See e.g. Thorhauer (2019), p. 569; Böse (2014), p. 112; Wörner and Wörner (2012), p. 209; Eser (2014), p. 170.

[28] Schulze-Fielitz (2008b), pp. 780–781. See also Remmert (2020), paras 23, 68.

[29] See e.g. Afshar (2015), p. 337 (footnote 59).

[30] See e.g. Böse (2014), pp. 114–115, 118–119; Meyer and Böse (2011), p. 342; In relation to Art 3 StGB see Van der Beken (1999), pp. 57–58.

With regard to the solution to these difficulties, it should be noted that the position that the applicability of a particular national criminal law should be foreseeable at the time of the offence, since otherwise the criminality of the conduct as well as its sanctions are not foreseeable, is generally rejected.[31] It has been argued that such a position increases the risk of forum shopping, since individuals will look for the state with the most lenient criminal system.[32] Hence, most legal scholars are of the opinion that the legality problems are solved when citizens could at the time of the offence have known that their conduct was criminal somewhere, meaning according to the law of a state.[33]

In light of the latter position, Ambos has stated that the criminality of certain behaviour does not always depend on the scope of application of the national criminal law, for instance, in cases of universally acknowledged criminal offences. In relation to these offences, the criminality of the behaviour remains clear, even if the applicability of the criminal law of which the offences are part is not.[34] In other words, the foreseeability of the applicability of a national criminal law and by extension the foreseeability of its criminal offences and sanctions is ensured because of the so-called obviousness of the criminality.[35]

Another way of ensuring foreseeability is setting the double criminality requirement as a condition for the applicability of the jurisdiction grounds, meaning that the act in question must also be a criminal offence according to the law of the state where it was committed.[36] The double criminality requirement in Articles 7(1) and 7(2) (nr. 1) StGB, of which the former establishes jurisdiction on the basis of the passive nationality principle, and the latter on the basis of the active nationality principle, also has this function. Especially in relation to the passive nationality principle, the double criminality requirement protects the individual who might be unaware at the time of the offence that he or she needs to abide by German law and who might for that reason be unfamiliar with the content—meaning the criminal acts and sanctions—of German criminal law.[37] However, not all requirements limiting the scope of the German jurisdiction rules are so clearly linked to the difficulties in foreseeing applicable national criminal laws. For instance, subsection 5(b) of Article 5 StGB restrict the exercise of extraterritorial jurisdiction with the dual requirement that the suspect has the German nationality and his main livelihood in Germany. Several legal scholars have stated that the justification for these additional requirements relates to the limited *Treupflicht* (duty of solidarity). The duty of solidarity and

[31] For this minority opinion see e.g. Oehler (1970), pp. 116–117. His point of view is summarized by Scholten (1995), p. 67.

[32] Eser (2012), pp. 566–567.

[33] Luchtman (2013), p. 23.

[34] Ambos (2018), pp. 5–6.

[35] For instance piracy or crimes against humanity. Böse (2014), p. 119; Ambos (2018), pp. 5–6.

[36] Scholten (1995), pp. 68–69.

[37] Another function of the double criminality requirement is the protection of state sovereignty. Werle and Jeßberger (2007c), p. 601.

regard for German national interests only binds German nationals with an additional link to Germany.[38]

Hence, it can be concluded that the *Gesetzlichkeitsprinzip*, in particular the *Bestimmtheitsgebot,* requires that criminal offences and sanctions are clearly described by law. Citizens should be able to foresee on the basis of the law for what kind of conduct they can be held criminally liable. The case law has not explicitly connected the *Bestimmtheitsgebot* to the rules of jurisdiction. In the legal literature, the problems concerning the foreseeability of the application of national criminal laws have been recognised, and the majority view is that Article 103(2) GG applies to jurisdiction rules, as well. However, the position that the national criminal law of a particular state must have been foreseeable is only a minority opinion. Most legal scholars consider it sufficient that citizens could have foreseen that their conduct was criminal somewhere.

6.2.4 *The Right to a Lawful Judge* (Gesetzliche Richter)

Article 101(1) GG embodies the equivalent of the right to a tribunal established by law. It states, '*Niemand darf seinem gesetzlichen Richter entzogen werden*', meaning that no individual may be removed from the jurisdiction of his or her lawful judge. This constitutional right reflects the principle of the separation of powers and aims to avoid arbitrary forum choices by, for instance, the executive on the national level.[39] In this light, the right imposes an obligation on the German legislator to adopt general laws which regulate the territorial and subject-matter jurisdiction of the courts.[40] More specifically, the law should determine which court and which judge are competent to decide a particular case in order to avoid concurring jurisdictions as much as possible.[41] However, as the regulation of certain aspects of a court's jurisdiction, such as the allocation of responsibilities by rigid general rules is simply impractical or hindering the effective administration of justice, the rules do not need to be very strict. They should be as clear as possible with regard to competent court and judge.[42]

The search for a balance between protection against forum manipulation and forum decisions in light of the effective administration of justice clearly surfaces in the discussions on Article 12(1) *Strafprozeßordnung* (German Code of Criminal

[38] Werle and Jeßberger (2007b), pp. 532–533. See also Fischer (2017), p. 40.

[39] BverfG 19 March 1959, 1 BvR 295/58 [13]; BVerfG 24 March 1964, 2 BvR 42, 83, 89/63 [14]; BVerfG 3 December 1975, 2 BvL 7/74 [13]; BVerfG 20 February 2018, 2 BvR 2675/17 [16]; BVerfG 22 March 2018, 2 BvR 780/16 [41, 49]; Lagodny (2001), p. 71; Eser (1995), p. 251.

[40] BVerfG 25 October 1966, 2 BvR 291, 2 BvR 656/64; Schulze-Fielitz (2008a), p. 660.

[41] BVerfG 3 December 1975, 2 BvL 7/74 [13]; Eser (1995), pp. 251–252.

[42] BverfG 19 March 1959, 1 BvR 295/58 [13]; BVerfG 24 March 1964, 2 BvR 42, 83, 89/63 [14]; Eser (1995), pp. 251–252.

Procedure, hereafter StPO). This provision states that in case more than one German court has local jurisdiction, priority is given to the court to which the case was brought first.[43] This almost unfettered discretion for the public prosecutor in making the forum decision has been criticised in light of Article 101(1) GG.[44] The case law of the BVerfG has however not settled this matter so far and the prevailing view still seems to be that the lack of a hierarchy between the different courts is not unconstitutional.[45] A strict and rigid ranking of the different competent courts hampers a fair consideration of the different interests affected by the choice of forum, among which the efficiency of the criminal proceedings and those of the prosecuted person. In that light, the lack of a strict system for forum choices in Article 12 StPO is not viewed as a violation of the Constitution.[46] In addition, the suspect has the possibility to issue an objection against the territorial jurisdiction of the court and a higher common court may on the basis of a request or *ex officio* decide to transfer the case to another court with territorial jurisdiction in case it has substantial reasons to do so.[47]

It can be concluded that contrary to *ius de non evocando* in the Dutch Constitution, the *gesetzliche Richter* in Article 101 GG explicitly covers the matter of case allocations. Its ratio is even to prevent arbitrary forum decisions by the executive. However, this does not mean that the German Constitution imposes the obligation of strict and rigid rules which leave no discretion to the judiciary or executive. Instead, the need for flexibility in order to make the best forum decision in the concrete case on the basis of a fair consideration of the different interests has also been recognised and demarcates the scope of Article 101 GG.

Still, even though the examination and conclusions regarding the *gesetzliche Richter* give an important insight into the views present in the German legal order regarding the need and way to regulate case allocations, it remains unclear to what extent these conclusions are relevant for the matter of forum choices in case of conflicts of national jurisdictions. The scope of Article 101 GG is limited to the national context and does not apply in case of conflicts of jurisdictions between states.[48] In other words, the German Constitution does not offer the right to

[43] According to Article 12(2) StPO only the common superior court may transfer the investigation and decision to another court.

[44] See Lagodny (2001), p. 71.

[45] Lagodny (2001), p. 70. The rulings of the BVerfG have been limited to provisions concerning subject-matter jurisdiction. See e.g. BVerfG 19 March 1959, 1 BvR 295/58.

[46] Classen (2010), pp. 939–940; BGH 18 March 1975, 1 StR 559/74; Schmitt (2017), p. 85. See also BGH 4 October 1956, 4 StR 294/56 in which the BGH decided that the discretion offered to the public prosecutor by the jurisdiction rules in the *Gerichtsverfassungsgesetz* (Courts Constitution Act) do not violate Article 101 GG.

[47] Art. 16 jo 12(2) StPO; Erb (2016), pp. 686–687. The place of residence of important witnesses or the state of health of one of the parties may be a reason to transfer the proceedings.

[48] Lagodny (2001), p. 114. This does not mean that a supranational or foreign court cannot be a lawful court as well. The CJEU has, for instance, been recognised as a lawful court in light of Article 101(2) GG. BVerfGE 22 October 1986, 2 BvR 197/83 [75]; BVerfG 24 May 1990, 2 BvL 12, 13/88, 2 BvR 1436/87 [129].

protection against arbitrary forum choices on the transnational level. Still, despite the limited application of Article 101 GG, it has been argued that the views on its application in the national setting could be guiding for the views on forum choices in the EU setting. The *gesetzliche Richter* has, for instance, been used as a yardstick in relation to discussions on the Council of Europe Convention on the transfer of criminal proceedings. This instrument has been criticised, because not all reasons in Article 8 for the transfer of proceedings represent a genuine link between the forum and the offence and suspect. According to Oehler, this clashes with Article 101 GG, since it makes it practically impossible for an individual to foresee which court will have jurisdiction.[49] According to Lagodny, the arguments in this discussion could further clarify the objections against forum shopping by prosecuting authorities on the international level.[50]

6.2.5 Interim Conclusion

On the basis of the above, it can be concluded that the German Constitutional Court has to some extent recognised the role of the EAW in relation to the difficulties in foreseeing the applicable national criminal laws, but only in light of Article 16 (2) GG, which exclusively protects German nationals. In other words, the need for some degree of protection against unforeseeable jurisdiction claims and the application of foreign criminal laws in the context of the EAW procedure has primarily been recognised on the basis of a constitutional safeguard which only protects German nationals and not on the basis of the generally applicable substantive legality principle. Furthermore, the recognition of the difficulties arising from unforeseeable jurisdiction claims in light of Article 103(2) GG is currently limited to the legal literature and there the prevailing view is not that the national criminal law of a *particular* state needs to be foreseeable at the time of the offence. Consequently, there are also no strong indications of the perspective that the EAW is a mechanism which could contribute to violations of Article 103(2) GG by facilitating the extradition of a citizen to a state whose jurisdiction claim is incompatible with the German substantive legality principle.[51]

In light of these conclusions, the next sections continue with the examination of the question what the views in the German legal order are on the role of the EAW in relation to the difficulties in foreseeing the applicability of national criminal laws in the AFSJ, but this time from the specific perspective of the extradition procedure itself. These sections will, for instance, show that the constitutional protection of German nationals against extradition in case of unforeseeable jurisdiction claims has

---

[49] Oehler (1983), p. 434. Oehler‘s point of view is criticised in Pappas (1996), pp. 136–137.

[50] Lagodny (2001), p. 70.

[51] If this had been the case, the follow-up question would be to what extent the German legal order is allowed to impose its own constitutional standards on other states. See also Sect. 5.2.5 and Case C-399/11 *Melloni* [2013] ECLI:EU:C:2013:107.

been integrated in the German extradition procedure. In fact Article 16(2) GG has had an immense influence on the EAW procedure in Germany. Not only was it part of the reason that the first EAW Act was declared unconstitutional, it has also influenced the interpretation and application of other refusal grounds. In other words, the protection of German nationals has an important place in the EAW procedure. In addition, the next sections examine whether—and, if so, for what reasons—the German legislator and the German executing and issuing judicial authorities have installed safeguards against the difficulties resulting from unforeseeable jurisdiction claims for non-German nationals as well.

The *gesetzliche Richter* in Article 101(1) GG covers forum choices on the national level. It requires that the law reflects a balance between protection against forum manipulation by the executive and flexibility to ensure that cases are allocated in light of the effective administration of justice. As the scope of Article 101(1) GG is limited to the national level, it is not possible to say whether the same point of view exists in relation to forum choices on the EU transnational level. However, in the legal literature some legal scholars have argued that the arguments regarding Article 101(1) GG and forum choices can be an inspiration for the discussion on the need to regulate forum decisions on the transnational level. The next sections explore to that extent this discussion has been held in the context of the extradition procedure itself. In other words, have the problems arising from the lack of a transparent EU system for forum choices played a role in the adoption and interpretation of the conditions for the execution and issuing of an EAW in German law?

6.3 Germany As the Executing State

6.3.1 Introduction to the Execution Procedure

The IRG and the Executing Authority

Two attempts were necessary to implement the FDEAW into German law. The First German European Arrest Warrant Act came into effect in 2004.[52] It was shortly afterwards declared unconstitutional by the BVerfG, among other reasons because of its lack of protection of German nationals.[53] The Second European Arrest Warrant Act of 2006 implemented the FDEAW in conformity with this ruling in what is now Chapter 8 of the IRG, more specifically Articles 78–83j.[54] However, Article 78 (1) IRG states that unless Chapter 8 contains specific regulations, the other provisions of the IRG apply to EAW procedures as well.[55] In addition, the rules in

[52] Europäisches Haftbefehlsgesetz *BGB* Part 1 (2004) 1748.

[53] BVerfG 18 July 2005, 2 BvR 2236/04.

[54] Article 1(4) IRG; Europäisches Haftbefehlsgesetz *BGB* Part 1 (2006) 1721.

[55] Art. 3 IRG on the double criminality requirement and Article 73 IRG containing a human rights refusal ground are examples.

Article 153–165 of the *Richtlinien für den Verkehr mit dem Ausland in strafrechtlichen Angelegenheiten* (Guidelines for Relations with Foreign Countries in Criminal Matters, hereafter RiVASt) provide guidelines for incoming and outgoing EAWs.[56]

The Federal Minister of Justice—and, as a result of delegation, the Ministries of Justice of the different *Bundesländer*—are the competent executing authorities in Germany.[57] The states have delegated this power to the *Staatsanwaltschaft beim Oberlandesgericht* (public prosecutors' offices at the higher regional courts, hereafter StAOLG) in whose jurisdiction the requested person is arrested.[58] We will see in the next paragraph which describes the different phases of the extradition procedure that the StAOLG shares its power and responsibility with the *Oberlandesgericht* (higher regional court, hereafter OLG).[59] An *Oberlandesgericht* is a court of appeal of which each *Bundesland* has at least one.[60]

It is important to note that despite the delegation, the StAOLG does not replace the Federal Minister of Justice as the competent authority, but merely executes the powers in his or her place. In other words, the execution of the competences is delegated, but not the competences themselves.[61] At the top of the hierarchy, the Federal Minister of Justice remains the so-called '*Herr des Verfahrens'* (master of the proceedings) and can accroach a case.[62] Both the Federal Minister of Justice and the Ministries of Justice of the *Bundesländer* may issue general or specific orders to the public prosecutors at the lower levels.[63] This appointment of political institutions as the official executing authorities can be explained on the basis of the fact that the German legislator views extradition on the basis of an EAW as 'relations with foreign states', which according to Article 32 GG are conducted by the Federation.[64]

[56] Richtlinien für den Verkehr mit dem Ausland in strafrechtlichen Angelegenheiten *Banz.* 10550.

[57] Art. 74(1) jo (2) IRG; Schönfelder W, Notification under Article 34(2) of the Framework Decision [2006] 12509/06.

[58] Art. 74(2) jo 14(1) IRG; Evaluation report on the fourth round of mutual evaluations 'The practical application of the European Arrest Warrant and Corresponding surrender procedures between Member States'—Report on Germany, 7058/2/09 REV 1 (2009), p. 16; Schönfelder W, Notification under Article 34(2) of the Framework Decision [2006] 12509/06.

[59] Art. 13 IRG.

[60] There are 24 in total. Some *Bundesländer* have more than one *Oberlandesgericht*. Contrary to the other ones, the OLG in Berlin is called *Kammergericht* Berlin.

[61] Schomburg and Hackner (2012), pp. 446–447.

[62] He or she can also be held responsible by Parliament for decisions taken on a lower level regarding international legal assistance, including the issuing and execution of EAWs. Schomburg and Hackner (2012), pp. 446–447; Böhm (2018b), para 725.

[63] Art. 146 and 147 Courts Constitution Act (*Gerichtsverfassungsgesetz*); Evaluation report on the fourth round of mutual evaluations 'The practical application of the European Arrest Warrant and Corresponding surrender procedures between Member States'—Report on Germany, 7058/2/09 REV 1 (2009), p. 5.

[64] BT Drucksage 15/1718 [10, 30]; BT Drucksage 16/1024 [11]; BVerfG 18 July 2005, 2 BvR 2236/04 (*Darkazanli*) [108]; Schomburg and Hackner (2012), p. 446.

However, this classification and the role of political bodies in the extradition procedure has been criticised in light of the fact that the FDEAW aims to establish a predominantly judicial procedure and intends to eliminate political elements which characterise the interstate extradition procedure.[65] In the case *AZ* the CJEU has prohibited the designation of public prosecutors as executing judicial authorities when they can be subjected to instructions from the executive power.[66] This ruling challenged the position of the StAOLG as the executive judicial authority, since public prosecutors could receive instructions from the executive. However, the ruling in *AZ* has not (yet) resulted in a clear change of the law. So far, the power of the Federal Minister of Justice to issue general or specific orders to the StAOLG has not been abolished.[67] As will be explained in the next section, the implications of the *AZ* case have primarily been picked up and integrated in the EAW procedure by the German courts. In addition, the CJEU case law has not (yet) resulted in an amendment of the IRG, which ensures that the Federal Minister of Justice can no longer be viewed as the official executing authority. However, in 2019 Germany amended its notification on the basis of Article 6(3) FDEAW as a result of the *OG & PI* case.[68] Contrary to the first notification, this notification does not appoint the Federal Minister of Justice as the official executing authority anymore. It only refers to the StAOLG (and the OLG).[69] Whether this means that the Federal Minister of Justice is no longer the official executing authority remains unclear as long as the relevant provisions in the IRG have not been amended.

A Twofold Procedure

The German procedure for the execution of an EAW consists *de facto* of three phases. In the first phase, the competent public prosecutors make a preliminary decision as to whether to apply one of the optional refusal grounds in Article 83b IRG. In case they intend not to apply any of them, they need to explain this decision to the OLG.[70] This explanation needs to show that the public prosecutor based the decision on the concrete circumstances of the case and that he or she did not ignore the interests of the prosecuted person.[71]

---

[65] Böse (2012a), p. 9; Von Bubnoff (2005), p. 63; Report from the Commission based on Article 34 of the Council Framework Decision on the European arrest warrant COM (2006) 8 final, p. 3.

[66] Case C-510/19 *AZ* [2020] ECLI:EU:C:2020:953.

[67] Art. 146 and 147 Courts Constitution Act (Gerichtsverfassungsgesetz). The 2021–2025 Coalition Agreement states that the execution of an EAW should become a judicial decision. The 2021–2025 Coalition Agreement states that the execution of an EAW should become a judicial decision. Coalition agreement 2021–2025 <https://www.spd.de/fileadmin/Dokumente/Koalitionsvertrag/Koalitionsvertrag_2021-2025.pdf>, last visited 5 March 2022.

[68] Case C-508/18, C-82/19 *OG & PI* [2019] ECLI:EU:C:2019:456.

[69] Thiemrodt I, Amendment to Germany's notification under Article 6(3) of the FDEAW [2019] 14444/19.

[70] Art. 79(2) IRG.

[71] Art. 79(2) IRG; Böse (2012a), pp. 15–16.

In the second phase, the OLG reviews the written statement of the public prosecutor, if one has been issued.[72] This review was introduced to comply with the judicial character of the EAW procedure as well as the right to effective judicial protection on the basis of Article 19(4) GG and the fact that the optional refusal grounds in Article 83b IRG aim to protect the interests of the individual.[73] However, the review by the OLG is a marginal one, since the court is only competent to examine the decision for errors in discretion and it may not conduct its own assessment on the merits.[74] An error in discretion occurs, for instance, when the public prosecutor did not consider important legal or factual aspects or based the decision on extraneous and irrelevant considerations.[75] Generally, the OLG assesses whether the public prosecutor considered all relevant objective aspects of a case when deciding on the application of one of the refusal grounds in Article 83b IRG, including the duty to execute an EAW, the availability of evidence, the place where the crime was committed, the place of residence of the victims and the individual interests of the requested person in being prosecuted either in Germany or in the requesting state.[76] However, as a result of the *AZ* case, it has been argued that the OLG should conduct a full judicial review of the decision of the public prosecutor.[77]

Next to this review, the OLG decides in the second phase on the *Zulassigkeit*, meaning the admissibility of the EAW, which includes a decision on the mandatory refusal grounds in Articles 80 and 81 IRG.[78] Only when the OLG finds the request admissible does the case move to the third phase, which is also referred to as the granting procedure or *Bewilligungsverfahren*. During this part of the procedure, the public prosecutor decides whether or not the extradition request will be granted.[79] In this phase, the optional refusal grounds in Article 83b IRG are considered. It should be noted that a preliminary decision not to apply any of these refusal grounds in the first phase does not prohibit the public prosecutor from changing his or her view when the case arrives at the third phase.[80]

[72] Art. 79((2) IRG. Böse suggests that the decision to apply one of the refusal grounds in Article 83b IRG ends the extradition procedure. Böse (2012a), pp. 13–14.

[73] BT Drucksache 16/1024 [12]; BVerfG 18 July 2005, 2 BvR 2236/04 (*Darkazanli*) [101–102]; OLG Stuttgart 6 March 2007, 3 Ausl 52/06, NJW 2007, 1702, StV 2007, 258.

[74] BT Drucksache 16/1024 [13]; OLG Dresden 20 June 2008, Ausl 51/08, StV 2008, 534; Böse (2012a), pp. 17–18.

[75] In addition to these errors the StAOLG can also be accused of *Ermessensunterschreitung*, meaning he or she only exercised part of his or her discretion, or *Ermessensuberschreitung*, which means that the public prosecutor exceeded the limits of his or her discretion. OLG Stuttgart 6 March 2007, 3 Ausl 52/06, NJW 2007, 1702, StV 2007, 258; OLG Dresden 20 June 2008, Ausl 51/08, StV 2008, 534; Böse (2012a), pp. 19–21.

[76] OLG Stuttgart 6 March 2007, 3 Ausl 52/06, NJW 2007, 1702, StV 2007, 258. These individual interests cover the expected length of the proceedings as well as the time the requested person would have to stay in pre-trial detention, the expected sentence and constitutional safeguards or fundamental rights such as those following from Article 16(2) GG and 6 GG.

[77] Böhm (2021), pp. 211–212; OLG Karlsruhe 24 February 2020, Ausl 301 AR 167/19.

[78] Art. 79(1) IRG.

[79] Art. 12 jo 13(2) IRG.

[80] BT Drucksache 16/1024 [14].

As discussed in greater detail later on, the division between the admissibility and granting procedure is based on the position that the decision to grant the extradition is 'in its core still a foreign policy decision of the federal government'.[81] Some of the optional refusal grounds in Article 83b IRG reflect situations of conflicts of jurisdictions, which are also regarded as foreign policy issues. According to the German legislator such matters should not be ruled on by a court, which also explains the limited judicial review by the OLG in the second phase, but by a public prosecutor who should be provided with flexible rules in determining which state is the most appropriate one for prosecution. However, as mentioned before, it is now being argued that a limited review of the decision of the public prosecutor is not compatible with EU law.[82]

Relevant Refusal Grounds

The following sections discuss the refusal grounds in the IRG which show a potential link to unforeseeable jurisdiction claims and forum choices in case of conflicts of national jurisdictions. Firstly, the refusal grounds applicable in the admissibility procedure before the OLG are examined, and secondly the refusal grounds in the granting procedure on which the public prosecutor decides. The refusal grounds which are explored in relation to the problems arising from unforeseeable jurisdiction claims are the double criminality requirement in Article 3 IRG and Articles 80 IRG and 83b (2) IRG on the protection of German nationals and foreigners residing in Germany. These are connected to the question according to whose law the conduct should be criminalised and to what extent requested persons should be protected against the unexpected application of foreign laws. Furthermore, the refusal ground in Article 83b (1)(a) IRG regarding domestic proceedings in Germany for the same offence offers the public prosecutor broad discretion in deciding on its application. Hence, it is examined to what extent this discretion must or is used to protect the requested person against extradition in case of unforeseeable jurisdiction claims.

In relation to the problems arising from the absence of a transparent EU system for forum choices, the refusal grounds in Articles 80 and 83b(1)(a) IRG are important. We will see that the German legislator has linked them to conflicts of national jurisdictions and the question which state is the better forum for the case at hand. In addition, the refusal ground in Article 83b(1)(c) IRG which covers concurring extradition requests could influence the underlying forum decision. The states whose extradition requests are not executed may as a result decide to discontinue their national criminal proceedings against the requested person. In addition, the human rights refusal ground in Article 73 IRG states that extradition requests should not be executed when this would result in a violation of the principles in Article 6 TEU. Consequently, the next sections also examine to what extent this refusal ground is used to avoid extraditions in case of a violation of Articles 49 or 47 CFR due to unforeseeable jurisdiction claims or forum choices that are not based on transparent rules.

[81] BT Drucksache 16/1024 [13].

[82] BT Drucksache 16/1024 [13]; BVerfG 18 July 2005, 2 BvR 2236/04 (*Darkazanli*) [109]; Böse (2012a), pp. 6–8; Böse (2012d), p. 6; Hackner (2007), pp. 193, 196–197. See also Case C-510/19 *AZ* [2020] ECLI:EU:C:2020:953.

6.3.2 Admissibility: The Double Criminality Requirement

Article 3(1) IRG codifies the double criminality requirement, which demands that the conduct is an unlawful act (*rechtswidrige Tat*) in Germany.[83] This requirement is satisfied when the acts or omissions on the EAW also constitute criminal offences under German law.[84] However, the qualification of the conduct may differ from the one on the EAW.[85] In compliance with Article 2(2) FDEAW, the OLG should refrain from conducting the double criminality test when the offence falls under one of the enumerated categories.[86]

It can be derived from the case law and legal literature that the application of the double criminality principle is not obligatory on the basis of Article 103(2) GG.[87] This conclusion also follows from the fact that the double criminality requirement is met when the act on the EAW did not constitute a criminal act according to German law at the time of the offence, but has been criminalised at the time of the decision on the extradition request.[88] Contrary to Article 80 IRG which is discussed in the next section, the double criminality requirement also does not aim to protect the trust of the prosecuted person that he will not be extradited.[89] Instead, the requirement correlates from the principle of reciprocity and as a result primarily protects the

---

[83] In principle, a criminal offense consists of three layers including the elements of the actus reus and mens rea in the description of the offense, the general unlawfulness of the conduct (*Rechtswidrigkeit*) and guilt (*Schuld*). The first two need to be assessed in light of the double criminality requirement. BT Drucksache 9/1338 [35]. Lagodny (2012), pp. 88–89.

[84] Article 3(1) IRG states that the double criminality requirement is also fulfilled when after *Sinngemäßer Umstellung des Sachverhalts* the act in question is criminalized under German law. *Sinngemäßer Umstellung des Sachverhalts* entails that after an analogous conversion or recharacterization of the facts, the conduct in question falls under a criminal offense in German criminal law. Such an exercise is required when the foreign offense contains elements relating to, for instance the nationality of the victim or the place where the crime was committed. So, if an EAW from France contains an offense which demands that the crime was committed against a French national, the German competent authority needs to consider whether the conduct would have been a criminal offense under German law if it had been committed against a German national. Lagodny (2012), p. 87.

[85] OLG Köln 18 September 2006, 6 Ausl.A 66/06 where unlawfully crossing the border under Polish law was classified as abuse of identity papers under German law. Kubiciel (2015), p. 170; Lagodny (2012), p. 88; Böhm (2018a), para 1078.

[86] Article 81(4) IRG.

[87] BVerfG 5 November 2003, 2 BvR 1243/03 [16]; OLG Stuttgart 28 January 2005, 3 Ausl. 1/05 [39]; BVerfG 18 July 2005, 2 BvR 2236/04 (*Darkazanli*) [98]; OLG Celle 16 December 2016, 1 AR (Ausl) 89/16 [16].

[88] OLG Celle 16 December 2016 1 AR (Ausl) 89/16 [16]. Under certain circumstances, the time of the actual extradition of the requested person can also be the reference point for the criminality of the behaviour according to German law. In addition, the BVerfG has also accepted the time of the receipt of the extradition request as the correct reference point. OLG Celle 27 February 2008, 1 ARs 23/07; OLG Celle 16 December 2016, 1 AR (Ausl) 89/16; BVerfG 5 November 2003, 2 BvR 1243/03 [16].

[89] OLG Celle 16 December 2016, 1 AR (Ausl) 89/16 [16].

interests of the German state.[90] Germany should not have to provide assistance to another foreign nation when the behaviour in question is not an offence according to German law and Germany would therefore, in the reversed position, not be able to request assistance.[91] Legal scholars have stated—both from the perspective of the protection of state interests and the protection of the fundamental rights of the individual[92]—that in general the purpose of the double criminality principle is to ensure that states are not forced to detain and extradite individuals who according to their laws and legal views are innocent.[93] Double criminality is in this light, also viewed as a legitimacy requirement for detention pending extradition.[94]

Contrary to the case law, the German legislator has not emphasised the link between double criminality and the principle of reciprocity. It has also not based the application of the requirement on the conviction that the use of coercive measures to ensure extradition to another state violates the rule of law when the conduct in question is not punishable in Germany.[95] Instead, the German legislator has stated in the past that the fact that Germany holds a different view on whether or not certain behaviour should be criminalised is in principle no reason to deny assistance to another state.[96] The perspective has been followed in the literature, with the restriction that solidarity towards other states should not extend to cases in which the conduct in question is not and cannot be punishable in Germany according to the German Constitution.[97] The German legislator based the inclusion of the double criminality principle in the IRG on the fact that its application was part of the normal practice of interstate assistance and the fact that the European Convention on Extradition allowed it.[98] In addition, the absence of the requirement would demand a broader 'ordre-public clause' to avoid any injustices (*Ungerechtigkeiten*) and such a refusal ground would be more difficult to apply.[99] Therefore, it can be concluded that neither the German legislator nor the case law has linked the double criminality

[90] BGH 31 March 1977, 4 ARs 8/77; OLG Frankfurt am Main 3 March 2011, 2 Ausl A 221/10; Kubiciel (2015), p. 169.

[91] Kubiciel (2015), p. 169.

[92] It has been argued that the fundamental rights dimension of the double criminality principle lies in the obligation of the requested state to refuse the extradition when the punishments in the requesting state are not in conformity with minimum fundamental rights standards. See Böse (2012c), pp. 14–15.

[93] Schünemann (2003), p. 189; Grützner (1956), p. 512. See also Meyer (2015), para 877; Peers (2004), p. 24; Böse (2012c), p. 13.

[94] Schünemann (2003), p. 189.

[95] The principle of reciprocity is also a separate refusal ground in Article 5 IRG. BT Drucksache 9/1338 [37]; BT Drucksache 15/1718 [17].

[96] BT Drucksache 9/1338 [37]; BT Drucksache 15/1718 [17].

[97] This would, for instance, be the case when the requesting state has criminalized the expression of 'harmless' opinions or could impose corporal punishments. Lagodny (2012), pp. 85–86; Lagodny (1989), pp. 996–997; Kubiciel (2015), pp. 169–170. See also BT Drucksache 15/1718 [17].

[98] BT Drucksache 9/1338 [37].

[99] BT Drucksache 9/1338 [37].

requirement to the need to protect citizens against extradition when the jurisdiction claim of the requesting state was difficult to foresee.

6.3.3 Admissibility: The Nationality Exception

6.3.3.1 An Introduction to Article 80 IRG

Article 80 IRG implements Articles 5(3) and 4(7)(a) FDEAW, but exclusively protects German nationals. Its current form and content are the result of the BVerfG case in which the first EAW Act was ruled unconstitutional in light of Article 16 (2) GG. According to the Constitutional Court, the German legislator had not used all the available discretion provided by the FDEAW, such as the refusal ground in Article 4(7)(a) FDEAW to protect German nationals against extradition. This legislative decision was criticised in light of Article 16(2) GG, which requires the legislator to protect the special bond which exists between the German state and its nationals.[100] Besides declaring the first EAW void, the BVerfG also enumerated different categories of situations in which extradition of German nationals is either viewed as allowed or prohibited according to Article 16(2) GG.[101] The German legislator has implemented these categories in Article 80 IRG, which covers extradition requests for the purpose of criminal prosecution.

The first category of situations prohibits the extradition of German nationals when the act has a substantial link to Germany, which is usually the case when the entire or essential parts of the act as well as an essential part of the consequences occurred in Germany.[102] These cases should be prosecuted in Germany.[103] This refusal ground aims to protect the legal certainty of German nationals and the trust they may have in their own legal system on the basis of Article 16(2) GG and the rule of law in Article 20(3) GG.

The second category of situations allows the extradition of German nationals when the requesting state guarantees that, in case of a conviction, any imposed custodial measure may be executed in Germany and the act has a substantial link to the requesting state.[104] The latter is usually the case when the entire or essential parts of the act, as well as an essential part of the consequences, occurred there.[105] In

---

[100] Or aboard a German vessel or aircraft or in places that are under German sovereign power. BVerfG 18 July 2005, 2 BvR 2236/04 (*Darkazanli*) [82–84].

[101] BVerfG 18 July 2005, 2 BvR 2236/04 (*Darkazanli*) [85–87].

[102] This follows from Art. 80(1) and (2) IRG.

[103] BVerfG 18 July 2005, 2 BvR 2236/04 (*Darkazanli*) [83–85]; BVerfG 9 November 2016, 2 BvR 545/16 [40]. Situations may occur in which according to the examples mentioned a substantial link to Germany exists, but this is *de facto* not the case—for instance, when the accused withholds a child from its parents who are abroad. Böse (2012b), pp. 17–18. In this case the situations fall under the third category in Article 80 IRG. BT Drucksache 16/1024 [16].

[104] Art. 80(1) IRG.

[105] BT Drucksache 16/1024 [16]; BVerfG 18 July 2005, 2 BvR 2236/04 (*Darkazanli*) [86]; BVerfG 9 November 2016, 2 BvR 545/16 [40]. BT Drucksache 16/1024 [16].

addition, the second category includes cases of serious cross-border crimes which are partially committed on the territory of the requesting state.[106] In these situations, German nationals cannot rely on the protection offered by Article 16(2) GG, since this could result in safe havens for German nationals who commit offences abroad and afterwards flee to Germany.[107] This category is, however, strictly interpreted, since a substantial link to the requesting state is already absent when not unessential parts of the crime were committed on German territory. To give an example, the BVerfG has once denied the existence of a substantial link to Poland as the requesting state, even though the crime itself was committed on Polish territory and the victim had the Polish nationality. The court based its decision on the fact that the crime was planned in Germany and had possibly started in Germany with the abduction of the victim.[108]

Denying a substantial link to the requesting state when there is no substantial link to Germany either automatically places the case in the third category of so-called *Mischfallen* (mixed cases or rest category).[109] This category can, for instance, cover situations in which both states or a third state can be designated as the place where the crime was committed or the situation in which the act itself was committed on German territory, but the results occurred abroad.[110] In such situations, the permissibility of the extradition of a German national is dependent on a double criminality test. In addition, this category requires a balancing exercise between the interests of the prosecuted person and the requesting state to determine whether the trust of the German national in his or her own legal system should be protected.[111] In essence, the OLG needs to decide which state is the best forum for prosecution by weighing the interests of the German national and those of the requesting state as well as the general need for effective crime-fighting efforts.[112] In this light, the OLG should assess the nature of the offence, the chances of an effective prosecution, which often

---

[106] BVerfG 18 July 2005, 2 BvR 2236/04 (*Darkazanli*) [86]. However, these cases also show a link to the German territory, which in principle places them in the third category. This category, therefore, only covers distinctive organized crimes, such as human trafficking and international terrorism, and not ‘simple’ cases of, for instance, gang violence. Böhm (2006), p. 2595.

[107] BT Drucksache 16/1024 [16]; BVerfG 9 November 2016, 2 BvR 545/16 [40]. BT Drucksache 16/1024 [16].

BVerfG 18 July 2005, 2 BvR 2236/04 (*Darkazanli*) [86].

[108] BVerfG 15 June 2016, 12 BvR 468/16 [21–23]. In another judgment the BVerfG concluded that no substantial link to Belgium, where a murder was committed, could be assumed to exist, since the alleged contribution of the requested person to the offense—he was accused of incitement to commit murder—took place on German territory. BVerfG 7 October 2015, 2 BvR 1860/15 [18].

[109] BVerfG 7 October 2015, 2 BvR 1860/15 [18]. In November 2016 the BVerfG in fact confirmed the existence of a substantial link to the requesting state, but still ordered the balancing act in Article 80(2) IRG. It based its decision on the fact that the case concerned an omission offense, which allowed both Germany, the state where the requested person resided at the time, and Poland, the state where the requested person should have acted, to be designated as *locus delicti.* BVerfG 9 November 2016, 2 BvR 545/16 [34–35, 42–44]; Böhm (2018a), p. 202.

[110] BT 16/1024 [14, 16–17]; BVerfG 18 July 2005, 2 BvR 2236/04 (*Darkazanli*) [87].

[111] BT Drucksache 16/1024 [16].

[112] Böse (2012b), p. 27.

relate to the availability of evidence, and the interests of the requested person while taking objectives relating to the establishment of 'a single European judicial area' into account.[113] In relation to the interests of the individual, the OLG should consider what difficulties the different procedural rules in the requesting state may bring about, as well as the right to family life and even humanitarian reasons for remaining in Germany.[114] In addition, the decision to initiate, not to initiate or to discontinue criminal proceedings in Germany should also be taken into account, as the interests of the requesting state in prosecution may have been partially or completely met by such decisions.[115]

6.3.3.2 Unforeseeable Jurisdiction Claims

As has been explained in Sect. 6.2.2, it follows from the BVerfG case law that Article 16(2) GG in combination with the rule of law aims to protect German nationals under certain circumstances against the application of foreign substantive criminal laws which they did not need to know at the time of the offence.[116] Hence, the BVerfGE has recognised that German nationals in the AFSJ may face difficulties in determining whose laws to obey. Article 80 IRG is a response to these concerns. However, the degree of protection offered by Article 80 IRG is strongly dependent on the territorial link which the criminal acts and their consequences have to Germany and/or the requesting state.[117] This is based on the position that a German national should know and abide the law of the state in which he or she is present.[118] Whether certain conduct constitutes a criminal offence and which sanctions can be imposed according to either German law or the law of the requesting state is considered foreseeable when both the essential part of the conduct and the consequences occur either on German territory or on the territory of the requesting state.[119]

Contrary to the double criminality requirement in Article 3 IRG, the application of the double criminality requirement in the third category aims to protect the trust of German nationals in the German legal order.[120] Even though this requirement applies to all cases falling within the third category, the legislator has primarily emphasised the

[113] Art. 80(2) IRG; BT Drucksache 16/1024 [16]; BVerfG 18 July 2005, 2 BvR 2236/04 (*Darkazanli*) [87]; BVerfG 9 November 2016, 2 BvR 545/16 [41]; BVerfG 7 October 2015, 2 BvR 1860/15 [18].

[114] Böse (2012b), p. 29; Böhm (2017), p. 81; Böhm (2018b), para 986.

[115] See Art. 83b(1) (nr. 1 and 2) IRG. These decisions are also optional refusal grounds, but the OLG should also consider them in light of Article 80 IRG. BT Drucksache 16/1024 [16–17]; Böse (2012b), pp. 32–33.

[116] BVerfG 18 July 2005, 2 BvR 2236/04 (*Darkazanli*) [85].

[117] BT Drucksache 16/1024 [16].

[118] Böhm (2006), p. 2594. See also Becker (2010), pp. 1574–1575.

[119] BVerfG 15 January 2016, 2 BvR 1860/15; Böhm (2018a), para 965; Böse (2012b), p. 19. He also states that the German jurisdiction rules will inform the individual when he or she may expect the application of foreign substantive criminal laws.

[120] See Böse (2012b), pp. 26–27.

situation in which there is a territorial link to Germany, but not a substantial one like in the first category. In these cases, the German national should be able to rely on the fact that his conduct is not criminal according to German law.[121] The double criminality requirement, therefore, aims to protect German nationals against extradition in case of an unexpected application of foreign substantive criminal law when the conduct at least in part occurred in Germany, but is not criminal according to German law.[122] Furthermore, several authors have argued that the double criminality requirement also covers the rules on jurisdiction, which means that the conduct in question must be criminal according to German law and one of the jurisdiction grounds should be applicable. This interpretation of the double criminality requirement would increase the protection against the broad extraterritorial jurisdiction of other states.[123] For example, if Germany receives an EAW from France, which exercises jurisdiction on the basis of the passive nationality principle over an offence over which Germany could not exercise extraterritorial jurisdiction, the double criminality requirement would not be fulfilled, and Article 80 IRG would prohibit extradition.

It follows clearly from the above that the BVerfG and Article 80 IRG strongly emphasise the protection of one's own, meaning German nationals, which is also a reflection of state sovereignty and national interests.[124] The nationality exception does not cover the position of other EU citizens or third-country nationals who may face the same foreseeability issues or who may be subjected to Germany's extraterritorial jurisdiction.[125] On the basis of Article 16(2) GG, the special connection between the German citizen and the German state is magnified, while the possibly similar relation between another EU citizen or third-country national and the German state is ignored.[126] This emphasis on the need to safeguard the trust which a German national may have in his or her own legal order has its roots in the events of the Second World War during which the institution of citizenship was devalued and replaced by a new 'national status' for those entitled to it.[127] The exclusive protection of German nationals has also been criticised in the legal literature, in which it is argued that not only German nationals can be subjected to the unexpected application of foreign national criminal laws and extensive foreign jurisdiction claims.[128]

[121] BT Drucksache 16/1024 [15, 17]; Böse (2012b), pp. 26–27.

[122] See Böse (2012b), p. 27.

[123] Böse (2012b), p. 26. See Lagodny (2012), pp. 87–88.

[124] BVerfG 18 July 2005, 2 BvR 2236/04 (*Darkazanli*); Luchtman (2017), p. 22.

[125] Luchtman (2017), p. 9.

[126] BVerfG 18 July 2005, 2 BvR 2236/04 (*Darkazanli*) [66–67].

[127] Deen-Racsmany (2006), p. 285; BVerfG 18 July 2005, 2 BvR 2236/04 (*Darkazanli*) paras [66]–[67].

[128] Some legal scholars, like Wasmeier are primarily in favour of more protection for foreigners who reside in Germany and are integrated. Others, such as Tinkl, do not seem to make this distinction and are in favour of extended protection for all individuals who are confronted with unexpected consequences of their actions. Vogel (2005), p. 805; Wasmeier (2006), p. 38; Tinkl (2010), p. 325. See also BVerfG 18 July 2005, 2 BvR 2236/04 (*Darkazanli*) [93]; Dissenting opinion of Judge Lübbe-Wolff BVerfG 18 July 2005, 2 BvR 2236/04 (*Darkazanli*) [157].

Hence, protection against extradition in these situations should not be made dependent on nationality, but should be based on Article 103(2) GG, more specifically the *Rückwirkungsverbot* (prohibition of a retroactive application of the law) and the *Bestimmtheitsgebot*.[129]

6.3.3.3 The Nationality Exception and Forum Choices

It follows from the above that the territoriality principle and the nationality of the accused are the lead criteria in determining whether the requested person should be extradited. Only when these do not appoint either Germany or the requesting state as the best forum for prosecution do the factors in Article 80(2) IRG need to be weighed against each other. The German legislator decided against an exhaustive list of factors with a clear hierarchy to ensure that the forum decision that is made in light of Article 80 IRG is made on the basis of the concrete facts of the case. Stricter rules could hamper the process of picking the best forum for prosecution.[130] In addition, the decision is made by a judicial authority, namely the OLG and not by the executive power, which according to some legal scholars may compensate for the lack of clarity in the law and reduce the risk of arbitrary decisions.[131]

On the basis of the above, it can be concluded that the German legislator has clearly linked the application of Article 80 IRG to the matter of forum choices on the transnational level, but from a purely German perspective in which the protection of German nationals is the starting point. In addition, neither the preparatory work to the IRG nor the case law clearly show that the possible risk of forum manipulations and arbitrary forum decisions in case of conflicts of national jurisdictions in the EU has played an important role in the establishment and interpretation of the nationality exception in Art. 80 IRG. Instead, the need for flexibility to choose the best forum for the concrete case is considered most important.

---

[129] Tinkl (2010), p. 325; Böse (2012b), pp. 9–10. See also Zimmerman who argues in favour of an extension of Article 16(2) GG to all EU citizens. Zimmerman (2017), p. 227. As explained before the BVerfGE did address the problems from the perspective of the substantive legality principle, but merely concluded that the extradition of a German for an act which has no substantial link to a foreign state and was not punishable in Germany when it occurred could be *tantamount* to a violation of the *Rückwirkungsverbot*. BVerfG 18 July 2005, 2 BvR 2236/04 (*Darkazanli*) [98].

[130] BT Drucksache 16/1024 [16–17]; Eurojust Annual Report (2004) 2005/00014 [98]. Böse states that the place where the crime was committed and the nationality of the suspect play a less important role in relation to the third category, because they were already considered and could not lead to a decision. The other criteria should be given more weight. Böse (2012b), pp. 28–29.

[131] Swart (1983), pp. 16–19.

6.3.4 *Admissibility: Human Rights Refusal Ground*

Article 73 IRG states that extradition requests should not be executed when doing so would result in a violation of the principles in Article 6 TEU.[132] This means that a violation of one of the sub-principles of the legality principle in Article 49 CFR by the requesting state could in fact block the extradition of the requested person.[133] However, the case law does not show a situation in which the extradition request was not granted on the basis of Article 49 CFR, because the jurisdiction claim of the requesting state, and therefore its criminal offences and sanctions, were not foreseeable.[134] The same goes for Article 47(2) CFR, which has not been interpreted in such a way that a lack of a transparent system of forum choices on the EU level should result in the inadmissibility of the extradition request. However, the fact that the OLG has not adopted this interpretation of the two fundamental rights can be explained in light of the fact that it is in principle for the CJEU to interpret EU law, including the fundamental rights in the CFR. As explained in Chap. 3, the CJEU has so far not explicitly considered the link between jurisdiction and Article 49 CFR or forum choices on the transnational level and Article 47 CFR.

In addition, the German courts have integrated the *Aranyosi* and *Câldâraru* and *LM* case in the executing procedure.[135] When the twofold test concerning a violation of the prohibition of inhuman and degrading treatment in Article 4 CFR or the right to an independent court in Article 47(2) CFR has been met the extradition request is inadmissible. The application of the twofold test has, however, not been extended to the right to a tribunal established by law in Article 47 CFR or the right to an accessible and foreseeable law in Article 49(1) CFR.

6.3.5 *Granting Procedure: Domestic Proceedings for the Same Offence*

Article 83b(1) IRG contains several optional refusal grounds. Subsection (a) transposes Article 4(2) FDEAW allowing the public prosecutor to refuse the extradition in case of domestic proceedings in Germany for the same offence. The scope of

[132] Article 73 IRG also states that extradition requests will not be granted when this would conflict with basic principles of the German legal system. This part of the provision applies to EAWs to the extent that EU law allows for it. Ambos and Poschadel (2015), para 77.

[133] Ambos and Poschadel (2015), para 89.

[134] On the application of Article 103(2) GG to the law of the requesting state in cases concerning requests from non-EU Member States, see e.g. BVerfG 20 November 2014, 2 BvR 1820/14 [11–14]; OLG Frankfurt am Main 22 January 2014, 2 Ausl A 104/13; OLG Koblenz GA 1987, 232 referred to in Lagodny (2012), p. 425.

[135] OLG Bremen 16 March 2020, 1 Ausl. A 78/19; OLG Düsseldorf 14 June 2019, 4 AR 38/19; OLG Köln 20 March 2018, 6 AuslA 203/17 – 14.

application of this refusal ground is not limited to situations in which the EAW is received, while criminal proceedings in Germany are already ongoing. Instead, the German legislator has explicitly stated that the information on the criminal offence provided by the EAW can be a reason for the German public prosecutor to assess the possibility of domestic criminal proceedings.[136] In some cases, there may even be a duty to prosecute the case in Germany on the basis of Article 152(2) StPO.[137] The application of this duty in a concrete case is in fact in itself sufficient for Article 83b (1)(a) IRG to apply, meaning that a formal initiation of criminal proceedings is not required.[138] In light of efficiency considerations, it is considered best that the public prosecutor decides on the application of the refusal ground before domestic proceedings are started. Making such a decision could require contact with the competent public prosecutor to prosecute the case in Germany to ask whether it is his or her intent to start domestic criminal proceedings.[139] If this is indeed the intent of the public prosecutor in the criminal case, the public prosecutor in the extradition procedure has a good reason to apply Article 83b(1)(a) IRG.[140] It can so far be concluded that Article 83b(1)(a) IRG has a broad scope of application and together with in particular the general duty to prosecute cases laid down in Article 152 (2) StPO it can even cause conflicts of national jurisdictions.

In relation to the matter of forum choices, it is also important to note that Article 83b(1)(a) IRG itself does not restrict the discretion granted to the public prosecutor and as explained before the OLG (in principle) only marginally assesses a decision of the public prosecutor not to apply any of the optional refusal grounds.[141] The reason for this broad discretion seems to be based on the position of the German legislator that this decision is closely related to a forum decision and that solving conflicts of jurisdictions is predominantly a foreign policy matter.[142] Consequently, not the OLG, but the public prosecutor is designated as the principal competent

[136] BT Drucksache 16/1024 [17]; BT Drucksache 15/1718 [21].

[137] Article 152(2) StPO is based on the principle of mandatory prosecution, also referred to as the legality principle (*Legalitätsgrundsatz*). BT Drucksache 16/1024 [17]; BT Drucksache 15/1718 [21]. However, in certain situations, for instance when the crime is committed abroad, the public prosecutor is not obliged to prosecute and is provided with prosecutorial discretion to make the decision. Articles 153c and 153f StPO.

[138] OLG Karlsruhe 11 May 2007, 1 AK 3/07; Böhm (2018b), para 1078.

[139] Böse (2012d), p. 4.

[140] Furthermore, in case the German public prosecutor competent to prosecute the case domestically formally decides not to do so, this may also result in a decision not to extradite the requested person, but this time on the basis of Article 83b(1)(b) IRG. This refusal ground allows the public prosecutor to refuse the extradition request in case of an official decision on the basis of, for instance, Article 153 StPO or Article 170(2) StPO not to initiate criminal proceedings in Germany for the same offense or to terminate ongoing criminal proceedings for the same offense. Böse (2012d), p. 4.

[141] Art. 79 (2) IRG; Böse (2012a), pp. 13–14. However, as explained before, in light of the developments in EU law, some German courts have argued that a full review of the decision of the public prosecutor should be conducted.

[142] BT Drucksache 16/1024 [12–13]; BT Drucksage 15/1718 [30]; Hackner (2007), pp. 193, 196–197; Böse (2012a), pp. 6–7.

authority to make the decision and he or she should be in a position to make the most appropriate forum choice for which flexibility and the absence of rigid rules is required.[143] Hence, the need for flexibility seems to take precedence over the need for strict rules regarding the allocation of cases on the transnational EU level to avoid forum manipulation. The latter has been a point of discussion in the legal literature, but not in the preparatory work to Article 83b IRG or in the case law.[144]

Even though the law itself does not limit the discretion of the public prosecutor, the parliamentary documentation does provide a non-limitative and non-hierarchal list of possible factors which match the ones that play a role in case of conflicts of jurisdictions between German courts.[145] These include the nationality and residence of the prosecuted person, the place where the crime was committed or the place where the '*Schwerpunkt*' (focus) of the offence is situated, the nationality and interests of the victims, the public interests of other states who wish to prosecute, the stage of the criminal proceedings in the competent states, and the availability of evidence.[146] Political or foreign policy considerations may still play a role, but they exist in addition to the interests of the individual in being prosecuted in either Germany or in the requesting state.[147] In relation to the interests of the individual, it follows from the case law that Article 83b(1)(a) IRG strongly focuses on the protection of the German national and Article 16(2) GG.[148] In fact, the combination of 83b(1)(a) IRG and Germany's broad (extra)territorial jurisdiction can serve as an escape-route to avoid unwanted extraditions, in particular for German nationals, where other refusal grounds fail.[149] For instance, when the extradition of a German national is not prohibited on the basis of Article 80 IRG, because the case has a substantial link to the requesting state, the public prosecutor should consider whether the interests of the prosecuted person require that domestic proceedings are initiated to avoid extradition.[150] As the constitutional protection offered by Article 16(2) GG is marked as an important consideration in the decision of the public prosecutor,[151]

[143] Böse (2012d), p. 6. See also Hackner (2007), pp. 193, 196.

[144] See Böhm (2018b), para 1077.

[145] BT Drucksache 16/1024 [13]; Arts. 7–12 StPO. In general, no hierarchy exists between these factors, but paras 159(1) jo 158(1) RiVASt emphasize the chances of an effective prosecution. Furthermore, Böse states that the similarities between these factors and the ones which need to be taken into account in the context of Article 80 IRG, means that the place where the crime was committed as well as the nationality or residence of the prosecuted person should be given important weight. Böse (2012d), p. 6. See also BT Drucksache 15/1718 [30].

[146] BT Drucksache 16/1024 [13].

[147] BT Drucksage 15/1718 [15]; BVerfG 18 July 2005, 2 BvR 2236/04 (*Darkazanli*) [95, 113].

[148] BVerfG 18 July 2005, 2 BvR 2236/04 (*Darkazanli*) [95]; OLG Stuttgart 6 March 2007, StV 2007, 258; OLG Karlsruhe 20 December 2006, 1 AK 46/06; Böhm (2018b), paras 974–975, 1078; Böse (2012d), pp. 5–6 who also refers to BT Drucksache 16/1024 [16].

[149] Von Bubnoff (2005), p. 78.

[150] OLG Karlsruhe 20 December 2006, 1 AK 46/06; OLG Karlsruhe 13 May 2013, 1 AK 63/12; OLG Karlsruhe 24 October 2014, 1 AK 90/14, BeckRS 2014, 22172; Böhm (2018a), p. 202.

[151] OLG Stuttgart 6 March 2007, StV 2007, 258; OLG Karlsruhe 20 December 2006, 1 AK 46/06.

protection against the unexpected application of foreign laws, which is part of this constitutional safeguard, also seems to have a role. However, this protection is limited to German nationals. No indications exist that Article 83b(1)(a) IRG also intends to offer protection against extradition to other EU citizens or third-country nationals when the applicability of the criminal law of the requesting state was difficult to foresee at the time of the offence.

6.3.6 Granting Procedure: Protection of Foreigners

In the first EAW Act, which was declared unconstitutional, and the first draft of the second EAW Act, the protection of foreigners who have their *gewöhnlicher Aufenthalt*[152] (habitual residence) in Germany against extradition for the purpose of prosecution was part of the mandatory refusal ground in Article 80 IRG.[153] The decision of the German legislator to transfer the protection of foreigners to the *Bewilligungsverfahren* was the result of extensive criticism voiced by the *Bundesrat* (Federal Council). This institution argued that a mandatory refusal ground could disproportionality burden the German law enforcement system, since foreign sentences for serious crimes would have to be executed in Germany, even though the foreigner would be deported after the execution of the sentence.[154] As the FDEAW does not demand that the protection of foreigners normally living in Germany is ensured by a mandatory refusal ground, the German legislator eventually included this protection in Article 83b(2)(1) IRG.[155] However, this decision has been criticised in light of the non-discrimination principle in Articles 18 TFEU and 21(2) CFR.[156]

The three categories which guide the decision on the basis of Article 80 IRG also apply in the context of Article 83b(2)(1) IRG.[157] As the protection of foreigners who normally live in Germany is optional, it is the public prosecutor who decides on the basis of the three categories to what extent the trust of these

[152] The requirement of '*gewöhnlichen Aufenthalts*' is a *Tatbestandmerkmal* which means that it does not fall within the discretion of the public prosecutor. In other words, when the requirement is not met, the public prosecutor does not move to the next phase in which he or she decides whether one of the categories in Article 80(1) and (2) IRG is applicable. Böhm (2018a), p. 202; OLG Frankfurt 10 May 2016, 2 AuslA 202/15.

[153] Böse (2012d), pp. 11–12; BT Drucksache 16/2015 [12–13].

[154] This criticism addressed an earlier version of the refusal ground in Article 80(4) IRG. This provision stated '*Die Absätze 1 bis 3 sind auf einen Ausländer entsprechend anwendbar, der im Inland mit einem deutschen Familienangehörigen oder Lebenspartner in familiärer oder lebenspartnerschaftlicher Lebensgemeinschaft lebt.*' BT Drucksache 16/1024 [22–23]. See also BT Drucksache 15/2905 [1–2].

[155] BT Drucksache 16/2015 [12–13].

[156] Meyer (2015), para 973.

[157] See Sect. 6.3.3.

foreigners in the German legal system needs to be protected.[158] As explained before, the trust which German nationals may have in the German legal system is connected to protection against the unexpected application of foreign laws.[159] Consequently, the reference to trust in the context of Article 83b(2)(1) IRG could mean that in some situations foreigners should receive the same protection in the context of the extradition procedure. However, even if this is the case, contrary to the mandatory refusal ground in Article 80 IRG, meeting the criteria in Article 83b(2)(1) IRG—the *gewöhnlichen Aufenthalts* and those in Article 80 (1) and (2) IRG—does not automatically offer protection against extradition.[160] The public prosecutor is competent to extradite the foreigner despite the fulfilment of the criteria in this provision.[161] Therefore, it is more difficult for foreigners living in Germany to receive protection against extradition in case of unforeseeable jurisdiction claims than for German nationals.[162]

6.3.7 Granting Procedure: Multiple Extradition Requests

The IRG does not contain a specific provision on the situation in which multiple EAWs are issued for the same offence. However, according to Böse Article 83b(1)(c) IRG covers both concurring extradition requests from EU Member States as well as concurring extradition requests from EU Member States and third states.[163] Similar to Article 83b(1)(a) IRG, the German legislator decided that flexible rules which allow for a decision on the basis of the concrete circumstances of the case should be prioritised over strict rules which contribute to legal certainty. In this light, the German legislator did not further restrict the discretion of the public prosecutor in Article 83b(1)(c) IRG itself, but merely stated in the preparatory work concerning this legal provision that the factors in Article 16 FDEAW and the ones considered in the context of Article 83b(1)(a) IRG should be taken into account.[164] However, in relation to concurring extradition requests from EU Member States and third states, the discretion of the German public prosecutor is restricted by the CJEU rulings in

[158] Schomburg (2012), p. 495; OLG Karlsruhe 11 May 2007, 1 AK 307; Kammergericht Berlin 10 January 2013, (4) 151 Ausl.A. 145/12 (216/12) [20].

[159] BVerfG 18 July 2005, 2 BvR 2236/04 (*Darkazanli*) [83, 85]. See also Sects. 6.2.2 and 6.3.3.

[160] Kammergericht Berlin 10 January 2013, (4) 151 Ausl.A. 145/12 (216/12) [20]; BT Drucksache 16/2015 [13].

[161] Some courts conduct a full review of the decision of the public prosecutor in relation to the application of the refusal rounds in Article 83b IRG. OLG Karlsruhe 24 February 2020, Ausl 301 AR 167/19.

[162] Meyer (2015), para 973.

[163] Böse (2012d), pp. 8–9. See also Sinn and Wörner (2008), p. 260.

[164] BT Drucksache 15/1718 [21]; Böse (2012d), pp. 8–9. Some courts conduct a full review of the decision of the public prosecutor in relation to the application of the refusal rounds in Article 83b IRG. OLG Karlsruhe 24 February 2020, Ausl 301 AR 167/19.

Petruhhin and *Pisciotti*.[165] This means that when Germany receives an extradition request for the purpose of prosecution from a third state for an EU citizen who is not a German national, it should first ask the state of nationality of the EU citizen whether it wishes to issue an EAW.[166] In case the latter decides to do so and the conditions for the execution of this EAW are met according to German law, its execution should be given priority over the extradition request from a third state.

6.3.8 Interim Conclusion

It can be concluded that contrary to the Dutch surrender procedure, the difficulties in foreseeing whose national criminal laws to obey at the time of the offence have been explicitly recognised in the context of the German extradition procedure, but primarily in relation to German nationals. On the basis of Article 16(2) GG which, as explained before, demands some protection against the unexpected application of foreign laws, the German legislator has adopted refusal grounds, such as Articles 80 and 83b(1)(a) IRG offering protection against extradition in such situations. Even though Article 83b(2) IRG is the equivalent of Article 80 IRG and, therefore, provides similar protection to foreigners who reside in Germany, its application is subject to more conditions and less certain due to the discretion allocated to the public prosecutor.[167]

In addition, it should be noted that German nationals are not provided with absolute protection against unforeseeable jurisdiction claims, meaning that extradition is prohibited whenever the law of the requesting state was not fully foreseeable. The three categories in Article 80 IRG show that the protection against unforeseeable jurisdiction claims is primarily intended for situations in which the offence in question has a substantial territorial link to Germany. The application of this refusal ground is, therefore, closely connected to the question where the criminal conduct and its consequences occurred. Hence, Article 80 IRG in combination with Article 83b(1)(a) IRG offers the strongest safeguards to static or non-moving German nationals.

In relation to the potential issues arising from the absence of a clear overarching EU system for forum choices it follows from the previous sections that conflicts of national jurisdictions are primarily dealt with in the *Bewilligungsverfahren*. This part of the extradition procedure provides room for foreign policy matters, which according to the German legislator include conflicts of national jurisdictions. In

[165] Case C-182/15 *Petruhhin* [2016] ECLI:EU:C:2016:630; Case C-191/16 *Pisciotti* [2018] ECLI:EU:C:2018:222; Böhm (2018a), paras 899, 1080.

[166] Before these rulings, certain German authors already argued in favour of prioritizing EAWs over extradition requests from third states in light of the restriction of Article 16(2) GG, free movement of persons and EU citizenship. Böse (2012d), pp. 8–9 (also for further references).

[167] This decision could be subject to review by the OLG. OLG Karlsruhe 24 February 2020, Ausl 301 AR 167/19.

that light, the public prosecutor is (still) competent to decide on the application of the relevant refusal grounds, most importantly those in Articles 83b(1)(a) and 83b(1)(c) IRG. In principle, the decision of the public prosecutor is not subjected to a full judicial review, but as a result of recent developments in EU law, some German courts have changed their position.

Furthermore, the German legislator has not explicitly discussed the potential risk of arbitrary forum choices arising from the lack of a transparent EU system to solve national conflicts of jurisdictions in the context of the *Bewilligungsverfahren*. Instead, the legislator has focused on the need for flexible rules. Its position seems to be that both on the national and transnational level rigid rules on case allocations interfere with the need to appoint the best forum for a case on the basis of the concrete circumstances.

The previous sections, in particular the ones on Article 80 IRG and Article 83b(1)(a) IRG, also show that the protection of German interests, including German nationals, has an important position in solving conflicts of national jurisdictions and could even justify the creation of conflicts of jurisdictions by the German public prosecutor. In the context of Article 83b(1)(a) IRG, the German legislator has explicitly acknowledged that the receipt of an EAW can trigger the obligation or possibility for the German public prosecutor to start domestic criminal proceedings in order to protect German prosecution interests and German nationals. In addition, in light of Article 80 IRG, a case should be prosecuted in Germany when it has a substantial territorial link to Germany and the suspect is German. Hence, Articles 80 and 83b(1)(a) IRG can be used to facilitate German criminal proceedings and by extension to protect German interests, including German nationals.

6.4 Germany As the Issuing State

6.4.1 The Issuing Procedure

This section examines to what extent the two complications with which an EU citizen can be confronted in the AFSJ have influenced the issuing procedure. Similar to the execution procedure, it seems that the Federal Minister of Justice is (still) officially the competent issuing authority. His or her competence has been delegated to the Ministries of Justice of the *Bundesländer*,[168] which appointed the public prosecutors' offices at the *Landgerichten* (regional courts) responsible for the underlying criminal proceedings as the competent authorities.[169] However, despite this

[168] Art. 74(1) jo (2) IRG; Schönfelder W, Notification under Article 34(2) of the Framework Decision [2006] 12509/06.

[169] There are over 100 *Landgerichten* in Germany. Schönfelder W, Notification under Article 34(2) of the Framework Decision [2006] 12509/06; Evaluation report on the fourth round of mutual evaluations 'The practical application of the European Arrest Warrant and Corresponding surrender procedures between Member States'—Report on Germany, 7058/2/09 REV 1 (2009), p. 6.

double delegation, the Federal Minister of Justice remained the so-called '*Herr des Verfahrens*', meaning that the public prosecutors merely executed powers in his or her place and were obliged to follow general or specific orders.[170] This duty to follow orders issued by the executive was recently criticised by the CJEU in the case *OG & PI*. The CJEU decided that under the current framework of rules, the German public prosecutor at the *Landgericht* cannot be classified as an issuing judicial authority in light of Article 6(1) FDEAW. It based this decision on the power of bodies of the executive to issue general or specific orders to public prosecutors, as a result of which the latter cannot be considered sufficiently independent.[171] As a result of this development, several German courts have adopted the position that a judicial power to issue an EAW can be derived from other provisions, such as Articles 131 and 162 StPO.[172] In addition, the amended notification on the basis of Article 6(3) FDEAW no longer refers to the Federal Minister of Justice as the official competent authority. It appoints the local, regional or higher regional courts as well the Federal Court of Justice as the competent issuing authorities.[173] However, without a clear amendment of the IRG, it remains unclear whether the Federal Minister of Justice is still the official issuing authority.

The issuing of an extradition request to another EU Member State is scarcely regulated in the IRG. Except for Article 83h IRG on speciality, Article 83i IRG on notification about delays, Article 83j IRG on legal counsel and several provisions in the RiVASt, which among other things prescribe the use of the EAW form, no substantive requirements have been laid down in the law.[174] It follows from other sources that the extradition request is subject to a proportionality test which in practice falls together with the proportionality assessment conducted in the context of the underlying domestic arrest warrant.[175] The lack of rules can be explained by the fact that the extradition request is in itself not viewed as a warrant for arrest, but as an extension of a domestic judicial arrest warrant. The extradition request is merely a search instrument, while the national arrest warrant is the official legal basis

---

[170] Art. 146 jo 147 GVG; Schomburg and Hackner (2012), pp. 446–447; Evaluation report on the fourth round of mutual evaluations 'The practical application of the European Arrest Warrant and Corresponding surrender procedures between Member States'—Report on Germany, 7058/2/09 REV 1 (2009), p. 5.

[171] Case C-508/18, C-82/19 *OG & PI* [2019] ECLI:EU:C:2019:456, paras 73–74; Case C-489/19 *NJ* [2019] ECLI:EU:C:2019:849, para 38.

[172] OLG Frankfurt am Main 12 September 2019, 2 Ws 60/19; Böhm (2021), p. 211. See also BVerfG 28 September 2020, 2 BvR 1435/20; Trüg and Ulrich (2019).

[173] Thiemrodt I, Amendment to Germany's notification under Article 6(3) of the FDEAW [2019] 14444/19.

[174] BT Drucksache 16/1024 [18]; Evaluation report on the fourth round of mutual evaluations 'The practical application of the European Arrest Warrant and Corresponding surrender procedures between Member States'—Report on Germany, 7058/2/09 REV 1 (2009), pp. 8, 39. See also para 162 RiVASt.

[175] Evaluation report on the fourth round of mutual evaluations 'The practical application of the European Arrest Warrant and Corresponding surrender procedures between Member States'—Report on Germany, 7058/2/09 REV 1 (2009), p. 8.

for arrest.[176] Consequently, an extradition request needs to be based on a domestic arrest warrant issued by an *Ermittlungsrichter* (investigative judge) at the *Amtsgericht* (local court).[177] A national arrest warrant may only be issued when on the basis of the facts of the case a strong suspicion of the commission of the offence and grounds for arrest can be established.[178]

In light of the above, it can be concluded that the rules regulating the issuing of an EAW are not explicitly influenced by the two complications with which EU citizens may be confronted in the EU. No indications exist which show that the German legislator considered either of the two problems when adopting the procedure for the issuing of an EAW. As the decision to issue an EAW and the decision to exercise jurisdiction in a concrete case are closely connected, the next section examines the rules regulating the latter decision, as well. The emphasis is on the question to what extent the public prosecutor has to take the foreseeability of the applicability of the German law and the need for a transparent system for forum decisions in case of conflicts of national jurisdictions into account when making the decision whether or not to prosecute. In other words: to what extent is the exercise of jurisdiction by Germany influenced by the question whether the suspect could have foreseen at the time of the offence that his conduct was punishable under German criminal law, and the need for a transparent EU system for forum choices?

6.4.2 The Rules Regulating the Power to Exercise Jurisdiction

In the German legal order, the *Legalitätsgrundsatz* (principle of mandatory prosecution) applies, which is codified in Article 152 StPO. This principle entails that the public prosecutor's office prosecutes a case and brings it before the court when sufficient factual indications exist.[179] Exceptions to the *Legalitätsgrundsatz* are laid down in Articles 153c and 153f StPO, which reflect the *Opportunitätsprinzip* (principle of opportunity) and provide the public prosecutor with prosecutorial discretion.[180] The next paragraphs will discuss in particular Articles 153c(1)(3) and 153f StPO, since they cover situations in which the criminal case has an extraterritorial dimension. The main question is to what extent the prosecutorial discretion granted by these provisions is demarcated by law and which factors bind

---

176 Sinn and Wörner (2007), p. 212; Sinn and Wörner (2008), pp. 255–256; Böhm (2018b), para 916.

177 Art. 114(1) StPO; Sinn and Wörner (2008), pp. 255–256. In some situations another court is competent. See e.g. Art. 169 StPO.

178 Art. 114(2) (nr. 3 and 4) StPO.

179 Art. 152(2) jo 170(1) StPO.

180 The StPO contains more legal provisions reflecting the *Opportunitätsprinzip*. See e.g. Article 153(1) StPO.

or guide the decision of the public prosecutor as to whether or not to exercise jurisdiction to prosecute. Before discussing these provisions in more detail, it should also be noted that, similar to the Netherlands, the territoriality principle has priority in Germany. Hence, when crimes are committed abroad, it is preferable to have the suspect prosecuted in the state of the *locus delicti* and, therefore, to have the public prosecutor use the discretion in Articles 153c StPO and 153f StPO.[181]

Article 153c(1) StPO allows the public prosecutor to refrain from bringing a case to court when the offence has been committed abroad.[182] This discretion is based on the position that in case of extraterritorial offences certain extrajudicial and political considerations may require the public prosecutor to refrain from prosecution.[183] In addition, it aims to control the workload of the public prosecutors' offices and recognises the often complicated nature of the investigation of extraterritorial crimes, which are also more time-consuming and costly.[184] In relation to the demarcation of the prosecutorial discretion granted by Article 153c(1) StPO it can be concluded that besides the *Richtlinien für das Strafverfahren und das Bußgeldverfahren* (Guidelines for Criminal Procedure and Procedure for Fines, hereafter RistBV) the use of the discretion is not further restricted.[185] These guidelines state that that the public prosecutor needs to consider whether the prosecution would cause unreasonable hardship, whether it serves a public interest, and whether the individual has already been convicted or acquitted for the same offence in another state.[186] In addition, it follows from the legal literature that in case of extraterritorial offences the public prosecutor needs to weigh prosecution interests, such as special and general prevention of crime and equal treatment of suspects against other public interests arguing against prosecution. The latter category covers political and diplomatic relations with other states, which are protected by not interfering with their sovereignty, and the prevention of conflicts of jurisdictions.[187]

The broad scope of the territoriality principle in Articles 3–9 StGB is counterbalanced by Article 153c(3) StPO on the basis of which no prosecution has to be initiated when the criminal act occurred abroad, but its consequences in Germany. This discretion is restricted, however, as it may only be exercised when prosecution interests are overruled by important public interests or when prosecution could cause serious harm to the German state—for instance, to its internal peace and

---

[181] Graf (2012), p. 2590. This also follows from the fact that when the German authorities discover that an individual who is present in Germany is suspected of having committed a crime abroad, they have to notify the competent German authorities, who could inform the foreign authorities and elicit an extradition request. The extradition of the suspect also allows the public prosecutor to drop any charges brought in Germany for the offence in question. See para 35 RiVASt; Van der Beken (1999), pp. 317–318.

[182] Art. 153c(1)(nr.1) StPO; Esser and Fischer (2010), p. 218.

[183] Beulke (2008), para 2; Peters (2016), para 30.

[184] Esser and Fischer (2010), p. 218; Peters (2016), paras 3, 15.

[185] RistBV *Banz.* 245, 22.

[186] Para 94(1) RistBV. See also para 94(2) RistBV; Esser and Fischer (2010), p. 218.

[187] Esser and Fischer (2010), p. 220.

security.[188] Article 153c(3) StPO was adopted to protect political interests in case the offence has both a territorial link to Germany and the requesting state.[189] Similar to Article 153c(1) StPO prosecution interests, such as the prevention of crime or equal treatment of suspects, need to be weighed against other public interests, such as the protection of state secrets which argue against prosecution.[190]

Article 153f StPO covers certain offences in the Code of Crimes against international law (*Völkerstrafgesetzbuch*). When these offences are committed abroad, the public prosecutor may only refrain from prosecution if the accused does not reside in Germany.[191] When the accused is a German national, a decision not to prosecute is only allowed when the offence is prosecuted by an international court of justice, the *locus delicti* or the state of nationality of the victim.[192] The purpose of these additional conditions is to balance the need to avoid impunity for serious crimes with the difficulties to investigate extraterritorial crimes and the risk of a work-overload for the German public prosecutor's offices. The starting point is that Germany prosecutes these crimes when international criminal courts—or more suitable foreign courts with a closer connection to the case in question—are unwilling or unable to prosecute.[193]

In addition to the above, it is important to note that the decision of the public prosecutor on the basis of Article 153c or 153f StPO is only in exceptional cases open to judicial review or appeal.[194] This is, for instance, the case when prosecution is terminated after the main proceedings (*Hauptverfahren*) have already started. The court is then competent to check whether the case indeed falls under Article 153c (1) or (3) StPO.[195] The limited possibility for a judicial check is justified on the basis of the political character of the decision to prosecute and the extrajudicial considerations which often need to be taken into account.[196]

It can be concluded that the foreseeability of the German law at the time of the offence does not seem to play an important role in the context of Articles 153c and 153f StPO. In addition, transparent forum choices in case of conflicts of national jurisdictions do not seem to claim an important role in the German prosecution

---

188 Diemer (2019), paras 14–15.

189 Beulke (2008), para 2; Peters (2016), para 22.

190 Peters (2016), paras 26, 28.

191 Art. 153f(1) StPO.

192 Art. 153f(1) StPO. Further exceptions to the obligation to prosecute can be found in Article 153 (f)(2) StPO.

193 Werle and Jeßberger (2007a), pp. 463, 487; BT Drucksache 14/8524 [37–38].

194 Werle and Jeßberger (2007a), p. 464. Art. 172 StPO allows victims to request the Higher Regional Court to order the public prosecutor to open an investigation, but it explicitly excludes this possibility in relation to decisions taken on the basis of Articles 153c and 153f StPO.

195 Peters (2016), para 8; Beulke (2008), para 30. In relation to Article 153f, the Oberlandesgericht Stuttgart decided that it was only allowed to review whether the public prosecutor had exercised its discretion and whether this has been done in an arbitrary manner OLG Stuttgart 13 September 2005, 5 Ws 109/05 [28].

196 Esser and Fischer (2010), p. 218; Peters (2016), para 10.

policy either. Articles 153c and 153f StPO allow the public prosecutor to refrain from prosecution when Germany would have to exercise extraterritorial jurisdiction. However, the prosecutorial discretion is primarily provided to make room for the protection of political and diplomatic interests and to protect the public prosecutors' office against an unmanageable workload.

6.5 Conclusion

The main question of this chapter is whether the two complications with which EU citizens can be confronted in the context of extradition proceedings are recognised as legal problems or even as legality problems in the German legal order. We have seen in Sect. 6.2 that extradition in case of unforeseeable jurisdiction claims has been recognised as problematic, but not in the context of the substantive legality principle in Article 103(2) GG. Instead, the link between extradition and the foreseeability of specific applicable national criminals laws at the time of the offence has been made in the context of Article 16(2) GG protecting exclusively German nationals. This focus on the German national is also clearly reflected in the conditions for the execution of an extradition request in the IRG. It follows from Sect. 6.3 that several refusal grounds, among which Articles 80 and 83b(1)(a) IRG, integrate the need for protection against the unexpected application of foreign laws correlating from Article 16 GG to some extent in the extradition procedure. In addition, Sect. 6.4 shows that the German rules on the issuing of an EAW and the exercise of jurisdiction to prosecute are not based on or shaped by the difficulties in knowing whose laws to obey in the AFSJ.

With regard to the position of the potential complications arising from the absence of an EU system for forum choices in the context of the extradition procedure, it can be concluded that it is not covered by the right to a lawful judge in Article 101 GG which only applies on the national level. It is, however, interesting to note that even though this constitutional safeguard aims to avoid arbitrary case allocations within Germany, it does not require rigid rules on forum choices. It follows from Sects. 6.3 and 6.4 that the same point of view is taken in relation to conflicts of national jurisdictions and forum choices on the transnational level, since the decision of the German public prosecutor to exercise (extraterritorial) jurisdiction, which can lead to the decision to issue an EAW, is hardly restricted by law. The same is true for the *Bewilligungsverfahren* in which the public prosecutor's power to apply the refusal grounds reflecting conflicts of jurisdictions is hardly demarcated by law to ensure flexibility in solving them. In addition, it also follows from the preparatory work to the IRG, the case law and the legal literature that the decision whether to apply refusal grounds, such as Articles 83b(1)(a) and 80 IRG is strongly coloured by sovereign German interests. In this light, Sect. 6.3 showed that the combination of the duty to prosecute in Article 152 StPO and the possibility to refuse extradition in case of domestic proceedings could even create conflicts of national jurisdictions, which are justified for the purpose of protecting German prosecution interests or German nationals.

It follows from the above that, in general, the protection of German (sovereignty) interests has an important role in the set-up and application of the extradition procedure. The two complications with which all EU citizens can be confronted in the context of the extradition procedure are only to a limited extent recognised. Furthermore, protection against extradition in case these issues occur is primarily offered to German nationals, in particular static German nationals.

References

Afshar F (2015) Der hinreichende Inlandsbezug für § 6 Nr. 5 StGB – Herleitung, Rechtsnatur und Grenzfälle. Onlinezeitschrift für Höchstrichterliche Rechtsprechung zum Strafrecht 8:332

Ambos K (2018) Internationales Strafrecht: Strafanwendungsrecht – Völkerstrafrecht – Europäisches Strafrecht – Rechtshilfe. Beck

Ambos K, Poschadel A (2015) § 73 IRG. In: Ambos K, König S, Rackow P (eds) Rechtshilferecht in Strafsachen. Nomos

Becker U (2010) §16 GG. In: Mangoldt/Klein/Starck Kommentar zum Grundgesetz. Verlag Franz Mahlen

Beulke W (2008) §153c StPO. In: Löwe/Rosenberg Die Strafprozeβordnung und das Gerichtsverfassungsgesetz Groβkommentar. Gruyter

Böhm K (2006) Das neue Europäische Haftbefehlsgesetz. NJW 36:2592

Böhm K (2017) Aktuelle Entwicklungen im Auslieferungsrecht. NStZ 2:77

Böhm K (2018a) Aktuelle Entwicklungen im Auslieferungsrecht. NStZ 4:197

Böhm K (2018b) Das Rechtshilfeverfahren. In: Ahlbrecht H et al (eds) Internationales Strafrecht. Auslieferung – Rechtshilfe – EGMR – internationale Gerichtshöfe. Müller

Böhm K (2021) Aktuelle Entwicklungen im Auslieferungsrecht. NStZ 4:209

Böse M (2012a) § 79 IRG. In: Grützner/Pötz/Kreß Internationaler Rechtshilfeverkehr in Strafsachen. Müller

Böse M (2012b) § 80 IRG. In: Grützner/Pötz/Kreß Internationaler Rechtshilfeverkehr in Strafsachen. Müller

Böse M (2012c) § 81 IRG. In: Grützner/Pötz/Kreß Internationaler Rechtshilfeverkehr in Strafsachen. Müller

Böse M (2012d) § 83b IRG. In: Grützner/Pötz/Kreß Internationaler Rechtshilfeverkehr in Strafsachen. Müller

Böse M (2014) Fundamental rights of the EU-charter. In: Böse M, Meyer F, Schneider A (eds) Conflicts of jurisdiction in criminal matters in the European Union. Volume II: Rights, principles and model rules. Nomos

Classen C (2010) 101 Abs. 1 GG. In: Mangoldt/Klein/Starck Kommentar zum Grundgesetz. Verlag Franz Mahlen

Deen-Racsmany Z (2006) The European Arrest Warrant and the surrender of nationals revisited: the lessons of constitutional challenges. EJCCLCJ 14:271

Diemer H (2019) §153c StPO. In: Hannich R (ed) Karlsruher Kommentar zur Strafprozessordnung mit GVG, EGGVG und EMRK. Beck

Erb V (2016) §12 StPO. In: Löwe/Rosenberg Die Strafprozeβordnung und das Gerichtsverfassungsgesetz Großkkomentar. Gruyter

Eser A (1995) Der "gesetzliche Richter" und seine Bestimmung für den Einzelfall. In: Eser A et al (eds) Straf- und Strafverfahrensrecht, Recht und Verkehr, Recht und Medizin, Festschrift für H. Salger. Carl Heymanns

Eser A (2012) Kritische Würdigung der Modellentwürfe eines Regelungsmechanismus zur Vermeidung von Jurisdiktionskonflikten. In: Sinn A (ed) Jurisdiktionskonflikte bei grenzüberschreitender Kriminalität. Ein Rechtsvergleich zum Internationalen Strafrecht. V&R unipress

Eser A (2014) Schönke/Schröder Strafgesetzbuch Kommentar. Beck

Esser R, Fischer T (2010) Strafvereitelung durch Überstellung von Piraterieverdächtigen an Drittstaaten? Strafrechtliche und strafprozessuale Folgen der EU-Operation Atalanta. JZ 5:217

Fischer T (2017) Strafgesetzbuch mit Nebengesetzen. Beck

Graf J (2012) Strafprozessordnung: Mit Gerichtsverfassungsgesetz und Nebengesetzen Kommentar. Beck

Grützner H (1956) Staatspolitik und Kriminalpolitik im Auslieferungsrecht. ZStW 68:502

Hackner T (2007) Probleme der Umsetzung des Rahmenbeschlusses über den Europäischen Haftbefehl in Deutschland. In: Lagodny O, Wiederin E, Winkler R (eds) Probleme des Rahmenbeschlusses am Beispiel des Europäischen Haftbefehls. NWV Verlag

Hecker B (2015) Europäisches Strafrecht. Springer

Kubiciel M (2015) §3 IRG. In: Ambos K, König S, Rackow P (eds) Rechtshilferecht in Strafsachen. Nomos

Lagodny O (1989) Grundkonstellationen des internationalen Strafrechts. Zugleich ein Rückblick auf das internationale Kolloquium über "International Cooperation in Criminal Matters" an der Harvard Law School. ZStW 101:987

Lagodny O (2001) Empfiehlt es sich, eine europäische Gerichtskompetenz für Strafgewaltskonflikte vorzusehen? Gutachten im Auftrag des Bundesministeriums der Justiz

Lagodny O (2012) § 3 IRG. In: Schomburg/Lagodny/Gleß/Hackner Internationale Rechtshilfe in Strafsachen. Beck

Luchtman M (2013) Choice of forum and the prosecution of cross-border crime in the European Union – what role for the legality principle? In: Luchtman M (ed) Choice of forum in cooperation against EU financial crime. Freedom, security and justice and the protection of specific EU-interests. Eleven International Publishing

Luchtman M (2017) Transnationale rechtshandhaving: Over fundamentele rechten in de Europese strafrechtelijke samenwerking, Boom

Meyer F (2013) Country report Germany. In: Böse M, Meyer F, Schneider A (eds) Conflicts of jurisdiction in criminal matters in the European Union. Volume I: National reports and comparative analysis. Nomos

Meyer F (2015) § 81 IRG. In: Ambos K, König S, Rackow P (eds) Rechtshilferecht in Strafsachen. Nomos

Meyer F, Böse M (2011) Die Beschränkung nationaler Strafgewalten als Möglichkeit zur Vermeidung von Jurisdiktionskonflikten in der Europäischen Union. ZIS 6:336

Oehler D (1970) Theorie des Strafanwendungsrechts. In: Oehler D, Pötz P-G (eds) Aktuelle Probleme des Internationalen Strafrechts. Heinrich Grützner zum 65. Geburtstag. Decker's Verlag

Oehler D (1983) Internationales Strafrecht: Geltungsbereich des Strafrechts, internationales Rechtshilferecht, Recht der Gemeinschaften, Völkerstrafrecht. Heymanns

Pappas C (1996) Stellvertretende Strafrechtspflege. Zugleich ein Beitrag zur Ausdehnung deutscher Strafgewalt nach § 7 As. 2 Nr. 2 StGB. Max-Planck-Institut für ausländisches und internationales Strafrecht

Peers S (2004) Mutual recognition and criminal law in the European Union: has the council got it wrong? Common Mark Law Rev 41:5

Peters S (2016) §153c StPO. In: Knauer C et al (eds) Münchener Kommentar zur StPO. Beck

Remmert B (2020) Art. 103 Abs. 2. In: Maunz/Dürig Kommentar Grundgesetz, 92nd edn

Schmitt B (2017) Vor § 7. In: Meyer-Goβner L, Schmitt B (eds) Strafprozessordnung, Gerichtsverfassungsgesetz, Nebengesetze und ergänzende Bestimmungen. Beck

Scholten H-J (1995) Das Erfordernis der Tatortstrafbarkeit in § 7 StGB. Ein Beitrag zur identischen Norm im transnationalen Strafrecht. Max-Planck-Institut für ausländisches und internationales Strafrecht

Schomburg W (2012) § 83b IRG. In: Schomburg/Lagodny/Gleß/Hackner Internationale Rechtshilfe in Strafsachen. Beck

Schomburg W, Hackner T (2012) § 74 IRG. In: Schomburg/Lagodny/Gleß/Hackner Internationale Rechtshilfe in Strafsachen. Beck

Schulze-Fielitz H (2008a) Art. 101. In: Dreier Grundgesetz Kommentar. Mohr Siebeck

Schulze-Fielitz H (2008b) Art. 103 II. In: Dreier Grundgesetz Kommentar. Mohr Siebeck

Schünemann B (2003) Europäischer Haftbefehl und EU-Verfassungsentwurf auf schiefer Ebene. Die Schranken des Grundgesetzes. Zeitschrift für Rechtspolitik 6:185

Sinn A, Wörner L (2008) Country report: Germany. In: Górski A, Hofmanski P (eds) The European Arrest Warrant and its implementation in the Member States of the European Union. Beck

Sinn A, Wörner S (2007) The European Arrest Warrant and its implementation in Germany – its constitutionality, laws and current developments. ZIS 5:204

Swart B (1983) Goede Rechtsbedeling en Internationale Rechtshulp in Strafzaken. Kluwer

Thorhauer N (2019) Jurisdiktionskonflikte im Rahmen transnationaler Kriminalität. Zur Koordination der Strafgewalten über natürliche Personen und Unternehmen in der Europäischen Union. Dike Verlag and Nomos

Tinkl C (2010) Die Ungleichbehandlung eigener und fremde Staatsbürger im deutschen Auslieferungsrecht. Verstoβ gegen das europäische Diskriminierungsverbot und gegen das grundgesetzliche Bestimmtheitsgebot. ZIS 4:320

Trüg G, Ulrich A (2019) Auf der Suche nach der verlorenen Kompetenz – Der Erlass Europäischer Haftbefehle. NJW 39:2811

Van der Beken T (1999) Forumkeuze in het internationaal strafrecht. Maklu

Vogel J (2005) Europäische Haftbefehl und deutsches Verfassungsrecht. JZ 17(801):805

Von Bubnoff E (2005) Der Europäische Haftbefehl, Auslieferung und Neuerungen des Gemeinschaftsinstruments. Ein Leitfaden für die Praxis. Muller

Wasmeier M (2006) Der Europäische Haftbefehl vor dem Bundesverfassungsgericht – Zur Verzahnung des nationalen und europäischen Strafrechts. ZEuS 9:23

Werle G, Jeßberger F (2007a) Vor par. 3 StGB. In: Laufhütte H, Saan R R-v, Tiedemann K (eds) Strafgesetzbuch, Leipziger Kommentar. De Gruyter

Werle G, Jeßberger F (2007b) par. 5 StGB. In: Laufhütte H, Saan R R-v, Tiedemann K (eds) Strafgesetzbuch, Leipziger Kommentar. De Gruyter

Werle G, Jeßberger F (2007c) par. 7 StGB. In: Laufhütte H, Saan R R-v, Tiedemann K (eds) Strafgesetzbuch, Leipziger Kommentar. De Gruyter

Wolswijk H (1998) Locus delicti en rechtsmacht. Gouda Quint

Wörner L, Wörner M (2012) Deutschland. In: Sinn A (ed) Jurisdiktionskonflikte bei grenzüberschreitender Kriminalität. Ein Rechtsvergleich zum Internationalen Strafrecht. V&R unipress

Zimmerman T (2017) Der Fall “Pisciotti” vor dem EuGH. ZIS 4:220

Chapter 7
The Legal Order of England and Wales: The Views on the Two Complications and Their Link to the EAW

7.1 Introduction

Like the previous two chapters on the Dutch and German legal order, this chapter examines to what extent the two complications with which EU citizens can be confronted in the context of the EAW procedure are recognised as legal problems or even as legality problems in the combined legal order of England and Wales. These two complications are the fact that in the AFSJ an EU citizen can be surrendered for the purpose of prosecution while the applicability of the national criminal law of the prosecuting state was not foreseeable at the time of the offence and the fact that surrender occurs without a complementary and transparent system of forum choices in case of conflicts of national jurisdictions. As explained in Chap. 1, an examination of the views on these complications in the English and Welsh legal order, hereafter referred to as England,[1] remains important, despite Brexit.[2] This is because the purpose of the chapters on the national legal orders is to illustrate how the two complications and their connection to the EAW are perceived on the national level which is an integral part of the overall EU legal order. In this light, an examination of the English legal order is important, since it has a long history of applying the EAW, was one of the few common law systems in the EU and in comparison to Germany represents the other side of the spectrum with regard to the recognition of an inextricable link between the state and its nationals.

To answer the main question of this chapter, Sect. 7.2 first examines to what extent the (pre-Brexit) influence of the EAW on the two complications was considered problematic in light of the equivalents in English (constitutional) law of the

[1] Any reference to England also includes Wales, unless stated otherwise.

[2] Agreement on the withdrawal of the United Kingdom of Great Britain and Northern Ireland from the European Union and the European Atomic Energy Community [2019] OJ C384I/1 (UK Withdrawal Agreement). For the current surrender procedure between the UK and the EU see Articles 76–112 of the EU-UK Trade and Cooperation Agreement [2020] OJ L444/14.

J. Graat, *The European Arrest Warrant and EU Citizenship*,
https://doi.org/10.1007/978-3-031-07590-2_7

nullum crimen sine lege principle in Article 49 CFR and the right to a tribunal established by law in Article 47 CFR. Hence, this section explores the possible triangular link between these fundamental rights, the EAW and the problems relating to jurisdiction and forum choices. For instance, was the issuing or execution of an EAW in case the two problems occurred viewed as a violation of one of these rights or was the surrender procedure perhaps perceived as a mechanism which could contribute to or enforce violations of these fundamental rights? Another option is that the possible triangular link has not been considered at all.

Sections 7.3 and 7.4 then discuss the EAW procedure as it was applicable in the English legal order before Brexit and examine to what extent the two complications played a role in the issuing and execution of EAWs. More specifically, Sect. 7.3 explains to what extent the conditions for the execution of an EAW intended to offer protection against the two complications. Section 7.4 conducts the same exercise for the rules regulating the issuing procedure. In light of the link between the issuing of an EAW and the decision to prosecute a case, the English rules on the exercise of jurisdiction are also discussed.

In relation to both Sects. 7.3 and 7.4, it is important to note that the EU-UK Trade and Cooperation Agreement 2020 regulates the surrender procedure between the EU and the UK since January 2021.[3] The rules on surrender following from the Agreement have been implemented in the Extradition Act 2003 of which Part 1, more specifically Sections 1–68, used to regulate the EAW procedure.[4] As most of this chapter was written before January 2021, it is primarily written in the present tense. However, it solely focuses on the EAW procedure as it used to be applicable in England and Wales before January 2021.[5] Furthermore, similar to the German legislator, the English legislator did not adopt most of the terminology of the FDEAW. The Extradition Act referred to 'extradition' instead of 'surrender' and to 'Part 1 warrants' from so-called 'Category 1 territories', which were incoming EAWs and 'Part 3 warrants', which were outgoing EAWs.[6] Category 1 territories are the EU Member States, Gibraltar, Norway and Iceland.[7] To avoid confusion, any reference to the Extradition Act and the extradition procedure in this chapter means the surrender procedure as regulated before Brexit, unless the text explicitly states otherwise. This chapter ends with a conclusion in Sect. 7.5.

[3] European Union (Future Relationship) Act 2020. It received royal assent on 31 December 2020. On the differences with the EAW see Wahl (2021).

[4] Extradition Act 2003 (Commencement and Savings) Order 2003, SI 2003/3103. The Extradition Act applies to all parts of the UK, subject to the exceptions in s 226 EA.

[5] The FDEAW still applies when an EAW was received before 1 January 2021 and the requested person was arrested before that date as well. Art. 62(1)(b) UK Withdrawal Agreement.

[6] Part 2 warrants are extradition requests from non-EU Member States with whom the UK has an extradition treaty.

[7] Extradition Act 2003 (Designation of Part I Territories) Order 2003, SI 2003/3333 as amended. See also Extradition Act 2003 (Amendments to Designations) Order 2020, SI 2020/265 which designates Norway and Iceland as Category 1 territories.

7.2 Protection Offered by Fundamental Rights and Principles

7.2.1 The Substantive Legality Principle

It was only with the adoption of the Human Rights Act 1998 (HRA) that the substantive legality principle was codified in the English legal order. The Human Rights Act makes Article 7 ECHR as well as other Convention rights and principles directly applicable.[8] English courts need to take the case law of the ECtHR into account when applying national law and legislation needs to be interpreted as far as possible in conformity with the ECHR.[9] However, the content and ratio of Article 7 ECHR were already recognised and applied in the national case law before the adoption of the HRA 1998, although not necessarily under the heading of the substantive legality principle or *nullum crimen sine lege* principle.[10] The same goes for the more specific right to an accessible and foreseeable law for criminal offences and sanctions, which was often linked to the principle of the rule of law and legal certainty.[11] In addition to the case law, the literature also frequently refers to the substantive legality principle in terms of 'the rule of law'. The latter requires that the law does not surprise or ambush individuals. Rather, the law should guide behaviour in order to avoid criminal liability and enable individuals to foresee the legal consequences of their conduct.[12] The rule of law is based on the principle of autonomy, which entails that a conviction is only fair when an individual has been informed of the criminality of his conduct by the law.[13]

As stated above, as a result of the Human Rights Act the sub-principles of Article 7 ECHR, including the right to an accessible and foreseeable law for offences and sanctions, are an integral part of the English legal order. As England is a common law jurisdiction, the concept of law in principle covers both offences recognised in the case law, also referred to as common law offences, and offences

[8] Ormerod et al. (2018), para A7.1.

[9] Human Rights Act 1998, ss 2–3. However, legislation that is considered incompatible with the Convention is not automatically invalid. In addition, s 6 HRA states that public authorities are not allowed to violate a Convention right.

[10] *R v Misra* [2004] EWCA Crim 2375, [2005] 1 Cr App R 21 [29]–[37] with references to further case law. This case was also referred to by Lord Bingham and Lord Rodger in *R v Rimmington* [2005] UKHL 63, [2006] 1 AC 459, 480–482, 489. See also Allgemeine Lehren des Strafrechts—Gesetzlichkeitsprinzip England und Wales (Max-Planck- Informationssystem für Strafrechtsvergleichung 2008) <http://infocrim.org/#!/reports?r=(eaw:II.A.1:de)&a=0> accessed 20 September 2021.

[11] *R v Misra* [2004] EWCA Crim 2375, [2005] 1 Cr App R 21 [37]; *Fothergill v Monarch Airlines Ltd*[1981] AC 251(HL) 279.

[12] Including for further references see Ashworth and Horder (2013), p. 56.

[13] Ashworth and Horder (2013), p. 56.

in statutes adopted by Parliament.[14] From the perspective of criminal law as a social defence mechanism, courts have in the past identified new criminal offences and punished individuals for these crimes.[15] This development of common law offences is restricted by the concept of precedent or *stare decisis*, which means that the lower courts are bound by the rulings of the higher courts and the latter are bound by their own decisions.[16] In the *Knuller* case, the competence of the courts to identify criminal offences was, however, considered to be a contradiction of democratic principles and therefore abolished.[17] Hence, since then, Parliament has in principle the exclusive competence to create new criminal offences.[18] However, within the parameters set by the case law of the ECtHR concerning Article 7 ECHR, courts are still allowed to develop common law offences in conformity with social changes.[19]

The law also needs to meet the quality requirements of accessibility and foreseeability. The former requires that an individual is provided 'with an indication that is adequate in the circumstances of the legal rules applicable to a given case'.[20] The latter requires that the law is sufficiently clear, which is ensured when citizens are able to know on the basis of the wording of the legal provision and, if necessary with the assistance of the courts' interpretation, for which acts or omissions they could be held criminally liable and what sanction could be imposed.[21] In the *Rimmington* case, these quality requirements were considered in relation to the crime of causing a public nuisance.[22] Lord Bingham stated that the existing common law principles set

[14]ECtHR 26 April 1979, 6538/74 (*Sunday Times/United Kingdom*) 47; Allgemeine Lehren des Strafrechts—Gesetzlichkeitsprinzip England und Wales (Max-Planck- Informationssystem für Strafrechtsvergleichung 2008) <http://infocrim.org/#!/reports?r=(eaw:II.A.3:de)&a=0> accessed 20 September 2021.

[15]*Shaw v DPP* [1962] AC 220 (HL) 268.

[16]For exceptions to the rule of judicial precedent, see e.g. the Practice Statement (Judicial Precedent) [1966] 3 All ER 77 (HL); *Willers v Joyce*[2016] UKSC 44, [2018] AC 843 [7].

[17]*R v Knuller Ltd*[1973] AC 435 (HL) 457–458; *R v Jones* [2006] UKHL 16, [2007] 1 AC 136 [28]–[29], [60].

[18]In addition, as a result of Parliamentary sovereignty, the common law rules may be changed by statute. Over the past decades, most common law offences have also been codified, but several important general legal principles determining criminal liability, such as certain defences are still regulated by common law. Allgemeine Lehren des Strafrechts—Gesetzlichkeitsprinzip England und Wales (Max-Planck- Informationssystem für Strafrechtsvergleichung 2008) <http://infocrim.org/#!/reports?r=(eaw:II.A.1:de)&a=0> accessed 20 September 2021.

[19]ECtHR 22 November 1995, 20166/92 (*SW/United Kingdom*) 34–47; ECtHR 22 November 1995, 20190/92 (*CR/United Kingdom*) 32–44. See also *Norris v USA* [2008] UKHL 16, [2008] 1 AC 920 [52]–[62].

[20]ECtHR 26 April 1979, 6538/74 (*Sunday Times/United Kingdom*) 49.

[21]ECtHR 11 November 1996, 17862/91 (*Cantoni/France*) 29; ECtHR 19 March 2006, 67335/01 (*Achour/France*) 41; ECtHR 25 May 1993, 14307/88 (*Kokkinakis/Greece*) 52.

[22]Lord Bingham in *R v Rimmington* [2005] UKHL 63, [2006] 1 AC 459, 482. Lord Rodger also applied Article 7 ECHR, but came to the conclusion that there was no violation. See also *R v Muhamad* [2002] EWCA Crim 1856, [2003] QB 1031, 1038–1039.

the same clarity and foreseeability requirements as Article 7 ECHR.[23] These common law principles are that 'no one should be punished under a law unless it is sufficiently clear and certain to enable him to know what conduct is forbidden before he does it; and no one should be punished for any act which was not clearly and ascertainably punishable when the act was done'.[24]

The quality requirements contribute to the prevention of the retroactive application of the law and extensive interpretations to the detriment of the accused, which are both sub-principles of the substantive legality principle.[25] The former prohibition entails that an individual may only be convicted for conduct that constitutes a criminal offence according to national or international law at the time it occurred.[26] The prohibition's rationale is linked to the concept of autonomous individuals and the rule of law requiring that an individual is able to rely on the law when shaping his or her life.[27] However, as stated above, the ECtHR has provided the national courts with some discretion in interpreting existing criminal offences in conformity with social developments if the interpretation is reasonably foreseeable.[28] In addition, the English case law has introduced the so-called 'thin-ice principle' which entails that in cases in which behaviour is clearly on the borderline of illegality, citizens should not be surprised if the law is interpreted in a way which pulls the conduct in question within its scope.[29] An extensive application of this thin-ice principle may, however, result in new criminal offences which were difficult to foresee at the time of their occurrence. In addition, an extensive application could clash with the prohibition of extensive interpretations of criminal offences law to the detriment of an accused.[30]

---

[23] This position was adopted by Lord Bingham and Lord Rodger in *R v Rimmington* [2005] UKHL 63, [2006] 1 AC 459, 482, 489.

[24] *R v Rimmington* [2005] UKHL 63, [2006] 1 AC 459, 482. Some authors have argued that only the second principle expresses the substantive legality principle whereas the first one covers the principle of fair warning and predictability. Both fall under the overarching principle of the rule of law, but the legality principle demands that criminal liability is determined by a rule of law and not a rule of officials. The fair waning principle has a different dimension as it requires that the legal rules offer individuals guidance in determining their actions. Other authors predominantly consider predictability and the fair warning function of the law part of the legality principle. Chan and Simester (2011), pp. 388–389; Ashworth and Horder (2013), pp. 63–65.

[25] ECtHR 25 May 1993, 14307/88 (*Kokkinakis/Greece*) 52.

[26] *R v Brown* [1994] 1 AC 212 (HL) 272. In relation to the application of the *lex mitior* rule as explained by the ECtHR see e.g. *R v Docherty* [2016] UKSC 62, [2017] 1 WLR 181.

[27] Ashworth and Horder (2013), p. 57.

[28] ECtHR 22 November 1995, 20166/92 (*SW/United Kingdom*) 36. See also *R v Rimmington* [2005] UKHL 63, [2006] 1 AC 459, 482.

[29] *R v Knuller Ltd*[1973] AC 435 (HL) 463; Ashworth and Horder (2013), p. 62; Chan and Simester (2011), p. 389.

[30] ECtHR 25 May 1993, 14307/88 (*Kokkinakis/Greece*) 52. Referred to in *R v Rimmington* [2005] UKHL 63, [2006] 1 AC 459, 483; Ashworth and Horder (2013), p. 62.

7.2.2 *The EAW: Outside the Scope of the Substantive Legality Principle?*

It is not completely clear to what extent the legality principle in fact applies to the extradition procedure.[31] Only some legal scholars have argued that in England the presumption could be that the substantive legality principle is also applicable to extradition procedures, including the EAW procedure.[32] This follows from the fact that the execution of an incoming extradition request from an EU Member State (incoming request) depends on the question whether the conduct constituted a criminal offence at the time of its commission according to both the law of the requesting state and English law.[33] This differs from the double criminality requirement in the German and Dutch legal order, where it is sufficient that the conduct constitutes a criminal act at the time of the offence, according to the law of the issuing state.

The English interpretation of the double criminality requirement follows from the *Pinochet* case decided by the House of Lords and has been consistently applied ever since. In *Pinochet*, Lord Browne-Wilkinson—with whom the other Lords agreed—stated that the provisions regulating the double criminality principle in the Extradition Act 1989 referred to the date at which the conduct occurred. This grammatical interpretation was complemented by the fact that the travaux prėparatoires for the European Extradition Convention and the departmental papers leading to the Extradition Act of 1989 did not mention the relevant date, nor did they disclose a discussion on replacing the date at which the conduct occurred with the date of the request for extradition. Lord Browne-Wilkinson concluded that it is unlikely that Parliament would make such a change without an investigation or a strong incentive.[34]

Lord Browne-Wilkinson did not refer to the substantive legality principle in his reasoning. However, in the legal literature, the point has been made that the interpretation of the double criminality requirement contributes to the warning function of substantive criminal law, inherent to the *nullum crimen sine lege* principle. Legal scholars have also criticised this interpretation from the perspective of the substantive legality principle, because they are of the opinion that this principle merely requires that the conduct was criminal at the time of its commission according to the law of the requesting state, which is the state that actually intends to prosecute and whose criminal law will apply.[35]

---

[31] On this discussion see Arnell (2018), p. 268; Arnell and Davies (2020).

[32] Van Sliedregt (2009), pp. 53–54.

[33] *Dabas v Spain* [2007] UKHL 6, [2007] 2 AC 31, 35; Jones and Doobay (2005), p. 140. The same interpretation was followed under the former Extradition Act of 1989. See *R v Metropolitan Stipendiary Magistrate, ex p Pinochet (No 3)* [2000] 1 AC 147 (HL) 195–196. For the other Lords see [2000] 1 AC 147 (HL) 198 and 230, 249, 265, 268, 279.

[34] *R v Metropolitan Stipendiary Magistrate, ex p Pinochet (No 3)* [2000] 1 AC 147 (HL) 193–196.

[35] Warbrick and McGoldrick (1999), p. 964; O'Keefe (2009), p. 11.

It can be concluded that it is not unambiguously established that the execution of an EAW in itself constitutes a violation of the *nullum crimen sine lege* principle as applicable in the English legal order when the applicability of the law of the issuing state was difficult to foresee at the time of the offence. Similar to the previous two chapters on the Dutch and German legal order, the next sections therefore discuss to what extent compliance with the substantive legality principle depends on the foreseeability of the applicability of a specific national criminal law at the time of the offence. In other words, these sections explore to what extent the accessibility and foreseeability of criminal offences and sanctions depends on the foreseeability of the applicability of the specific national criminal law to which these offences and sanctions belong. The consequences of the outcome of this examination for the extradition procedure are discussed afterwards. For example, in case it can be concluded that compliance with the *nullum crimen sine lege* principle requires that the law of a particular state was foreseeable at the time of the offence, the follow-up question could be whether this also means that the EAW is generally viewed as a mechanism which could transfer citizens to a state whose jurisdiction claim is not in compliance with this principle? In other words, is the EAW perceived as a procedure which could contribute to violations of the English substantive legality principle by extraditing a person to the state where the violation occurs?

7.2.3 *The Substantive Legality Principle and Rules of Jurisdiction*

7.2.3.1 Rules on the (Extra)territorial Scope of English Criminal Law: All Crime Is Local!

Unlike the Netherlands and Germany, England does not have a criminal code or statute in which it generally regulates the ambit of English criminal law. The general rule is that English criminal law applies to the realm of England and Wales and those present within that realm.[36] This also means that officially neither common law offences nor statutes have an extraterritorial ambit. However, parliamentary sovereignty allows Parliament to adopt specific statutory provisions establishing extraterritorial jurisdiction over certain offences.[37]

Whenever Parliament decides to use this power, it is the custom to exclusively extend the ambit of English criminal law on the basis of the active nationality

[36] *Macleod v AG for New South Wales* [1891] UKPC 31, [1891] AC 455, 458; *Cox v Army Council* [1963] AC 48 (HL) 67; *Treacy v DPP* [1971] AC 537 (HL) 552; Hirst (2003), p. 3. For rules on immunity, see Ormerod et al. (2018), para A8.25.

[37] *Treacy v DPP* [1971] AC 537 (HL) 552; Ormerod et al. (2018), paras A8.1–A8.2; Hirst (2003), p. 3.

principle and sometimes the domicile principle.[38] Except for exceptional cases, a strong presumption exists that no jurisdiction is established over offences committed by foreigners while abroad.[39] Exceptional circumstances could arise in case consensus exists among states that universal jurisdiction may be exercised over certain serious crimes or in case of treaty or international obligations.[40] The latter was also the reason to establish jurisdiction on the basis of the passive nationality principle over certain terrorism offences, even though this ground for extraterritorial jurisdiction is not commonly accepted in England.[41]

As extraterritorial jurisdiction constitutes a deviation from the general rule of territoriality, the statutory provisions need to reveal Parliament's intention to establish extraterritorial jurisdiction in unambiguous and express terms.[42] As Lord Diplock stated in *Air-India*, the statute should be 'so clear and specific as to be incapable of any other meaning'.[43] Over the decades Parliament has often used this competence, which has resulted in a complex patchwork of statutory provisions, which in itself threatens the legal certainty of citizens.[44] Furthermore, as discussed later on, the case law shows a broad interpretation of when an offence is considered to have occurred within the English realm.

It follows from the above that whether certain behaviour constitutes a criminal offence under English law depends on whether it occurred on English territory or the existence of a clear legal basis providing an offence with an extraterritorial scope.[45] As argued by Hirst, jurisdiction therefore seems determinative for the criminality of particular behaviour.[46] However, subsections (b) and (c) explain that the link between the criminality of conduct and the applicability of English law is not explicitly based on the substantive legality principle and the conviction that individuals should be able to foresee at the time of the offence which specific criminal law is applicable to them. However, a discussion on the foreseeability of English law is not completely absent. Subsection (d) will set out the discussion in the legal literature in which the double criminality requirement has been described as a safeguard against unwanted or unexpected prosecutions in cases with a foreign element.

---

[38] Klip and Massa (2010), pp. 57, 70; Van der Beken (1999), p. 97; Ormerod et al. (2018), para A8.20; Hirst (2013), pp. 42–43. See also *Halsbury's Laws* (5th edn, 2018) vol 61, para 215.

[39] *Air India v Wiggins*[1980] 2 All ER 593 (HL) 596.

[40] Ormerod et al. (2018), para A8.20.

[41] The Crime (International Cooperation) Act 2003 implements jurisdiction rules following from the Framework Decision on Combating Terrorism and establishes jurisdiction on the basis of the passive personality principle over terrorism offences. *Halsbury's Laws* (5th edn, 2018) vol 61, para 218.

[42] *Air India v Wiggins*[1980] 2 All ER 593 (HL) 596; *Treacy v DPP* [1971] AC 537 (HL) 552.

[43] *Air India v Wiggins*[1980] 2 All ER 593 (HL) 596.

[44] Hirst (2013), p. 27; Hirst (2003), p. 5.

[45] See also *R v Abu Hamza* [2006] EWCA Crim 2918, [2007] QB 659 [28ff].

[46] Hirst (2013), p. 27. See also Ormerod et al. (2018), para. A8.1.

7.2.3.2 The Influence of the Rules of Venue on the Ambit of English Criminal Law

Before elaborating on this influence, it is important to understand the difference between rules of venue, which are procedural in nature, and the rules regulating the ambit of English criminal law, which are part of substantive criminal law.[47] The rules of venue are concerned with the jurisdiction to adjudicate and cover the competence of a certain court to try a particular case.[48] In England, courts often have almost unlimited territorial competence.[49] According to Section 46(2) Senior Courts Act 1981, 'The jurisdiction of the Crown Court with respect to proceedings on indictment shall include jurisdiction in proceedings on indictment for offences wherever committed, and in particular proceedings on indictment for offences within the jurisdiction of the Admiralty of England.' Magistrates' courts have similar broad competences.[50] The reason why a particular case cannot be tried before the court in England is, therefore, often not a lack of jurisdiction to adjudicate, but the fact that the conduct is not a criminal act or omission under English law. In other words, the conduct does not fall within the ambit of English criminal law. To illustrate this, in *Treacy* the appellant sent a blackmail letter from England to a victim living in Frankfurt. Lord Diplock clarified that the question whether the demand was made in the UK or Germany was not one of venue, and therefore not whether the English criminal courts had jurisdiction to adjudicate. Instead, the place where the demand was made determined whether the facts constituted a criminal offence under English law or not.[51] Hence, the decision in *Treacy* relates to the second form of jurisdiction, the rules on the ambit of English criminal law.

Even though the rules on the ambit of English law and the rules of venue constitute two sets of rules, the latter have strongly influenced the former. The general rule that all crime is local primarily correlates from the ancient common law rules of venue, which are procedural in nature and connected to the development of the jury-trial. In medieval England, offences had to be tried by a jury made up of residents of the country in which the conduct had occurred.[52] These residents were assumed to have local knowledge of the acts which occurred in their county and were assumed not to possess knowledge of conduct which occurred in another county.[53] In light of the fact that actions should be tried in the country where they had

---

[47] *R v Smith*[2004] EWCA Crim 631, [2004] QB 1418, 1438.

[48] Farmer (2013), p. 230.

[49] Ormerod (2018), para A8.1; Hirst (2013), p. 27.

[50] Magistrates' Courts Act 1980, s 2(1).

[51] *Treacy v DPP* [1971] AC 537 (HL) 559. Following case law refers interchangeably to the criminality of certain behaviour according to English law and the jurisdiction of English courts. See e.g. *Doot*, in which the Lords sometimes question of whether the behaviour constitutes a conspiracy and sometimes whether this case can be tried in English courts. *DPP v Doot* [1973] AC 807 (HL).

[52] *Treacy v DPP* [1971] AC 537 (HL) 559; Hirst (2003), p. 30.

[53] Lew (1987), p. 168; Hirst (2003), pp. 32–33.

occurred, it was considered illogical to criminalise conduct that occurred outside a county, or even in another state.[54] So, the strict doctrine on venue created or largely contributed to the primacy of the territoriality principle in determining the ambit of English criminal law.[55]

Not surprisingly, the strict rules on venue resulted in difficulties when, for instance, the conduct and consequences occurred in different places. These were solved by the adoption of statutes which allowed a murder trial to be held in the place where the consequences of the conduct—meaning the death of the victim—occurred.[56] However, the slow abolition of the strict venue doctrine by different statutory exceptions and its further abrogation by the Courts Act 1971[57] was not accompanied by the abrogation of the strict adherence to the territoriality principle.[58] Even though numerous statutory provisions establish extraterritorial jurisdiction over certain offences, the initial presumption is still that English criminal law does not apply to offences committed abroad.[59] In parliamentary discussions, the establishment of extraterritorial jurisdiction is also still referred to as a major step or exceptional measure.[60]

The case law and literature provide several explanations for the survival of the reticent approach towards extraterritorial jurisdiction, in the sense that despite the numerous statutory exceptions, Parliament has not created a more generalised doctrine of extraterritorial jurisdiction. Firstly, the law of nations and principle of territorial sovereignty is often named in the sense that offences committed on the territory of a particular state are primarily the concern of that state.[61] In this light, Lord Russell stated in *Jameson* that the rule that all crime is local is 'based on international law by which one sovereign power is bound to respect the subjects and the rights of all other sovereign powers outside its own territory'.[62] The sovereignty of states and international relations with other states is also the reason why certain limitations are included in statutory provisions establishing universal jurisdictions.

[54] *R v Page* [1954] 1 QB 170 (CA) 175; Hirst (2003), pp. 32–33; Hirst (2013), p. 29.

[55] Hirst (2013), p. 49.

[56] Lew (1978), p. 233; Hirst (2003), p. 31.

[57] This Act provided the Crown Court with jurisdiction over indictable offences committed anywhere.

[58] Hirst (2003), p. 34.

[59] Hirst (2013), p. 49.

[60] HC Deb 1 July 2008, vol 478 (W); Counter-Terrorism and Border Security Bill Deb 3 July 2018, col 100.

[61] *Macleod v AG for New South Wales* [1891] UKPC 31, [1891] AC 455, 458; *R v Page* [1954] 1 QB 170 (CA) 175; *Treacy v DPP* [1971] AC 537 (HL) 561, 564. See also Mulan (1997), p. 28; Hirst (2003), pp. 11, 34–35, 43, 56. See also Allgemeine Lehren des Strafrechts—Internationaler Geltungsbereich des Strafrechts England und Wales (Max-Planck- Informationssystem für Strafrechtsvergleichung 2008) <http://infocrim.org/#!/reports?r=(eaw:II.B.1:de)&a=0> accessed 20 September 2021; Marshall (2004), p. 355.

[62] *The Queen v Jameson*[1896] 2 QB 425 (QB) 430.

The ICC Act constitutes such an example, as it extends criminal jurisdiction to residents of the UK, but excludes short-term visitors.[63]

Secondly, practical considerations play an important role. Even though the rules on the admissibility of foreign evidence have been relaxed and accessibility to foreign evidence, including witnesses abroad, has improved, prosecuting a case on the basis of extraterritorial jurisdiction is more difficult and costly.[64] In this light, the decision of the English legislator to deviate from the exclusive application of the territoriality principle often also seems to be the outcome of a balancing act, primarily between the practical difficulties in prosecuting extraterritorial offences and policy considerations in favour of extending the ambit of English criminal law.[65] Convincing reasons for extending extraterritorial jurisdiction are the increase of cross-frontier criminality, EU or international treaty obligations and threats to national security.[66]

7.2.3.3 A Flexible Interpretation of the Territoriality Principle: Terminatory and Inclusive Approach

The fact that the link between jurisdiction and the criminal offence is not based on the right to an accessible and foreseeable law correlating from the *nullum crimen sine lege* principle is also illustrated by the case law showing a flexible interpretation of the territoriality principle. In this light, the terminatory interpretation is the oldest one and establishes territorial jurisdiction when the crime is completed in England, meaning that the last constituent element of the crime occurred on English territory.[67] In case of conduct-offences, the crime is completed in England when the criminal conduct occurred in England, regardless of where the consequences occurred.[68] In case of result-offences, jurisdiction is established when the specified result occurs in England, regardless of where the conduct leading to the results occurred.[69] This terminatory approach has in the past resulted in unwanted situations in which the case could not be prosecuted due to a lack of jurisdiction.[70] The development and increase of cross-frontier crimes, including cross-frontier fraud

---

[63] Williams (2012), p. 375.

[64] Mulan (1997), p. 28; *Halsbury's Laws* (5th edn, 2018) vol 61, para 210; Farmer (2013), pp. 232–233; Hirst (2003), pp. 55–56; Klip and Massa (2010), pp. 70–71.

[65] See e.g. HC Written Statement on Arrest Warrants—Universal Jurisdiction 22 July 2010, vol 514 <https://hansard.parliament.uk/commons/2010-07-22/debates/10072238000038/ArrestWarrants%E2%80%94UniversalJurisdiction> accessed 20 September 2021; HC Deb 2 February 1996, vol 270, cols 1249–1250.

[66] Farmer (2013), p. 236; Lew (1978), pp. 180–181; Hirst (2003), pp. 28–29, 41; Klip and Massa (2010), p. 56.

[67] *R v Smith*[2004] EWCA Crim 631, [2004] QB 1418, 1432; Lew (1978), p. 170.

[68] *Treacy v DPP* [1971] AC 537 (HL); Ormerod et al. (2018), para. A8.5.

[69] *R v Smith*[2004] EWCA Crim 631, [2004] QB 1418, 1432.

[70] *R v Smith*[2004] EWCA Crim 631, [2004] QB 1418, 1432; Lew (1978), p. 170.

offences, forced the English courts into the often difficult exercise of determining where the offence was completed.[71] Consequently, the inclusive approach was developed as an alternative to the terminatory approach. This inclusive approach establishes territorial jurisdiction when substantial parts of the crime occur on English territory unless international comity demands that the offence is prosecuted in another state.[72] The court acknowledged that this new interpretation of territoriality was difficult to appropriately substantiate in light of the legal certainty of the individual. However, the court justified its decision on the basis of the need to adjust the law in conformity with important changes in society and the increasing cross-frontier nature of crimes. In addition, it stated that despite their official classification as rules of substantive law, the jurisdiction rules establishing the ambit of English law *de facto* have a procedural character.[73]

Legal scholars have argued that both approaches come with a risk of prosecution, while the applicability of English criminal law and therefore the criminality of certain conduct under English law was difficult to foresee at the time of the offence.[74] With regard to the terminatory approach, this is exemplified by cases like *R v Perrin*,[75] concerning the conviction of a French citizen on the basis of the Obscene Publications Act 1959. A police officer in London had downloaded the content of the appellant's USA-based website, and for that reason the material was considered to be 'published' in London. Consequently, the results of the conduct occurred in England, providing it with jurisdiction and rendering the conduct criminal. This case has been used as an example to prove that the results of one's actions may occur in unexpected or random states resulting in unexpected criminal liability.[76] This risk of prosecution by England while the manifestation of the consequences of the crime on English territory was difficult to predict may be a bit more limited when the inclusive approach is used, which focuses on the question whether a substantial part of the crime occurred in England. Had this interpretation been applied in the case *R v Perin,* England would probably not have had jurisdiction, because most parts of the crime occurred in other states. However, when the inclusive approach is used, the situation may still arise that the majority of the results

[71] *R v Smith* [1996] 2 BCLC 109 (CA) 126. See also *Liangsiriprasert v USA* [1990] 2 All ER 866 (PC Hong Kong) 877–878.

[72] This approach was introduced by the Crime Justice Act 1993. Later on it was extended to offenses outside the scope of this Act. *R v Smith* [1996] 2 BCLC 109 (CA); *R v Smith*[2004] EWCA Crim 631, [2004] QB 1418; *R v Sheppard*[2010] EWCA Crim 65, [2010] 2 All ER 850; *R v Burns*[2017] EWCA Crim 1466, [2017] 9 WLUK 71. See also Ormerod et al. (2018), para A8.5; Hirst (2013), pp. 32–33.

[73] *R v Smith*[2004] EWCA Crim 631, [2004] QB 1418, 1438. The procedural character of the jurisdiction rules, which are officially part of substantive law, allowed for a more lenient application of the rule on precedence in comparison to other rules of substantive criminal law.

[74] Ormerod et al. (2018), para A8.6; Hirst (2013), p. 33.

[75] *R v Perrin*[2002] EWCA Crim 747, [2002] 3 WLUKspiepr146 691.

[76] Ormerod et al. (2018), para A8.6; Hirst (2013), p. 33.

occur by chance on English territory.[77] In relation to both approaches, Lews has stated that the courts need to avoid the exercise of excessive criminal jurisdiction. In his view, citizens can only be expected to know and comply with the laws of the place where they act whereas they cannot be expected to know the laws of the country in which the consequences of their actions may accidentally occur. Any other opinion would violate state sovereignty, but also 'place an instrument of oppression in the hands of a government'.[78] In this light, it can be concluded that neither the terminatory nor the inclusive interpretation of the territoriality principle aims to protect citizens against the unforeseeable application of English criminal law. In fact, both interpretations also facilitate the prosecution of offences while the application of English law was difficult to foresee at the time of the offence.

7.2.3.4 The Double Criminality Requirement As a Safeguard?

Even though the reason for a more restrictive approach to extraterritorial jurisdiction seems primarily based on principles regulating interstate relations and practical difficulties, the applicability of the double criminality requirement has in the legal literature been discussed in light of legal certainty and the legality principle. It has been argued that the exclusion of the double criminality requirement in rules on extraterritorial jurisdiction threatens the legal certainty of individuals who will not always be able to know the criminality of certain conduct. An example concerns the Proceeds of Crime Act 2002 (POCA).[79] Until 2005, the POCA criminalised money laundering without subjecting the predicate offence to a double criminality requirement, which meant that an individual could be prosecuted for money laundering in the UK, even though the predicate conduct was not criminal *de lege loci*.[80] In addition, property gained as a result of acts abroad could be confiscated, even though the predicate conduct was only criminal according to English law.[81] This also created problems in relation to the obligation to report suspicions of money laundering abroad, of which the failure to do so could result in criminal charges and

[77] Ormerod et al. (2018), para A8.6; Hirst (2013), p. 33.

[78] Lew (1978), pp. 171, 178–179.

[79] Another example is the abolishment of the double criminality requirement in the Sexual Offences Act 2003, which aims to increase the prevention and discouragement of sex tourism abroad. This abolition has been criticized in light of legal certainty, as it allows for the prosecution of a British national in the UK, even one who has always resided abroad, for conduct which is not criminal according to the law of other no less civilized jurisdictions. Criminal Justice and Immigration Bill 2008. HC 1 July 2008, vol 478 (written answers) <https://hansard.parliament.uk/commons/2008-07-01/debates/08070177000029/SexualOffencesJurisdiction> accessed 20 September 2021; Saxby (2008), pp. 281–282. See also Hirst (2013), p. 45.

[80] S 102 Serious Organised Crime and Police Act 2005 (SOCA) amended the money laundry offenses by adding a double criminality requirement to the predicate conduct.

[81] Carr and Goldby (2011), p. 180.

which *de facto* required the addressees to apply English law to acts abroad.[82] Legal scholars have criticised the lack of a double criminality requirement with regard to the predicate conduct in money laundry offences in light of the international rules on comity, more specifically state sovereignty, as well as the legal certainty and legality principle.[83] It has been argued that the offence of money laundering requires that proceeds are derived from criminal conduct and that it would fall foul of the legality principle if the criminality of conduct was determined according to the law of any other state than the place where the predicate conduct occurred.[84]

7.2.4 The Right to a Lawful Judge

In the English legal order, the idea behind the right to a lawful judge, which is the prohibition for the sovereign of the state to establish prerogative courts, seems endorsed.[85] However, contrary to many continental legal orders, which have included the right to a lawful judge in their constitutions, be it under different names and with some differences in their content, this right does not have a prominent position in the English legal order.[86] The issues which civil law countries sometimes link to the right to a lawful judge have also been discussed in light of other rights or concepts. For instance, the opaqueness of the composition of a judicial panel has been a subject of discussion in the context of the scope of judicial accountability.[87]

In addition, the right to a tribunal established by law in Article 6 ECHR is nowadays part of the English legal order as a result of the Human Rights Act 1998. For quite some time, this right did not seem to have a very prominent position in the English legal order. This follows, for instance, from the fact that the main commentaries, such as Blackstone, extensively explain Article 6 ECHR, but pay no attention to the meaning of a tribunal established by law or its place in the English legal order.[88] However, a relatively recent comparative survey conducted by the ECtHR in one of its cases shows that the scope of the right to a tribunal established by law in the UK covers the composition of the court and the procedure for the

---

[82] See Marshall (2003).

[83] Marshall (2004), p. 355.

[84] Stessens (2000), p. 227. An exception is made in cases in which the state prosecuting for money laundering also has extraterritorial jurisdiction over the predicate offenses.

[85] Müßig (2006), pp. 20–21; Luchtman (2011), p. 85. The Royal Commission on Extradition also casually refers to the natural judge in the discussion on the inclusion of a nationality bar. It states that an argument in favour of such a refusal ground is that the extradition of nationals would rob them of their natural judge. *Report of the Royal commission on Extradition* (Cmd 2039, 1878).

[86] Müßig (2006), pp. 20–21; Luchtman (2011), p. 85; Kosař (2013), p. 247.

[87] Woodhouse (2006), pp. 137–138.

[88] Ormerod et al. (2018), para A7.52.

appointment of judges.[89] In relation to the former, the composition of a bench does not have to be regulated by statutory law, but may be left to the discretion of the judiciary.[90]

It follows from the above that, in the English legal order, there is no right to a lawful judge or tribunal established by law, which demands that citizens are protected against arbitrary forum choices in case of conflicts of national jurisdictions. In other words, the issue of forum choices on the EU level is not clearly linked to the right to a lawful judge and tribunal established by law.

7.2.5 *Interim Conclusion*

It can be concluded that, in the English legal order, the question whether certain conduct constitutes a criminal offence under English law depends on the question whether the conduct falls within English jurisdiction, meaning the ambit of English criminal law. The general rule is that English criminal law applies in England and not to acts committed abroad. This link between jurisdiction and criminal offences and the primacy of the territoriality principle are not based on the substantive legality principle as applicable in the English legal order or the conviction that the application of English criminal law should be foreseeable at the time of the offence. Instead, the old rules of venue, the protection of state sovereignty and the practical cost-benefit assessments constitute the basis for the restrictive approach towards extraterritorial jurisdiction. However, the double criminality requirement has in the legal literature been described as a safeguard against unexpected prosecutions in cross-border cases. In addition, the right to a lawful judge and tribunal established by law as applicable in the English legal order do not include protection against arbitrary forum decisions on the European level. In other words, these rights do not demand that citizens are protected against the risk of forum manipulation in case of conflicts of national jurisdictions.

It follows from the above that the problems arising from unforeseeable jurisdiction claims and the absence of an overarching EU system for forum choices are not explicitly recognised as legality issues. By extension, no clear indications exist of the view that the extradition procedure constitutes a mechanism which could contribute to violations of the English legality principle by transferring citizens to the issuing state where the violation occurs. In other words, from the perspective of the legality principle in the English legal order, there is no reason to assume that the extradition procedure is considered to be a procedure which can enforce violations of the English legality principle by transferring a person to a state when one of the two complications occurs. In light of these conclusions, Sects. 7.3 and 7.4 will now examine to what extent the problems relating to jurisdiction and forum choices have

---

[89] ECtHR 1 December 2020, 26374/18 (*Guðmundur Andri Ástráðsson/Iceland*) paras 150–152.

[90] See Thorhauer (2015), p. 94.

influenced the extradition procedure in the English legal order. In other words, have the English legislator implementing the FDEAW and the national authorities applying it recognised the two problems at hand—perhaps even as possible legality issues—and installed safeguards to prevent surrender in these situations?

7.3 England As the Executing State

7.3.1 An Introduction to the Execution Procedure

Sections 7.3 and 7.4 describe the surrender procedure on the basis of the FDEAW before January 2021. Until that date the FDEAW was implemented in Part 1 of the Extradition Act 2003 (EA), more specifically Sections 1–68, which entered into force on 1 January 2004.[91] This Act intended to modernise and streamline extradition proceedings and at the same time implement the FDEAW.[92] Like the German legislator, the UK legislator decided to include the EAW and the extradition procedure in the same Act. A possible explanation for this decision is the position taken by the Under-Secretary of State at the time of the implementation of the FDEAW, who stated on behalf of the Government that the FDEAW does not abolish the extradition process between states. The EAW procedure should be viewed as a process in which one state sends a person to another state and which therefore does not fundamentally differ from extradition.[93] In addition, similar to the German IRG, the Extradition Act does not use the terminology of the FDEAW.[94] In that light, Part 1 warrants coming from EU Member States, which are all designated as Category 1 territories, will from now on be referred to as 'incoming warrants'. Part 3 warrants, which constitute extradition requests to both Category 1 and Category 2 territories, meaning states outside the EU, will be referred to as 'outgoing warrants'.[95] Both the decision to include the surrender procedure and extradition procedure in the same Extradition Act and the decision not to use the terminology of the FDEAW have been viewed as

[91] Extradition Act 2003 (Commencement and Savings) Order 2003, SI 2003/3103.

[92] Padfield (2007), p. 255; Scott Baker, David Perry and Anand Doobay, A Review of the United Kingdom's Extradition Arrangements (2011) <https://www.gov.uk/government/publications/independent-review-of-the-united-kingdoms-extradition-arrangements> accessed 20 September 2021, para 2.7 (hereafter referred to as the Baker report).

[93] HL Deb 3 June 2003, vol 648, col 120.

[94] Lord Bingham stated in Armas that Part 1 of the 2003 Act does not on the whole use the language of the FDEAW. He and Lord Hope agreed that any differences between the FDEAW and the Extradition Act should be viewed as Parliamentary endeavours to afford the necessary protection against unlawful interferences with the right to liberty. *Officer of the King's Prosecutor (Brussels) v Armas* [2005] UKHL 67, [2006] 2 AC 1 [24]–[28].

[95] Upon approval by Parliament the Home Secretary is competent to designate other states as 'Category 1 territories' as well. Extradition Act 2003, ss 223 (5–6) (8) and 1(1). According to s 1(3) EA a non-EU Member State may become a first category state, provided it does not impose the death penalty. Ormerod et al. (2018), para D31.1.

a hindrance to the adoption of a new system for the transfer of citizens on the basis of the FDEAW.[96] It has been argued that these decisions ignore the different character of the surrender procedure.[97] In the House of Lords, the point was made that by not referring to 'surrender' and by emphasising the need to increase the speed and efficiency of extradition, the government was trying to 'slide the significant consequences of the Bill past the country'.[98] Consequently, an amendment was introduced which forced the government to recognise the true intention of the Extradition Bill, which was to contribute to the establishment of an AFSJ and not merely to speed up the existing extradition process.[99] However, the amendment did not pass.

Historically, the extradition process was the responsibility of both the court and the executive, meaning the Home Secretary, who had the last say. The role of the Home Secretary and his or her power to prevent the extradition of a person signified extradition as an act of sovereignty in which the final decision was made by the executive.[100] It was within the power of the Home Secretary to prohibit extradition in cases in which all the formal legal requirements were met, but the transfer of the person would be unjust, oppressive or unfair.[101] With the implementation of the FDEAW, the powers of the Home Secretary were restricted in relation to incoming warrants. His or her role was limited to deciding between competing Part 1 and Part 2 requests for extradition and preventing extradition in case of national security matters.[102] The Westminster Magistrates' Court is the solely designated executing authority for England and Wales.

Even though the Westminster Magistrates' Court is the official executing authority, the National Crime Agency (NCA) is the first authority to receive the EAW. The NCA assesses whether the issuing authority is a judicial authority as required by the

[96] Mackarel (2007), p. 380; Spencer (2009), p. 535; Evaluation report on the fourth round of mutual evaluations 'The practical application of the European Arrest Warrant and Corresponding surrender procedures between Member States'—Report on the United Kingdom, 9974/2/07 REV 2 EXT 1 (2007), pp. 57–58.

[97] Evaluation report on the fourth round of mutual evaluations 'The practical application of the European Arrest Warrant and Corresponding surrender procedures between Member States'—Report on the United Kingdom, 9974/2/07 REV 2 EXT 1 (2007), p. 58.

[98] HL Deb 3 June 2003, vol 648, cols 118–119.

[99] 'Lord Hodgson of Astley Abbotts moved Amendment No. 1: Before Clause I, insert the following new clause—PURPOSE OF THIS ACT The purpose of this Act is to make provision about extradition and to give effect to the Council Framework Decision of 13th June 2002, on the European arrest warrant and the surrender procedures between Member States. The noble Lord said: Amendment No. 1 would introduce a new purpose clause and, in doing so, make clearer what the Government intend by the proposals in the Bill.' HL Deb 3 June 2003, vol 648, cols 117–119, 121, 127, 131.

[100] Baker report (2011), para 3.32.

[101] *R v Secretary of State for the Home Department ex p Launder (No 2)* [1997] 1 WLR 839, 844–845; Jones and Doobay (2005), p. 229.

[102] Extradition Act 2003, ss 179 EA and 208A. In addition, the Home Secretary is responsible for designating states as Category 1 or 2 states and may nominate the authority through which incoming EAWs are received. Ormerod et al. (2018), para D31.1; Padfield (2007), pp. 257–258.

FDEAW and conducts a proportionality check to avoid that trivial or minor cases reach the court.[103] If the NCA certifies the request, it forwards it to the Westminster Magistrates' Court for England and Wales where the case is decided by a District Judge (DJ)[104] specialised in extradition proceedings[105]. In these proceedings, the Crown Prosecution Service (CPS) represent the judicial authorities of the requesting Member State.[106] The District Judge considers the validity of the incoming warrant, whether the warrant covers an extradition offence, whether any bars to extradition apply, whether extradition would violate the ECHR, whether extradition is proportionate and whether the requested person should receive an adjournment or discharge of extradition proceedings, because his physical or mental state would render extradition unjust or oppressive.[107] Both the prosecutor and the defence may issue an appeal against the decision of the District Judge to the Administrative Division of the High Court.[108] With the leave of the High Court or the Supreme Court, an appeal to the Supreme Court is possible.[109]

The following sections discuss the conditions for the execution of an incoming warrant which have a potential link to unforeseeable jurisdiction claims and forum choices in case of conflicts of national jurisdictions. This examination includes the double criminality requirement, implemented in Section 64 EA, since it touches upon the question according to whose national criminal laws the conduct should be criminalised. In addition, the forum bar in Section 19B EA as well as the possibility to adjourn the extradition procedure in case of domestic proceedings for the same offence and the possibility to suspend domestic proceedings to facilitate extradition in Sections 8A and 22 EA are discussed. The main question is whether these provisions aim to grant the English competent authorities the power to protect citizens against extradition in case of unforeseeable jurisdiction claims or to influence the forum where the case is eventually prosecuted and tried. Furthermore, the human rights ground in Section 21A EA and the provisions regulating concurrent extradition requests for the same person and the same offence are examined. The human rights ground is important because it follows from the case law that it provides a context within which the requested person can challenge the jurisdiction

[103] Regarding the competence of the issuing authority see Extradition Act 2003, ss 2(7–8); *Lithuania v Bucnys*[2013] UKSC 71, [2014] AC 480 [33]. Extradition Act 2003, ss 2(7A) and (7C) cover the proportionality check.

[104] Extradition Act 2003, s 67(1)(a) Ormerod et al. (2018), para D31.3.

[105] Extradition Act 2003, s 139(1) EA; Baker report (2011) paras 10.37–10.38.

[106] The CPS may, for instance, appeal a decision to grant bail to the High Court on behalf of the requesting territory, if it also argued against the grant of bail before the magistrates' court. Bail (Amendment Act) 1993, ss 1A) and 1C(3); Ormerod et al. (2018), para D31.3; Padfield (2007), p. 258.

[107] In case the EAW concerns a conviction, the court should consider the *in absentia* rules.

[108] Extradition Act 2003, ss 26 and 28. Evaluation report on the fourth round of mutual evaluations 'The practical application of the European Arrest Warrant and Corresponding surrender procedures between Member States'—Report on the United Kingdom, 9974/2/07 REV 2 EXT 1 (2007), p. 47.

[109] Extradition Act 2003, s 32.

claim of the requesting state. The provisions on concurrent extradition requests could have an indirect influence on the eventual forum decision, since the states whose extradition request is not executed may decide not to continue their own criminal proceedings.

7.3.2 *Extradition Offences*

Section 64 EA regulates when an offence constitutes an 'extradition offence' in case of accusation warrants, which are warrants issued for the purpose of prosecution.[110] The double criminality requirement is part of this provision and therefore does not constitute a separate bar to extradition.[111] A conduct-based test decides whether the substantive double criminality requirement is fulfilled. In other words, the District Judge needs to examine whether the conduct in the warrant would be an offence under UK law if it would occur in the UK.[112] This means that the elements of the foreign offence do not need to correspond one-on-one to an offence under the law of the UK.[113] In other words, the legal classification of the conduct under the law of the UK and that of the requesting state may differ.[114] A failure to fulfil the double criminality requirement means that the offence is not an extradition offence, which in turn means that the requested person needs to be discharged from the extradition proceedings.[115]

In principle, the double criminality requirement needs to be fulfilled in all cases, unless the offence falls under one of the categories listed in Article 2(2) FDEAW.[116] However, Section 64 EA states that an exception to the exception needs to be made in two types of circumstances, which mirror the situations laid down in Articles 4(7)(a) and 4(7)(b) FDEAW. Firstly, the double criminality requirement applies in case of list-offences when the conduct is not criminalised under UK law and part of it

[110] Section 64 also includes the situation in which the requested person has been convicted in the requesting state, but no sentence has been imposed yet. Section 65 covers conviction warrants.

[111] For the bars to extradition see Extradition Act 2003, s 11.

[112] Similar to Germany and the Netherlands, the District Jude needs to conduct a transposition exercise of the case when the offence on the warrant refers to the territory of the requesting state. This means that the District Judge needs to answer the double criminality question by substituting England for the requesting state. Baker report (2011), para C.36. This report refers to several cases decided under the Extradition Act 1870.

[113] *Norris v USA* [2008] UKHL 16, [2008] 1 AC 920 [63]–[91]. This case concerned an incoming warrant from a third state (Part 2 warrant) but the House of Lords stated that the conduct test should be applied consistently throughout the Extradition Act.

[114] According to the case law, the *actus reus* of an offence under English law needs to be proven, while the *mens rea* can be inferred from the description of the conduct in the incoming warrant. *Hertel v Canada* [2010] EWHC Admin 2305, [2010] 9 WLUK 305 [48]; *Assange v Sweden* [2011] EWHC Admin 2849, [2011] 11 WLUK 63 [57].

[115] Extradition Act 2003, s 10(3).

[116] Article 2(2) FDEAW is copied into Schedule 2of the Extradition Act 2003.

occurred in the UK.[117] In such situations, extradition has been viewed as unjust.[118] Secondly, if the criminal conduct occurred outside the territory of the requesting state, the conduct in question must under corresponding circumstances constitute an extraterritorial offence according to the law of the relevant part of the UK.[119] This means that the facts must not only constitute offences under in this case English law, but in a similar situation England should have extraterritorial jurisdiction over the facts as well.[120]

This double criminality requirement seems to have a multi-part goal. It reflects the principle of reciprocity, protecting the equality of states. It ensures that a state does not have to provide assistance to a state, which would in the reversed situation not be able to provide assistance. It is also considered undesirable to force a state to cooperate when the conduct in question is not punishable in its own legal order.[121] In addition, in the case law and the parliamentary debates the double criminality requirement has been linked to legal certainty and the protection of citizens against exorbitant jurisdiction claims.[122] During the parliamentary debate on the Extradition Act 2003, some members of parliament (MPs) raised the point that individuals should not be subjected to foreign laws when the facts are not criminal according to UK law.[123] Johnson stated in relation to the double criminality assessment that 'when people are in Britain, they should have the legal certainty that the laws of this

[117] In *Armas* the Divisional Court declared this exception compatible with Article 4(7)(a) FDEAW, which allows Member States to refuse the execution of an EAW when the facts occurred wholly or partially on their territory. *Office of the King's Prosecutor, Brussels v Cando Armas*[2005] UKHL 67, [2006] 2 AC 1 [32].

[118] Explanatory Notes to the Anti-Social Behaviour, Crime and Policing Act 2014, para 485; Baker report (2011), para C.30; HL Deb 1 July 2003, vol. 650, col GC202.

[119] Explanatory Notes to the Anti-Social Behaviour, Crime and Policing Act 2014, para 486.

[120] HL Deb 19 June 2003, vol 649, col GC399. This situation reflects the content of Article 4(7)(b) FDEAW which allows the executing state to refuse the EAW if the issuing state exercises extraterritorial jurisdiction, while the executing state would in a similar situation not be able to do so. In practice, the courts also conduct the dual check concerning the criminality of the act and jurisdiction. See e.g. *Taylor v Germany* [2012] EWHC Admin 475, [2012] WLUK 373 [23–26]; *Surico v Italy* [2018] EWHC Admin 401, [2018] 3 WLUK 73. Extradition Act 2003, s 10(3).

[121] HL Deb 19 November 2001, vol 628, col 964; *R v Metropolitan Stipendiary Magistrate, ex p Pinochet (No 3)* [2000] 1 AC 147 (HL) 184; Baker report (2011), paras 3.25–3.26.

[122] In addition, Lord Lamon stated that the double criminality requirement is a safeguard against the procedural disadvantages of standing trial abroad. These include the fact that suspects may be subjected to stricter rules of pre-trial detention and bail as well as language difficulties. He also stated that one of the goals of double criminality is to protect individuals against harsh and repressive foreign laws. However, in the EU, this is no longer necessary. Furthermore, the *Norris* judgment states that the rationale of the double criminality requirement is to protect the right to liberty of the requested person in the sense that this right should not be restricted in relation to conduct which does not constitute a criminal act according to the law of the requested state. HL Deb 12 November 2003, vol 654, col 1428; *Norris v USA* [2008] UKHL 16, [2008] 1 AC 920 [88]; *R (on the Application of the United States of America) v Nirvana* [2018] EWHC Admin 706, [2018] 3 WLUK 377 [5].

[123] HC Deb 9 December 2002, vol 396, col 90; HC Deb 25 March 2003, vol 402, col 201.

country, not those of another community country, will apply to them'.[124] Others argued that it is unreasonable to expect from citizens when travelling abroad that they know and understand the criminal law of another state, including all minor or trivial offences.[125] Furthermore, as explained above when an EU Member State exercises extraterritorial jurisdiction over acts completely committed abroad, the double criminality requirement is only satisfied when England would be able to exercise such jurisdiction in corresponding circumstances.[126] This extension of the scope of the double criminality test to include jurisdiction been linked to the protection of citizens against extradition to states exercising extravagant jurisdiction claims.[127]

It can be concluded that the double criminality requirement in the Extradition Act 2003 does not exclusively protect the sovereignty of the UK as a state. The case law and parliamentary debates have linked the requirement to legal certainty and the need to offer protection against exorbitant jurisdiction claims. During the debates on the implementation of the FDEAW, some MPs even raised the point that individuals should only have to abide by and fear English law while they are on English territory. The argument was made that it is unreasonable to expect individuals to know and understand the law of all the states to which they travel. However, despite these arguments, which touch upon the foreseeability of the application of national criminal laws, and the discussions on protection against exorbitant jurisdiction, it remains unclear to what extent the double criminality was in the end actually based on the commonly accepted position that citizens should not be extradited when the application of the law of the requesting state was difficult to foresee at the time of the offence. Such a position does not follow from the case law or the parliamentary debates, which also lack a more general discussion on the problems arising from unforeseeable jurisdiction claims. In addition, the need for protection against exorbitant jurisdiction has not been unambiguously linked to the position that the application of a particular substantive criminal law should be foreseeable at the time of the offence.

[124] HC Deb 25 March 2003, vol 402, col 200.

[125] HL Deb 27 October 2003, vol 654, cols 66–67; HL Deb 1 July 2003, vol 650, cols GC208-GC209, GC211–GC212.

[126] *Kalinowski v Poland* [2019] EWHC Admin 3734, [2019] 12 WLUK 263.

[127] The double criminality requirement also included jurisdiction in the former Extradition Act 1989 with the intent to avert assistance in case of exorbitant jurisdiction claims. HL Deb 19 November 2001, vol 628, cols 993–994; *R (on the application of Al-Fawwaz) v Governor of Brixton Prison* [2001] UKHL 69, [2002] 1 AC 556 [95], [105]. See also Arnell and Davies (2020), p. 153.

7.3.3 *Domestic Proceedings for the Same Offence*

7.3.3.1 Unforeseeable Jurisdiction Claims

Sections 8A and 22 EA state that extradition proceedings need to be adjourned when the judge—either before or during the extradition hearing—discovers that the person is charged with an offence—either the same one as the extradition offence or another offence—in the UK. The extradition proceedings need to be adjourned until, for instance, the domestic charge is withdrawn, disposed of or proceedings are discontinued.[128] In these situations, the extradition proceedings are continued, unless this is prohibited by the double jeopardy rule in Section 12 EA.[129] In addition, Section 36A EA sets the same obligation to adjourn the extradition proceedings when, after the end of an extradition hearing, the judge is informed about domestic proceedings against the requested person. This provision ensures that England is in a position to prosecute the prosecuted person for serious offences committed during, for instance, his release on bail, pending the extradition procedures.[130]

The rationale of the possibility to adjourn the extradition proceedings seems to be the protection of state sovereignty and territoriality. In the *Ostuna* case, Section 22 EA was linked to the right of the state to bring a prosecution for acts occurring within its own jurisdiction.[131] In a judgement of the Scottish High Court of Justiciary, the provisions are linked to the rationale of Article 4(7)(a) FDEAW, which is the protection of the primacy of domestic jurisdiction.[132] Hence, the case law does not indicate that Sections 8A, 22 and 36A EA predominantly aim to protect citizens against extradition to states whose jurisdiction claim was not foreseeable at the time of the offence. This also follows from the fact that they do not bar extradition but merely postpone it. Instead, it is the double jeopardy bar which, after the conclusion of the domestic proceedings, may offer the necessary protection against extradition.[133]

Even though it is not its rationale, the power to start domestic proceedings for the same criminal offence could in practice be used to avoid extradition when the jurisdiction claim of the requesting state was difficult to foresee. However, it seems unlikely that it is used for this purpose, since the obligation to adjourn

[128] Extradition Act 2003, s 22(2). For the definition of a disposal of charges, see Section 214.

[129] Extradition Act 2003, ss 8A(2) and 22(2)(4) and 214. Doobay (2015), p. 77.

[130] Explanatory notes to the Anti-Social Behaviour, Crime and Policing Act 2014, para 478.

[131] *Edwin Osunta v The Public Prosecutor's Office in Dusseldorf* [2007] EWHC 1562 (Admin) para. 27.

[132] However, Section 22 EA differs from the territoriality exception in the FDEAW in the sense that it only applies when jurisdiction is in fact being exercised by the UK and that it can also apply in cases in which the UK exercises extraterritorial jurisdiction as well. In addition, Sections 8A, 22 and 36A have also been described as reflections of Article 4(2) and 24(1) FDEAW. *La Torre (Antonio) v HM Advocate* [2006] HCJAC 56, [2008] JC 23 [101]; *Governor of Wandsworth Prison v Kinderis* [2007] EWHC Admin 998, [2008] QB 347 [44]–[45], [50]; Baker report (2011), paras 5.240, B11.

[133] *Augusciak v Poland* [2014] EWHC Admin 420, [2014] WLUK 703 [14].

extradition proceedings only arises when the requested person has been charged in the domestic case.[134] If the public prosecutor still needs to conduct the investigation on which a charge can be based, charging a person before the end of the extradition proceedings might not be possible. In other words, starting domestic proceedings to avoid extradition in case of extravagant and unforeseeable jurisdiction claims will probably only work when the public prosecutor has already finished the investigation.

7.3.3.2 A Need for a Transparent System for Forum Choices?

The obligatory adjournment of the extradition procedure in case of domestic proceedings can in the end prevent extradition when the domestic proceedings trigger the double jeopardy bar. The prosecutorial discretion in deciding on the initiation of domestic charges in the context of extradition proceedings has to a certain extent been limited by guidelines. In case of (future) concurrent proceedings for the same offence in different EU Member States, relevant guidance is laid down in the Director's Guidance on the handling of cases where the jurisdiction to prosecute is shared with prosecuting authorities overseas, hereafter Director's Guidance on concurrent jurisdictions, and the Legal Guidance on Jurisdiction for the Crown Prosecution Service.[135] These guidelines are formally not binding, but followed in practice.[136] Both Guidances recommend early consultations with foreign colleagues to find the best place for prosecution. With regard to the criteria on the basis of which the forum decision should be made, both instruments enumerate a few and refer to the Eurojust Guidelines of 2016. A certain ranking between the different factors or principles follows from the wording of the Director's Guidance on concurrent

[134] An example of a case in which the UK initiated a prosecution after the receipt of an extradition request is *Abu Hamza*, which concerned an extradition request from the USA. In that case, the UK had previously investigated the case, but this had not resulted in a prosecution. After the receipt of the extradition request, they decided to prosecute for some offences after all. This was probably to avoid a public backlash for not prosecuting terrorist activities. After being prosecuted and convicted in the UK, extradition proceedings were resumed and Abu Hamza was extradited to the USA for other (related) offences. Initiating a prosecution after the receipt of the extradition request was also not classified as an abuse of process. *R v Abu Hamza* [2006] EWCA Crim 2918, [2007] QB 659 [74]. See also *Hamza v Secretary of State for the Home Department* [2012] EWHC Admin 2736, [2012] 10 WLUK 171 [8].

[135] The Director of Public Prosecutions (DPP) is the head of the CPS. Director's Guidance on the handling of cases where the jurisdiction to prosecute is shared with prosecuting authorities overseas (17 July 2013) <https://www.cps.gov.uk/publication/directors-guidance-handling-cases-where-jurisdiction-prosecute-shared-prosecuting> accessed 20 September 2021; Legal Guidance on jurisdiction (26 July 2021) <https://www.cps.gov.uk/legal-guidance/jurisdiction> accessed 3 March 2022; Ormerod et al. (2018), para A9.25.

[136] Deviations should only occur in exceptional circumstances and can be challenged whey they appear unreasonable. HC Written Statement on Concurrent Jurisdiction 17 July 2013, vol 566 <https://hansard.parliament.uk/Commons/2013-07-17/debates/13071774000018/ConcurrentJurisdiction#contribution-13071774000043> accessed 20 September 2021.

jurisdictions, which favours the territoriality principle.[137] However, for some factors, it is not clear how much weight should be allocated to them nor how they should be balanced against other factors. One of these factors is the connection of the accused to the UK, even though the Scott Baker report stated that any guidelines should 'specifically address the significance to be accorded to the nationality or residence of a suspect'.[138] The lack of an explanation on the role British nationality and residence should have in the decision of the public prosecutor fits with the general position that British nationality should not be a bar to extradition.

It follows from the above that even though the weight and position of each factor in the decision-making process to start domestic proceedings has not been clarified, the two Guidances do limit the discretion of the domestic public prosecutor in deciding whether a case can best be prosecuted in the UK or elsewhere. Their existence reflects a recognition of the need for a transparent system for forum choices in case of conflicts of national jurisdictions. The Director's Guidance on concurrent jurisdictions was also a response to the findings of the Scott Baker report, which reviewed the UK extradition rules. This report states that even though public prosecutors generally carefully consider all relevant circumstances in cases of conflicts of national jurisdictions, the decision is not made on the basis of a transparent process, nor on the basis of formally and nationally agreed criteria.[139]

However, it is important to note that the Director's Guidance on concurrent jurisdictions only covers the situation of cross-frontier offences, which are partially committed in the UK and partially abroad. The Director's Guidance therefore neglects cases in which the crime occurred wholly abroad.[140] No specific guidelines for the latter situation seem to exist, which could be explained by the fact that such prosecutions rarely occur considering the difficulties in collecting foreign evidence, the high costs of investigations abroad and the preference for prosecution by states with a strong territorial claim.[141] In relation to the latter, the 1878 report of the Royal Commission on Extradition already stated that there is no discussion necessary on the best forum, since this is the state on whose territory the crime was committed. Individuals owe obedience to the law of the state in which they find themselves in

[137] It follows, for instance, from the Director's Guidance on concurrent jurisdictions that the possibility to concentrate all prosecutions in one place should be considered if this does not clash with the territoriality principle and the possibility to gain access to foreign evidence. Potential delays as a result of proceedings in one state or the other as well as costs and resources may be considered where all other factors are 'finely balanced'.

[138] Baker report (2011), para 1.18.

[139] Baker report (2011), paras 1.18–1.19, 6.43, 6.71–6.74;Doobay (2015); HC Deb 16 October 2012, vol 551, col 165.

[140] Director's Guidance on the handling of cases where the jurisdiction to prosecute is shared with prosecuting authorities overseas (17 July 2013) <https://www.cps.gov.uk/publication/directors-guidance-handling-cases-where-jurisdiction-prosecute-shared-prosecuting> accessed 20 September 2021, para 11. The Legal Guidance on Jurisdiction, which refers to the Director's Guidance, does not clearly state whether it also applies in case the complete criminal act was committed abroad.

[141] HL Deb 26 October 2009, vol 713, col 1071; Klip and Massa (2010), p. 56; Hirst (2003), p. 203.

exchange for the protection offered by the law of that state as if he or she is one of its own subjects.[142]

Additionally, protection against random or unreasonable forum decisions is to a certain extent also offered by the fact that in principle, both the decision to prosecute in the UK and the decision not to do so are open to judicial review.[143] It, however, follows from the case law that this is an exceptional remedy which hardly ever succeeds.[144] The judiciary finds the decision to prosecute one that should remain as much as possible with the public prosecutor.[145] Judicial review could for instance be successful if it is proven that the public prosecutor used his or her powers in bad faith.[146]

7.3.4 The Forum Bar

7.3.4.1 An Introduction

The Crime and Courts Act 2013 inserted a forum bar in the Extradition Act 2003, which aims to prevent extradition when this is not in the interest of justice.[147] Section 19B (1–3) EA states the following:

> (1) The extradition of a person ("D") to a category 1 territory is barred by reason of forum if the extradition would not be in the interests of justice.
> (2) For the purposes of this section, the extradition would not be in the interests of justice if the judge—
>
> (a) decides that a substantial measure of D's relevant activity was performed in the United Kingdom; and
> (b) decides, having regard to the specified matters relating to the interests of justice (and only those matters), that the extradition should not take place.
>
> (3) These are the specified matters relating to the interests of justice—

---

[142] *Report of the Royal commission on Extradition* (Cmd 2039, 1878).

[143] Baker report (2011), para 6.55 (viii).

[144] *Sharma v Brown-Antoine* [2006] UKPC 57, [2007] 1 WLR 780 [14]; *R (on the application of Bermingham) v Director of the Serious Fraud Office* [2006] EWHC Admin 200, [2007] QB 727 [63]; Hirst (2013), p. 60; Baker report (2011), para 6.55. In *Sharma*, the court stated that the decision not to prosecute may have a slightly higher chance of being successfully challenged, since the aggrieved person cannot raise this complaint during the criminal trial. Judicial review is therefore the only available remedy.

[145] *Poland v Celinksi*[2015] EWHC Admin 1274, [2016] 1 WLR 551 [11]; *Mohit v DPP of Mauritius* [2006] UKPC 20, [2006] 1 WLR 3343 [17]; *Sharma v Brown-Antoine* [2006] UKPC 57, [2007] 1 WLR 780 [14]. See also Arnell and Davies (2020), p. 154.

[146] *R v DPP ex p Kebilene* [2000] 2 AC 326 (HL) 371; *Halsbury's Laws* (5th edn, 2018) vol 61A, para 1.

[147] Crime and Courts Act 2012, sch 20, paras 2–3; Extradition Act 2003, ss 19B–19F.

(a) the place where most of the loss or harm resulting from the extradition offence occurred or was intended to occur;
(b) the interests of any victims of the extradition offence;
(c) any belief of a prosecutor that the United Kingdom, or a particular part of the United Kingdom, is not the most appropriate jurisdiction in which to prosecute D in respect of the conduct constituting the extradition offence;
(d) were D to be prosecuted in a part of the United Kingdom for an offence that corresponds to the extradition offence, whether evidence necessary to prove the offence is or could be made available in the United Kingdom;
(e) any delay that might result from proceeding in one jurisdiction rather than another;
(f) the desirability and practicability of all prosecutions relating to the extradition offence taking place in one jurisdiction, having regard (in particular) to—
(g) the jurisdictions in which witnesses, co-defendants and other suspects are located, and
(h) the practicability of the evidence of such persons being given in the United Kingdom or in jurisdictions outside the United Kingdom;
(i) D's connections with the United Kingdom.

The forum bar is only applicable to accusation warrants[148] and has a purely domestic origin,[149] meaning that it was not derived from the FDEAW. It is one of the provisions of the Extradition Act which reflect the UK's willingness to cooperate on the basis of the FDEAW, but on its own terms and its own set of safeguards.[150]

The forum bar shows similarities to Article 4(7)(a) FDEAW, since the first of the two cumulative criteria for its application requires that a substantial degree of the relevant activity occurred in the UK.[151] The second criterion constitutes on overall value judgement whether extradition is in the interest of justice. This judgement should be based on the factors enumerated in Section 19B(3) EA.[152] In this light, the court often makes a comparison between prosecution in the UK and prosecution in the requesting state. However, the decision to apply the forum bar does not constitute a forum decision in the strict sense of the word, since the

[148] Conviction warrants are excluded, including those issued in cases in which the requested person has a right of retrial upon his surrender. *Belbin v France* [2015] EWHC Admin 149, [2015] 1 WLUK 723 [35]–[41]; *Bagri v France* [2014] EWHC Admin 4066 (Admin) [2014] 12 WLUK 519 [39].

[149] *Atraskevic v Lithuania* [2015] EWHC Admin 131, [2016] 1 WLR 2762 [10].

[150] Other examples are the former hostage bar in Section 16 EA and Section14 EA, which prohibits extradition when this would be unjust or oppressive as a result of the passage of time. The latter allows the District Judge to examine to some extent the merits of the underlying case to the EAW and the conduct of the issuing state, which is at odds with the principle of mutual recognition. Spencer (2009), p. 535; Evaluation report on the fourth round of mutual evaluations 'The practical application of the European Arrest Warrant and Corresponding surrender procedures between Member States'—Report on the United Kingdom, 9974/2/07 REV 2 EXT 1 (2007), pp. 46, 65; Jones and Doobay (2005), pp. 221–222.

[151] Relevant activity means 'activity which is material to the commission of the extradition offence and which is alleged to have been performed by ... [the person]'. Extradition Act 2003, s 19B(6).

[152] Extradition Act 2003, 19B(2); *Atraskevic v Lithuania* [2015] EWHC Admin 131, [2016] 1 WLR 2762 [13]—[14]. On the review of the value judgment on appeal see also *Shaw v Government of the USA* [2014] EWHC Admin 4654, [2014] 11 WLUK 488 [42].

decision that the UK is the more appropriate forum does not oblige the CPS to prosecute the case in England.[153] The case *Scott* also states that the primary focus of the court is on a choice between the UK and the requesting state, but that in certain cases the choice may even be between prosecution in the requesting state and no prosecution at all.[154] So, the forum bar does not necessarily determine where the citizen will be prosecuted.

The forum bar as explained above shows similarities to the previously discussed possibility to adjourn the extradition proceedings as a result of domestic proceedings in England for the same offence. However, Section 19B EA differs from Sections 8A and 22 EA in several ways. Firstly, the forum bar will actually block extradition to the requesting state, whereas Sections 8A and 22 EA only grant the power to adjourn the extradition proceedings until the domestic ones are concluded. Secondly, the forum bar can also apply when the suspect has not yet been charged in England for the same criminal actions, whereas the extradition proceedings cannot be adjourned until the suspect is officially charged. Thirdly, as follows from the *Scott* case, in some situations the actual decision is not between prosecution in the UK or the requesting state, but between prosecution and no prosecution.

7.3.4.2 Unforeseeable Jurisdiction Claims

The forum bar has a relatively long history. It was first introduced in the Police Act of 2006 as a reaction to cases such as *NatWest Three*, in which British citizens were extradited to the USA while they could—at least in theory—also be prosecuted in the UK.[155] However, that forum bar never entered into force, as it was considered too complicated and a threat to the speed of extradition proceedings.[156] A few years later, similar cases to the *NatWest Three* case occurred, concerning once again extradition requests from the USA for British nationals who could in principle also be prosecuted in the UK. This resulted in public and parliamentary concern, in

---

[153] The case law is a bit blurry in formulating the 'interest of justice' test. In *Shaw*, the court states that it is not a question of whether prosecution should take place in the UK or the requesting state, but whether it is in the interest of justice to extradite the person to the requesting state. However, in *Scott*, the court states that the forum bar primarily concerns the question of whether prosecution should take place in the UK or in the requesting state. Furthermore, the concern that the application of the forum bar would allow the suspect to walk away 'scot-free', since its application is not complemented by an obligation to prosecute the case in England was one of the concerns raised during the Parliamentary debates. *Shaw v Government of the USA* [2014] EWHC Admin 4654, [2014] 11 WLUK 488 [41]; *Scott v USA* [2018] EWHC Admin 2021, [2019] 1 WLR 774 [34]; HL Deb 25 March 2013, vol 744, cols 898–899.

[154] This also affects the weighing of the factors, since some factors inherently require a comparison between prosecution in the UK and prosecution in the requesting state. *Scott v USA* [2018] EWHC Admin 2021, [2019] 1 WLR 774 [34]–[35]; Grange (2018).

[155] *R (on the application of Bermingham) v Director of the Serious Fraud Office* [2006] EWHC Admin 200, [2007] QB 727;Grange (2018); Arnell and Davies (2020), p. 147.

[156] HL Deb 25 March 2013, vol 744, cols 895–896.

particular about the UK/USA agreement.[157] The perceived excessive exercise of jurisdiction by the USA, which was also the result of the very vocal campaigns held by those subjected to the extradition requests,[158] as well as the differences in the standard of proof that each country had to meet gave rise to a demand for more protection against extradition.[159] The driver behind the forum bar was, therefore, not exorbitant and unforeseeable jurisdiction exercised by EU Member States, but extradition requests for British nationals from the USA which was considered to exercise extravagant jurisdiction. In 2012, then-Home Secretary Theresa May announced her intent to introduce a forum bar, which later on became part of the Crime and Courts Bill 2013.[160] However, despite the public outcry for more protection of British nationals, the forum bar which was adopted does not exclusively apply to British nationals.[161] This can be explained on the basis of the fact that any bar to extradition which *de facto* would constitute a nationality bar does not fit in a legal system that historically does not oppose the extradition of its own nationals. Contrary to several civil law states, especially Germany, the protection of British nationals in extradition procedures has never gained an important place in the Anglo-Saxon legal tradition.[162] In the UK, the predominant opinion is that when it comes to extradition, the public prosecutor and judge are blind towards nationality.[163] This position is also reflected in the decision not to implement Article 4(6) and 5(3) FDEAW into the Extradition Act 2003.

Since its introduction, the forum bar has not yet barred extradition to an EU Member State, but it has been successful twice in relation to incoming Part 2 warrants from third states.[164] In the case law on several incoming Part 2 warrants, the forum bar is described as an individual safeguard. It aims to complement the protection already offered by the human rights refusal ground, discussed later on, by preventing extradition when this is not in the interest of justice and the offence could be fairly and effectively tried in the UK.[165] Some legal scholars have argued that courts

[157] HL Deb 25 March 2013, vol 744, col 888; HC Deb 5 December 2011, vol 537, col 109; HC Deb 24 November 2011, vol 536, cols 161WH, 172WH; HC Deb 16 October 2012, vol 551, col 174; Grange (2018);Vamos (2018); Arnell and Davies (2020), p. 147.

[158] Baker report (2011), para 6.11; Home Affairs Select Committee, *The US-UK Extradition Treaty* (HC 2010–12, 64-I) 11; Arnell and Davies (2020), pp. 142, 145.

[159] HC Deb 20 March 2012, vol 542, cols 644–645; HC Deb 15 July 2009, vol 496, col 355; HC Deb 16 October 2012, vol 551, col 165. See also Grange (2018).

[160] HC Deb 16 October 2012, vol 551, cols 164–165.

[161] HC Deb 24 November 2011, vol 536, col 162WH, 164WH; HC Deb 16 October 2012, vol 551, cols 174, 176; Grange (2018).

[162] *Report of the Royal commission on Extradition* (Cmd 2039, 1878).

[163] HL Deb 25 March 2013, vol 744, col 899. See also HC Deb 5 December 2011, vol 537, col 121; Arnell and Davies (2020), p. 161.

[164] *Love v USA* [2018] EWHC Admin 172, [2018] 1 WLR 2889; *Scott v USA* [2018] EWHC Admin 2021, [2019] 1 WLR 774. See also Arness and Davies (2020), p. 149.

[165] *Love v USA* [2018] EWHC Admin 172, [2018] 1 WLR 2889 [22]; *Ejinyere v USA* [2018] EWHC Admin 2841, [2018] 10 WLUK 448 [14].

should have the power to protect a person against extradition to a foreign state when the conduct primarily occurred on UK soil, especially when the suspect in question has not even left the UK. To avoid disproportionate disruptions to the daily life of the accused, prosecution in the UK serves the interest of justice.[166] Hence, the forum bar could protect against excessive foreign jurisdiction claims.[167]

It follows from the above that the forum bar does not aim to protect the sovereignty of the UK. Instead, it is an individual safeguard aiming to protect individuals against extravagant jurisdiction claims, in particular from the USA. However, the introduction of the forum bar is not explicitly or generally linked to the issue of the foreseeability of a jurisdiction claim. Nothing indicates that the UK legislator or the courts interpret exorbitant jurisdiction claims as jurisdiction claims which were not foreseeable at the time of the offence.

7.3.4.3 A Need for a Transparent System for Forum Choices?

The Situation Before the Forum Bar

Before elaborating on the question whether the forum bar is in one way or another linked to the position that forum choices on the EU level require a transparent set of rules, it is important to note that, for a long time, the starting point in the English legal order was that the ability of the UK to prosecute the requested person itself should not be allocated a role beyond Sections 8A and 22 EA discussed above. In the case law, judges have taken the position that extradition should not become a forum for a discussion on the best place for prosecution.[168] In several judgements on incoming warrants from third states, the point is also made that England's jurisdiction to prosecute should not significantly influence the court's decision on extradition. In other words, the case law shows the general position that forum decisions should be made outside the context of the extradition procedure. This separation between forum decisions, more specifically the assessment of the possibility of prosecuting the case in England and the extradition procedure, is based on the potential adverse effect which this assessment could have for international cooperation and relations, as well as on efficiency considerations such as avoiding unnecessary duplication of efforts and a waste of resources.[169]

The possibility of prosecution in England was not completely excluded from the extradition procedure, but strongly minimalised. Until the adoption of the forum bar,

---

[166] Baker report (2011), para 6.11; Doobay (2015), pp. 76–77. See also HC Deb 5 December 2011, vol 537, col 117.

[167] Arnell (2015), pp. 709–710.

[168] *Norris v USA*[2010] UKSC 9, [2010] 2 AC 487 [67]. Referred to in *Atraskevic v Lithuania* [2015] EWHC Admin 131, [2016] 1 WLR 2762 [45].

[169] *Hashmi v USA* [2007] EWHC Admin 564, [2007] 3 WLUK 519 [31]–[32]; *R (on the application of Bermingham) v Director of the Serious Fraud Office* [2006] EWHC Admin 200, [2007] QB 727 [126]. The *Bermingham* case also refers to *Wright v Scottish Ministers* [2004] SLT 823, [2004] 7 WLUK 293 [28].

it could only play a role in the context of Sections 8A and 22 EA or the decision on the human rights ground in Article 21A EA, which is further discussed in the next section. In relation to the latter, the possibility of an English prosecution could be considered by the court when it had to determine whether extradition would be a disproportional infringement of the right to private and family life in Article 8 ECHR. More concretely, it was accepted in the case law, including case law on incoming warrants from EU Member States, that in certain circumstances the possibility of domestic criminal proceedings could 'tip the balance of judgement in favour of a disproportionate interference with Article 8 ECHR'.[170] In *Norris*, Lord Phillips stated, 'Rarely, if ever, on an issue of proportionality, could the possibility of bringing criminal proceedings in this jurisdiction be capable of tipping the scales against extradition in accordance with this country's treaty obligations. Unless the judge reaches the conclusion that the scales are finely balanced he should not enter into an enquiry as to the possibility of prosecution in this country.'[171]

As a result of the introduction of the forum bar, the scope of the argument that the requested person could be prosecuted in the UK in light of Article 8 ECHR 'is reduced almost to vanishing point'.[172] In *Bagri*, the court decided that forum considerations in light of Article 8 ECHR can still play a role in case of a conviction warrant when the requested person has an unconditional right to a retrial after this surrender.[173] More importantly, the introduction of the forum bar has to some extent eroded the general position that the possibility of domestic criminal proceedings should not play an important role in the extradition procedure and that forum decisions should in principle not play a role in the extradition procedure. The discussion in the next paragraphs will show that in the context of the application of the forum bar, the court often assesses whether the case could better be prosecuted in the UK or in the requesting state.

Parliamentary Debates on the Forum Bar

During the parliamentary debates on the forum bar, several speakers, including the Home Secretary, stated that it would provide the necessary transparency regarding the

[170] *Atraskevic v Lithuania* [2015] EWHC Admin 131, [2016] 1 WLR 2762 [44]–[45], [47]; *R (on the application of Bermingham) v Director of the Serious Fraud Office* [2006] EWHC Admin 200, [2007] QB 727 [121]; *Hashmi v USA* [2007] EWHC Admin 564, [2007] 3 WLUK 519 [39]. These cases concern Part 2 warrants, but the relevant provisions are quoted in cases on incoming warrants from EU Member States warrants. *Bagri v France* [2014] EWHC Admin 4066 (Admin) [2014] 12 WLUK 519.

[171] *Norris v USA*[2010] UKSC 9, [2010] 2 AC 487 [67]. See also *H v Lord Advocate* [2012] UKSC 24, [2013] 1 AC 413 [62]–[64]; *Diri v USA* [2015] EWHC Admin 2130, [2015] WLUK 751 [46]–[47].

[172] *Atraskevic v Lithuania* [2015] EWHC Admin 131, [2016] 1 WLR 2762 [45]. See also *Bagri v France* [2014] EWHC Admin 4066 (Admin) [2014] 12 WLUK 519 [43]; *Diri v USA* [2015] EWHC Admin 2130, [2015] WLUK 751 [46]–[47].

[173] However, the limits imposed by Norris would apply, meaning that this possibility may only play a role if the judge concludes that all other factors are finely balanced. *Bagri v France* [2014] EWHC Admin 4066 (Admin) [2014] 12 WLUK 519 [43], [49].

decision on whether prosecution should take place in the UK or abroad.[174] Lord Hodgson was of the opinion that the forum bar 'will end the unattractive process of forum shopping, which is a search for judicial procedures that offer the greatest chance of conviction and the highest possible penalties'.[175] The forum bar was, therefore, viewed by some as a mechanism for opening the black box in which public prosecutors now make forum decisions, which increases the risk of arbitrary decision-making or decisions based on pure political motives or political pressure.[176] It has also been argued that the forum bar required the CPS to carefully consider the forum for prosecution, as it might be an issue that can come up in court.[177] The opponents of the forum bar stated that the decision whether to prosecute and where to prosecute should fall to the public prosecutors and not to the court. Contrary to the courts, public prosecutors are familiar with the availability or non-availability of evidence, the particular facts of the case and the viability of prosecution in one jurisdiction or the other.[178]

A Closer Look at the 'Interest of Justice' Test

The second step of the forum bar constitutes the 'interest of justice test' which requires an assessment of the factors enumerated in Section 19B(3) EA covering (a) where most of the loss or harm occurred or was intended to occur, (b) the interests of the victims, (c) the belief of a public prosecutor that the UK is not the most appropriate jurisdiction for prosecution,[179] (d) whether the necessary evidence could be made available in the UK in case of prosecution, (e) any delay that might result from criminal proceedings in either state, (f) the desirability and practicability of conducting all prosecutions relating to the extradition offence in one jurisdiction, having regard to the jurisdictions in which witnesses, co-defendants and other suspects are located and the practicability of the evidence of such persons being given in the UK or in states outside the UK and (g) the connection of the prosecuted person to the UK. The connection to the UK is not solely determined by nationality or permanent residency, but also by, for instance, family ties, property in the UK and employment.[180] In addition, in *Atraskevic*, the court emphasised that this factor should also be read in light of the connection to the requesting state.[181]

[174] HC Deb 16 October 2012, vol 551, cols 176, 178; HC Deb 11 February 2013, vol 558, col 564; HC Deb 24 November 2001, vol 536, col 194WH; HC Deb 5 December 2011, vol 537 col 84; HL Deb 25 March 2013, vol 744, col 898.

[175] HL Deb 16 October 2012, vol 739, col 1381. See also HL 25 March 2013, vol 744, col 888.

[176] See also HL Deb 25 March 2013, vol 744, col 899; HC Deb 5 December 2011, vol 537, col 109.

[177] HL Deb 25 March 2013, vol 744, col 888; Davies (2018), p. 300.

[178] Other arguments put forward were that the forum bar would cause significant delays and would violate the principle of mutual recognition. HL Deb 20 October 2009, vol 497, col 603; HL Deb 25 March 2013, vol 744, col 888; Baker report (2011), paras 6.63, 6.69. See also Arnell and Davies (2020), p. 157.

[179] This requirement is explained in *Shaw v Government of the USA* [2014] EWHC Admin 4654, [2014] 11 WLUK 488. The case concerns a Part 2 warrant.

[180] *Love v USA* [2018] EWHC Admin 172, [2018] 1 WLR 2889 [40]–[41].

[181] *Atraskevic v Lithuania* [2015] EWHC Admin 131, [2016] 1 WLR 2762 [41]. See also *Yilmaz v Turkey* [2017] EWHC Admin 1617, [2017] 3 WLUK 510 [53].

Section 19B(3) provides an exhaustive list, meaning that, for instance, sentencing guidelines in the requesting state do not carry any weight unless they should be considered in light of one of the other factors.[182] As all factors need to be considered, the District Judge first needs to establish whether a factor is present and, on the assumption that it is, weigh it against other present factors.[183] In *Love*, the court stated that an exhaustive list of relevant factors prevents the court from entering into a vague assessment of what is just.[184] English law also provides the possibility to appeal the decision of the District Judge in which the conclusions with regard to the interest of justice test can be reviewed.[185]

No hierarchy exists between the enumerated factors and the weight given to each of them may vary depending on the circumstances of each case.[186] The case law provides some indications as to how the factors should be balanced. In *Love*, the court stated that the place where most of the loss or harm took place is usually an important one.[187] Furthermore, the concentration of all prosecutions in one state is primarily important when there are co-defendants, since it is considered advantageous to try all defendants before the same courts and under the same law and sentencing regime.[188] The factor primarily highlights the advantages of a single trial in terms of the availability of all relevant evidence, consistency of decision-making and efficiency.[189] In addition, the case law states that when the public prosecutor has issued no statement of belief that the UK is not the better forum, this factor may not

[182] *Atraskevic v Lithuania* [2015] EWHC Admin 131, [2016] 1 WLR 2762 [14]; *Love v USA* [2018] EWHC Admin 172, [2018] 1 WLR 2889; Ormerod et al. (2018), para D31.28. Extradition Act 2003, s 19B(4) contains an exception.

[183] This also means that when the factor is not present, this conclusion is the only regard the District Judge can have for it. *Atraskevic v Lithuania* [2015] EWHC Admin 131, [2016] 1 WLR 2762 [14], [36]. See also *Shaw v Government of the USA* [2014] EWHC Admin 4654, [2014] 11 WLUK 488 [40].

[184] *Love v USA* [2018] EWHC Admin 172, [2018] 1 WLR 2889 [22].

[185] However, the appeal court may not conduct a complete reassessment of all the facts or weight that should be given to the different factors in Section 19B, 'unless it is established that the judge at the extradition hearing: (1) misconstrued the statutory wording; (2) erred in respect of some applicable principle of law; (3) failed to take into account a relevant factor, or took into account an irrelevant factor; or (4) reached an irrational or perverse conclusion on the issue as a whole'. As follows from the cases *Love* and *Scott*, an appeal may be successful when the DJ did not sufficiently emphasize particular factors, such as the connection to the UK. *Atraskevic v Lithuania* [2015] EWHC Admin 131, [2016] 1 WLR 2762 [34].

[186] *Ejinyere v USA* [2018] EWHC Admin 2841, [2018] 10 WLUK 448 [17]; *Dibden v France* [2014] EWHC Admin 3074, [2014] 7 WLUK 739 [18], [25]; *Atraskevic v Lithuania* [2015] EWHC Admin 131, [2016] 1 WLR 2762 [25].

[187] *Ejinyere v USA* [2018] EWHC Admin 2841, [2018] 10 WLUK 448 [20]; *Love v USA* [2018] EWHC Admin 172, [2018] 1 WLR 2889 [28]. *A contrario Dibden v France* [2014] EWHC Admin 3074, [2014] 7 WLUK 739 [25].

[188] *Ejinyere v USA* [2018] EWHC Admin 2841, [2018] 10 WLUK 448 [20]; *Love v USA* [2018] EWHC Admin 172, [2018] 1 WLR 2889 [39].

[189] *Scott v USA* [2018] EWHC Admin 2021, [2019] 1 WLR 774 [55]–[56]; *Ejinyere v USA* [2018] EWHC Admin 2841, [2018] 10 WLUK 448 [38].

be used as an argument in favour of extradition.[190] The prosecutor cannot be compelled to issue such a statement, which correlates from the rule that the decision of the domestic authorities not to investigate or prosecute a case may only be judicially reviewed in exceptional circumstances.[191] Inquiries into the basis of the belief are allowed when appropriate,[192] but Section 19B(3)(c) EA is not intended as a possibility to judicially review the decision of the public prosecutor on the more appropriate forum on other grounds than irrationality.[193]

In *Love*, the court emphasised the potential importance of the last factor, which is the connection to the UK. As explained before, this connection is not solely determined on the basis of nationality, but also by, for instance, employment in the UK. In addition, in *Love*, the special medical conditions of Mr. Love were taken into account in light of this factor. The court decided that even though health issues should actually not be taken into account to determine the connection to the UK, an exception is made when there is something special about the nature of the health issues that connects the necessary treatment to the UK.[194] Such medical conditions and necessary treatment make the connection to the UK stronger.[195]

Interim Conclusion

It can be concluded that the forum bar was introduced to avoid extradition in case of excessive jurisdiction claims and to increase transparency in relation to the decision whether and where a case should be prosecuted. With the forum bar, the UK legislator has aimed to provide more clarity and guidance in relation to the decision-making process of whether a case should be prosecuted and where in case of conflicts of national jurisdictions. Both the forum bar and its rationale show that the risk of arbitrary forum choices due to a lack of a transparent EU or international system for forum choices is to some extent recognised in the English legal order. This also follows from the parliamentary debates on the forum bar.

It is also true that the lack of a hierarchy among the different factors in the 'interest of justice test', and the fact that the forum bar seems limited to a choice between the UK and the requesting state or prosecution and no prosecution, argue against the forum bar as a mechanism which ensures a transparent system for forum

---

[190] *Atraskevic v Lithuania* [2015] EWHC Admin 131, [2016] 1 WLR 2762 [39]. See *a contrario Love v USA* [2018] EWHC Admin 172, [2018] 1 WLR 2889 [34]–[35] in which the court stated that the absence of a prosecutor's belief should be considered a factor modestly favouring the application of the forum bar. The interpretation in Atraskevic was, however, confirmed in *Scott v USA* [2018] EWHC Admin 2021, [2019] 1 WLR 774 [31]; *Balog v Czech Republic* [2019] EWHC Admin 3528, [2019] 12 WLUK 376 [16], [39]. See also Arnell and Davies (2020), p. 151.

[191] *Atraskevic v Lithuania* [2015] EWHC Admin 131, [2016] 1 WLR 2762 [37].

[192] *Piotrowicz v Poland* [2014] EWHC Admin 3884, [2014] 10 WLUK 853 [25]; Ormerod et al. (2018), para D 31.28.

[193] *Dibden v France* [2014] EWHC Admin 3074, [2014] 7 WLUK 739 [35].

[194] Mr. Love required the stability and care provided by his parents, which could not be provided abroad. *Love v USA* [2018] EWHC Admin 172, [2018] 1 WLR 2889 [40]–[41], [43].

[195] *Ejinyere v USA* [2018] EWHC Admin 2841, [2018] 10 WLUK 448 [43]; *Scott v USA* [2018] EWHC Admin 2021, [2019] 1 WLR 774 [57].

choices in light of the proper administration of justice in case of concurrent jurisdictions. In the legal literature, the point has been made that the forum bar aims to determine whether extradition in the specific situation is in the interest of justice. It does not necessarily appoint the most appropriate forum for prosecution as such.[196]

However, it needs to be kept in mind that the FDEAW itself is also not an instrument for forum decisions and that it is questionable whether the EAW procedure is the right procedure for making such a decision.[197] In this light, it is not the responsibility or task of the UK to set up a clear system for forum choices in its Extradition Act 2003 or more generally to install a general transparent system for forum choices in case of conflicts of national jurisdictions in its national law. In fact, it is also questionable whether the forum bar is in compliance with the FDEAW, since it goes beyond the refusal grounds enumerated in Articles 3 and 4 FDEAW. The main point remains that the introduction of the forum bar shows that in the English legal order the potential problems arising from the absence of a clear EU system for forum choices are to some extent recognised and integrated in the context of the extradition procedure.

7.3.5 *The Human Rights Ground*

Before the implementation of the FDEAW, the Secretary of State, who is a member of the government, was provided with the power to offer protection against exorbitant extraterritorial jurisdiction by using his or her discretion to prevent extradition in a concrete case.[198] In *Al-Fawwaz,* which was decided under the former Extradition Act 1989, Lord Rodger stated that protection against exorbitant jurisdiction is primarily the responsibility of the state. Governments should only conclude treaties with states who have a correct and appropriate approach to the exercise of (extra)-territorial jurisdiction for the purpose of prosecution.[199] As a result of the FDEAW the role of the Secretary of State has been limited and he or she is no longer competent to prevent extradition in case of exorbitant jurisdiction claims. To compensate for this, the matter of exorbitant jurisdiction claims can now be raised in the context of the human rights ground. Section 21A(1)(a) EA states that the District Judge should assess whether extradition is compatible with the Convention rights within the meaning of the Human Rights Act 1998.[200] It follows from the case law

---

[196] Arnell and Davies (2020), p. 151.

[197] This will be further elaborated on in Chaps. 10 and 13.

[198] *R (on the application of Al-Fawwaz) v Governor of Brixton Prison* [2001] UKHL 69, [2002] 1 AC 556 [39], [105].

[199] *R (on the application of Al-Fawwaz) v Governor of Brixton Prison* [2001] UKHL 69, [2002] 1 AC 556 [95], [148]–[149].

[200] Extradition Act 2003, s 87 codifies the human rights bar for Part 2 warrants. The case law on Section 87 EA is relevant for Section 21A EA and vice versa. *Hashmi v USA* [2007] EWHC Admin 564, [2007] 3 WLUK 519 [25]–[26].

that extravagant jurisdiction claims can be a relevant factor in light of the proportionality assessment conducted in case of a violation of Article 8 ECHR. This proportionality assessment covers the question whether the interference with privacy and family life caused by extradition is outweighed by the public interests served by extradition.[201]

Cases in which the requesting state is considered to exercise exorbitant jurisdiction are likely to be rare.[202] It follows from the English jurisprudence that the requesting state only exercises exorbitant jurisdiction when it has a tenuous connection to the criminal offence in the extradition request.[203] An example could be the exercise of jurisdiction in a cross-border fraud case, while the only link to the prosecuting state is the fact that an email was routed through a server in that state.[204] Furthermore, meeting the double criminality requirement in Article 64 EA strongly demonstrates that the requesting state does not exercise exorbitant jurisdiction.[205]

In addition, exorbitant jurisdiction is merely one of the factors which can be taken into account in light of the proportionality assessment of Article 8 ECHR and the case law sets a high threshold for refusing extradition on the basis of Article 8 ECHR. Quite exceptionally compelling circumstances need to exist for extradition to be considered in light of the right to family life.[206] In practice, the argument of exorbitant jurisdiction does not have an important role, and a search of the case law does not show any judgements discharging the requested person on the basis of Article 8 ECHR, because of exorbitant jurisdiction claims.[207]

So, protection against exorbitant jurisdiction may be a relevant factor in determining the proportionality or disproportionality of the interference with the right to private and family life in Article 8 ECHR caused by extradition. However, the case law on Article 21A EA does not show a link between exorbitant jurisdiction claims, and the view that the applicability of the requesting state should have been foreseeable at the time of the offence. In addition, the case law on Article 21A EA does not

[201] *Atraskevic v Lithuania* [2015] EWHC Admin 131, [2016] 1 WLR 2762 [43]; *Boudhiba v Spain*, [2006] EWHC Admin 167, [2007] 1 WLR 124 [44]; *Hashmi v USA* [2007] EWHC Admin 564, [2007] 3 WLUK 519 [26].

[202] *Hashmi v USA* [2007] EWHC Admin 564, [2007] 3 WLUK 519 [34]. The court decided that the USA did not exercise exorbitant jurisdiction when it charged the requested person for agreeing to provide military gear to Al Qaeda as well as the act of attempting to provide it. These actions occurred in London, but the allegation was that the material was intended to fight US forces.

[203] *Boudhiba v Spain*, [2006] EWHC Admin 167, [2007] 1 WLR 124 [44]; *Louca v Germany* [2008] EWHC Admin 2907, [2008] 11 WLUK 726 [48]–[50].

[204] Baker report (2011), para 6.45. In *R (on the application of Bermingham v Director of the Serious Fraud Office* [2006] EWHC Admin 200, [2007] QB 727 [129] in which the court stated 'The United States dimension does not arise from the contingency that a telephone call or an e-mail happened to be received in that jurisdiction.'

[205] *Boudhiba v Spain*, [2006] EWHC Admin 167, [2007] 1 WLR 124 [44].

[206] *Bagri v France* [2014] EWHC Admin 4066, [2014] 12 WLUK 519 [46]. See also *Norris v USA* [2010] UKSC 9, [2010] 2 AC 487; Ormerod et al. (2018), para D31.35.

[207] Search on Westlaw and LexisNexis using the terms 'exorbitant jurisdiction' and 'exorbitant'.

include any important judgements in which the requested person was discharged, because extradition would constitute a violation of the right to a tribunal established by law laid down in Articles 6 ECHR and 47 (2) CFR.

The English courts also refer to the cases *Aranyosi* and *Câldâraru* and *LM* in their rulings on extradition requests.[208] On the basis of these two CJEU rulings, the requested person will not be surrendered to the issuing state when the twofold test has been met. However, as stated before in Chaps. 3 and 4, the two-step test for now only applies in relation to the prohibition of torture and inhuman and degrading treatment in Article 4 CFR and the right to an independent judge in Article 47 (2) CFR. The English courts have also limited the application of the CJEU case law to these two fundamental rights and have therefore not taken the liberty to extend the scope of the twofold test to other fundamental rights, such as Article 49 CFR or the right to a tribunal established by law. As explained before in Chaps. 5 and 6, this can be explained in light of the fact that the interpretation of EU law, including the fundamental rights in the Charter, falls within the competence of the Court of Justice of the European Union. Member states are, therefore, less likely to decide on their own accord that the substantive legality principle in Article 49 CFR and the right to a tribunal established by law in 47 CFR cover jurisdiction and forum choices on the EU level and that the twofold test should also be applied in relation to these two fundamental rights.

7.3.6 Multiple Extradition Requests

Section 44 EA covers the situation in which Westminster Magistrates' Court receives multiple warrants from EU Member States for the same person and the same offence.[209] The court's decision regarding which warrant should be given precedence has to be based on the same criteria as those in Article 16 FDEAW, which are the seriousness of the offences, the place whether the crime was committed or alleged to have been committed, the dates on which the EAWs were issued and whether the EAW is for the purpose of prosecution or enforcement.[210] In relation to the place where the crime was committed, priority should be given to the warrant issued by the state exercising territorial jurisdiction.[211] The list is not exhaustive in order to ensure that all important factors in a specific situation can be taken into account and does not set a pecking order.[212] As a result of the lack of a

[208] See e.g. *Kirchanov v Bulgaria* [2017] EWHC Admin 1285, [2017] 5 WLUK 494; *Bartulis v Lithuania* [2019] EWHC Admin 3504, [2019] 12 WLUK 388; *Lis v Poland (No 1)*[2018] EWHC Admin 2848, [2018] 10 WLUK 450; *Lis v Poland (No 2)* [2019] EWHC Admin 674, [2019] 3 WLUK 385.

[209] *R (on the application of Caldarelli) v City of Westminster Magistrates' Court* [2009] EWHC 107, [2009] 1 WLUK 483 [42].

[210] Extradition Act 2003, s 44(7).

[211] HL Deb 10 July 2003, vol 651, col 126GC.

[212] HL Deb 10 July 2003, vol 651, col 126GC.

hierarchy and the limited amount of reported case law on how to balance the different factors, it is unclear how much weight should be allocated to each individual factor.[213]

In case of competing warrants from EU Member States and third states, the Secretary of State is the competent authority to make the decision. Section 179 (3) EA provides the same non-exhaustive list of factors as Section 44 EA and is also without a clear hierarchy. It is questionable to what extent the discretion of the Secretary of State is restricted by the CJEU rulings in *Petruhhin* and *Pisciotti*.[214] It follows from these cases that when an EU Member State receives an extradition request for the purpose of prosecution from a third state for an EU citizen who has exercised the right to free movement and is not a national of the requested state, it should first ask the state of nationality of the EU citizen whether it wishes to issue an EAW. However, the CJEU issued these rulings in cases in which the national law of the requested states exclusively protected their own nationals against extradition. As English law allows for the extradition of Englishmen, the CJEU ruling in *Petruhhin* and *Pisciotti* may not be applicable.

As explained before, the decision for a particular warrant could influence the eventual forum decision. The state whose warrant is rejected may for that reason decide not to prosecute or to suspend its prosecution. However, neither Sections 44 and 179 EA nor the case law indicates that the rules regulating concurrent warrants are influenced by the opinion that the decision on the forum for prosecution and trial should be made on the basis of a transparent and clear set of rules. In other words, the potential problems arising from the absence of a transparent EU system for forum choices, in particular the risk of arbitrary forum decision, do not seem to play a role in the context of the rules regulating the situation of competing warrants. This also follows from the fact that the list of factors enumerated in the applicable provisions are not exhaustive nor hierarchical, which diminishes the legal certainty of individuals and increases the risk of arbitrary decisions. An explanation for this flexibility is that it allows the competent authority to choose the best state for prosecution in the concrete case.[215] However, in case of competing warrants from EU Member States, the risk of a random decision for a particular warrant, which can also influence the eventual forum decision, is to a certain extent remedied by the fact that it is not a member of the executive, but a judge who decides which warrant will be executed. In addition, the decision of the District Judge can be appealed.[216]

---

[213] Jones and Doobay (2005), p. 300. The decisions taken in first instance are not reported, so it is not possible to verify whether the criteria are generally weighed in the same manner.

[214] Case C-182/15 *Petruhhin* [2016] ECLI:EU:C:2016:630; Case C-191/16 *Pisciotti* [2018] ECLI: EU:C:2018:222.

[215] HL Deb 10 September 2003 vol 652, cols 14GC-16GC.

[216] In relation to competing warrants from EU Member States and third states, a request for judicial review of the decision of the Secretary of State can be made to the court. However, this is a more complicated route, as also follows from the Civil Procedure Rules (CPR) <https://www.justice.gov.uk/courts/procedure-rules/civil/rules> accessed 20 September 2021, rr 54.1 and 54.4.

7.4 England As the Issuing State

7.4.1 An Introduction

This section examines to what extent the two complications with which an EU citizen may be confronted in the AFSJ have been recognised as problems in the context of the issuing procedure. The third part of the Extradition Act, more specifically Sections 142–149 EA, and the Legal Guidance on Extradition for the CPS regulate the issuing procedure.[217] The Extradition Act 2003 refers to outgoing EAWs as Part 3 warrants and this term will, therefore, be used in the next section.[218] Furthermore, the English rules regulating the decision to issue a Part 3 Warrant refer to the rules regulating the underlying decision to prosecute a case. These are the Code for Crown Prosecutors (CCPS) and the previously discussed Director's Guidance on concurrent jurisdictions and the Legal Guidance on jurisdiction for the CPS.[219] In light of the link between the rules regulating the issuing procedure and the rules on the decision to prosecute, these are discussed together. The main emphasis is on the question to what extent these rules reflect the position that a suspect should have been able to foresee the applicability of English law at the time of the offence and that a transparent system for preventing or solving national conflicts of jurisdictions is required.

7.4.2 The Issuing Procedure and the Rules Regulating the Power to Exercise Jurisdiction

In England, the authorities which are officially competent to issue a Part 3 Warrant are District Judges at the Magistrates' Courts, a justice of the peace or a judge entitled to exercise the jurisdiction of the Crown Court.[220] In practice, the Westminster Magistrates' Court issues the Part 3 warrants for Wales and the southern parts of England, while Leeds Magistrates' Court issues them for persons wanted in the north

[217] Legal Guidance on Extradition (12 May 2020) <https://www.cps.gov.uk/legal-guidance/extradition> accessed 20 September 2021.

[218] The Extradition Act 2003 also calls outgoing extradition requests to third states Part 3 warrants. However, Sect. 7.4.2 will only cover Part 3 warrants to EU Member States.

[219] Code for Crown Prosecutors (2018) <https://www.cps.gov.uk/sites/default/files/documents/publications/Code-for-Crown-Prosecutors-October-2018.pdf> accessed 20 September 2021; Director's Guidance on the handling of cases where the jurisdiction to prosecute is shared with prosecuting authorities overseas (17 July 2013) <https://www.cps.gov.uk/publication/directors-guidance-handling-cases-where-jurisdiction-prosecute-shared-prosecuting> accessed 20 September 2021; Legal Guidance on jurisdiction (26 July 2021) <https://www.cps.gov.uk/legal-guidance/jurisdiction> accessed 3 March 2022.

[220] Extradition Act 2003, ss 142(1) and 149(1)(a).

of England.[221] These courts issue Part 3 warrants on the request of a police officer or a public prosecutor in England and Wales.[222] In most cases the official application for a Part 3 Warrant is made by the public prosecutor who deals with the underlying case.[223] The District Judge considers, amends if necessary and signs the EAW, which in practice often means a rubber-stamping of the application.[224] The CJEU string of case law on the competent issuing judicial authority starting with *OG & PI* has not resulted in changes to this division of tasks. In this light, the Framework agreement between the Law Officers and the Director of Public Prosecutions states that the CPS acts independently from the executive when deciding whether or not to prosecute.[225]

The public prosecutor is competent to make an application for a Part 3 Warrant to the court under the following conditions. Firstly, a domestic arrest warrant must have been issued for the offence in question and there need to be reasonable grounds for believing that the person in question has committed the extradition offence.[226] Secondly, the Part 3 Warrant needs to meet the proportionality requirement, since it interferes with the right to liberty and could require the use of considerable resources. To avoid extradition requests in trivial cases, the public prosecutor should consider the seriousness of the offence, the penalty which will likely be imposed and the interests of the victim.[227] Thirdly, the Extradition Act and Legal Guidance on

[221] Evaluation report on the fourth round of mutual evaluations 'The practical application of the European Arrest Warrant and Corresponding surrender procedures between Member States'—Report on the United Kingdom, 9974/2/07 REV 2 EXT 1 (2007), p. 5.

[222] Extradition Act 2003, s 142(1)(a) jo (9); Legal Guidance on Extradition (12 May 2020) <https://www.cps.gov.uk/legal-guidance/extradition> accessed 20 September 2021; Padfield (2007), p. 257.

[223] Legal Guidance on Extradition (12 May 2020) <https://www.cps.gov.uk/legal-guidance/extradition> accessed 20 September 2021.

[224] Presence is only required if the issuing of the domestic warrant is part of the application. Evaluation report on the fourth round of mutual evaluations 'The practical application of the European Arrest Warrant and Corresponding surrender procedures between Member States'—Report on the United Kingdom, 9974/2/07 REV 2 EXT 1 (2007), p. 17.

[225] However, in some situations, the public prosecutor needs the consent of the Attorney General, who then acts independently of the government. In some exceptional cases, the Director of Public Prosecutors or Attorney General may deem it desirable to ask the advice of the government on public interest considerations. However, the eventual prosecution decision remains with the prosecutor. Framework agreement between the Law Officers and the Director of Public Prosecutions (2020) <https://www.gov.uk/government/publications/framework-agreement-between-the-law-officers-and-the-director-of-public-prosecutions-cps> accessed 3 March 2022, ss 46–56. See also Code for Crown Prosecutors (2018) <https://www.cps.gov.uk/sites/default/files/documents/publications/Code-for-Crown-Prosecutors-October-2018.pdf> accessed 20 September 2021, paras 2.1 and 3.8.

[226] Extradition Act 2003, s 142 (2)(a)(b) jo (8) jo (8A) EA. Section 148 EA defines the meaning of 'extradition offense'.

[227] According to the Evaluation report, this proportionality assessment is part of the public interest test conducted by the public prosecutor when deciding whether to start a domestic prosecution. Evaluation report on the fourth round of mutual evaluations 'The practical application of the

Extradition state that the Part 3 Warrant may not be issued for any other reason than for the purpose of prosecuting a person who has been officially accused of committing the offences in the warrant.[228] In general, this means that the public prosecutor needs to be trial-ready when requesting the court to issue a Part 3 Warrant.[229] Lastly, in light of the link between the decision to prosecute and the issuing of a Part 3 Warrant, the Legal Guidance on Extradition states that an extradition request may only be issued when the requirements of the Full Code Test in the Code for Crown Prosecutors is met.[230] It consists of an evidential stage followed by the public interest stage, which entails that criminal proceedings should not continue if the evidence does not show a realistic prospect of conviction.[231] In relation to the public interest test, the Code for Crown Prosecutors includes a non-exhaustive and non-hierarchical list of factors which should be taken into consideration.[232] Furthermore, in case of conflicts of national jurisdictions the factors in the Director's Guidance on concurrent jurisdictions and the CPS Legal Guidance on jurisdiction should also be taken into account when deciding whether to prosecute a case in England and issue a Part 3 Warrant for that purpose.[233] However, neither the factors

European Arrest Warrant and Corresponding surrender procedures between Member States'—Report on the United Kingdom, 9974/2/07 REV 2 EXT 1 (2007), p. 13. See also Legal Guidance on Extradition (12 May 2020) <https://www.cps.gov.uk/legal-guidance/extradition> accessed 20 September 2021.

[228] Extradition Act 2003, s 142(4).

[229] Legal Guidance on Extradition (12 May 2020) <https://www.cps.gov.uk/legal-guidance/extradition> accessed 20 September 2021.

[230] In exceptional circumstances, the Threshold Test applies when the requirements of the Full Code Test are not met. On the basis of the Threshold Test, a person can be charged when the prosecutor only has enough evidence to conclude that reasonable grounds exist that the suspect has committed the offence. However, the use of the Test is restricted by five cumulative criteria, of which the public interest test is one as well. Legal Guidance on Extradition (12 May 2020) <https://www.cps.gov.uk/legal-guidance/extradition> accessed 20 September 2021; Code for Crown Prosecutors 2018, paras 4.1–4.14 and 5.1–5.10.

[231] For the evidentiary standard to be met, the evidence should be reliable and credible or in other words, admissible in court. Code for Crown Prosecutors (2018) <https://www.cps.gov.uk/sites/default/files/documents/publications/Code-for-Crown-Prosecutors-October-2018.pdf> accessed 20 September 2021, paras 4.4 and 4.6–4.8.

[232] Code for Crown Prosecutors (2018) <https://www.cps.gov.uk/sites/default/files/documents/publications/Code-for-Crown-Prosecutors-October-2018.pdf> accessed 20 September 2021, paras 4.11–4.14. However, para 4.14 states 'The cost to the CPS and the wider criminal justice system, especially where it could be regarded as excessive when weighed against any likely penalty. Prosecutors should not decide the public interest on the basis of this factor alone. It is essential that regard is also given to the public interest factors identified when considering the other questions in paragraphs 4.14 a) to g) but cost can be a relevant factor when making an overall assessment of the public interest.'

[233] The Legal Guidance on Extradition 2020 states, 'Prosecutors should also consider whether the offending gives rise to concurrent jurisdiction in all cases where the conduct took place in more than one Member State, or where another Member State has extra-territorial jurisdiction to prosecute the matter. In such cases, prosecutors should refer to the Legal Guidance on Jurisdiction and the .' Legal Guidance on Extradition (12 May 2020) <https://www.cps.gov.uk/legal-guidance/extradition>

in the Full Code Test nor the factors in the Director's Guidance on concurrent jurisdictions and CPS Jurisdiction Guidance mention the foreseeability of the application of English law at the time of the offence as an important consideration. These factors reflect a clear preference for prosecution by the *locus delicti*, which is facilitated by the possibility to extradite British subjects, but this preference is not based on 'foreseeability' considerations. Hence, the position that the applicability of English law should have been foreseeable at the time of the offence has not significantly influenced the procedure for the issuing of a Part 3 Warrant.

In relation to the problems arising from the absence of a transparent EU system for forum choices, Sect. 7.3.3.2 already discussed the most important points. It explained that the Legal Guidance on jurisdiction and the Director's Guidance on concurrent jurisdictions address the matter of conflicts of national jurisdictions, even though at least the latter only covers cases in which the offence is partially committed in the UK and partially abroad. The Director's Guidance on concurrent jurisdictions was in fact a response to the findings of the Scott Baker report reviewing the UK's extradition arrangements, which concluded that the process leading to a decision to prosecute in case of conflicts of national jurisdictions was not sufficiently transparent or based on formally agreed upon criteria.[234] The Director's Guidance on concurrent jurisdictions states that in case of cross-frontier offences the sharing of information and early consultation with foreign colleagues is recommended to find the best place for prosecution.[235] The Legal Guidance on Extradition also refers to this Director's Guidance on concurrent jurisdictions. Hence, in the English legal order, emphasis has been put on the need for a transparent system for forum decisions in case of conflicts of national jurisdictions.

7.5 Conclusion

The main question of this chapter was whether the two complications with which EU citizens can be confronted in the context of the EAW procedure are recognised as legal problems or even as legality problems in the combined legal order of England and Wales. In relation to unforeseeable jurisdiction claims, we have seen in Sect. 7.2 that the criminality of conduct under English law also depends on the question

accessed 20 September 2021. See also Code for Crown Prosecutors (2018) <https://www.cps.gov.uk/sites/default/files/documents/publications/Code-for-Crown-Prosecutors-October-2018.pdf> accessed 20 September 2021, para 4.11.

[234] Baker report (2011), paras 1.18–1.19, 6.43, 6.71–6.74; Doobay (2015); HC Deb 16 October 2012, vol 551, col. 165.

[235] Even though it is considered a rare situation, the decision for a particular jurisdiction should be revisited in case a change of circumstances requires this. Director's Guidance on the handling of cases where the jurisdiction to prosecute is shared with prosecuting authorities overseas (17 July 2013) <https://www.cps.gov.uk/publication/directors-guidance-handling-cases-where-jurisdiction-prosecute-shared-prosecuting> accessed 20 September 2021, para 9.

whether it falls within its ambit. The general rule on the ambit of English criminal law is that English law exclusively applies on the territory of England and Wales and to all individuals within its realm, unless a specific statutory provision established extraterritorial jurisdiction. Even though the primacy of the territoriality principle could very well be based on the position that citizens should be protected against the unexpected application of foreign laws, especially in an AFSJ in which EU citizens are provided with the right to free movement, this is not the case. Instead, the general rule that all crime is local is based on old procedural rules of venue and aims to protect state sovereignty.

Section 7.3 explained that some of the conditions for the execution of an incoming warrant, in particular the double criminality requirement, forum bar and human rights ground, aim to protect citizens against exorbitant jurisdiction claims. Some MPs even stated during the debate on the double criminality requirement that those who travel to another state cannot be expected to always know and understand the national criminal laws of those states. Still, it also follows from Sect. 7.3 that exorbitant jurisdiction has in the case law been defined as the existence of a mere tenuous connection to the prosecuting state without any reference to the foreseeability of the jurisdiction claim. Furthermore, it follows from the examination of the forum bar that the concerns for extravagant jurisdiction claims primarily exist in relation to third states, such as the USA. Hence, it can be concluded that the protection against exorbitant jurisdiction claims offered by conditions for the execution of an incoming warrant are not explicitly and clearly based on the view that individuals should not be extradited when they were not able to foresee at the time of the offence which particular national criminal law was applicable to them. A similar conclusion can be drawn in relation to the conditions for the issuing of a Part 3 Warrant discussed in Sect. 7.4. The foreseeability of English criminal law at the time of the offence does not play a prominent role in the decision to issue an EAW and the underlying decision to prosecute a case in England.

Despite these conclusions, it is interesting to note that contrary to Germany, which almost exclusively focuses on the protection of Germans against extraterritorial jurisdiction, the UK recognises the problem of extravagant jurisdiction claims for all individuals subjected to an extradition procedure. This more open attitude of the UK has, however, not explicitly been explained in light of the concept of EU citizenship, free movement or the adoption of new measures for judicial cooperation in the EU. This also follows from the fact that in case law preceding the FDEAW, such as the 2001 *Al-Fawwaz* case, protection against exorbitant jurisdiction was already considered the responsibility of the state, which should not conclude treaties with states who are likely to exercise extravagant jurisdiction. Instead, the more open attitude of England fits with the long existing tradition to extradite British nationals and foreigners alike as well as the position that crimes should be prosecuted in the state where they occurred.

Contrary to the complications arising from unforeseeable jurisdiction claims, the difficulties arising from the absence of a transparent EU or international system for forum choices have a more prominent position in the English legal order. Concerns regarding the transparency of the use of prosecutorial discretion in case of conflicts of national jurisdictions have resulted in the forum bar and in the Director's Guidance on concurrent jurisdictions. Both aim to provide more openness as to how a decision to prosecute a case in England or abroad is being made. Hence, contrary to the Netherlands and Germany, England has put more emphasis on the need for a transparent system for forum decisions in case of conflicts of national jurisdictions.

References

— Halsbury's Laws (5th edn, 2018) vol 61
Arnell P (2015) Lessons from the case of Abu Hamza. Crim Law Justice Weekly 179:709
Arnell P (2018) What an extradition hearing is and why it matters. Jur Rev 4:250
Arnell P, Davies G (2020) The forum bar in UK extradition law: an unnecessary failure. J Crim Law 84:142
Ashworth A, Horder J (2013) Principles of criminal law. Oxford University Press
Carr I, Goldby M (2011) Recovering the proceeds of corruption: UNCAC and anti-money laundering standards. J Bus Law 170
Chan W, Simester A (2011) Four functions of mens rea. Camb Law J 70:381
Davies G (2018) Extradition, forum bar and concurrent jurisdiction: is the case of Love a precedent for trying hackers in the UK? J Crim Law 82:296
Doobay A (2015) Forum in criminal proceedings: practice and procedure. Crim Law Justice Weekly 179:76
Farmer L (2013) Territorial jurisdiction and criminalization. Univ Toronto Law J 63:225
Grange E (2018) Love changes everything? Law Society Gazette. https://www.lawgazette.co.uk/commentary-and-opinion/love-changes-everything/5064754.article. Accessed 20 Sept 2021
Hirst M (2003) Jurisdiction and the ambit of the criminal law. Oxford University Press
Hirst M (2013) Country report England and Wales. In: Böse M, Meyer F, Schneider A (eds) Conflicts of jurisdiction in criminal matters in the European Union. Volume I: National reports and comparative analysis. Nomos
Jones A, Doobay A (2005) Jones and Doobay on extradition and mutual assistance. Sweet & Maxwell
Klip A, Massa A-S (2010) Communicerende grondslagen van extraterritoriale rechtsmacht. Maastricht University
Kosař D (2013) The least accountable branch. Int J Constitutional Law 11:234
Lew J (1978) The extra-territorial criminal jurisdiction of English Courts. Int Comp Law Q 27:168
Luchtman M (2011) Choice of forum in an area of freedom, security and justice. ULR 7:74
Mackarel M (2007) Surrendering the fugitive – The European Arrest Warrant and the United Kingdom. J Crim Law 71:362
Marshall P (2003) Criminal conduct under Part 7 of the Proceeds of Crime Act 2002: a requirement for double criminality? J Int Bank Financ Law 18:233
Marshall P (2004) Risk and legal uncertainty under the Proceeds of Crime Act 2002 – the results of legislative oversight. Company Lawyer 354
Mulan G (1997) The concept of double criminality in the context of extraterritorial crimes. Crim Law Rev 17
Müßig U (2006) Gesetzlicher Richter ohne Rechtsstaat? Eine historisch-vergleichende Spurensuche. De Gruyter
O'Keefe R (2009) Case comment: double-plus good or double trouble? Camb Law J 68:9
Ormerod D et al (eds) (2018) Blackstone's Criminal Practice 2019. Oxford University Press

Padfield N (2007) The European Arrest Warrant: between trust, democracy and the rule of law. The implementation of the European Arrest Warrant in England and Wales. Eur Constitutional Law Rev 3:253

Saxby S (2008) Child protection activity is stepped up on both sides of the Atlantic. Comput Law Secur Rep 24:281

Spencer J (2009) Mutual recognition of decisions in criminal justice and the United Kingdom. In: Tiggelen GV-V et al (eds) The future of mutual recognition in criminal matters in the European Union. University of Brussel

Stessens G (2000) Money laundering: a new international law enforcement model. Cambridge University Press

Thorhauer N (2015) Conflicts of jurisdiction in cross-border criminal cases in the area of freedom, security, and justice. Risks and opportunities from an individual rights-oriented perspective. NJECL 6:78

Vamos N (2018) A forum for debate about extradition? The barrister 2018. https://www.barristermagazine.com/a-forum-for-debate-about-extradition/. Accessed 20 Sept 2021

Van der Beken T (1999) Forumkeuze in het internationaal strafrecht. Maklu

Van Sliedregt E (2009) The dual criminality requirement. In: Keijzer N, van Sliedregt E (eds) The European Arrest Warrant in practice. Asser

Wahl T (2021) Brexit: EU-UK trade and cooperation agreement – impacts on PIF and JHA in a Nutshell. eucrim. https://eucrim.eu/news/brexit-eu-uk-trade-and-cooperation-agreement-impacts-on-pif-and-jha-in-nutshell/. Accessed 20 Sept 2021

Warbrick C, McGoldrick D (1999) Case comment: extradition law aspect of Pinochet 3. Int Comp Law Q 48:958

Williams S (2012) Arresting developments? Restricting the enforcement of the UK's universal jurisdiction provisions. Mod Law Rev 75:368

Woodhouse D (2006) Judicial independence and accountability in the United Kingdom's New Constitutional Settlement. In: Canivet G, Andenas M, Fairgrieve D (eds) Independence, accountability and the judiciary. British Institute of International and Comparative Law

Chapter 8
The Synthesis: The Current Recognition of a Triangular Link Between the EAW, the Legality Principle and Foreseeability Risks

8.1 Introduction

On the basis of the conclusions drawn in Chaps. 3–7, this chapter aims to answer the first part of the main research question concerning the existence and recognition of foreseeability problems of jurisdiction claims and forum choices citizens may be faced with in the context of the EAW.[1] The previous five chapters have examined the current perspective on the existence of a triangular relationship between jurisdiction claims and forum choices, the legality principle and the EAW in the EU and national legal practice, in particular on the legislative and judicial level. They have discussed to what extent the two complications relating to jurisdiction and forum decisions have been classified as legality problems and what that means for the role of the EAW in relation to these two complications. Consequently, they provide the basis for an answer to the question whether the EAW is recognised on the EU and the national level as a mechanism which can contribute to the materialisation of violations of the *nullum crimen sine lege* principle and right to a tribunal established by law when it surrenders EU citizens to a state whose jurisdiction claim was not foreseeable and whose decision to prosecute was not based on a clear EU system preventing or solving conflicts of jurisdictions. More specifically, Chap. 2 has set out the foreseeability problems which could arise from the current state of art of applicable jurisdiction rules and rules on forum choices in the EU. With regard to the EU level, Chap. 3 has examined to what extent the problem of unforeseeable jurisdiction claims and the potential issues arising from the lack of an EU system for forum choices have been recognised as legality problems in light of Articles 49 and 47 CFR and what this means for the role of the EAW in relation to these issues. In Chap. 4, the current level of protection offered by the EU legislator and CJEU against the foreseeability problems in the procedure for the issuing and execution of

[1] The second part of the main research question concerns the extent to which EU citizenship could help to address foreseeability problems. This part is examined and answered in Chaps. 10–12.

J. Graat, *The European Arrest Warrant and EU Citizenship*,
https://doi.org/10.1007/978-3-031-07590-2_8

an EAW has been set out. Chapters 5, 6 and 7 have explored for three national legal orders to what extent the two foreseeability issues have been recognised as legality problems and the EAW as a mechanism, which in itself does not cause these problems, but contributes to their enforcement.

To provide a clear answer to the first part of the central research question, this chapter is structured in the following way.[2] Section 8.2 will repeat the possible problems arising from the operation of the EAW in an AFSJ in which jurisdiction claims are often not foreseeable to EU citizens and no transparent system preventing or solving conflicts of national jurisdictions has been adopted. Section 8.3 then answers the twofold question to what extent unforeseeable jurisdiction claims have on the EU and national level been linked to the requirement of an accessible and foreseeable law for offences and sanctions, and to what extent the EAW is viewed as a mechanism enforcing violations of this fundamental right by transferring EU citizens, while the jurisdiction claim of the issuing state was not foreseeable at the time of the offence. For this purpose, Sect. 8.3.1 compares the conclusions in Chapters 3 and 5–7 regarding the scope of the *nullum crimen sine lege* principle. Sections 8.3.2 focuses on the protection offered against unforeseeable jurisdiction claims in the issuing procedure on the EU and national level. Section 8.3.3 has the same focus in relation to the conditions in the executing procedures. Section 8.4 discusses the twofold question to what extent the absence of a transparent EU system preventing or solving conflicts of national jurisdictions has been recognised as a violation of the right to a tribunal established by law on the EU and national level and to what extent the EAW is viewed as a mechanism which could contribute to such violations by transferring EU citizens, while the jurisdiction claim of the issuing state is not based on a transparent system for forum choices in case of conflicts of national jurisdictions. For this purpose, Sect. 8.4.1 compares the scope of application of the right to a tribunal established by law as applicable on the EU and the national level. Section 8.4.2 then discusses the recognition of the possibility of arbitrary forum choices in the context of the issuing procedure. Section 8.4.3 conducts the same comparison for the executing procedure. Section 8.5 then provides the conclusion and will indicate to what extent there are signs that the two problems and the role of the EAW therein have been discussed and are perhaps even recognised as legality problems on the EU and national level.

8.2 A Recap of the Two Problems and the Role of the EAW

As this chapter aims to provide an answer to the first part of the main research question, this section briefly reiterates the role of the EAW in relation to two potential problems with which EU citizens can be confronted due to the lack of

[2] Like in Chap. 7, references to the EAW procedure in England and Wales cover the situation before January 2021.

EU rules which fully harmonise jurisdiction and an adequate EU system preventing or solving conflicts of jurisdictions. As explained in Chap. 2, most Member States have extended the scope of application of their national substantive criminal laws to crimes committed abroad. This was a response to the increased risk of cross-border criminality brought about by the common goal to remove internal borders in the AFSJ and the right to free movement provided to EU citizens.[3] As a result, most Member States are now competent to prosecute and try suspects for crimes committed outside their own territory. Within this picture, the EAW is a mechanism which national competent authorities can use to ensure the enforcement of their own national criminal laws, as it provides them with the possibility to bring suspects to their territory for prosecution and trial. It compensates for the Member States' lack of extraterritorial jurisdiction to enforce, since states are under international law prohibited from conducting investigatory actions, including arrests, on the territory of other states without permission. Hence, the EAW, which is more speedy and efficient in comparison to extradition procedures, is also viewed as the extended (extraterritorial) enforcement arm of national prosecution authorities.

Article 3(2) TEU states that the EU should offer its citizens an AFSJ in which both free movement and security are guaranteed. The combination of the Member States' broad extraterritorial jurisdiction and the EAW is an asset to the security dimension of the AFSJ, but it can also cause complications for EU citizens, especially for those exercising their right to free movement and those confronted with someone who exercises the right to free movement. The first complication arises from the fact that due to the broad extraterritorial jurisdiction of the Member States, EU citizens could be subjected to multiple national criminal laws.[4] As a result of the broad use of jurisdiction grounds, such as the effects doctrine correlating from the territoriality principle and the passive nationality principle, it can become quite difficult for EU citizens to know which particular national criminal laws to obey at a particular time in the AFSJ. The effects doctrine can be problematic, because the consequences of a criminal offence may occur in unanticipated places, and the passive nationality principle because the alleged offender may at the time of the offence be unaware of the nationality of the victim.

From the perspective of the EU citizen, this foreseeability issue is problematic, because the substantive criminal laws of the Member States still differ to a large extent. As a result, moving EU citizens can be exposed to unexpected criminal liability, prosecution for more serious offences or heavier sanctions. The role of the EAW in this setting is that it provides a fast and more efficient surrender mechanism for the purpose of prosecution and could, therefore, aid prosecution by a state while the applicability of its national criminal law was difficult to foresee at the time of the offence. Hence, the EAW can facilitate the transfer of EU citizens, even though they are confronted with this foreseeability problem in the underlying criminal cases.

[3] See Sects. 2.3 and 2.4.

[4] This problem and the question which it raises are discussed in Sect. 2.5.

The complication set out above raises questions in light of the accessibility and foreseeability requirement correlating from the substantive legality principle as codified in Article 49 CFR and Article 7 ECHR. More specifically, the question arises: are citizens provided with an adequate indication as to the applicable criminal rules, and are they able to foresee the possibility of criminal liability and sanctions on the basis of the law when they could not have known at the time of the offence which specific national criminal codes to obey? In relation to the role of the EAW, the question becomes whether its current legal framework forces the executing judicial authority to surrender the requested person, while the validity of the jurisdiction claim of the issuing state, due to its lack of foreseeability, raises concerns in light of Article 49 CFR.

The second potential foreseeability complication with which EU citizens can be confronted is also based on the fact that the FDEAW is not complemented by EU rules, which generally regulate the Member States' jurisdiction to prescribe and forum choices in light of the good administration of justice.[5] Even though it was not adopted for this purpose, the *ne bis in idem* principle is currently the only *de facto* forum rule in the AFSJ. This means that parallel criminal procedures for the same act and against the same person are allowed until one state has adopted a final decision in the case. The lack of an overarching EU system for forum choices complementing the *ne bis in idem* principle provides the national competent authorities with broad discretion in deciding whether to prosecute a case and where. It provides the possibility of uncoordinated and coordinated forum decisions. In case of the former, the forum decision is largely left to chance and in no way guarantees that the best forum for the concrete case is chosen either from the perspective of the EU citizen as a suspect, the states, the victim or the general interest of justice. In case of coordinated forum decisions, the forum decision is made in a so-called black box without clear rules for the decision-making process and without the (obligatory) input of other actors, such as the accused, even though the legal position of these outsiders is often affected by the decisions made. By the time the accused becomes aware of such a coordination decision—if he or she becomes aware of it—it may be too late to challenge the decision before a judge.

This broad discretion of the national competent authorities, often public prosecutors, to decide whether to prosecute a case and where can be beneficial to the EU citizen, who can even try to manipulate the forum decision by committing the crime in the state with the most favourable criminal law. However, the absence of a transparent EU system solving or preventing conflicts of jurisdictions on the basis of the proper administration of justice can also be detrimental to the interests of EU citizens. EU citizens can be subjected to parallel proceedings in different Member States. In that light, EU citizens can be exposed to the same investigatory measures in different states and forced to establish multiple defence strategies, which is both complicated and costly. In addition, the states may agree for unclear, unknown and even unfair reasons to prosecute the EU citizen in the state which can impose the

[5] This problem and the question which it raises are discussed in Sect. 2.6.

highest sanctions and which has the most stringent procedural rules regarding investigatory measures, pre-trial detention and rules on evidence. In other words, the broad discretion of the national competent authorities comes with a risk of abuse of power and arbitrary forum choices. Similar to the first problem, the EAW could contribute to the materialisation of these problems in practice as it facilitates the transfer of the suspect to the 'randomly' chosen forum.

The situation set out above raises questions in light of the right to a tribunal established by law as, for instance, laid down in Article 47(2) CFR. This right demands protection against arbitrary decisions by the executive and judiciary when it comes to the judicial organisation of a state. The judicial organisation should therefore be established by laws emanating from Parliament.[6] More concretely, the question arises whether a national court or tribunal is 'established by law' when the national jurisdiction of which this court or tribunal is part has not been appointed on the basis of a clear and transparent set of rules as the best jurisdiction for prosecution in light of the proper administration of justice. In addition, due to the absence of a clear system preventing or solving conflicts of jurisdiction on the basis of the proper administration of justice, the operation of the EAW is also not guided by this yardstick. Hence, the EAW is currently not a mechanism which aims to ensure and ensures prosecution by the state appointed as the most appropriate one on the basis of a clear set of rules. In this light, the main question is whether the EAW presently functions as a mechanism which could—so to say—worsen the problems arising from the absence of a clear EU system for forum choices or contribute to violations of Article 47 CFR, since it can facilitate the transfer of citizens to a state while concerns exist with regard to the compatibility of the state's jurisdiction claim with Article 47 CFR.

In addition, as also explained in Chaps. 1 and 2, the potential foreseeability problems and the additional dimension of the EAW are not unique for the AFSJ, as they also occur in the outer-EU setting where the transfer of suspects is regulated by extradition agreements. In this broader international context, these complications and the role of extradition procedures therein have not occupied an important role or resulted in solutions. However, whereas extradition procedures occur in a context in which the state is the central actor, the EAW operates in an AFSJ consisting of states and EU citizens who are provided with free movement rights. It is also precisely the exercise of these free movement rights which could cause the materialisation of the two foreseeability complications and the issuing of EAWs. In light of these differences, the question arises whether contrary to the outer-EU setting, these problems are currently in the AFSJ recognised as fundamental rights problems and the EAW as a mechanism which could facilitate the surrender of EU citizens to states whose jurisdiction claim and decision to prosecute are questionable in light of the *nullum*

[6] EcHR 12 October 1978, 7360/76 (*Leo Zand/Austria*) para 69; ECtHR 22 June 2000, 32,492/96, 32,547/96, 32,548/96, 33,209/96, 33,210/96 (*Coëme and others/Belgium*) para 98. See also Joined Cases C-542/18 RX-II and C-543/18 RX-II *Simpson v Council of the European Union and HG v European Commission* [2020] ECLI:EU:C:2020:232, para 73.

crimen sine lege principle and right to a tribunal established by law. Chapters 3–7 provide the required information to answer this question, as they describe the current level of protection against the two foreseeability complications in the context of the surrender procedure and their recognition as legality problems on the EU and the national level.

8.3 The Surrender of a Citizen in Case of Unforeseeable Jurisdiction Claims: Legality Issues and the Level of Protection Offered?

8.3.1 The Scope of the Substantive Legality Principle

8.3.1.1 The EU Level

The right to an accessible and foreseeable law for criminal offences and sanctions correlates from the substantive legality principle codified in Articles 49(1) CFR and 7 ECHR. The accessibility requirement entails that an individual must be provided with an adequate indication of the applicable legal rules in a given case.[7] The foreseeability requirement demands that the individual is able to understand from the wording of the legal provision, and if necessary with the assistance of the court's interpretation of the legal provision, for what kind of conduct, including acts and omissions, he or she can be held criminally liable and what penalties can be imposed.[8] As explained in Sect. 3.3.3, the ECtHR has in its case law decided that the *nullum crimen sine lege* principle is not applicable to extradition and surrender procedures, since the goal of these procedures is to aid or assist prosecution and the enforcement of sanctions.[9] The Strasbourg court ruled that the decision to surrender or extradite a person does not constitute a penalty or an intrinsic part of the underlying criminal case.[10] According to Article 52(3) CFR, Article 49 CFR has in principle the same content and scope as Article 7 ECHR, but it may provide a higher level of protection as well. However, up until this point, the CJEU has not adopted a different position with regard to the question whether the EAW falls

---

[7] ECtHR 26 April 1979, 6538/74 (*Sunday Times/UK*) para 49.

[8] Case C-42/17 *M.A.S., M.B* [2017] ECLI:EU:C:2017:936 (*Taricco II*), para 56; Case C-72/15 *Rosneft* [2017] ECLI:EU:C:2017:236, para 162; Case C-303/05 *Advocaten voor de Wereld* [2007] ECLI:EU:C:2007:261, paras 49–50; ECtHR 11 November 1996, 17,862/91 (*Cantoni/France*) para 29; ECtHR 19 March 2006, 67,335/01 (*Achour/France*) para 41.

[9] EcHR 6 July 1976, 7512/76 (*X/The Netherlands*) paras 185–186; ECtHR 7 October 2008, 41,138/05 (*Monedero Angora/Spain*); ECtHR 23 October 2012, 1997/11 (*Giza/Poland*) paras 30–31.

[10] ECtHR 7 October 2008, 41,138/05 (*Monedero Angora/Spain*); Case C-303/05 *Advocaten voor de Wereld* [2006] ECLI:EU:C:2006:552, Opinion of AG Ruiz-Jarabo Colomer, paras 102–105.

within the scope of the *nullum crimen sine lege* principle in Article 49 CFR.[11] Hence, it follows from this examination that neither Article 49 CFR nor Article 7 ECHR demands that the surrender procedure meets the requirements of accessibility and foreseeability. The issuing or execution of an EAW can in itself not violate the substantive legality principle, including in the situation in which the jurisdiction claim of the issuing state was not foreseeable at the time of the offence.

Another way in which the surrender of an EU citizen to a state whose jurisdiction claim was not foreseeable can be connected to the substantive legality principle is by arguing that the criminal offences and sanctions of a state do not meet the legality requirements of accessibility and foreseeability, because the applicability of the national criminal law of that particular state was not foreseeable at the time of the offence. In this scenario, the issuing of an EAW while the jurisdiction claim of the issuing state was not foreseeable is in itself not a violation of the substantive legality principle, but it could contribute to the materialisation of such a violation. The EAW would be classified as a mechanism which can enforce violations of Article 49 CFR by transferring EU citizens to states who, due to their unforeseeable jurisdictions claims, are not in compliance with the requirements of accessibility and foreseeability for criminal offences and sanctions.

This conclusion requires that Article 49 CFR and 7 ECHR link the fulfilment of the requirement of an accessible and foreseeable law for criminal offences and sanctions to the foreseeability of the application of the national criminal law of which the offences and sanctions are part. However, as explained in Chap. 3, the link between jurisdiction and the *nullum crimen sine lege* principle has only been touched upon in a small amount of cases.[12] In the *Taricco* rulings, the CJEU determined that the decision not to apply Italian statutory rules of limitation, which would have extended the possibility of effective criminal proceedings for certain offences, would in principle not violate the prohibition of a retroactive application of the law.[13] Considering the similarities between statutory rules of limitation and rules of jurisdiction, which both determine whether offences and sanctions apply in a certain case, the chance exists—this remains mere speculation—that the CJEU would decide that rules of jurisdiction do not clearly fall within the scope of Article 49 CFR, either.

Other important examples are *Camilleri/Malta* and *Seychell/Malta*, which cover Article 7 ECHR.[14] In these cases, the ECtHR concluded that the unfettered discretion of the Advocate General in Malta to decide before which national court the accused will be tried violates the foreseeability requirement in Article 7 ECHR, because the competent courts apply penalty brackets with different minimum and

[11] Section 3.3.3. See also Case C-717/18 *X* [2019] ECLI:EU:C:2019:1011, Opinion of AG Bobek, paras 92–100.

[12] Sections 3.3.4.1 and 3.3.4.2.

[13] See also Case C-105/14 *Taricco I* [2015] ECLI:EU:C:2015:555, paras 54–58; C-42/17 *M.A.S., M. B* [2017] ECLI:EU:C:2017:936 (*Taricco II*), para 42.

[14] Section 3.3.4.2.

maximum sentences.[15] These judgements show that the ECtHR does not prohibit overlapping sets of criminal offences and penalties as such. The court does, however, demand that the power of the authority competent to decide on the applicable set of rules in a concrete case is sufficiently restricted by law in order to avoid arbitrary prosecutions, convictions and sanctions. Still, this conclusion can only be drawn in relation to overlapping sets of criminal offences and sanctions within one state. The ECtHR has not yet determined whether it holds the same view in relation to overlapping national criminal laws on the transnational EU level. It has, therefore, adopted a very 'state-focused' interpretation of the accessibility and foreseeability requirement in Article 7 ECHR.

8.3.1.2 The National Level

None of the three national legal orders has unambiguously adopted the position that the scope of their national substantive legality principle extends to the surrender procedure.[16] Hence, similar to Articles 7 ECHR and 49 CFR the issuing and execution of an EAW in a certain set of circumstances cannot constitute a violation of the *nullum crimen sine lege* principle. It should be noted, however, that the German legal order offers constitutional protection against surrender in case of unexpected jurisdiction claims, but not on the basis of the substantive legality principle in Article 103(2) GG.[17] This protection is based on Article 16(2) GG, which prohibits the extradition of German nationals and whose personal scope is, therefore, limited to German nationals.

From the three national legal orders, the Dutch and German legal system show some indications of a connection between jurisdiction and criminal offences and sanctions in light of the substantive legality principle.[18] On the Dutch legislative level, the existence of such a link was on a few occasions recognised during the 2013 review of the rules on extraterritorial jurisdiction, in particular in the discussion on the double criminality principle as a limitation to extraterritorial jurisdiction and the possible retroactive application of the new jurisdiction rules. It follows from several statements made by the Minister of Justice and Security at the time that citizens should at the time of the offence be able to foresee that their conduct was criminal somewhere, meaning according to the law of a state. This can, for instance, be achieved by restricting an extraterritorial ground of jurisdiction with the double criminality requirement, which demands that the actions are criminal according to the law of the state where they occurred and the law of the prosecuting state.[19] In

[15] ECtHR 22 January 2013, 42931/10 (*Camilleri/Malta*) para 40; ECtHR 28 August 2018, 43328/14 (*Seychell/Malta*) para 47.

[16] Sections 5.2.2, 6.2.2, and 7.2.2.

[17] Section 6.2.2.

[18] Sections 5.2.3 and 6.2.3.

[19] Section 5.2.3.1.

addition, the Dutch Supreme Court has decided that the prohibition of a retroactive application of the law applies to jurisdiction grounds, but it allowed for exceptions in certain circumstances. Lower courts have on occasion connected jurisdiction rules to other sub-principles of legality, including the prohibition of analogous interpretations.[20]

Similar to the Dutch Supreme Court, the German courts have also linked the prohibition of the retroactive application of the law to jurisdiction grounds. This means that even when the act or omission was criminalised by German law at the time it occurred, a citizen cannot be held criminally liable when German law did not establish jurisdiction at the time of the offence as well.[21] In addition, the double criminality requirement in Articles 7(1) and 7(2) (nr. 1) StGB has the dual goal of protecting state sovereignty and the individual who at the time of the offence may have been unaware of and unfamiliar with the applicability of German substantive criminal law.[22]

Still, even though neither the Dutch nor the German legal order has strictly separated rules on jurisdiction from the *nullum crimen sine lege* principle, they have not unambiguously connected jurisdiction to the Dutch *lex certa* requirement and the German *Bestimmtheitsgebot*, either. Currently, no strong indications exist that, in these legal orders, compliance with the *lex certa* requirement and *Bestimmtheitsgebot* applicable to criminal offences and sanctions depends on the foreseeability of the application of the specific national criminal law of which these offences and sanctions are part. It also follows from Chaps. 5 and 6 that in the legal literature, the opinion that the law of a particular Member State must be foreseeable at the time of the offence constitutes a minority opinion in both states.[23]

This conclusion can possibly be explained by the fact that in Germany, jurisdiction grounds are classified as *objektive Bedingungen der Strafbarkeit* (preconditions for criminal liability), and in the Netherlands jurisdiction is still primarily referred to as a *vervolgingsvoorwaarde* (condition for prosecution), not as a factor determining criminality.[24] Hence, in both legal orders, jurisdiction is necessary to establish criminal liability, but the rules on jurisdiction do not clearly affect or co-determine the wrongfulness of the conduct. In other words, murder remain a criminal offence, regardless of the question whether jurisdiction exists to prosecute the case.

Furthermore, in the English legal order, the meaning of the substantive legality principle follows that of Article 7 ECHR, but this principle already applied—albeit under different names, such as the rule of law—before the adoption of the Human Rights Act. In comparison to the Dutch and German legal order, the English legal order tells a slightly different story with regard to the link between jurisdiction and criminal offences. It follows from Sect. 7.2.3 that the main rule is that only acts and

[20] Section 5.2.3.2.

[21] Section 6.2.3.

[22] Section 6.2.3.

[23] Sections 5.2.3 and 6.2.3.

[24] Section 6.2.3.

omissions that occurred within the English realm can constitute criminal offences.[25] The question whether certain conduct can be classified as a criminal offence is, therefore, partially determined by the ambit of English criminal law, which is in principle limited to the territory of the UK. The link between the territorial ambit of English criminal law and the criminality of certain behaviour could very well have been based on the substantive legality principle, in particular foreseeability considerations. As a result of this link, citizens should in principle only have to abide by the law of the state in which they act, and they are therefore less likely to be surprised by the criminality of their actions according to the national criminal laws of other states, which have extraterritorial application. However, the general rule that all crime is local is in fact not based on foreseeability concerns or the substantive legality principle in general. Instead, it aims to protect territorial sovereignty and avoid time-consuming and costly investigations into acts committed abroad. This indicates that, similar to the Netherlands and Germany, there is no strong conviction in the English legal order that in light of the substantive legality principle, citizens should be able to foresee at the time of the offence that a particular national criminal law is applicable to them.

8.3.1.3 Interim Conclusion

It follows from the above that the current interpretation of Articles 7 ECHR and 49 CFR is very state-focused, since the case law of the ECtHR and CJEU covers exclusively substantive legality problems which occur within the borders of one state. Neither court has so far clearly and unambiguously answered the question whether the rulings in the *Camilleri* and *Seychell* case also apply to overlapping national criminal codes on the EU level. More generally, the courts have not (yet) addressed from the perspective of Articles 49 CFR and 7 ECHR the matter that EU citizens who are encouraged to exercise their free movement rights can in the AFSJ be confronted with the challenge of unforeseeable jurisdiction claims. Due to the unanswered questions on the link between jurisdiction and the requirements of accessibility and foreseeability, there are from the perspective of the *nullum crimen sine lege principle* also no strong indications that the EAW is viewed as a mechanism which could transfer citizens to a state whose jurisdiction claim is not in compliance with the EU substantive legality principle as the application of its national criminal law was not foreseeable at the time of the offence.

The examination of the national legal orders does not provide a different conclusion. It follows from Chap. 5 that the Dutch requirement of *lex certa* is not linked to the foreseeability of a specific jurisdiction claim, nor is the surrender of a person when the jurisdiction claim of the issuing state was not foreseeable clearly marked as problematic in light of the Dutch substantive legality principle. In the English legal order, the general rule that all crime is local could in theory have been based on the

[25] Exceptions to this rule should be laid down in clear and precise statutory provisions.

argument that citizens should be protected against the unforeseeable application of foreign criminal laws in light of the substantive legality principle, but this is not the case in practice. In the German legal order, the surrender of citizens while the applicable foreign law of the issuing state was not foreseeable has been recognised, but not on the basis of the substantive legality principle. Instead, it is based on Article 16(2) GG, which exclusively protects German nationals. This also shows that the protection is not strongly based on EU citizenship arguments or more specifically the point of view that EU citizens provided with free movement rights should be protected against the negative effects of the combination of overlapping national criminal jurisdictions and the EAW.

8.3.2 *Protection Offered in the Procedure for the Issuing of an EAW*

8.3.2.1 The EU Level

The provisions of the FDEAW primarily focus on the procedure for the execution of an EAW and leave the Member States with ample discretion in determining the issuing procedure. The most important conditions in relation to the problems arising from unforeseeable jurisdiction claims and Article 49 CFR are the double criminality requirement in Article 2(4) FDEAW, the requirement of an underlying national arrest warrant in Article 8(1)(c) FDEAW and the requirement that the EAW is issued by a judicial authority in Article 6(1) FDEAW. These three provisions have in the last few years also been the subject of multiple preliminary rulings of the CJEU which have put more flesh on the bones of the issuing procedure.[26]

It follows from the preparatory work to the FDEAW and the CJEU case law that the primary aim of the double criminality requirement, which demands that the conduct constitutes a criminal offences according to the law of the issuing and executing state, is to protect state sovereignty.[27] The general position is that states should not have to assist foreign prosecutions for acts and omissions which they do not view as criminal behaviour. The discussion of the double criminality requirement in Sects. 4.2.2 and 4.3.2 shows that it is not a corollary of the *nullum crimen sine lege* principle and that its purpose is not to prevent states from issuing an EAW when the application of their national criminal law was at the time of the offence not foreseeable to the requested person.

In relation to Article 8(1)(c) FDEAW, the CJEU has decided that an EAW needs to be based on a separate national arrest warrant that is issued or confirmed by a

[26] See Sect. 4.3.

[27] See Sections 4.2.2 and 4.3.2. See also FDEAW, art 2(2); Case C-303/05 *Advocaten voor de Wereld* [2007] ECLI:EU:C:2007:261; Case C-717/18 *X* [2020] ECLI:EU:C:2020:142.

national authority participating in the administration of justice.[28] This decision was based on the argument that the requested person should be provided with a dual level of fundamental rights protection, meaning both at the level of the national arrest warrant and at the level of the EAW.[29] The CJEU has, however, not explicitly linked the requirement of an underlying national arrest warrant or equivalent judicial decision to Article 49 CFR and the need to protect EU citizens against surrender in case the jurisdiction claim of the issuing state was not foreseeable at the time of the offence.

The national authority competent to issue an EAW, referred to in Article 6(1) FDEAW, needs to be an authority participating in the administration of justice, which excludes members of a state's government and the police.[30] The competent issuing judicial authority should also be objective when deciding whether or not to issue an EAW, meaning that it needs to take all exculpatory and incriminatory evidence into account, as well as independent, meaning that it is not obliged to follow instructions of the executive.[31] In addition, in the case law regarding Article 6(1) FDEAW, the CJEU has also introduced other conditions for the issuing procedure which are not determinative for the question whether the EAW was issued by the right authority.[32] For instance, because the EAW could infringe upon the right to liberty and because the surrender procedure is based on a twofold level of fundamental rights protection, a court or judge should be involved during either the issuing of the national arrest warrant or the issuing of the European Arrest Warrant.[33] Furthermore, when the decision to issue an EAW is not made by a court or judge, it should be possible for the requested person to challenge it in a procedure which meets the requirements of effective judicial protection in the issuing state.[34] As explained in Sect. 4.3.4, the case law of the CJEU does, however, not suggest in any way that such a court procedure should be viewed as or was intended as a possibility for the requested person to address the foreseeability of the jurisdiction claim of the issuing state. The CJEU specifically states that during this procedure the requested person should have the chance to question the decision to issue an EAW. While the scope of application of a state's substantive criminal law is, in principle, important for the question whether an EAW for the purpose of prosecution can be issued, it is not officially part of the conditions for the issuing of an EAW nor is it regulated by the FDEAW. Hence, it can be concluded that despite the

---

[28] See Sect. 4.3.3; Case C-241/16 *Bob-Dogi* [2016] ECLI:EU:C:2016:385, para 48; Case C-453/16 *Özçelik* [2017] ECLI:EU:C:2016:860, para 33.

[29] Case C-241/15 *Bob-Dogi* [2016] ECLI:EU:C:2016:385, paras 55–56.

[30] Section 4.3.4; Case C-477/16 *Kovalkovas* [2016] ECLI:EU:C:2016:861, paras 41–42; Case C-452/16 *Poltorak* [2016] ECLI:EU:C:2016:858, para 33.

[31] Joined Cases C-508/18 & C-82/19 *OG & PI* [2019] ECLI:EU:C:2019:456, para 73.

[32] Joined Cases C-566/19 & C-626/19 *JR & YC* [2019] ECLI:EU:C:2019:1077, paras 48–49.

[33] Joined Cases C-508/18 & C-82/19 *OG & PI* [2019] ECLI:EU:C:2019:456, paras 68–69; Case C-489/19 *NJ* [2019] ECLI:EU:C:2019:849, para 35.

[34] Joined Cases C-508/18 & C-82/19 *OG & PI* [2019] ECLI:EU:C:2019:456, para 75; Joined Cases C-566/19 & C-626/19 *JR & YC* [2019] ECLI:EU:C:2019:1077, paras 62–63.

explicit focus on the protection of the requested person and fundamental rights, none of the above-mentioned requirements for the issuing of an EAW were introduced in light of the substantive legality principle in Article 49 CFR or for the specific purpose of avoiding surrender in cases of unforeseeable jurisdiction claims.

8.3.2.2 The National Level

Chapters 5–7 provide a simple and uniform answer to the question to what extent the difficulties for EU citizens, in particular moving ones, to foresee whose national criminal laws to obey have been recognised in the context of the issuing procedure.[35] None of the national legal orders examined reveals a discussion or clear recognition of the risk that the EAW could function as a mechanism which enforces unforeseeable jurisdiction claims on either the legislative level or in the case law. The same conclusion can be drawn in relation to the rules regulating the power to exercise jurisdiction, which is closely related to the decision to issue an EAW.[36] It follows from the chapters on the national legal orders that in the Netherlands the 2021 Instruction on grounds of dismissal enumerates the reasons on the basis of which the public prosecutor can refrain from prosecution in light of the public interest. However, the foreseeability of the application of Dutch law at the time of the offence is not mentioned as a valid reason. The same goes for the criteria in Articles 153c and 153f StPO, which restrict the power of the German public prosecutor to refrain from exercising extraterritorial jurisdiction, and the Guidelines for Criminal Procedure and Procedure for Fines, which apply in relation to Article 153c(1) StPO. None of these criteria or factors covers the foreseeability of German criminal law at the time of the offence or is explicitly based on the position that citizens should be able to foresee which specific national criminal laws are applicable to them in a particular situation. Furthermore, the English legal order is the only one in which the decision to issue an EAW has been more explicitly linked to the decision to prosecute when the crime occurred on both English and foreign territory.[37] However, the factors in the Director's Guidance on concurrent jurisdictions and those in the Code for Crown Prosecutors, which regulate the decision to exercise jurisdiction, do not refer to the foreseeability of the application of English law at the time of the offence as an important consideration. Consequently, it can be concluded that in none of the three national legal orders the national rules regulating the decision to exercise jurisdiction mention the foreseeability of the national criminal law as an important factor. Instead, the national rules are often the result of practical

[35] Sections 5.4.2, 6.4.1 and 7.4.2.

[36] Sections 5.4.3, 6.4.2 and 7.4.2.

[37] See Sect. 7.4.2 and the Legal Guidance on Extradition (12 May 2020) <https://www.cps.gov.uk/legal-guidance/extradition> accessed 20 September 2021.

considerations, such as the difficulties of investigating and prosecuting crimes abroad or the protection of diplomatic relations.[38]

8.3.2.3 Interim Conclusion

On the basis of the above it can be concluded that the drafters of the FDEAW did not elaborately discuss and consider the possible link between the issuing of an EAW and the enforcement of unforeseeable jurisdiction claims. No specific attention was paid to the question whether the EAW could in practice come to facilitate the transfer of a person to the issuing state while the application of its national substantive criminal law and, therefore, its offences and sanctions were difficult to foresee at the time of the offence. In addition, no protection against this possible risk has been integrated in the issuing procedure by the CJEU. This does, however, not necessarily mean that the CJEU definitely does not recognise the problem of unforeseeable jurisdiction claims and the role which the EAW could have in relation to this problem. As explained before, the possibility for the CJEU to interpret EU law in a concrete case depends to a large extent on preliminary questions issued by national courts. So far the CJEU has simply not yet been confronted with a preliminary question specifically addressing the link between the EAW, problems arising from unforeseeable jurisdiction claims and Article 49 CFR.

Similar to the issuing procedure as laid down in the FDEAW and the complementary CJEU case law, the issuing procedure on the national level does not include conditions which aim to protect EU citizens against surrender when the jurisdiction claim of the issuing state was at the time of the offence not foreseeable. In addition, the foreseeability of the applicability of the Dutch, German and English law is not a major consideration in the national rules guiding the decision of the public prosecutor whether or not to exercise jurisdiction. In other words, these national rules do not reflect a recognition of the risk that the EAW could in practice function as a mechanism enforcing unforeseeable jurisdiction claims either.

8.3.3 Protection Offered in the Procedure for the Execution of an EAW

8.3.3.1 The EU Level

In Chap. 4 the conditions for the execution of an EAW which show a potential link to the problems arising from unforeseeable jurisdiction claims were discussed. These are the double criminality requirement in Article 4(1) FDEAW and the territoriality

[38] See eg Sect. 6.4.2.

exception in Article 4(7)(a) FDEAW.[39] In relation to the double criminality requirement, the preparatory work to the FDEAW and the CJEU case law show that its main rationale is the protection of state sovereignty.[40] The executing state should not be forced to aid foreign investigations and prosecutions when the conduct in question does not constitute a criminal offence under its own domestic law. In *Advocaten voor de Wereld*, the CJEU also clearly pointed out that the substantive legality principle in Article 49 CFR does not demand the application of the double criminality requirement in the surrender procedure.[41] Hence, this requirement is not based on the *nullum crimen sine lege* principle and it does not intend to protect citizens against surrender when the jurisdiction claim of the issuing state was at the time of the offence not foreseeable. This conclusion has been endorsed by some legal scholars. They have, for instance, argued that the criminality of the conduct according to the law of the executing state does not necessarily contribute to the foreseeability of the criminality of the behaviour according to foreign laws, since the criminal case may not have any connection to the executing state.[42] Still, a few legal scholars have also criticised the ruling of the CJEU in *Advocaten voor de Wereld*. Their reasoning is that the double criminality requirement may in the context of the surrender procedure on occasion offer some protection against the theoretical obligation to know and obey the laws of all Member States, which is considered unreasonable.[43]

In relation to the territoriality exception, it follows from Chap. 4 that the preparatory work to the FDEAW and CJEU case law remain silent on its ratio.[44] In the legal literature this refusal ground, which allows states to refuse the execution of an EAW when the crime was at least partially committed on their territory, is often connected to the protection of state sovereignty. The argumentation is that the state on whose territory the act occurred should have the first say on whether the conduct constitutes a criminal offence. This makes the territoriality exception a compensation mechanism for the partial abolition of the double criminality principle. If the conduct constitutes a criminal offence in the executing state, this state should also have the first say on how the case should be dealt with.

In its capacity as a compensation mechanism for the double criminality requirement, the territoriality exception has in the legal literature and in some national parliamentary discussions been connected to the legality principle and legal certainty of the requested person, but from a more procedural point of view.[45] In this light, Article 4(7)(a) FDEAW intends to protect the trust which citizens may have that when they act in compliance with the law of the executing state, its authorities will

---

[39] Section 4.2.1.

[40] Section 4.2.2.

[41] Case C-303/05 *Advocaten voor de Wereld* [2007] ECLI:EU:C:2007:261.

[42] Section 4.2.2; Glerum (2013), pp. 336–337.

[43] See Section 4.2.2.

[44] Section 4.2.3.1.

[45] Section 4.2.3.1. See also Glerum (2013), pp. 338–339; *Kamerstukken II* 2003/04, 29,451, nr. 1, p. 9, 11 (notitie *Dubbele strafbaarheid in het Nederlandse strafrecht*).

not subject them to coercive measures. Hence, this reasoning does not so much focus on the foreseeability of the national criminal law of the issuing state, but on the link between the criminality of one's actions according to the law of the state where the conduct occurred and the exercise of coercive procedural powers by that state.

In addition, Chap. 4 has also examined to what extent the fundamental rights exception introduced by Opinion 2/13 provides the possibility to prevent the execution of an EAW on the basis of Article 49 CFR due to the unforeseeable jurisdiction claim of the issuing state.[46] The conclusion was that the current CJEU case law shows that the court did not intend to establish a general human rights refusal ground. So far the CJEU has only allowed exceptions to mutual trust when concerns arise in relation to the prohibition of torture and inhuman treatment in Article 4 CFR, which constitutes an absolute fundamental right, and in relation to the right to an independent judge in Article 47(2) which is a fundamental aspect of the rule of law on which the EU is founded.[47] It is, therefore, questionable to what extent the CJEU would allow the risk of violations of Article 49 CFR in the issuing state to be a barrier to surrender. In addition, besides the question whether a violation of Article 49 CFR could in the first place justify an additional exception to the principle of mutual trust on which the FDEAW is based, the CJEU would also have to answer the interlinked question whether the foreseeability of the jurisdiction claim of the issuing state in fact affects the accessibility and foreseeability of its criminal offences and sanctions.[48]

It follows from the above that neither the preparatory work to the FDEAW nor the CJEU case law links the double criminality requirement, the territoriality exception and the fundamental rights barrier to the substantive legality principle or the requirements of foreseeability and accessibility. These conditions for the execution of an EAW were not introduced with the intent to protect citizens against surrender in case of unexpected foreign jurisdiction claims and they are not based on the view that the EAW could potentially function as an enforcement mechanism for unforeseeable jurisdiction claims. Instead, the primary goal of Articles 4(1) and 4(7)(a) FDEAW is to protect the sovereignty of the executing Member State, while the fundamental rights exception is limited to concerns arising in relation to Article 4 CFR and the right to an independent judge in Article 47 CFR.

8.3.3.2 The National Level

It follows from the examination of the executing procedure in the three national legal orders that only a few refusal grounds relate to the jurisdiction claim of the issuing state and even fewer specifically to the foreseeability of a foreign substantive

[46] Section 4.2.6; Opinion 2/13 [2014] ECLI:EU:C:2014:2454, paras 191–192.

[47] Joined Cases C-404/15 & C-659/15 *Aranyosi & Căldăraru* [2016] ECLI:EU:C:2016:198; Case C-216/18 *LM* [2018] ECLI:EU:C:2018:586.

[48] As explained in Chap. 3, this question has not yet been answered by the CJEU or ECtHR.

criminal law and the need for protection against unforeseeable jurisdiction claims. This section first discusses the clearest examples which are the German nationality exception in Article 80 IRG and the refusal ground in case of domestic proceedings in Article 83b(1)(a) IRG. Afterwards it will have a closer look at the human rights refusal ground and forum bar in the UK Extradition Act 2003. Lastly, it will analyse the double criminality requirement in the Dutch and English legal order as well as the territoriality exception in the Dutch Surrender Act in relation to which the problems arising from unforeseeable jurisdiction claims have to some extent been discussed.

Articles 80 and 83b(1)(a) IRG

The nationality exception in Article 80 IRG constitutes the most prominent example of protection against unforeseeable jurisdiction claims in the context of the surrender procedure.[49] This refusal ground correlates from the constitutional protection against extradition which German nationals enjoy on the basis of Article 16(2) GG. In that light, Article 80 IRG aims to protect the trust which German nationals may have in the German legal order, including protection against foreign substantive criminal laws whose application they did not need to foresee. As explained in Sect. 6.3.3 this protection is the strongest when the offence has a substantial territorial link to Germany and the weakest when it has a substantial territorial link to the issuing state. When no substantial link exists to either Germany or the issuing state, the application of Article 80 IRG depends on a balancing exercise of the different interests and on the question whether the double criminality requirement is met. In this context the purpose of the double criminality requirement is also to protect German nationals against extradition in case of unforeseeable jurisdiction claims when the conduct at least in part occurred in Germany, but is not criminal according to German law.

Article 80 IRG exclusively protects German nationals, but in certain situations the IRG also protects the trust which some foreigners who reside in Germany may have in the German legal system.[50] However, this protection is more restricted, since it is part of the granting procedure in which the public prosecutor is competent to surrender the foreigner despite the fulfilment of the mandatory criteria in Article 83b(2)(1) IRG. It is, therefore, more difficult for foreigners living in Germany to receive protection against extradition in case of unforeseeable jurisdiction claims than it is for German nationals on the basis of Article 80 IRG.

The protection offered by Article 80 IRG is complemented by Article 83b(1)(a) IRG which allows the public prosecutor to refuse the EAW when domestic proceedings for the same offence are conducted in Germany.[51] Whereas the equivalents of Article 83b(1)(a) IRG in the Dutch and English legal order aim to protect

[49] Sections 6.3.3.1 and 6.3.3.2.

[50] Section 6.3.6.

[51] Section 6.3.5.

state sovereignty,[52] in Germany public prosecutors are required to base their decisions regarding the application of this refusal ground on an assessment of all interests. In that light, they have to pay specific attention to the constitutional protection of German nationals against extradition.[53] As explained in Sect. 6.3.5 the possibility to start domestic proceedings after the receipt of the EAW and Germany's broad extraterritorial jurisdiction in fact provide an additional route to the protection of German nationals against unforeseeable jurisdiction claims when other refusal grounds, such as Article 80 IRG fail.

The strong protection offered to German nationals by Articles 80 and 83b(1)(a) IRG is unique for the German legal order. These refusal grounds signify the strong bond between the German national and the German state which also follows from Article 16(2) GG. As explained in Chaps. 5 and 7 the Dutch and English legal order do not offer similar protection to their own nationals. In the Netherlands Article 5(3) FDEAW has been implemented in Article 6 SA, which covers both Dutch nationals and permanent residents. Its main goal is to contribute to the chances of reintegration and not to protect citizens against surrender in case of unforeseeable jurisdiction claims.[54] Furthermore, it follows from Sect. 5.3.5 that whereas Article 83b(1)(a) IRG allows domestic proceedings to start after the receipt of an EAW in order to protect in particular German nationals against the unexpected application of foreign laws, it has not been explicitly determined whether the Dutch implementation of Article 4(2) FDEAW may be used in the same way and for the same purpose. In addition, the tradition in the English legal order is to extradite foreigners and British nationals alike as a result of which Article 5(3) FDEAW is not implemented at all. It also follows from Chap. 7 that in light of this tradition any protection which the Extradition Act 2003 offers against exorbitant jurisdiction claims is provided to all citizens and not just to British nationals.

The Human Rights Ground and Forum Bar in the English Legal Order

With regard to the applicable national fundamental rights bars, only the provisions in the UK Extradition Act 2003 are relevant.[55] It follows from Sect. 7.3.5 that extravagant jurisdiction claims can be a factor in the decision of the English court whether the execution of the EAW constitutes a justified interference with Article 8 ECHR. More specifically the argument that the jurisdiction claim of the issuing state is exorbitant, meaning that it only has a tenuous connection to the criminal offence, can be considered in light of the proportionality assessment conducted in case of a violation of the right to privacy and family life. However, exorbitant jurisdiction

[52] See Sects. 5.3.5 and 7.3.3.1.The UK Extradition Act 2003 does not classify domestic proceedings for the same offense as a refusal ground, but merely as a reason to adjourn the extradition proceedings. However, on the basis of the *ne bis in idem* principle such domestic proceedings can later on result in a refusal of the EAW.

[53] Section 6.3.5.

[54] Section 5.3.1.

[55] For the discussion of the fundamental rights exception in the Dutch and German legal order see Sections 5.3.6 and 6.3.4.

claims are merely one of the many factors that the English court can take into account and a search of the English case law suggests that this factor has not claimed an important role in practice. Furthermore, the possibility to raise the argument of exorbitant jurisdiction claims in the context of the human rights bar has not been based on the position that for the criminal offences and sanctions of the issuing state to be foreseeable at the time of the offence, the jurisdiction claim of the issuing state needs to have been foreseeable as well by either the UK legislator or the courts. In other words, the role of exorbitant jurisdiction claims is not based on a recognition of the problem of unforeseeable jurisdiction claims in the AFSJ.

In addition, the UK Extradition Act 2003 is the only Act implementing the FDEAW which includes a forum bar. This bar aims to prevent the execution of an EAW when this is not in the interest of justice.[56] Its introduction was a response to the public outcry and vocal campaigns regarding extradition in cases in which the requesting state was considered to exercise excessive jurisdiction. However, the concerns raised covered solely extradition cases in which extravagant jurisdiction was exercised by third states, in particular the USA. Furthermore, as also explained in the previous paragraph, the English case law defines exorbitant jurisdiction claims as claims which only have a tenuous connection to the prosecuting state. This interpretation does not show a 'foreseeability' perspective in the sense that it is explicitly based on the view that in an AFSJ in which EU citizens are granted the right to free movement protection should be offered against surrender when these EU citizens could at the time of the offence not know precisely whose national criminal laws to obey.

The Double Criminality Requirement

The main conclusion that can be drawn on the basis of the discussion of the double criminality requirement in Chaps. 5–7 is that this requirement is in none of the three national legal orders introduced for the primary purpose of protecting citizens against surrender when the jurisdiction claim of the issuing state was difficult to foresee at the time of the offence. This follows most clearly from the examination of the German legal order, since neither the German legislator nor the national courts have even designated the double criminality requirement as a safeguard for the citizen protecting his or her legal certainty. It was in fact the opinion of the German legislator that differing views on what conduct should or should not be criminalised should not be a reason to refuse assistance to other states.[57] This is different in the Netherlands and the English legal order in which the double criminality requirement aims to protect both the sovereignty of the executing state and the citizen.[58] More specifically, in the English legal order, the double criminality requirement prevents the surrender of citizens in case of exorbitant jurisdiction claims, while in the Netherlands both the double criminality requirement and the territoriality exception

[56] Section 7.3.4.1.

[57] Section 6.3.2.

[58] Sections 5.3.2 and 7.3.2.

in Article 13 SA have been linked to the principle of legal certainty. This means that they aim to protect citizens against coercive actions by Dutch authorities on the request of foreign nations for conduct which is not a criminal offence according to Dutch law.[59] However, despite its purpose as an individual safeguard, the double criminality requirement has in neither of the two legal orders been explicitly linked to the substantive legality principle or the need to protect citizens against surrender in case of unforeseeable jurisdiction claims. The same goes for the Dutch territoriality exception.

Despite the conclusion that the actual ratio of the double criminality requirement, even in its capacity as an individual safeguard, is not to protect EU citizens against surrender in case of unforeseeable jurisdiction claims, this matter has to some extent been discussed during the parliamentary debates on the implementation of the double criminality requirement in the English and Dutch legal order.[60] During the parliamentary debates in the English legal order, the point was, for instance, made that, while in the UK, individuals should only have to fear the law of the UK. In addition, they cannot always be expected to know the criminal law of the state to which they travel. In the Netherlands, the parliamentary debates on the double criminality requirement show that some members of Dutch Parliament were of the opinion that it can hardly be expected of EU citizens to know the laws of all EU Member States and that the partial abolition of the double criminality requirement for what they considered a vague list of offences constitutes a violation of the *lex certa* principle. However, in his response to this criticism, the then-Dutch Minister of Justice and Security adopted a more 'state-focused' interpretation of the principle of legal certainty. He stated that the exclusion of the double criminality requirement does not harm legal certainty, since an individual can always know what conduct is criminal in a certain state. Hence, he did not seem to consider the theoretical obligation of citizens to know the laws of all EU Member States as a problem or a reason to not limit the scope of application of the double criminality requirement. It follows from the above that even though the double criminality does not primarily aim to offer protection against surrender in case of unforeseeable jurisdiction claims, this matter has at least been discussed in the English and Dutch implementation process.

8.3.3.3 Interim Conclusion

On the basis of the previous sections, it can be concluded that on the EU level, the conditions for the execution of an EAW have not been linked to the view that in an AFSJ in which EU citizens are provided with the right to free movement they should also be protected against the application of national criminal laws which were

[59] See Sects. 5.3.2 and 5.3.3.2.

[60] Sections 5.3.2 and 7.3.2.

difficult to foresee at the time of the offence. Neither the preparatory work to the FDEAW nor the CJEU case law shows that any of the conditions in the executing procedure were installed to protect EU citizens against surrender in case of unforeseeable jurisdiction claims. Instead, the protection of state sovereignty is often the primary ratio.

A similar conclusion can be drawn on the basis of the discussion of the relevant conditions for the execution of an EAW in the national legal orders. The protection of state sovereignty occupies an important position in the national executing procedures, whereas the foreseeability of foreign substantive criminal laws has a relatively small role. It follows from the previous sections and Chaps. 5–7 that the problems which can arise from extraterritorial jurisdiction claims are primarily reflected in the executing procedure in the English and German legal order. However, only in the German legal order has the foreseeability of the applicable national criminal laws been explicitly recognised as problematic and resulted in protection that is specifically offered for this purpose. This recognition and protection is derived from the special bond which exists between the German national and the state. In that light, it is also not based on the substantive legality principle in Article 103(2) GG, but on the constitutional protection of Germans against extradition in Article 16(2) GG. Hence, the protection against unforeseeable jurisdiction claims offered in Articles 80 and 83b(1)(a) IRG also has a strong 'state interest' and 'state sovereignty' dimension reflected by the strong focus on the protection of German nationals.[61]

In relation to the English legal order, the most important conclusion is that it recognises the problem of exorbitant jurisdiction claims and offers protection against this specific problem in the executing procedure. Contrary to Germany, this protection is not limited to British nationals, but, similar to Germany, it is not based on the substantive legality principle or the general view that an EU citizen with free movement rights should be protected against surrender in case of unforeseeable jurisdiction claims. The definition of exorbitant jurisdiction claims in the English case law has also not been linked to the foreseeability of a jurisdiction claim and the effect which this could have on the foreseeability of criminal offences and sanctions. Instead, the role of exorbitant jurisdiction claims in the executing procedure can be explained by the primacy of the territoriality principle in the UK reflected in the general rule that in principle all crime is local and that extraterritorial jurisdiction should only be established and exercised in exceptional circumstances.

[61] Sections 6.3.3.2 and 6.3.5.

8.4 The Problems Arising from the Functioning of the FDEAW Without a Complementary EU System for Forum Choices: Legality Issues and the Level of Protection Offered?

8.4.1 The Scope of the Right to a Tribunal Established by Law: The EU and National Level

As explained in Sect. 3.4, the right to a tribunal established by law in Articles 6 ECHR and 47(2) CFR, also referred to as the procedural legality principle, aims to protect citizens against arbitrary decisions by the executive and judiciary in the context of the judicial organisation of a state.[62] In that light, the right demands that a state's judicial organisation is in principle regulated by a law emanating from Parliament and that the judiciary and executive are not provided with excessive discretion when they are allocated a particular task in the establishment of this organisation.[63] In relation to the specific topic of forum choices, the scarce case law of the EcHR and ECtHR shows that the right to a tribunal established by law does not include the right to choose a particular court. The foreseeability requirement included in the concept of 'law' demands that the rules regulating the procedure before a court are sufficiently clear to guarantee the possibility of an effective preparation for the defence, but not that an individual is at the time of the offence able to foresee which national procedural rules—of which states—apply.[64] In addition, it follows from several cases that when a national legislator has regulated forum decisions within its own state, the competent authority in the state in question is obliged to make a reasonable decision on the basis of the applicable rules.[65] However, these cases solely concern conflicts of jurisdiction and forum decisions on the national level, meaning that they occur within one Member State. Neither the ECtHR nor the CJEU has so far decided whether the right to a tribunal established by law in Articles 6 ECHR and 47 CFR imposes the obligation to limit the broad discretion of the national competent authorities, which are often public prosecutors, to make forum decisions in case of conflicts of national jurisdictions on the cross-border EU level.

The right to a tribunal established by law also exists in the three national legal orders, but under different names and with a different scope.[66] In the English legal

[62]ECtHR 22 June 2000, 32492/96, 32547/96, 32548/96, 33209/96, 33210/96 (*Coëme and others/ Belgium*) para 98; Böse (2014), p. 125.

[63]See Sect. 3.4.1; EcHR 18 December 1980, 8603/79, 8722/79, 8723/79 & 8729/79 (*Crociani and others/Italy*) page 219; ECtHR 20 January 2005, 30,598/02 (*Accardi and others/Italy*); EcHR 12 October 1978, 7360/76 (*Leo Zand/Austria*) para 69.

[64]Section 3.4.2.1. See also ECtHR 12 July 2007, 74613/01 (*Jorgic/Germany*) para 65; ECtHR 28 April 2009, 17214/05, 20329/05, 42113/04 (*Savino and others/Italy*).

[65]Section 3.4.2.2. See also EcHR 10 October 1990, 16875/90 (*G/Switzerland*).

[66]Sections 5.2.4, 6.2.4 and 7.2.4.

order, this right does not occupy a strong position, but the idea behind it is endorsed, namely the prohibition of the sovereign to establish prerogative courts. It also follows from Sect. 7.2.4 that, similar to the Netherlands, the right to a tribunal established by law in the English legal order does not require that the *ad hoc* composition of a bench is laid down in statutory law. Instead, the composition of the bench falls within the discretion of the judiciary.

In the Netherlands and Germany, the right to a tribunal established by law is a constitutional safeguard, but it occupies the most prominent position in Germany. This follows, for instance, from the fact that *ius de non evocando* in Article 17 of the Dutch Constitution primarily requires that Dutch courts are established by Acts of Parliament.[67] In addition, during discussions on the Dutch legislative level with regard to the legal framework for the transfer of criminal proceedings to other states, the position was taken that *ius de non evocando* does not require that the competent judge in a concrete case is specifically regulated by law. Furthermore, this constitutional right does not prohibit prosecution authorities from deciding whether the case should be brought before a Dutch or a foreign court. Interestingly enough, members of the government also pointed out during these discussions that public prosecutors must make reasonable decisions and avoid arbitrary forum choices, but this point was just not based on Article 17 of the Constitution.

The lack of a connection between forum choices and *ius de non evocando* in the Dutch legal order is in sharp contrast with the German legal order, where the right to a lawful judge (*gesetzliche Richter*) is codified in Article 101(1) GG.[68] This constitutional right requires that the German law regulates the allocation of cases and even the composition of the bench to prevent arbitrary forum choices by the executive.[69] However, the scope of the German constitutional right to a tribunal established by law is limited to the national level. This means that the *gestzliche Richter* does not protect citizens in case of conflicts of national jurisdictions against prosecution by a state which has not been appointed as the most appropriate forum in light of the proper administration of justice on the basis of a clear EU or international system for forum choices. However, it also follows from Sect. 6.2.4 that, in the legal literature, the absence of clear rules covering forum decisions made in the context of the transfer of criminal proceedings to other states has been criticised in light of Article 101(2) GG. It has been argued by some legal scholars that the arguments in this discussion could also be relevant for the discussion on the absence of an EU or international mechanism for forum choices and the risk of forum shopping which this brings about.

It can be concluded that the absence of a transparent EU mechanism for forum choices in light of the proper administration of justice has in the legal literature been

---

[67] For the Dutch legal order see Sect. 5.2.4.

[68] For the German legal order see Sect. 6.2.4.

[69] As explained in Sect. 6.2.4, Article 101(1) GG does not require a strict system for forum choices in order to provide the necessary flexibility that allows for forum decisions which serve the effective administration of justice.

addressed from the perspective of the EU or national procedural legality principle. However, it has neither on the legislative level nor in the case law been explicitly recognised or classified as problematic in light of the right to a tribunal established by law as applicable on the EU level and in the national legal orders. Similar to the European and national substantive legality principle discussed in Sect. 8.3.1, the codifications of the right to a tribunal established by law whose scope includes forum decisions, such as Article 47(2) CFR and Article 101(1) GG have a very state-focused interpretation. They apply to the national level and solely address situations within one national legal order. Consequently, as the absence of a transparent EU system preventing or solving conflicts of jurisdictions in light of the proper administration of justice has not been clearly classified as a legality problem there are also no strong indications suggesting that the fact that the EAW currently operates without such a system is problematic in light of the right to a tribunal established by law. In other words, the current scope of this right does not send the signal that the EAW could be viewed as a mechanism which can facilitate forum decisions which are themselves due to the absence of clear EU rules on forum choices not in compliance with the right to a tribunal established by law.

8.4.2 *Protection Offered in the Procedure for the Issuing of an EAW*

8.4.2.1 The EU Level

As already mentioned in Sect. 8.3.2.1, the FDEAW offers ample discretion to the national legislators in setting the conditions for the issuing of an EAW.[70] The preparatory work to the FDEAW does not show a discussion of the possible risk that the combination of this broad discretion and the absence of a clear EU system for forum choices could in practice turn the EAW into a mechanism facilitating prosecution by a state or states which are not appointed on the basis of a transparent set of rules as the best forum for prosecution in light of the proper administration of justice. In other words, the risk that the EAW could without a complementary EU system solving conflicts of jurisdictions come to function as a mechanism which, so to speak, facilitates or enforces arbitrary forum choices was not explicitly considered when the rules for the issuing procedure were adopted.

During the last few years, the most important conditions for the issuing of an EAW have been more closely defined and interpreted in preliminary rulings from the CJEU. As explained before, Articles 2(4), 6(1) and 8(1)(c) FDEAW codify these conditions, which are the double criminality requirement, an underlying national arrest warrant and the appointment of a judicial authority for the issuing of an

[70] See also Sect. 4.3.

EAW.[71] As a result of the preliminary rulings on these conditions, the broad discretion of the Member States in establishing the issuing procedure has become a bit more demarcated.[72] Furthermore, the interpretations adopted by the CJEU often have a strong basis in the protection of fundamental rights. For instance, the requirement that the EAW needs to be based on a national arrest warrant or equivalent enforceable judicial decision was based on the argument that the requested person should be provided with a dual level of fundamental rights protection, meaning during the issuing of the national arrest warrant and EAW.[73] In addition, in light of this dual level of protection and the fact that the EAW can infringe upon the right to liberty, the CJEU decided that a court or a judge should be involved in either the issuing of the national arrest warrant or the issuing of the European Arrest Warrant. In case the decision to issue an EAW is not made by a court or a judge, the requested person should also be allowed to challenge this decision in a procedure in the issuing state which meets the requirements of effective judicial protection, meaning a court or tribunal *stricto sensu*.[74] As explained in Sect. 4.3.4 the case law of the CJEU does, however, not suggest in any way that such a court procedure should be viewed as or was intended as a possibility for the requested person to address the reasonableness or possible arbitrariness of the underlying forum decision of the issuing state. The Luxembourg court specifically states that during this procedure, the requested person should have the chance to question the decision to issue an EAW. While a state's decision to prosecute is closely related to this decision, it is not officially part of the conditions for the issuing of an EAW, nor is it regulated by the FDEAW.

It can be concluded that the limitations which the CJEU case law imposes on the broad discretion of national legislators to regulate the issuing procedure are not based on the concern that, due to this broad discretion, the EAW could contribute to prosecution by a state which is not appointed on the basis of a transparent set of rules and is not necessarily the best forum in light of the proper administration of justice. Even though the CJEU regularly refers to fundamental rights protection and effective judicial protection in its interpretation of the separate conditions, none of these were installed for the specific purpose of avoiding the enforcement of arbitrary form choices by the EAW in light of Article 47(2) CFR. So, neither the preparatory work to the FDEAW nor the case law of the CJEU on the issuing procedure reveals a strong discussion of the fact that, due to the absence of a clear EU system for forum choices, the risk arises that in practice the EAW contributes to the enforcement of forum choices which are not based on a transparent set of rules and do not serve the proper administration of justice.

---

[71] See Sect. 8.3.2.1.

[72] See Sect. 4.3.

[73] Section 4.3.3. See also Case C-241/15 *Bob-Dogi* [2016] ECLI:EU:C:2016:385, paras 55–56.

[74] Section 4.3.4. See also Joined Cases C-508/18 & C-82/19 *OG & PI* [2019] ECLI:EU:C:2019: 456, paras 68, 75; Case C-489/19 *NJ* [2019] ECLI:EU:C:2019:849, para 35; Joined Cases C-566/19 & C-626/19 *JR & YC* [2019] ECLI:EU:C:2019:1077, paras 62–63.

8.4.2.2 The National Level

It follows from Chaps. 5 and 6 that the Dutch and German issuing procedures leave the issuing judicial authority with ample discretion in deciding whether or not to issue an EAW.[75] The few conditions for the issuing of an EAW in the IRG and Dutch Surrender Act are also not concretely linked to the decision to prosecute the underlying case. They are not based on the position that the power to issue an EAW in case of conflicts of jurisdictions should be limited to such an extent that it could not result in the surrender of an EU citizen, while the decision to prosecute of the Dutch and German public prosecutor was not based on a transparent set of forum rules and does not serve the proper administration of justice. So, neither the Dutch nor the German issuing procedure seems to be influenced by a recognition of the risk on the legislative and judicial level that in the absence of an EU system for forum choices complementing the FDEAW, the EAW could in practice function as a mechanism for the enforcement of arbitrary forum choices.

The same conclusion can be drawn in relation to the German and Dutch rules regulating the discretion of the public prosecutor to prosecute a case when more than one state is competent.[76] As already explained in Sect. 8.3.2.2, the discretion granted to the German public prosecutor to refrain from exercising extraterritorial jurisdiction aims to protect political interests and avoid a work-overload. The limits which the German legislator set to the use of this discretion were not based on the opinion that the decision to prosecute in cases in which more states are competent should be based on a transparent set of rules to avoid arbitrariness. The lack of a strict set of rules regulating the decision to prosecute in case of conflicts of national jurisdictions in the German legal order could be explained on the basis of the position of the German legislator—expressed in the context of the procedure for the execution of an EAW—that conflicts of national jurisdictions are foreign policy matters which should preferably be solved by the public prosecutor. In that light, the public prosecutor should also be provided with the necessary flexibility to choose the best state on the basis of the concrete circumstances of the case.[77]

The Dutch legislator has stated during the 2013 review of the Dutch jurisdiction rules that forum decisions in case of conflicts of jurisdictions should serve the proper administration of justice, which will often mean prosecution by the *locus delicti*.[78] In that light, the Dutch public prosecutor should only exercise extraterritorial jurisdiction in case serious crimes would otherwise go uninvestigated. However, this position was taken during a debate. The actual rules demarcating the discretion of the public prosecutor, most importantly the 2021 Instruction on the use of grounds of dismissal, and the Instruction implementing Framework Decision 2009/948/JHA on conflicts of jurisdiction, do not provide clear and strict criteria guiding the decision to

[75] Sections 5.4.2 and 6.4.1.

[76] Sections 5.4.3 and 6.4.2.

[77] See also Sect. 6.3.5.

[78] Section 5.4.3.

exercise jurisdiction.[79] For instance, they do not prohibit the exercise of extraterritorial jurisdiction when the state where the crime occurred could also prosecute. In addition, these instructions were not adopted for the purpose of limiting the risk that in case of conflicts of national jurisdictions, the Dutch decision to prosecute would be viewed as an arbitrary forum decision. In other words, these rules are not based on the position that the decision to prosecute in case of conflicts of jurisdictions should be based on a transparent set of rules.

Contrary to the Dutch and German legal order, the issuing procedure has to some extent been connected to conflicts of jurisdictions in the English legal order.[80] The Legal Guidance on Extradition refers to the Director's Guidance on concurrent jurisdictions, which states that the English public prosecutor should consult foreign colleagues to solve conflicts of jurisdictions at an early stage.[81] The Director's Guidance on concurrent jurisdictions also specifically aims to increase the transparency of the decision-making process of the public prosecutor in case of conflicts of national jurisdictions.[82] For that purpose, the Guidance lists relevant factors for the forum decision and even establishes some hierarchy among them. Hence, in the English legal order, transparent forum decisions in case of conflicts of national jurisdictions have been linked to the issuing procedure and are generally recognised as an important interest.

Lastly, all three national legal orders provide in one way or another the possibility to challenge the decision (not) to prosecute a case domestically before a court.[83] However, it may for several reasons be difficult to issue a successful objection to such a decision before a Dutch, German or English court from the perspective of the best forum for the case at hand. Firstly, suspects are not provided with an all-embracing EU or international system for case allocations on which they can base their arguments in a national court. Secondly, the legal exit to domestic proceedings or the power of the court to order a domestic prosecution are often absent when national courts are confronted with arguments regarding the most suitable forum. A national court normally determines whether it may try a case on the basis of the rules regulating its territorial and material competences. Such a

[79] Aanwijzing sepot en gebruik sepotgronden (*Stcrt.* 2020, 62570); Aanwijzing rechtsmachtgeschillen bij strafprocedures (*Stcrt.* 2012, 11716).

[80] Section 7.4.2.

[81] The Director's Guidance only covers situations in which part of the criminal act occurred in the UK.

[82] It is interesting that the English legal order has the most elaborate set of rules guiding the decision to prosecute in case of conflicts of jurisdictions, while it is the only state that is not bound by Framework Decision 2009/948/JHA on conflicts of jurisdiction.

[83] Sections 5.4.3, 6.4.2 and 7.3.3.2. In addition, if it is allowed under national law, suspects can before or during the actual criminal trial raise the matter of forum choices before the court trying their case. This could trigger the national court to look for ways to have the case prosecuted somewhere else if this is possible. International and EU instruments for judicial cooperation, such as the EAW could help in these situations.

determination may not require that the court considers whether the national jurisdiction of which it is part is the best forum for the case at hand.[84]

8.4.2.3 Interim Conclusion

It follows from the above that, both on the EU level and in the Dutch and German legal order, the risk that the restricted regulation of the power to issue an EAW and the absence of an EU system for forum choices could in practice turn the EAW into a mechanism enforcing arbitrary forum choices has not been an important point of discussion in the context of the adoption and development of the issuing procedure. However, in the English legal order, the existing lack of transparency in the decision-making process of the English public prosecutor, including in cases of conflicts of jurisdictions, was precisely the reason why the Director's Guidance on concurrent jurisdictions with a clear set of criteria was adopted. This Director's Guidance also has to be considered in the context of the issuing procedure. In this light, it can be concluded that in the English legal order, the issuing procedure seems to be more connected to forum decisions in case of conflicts of jurisdictions and the need for a transparent set of rules on the basis of which the decision to prosecute should then be made.

8.4.3 Protection Offered in the Procedure for the Execution of an EAW

8.4.3.1 The EU Level

As explained in Chap. 4, the FDEAW is not a model for forum choices and it was also never intended as such.[85] Still, the refusal grounds in Articles 4(2) 4(7)(a) and (b) FDEAW as well as the rules on concurrent EAWs in Article 16 FDEAW reflect situations of potential conflicts of national jurisdictions. The decision of the executing judicial authority whether or not to apply any of these refusal grounds and the decision for a particular EAW do not constitute forum decisions *sensu stricto,* since, for instance, the decision to refuse an EAW does not oblige the issuing state to refrain from prosecution or the executing state to prosecute the requested person instead. However, these conditions for the execution of an EAW can influence forum choices made on the national level in case of conflicts of jurisdictions, since a decision not to surrender the requested person could convince the issuing state to stop its own criminal proceedings against the requested person. In other words, their application can *de facto* have the effect of settling conflicts of jurisdictions.

[84] Böse et al. (2013), p. 459.

[85] Section 4.2.1.

One of the clearest examples of a situation in which the EAW could influence eventual forum decisions is laid down in Article 16 FDEAW.[86] The Eurojust Guidelines on competing EAWs even explicitly state that the decision for one of the competing EAWs essentially constitutes a decision on the forum for prosecution.[87] However, it follows from Sect. 4.2.7 that the discretion of the executing judicial authority is hardly restricted by Article 16 FDEAW itself or soft law, such as the Eurojust Guidelines. Furthermore, except for the fact that the Commission Handbook on the issuing and execution of an EAW states in light of Article 16 FDEAW that 'first-come, first-served' forum decisions should be avoided, which implies to some extent a recognition of the risk that the EAW can facilitate unwanted and more arbitrary forum decisions, the risk of the EAW as a potential mechanism for the enforcement of arbitrary forum decisions is not discussed in the context of the discretion granted to the executing judicial authority by Article 16 FDEAW.[88] Neither the EU legislator nor the CJEU has linked the rules on competing EAWs to the need to protect the requested person to some extent against prosecution by states which have not been appointed as the most appropriate forum for prosecution in light of the proper administration of justice and on the basis of a transparent set of rules. Instead, the emphasis which Article 16 FDEAW and the rules of soft law put on a decision on the basis of the concrete circumstances of the case suggests that flexibility and broad discretion are in fact favoured over stricter rules to allow the executing judicial authority to execute the EAW of the state which in the concrete case constitutes the best forum.[89]

The refusal ground in Article 4(2) FDEAW allows the executing state to give priority to its own domestic criminal proceedings for the same criminal conduct as on the EAW.[90] In other words, the executing judicial authority may decide that its domestic prosecution should take precedence over prosecution in the issuing state. The existence of this refusal ground has in the legal literature been explained in light of the absence of EU rules fully harmonising the Member States' jurisdiction and a transparent EU system to solve conflicts of national jurisdictions.[91] However, nothing suggests that the EU legislator or CJEU have based this refusal ground on the position that EU citizens should be protected against surrender when the issuing state's decision to prosecute is not made on the basis of a transparent set of rules regulating forum decisions in light of the proper administration of justice. Instead, in the legal literature, the predominant opinion is that Article 4(2) FDEAW protects the sovereignty of the executing state against the fact that the FDEAW is not

[86] Section 4.2.7.

[87] Eurojust Guidelines for deciding on competing requests for surrender and extradition (2019), p. 10.

[88] Handbook on how to issue and execute a European arrest warrant (European Commission Notice) [2017] OJ C335/1, p. 53.

[89] Section 4.2.7.

[90] Section 4.2.5.

[91] See Glerum (2013), pp. 149, 559–560. Discussed in Sect. 4.2.5.

complemented by a clear system for forum decisions.[92] The executing state should not be forced to cooperate with the issuing state if it holds a different opinion with regard to the better forum for the case—itself or the issuing state—or when its own national interests require prosecution in the executing state. Simply put, the executing states should not be forced to put the interests or opinion on the better forum of the issuing state above their own. In addition, the conclusion that Article 4(2) FDEAW is not intended as a safeguard against prosecution in case of arbitrary forum decisions is endorsed by the fact that this legal provision does not prescribe the factors which the executing state needs to take into account when deciding where they believe the case should be prosecuted. In fact, the decision of the executing state may also be the result of a process in which the issuing and executing state decided among each other and outside the view of the other relevant parties, such as the suspect who should prosecute the case.[93]

As explained before in Sect. 8.3.3.1, the main ratio of the territoriality exception in Article 4(7)(a) FDEAW is also to protect state sovereignty. It is based on the position that the executing state should not be obliged to aid the issuing state's prosecution when it disagrees with the criminalisation of the behaviour in question and that the executing state should have the first say in deciding how the case should be handled. Neither the preparatory work to the FDEAW nor the CJEU case law indicate that the discretion of the executing state to refuse the execution of the EAW is based on the position that EAW should not have the effect of enforcing arbitrary forum decisions. In other words, the territoriality exception does not intend to protect the requested person against surrender, because the decision to prosecute of the issuing state is viewed as arbitrary due to the absence of a clear set of rules regulating forum choices in case of conflicts of jurisdictions. Similar to Article 4(2) FDEAW, this conclusion is endorsed by the fact that the discretion of the executing state to apply the territoriality exception is hardly delineated. Hence, the decision of the executing judicial authority is not guided by clear criteria which aim to contribute to a prosecution of the cases by the most appropriate forum.[94]

The same conclusion can be drawn in relation to the extraterritoriality exception in Article 4(7)(b) FDEAW.[95] This refusal ground allows the executing state to refuse the EAW when it concerns an offence which has been committed outside the territory of the issuing Member State and the executing state would itself be unable to prosecute the case if the same offence had been committed outside its own territory. The extraterritoriality exception was adopted to protect state sovereignty and reflects the principle of reciprocity, which protects the equality of states. In this light, the extraterritoriality exception intends to ensure that the executing state is not forced to assist another state in the enforcement of its national criminal law if it could not request assistance in a similar case. Neither the preparatory work to the FDEAW

[92] See Glerum (2013), pp. 149, 559–560.

[93] Section 4.2.5.

[94] Section 4.2.3.2.

[95] Section 4.2.4.

nor the CJEU case law link this refusal ground to the position that, without clear rules on forum choices, the EAW could become a mechanism for the enforcement of arbitrary forum decisions.

Lastly, Chap. 4 also examined to what extent the fundamental rights exception introduced by Opinion 2/13 offers the possibility to refuse the execution of an EAW, because of a potential violation of the right to a tribunal established by law due to the decision to prosecute of the issuing state which is not based on a transparent set of rules preventing or solving conflicts of jurisdictions in the EU.[96] Similar to a possible violation of Article 49 CFR due to unforeseeable jurisdiction claims as discussed in Sect. 8.3.3.1, it is difficult to say whether a decision not to execute an EAW is allowed in such a situation, since the CJEU has so far only allowed additional exceptions to the principle of mutual trust in case of a risk of a violation of Article 4 CFR and the right to an independent court in Article 47 CFR. Furthermore, even if the CJEU would reach the conclusion that the risk of a violation of the right to a tribunal by law in the issuing state could also justify an additional exception to the principle of mutual trust, it would in addition have to clarify whether the lack of a clear EU system for forum choices regulating the Member States' decision to prosecute in case of conflicts of jurisdictions in fact violates the right to tribunal established by law. As explained in Chap. 3, this last question has not been answered yet.

8.4.3.2 The National Level

It follows from Chaps. 5–7 that only in the English legal order a few of the conditions for the execution of an EAW are to some extent based on the view that a state's decision to prosecute when more states are competent should be based on a transparent set of forum rules. The most important conditions in this light are those in Sections 8 and 22 of the Extradition Act 2003, in relation to which Director's Guidance on concurrent jurisdictions is important, and the forum bar in Section 19B. Both the Director's Guidance and the forum bar were adopted as a response to the Scott Baker report reviewing the UK's extradition arrangements. This report concluded that the process leading to a decision to prosecute in case of conflicts of national jurisdictions was not sufficiently transparent or based on formally agreed upon criteria.[97]

It follows from Sect. 7.3.3. that Article 4(2) FDEAW has not been implemented as a refusal ground in the Extradition Act 2003. Instead, Westminster Magistrate's Court is, on the basis of Sections 8 and 22 EA, only competent to adjourn the extradition procedure in case of domestic charges. The interconnected power of the domestic public prosecutor to initiate these domestic charges can only prevent the execution of an EAW, when the domestic proceedings result in a final decision

[96] Section 4.2.6. See Opinion 2/13 [2014] ECLI:EU:C:2014:2454, paras 191–192.

[97] Sects. 7.3.3.2, 7.3.4.1 and 7.3.4.3.

triggering the application of the double jeopardy bar. However, using the power to charge the requested person, which triggers the adjournment of the extradition proceedings, in order to influence the eventual forum decision is not an easy task, since the decision to charge needs to be based on an investigation of the criminal offence, which may not be finished before the end of the extradition proceedings. In addition, the power of the public prosecutor to start domestic proceedings is delineated by the Director's Guidance on concurrent jurisdictions and the Legal Guidance on jurisdiction for the CPS. These guide the decision of the public prosecutor in several cases in which (possible) conflicts of national jurisdictions arise.[98] They, for instance, provide different factors with a certain pecking order, which should be taken into account in the decision-making process. Hence, together with Sections 8 and 22 EA these Guidances imply that in the English legal order the EAW is to some extent viewed as a mechanism which should be used to surrender the requested person to the most appropriate state. The decision of which state is the most appropriate forum should in addition be based on a set of transparent and formally agreed on rules.

The forum bar applies when part of the crime occurred in the UK and the execution of the EAW is not in the interest of justice. In relation to the latter requirement, the court needs to determine whether the UK or the issuing state is the better forum. However, the case law also shows that even when the UK is considered the better forum, this does not mean that the case will also be prosecuted in the UK. The interest of justice test is demarcated by an exhaustive, but non-hierarchical set of factors which the court needs to take into account. This way, the UK legislator aimed to provide more transparency in relation to the decision on the most appropriate forum.[99]

Contrary to the English legal order, the risk of arbitrary forum decisions due to the absence of a transparent EU system and the risk that the EAW constitutes a mechanism enforcing such arbitrary forum decisions is hardly reflected or recognised in the German and Dutch executing procedure. As explained in Sect. 6.2.4 Germany has a relatively strong constitutional right to a lawful judge of which the ratio is to protect citizens against arbitrary forum decisions. Its scope of application is, however, limited to the national level and also in that context the protection against forum manipulation is not absolute. The case law of the German Constitutional Court reflects the need for a balance between strict forum rules which limit the chances of arbitrary decisions and flexible rules which facilitate the appointment of the best forum for the concrete case.[100] The discussion of the refusal grounds in the IRG shows that with regard to forum decisions on the EU or international level, the German legislator puts the focus on flexible rules preventing or solving conflicts of national jurisdictions.

---

[98] Sections 7.3.3.1 and 7.3.3.2.

[99] Sections 7.3.4.1 and 7.3.4.3.

[100] BverfG 19 March 1959, 1 BvR 295/58 [13]; BVerfG 24 March 1964, 2 BvR 42, 83, 89/63 [14]. See also Eser (1995), pp. 251–252.

This follows from the division between the admissibility procedure, in which the *Oberlandesgericht* (Higher Regional Court) decides on the application of the mandatory refusal grounds in Article 80 and 81 IRG, and the granting procedure, in which the public prosecutor decides on the optional refusal grounds in Article 83b IRG. Most of the refusal grounds which reflect conflicts of national jurisdictions were included in the granting procedure, because the German legislator was of the opinion that they constitute foreign policy issues which should be solved by a public prosecutor and not a court.[101] The former should also not be subjected to strict rules, but be provided with broad discretion to make the best decision on the basis of the concrete circumstances of the case.[102] In this light, Article 83b(1)(a) and (c) IRG, which provide the power to refuse the EAW in case of German proceedings for the same offence and the power to make a decision in case of concurring EAWs, have intentionally not been subjected to additional criteria or been complemented by other guidelines.[103]

The nationality exception in Article 80 IRG is an exception to the common position that conflicts of national jurisdictions are at their core foreign policy matters, which should be solved by public prosecutors. The *Oberlandesgericht* decides on the application of this refusal ground and its discretion in this matter is a bit more restricted than the discretion offered to public prosecutors by Article 83b IRG. As explained in Sect. 6.3.3.1 the power of the court is demarcated by the three categories of situations which follow from the case *Darkazanli* and Article 80 IRG itself. The third category of *Mischfallen* (mixed cases or rest category), in which the case has no substantial link to either Germany or the issuing state, the discretion of the court is relatively broad for the same reasons as the public prosecutor is provided with broad discretion in the granting procedure. The German legislator decided that restricting the compulsory balancing act of the different interests by a hierarchical and exhaustive list of factors would hamper the possibility of picking the best forum for prosecution.[104]

It follows from Chap. 5 on the Dutch legal order that the conditions for the execution of an EAW, which can indirectly affect forum choices, provide broad discretion to different authorities, including the Amsterdam District Court, the public prosecutor and the Minister of Justice and Security. Only Article 26(3) SA on

---

[101] However, as explained, in light of recent EU case law, some German courts have decided to conduct a full review of the decision of the public prosecutor when he or she decides not to apply the refusal grounds in Article 83b IRG.

[102] Sections 6.3.1 and 6.3.5.

[103] The same goes for Article 83b(2)(1) IRG. This provision only sets a few conditions and even when these are met the public prosecutor has the discretion to surrender the requested person anyway. See Sects. 6.3.5–6.3.7. In addition, as explained in Sect. 6.3.5 the combination of the general duty to prosecute in Article 152 StPO, which obliges the public prosecutor to prosecute in case of sufficient evidence, and the possibility to apply Article 83b(1)(a) IRG when domestic proceedings are initiated after the receipt of an EAW could even cause conflicts of national jurisdictions.

[104] Section 6.3.3.3.

concurring EAWs explicitly states that the decision of the public prosecutor should be made in light of the proper administration of justice. In this light, it also provides a non-hierarchical and non-exhaustive list of factors that should be considered.[105] In addition, the proper administration of justice criterion should also guide the decision of the Minister of Justice and Security whether to suspend domestic proceedings for the same offence, which would block the application of the refusal ground in Article 9(1)(a) SA. However, nowhere has the meaning of the proper administration of justice been clearly defined, but the Dutch legislator did state in relation to Article 9(1)(a) SA that the best forum should be chosen on the basis of the concrete circumstances of the case.[106] So, similar to the German IRG, the Dutch Surrender Act provides broad discretion to the competent authorities deciding on refusal grounds and concurring EAWs which could indirectly influence forum decisions. However, contrary to the German legislator, the Dutch legislator has not unambiguously explained why it chooses broad discretion over rigid rules. Only the preparatory work on Article 9(1)(a) SA suggests that this is to ensure the necessary flexibility to facilitate prosecution by the most appropriate forum.

8.4.3.3 Interim Conclusion

It can be concluded that the problems which can arise from the fact that the EAW is not complemented by a transparent EU mechanism for forum choices have on the EU level and in the German and Dutch legal order hardly been discussed in the context of the executing procedure. With regard to the EU level, the problems which can arise due to the absence of clear EU rules preventing or solving conflicts of national jurisdictions have only been mentioned in relation to Article 16 FDEAW on concurring EAWs. In this light, the point was made that the decision for a particular EAW should avoid 'first-come, first-served' forum decisions. However, the discretion offered by Article 16 FDEAW has not been strictly delineated. With regard to the German and Dutch legal order, the examination of the conditions for the execution of an EAW which could indirectly influence forum decisions show that these legal orders prioritise flexibility over rigid rules. In Germany, the legislator has also clearly stated that the public prosecutor should be provided with broad discretion when deciding on the application of refusal grounds which have a link to conflicts of national jurisdictions. In the Netherlands, the legislator has not substantiated the lack of rigid rules as clearly as the German legislator, but the preparatory work on Article 9 SA suggests that it also holds the opinion that flexibility contributes to forum decisions in light of the proper administration of justice.

The examination of the English legal order leads to a different conclusion. The forum bar and Director's Guidance on concurrent jurisdictions were introduced to

[105] Section 5.3.7. The decision of the public prosecutor is subject to a marginal review by the Amsterdam District Court, which checks its reasonableness.

[106] Section 5.3.5.

increase the transparency of forum decisions in case of conflicts of jurisdictions. The scope of application of these instruments is, however, limited to cases in which the crime was partially committed on the territory of the UK. Still, their adoption does reflect a certain recognition of the risk that without a complementary transparent system for forum choices in light of the proper administration of justice, the EAW could in practice become a mechanism for the enforcement of arbitrary forum decisions.

8.5 Conclusion

On the basis of the previous sections, an answer can be formulated to the first part of the main research question. For this purpose, Sect. 8.2 has once more explained the foreseeability complications with which EU citizens can be confronted and the additional dimension of the EAW to these problems. It follows from this section that while the Member States have established broad extraterritorial jurisdiction, the operation of the EAW is currently not complemented by an EU system preventing or solving conflicts of jurisdictions. As a result, EU citizens can be confronted with the risk of being surrendered to a state whose jurisdiction claim was not foreseeable at the time of the offence and which has not been appointed on the basis of a transparent set of rules as the most appropriate forum for prosecution in light of the proper administration of justice. A similar risk exists in the outer-EU setting, in which extradition agreements are not complemented by an overarching international framework regulating forum choices. In this broader international setting, this risk has a limited role and so far has not resulted in a solution. This can possibly be explained on the basis of the central position of the state in extradition agreements and the limited role for the individual. However, contrary to the outer-EU context, the EAW operates in an AFSJ in which EU citizens have a prominent position and are provided with specific free movement rights. It is also precisely the exercise of these free movement rights which could cause the materialisation of the two foreseeability complications and the issuing of EAWs. This unique EU citizenship and free movement dimension of the AFSJ, therefore, constitutes the foundation of and justification for the question to what extent the two foreseeability problems are recognised as fundamental rights problems and to what extent protection against them is offered under the operation of the EAW.

In addition, on the basis of the examination of the substantive and procedural legality principle on the EU and national level in Sects. 8.3.1 and 8.4.1, the conclusion can be drawn that the scope of these principles is still very 'state-focused'. It follows from the European and national case law that the substantive legality principle exclusively covers problems which occur within the borders of a particular Member State. In this light, the right to an accessible and foreseeable law for criminal offences and sanctions in Article 49 CFR, as well as its equivalent in the national legal orders, has not been unambiguously connected to the foreseeability of a particular national criminal law. To put it differently, compliance with the requirement of an accessible and foreseeable law for criminal offences and sanctions has not explicitly been made dependent on the question to what extent the application of the national law of which the criminal offences and sanctions are part was foreseeable at the time of the offence. However, it should be noted that even though in the German legal order the unexpected application of foreign criminal laws is not recognised as a problem in light of the German substantive legality principle, protection against surrender in these situations is provided by Article 16(2) GG, which protects German nationals against extradition. Hence, in the German legal order, the problems arising from unforeseeable jurisdiction claims and the possibility of surrender in these situations is recognised as a fundamental rights problem, just not specifically as a legality issue.

With regard to the right to a tribunal established by law, the case law of the CJEU and ECtHR also shows a state-focused interpretation. This jurisprudence only discusses conflicts of jurisdictions within one particular state. Furthermore, in the national legal orders, the scope of the right to a tribunal established by law is also limited to the national level. Hence, it does not demand that the discretion of the national competent authorities, often public prosecutors, to make a forum decision in case of conflicts of national jurisdictions is sufficiently restricted by law to avoid arbitrary case allocations.

It follows from Sects. 8.3.2 and 8.4.2 that the rules regulating the decision to issue an EAW and the underlying decision to prosecute a particular case do not provide strong protection against the two central problems, either. On the EU level, neither the preparatory work to the FDEAW nor the CJEU case law link the conditions in the issuing procedure to one of the two problems. A discussion of the risk that the EAW could in practice possibly function as a mechanism for the enforcement of unforeseeable jurisdiction claims and arbitrary forum choices is absent. The only relatively clear opening to integrate the two problems in the issuing procedure was provided by the decision of the CJEU that the requested person should have the possibility to challenge the decision to issue an EAW before a court or judge when the issuing judicial authority is, for instance, a public prosecutor. However, it is unlikely that the CJEU intended this possibility of judicial review to be an opportunity to also challenge the underlying jurisdiction claim and decision to prosecute of the issuing state, since the application of a state's substantive criminal law and decision to prosecute are not part of the conditions for the issuing of an EAW laid down in the FDEAW. In addition, only the English legal order shows some form of recognition of the problems arising from the operation of the EAW without a complementary EU system for forum choices. This follows from the adoption of the Director's Guidance on concurrent jurisdictions as a response to the critique that the decision of the English public prosecutor to prosecute a case and issue an EAW when more states are competent was not based on sufficiently transparent rules.

In relation to the executing procedure, it follows from Sects. 8.3.3 and 8.3.4 that the conditions for the execution of an EAW as codified in the FDEAW and interpreted by the CJEU primarily protect state sovereignty. The same conclusion can be drawn in relation to the executing procedure on the national level, but some exceptions exist. Two of these exceptions are the nationality bar in Article 80 IRG and 83b(1)(a) IRG, which allows the German public prosecutor to refuse the EAW in case of domestic proceedings. These refusal grounds integrate the constitutional protection against extradition offered to German nationals by Article 16(2) GG and aim to protect Germans in certain situations against surrender when the application of a foreign criminal law was difficult to foresee. In addition, the UK legislator has installed protection against exorbitant jurisdiction claims in the UK Extradition Act 2003, but the definition of 'exorbitant' is not linked to the foreseeability of the jurisdiction claim at the time of the offence. However, the forum bar and previously mentioned Director's Guidance on concurrent jurisdictions were adopted for the specific purpose of increasing the transparency of the decision-making process in case of conflicts of national jurisdictions.

On the basis of these findings, it can be concluded in light of the first part of the main research question that the current level of fundamental rights protection is very state-focused. Difficulties which occur at the interface of national legal orders, such as being able to foresee which specific national substantive criminal laws to obey and the lack of a clear set of rules ensuring forum choices in light of the proper administration of justice, have as a result not been uniformly classified as fundamental rights problems, more specifically legality problems, on the legislative and judicial level. In this light, no strong indications exist either that the EAW is currently viewed as a mechanism which can contribute to or enforce violations of the legality principle by surrendering EU citizens while they are in the underlying criminal cases confronted with unforeseeable jurisdiction claims and forum decisions. However, despite this conclusion, there are subtle signs of some form of recognition of the problems and the role of the EAW therein, in particular in the German and English legal order. In Germany, this recognition is, for instance, based on other constitutional safeguards than the substantive legality principle and in England the lack of a transparent system for forum choices in case of conflicts of jurisdictions has resulted in guidelines for the English public prosecutor. Still, it should also be noted that this limited amount of recognition and protection offered in the two national legal orders is not based on the position that in an AFSJ in which EU citizens are provided with free movement rights they should be protected against the negative effects of the combination of the EAW and broad extraterritorial jurisdiction. This follows from the fact that, in Germany, the existing protection focuses on German nationals, while in the English legal order the protection against exorbitant jurisdiction claims is not linked to foreseeability considerations and the protection of EU citizens, but to the general rule that all crime is local. Hence, the EU citizenship and free movement dimensions of the AFSJ have so far not significantly influenced the scope of the EU and national legality principle, which still have a state-focused interpretation. EU citizenship and free movement have also not resulted in strong protection against surrender in case of unforeseeable jurisdiction claims and forum choices that are not based on a transparent set of rules. The next chapter follows up on this conclusion by providing an explanation for the limited attention for the foreseeability problems with which EU citizens can be confronted and the fact that they are not generally recognised as legality issues.

References

Böse M (2014) Fundamental rights of the EU-charter. In: Böse M, Meyer F, Schneider A (eds) Conflicts of jurisdiction in criminal matters in the European Union. Volume II: rights, principles and model rules. Nomos

Böse M, Meyer F, Schneider A (2013) Comparative analysis. In: Böse M, Meyer F, Schneider A (eds) Conflicts of jurisdiction in criminal matters in the European Union. Volume I: national reports and comparative analysis. Nomos

Eser A (1995) Der "gesetzliche Richter" und seine Bestimmung für den Einzelfall. In: Eser A et al (eds) Straf- und Strafverfahrensrecht, Recht und Verkehr, Recht und Medizin, Festschrift für H. Salger. Carl Heymanns

Glerum V (2013) De weigeringsgronden bij uitlevering en overlevering – Een vergelijking en kritische evaluatie in het licht van het beginsel van wederzijdse erkenning. Wolf Legal Publishers

Chapter 9
The Intergovernmental Perspective on the EAW

9.1 Introduction

The previous chapter explained that the possible foreseeability complications with which EU citizens can be confronted, arising from the broad extraterritorial jurisdiction of the Member States and the lack of a clear EU system for forum choices, are currently not recognised as fundamental rights problems or more specifically as legality issues. By extension, no strong indications exist on the EU or national level that the EAW is viewed as a mechanism which can contribute to violations of the legality principle by surrendering EU citizens to states despite an unforeseeable jurisdiction claim or decision to prosecute which is not based on a transparent set of rules. In fact, the complications which EU citizens may face as a result of the operation of the EAW in an AFSJ, in which Member States have broad extraterritorial jurisdiction and no clear EU mechanism for forum choices exists, are only to a very limited extent recognised or discussed as problems at all. In addition, the limited recognition and protection which has been installed, in particular in the German and English legal order, does not have a strong basis in the EU citizenship dimension of the AFSJ. This chapter aims to offer an explanation for these conclusions.

As mentioned before in Chap. 2, whether the current state-focused interpretation of the legality principle and the lack of attention for the problems at hand, despite the EU citizenship dimension of the AFSJ, are understandable and acceptable depends, in my opinion, on the question of how one views the EAW.[1] In this light, two different perspectives on the surrender procedure can, in my view, be derived from the examination of the legality principle and surrender procedure on the EU and national level in Chaps. 3–7. These are the intergovernmental and transnational perspective. The former views the EAW as a form of cooperation which is not fundamentally different from the traditional extradition procedure whereas the latter

[1] Section 2.7.

J. Graat, *The European Arrest Warrant and EU Citizenship*,
https://doi.org/10.1007/978-3-031-07590-2_9

is based on the opposite position. This chapter focuses on the intergovernmental perspective and the effects which it can have on the role of fundamental rights and citizenship in judicial cooperation procedures in the AFSJ. We will see that in intergovernmental extradition procedures in which the state is the main actor, a restrictive role is allocated to fundamental rights while the role of citizenship, if there is any, is often limited to national citizenship. In this light, the intergovernmental perspective can possibly explain the conclusions drawn in Chap. 8. Chapter 10 then discusses the transnational perspective, which does not explain, but questions the acceptability of the current status quo of fundamental rights protection, as well as the intergovernmental perspective as an explanation for this status quo.

This chapter is structured in the following way. Section 9.2 introduces the intergovernmental perspective and its most important characteristics. This is followed by an examination of the possible consequences of this perspective for the role of fundamental rights and the position of the EU citizen in judicial cooperation procedures in the AFSJ in Sect. 9.3. Sections 9.4 and 9.5 then discuss to what extent the intergovernmental perspective is adhered to in the EU and national legal orders. More specifically, these sections examine to what extent indications of the intergovernmental perspective and its consequences exist in the legal practice, including the legislative and judicial level and academic debate, of the EU and national legal orders. This discussion is largely based on the information gathered in Chaps. 3–7, but is complemented by additional research. This chapter ends with a conclusion in Sect. 9.5.

9.2 The Intergovernmental Perspective Introduced

The extradition procedure constitutes a form of intergovernmental or interstate cooperation which is generally perceived as a matter between states. The treaties or agreements in which the extradition procedures are laid down are concluded between the governments of different states, which act from an independent position and try to serve their own national interests.[2] For the application of the extradition rules in practice, some states have introduced two layered procedures in which the courts and government representatives, such as the Minister of Justice or Foreign Affairs share the responsibility for the final decision.[3] The competent authorities in the requested state, which is the state receiving the extradition request, decide on a

[2] An example is the European Convention on Extradition [1957] ETS No 024. Case C-303/05 *Advocaten voor de Wereld* [2006] ECLI:EU:C:2006:552, Opinion of AG Ruiz-Jarabo Colomer, paras 42, 45.

[3] Such a system has, for instance, been established in the Dutch Extradition Act. The Dutch Minister of Justice and Security decides whether refusal grounds with a political or diplomatic character, like the nationality exception, are applicable. European Commission, 'Proposal for a Council Framework Decision on the European arrest warrant and the surrender procedures between the Member States' COM (2001) 522 final, pp. 2, 5; Glerum (2013), p. 5; Luchtman (2020), p. 18.

case-by-case basis whether to execute the request. In this context, they consider both legal conditions as well as the possible implications of a certain decision for diplomatic relations with the requesting state.[4] Hence, extradition procedures often have a strong political character and allocate an important role to members of the government.

The central role of the state is also reflected in several principles of international law which influence the substantial and procedural requirements of extradition. The first one is the principle of state sovereignty on which many exceptions to the obligation to extradite, including the double criminality requirement, are founded. It primarily aims to protect the state as the main actor in intergovernmental procedures, instead of the individual who is subjected to an extradition request. The latter is, therefore, only to a limited extent or not at all able to rely the principle of state sovereignty before the national courts.[5] In relation to the protection of states, the principle of sovereignty is on the one hand closely connected to the principle of non-interference, since it prohibits the authorities of one state to arrest individuals on the territory of another state or to subject them to other coercive measures.[6] On the other hand, the principle of sovereignty entails that states are competent to decide what actions are taken in case an offence is committed on their territories. They should have the power and first say in the decision whether or not to arrest suspects, to prosecute them, extradite them or to transfer the proceedings to other states.[7] In addition, the principle of sovereignty is mirrored in other principles of international law, which also confirm the state as the key player in intergovernmental procedures. One example is the principle of reciprocity, from which it follows that all states are equal and have equal obligations towards each other. More concretely, this principle entails that when State A refuses to extradite suspects who are under the age of 16 to State B, the latter is also not obliged to extradite these type of suspects to State A.[8]

In addition to the principles of sovereignty and reciprocity, the principle of mutual trust plays an important role in extradition procedures, as well. In this context, the principle of mutual trust has two dimensions; a conditional and a limitative one.[9] The former presents mutual trust as a condition for the conclusion of extradition treaties. For that purpose, the participating states should have a certain degree of trust in the fairness of each other's legal systems and believe that individuals will receive a fair trial in other states and be treated in conformity with

[4] Case C-303/05 *Advocaten voor de Wereld* [2006] ECLI:EU:C:2006:552, Opinion of AG Ruiz-Jarabo Colomer, paras 42, 45.

[5] Glerum and Rozemond (2015), p. 169.

[6] States are also only obliged to extradite an individual when they have decided to become party to a treaty imposing such an obligation. Glerum and Rozemond (2015), p. 169.

[7] Glerum and Rozemond (2015), p. 170.

[8] See European Convention on Extradition, art 26(3). It reflects the principle of reciprocity.

[9] De Groot (2005), pp. 83–84. See also Kraniotis (2016), p. 41.

fundamental rights standards.[10] The limitative dimension of mutual trust means that signing an extradition treaty, which is the *in abstracto* expression of trust, often also implies an obligation to take a reticent approach in assessing a *concrete* request for cooperation from another state.[11]

9.3 Consequences of this Perspective for Fundamental Rights and the Position of EU Citizenship

This section explains the most likely consequences of the intergovernmental approach to the EAW for the view on the position of fundamental rights and EU citizenship in judicial cooperation procedures. We will see that these consequences also explain the conclusions of the previous chapter concerning the current state-focused interpretation of fundamental rights, in particular Article 49 and 47(2) CFR, and the limited influence of the EU citizenship dimension on the scope of these fundamental rights as well as the existing level of protection against the two risks with which EU citizens can be confronted in the AFSJ. Firstly, with regard to the role of fundamental rights in intergovernmental extradition procedures, the previously discussed principle of mutual trust is important. It explains the two most important functions of fundamental rights in extradition procedures, of which the first is the establishment and proof of trust between states entering into an agreement.[12] Their second role is to block extradition in case of a risk of fundamental rights violations in the requesting state.[13] In light of the trust established when the extradition treaty was concluded, the second role is often more limited, which is illustrated by the high standard of proof set by the ECtHR for fundamental rights restrictions in concrete extradition cases. For instance, Article 3 ECHR only prohibits extradition in case of substantial grounds proving a real risk of torture or inhuman and degrading treatment in the requesting state and in relation to the right to a fair trial in Article 6 ECHR the extradition must result in a flagrant denial of justice.[14]

It follows from the above that fundamental rights protection in intergovernmental extradition procedures focuses on the existence and enforcement of adequate fundamental rights standards within the borders of a particular state. In other words, mutual trust between states and protection of individuals in extradition procedures

[10]This trust can also be derived from, for instance, membership to a general human rights convention. De Groot (2005), p. 85; Glerum and Rozemond (2015), pp. 171–172.

[11]Kraniotis (2016), pp. 70–71.

[12]Luchtman (2017), p. 9; Luchtman (2020), p. 16.

[13]When a state is bound by an extradition agreement and the ECHR, it needs to follow the ECtHR case law on the role of fundamental rights in extradition proceedings. See eg ECtHR 7 July 1989, 14038/88 (*Soering/United Kingdom*).

[14]ECtHR 7 July 1989, 14038/88 (*Soering/United Kingdom*) paras 88, 133. See also ECtHR 16 October 2001, 71555/01 (*Einhorn/France*) para 25; ECtHR 4 February 2005, 46827/99 and 46951/99 (*Mamatkulov and Askarov/Turkey*).

requires that fundamental rights safeguards are established and complied with in each separate Member State. This view on the role of fundamental rights explains the 'state-focused' interpretation of the right to an accessible and foreseeable law in Article 49 CFR and the right to a tribunal established by law in Article 47(2) CFR as well as their equivalents in the ECHR and national legal orders.[15] This perspective clarifies why these fundamental rights do not cover the difficulties discussed in the previous chapters with which EU citizens can be confronted due to the combination of the broad extraterritorial jurisdiction of the Member States and the EAW as a compensation mechanism for their lack of extraterritorial jurisdiction to enforce. These potential difficulties go beyond compliance with fundamental rights within a particular Member State as they occur at the interface of national legal orders. In other words, these complications may arise even though the legal system of each state involved in the cooperation procedure meets the standards of the substantive legality principle and the right to a tribunal established by law.

So, more specifically with regard to the substantive legality principle as laid down in the EU Charter of Fundamental Rights and national laws, it is in the intergovernmental context sufficient that the offences and sanctions in each national substantive criminal law meet the requirements of accessibility and foreseeability. The compliance of the law codifying criminal offences and sanctions with the substantive legality principle is therefore not dependent on the foreseeability of the applicability of the specific national criminal law at the time of the offence. With regard to the right to a tribunal established by law, it is sufficient that within each Member State all courts and tribunals meet the requirements correlating from this right as applicable on the EU level and in the national legal order.

In relation to the position of EU citizenship, the previous chapter explained that the German and English legal order have to some extent integrated protection against unforeseeable jurisdiction claims and forum decisions that are not based on a transparent set of rules in the surrender procedure. This protection is, however, in the English legal order strongly derived from the traditional view that all crime is local, whereas in Germany it is almost exclusively provided to German nationals. Hence, the safeguards provided in the IRG and the Extradition Act 2003 have a strong basis in sovereignty considerations and are not based on the view that in an AFSJ in which EU citizens are provided with free movement rights, they should be protected against complications which may be a direct result of the decision to move to another state. In the context of the intergovernmental perspective, this conclusion can be explained in light of the fact that in intergovernmental extradition proceedings, the state is the central actor, and the interests and position of the requested person play a secondary role.[16] In addition, in light of the fact that the protection of one's nationals is viewed

[15]The limited scope of the fundamental rights and principles in the ECHR can be explained by the fact that this instrument was adopted at a time in which the Westphalian national state was the main actor in the international community as well as its purpose, which is to protect fundamental rights *within* national criminal justice systems. Meyer (2014), p. 206.

[16]The attention for the position of the individual has, however, increased over time. Eser et al. (2002), pp. 697ff.

as an expression of state sovereignty, safeguarding the interests of individuals in interstate cooperation procedures is traditionally presumed to be the primary prerogative and responsibility of the state of nationality.[17] Consequently, it is national citizenship which has a relatively important role in extradition procedures.

This focus on national citizenship in traditional extradition procedures which correlates from the central position of the state, state sovereignty and state interests explains why the full concept of EU citizenship, including its free movement dimension, which is often the cause of the complications which EU citizens may face, has not resulted in a strong discussion on the acceptability of the current state-focused interpretation of fundamental rights. As the free movement dimension of EU citizenship does not have an important role, it is also not likely to trigger a reconsideration of the adequacy of the current scope of fundamental rights protection in the AFSJ. In addition, the emphasis on sovereignty and the national citizen explains why the protection which has in the national legal orders been installed against surrender in case of unforeseeable jurisdiction claims and forum decisions that are not based on a transparent set of rules does not have a strong basis in the comprehensive status of EU citizenship.

To sum up, the intergovernmental perspective places the state—and therefore national interests—at the centre. In this context, fundamental rights constitute the basis for the necessary trust between states to enter into an extradition agreement, and they can function as a barrier to extradition in concrete cases. This twofold function of fundamental rights focuses on the establishment of adequate standards and compliance with these standards within the borders of the Member States and can, therefore, explain the current state-focused interpretation of the substantive legality principle and right to a tribunal established by law. In addition, the focus on national citizenship in extradition procedures can be the reason for the current state-focused interpretation of fundamental rights, despite the EU citizenship and free movement dimension of the AFSJ, as well as the fact that the existing level of protection against problems occurring at the interface of the national legal orders does not have a strong basis in the all-encompassing concept of EU citizenship. Hence, the position of national citizenship limits the current and most likely also the future role of EU citizenship in extradition procedures to primarily a symbolic status that is granted to all nationals of the Member States, while the right to free movement which comes with this status does not occupy an important position or have a significant influence.[18]

---

[17] Luchtman (2013), p. 12; Luchtman (2017), p. 9; Coutts (2014), pp. 99–100.

[18] See also Herlin-Karnell (2012), p. 104.

9.4 Indications of the Intergovernmental Perspective and Its Consequences in the Legal Practice of the EU Legal Order

9.4.1 The Surrender Procedure is (Just) a (Modern) Extradition Procedure

Arguments in favour of the perspective that the EAW is not and was never intended to be a fundamentally different procedure for cooperation can be derived from the remaining similarities or the lack of differences between the FDEAW and the extradition procedure. The similarities can primarily be found in the effect of the extradition and surrender procedure, which in both cases is the transfer of the individual, and the applicable refusal grounds. Whereas several of the 'typical' extradition refusal grounds—including the double criminality test, the nationality exception and those based on domestic criminal proceedings for the same act—were excluded in the original European Commission proposal for a FDEAW, many were also completely or partially restored during the legislative negotiations.[19] In the final version of the FDEAW, the most important differences with the extradition procedure are the abolition of the refusal grounds for fiscal, political and military offences, the partial abolition of the double criminality requirement and the restricted possibility to exclusively protect one's nationals.[20] This means that most of the classical refusal grounds in extradition procedures are also part of the surrender procedure, including the double criminality requirement, territoriality exception, extraterritoriality exception and possibility to give priority to domestic criminal proceedings. This survival of quite a few refusal grounds, which aim to protect state sovereignty, clashes with the idea of the EAW as a new form of cooperation on the basis of mutual recognition and mutual trust in an AFSJ consisting of both states and EU citizens.[21]

Two other important arguments in favour of the intergovernmental perspective on the EAW are provided by Keijzer and Plachta. The former legal scholar has stated that the goal of the FDEAW is merely to speed up extradition procedures, as follows from the first paragraph of the preamble. In light of this purpose, the FDEAW

---

[19] COM (2001) 522 final; Luchtman (2017), p. 23. See also Plachta (1999), pp. 99–100.

[20] In relation to the double criminality requirement, which in the proposal was completely abolished, the current FDEAW allows its application unless the EAW is issued for one of the offenses listed in Article 2(2) FDEAW. In subsequent mutual recognition instruments on judicial cooperation other tradition cooperation features, such as the double criminality requirement were completely reinstated for the protection of sovereignty. Taupiac-Nouvel (2012), p. 238. See eg Council Framework Decision 2008/909/JHA of 27 November 2008 on the application of the principle of mutual recognition to judgments in criminal matters imposing custodial sentences or measures involving deprivation of liberty for the purpose of their enforcement in the European Union [2008] OJ L327/27.

[21] Glerum (2013), pp. 793–794; Barents (2006), p. 363.

constitutes an extradition treaty *sui generis*.[22] Plachta has argued that if the EU legislator had really intended to establish a new surrender procedure, then contrary to the extradition procedure, all procedural safeguards in Article 5 ECHR, which codifies the right to liberty, would have been fully applicable.[23] However, according to the European Commission proposal for the FDEAW, the EAW should be treated as an equivalent of extradition in relation to Article 5 ECHR, which means that the protection offered by this fundamental right in the surrender procedure is subjected to the same limitations as the protection offered in the extradition procedure.[24] Hence, as the drafters of the FDEAW most likely did not intend to circumvent the current limitations set by the ECtHR to the scope of protection of Article 5 ECHR in extradition procedures, it is most likely that surrender was intended to be the same as extradition in 'all purposes' and not just in relation to the scope of protection of Article 5 ECHR.[25]

On the basis of the arguments set out above, several legal scholars have in primarily the older legal literature come to the conclusion that the EU legislator did not set up a new system for judicial cooperation in criminal matters.[26] Others have concluded that the EAW is just one step in the process of replacing the extradition procedure with a new system of surrender on the basis of the principle of mutual recognition. The latter opinion was, for instance, taken by AG Bot in the case *Bob-Dogi*. The Advocate General stated that the limitation of the double criminality requirement, the abolition of the rule prohibiting the extradition of nationals and the judicialisation of the procedure distinguish the EAW from extradition, but do not establish a full-fledged mutual recognition procedure which fundamentally differs from extradition.[27] A similar position is taken by Glerum, who argues on the basis of his comparison of the refusal grounds in extradition and surrender proceedings that the surrender procedure constitutes 'extradition in transition', meaning that it is 'merely' an important step towards cooperation on the basis of mutual recognition.[28]

9.4.2 A State-Focused Interpretation of Fundamental Rights

As explained before, the role of fundamental rights in intergovernmental extradition procedures is primarily to establish the necessary trust between states entering into a

[22] Keijzer (2005), p. 139.

[23] Plachta (2003), p. 193.

[24] Article 5(3) ECHR does not apply in extradition procedures. COM (2001) 522 final, p. 5.

[25] Plachta (2003), p. 193.

[26] Plachta (2003), pp. 184–192; Conway (2005), p. 255. See also Deen-Racsmany (2006), p. 171.

[27] Case C-241/15 *Bob-Dogi* [2016] ECLI:EU:C:2016:131, Opinion of AG Bot, paras 47–48.

[28] Glerum (2013), pp. 794, 795. See also Van Sliedregt (2009), p. 67; Lagodny (2005), pp. 40–42, 45; Satzger (2019), pp. 51–52. Satzger also refers to Mathisen (2010), p. 2.

cooperation agreement and to block extradition in a concrete case when there is a strong suspicion that the fundamental rights protection provided by the requesting state is insufficient. In this light, the focus is on fundamental rights standards and compliance with these standards within the separate contracting states, meaning that the law of each of these states needs to be in compliance with fundamental rights obligations. In relation to measures for judicial cooperation on the basis of mutual recognition, of which the EAW is one, the EU level also shows signs of the more classical view on the role of fundamental rights and their state-focused interpretation.

The state-focused interpretation of fundamental rights, already illustrated by the analysis of the current scope of the EU legality principle in Chap. 3, also follows from Opinion 2/13, in which the CJEU advised against the adoption of the draft agreement on the accession of the EU to the ECHR. Paragraphs 191 and 192 of this Opinion state:

> The principle of mutual trust] requires, particularly with regard to the area of freedom, security and justice, each of those States, save in exceptional circumstances, to consider all the other Member States to be complying with EU law and particularly with the fundamental rights recognised by EU law...Thus, when implementing EU law, the Member States may, under EU law, be required to presume that fundamental rights have been observed by the other Member States, so that not only may they not demand a higher level of national protection of fundamental rights from another Member State than that provided by EU law, but, save in exceptional cases, they may not check whether that other Member State has actually, in a specific case, observed the fundamental rights guaranteed by the EU.

This definition of mutual trust and its consequences for the Member States emphasise the need for adequate fundamental rights standards and enforcement of these standards within the borders of each Member State. In this Opinion, the CJEU does not hint towards the need for a different interpretation of fundamental rights in an AFSJ characterised by EU citizenship and judicial cooperation on the basis of mutual recognition, meaning an interpretation which goes beyond the obligation for each state to organise its own legal system in compliance with fundamental rights. In other words, while the CJEU does clearly indicate that it is of the opinion that judicial cooperation in the AFSJ differs from cooperation in the outer-EU context in important ways, it does not connect this conclusion to the belief that the current scope of fundamental rights protection is insufficient and should be adapted in in light of these differences, of which EU citizenship and free movement are important ones.[29]

In addition, the statement in paragraphs 191 and 192 of Opinion 2/13 that in 'exceptional cases' states may make an exception to the presumption of mutual trust and check the fundamental rights compliance of another state also reflects an intergovernmental perspective on the role of fundamental rights in judicial cooperation procedures on the basis of mutual recognition. In that light, it is important to note that before Opinion 2/13 was issued, fundamental rights concerns could,

[29] See eg Opinion 2/13 [2014] ECLI:EU:C:2014:2454, paras 157–172.

contrary to many extradition procedures, not block the execution of an EAW. A human rights refusal ground in the FDEAW was deemed unnecessary in light of the high level of trust between the EU Member States as well as contrary to the goal of speedy judicial cooperation on the basis of mutual recognition.[30] The opening for fundamental rights exceptions in the surrender procedure offered by Opinion 2/13 and the use of this opening in subsequent CJEU case law made a dent in the strong presumption of mutual trust, which has also been referred to as blind trust.[31] In the cases *Aranyosi and Căldăraru* and *LM*, the CJEU introduced a twofold test on the basis of which the executing judicial authority should determine whether it is prohibited from executing the EAW because of a risk of inhuman and degrading detention conditions in the issuing state or a violation of the right to be tried by an independent court.[32] This twofold test has been explained in Sect. 4.2.6 and requires that after the conclusion that a general risk of a violation of either fundamental right exists in the issuing state, it needs to be examined whether there are substantial grounds to believe that the surrender of the requested person will expose him or her to a real risk of such a violation in the concrete case. These accepted exceptions to the strong presumption of mutual trust, on which mutual recognition instruments like the EAW are based, reduce the differences between the surrender and extradition procedure, which existed before Opinion 2/13 was issued.[33] In other words, the official introduction of the possibility to block the surrender of requested persons in case of a risk that they be subjected to fundamental rights violation in the issuing state increases the similarities between the role of fundamental rights in the surrender procedure and in the extradition procedure.

Furthermore, the day before the entry into force of the Treaty of Lisbon, a Council Resolution with a Roadmap for strengthening procedural rights of suspects and accused persons in criminal proceedings was adopted.[34] The Roadmap states that the facilitation of the right to free movement in the AFSJ also requires that EU citizens can count on the fact that the right to a fair trial is respected when they are subjected to criminal proceedings in one or more Member States.[35] This Roadmap seems to collide with the intergovernmental view, since it approaches fundamental rights from the perspective of EU citizens' right to free movement. However, the six

---

[30] COM (2001) 522 final, art 49.

[31] See also Xanthopoulou (2018), pp. 492–494.

[32] This test has been further elaborated on in eg Case C-220/18 *ML* [2018] ECLI:EU:C:2018:589; Case C-128/18 *Dorobantu* [2019] ECLI:EU:C:2019:857; Joined Cases C-354/20 & C-412/20 [2020] *L and P* ECLI:EU:C:2020:1033.

[33] For an assessment and comparison of the standard for fundamental rights exceptions in surrender and extradition procedures set by the CJEU and ECtHR case law see Przemyslaw (2017), p. 931ff.

[34] The Council also links the need for harmonization measures regarding procedural safeguards to the smooth operation of mutual recognition instruments which contribute to security. Resolution of the Council of 30 November 2009 on a Roadmap for strengthening procedural rights of suspected or accused persons in criminal proceedings [2009] OJ C295/1, paras 6, 8.

[35] Resolution of the Council of 30 November 2009 on a Roadmap for strengthening procedural rights of suspected or accused persons in criminal proceedings [2009] OJ C295/1, paras 3–5, 10.

Drectives which were subsequently adopted and harmonise different procedural safeguards hardly reflect this free movement perspective.[36] The preambles of the Directives do not present EU citizenship or free movement as the actual or main driving forces behind the adoption of the Directives.[37] Even though some of the preambles state that common rules should or may remove obstacles to the exercise of free movement,[38] the strengthening of mutual trust to facilitate mutual recognition and effective cooperation is the main reason for the adoption of these instruments.[39] Hence, the harmonisation directives primarily focus on the trust that Member States

---

[36] Directive 2010/64/EU of the European Parliament and of the Council of 20 October 2010 on the right to interpretation and translation in criminal proceedings [2010] OJ L280/1; Directive 2012/13/EU of the European Parliament and of the Council of 22 May 2012 on the right to information in criminal proceedings [2012] OJ L142/1; Directive 2013/48/EU of the European Parliament and of the Council of 22 October 2013 on the right of access to a lawyer in criminal proceedings and in European arrest warrant proceedings, and on the right to have a third party informed upon deprivation of liberty and to communicate with third persons and with consular authorities while deprived of liberty [2013] OJ L294/1; Directive (EU) 2016/343 of the European Parliament and of the Council of 9 March 2016 on the strengthening of certain aspects of the presumption of innocence and of the right to be present at the trial in criminal proceedings [2016] OJ L65/1; Directive (EU) 2016/800 of the European Parliament and of the Council of 11 May 2016 on procedural safeguards for children who are suspects or accused persons in criminal proceedings [2016] OJ L132/1; Directive (EU) 2016/1919 of the European Parliament and of the Council of 26 October 2016 on legal aid for suspects and accused persons in criminal proceedings and for requested persons in European arrest warrant proceedings [2016] OJ L297/1.

[37] The same point has been made in relation to security measures, such as the FDEAW. Meyer (2014).

[38] See eg Directive 2013/48/EU of the European Parliament and of the Council of 22 October 2013 on the right of access to a lawyer in criminal proceedings and in European arrest warrant proceedings, and on the right to have a third party informed upon deprivation of liberty and to communicate with third persons and with consular authorities while deprived of liberty [2013] OJ L294/1, recital 8; Directive (EU) 2016/343 of the European Parliament and of the Council of 9 March 2016 on the strengthening of certain aspects of the presumption of innocence and of the right to be present at the trial in criminal proceedings [2016] OJ L65/1, recital 10; Directive (EU) 2016/800 of the European Parliament and of the Council of 11 May 2016 on procedural safeguards for children who are suspects or accused persons in criminal proceedings [2016] OJ L132/1, recital 2.

[39] See eg Directive 2010/64/EU of the European Parliament and of the Council of 20 October 2010 on the right to interpretation and translation in criminal proceedings [2010] OJ L280/1, recitals 1–9; Directive 2012/13/EU of the European Parliament and of the Council of 22 May 2012 on the right to information in criminal proceedings [2012] OJ L142/1, recitals 2–10; Directive 2013/48/EU of the European Parliament and of the Council of 22 October 2013 on the right of access to a lawyer in criminal proceedings and in European arrest warrant proceedings, and on the right to have a third party informed upon deprivation of liberty and to communicate with third persons and with consular authorities while deprived of liberty [2013] OJ L294/1, recitals 4–8; Directive (EU) 2016/343 of the European Parliament and of the Council of 9 March 2016 on the strengthening of certain aspects of the presumption of innocence and of the right to be present at the trial in criminal proceedings [2016] OJ L65/1, recitals 3,-5, 7, 10; Directive (EU) 2016/1919 of the European Parliament and of the Council of 26 October 2016 on legal aid for suspects and accused persons in criminal proceedings and for requested persons in European arrest warrant proceedings [2016] OJ L297/1, recitals 2–5. See also Tampere Programme 1999, para 37.

should have in each other's legal systems and fundamental rights standards for the purpose of efficient judicial cooperation in criminal matters.

9.4.3 The Importance of National Citizenship

With regard to the position of EU citizenship in the surrender procedure, the previous sections explained that when viewed from the intergovernmental perspective the current and probably also the future role of EU citizenship is more strongly restricted to being a status granted to all nationals of the Member States, since the national citizen has the most prominent position in intergovernmental extradition procedures. Consequently, the free movement dimension of EU citizenship does not and most likely will not have a significant influence on the surrender procedure, more specifically the role which the EAW has in relation to the two problems discussed which arise at the interface of national legal orders. Indications of this intergovernmental view on the position of EU citizenship and the more prominent position of national citizenship in the EAW procedure follow, for instance, from the preambles of the EU directives harmonising several procedural safeguards, discussed above. As explained, the preambles do not link the need for fundamental rights safeguards to the protection of the right to free movement of the EU citizen.

Furthermore, indications of the intergovernmental perspective on EU citizenship can be derived from the legislative discussions on what are now Articles 4(6) FDEAW and 5(3) FDEAW, as well as the early CJEU case law on these legal provisions. Article 4(6) FDEAW constitutes an optional refusal ground which allows the executing state to refuse an execution EAW issued for its nationals, residents or persons staying on its territory. Article 5(3) FDEAW covers prosecution EAWs and grants the executing state the discretion to demand a return guarantee for these persons when a custodial sanction is imposed in the issuing state. However, it should be noted beforehand that in more recent preliminary rulings on the interpretation of the conditions in Articles 4(6) and 5(3) FDEAW the CJEU has reconsidered its earlier position with regard to the protection of nationals. As a result of this the possibility for Member States to reintroduce a nationality exception in the surrender procedure via the backdoor has been restricted. These preliminary rulings are discussed in more detail in Chap. 10.

The European Commission proposal for the FDEAW in fact showed a strong goodbye to the focus on national citizenship that characterises extradition procedures. This follows from the preamble of the proposal which stated, 'Since the European Arrest Warrant is based on the idea of citizenship of the Union as provided in Articles 17 to 22 TEC, the exception provided for a country's nationals, which existed under traditional extradition arrangements, should not apply within the Common Area of Freedom, Security and Justice. A Citizen of the Union should face being prosecuted and sentenced wherever he or she has committed an offence within the territory of the European Union, irrespective of his or her nationality.'[40] So, EU citizenship was explicitly recognised as a basis for the FDEAW. In this light, the classical nationality exception was replaced by an refusal ground for execution EAWs and the power to demand a return guarantee in case of prosecution EAWs which would be applicable in all situations in which EU citizens would have a better chance of reintegration in the executing state.[41] In other words, the chance of a successful reintegration in society was established as the criterion on the basis of which the executing judicial authority should determine whether an execution EAW should be refused or a return guarantee should be demanded in case of a prosecution EAW. These replacements of the nationality exception clearly reflect the idea of an EU citizen who is provided with free movement rights and may decide to reside in another state than his or her state of nationality.[42] Hence, the European Commission proposal plainly integrated the full concept of EU citizenship, including its free movement dimension, in the surrender procedure.

However, the final version of the FDEAW shows that this integration was downplayed during the consecutive legislative negotiation process. The preamble no longer refers to EU citizenship as the basis for the FDEAW and Articles 4(6) and 5(3) FDEAW do not mention reintegration as the main criterion for deciding whether or not the execution EAW should be refused or the prosecution EAW should be made dependent on a return guarantee. The criterion of reintegration was to some extent reintroduced in the first preliminary rulings on these legal provisions in which the CJEU stated that one of the main objectives of Articles 4(6) and 5(3) FDEAW is to increase the chances of resocialisation.[43] Still, in this early jurisprudence, in particular in the *Wolzenburg* case, the CJEU also interprets the conditions in the two provisions in a way which gives rise to the idea that the classical nationality exception has to a large extent survived. In *Wolzenburg*, the court ruled that the objective of reintegration justifies the Dutch implementation of Article 4(6) FDEAW on the basis of which the surrender of Dutch nationals is automatically refused while the refusal of the surrender of foreigners is linked to a five-year residence requirement.[44] This ruling allows Member States to preserve a strong protection of their own nationals, which is a competence which they also had in extradition law, and provide a more restricted level of protection to foreigners.

---

[40] COM (2001) 522 final, recital 12.

[41] COM (2001) 522 final, pp. 5–6, recital 12 and arts 33 and 36; Glerum and Rozemond (2008), pp. 820–822, 831.

[42] COM (2001) 522 final, p. 5.

[43] Case C-66/08 *Kozlowski* [2008] ECLI:EU:C:2008:437, para 45; Case C-123/08 *Wolzenburg* [2009] ECLI:EU:C:2009:616, para 67; Case C-306/09 *IB* [2010] ECLI:EU:C:2010:626, para 52.

[44] Article 6(5) (old) SA covers both EU citizens with another nationality and third-country nationals. In comparison the latter category is subjected to even more conditions, including the possession of a permanent residence permit. This is not required of EU citizens. See Case C-123/08 *Wolzenburg* [2009] ECLI:EU:C:2009:616; Rb. Amsterdam 3 January 2012, ECLI:NL:RBAMS:2012:BV1119 (Amsterdam District Court); Rb. Amsterdam 12 October 2012, ECLI:NL:RBAMS:2012:BY2645 (Amsterdam District Court).

The decision of the CJEU in *Wolzenburg* seems to be based on the twofold presumption that a national of the executing state is, due to his or her nationality, by definition sufficiently integrated in the executing state, and that EU citizens with another nationality who have not resided for a certain period of time in the executing state—in this case, 5 years—have a comparatively stronger connection to their state of origin.[45] The first presumption has, however, been rebutted in the *Poplawski* case, in which the CJEU decided that the executing judicial authority should always have some degree of discretion when deciding whether or not to apply the refusal ground in Article 4(6) FDEAW.[46] This suggests that the CJEU finds an automatic refusal of the surrender of nationals no longer acceptable, which weakens the role of national citizenship in the surrender procedure.[47] Still, the second presumption has so far not been rebutted, meaning that the court has not changed its position with regard to the acceptability of the five-year residence requirement for foreigners, which does not apply to nationals of the executing state. The acceptance of this residence requirement in light of the reintegration objective of Article 4(6) FDEAW does not necessarily strongly contribute to the position of the national citizen, but in my opinion, it does raise questions from the perspective of the EU citizen with free movement rights. This is because the CJEU could also have ruled that the executing judicial authority is obliged to apply the *Kozlowski* test in cases in which the five-year residence requirement is not met.[48] The *Kozlowski* case preceded *Wolzenburg* and states that the determination whether the requested person is 'staying in' the executing state requires an assessment of the individual circumstances and objective factors, such as the length, nature and conditions of the presence of the requested person on the territory of the executing state as well as his or her family and economic connections.[49] Had the CJEU delineated its acceptance of the five-year residence requirement with the demand that the *Kozlowski* criteria are applied when the residence requirement is not met, the *Wolzenburg* case would have shown a much stronger recognition and integration of the free movement dimension of EU citizenship in the surrender procedure.

Other cases which have been criticised for strengthening the nationality exception and, therefore, the position of national citizenship over supranational EU

[45] Case C-123/08 *Wolzenburg* [2009] ECLI:EU:C:2009:616, paras 68, 70. See also Glerum (2013), p. 402.

[46] Case C-579/15 *Poplawski* [2017] ECLI:EU:C:2017:503, para 21. The Dutch Surrender Act has been amended in 2021. The Dutch legislator has changed turned the obligation for the Amsterdam District Court to refuse the surrender of all Dutch nationals into a discretionary power. See art 6a (1) SA.

[47] In *Poplawski II*, the CJEU clarified that when the national courts are incapable of explaining the national law in full compatibility with EU law, because this would, for instance, constitute a *contra legem* interpretation, they should at least interpret the national law in such a way that it fulfills the objective of the EU instrument. Case C-573/17 *Poplawski II* [2019] ECLI:EU:C:2019:530, paras 104–107.

[48] Mitsilegas (2016), p. 218.

[49] Case C-66/08 *Kozlowski* [2008] ECLI:EU:C:2008:437, para 48.

citizensahip are *Petruhhin, Pisciotti* and *BY*.[50] All cases concerned extradition requests received by EU Member States for EU citizens who had exercised their right to free movement and did not have the nationality of their host states.[51] In this setting, the CJEU was confronted with the question whether the protection offered by an EU Member State to its own nationals in extradition agreements with third states should also be offered to EU citizens who are nationals of another Member State. The court decided that rules which exclusively protect a state's nationals against extradition violate the prohibition of discrimination on the basis of nationality and hamper the exercise of free movement rights.[52] However, where the state with a nationality exception in its extradition law usually also has jurisdiction to prosecute its nationals for the offence committed abroad, it may not have jurisdiction to prosecute an EU citizen with another nationality for extraterritorial crimes. Avoiding impunity may, therefore, constitute a justification for discrimination on the basis of nationality.[53] In relation to this reasoning, the CJEU stated in *BY* that even if the national law of the host state would allow for the prosecution of the EU citizen in the host state, the latter is not obliged to refuse the extradition request and prosecute the case itself. Such an obligation would infringe upon the limits that EU law may enact on the sovereignty of the Member States and their discretion in deciding whether or not it is appropriate to prosecute a case.[54] However, in light of the proportionality requirement, the host Member State which receives the extradition request is obliged to contact the state of nationality of the EU citizen and allow it to issue an EAW, provided that this state can exercise jurisdiction. If an EAW is issued which can be executed according to the law of the host state, it should be given priority over the execution of the extradition request.[55] The obligation to solely inform the state of nationality and allow it to issue an EAW has been criticised in the legal literature for strengthening the notion of nationality and weakening the notion and relevance of EU citizenship.[56] It has been argued that the decision that only the state of nationality should be informed draws from the nationality exception

[50] Case C-182/15 *Petruhhin* [2016] ECLI:EU:C:2016:630; Case C-191/16 *Pisciotti* [2018] ECLI:EU:C:2018:222; Case C-398/19 *BY* [2020] ECLI:EU:C:2020:1032.

[51] In *BY*, the person in question had only acquired the Romanian nationality and, therefore, EU citizenship, after travelling from Romania to Germany. The CJEU decided that the fact that the right to free movement was exercised before BY had official become an EU citizen did not lead to the conclusion that the case fell outside the scope of EU law. A different conclusion would prevent an EU citizen from enjoying his or her EU citizenship rights, which would undermine the effectiveness of this status. Case C-398/19 *BY* [2020] ECLI:EU:C:2020:1032, paras 30–31.

[52] TFEU, art 18.

[53] Case C-182/15 *Petruhhin* [2016] ECLI:EU:C:2016:630, paras 32–34, 37–38; Case C-191/16 *Pisciotti* [2018] ECLI:EU:C:2018:222, paras 45, 47–48; Case C-398/19 *BY* [2020] ECLI:EU:C:2020:1032, paras 39–42.

[54] Case C-398/19 *BY* [2020] ECLI:EU:C:2020:1032, para 65.

[55] Case C-182/15 *Petruhhin* [2016] ECLI:EU:C:2016:630, paras 48, 50; Case C-191/16 *Pisciotti* [2018] ECLI:EU:C:2018:222, para 51; Case C-398/19 *BY* [2020] ECLI:EU:C:2020:1032, para 43.

[56] Klip (2017), p. 201.

and the idea that Member States protect their own nationals while leaving the protection of other EU citizens to their own states of nationality.[57] This link between the 'return to national citizenship' and the devaluation of supranational EU citizenship is not limited to the area of extradition and surrender. It is, for instance, also made in the legal literature on free movement and social EU citizenship. It is argued that the responsibility which is still imposed on the home Member State—Member State of nationality—in protecting the right to free movement as well as social and welfare rights of moving EU citizens is a reiteration of national citizenship at the expense of supranational EU citizenship.[58]

9.5 Indications of the Intergovernmental Perspective and Its Consequences in the Legal Practice of the National Legal Orders

The examination of the three national legal orders in Chaps. 5–7 reveals several indications of the intergovernmental perspective and its consequences for fundamental rights and EU citizenship. With regard to the intergovernmental perspective on the EAW itself, the analysis of the implementation process in the national legal orders shows that all national legislators have referred to the EAW as a form of extradition. The German legislator has, for instance, stated during the discussions on the first Act implementing the FDEAW, 'Die Regelungen des RbEuHb ersetzen zwar die bestehenden Verfahren zur Aus- und Durchlieferung zwischen den Staaten der Europäischen Union. Der RbEuHb greift diese im Wesentlichen jedoch auf und modifiziert sie punktuell zur Beschleunigung und Erleichterung der Zusammenarbeit, etwa durch die Reduzierung der Verweigerungsgründe, die zu einer Ablehnung des Verfahrens berechtigen, oder durch die Einführung von Fristen.'[59] The same intergovernmental view is later on adopted by the German Constitutional Court in the case *Darkazanli*, in which the first implementation Act was ruled unconstitutional. The court emphasised that the FDEAW was adopted in the context of the third pillar, which is primarily intergovernmental, and falls outside the supranational framework of community law.[60] Furthermore, it concluded that the decision to adopt a FDEAW based on a restricted level of mutual recognition instead of EU measures harmonising the criminal law of the Member States in fact protects national identity and statehood.[61] Similar to the German legislator and BVerfG, the

[57] Klip (2017), p. 201; João Costa (2017), pp. 196–198.

[58] Spaventa (2017), pp. 215–216; O'Brien (2017), p. 243; Strumia (2020), p. 512.

[59] BT Drucksache 15/1718 [11].

[60] BVerfG 18 July 2005, 2 BvR 2236/04 (*Darkazanli*) [81]. The Treaty of Lisbon has dissolved the pillar structure as a result of which criminal justice measures now also fall within the supranational framework of the EU.

[61] BVerfG 18 July 2005, 2 BvR 2236/04 (*Darkazanli*) [76].

Dutch legislator has classified surrender as international cooperation in criminal matters which is in principle the same as extradition.[62] With regard to the English legal order, legal scholars have argued that the fact that the EAW is implemented in the Extradition Act 2003 which also regulates extradition from and to non-EU Member States means that the UK legislator does not consider the surrender procedure to be a *sui generis* procedure.[63]

The intergovernmental perspective on the EAW also follows from the way in which specific aspects of the executing and issuing procedure have been implemented in the national legal orders. Firstly, in the German and English legal order the surrender procedure and extradition procedure are regulated in the same national act in which the terminology of the FDEAW is not completely adopted, even though it differs from the jargon typically used in extradition agreements.[64] Furthermore, the UK's Home Secretary and the German Federal Minister of Justice,[65] have been provided with powers which are in contrast with the spirit of the FDEAW. As explained in Chap. 7, the role of the Home Secretary is more limited in EAW procedures than in classical extradition procedures, but he or she is allowed to designate non-EU Member States as Category 1 territories.[66] This contradicts the idea that the EAW establishes a new system for cooperation based on the principle of mutual recognition and a unique form of trust in the fundamental rights standards of fellow EU Member States.[67] As explained in Chap. 6, the power to execute an EAW is officially still shared between the public prosecutor and the OLG.[68] However, the power of the Federal Minister of Justice to issue instructions to the public prosecutor has not been abolished. This clashes with the case law of the CJEU which states that the executing judicial authority should be independent and may not be obliged to comply with orders issued by the executive. In addition, as long as the IRG is not amended, the Federal Minister of Jusitce seems to remain the official issuing and executing authority. This position for the Minister is the result of the view that the

[62] *Kamerstukken II* 2002/03, 29 042, nr. 3, p. 5.

[63] Zagaris (2003); Plachta (2003), p. 194. See also HL Deb 3 June 2003, vol 648, col 120.

[64] See Evaluation report on the fourth round of mutual evaluations 'The practical application of the European Arrest Warrant and Corresponding surrender procedures between Member States'—Report on Germany, 7058/2/09 REV 1 (2009), p. 35; Case C-220/18 *ML* [2018] ECLI:EU:C:2018:547, Opinion of AG Campos Sánchez-Bordona, fn 53; Sinn and Wörner (2008), p. 249; Mackarel (2007), p. 380; Spencer (2009), p. 535; Evaluation report on the fourth round of mutual evaluations 'The practical application of the European Arrest Warrant and Corresponding surrender procedures between Member States'—Report on the United Kingdom, 9974/2/07 REV 2 EXT 1 (2007), pp. 57–58.

[65] On the Federal Minister of Justice as the official competent authority to issue and execute an EAW, see Sects. 6.3.1 and 6.4.1.

[66] Section 7.3.1; Extradition Act 2003, ss 1(1) and 223 (5–6), (8).

[67] Mackarel (2007), p. 374; Spencer (2009), p. 535. See also Jones and Doobay (2005), pp. 130–131; Committee on Home Affairs, *Extradition Bill* (HC 2002-03, 138, 475 Government Response); HC Deb 25 March 2003, vol 402, cols 225, 227.

[68] Some German courts have, however, decided to conduct a full judicial review of the decision of the public prosecutor. See Sect. 6.3.1.

surrender procedure covers relations between the German state and foreign states which according to Article 32 GG are conducted by the Federation.[69] In this light, the role of the Federal Minister of Justice both fits with the intergovernmental perspective in which the state is the main actor and clashes with the objective of the FDEAW to establish a system of surrender in which judicial authorities cooperate directly with one another and make decisions independently of the executive.[70]

Secondly, the intergovernmental perspective, in particular its focus on the state as the central actor and the role of political and diplomatic interests, is strongly reflected in the decision of the German legislator to divide the surrender procedure into a decision on the admissibility and the granting of an EAW. The latter decision is in traditional extradition procedures in Germany classified as a foreign policy decision in which political and diplomatic interests may play a role. While the goal of the FDEAW is to exclude the political and diplomatic elements from the surrender procedure, the German legislator has preserved such elements by not abolishing the granting decision, which also in the surrender procedure constitutes at its core a foreign policy decision in the context of which political and diplomatic considerations may play a role.[71]

Lastly, whereas intergovernmental extradition agreements normally allow states to add certain refusal grounds via declarations and reservations this possibility does not exist in relation to the FDEAW which exhaustively enumerates the refusal grounds that may be applied.[72] Despite this fact, the three national legal orders have adopted refusal grounds which do not appear in the FDEAW and even clash with its underlying principles. For example, even though the decision on guilt or innocence is not part of the surrender procedure as regulated by the FDEAW and should be left to the issuing state, similar to the Dutch Extradition Act the Dutch Surrender Act demands that the execution of the EAW is refused when requested persons can prove their innocence.[73] Other examples are provided by the IRG, which includes a refusal ground protecting the principle of reciprocity, which is closely related to state sovereignty, and a refusal ground which bars surrender in case of a violation of the basic principles of the German legal system.[74] These two refusal grounds apply in both the German extradition and surrender procedure, even though

[69] Sections 6.3.1 and 6.4.1.

[70] Case C-477/16 *Kovalkovas* [2016] ECLI:EU:C:2016:861, paras 41–42; Joined Cases C-508/18 & C-82/19 *OG & PI* [2019] ECLI:EU:C:2019:456, paras 73–74; Case C-489/19 *NJ* [2019] ECLI:EU:C:2019:849, para 38; Case C-510/19 *AZ* [2020] ECLI:EU:C:2020:953. So far, Germany has not changed the provisions in the IRG appointing the Federal Minister as the competent authority for the issuing and execution of EAWs in light of this case law.

[71] Section 6.3.1; BT Drucksache 16/1024 [13].

[72] See eg Case C-123/08 *Wolzenburg* [2009] ECLI:EU:C:2009:616, para 57; Case C-396/11 *Radu* [2013] ECLI:EU:C:2013:39, para 36.

[73] Art 28(2) Extradition Act; Article 28(2) SA.

[74] Article 83b(1)(d) and Article 73 IRG. Evaluation report on the fourth round of mutual evaluations 'The practical application of the European Arrest Warrant and Corresponding surrender procedures between Member States'—Report on Germany, 7058/2/09 REV 1 (2009), pp. 25, 44.

their application clashes with EU law. In addition, the UK Extradition Act contains several refusal grounds that are of domestic origin as illustrated by Section 14 EA. This refusal ground prohibits the execution of an EAW when this would be unjust or oppressive as a result of the passage of time. It also allows the District Judge to examine the merits of the underlying criminal case and the conduct of the issuing state, which clashes with the principle of mutual recognition.[75]

Besides indications of the intergovernmental perspective on the EAW, the national legal orders also show signs of the intergovernmental view on the role of fundamental rights and the prominent position of national citizenship in the surrender procedure. The former follows, for instance, from the fact that even though it is not in conformity with the FDEAW and the presumption of mutual trust, all three national legal orders have a general human rights refusal ground in their surrender procedure.[76] In other words, similar to the national extradition procedures, these national surrender procedures already granted the possibility to refuse the execution of an EAW due to doubts about the issuing state's compliance with fundamental rights standards before Opinion 2/13 was issued by the CJEU, which officially allowed some fundamental rights exceptions.[77] Hence, the three national legal orders do not seem to fully believe in a level of mutual trust regarding fundamental rights standards in all EU Member States which makes fundamental rights as a protection mechanism for the individual in concrete extradition cases obsolete for the surrender procedure.[78]

With regard to the position of national citizenship, it follows from Chap. 7 that, in the UK, British citizenship does not have an important role in either the surrender or extradition procedure.[79] However, the opposite conclusion follows from Chap. 6 on the German legal order. In the case *Darkazanli*, the German Constitutional Court emphasised the 'additional' status of EU citizenship to national citizenship and stated that the latter is not devalued by the former.[80] In the same case, the BVerfG declared the First EAW Implementation Act unconstitutional because the German legislator had not used all the discretion provided by the FDEAW to protect German nationals against surrender. On the basis of Article 16(2) GG, the court focused on the protection of Germans against surrender in cases in which the application of foreign substantive criminal laws would not be foreseeable while the protection of

[75] Evaluation report on the fourth round of mutual evaluations 'The practical application of the European Arrest Warrant and Corresponding surrender procedures between Member States' – Report on the United Kingdom, 9974/2/07 REV 2 EXT 1 (2007), pp. 46, 65. On this extradition bar see Jones and Doobay (2005), pp. 221–222.

[76] Art 11 SA; art 73 IRG; Extraditon Act 2003, s 21A.

[77] Opinion 2/13 [2014] ECLI:EU:C:2014:2454.

[78] See eg *Kamerstukken II* 2003/04, 29,042, nr. 5, p. 12–15.

[79] Section 7.3.4. In relation to the English legal order see *Report of the Royal commission on Extradition* (Cmd 2039, 1878); HL Deb 20 June 2018, vol 791, cols 2025–2026.

[80] BVerfG 18 July 2005, 2 BvR 2236/04 (*Darkazanli*) [74]–[75].

other EU citizens who could be confronted with this problem was ignored.[81] Hence, the special relationship between the German citizen and the German state was magnified, while the possibility of a similar relationship between an EU citizen with another nationality and the German state was neglected.[82] This special bond between the German and the German state has also been integrated in the refusal grounds of the executing procedure, in particular in Article 80 IRG, which is largely based on the ruling in *Darkazanli.*[83]

At least until the 2021 amendments to the Surrender Act were adopted, the Dutch legal order showed in comparison to the English and German one a more intermediate position regarding the importance of national citizenship in the surrender procedure. This position followed from the way in which Articles 4(6) and 5(3) FDEAW were implemented in the Dutch Surrender Act. Before the 2021 amendments, the Amsterdam District Court was obliged to refuse execution EAWs and demand a return guarantee for prosecution EAWs when these were issued for Dutch nationals.[84] Hence, Dutch nationality was in itself sufficient to consider the requested person 'integrated' in Dutch society and to trigger the mandatory protection, while the same protection for other EU citizens and foreigners was subject to a five-year residence requirement.[85] In other words, Dutch nationals who had never really resided in the Netherlands would be protected, whereas EU citizens who had lived in the Netherlands for less than 5 years but had strong economic and family ties to the country were not. This strict interpretation of 'integration', which was decisive for the decision whether the protection in Article 6 SA would be offered, shows a relatively strong position for the Dutch national and puts the EU citizen with free movement rights in the background. However, as mentioned before in 2021, the Dutch legislator amended the implementation of Articles 4(6) and 5(3) FDEAW. As a result, Articles 6 and 6a in the current Surrender Act no longer oblige and allow the Amsterdam District Court to provide automatic protection to Dutch nationals, which to some extent diminishes the position of the national citizen in the surrender procedure. Still, the Dutch legislator did not abolish the obligator five-year residence requirement for foreigners, which does not apply to requested persons with the Dutch nationality.

[81] BVerfG 18 July 2005, 2 BvR 2236/04 (*Darkazanli*) [85]. See also BVerfG 3 September 2009, 2 BvR 1826/09 [14]–[15]; BVerfG 9 November 2016, 2 BvR 545/16 [36]; Luchtman (2017), p. 9.

[82] BVerfG 18 July 2005, 2 BvR 2236/04 (*Darkazanli*) [66]–[67]; BVerfG 9 November 2016, 2 BvR 545/16 [36].

[83] See Sect. 6.3.3.

[84] Art 6(1)(2)(5) SA (old).

[85] See Sect. 5.3.1; Glerum and Rozemond (2010), pp. 271–302. In 2021 the Dutch legislator amended the implementation of Articles 4(6) and 5(3) FDEAW. Articles 6 and 6a SA no longer oblige the Amsterdam District Court to provide automatic protection to Dutch nationals, but they are still not subjected to the same five-year residence requirement as other EU citizens.

9.6 Conclusion

The purpose of this chapter was to provide an explanation for the answer to the first part of the research question presented in Chap. 8. The main conclusion of that chapter was that the EU citizenship dimension of the AFSJ has not (yet) resulted in a full rejection of the 'state-focused' interpretation of the substantive legality principle and right to a tribunal established by law on the EU and national level. Due to this 'state-focused' interpretation, no strong indications exist that the problems with which EU citizens may be confronted, which occur at the interface of national legal orders and arise from the operation of the EAW without a complementary EU system for forum choices in light of the proper administration of justice are recognised as legality problems. Consequently, the position that the EAW is a mechanism which can contribute to or enforce violations of the legality principle by surrendering EU citizens while they are in the underlying criminal cases confronted with unforeseeable jurisdiction claims or arbitrary forum decisions is not strongly reflected on the EU and national level.

This chapter has presented the intergovernmental perspective on the EAW as an explanation for this 'state-focused' interpretation of the *nullum crimen sine lege* principle and the right to a tribunal established by law, as well as the largely absent recognition of the EAW as a mechanism which can worsen problems arising from unforeseeable jurisdiction claims and the absence of an EU system for forum choices by transferring EU citizens to states while these problems occur in the underlying criminal cases. In the intergovernmental perspective, the EAW is viewed as a classical intergovernmental extradition procedure, in which the state and state sovereignty occupy a central position. In this context, fundamental rights often have a relatively restricted role, as they primarily establish and verify the existence of mutual trust between states, which is a necessary requirement for successful cooperation. As follows from the ECtHR case law, fundamental rights can also block extradition in cases in which there is a strong suspicion of fundamental rights violations in the requesting state. This twofold function of fundamental rights in the intergovernmental perspective is satisfied when each separate state establishes adequate fundamental rights standards and complies with them. It therefore also explains the current 'state-focused' interpretation of the substantive legality principle and the right to a tribunal established by law, as well as why the problems discussed in this book are not recognised as legality problems. As explained, these problems occur at the interface of national legal orders, meaning that they can arise even though the separate national laws of all the contracting states in the extradition procedure comply with the substantive and procedural legality principle. In addition, in the intergovernmental perspective the national citizen has the most prominent role. It is considered the prerogative and responsibility of the state of nationality to protect its nationals when this is considered to be a national state interest. This focus on the national citizen could explain why the comprehensive concept of EU citizenship, including its free movement dimension which puts the emphasis on the state of residence instead of the state of nationality, has not resulted in the abandonment of the 'state-focused' interpretation of the legality principle or a clear recognition of the problems with which in particular moving EU citizens can be confronted arising from the combination of the EAW with the broad extraterritorial jurisdiction of the Member States.

Signals or evidence of this intergovernmental perspective on the EAW, fundamental rights and EU citizenship can predominantly be found in the national legal orders. The national legislators responsible for implementing the FDEAW have all adopted the view that the surrender procedure is a modern extradition procedure. This view is also reflected in the decisions regarding the implementation of specific aspects of the FDEAW, such as its refusal grounds, and its terminology. In addition, the Dutch legal order and in particular the German legal order emphasise the bond between the state and its nationals in the surrender procedure. In Germany, protection is often almost exclusively offered to German nationals as illustrated by the case law of the BVerfG and the nationality exception in Article 80 IRG. Besides the national level, some signs of the intergovernmental perspective can also be found on the EU level. It is primarily reflected in the survival of many typical extradition refusal grounds as well as in the focus on the national citizen in the *Wolzenburg* case and the *Petruhhin* string of case law. Furthermore, in Opinion 2/13 and subsequent case law, the CJEU explained the principle of mutual trust in a way which resembles the twofold function of fundamental rights in extradition procedures. However, despite these clear indications of the intergovernmental perspective on the EU and the national level, both levels also show signs which contradict the intergovernmental perspective and in fact point at the existence of another way to view the EAW. The next chapter elaborates on this by presenting two strings of arguments which both question the validity of the conclusions of Chap. 8 as well as the intergovernmental perspective as their explanation, and constitute the foundation of the alternative transnational perspective on the surrender procedure.

References

Barents R (2006) De denationalisering van het strafrecht. Preadvies voor de NVER-vergadering van 24 november 2006. SEW 358

Conway G (2005) Judicial interpretation and the third pillar: Ireland's acceptance of the European arrest warrant and the Gözütok and Brügge case. Eur J Crime Crim Law Crim Just 13:255

Coutts S (2014) Citizenship of the European Union. In: Arcarazo DA, Murphy C (eds) EU security and justice law: after Lisbon and Stockholm. Hart

Deen-Racsmany Z (2006) The European arrest warrant and the surrender of nationals revisited: the lessons of constitutional challenges. Eur J Crime Crim Law Crim Just 14:271

De Groot S (2005) Mutual trust in (European) extradition law. In: Blekxtoon R, van Ballegooij W (eds) Handbook on the European arrest warrant. Asser

Eser A, Blakesly C, Lagodny O (eds) (2002) The individual as subject of international cooperation in criminal matters – a comparative study. Nomos

Glerum V (2013) De weigeringsgronden bij uitlevering en overlevering – Een vergelijking en kritische evaluatie in het licht van het beginsel van wederzijdse erkenning. Wolf Legal Publishers

Glerum V, Rozemond N (2008) Overlevering van Nederlanders: copernicaanse revolutie of uitlevering in overgang? DD 816

Glerum V, Rozemond N (2010) Het Wolzenburg-arrest, de interpretatie van het Kaderbesluit betreffende het Europees aanhoudingsbevel en de gevolgen voor de Nederlandse overleveringspraktijk. DD 271

Glerum V, Rozemond N (2015) Uitlevering. In: van Elst R, van Sliedregt E (eds) Handboek Internationaal Strafrecht – Internationaal en Europees strafrecht vanuit Nederlands perspectief. Wolters Kluwer

Herlin-Karnell E (2012) In: Dougan M, Shuibhne NN, Spaventa E (eds) Is the citizen driving the EU's criminal law agenda?, Empowerment and disempowerment of the European Citizen, Hart

João Costa M (2017) The emerging EU extradition law. Petruhhin and beyond. New J Eur Crim Law 8:192

Jones A, Doobay A (2005) Jones and Doobay on extradition and mutual assistance. Sweet & Maxwell

Keijzer N (2005) The double criminality requirement. In: Blekxtoon R, van Ballegooij W (eds) Handbook on the European arrest warrant. Asser

Klip A (2017) Europeans First! Petruhhin, an unexpected revolution in extradition law. Eur J Crime Crim Law Crim Just 25:195

Kraniotis T (2016) Het vertrouwensbeginsel bij de interstatelijke samenwerking in strafzaken. Kluwer

Lagodny O (2005) Extradition without a granting procedure: the concept of surrender. In: Blekxtoon R, van Ballegooij W (eds) Handbook on the European arrest warrant. Asser

Luchtman M (2013) Choice of forum and the prosecution of cross-border crime in the European Union – what role for the legality principle? In: Luchtman M (ed) Choice of forum in cooperation against EU financial crime. Freedom, security and justice and the protection of specific EU-interests. Eleven International Publishing

Luchtman M (2017) Transnationale rechtshandhaving: Over fundamentele rechten in de Europese strafrechtelijke samenwerking. Boom

Luchtman M (2020) Transnational law enforcement cooperation – fundamental rights in European cooperation in criminal matters. Eur J Crime Crim Law Crim Just 28:14

Mackarel M (2007) Surrendering the fugitive – the European arrest warrant and the United Kingdom. J Crim Law 71:362

Mathisen G (2010) Nordic cooperation and the European arrest warrant: intra-Nordic extradition, the Nordic arrest warrant and beyond. Nordic J Int Law 79:1

Meyer F (2014) An area of freedom, security and justice. In: Böse M, Meyer F, Schneider A (eds) Conflicts of jurisdiction in criminal matters in the European Union. Volume II: rights, principles and model rules. Nomos

Mitsilegas V (2016) EU criminal law after Lisbon: rights, trust and the transformation of justice in Europe. Hart Publishing

O'Brien C (2017) Unity in adversity: EU citizenship, social justice and the cautionary tale of the UK. Bloomsbury Publishing

Plachta M (1999) (Non-)extradition of nationals: a neverending story? Emory Int Law Rev 13:77

Plachta M (2003) European arrest warrant: revolution in extradition. Eur J Crime Crim Law Crim Just 11:178

Przemyslaw T (2017) After the dust has settled: how to construct the new accession agreement after opinion 2/13 of the CJEU. German Law J 18:919

Satzger H (2019) Is mutual recognition a viable general path for cooperation? New J Eur Crim Law 10:44

Sinn A, Wörner L (2008) Country report: Germany. In: Górski A, Hofmanski P (eds) The European arrest warrant and its implementation in the member states of the European Union. Beck

Spaventa E (2017) Earned EU citizenship – understanding union citizenship through its scope. In: Kochenov D (ed) EU citizenship and federalism: the role of rights. Cambridge University Press

Spencer J (2009) Mutual recognition of decisions in criminal justice and the United Kingdom. In: Gisèle Vernimmen-Van Tiggelen et al. (eds) The future of mutual recognition in criminal matters in the European Union University of Brussel
Strumia F (2020) Supranational citizenship enablers. Free movement from the perspective of home Member States. Eur Law Rev 45:507
Taupiac-Nouvel G (2012) The Prinicple of mutual recognition in criminal matters: a new model of judicial cooperation within the European Union. Eur Crim Law Rev 2:236
Van Sliedregt E (2009) The dual criminality requirement. In: Keijzer N, van Sliedregt E (eds) The European arrest warrant in practice. Asser
Xanthopoulou E (2018) Mutual trust and rights in EU criminal and asylum law: three phases of evolution and the uncharted territory beyond blind trust. Common Mark Law Rev 55:489
Zagaris B (2003) Blair administration introduces bill to simplify extradition. Int Enforcement Law Reporter 19:13

Chapter 10
Does the Intergovernmental Shoe Still Fit? The Rise of an Alternative Perspective: Transnational Cooperation in a Shared Legal Order

10.1 Introduction

The previous chapter presented the intergovernmental perspective on the EAW and its possible consequences for the position of fundamental rights and EU citizenship as an explanation for the conclusions drawn in Chap. 8. It also explained to what extent this intergovernmental perspective is currently reflected on the EU level and in the national legal orders. However, as already mentioned in Chap. 2, it has been argued in the legal literature that this intergovernmental perspective on the surrender procedure is not the only one or the most suitable one.[1] The development of the operation of the EAW in the context of the AFSJ, including the EU and the national level, also shows signs of a perspective which views the EAW as a form of transnational cooperation which takes place in a shared legal order consisting of both states and EU citizens and which is founded on common values, including the rule of law and fundamental rights.

Sections 10.2–10.5 set out two strings of arguments that can be derived from the operation of the EAW on the EU level which challenge the validity of the intergovernmental perspective and which solidify the transnational perspective. Section 10.2 discusses the first string of arguments. It is based on the way in which the EAW is presented in the text of the FDEAW as well as the differences between the substantive conditions and the procedural aspects laid down in the FDEAW and extradition agreements, such as the European Convention on Extradition.[2] Hence, this string of arguments considers the EAW in isolation from the AFSJ as the normative context within which it functions. Sections 10.3–10.5 discuss the second string of arguments, which emphasises the differences between the normative contexts within which the EAW and extradition agreements function. To give an example, contrary to the intergovernmental context within which extradition agreements operate, the

[1] See Sect. 2.7.3.

[2] European Convention on Extradition [1957] ETS No 024.

J. Graat, *The European Arrest Warrant and EU Citizenship*,
https://doi.org/10.1007/978-3-031-07590-2_10

EAW aims to contribute to the establishment of a common judicial area, referred to as the AFSJ, which has an EU citizenship and free movement dimension. Section 10.6 then examines to what extent the legislation and case law of the national legal orders also shows signs which contradict the adoption of the intergovernmental perspective on the national level. This is followed by Sect. 10.7, in which the question is answered to what extent the intergovernmental perspective can be a valid explanation and justification for the conclusions drawn in Chap. 8.

Section 10.8 then discusses the transnational perspective which is to a large extent founded on the same arguments as the ones against the intergovernmental perspective. It is followed up by a conclusion in Sect. 10.9. The possible consequences of the transnational perspective for the acceptability of the conclusions drawn in Chap. 8, including the acceptability of the current 'state-focused' interpretation of the legality principle, the position of the EU citizen and the need for EU or national action to solve the problems arising at the interface of national legal orders with which EU citizen can be confronted are discussed in the next chapters. Chapter 11 will analyse how the transnational perspective can trigger the need for a transnational interpretation of the legality principle and what consequences the adoption of such an interpretation could have for the functioning of the EAW as well as the need for action on the EU and/or national level to solve these consequences. Chapter 12 then elaborates on the role which the EU citizen can and should play in realising any required changes to the role of fundamental rights and the operation of the EAW in the AFSJ in the context of the transnational perspective.

10.2 The First String of Arguments: The Text of the FDEAW

As explained in the previous section, the first string of arguments is derived from the way in which the EAW is described in the Framework Decision and the differences between the final version of the FDEAW and classical extradition agreements, such as the European Convention on Extradition. In relation to the former, the preamble of the FDEAW describes the surrender procedure as a new procedure, which replaces all extradition agreements between EU Member States.[3] This characterisation also follows from earlier versions of the FDEAW, including the European Commission's proposal.[4] In fact, in this proposal the European Commission clearly based the introduction of the surrender procedure on the position that extradition procedures, which have a political dimension and are often slow and complex, are not suitable

[3] FDEAW, recitals 5, 11.

[4] European Commission, 'Proposal for a Council Framework Decision on the European arrest warrant and the surrender procedures between the Member States' COM (2001) 522 final, recital 4; Council, 'Proposal for a Council Framework Decision on the European arrest warrant and the surrender procedures between the Member States' [2001] 14867/1/01, recital 5.

for an AFSJ without internal borders in which a high degree of confidence exists between Member States.[5] Hence, the legislative process leading to the adoption of the FDEAW and the recitals of the final version reveal the view that the surrender procedure should not be placed on equal footing with the extradition procedure. The intent was and is to get rid of the political and diplomatic character of the extradition procedure and replace it with a new surrender procedure in which judicial authorities are required to directly cooperate with one another.[6] This intent is also confirmed by the CJEU, which in its case law consistently states that the FDEAW replaces the extradition procedure with a new surrender procedure.[7] The court has also prohibited the appointment of a member of the executive as the issuing and executing judicial authority as well as the appointment of authorities which can receive instructions from the executive branch. These prohibitions reflect the position that the goal of the surrender procedure is to break with the political and diplomatic character of the extradition procedure.[8]

In addition, whereas legal scholars who adhere to the intergovernmental perspective logically focus on the similarities between the FDEAW and extradition agreements, those who consider this perspective outdated or incorrect stress their differences.[9] The first important difference that is often referred to is the same one as mentioned in the previous paragraph. The FDEAW intends to restrict the role of the government and political considerations which characterise classical extradition procedures. The legislative history of the FDEAW and the CJEU case law emphasise the introduction of a procedure of direct cooperation between judicial authorities of the Member States who need to make the issuing and execution decisions in the surrender procedure.[10] Secondly, whereas cooperation outside the context of the EU often takes a request-based approach, the EAW is an order to surrender the requested person, which is generally viewed as more imperative.[11] Thirdly, the FDEAW

---

[5] COM (2001) 522 final, p. 2 and recital 4.

[6] FDEAW, recitals 5, 11.

[7] See e.g. Joined Cases C-404/15 & C-659/15 *Aranyosi & Căldăraru* [2016] ECLI:EU:C:2016:198, para 75; Case C-477/16 *Kovalkovas* [2016] ECLI:EU:C:2016:861, para 25. See also Case C-551/18 *IK* [2018] ECLI:EU:C:2018:890, Opinion of AG Sharpston, para 40.

[8] See e.g. Case C-477/16 *Kovalkovas* [2016] ECLI:EU:C:2016:861, paras 41–42; Cases C-508/18 & C-82/19 *OG & PI* [2019] ECLI:EU:C:2019:456, paras 64–65; Case C-510/19 *AZ* [2020] ECLI:EU:C:2020:953, paras 48, 54.

[9] AG Colomer has stated in the case *Advocaten voor de Wereld* that, except for their intended result, which is the transfer of a person for the purpose of prosecution or the execution of a sentence, the two systems are completely different. Case C-303/05 *Advocaten voor de Wereld* [2006] ECLI:EU:C:2006:552, Opinion of AG Ruiz-Jarabo Colomer, paras 40–41, 46. See also European Commission, 'Report on the implementation of Council Framework Decision of 13 June 2002 on the European arrest warrant and the surrender procedures between Member States' COM (2020) 270 final, para 1.2.

[10] COM (2001) 522 final, pp. 2, 5; Cases C-508/18 & C-82/19 *OG & PI* [2019] ECLI:EU:C:2019:456, paras 64–65; Case C-303/05 *Advocaten voor de Wereld* [2006] ECLI:EU:C:2006:552, Opinion of AG Ruiz-Jarabo Colomer, paras 43–45; Van Sliedregt (2007), p. 248; Glerum (2013), p. 5.

[11] Kraniotis (2016), p. 254; Borgers (2010); Spencer (2013), p. 63.

provides a standard form for the issuing of an EAW and subjects the executing judicial authority to relatively strict deadlines for making a decision.[12] Fourthly, the FDEAW contains in principle an exhaustive list of refusal grounds and guarantees to which states may not add by issuing declarations or reservations.[13] The list in Articles 3–5 FDEAW also excludes several typical extradition refusal grounds, such as those for political, military and fiscal offences. Furthermore, it limits the application of the double criminality requirement and replaces the nationality exception with a refusal ground and guarantee which oblige the executing state to offer equal protection to its own nationals and EU citizens residing or staying in the executing state.[14] Lastly, the restriction of the double criminality requirement as well as the existence of primarily optional refusal grounds in the FDEAW diminish the effect of the principle of reciprocity, which characterises extradition procedures.[15] The executing state might have to surrender a person for acts or omissions it does not classify as criminal offences under its own national criminal law and in relation to which it could, therefore, not ask the assistance of the issuing state in the reversed situation. In addition, State A may have to surrender a person to State B who in the reversed situation would refuse the execution of the EAW, because it has implemented an optional refusal ground which State A has not.[16]

10.3 The Second String of Arguments: The Normative Context of the AFSJ

Whereas the first string of arguments describes the differences between the substantive and procedural conditions of the extradition and surrender procedure, the second string of arguments focuses on the differences between the normative context of the AFSJ in which the EAW operates and the normative context in which extradition agreements operate.[17] On the overall level, it follows from the treaties and the CJEU case law that the EU is supposed to be a 'new legal order of international law for the benefit of which the states have limited their sovereign rights, albeit within limited fields, and the subjects of which comprise not only the Member States but also their

[12]FDEAW, art 17.

[13]Case C-123/08 *Wolzenburg* [2009] ECLI:EU:C:2009:616, para 57.

[14]FDEAW, arts 4(6) and 5(3); Case C-551/18 *IK* [2018] ECLI:EU:C:2018:890, Opinion of AG Sharpston, para 39.

[15]Glerum (2013), p. 759; Case C-303/05 *Advocaten voor de Wereld* [2006] ECLI:EU:C:2006:552, Opinion of AG Ruiz-Jarabo Colomer, paras 42, 45.

[16]Glerum (2013), p. 759.

[17]See eg Case C-303/05 *Advocaten voor de Wereld* [2006] ECLI:EU:C:2006:552, Opinion of AG Ruiz-Jarabo Colomer, paras 40–46; Case C-551/18 *IK* [2018] ECLI:EU:C:2018:890, Opinion of AG Sharpston, paras 37–47.

nationals'.[18] Hence, contrary to international treaties, the EU treaties aim to establish an EU legal order *sui generis* stemming from an independent source of law, with its own institutions and in which both states and EU citizens occupy an important position.[19] Contrary to the outer-EU setting, the EU legal order is also founded on common values shared by the Member States, including the rule of law and fundamental rights.[20]

Many of these unique characteristics of the EU legal order also characterise the AFSJ, the establishment of which is a common objective of the EU.[21] The EAW operates in the context of this AFSJ, which already marks an important difference between the normative context of judicial cooperation on the basis of the FDEAW and extradition.[22] In the intergovernmental setting, extradition agreements often contribute to crime-fighting efforts and are based on the coming together of separate individual interests of states. The FDEAW goes beyond this, as its main purpose is to contribute to the establishment and maintenance of the common AFSJ.[23] Hence, whereas extradition in nature constitutes contact between states, acting from independent positions, the surrender procedure is one of the building blocks of a common objective shared by the Member States, which is the establishment of an AFSJ.[24] On top of that, Article 3(2) TEU explicitly links the objective of the AFSJ to EU citizenship, as it states that EU citizens are the primary beneficiaries of the AFSJ. Both this EU citizenship dimension and the ambition to establish common areas such as the AFSJ are usually not part of intergovernmental agreements.[25]

Moreover, it follows from Articles 3(2) TEU and 67(1) TFEU that the goal of the AFSJ is not limited to security,[26] but includes free movement as well. Furthermore, the power to adopt measures to realise this twofold purpose is demarcated by the obligation to respect fundamental rights and the national legal systems of the

[18]Case C-26/62 *Van Gend & Loos* [1963] ECLI:EU:C:1963:1, p. 12; Opinion 2/13 [2014] ECLI:EU:C:2014:2454, para 157; Case C-6/64 *Costa* [1964] ECLI:EU:C:1964:66, p. 593; Opinion 1/09 [2011] ECLI:EU:C:2011:123, para 65.

[19]Case C-6/64 *Costa* [1964] ECLI:EU:C:1964:66, p. 594; Opinion 2/13 [2014] ECLI:EU:C:2014:2454, paras 157, 166.

[20]TEU, art 2.

[21]TEU, art 3(2).

[22]Taupiac-Nouvel (2012), p. 237.

[23]Case C-303/05 *Advocaten voor de Wereld* [2006] ECLI:EU:C:2006:552, Opinion of AG Ruiz-Jarabo Colomer, para 42; Klip (2007), para 24.

[24]See Klip (2007), para 24; Case C-303/05 *Advocaten voor de Wereld* [2006] ECLI:EU:C:2006:552, Opinion of AG Ruiz-Jarabo Colomer, paras 42, 45; Van Sliedregt (2007), p. 248.

[25]The same goes for the common objective of establishing an internal market. TEU, art 3(2–3); Opinion 2/13 [2014] ECLI:EU:C:2014:2454, para 172.

[26]Prosecution of (serious) crimes in an area without borders needs to be facilitated, since prosecution is not only in the interest of the states who are in one way or another affected by the crime, but by all Member States which are part of the AFSJ. Case C-303/05 *Advocaten voor de Wereld* [2006] ECLI:EU:C:2006:552, Opinion of AG Ruiz-Jarabo Colomer, paras 42, 45. See also Glerum, who states that Member States conclude extradition treaties, because they themselves may need the help of another state for the purpose of extradition 1 day. Glerum (2013), p. 13.

Member States.[27] These fundamental rights are laid down in the Charter of Fundamental Rights which occupies an equal position to the two treaties and is therefore part of the constitutional framework of the EU. It binds the EU institutions in their actions and decisions as well as the Member States when implementing EU law.[28]

In addition, two other important differences which separate the AFSJ from the outer-EU context are its institutional framework—in particular the preliminary ruling procedure before the CJEU—and the role of national judicial authorities. The preliminary ruling procedure contributes to the harmonisation of the surrender procedure, resulting in the establishment of a common framework within which the EAW operates. It also provides the CJEU with the power to influence the obligations and actions of national judicial authorities.

To sum up, what separates the AFSJ as the normative context in which the FDEAW operates from the outer-EU context is its EU citizenship dimension, its institutional framework and the role allocated to national judicial authorities, its twofold objective to ensure security and free movement, as well as the explicit obligation to respect fundamental rights in the process of attaining the twofold objective. This normative context with its defining characteristics is eloquently reflected in a speech of Michel Barnier, who was the EU Chief negotiator during the Brexit negotiations, in which he discussed the possibility of the UK to remain a party to the EAW:

Is there another region where sovereign states build together a common area without internal border controls? Where citizens enjoy free movement and security, and can avail of shared institutions to ensure their fundamental rights are protected. This cooperation is both unique and unprecedented. And it is made possible by the trust between Member States. This trust does not fall from the sky! There is no magic wand... [T]his trust is founded on an "ecosystem" based on common rules and safeguards, shared decisions, joint supervision and implementation and a common court of justice... The European Arrest Warrant is linked to the free movement of people. It works well because it is based on mutual trust between Member States. This trust is underpinned by shared respect for fundamental rights as set out in the Charter of Fundamental Rights; by certainty that other Member States enforce and apply the rules the same way, under the jurisdiction of the European Court of Justice; and by the concept of EU citizenship, which allows Member States to lift the constitutional ban on the extradition of their own nationals. Yet today we know that the UK is not ready to accept the free movement of people, the jurisdiction of the Court and the Charter of Fundamental Rights—for the Charter, this was confirmed last week by the House of Commons. This means that the UK cannot take part in the European Arrest Warrant.[29]

---

[27] TEU, art 3(2) and TFEU, art 67(1).

[28] CFR, art 51(1).

[29] Michel Barnier, *Speech at the European Union Agency for Fundamental Rights* [2018] <https://ec.europa.eu/commission/presscorner/detail/en/SPEECH_18_4213> accessed 20 September 2021.

On paper, the normative context of the AFSJ as set out above shows many fundamental differences with the outer-EU context, but the fact remains that the establishment and maintenance of an AFSJ with its unique characteristics constitutes both a *status quo* and *status quem*. Hence, the AFSJ is a goal which is in the process of being achieved.[30] The question is, therefore, to what extent its unique characteristics are not primarily promises made and goals set by the EU treaties, but have also taken shape in the current legal practice on the EU level. The next part will delve into this question by describing the development of judicial cooperation in criminal matters, in particular the FDEAW, in the AFSJ and the indications which it offers for the realisation of the normative context as described above and in that light, against the intergovernmental perspective. It will set out to what extent over time on the EU level actions have been taken to achieve the establishment of an AFSJ as described by the treaties, in particular its EU citizenship dimension, free movement dimension and the position of fundamental rights. The analysis of the development of the AFSJ as the normative context in which the EAW operates is divided into two time-periods of which the first one covers the time before the entering into force of the Treaty of Lisbon, while the second one covers the subsequent years.

10.4 Development of Judicial Cooperation in the AFSJ: Pre-Lisbon

10.4.1 From the Tampere Programme to the Roadmap on Procedural Safeguards: The Development of the Free Movement Dimension

Both the Tampere Programme of 1999 and The Hague Programme of 2004, in which the European Council sets out the EU's priorities for the coming 5 years, refer to the interests of the EU citizen and free movement, but predominantly from a security angle. They place the main emphasis on the establishment of an area of security and the fight against the risk of increasing cross-border criminality resulting from the slow abolishment of internal borders.[31] The argument is that the facilitation of the right to free movement requires measures which limit the chance of impurity and safe havens for criminals in the AFSJ.[32]

However, as explained in Sect. 9.4.2, a Council Resolution with a Roadmap for strengthening procedural rights of suspects and accused persons in criminal

[30]Merkel and Scheinfeld (2012), p. 210.

[31]European Council, Presidency Conclusions 1999 (Tampere Programme) <https://www.europarl.europa.eu/summits/tam_en.htm> accessed 20 September 2021, paras 5, 6; European Council, The Hague Programme: strengthening freedom, security and justice in the European Union (The Hague Programme) [2005] OJ C53/1, 1; Mitsilegas (2016), p. 125; Luchtman (2013), p. 12.

[32]Tampere Programme 1999, paras 5–6.

proceedings was adopted briefly before the Treaty of Lisbon entered into force. This Roadmap shifts the emphasis from security to a balance between security and fundamental rights.[33] It reflects the position that an AFSJ in which internal borders are slowly eliminated and in which EU citizens are provided with free movement rights requires an appropriate balance between security measures, like the FDEAW, and measures protecting the rule of law and specific procedural rights. In that light, the Roadmap states that the facilitation of the right to free movement in the AFSJ requires adequate fundamental rights standards in the Member States.[34]

So, The Hague and Tampere Programme as well as the Roadmap show that the right to free movement is not intended to be a symbolic right. They reveal the intent of the European Council, whose five-year programmes guide the actions of the European Commission which has the right of initiative in the legislative procedure for criminal justice measures, to strengthen EU citizens' right to free movement. The Roadmap also recognises that this does not only require the adoption of security measures such as the EAW, but also of EU instruments regulating the protection of fundamental rights and procedural safeguards.[35]

10.4.2 The Case Law of the CJEU

10.4.2.1 *Kozlowski* and *Wolzenburg*: Establishing a Common Framework for the Surrender Procedure

Two years before the entering into force of the Treaty of Lisbon, the CJEU issued the *Kozlowski* and *Wolzenburg* judgements.[36] *Kozlowski* was the first step towards the establishment of a *lingua franca* for the operation of the EAW. As explained in Chap. 4, the CJEU decided in that case that Article 4(6) and 5(3) FDEAW have in particular the goal of 'enabling the executing judicial authority to give particular

[33] The Council also links the need for harmonization measures regarding procedural safeguards to the smooth operation of mutual recognition instruments which contribute to security. Resolution of the Council of 30 November 2009 on a Roadmap for strengthening procedural rights of suspected or accused persons in criminal proceedings [2009] OJ C295/1, paras 6, 8.

[34] Resolution of the Council of 30 November 2009 on a Roadmap for strengthening procedural rights of suspected or accused persons in criminal proceedings [2009] OJ C295/1, paras 3–5, 10.

[35] However, as also explained in Sect. 9.4.2, despite the fact that the Roadmap focuses on the link between fundamental rights and the right to free movement, the subsequently adopted Directives harmonizing procedural safeguards do not. The preambles of the different Directives adopted in the post-Lisbon era, primarily link the harmonization of procedural safeguards to the goal of effective judicial cooperation. Hence, the free movement perspective on fundamental rights is largely absent in the Directives adopted in the post-Lisbon era which implement the Roadmap. See also Sect. 10.5.2; Europan Commission, 'EU Citizenship Report 2010 Dismantling the obstacles to EU citizens' rights' COM (2010) 603 final, pp. 5–7.

[36] Case C-66/08 *Kozlowski* [2008] ECLI:EU:C:2008:437; Case C-123/08 *Wolzenburg* [2009] ECLI:EU:C:2009:616.

weight to the possibility of increasing the requested person's chances of reintegrating into society when the sentence imposed on him expires'.[37] In light of this objective and for the purpose of a uniform application of community law—now Union law—the CJEU has adopted an autonomous interpretation of the terms 'staying in' and 'resident' in Article 4(6) FDEAW.[38] Requested persons are residents if they have established their actual place of residence in the executing state. They are staying in the executing state if they have after a stable period of presence developed a connection to the executing state that is similar to that of a resident. If the national law implementing Article 4(6) FDEAW does not provide for specific conditions to determine the existence of such a connection, the executing judicial authority needs to make an overall assessment of several factors, including the requested person's family and economic connections to the executing Member State.[39] In *Wolzenburg*, the CJEU added that Member States may interpret 'staying in' in a way which limits the scope of application of Article 4(6) FDEAW to foreigners who have been living in their state for 5 years or more.[40] This autonomous interpretation of the conditions in Article 4(6) FDEAW, which is also relevant for the conditions in Article 5(3) FDEAW, marks the start of the harmonisation process of the surrender procedure, which contributes to a common framework for the operation of the EAW.[41] Such a common framework, which contributes to a consistent and uniform application of the EAW, avoids the 'Wild West scenario', which often characterises extradition procedures in which different interpretations of terms or provisions decrease legal certainty.[42]

10.4.2.2 The Development of the Right to Free Movement Into an *Abwehrrecht*

In its case law, the CJEU has relied on the prohibition of discrimination on the basis of nationality in Article 18 TFEU to limit the criminal law competences of the Member States in order to protect the free movement of EU citizens. The cases concern nationals of Member States who have used one of their free movement

---

[37] Case C-66/08 *Kozlowski* [2008] ECLI:EU:C:2008:437, para 45. See also Case C-123/08 *Wolzenburg* [2009] ECLI:EU:C:2009:616, para 67; Case C-306/09 *IB* [2010] ECLI:EU:C:2010:626, para 52.

[38] Case C-66/08 *Kozlowski* [2008] ECLI:EU:C:2008:437, paras 42–43.

[39] Case C-66/08 *Kozlowski* [2008] ECLI:EU:C:2008:437, paras 46, 48.

[40] Case C-123/08 *Wolzenburg* [2009] ECLI:EU:C:2009:616, paras 57–74.

[41] In the legal literature, the question has been raised whether the CJEU is the right authority to autonomously define the terms in the FDEAW. In light of the principle of mutual recognition, it can also be argued that this is a task for the Member States. See eg Van den Brink and Marguery (2018); Fichera (2011).

[42] However, more generally autonomous interpretation is not completely absent in the outer-EU context. For instance, such an interpretation appears in the case law of the ECtHR. Mitsilegas (2020), p. 46.

rights and encounter unequal treatment in the host state when they become accused of or are victims of crimes.[43] One example is the case *Bickel* and *Franz*, in which the CJEU ruled that the refusal of the Italian authorities to conduct the criminal proceedings of two German nationals in German, while this right was granted to Italian nationals, violated the prohibition of discrimination. Such unequal treatment is in turn liable to hamper the exercise of free movement rights.[44] This case law shows that the right to free movement is developed into an *Abwehrrecht*, since it leads to the prohibition of national measures and actions which hamper free movement.[45] This emphasis on the protection of free movement rights of EU citizens once again shows that these rights are not merely symbolic ones.

10.4.2.3 The Development of the *Ne Bis In Idem* Principle in the Context of the AFSJ

The case law in which the CJEU interprets the conditions for the application of the *ne bis in idem* principle codified in Article 54 Convention implementing the Schengen Agreement (CISA) also contradicts the intergovernmental perspective as the only and most fitting perspective on judicial cooperation in the AFSJ. Article 54 CISA states, 'A person whose trial has been finally disposed of in one Contracting Party may not be prosecuted in another Contracting Party for the same acts, provided that if a penalty has been imposed, it has been enforced, is actually in the process of being enforced or can no longer be enforced under the laws of the sentencing Contracting Party.'[46] It was initially adopted outside the context of the EU, but the introduction of the AFSJ as the next step in European integration by the Treaty of Amsterdam came with the realisation that pursuing the free movement of persons increases the risk of consecutive prosecutions and punishments for the same act by multiple states.[47] Consequently, the Schengen acquis was integrated into the legal framework of the EU by the Treaty of Amsterdam.[48]

[43] See e.g. Case C-186/87 *Cowan* [1989] ECLI:EU:C:1989:47, paras 15, 19. Cowan was a British national who became the victim of a crime in France. The French authorities did not want to pay him victim-compensation, since he was not a French national. The CJEU considered this rule to be in violation of the prohibition of discrimination on the basis of nationality.

[44] The CJEU decided that the freedom to receive services had been exercised by the two defendants. Case C-274/96 *Bickel and Franz* [1998] ECLI:EU:C:1998:563, paras 16–19. See also Case C-186/87 *Cowan* [1989] ECLI:EU:C:1989:47.

[45] See Sect. 2.2.2.

[46] See also CISA, arts 55–58. These legal provisions regulate and demarcate the *ne bis in idem* principle.

[47] Satzger (2018), pp. 149–150; Council and the European Commission, 'Action Plan of the Council and the Commission on the implementation of the area of Freedom, Security and Justice' [1999] OJ C19/1, para 49(e); Ouwerkerk (2011), p. 1688.

[48] Protocol (No 19) on the Schengen acquis integrated into the framework of the European union [2012] *OJ C326/290.*

The pre-Lisbon case law on Article 54 CISA reveals how the CJEU started to adapt the *ne bis in idem* principle in conformity with the unique characteristics of the AFSJ, in particular the objective of free movement as laid down in Article 3(2) TEU, and in that light, moved away from the intergovernmental perspective. The first case before the CJEU was *Gözütok* and *Brügge*, in which the court established free movement of persons—in close combination with the protection of legal certainty and legitimate expectations—as the rationale of the *ne bis in idem* principle.[49] It decided that those who have been prosecuted for a certain act and have their cases finally disposed of in a Member State should be able to use their free movement rights without the risk of being prosecuted for the same act in another Member State.[50] While the protection of legal certainty is a common rationale of the *ne bis in idem* principle, the protection of free movement was added, because of the application of this principle in the specific context of the AFSJ.[51]

In addition, the CJEU has also interpreted the *bis* element—final disposal of a case—in light of the free movement rationale of the *ne bis in idem* principle. In *Gözütok* and *Brügge*, this follows from the fact that the Dutch transaction, which is an out-of-court settlement, should be classified as a final decision.[52] The CJEU stated that restricting the scope of the principle of *ne bis in idem* to final decisions delivered by a criminal court after a full trial would limit the protection of free movement of persons to those convicted of more serious crimes for which out-of-court settlements are not an option.[53] In the case law following *Gözütok* and *Brügge*, the *bis* element has been extended for the purpose of the protection of free movement and legal certainty to, for instance, acquittals due to a lack of evidence and time-barred prosecutions.[54] Furthermore, with regard to the *idem* element, the CJEU has decided

[49] Joined Cases C-187/01 & C-385/01 *Hüseyin Gözütok & Klaus Brügge* [2003] ECLI:EU:C:2003:87, paras 38, 40. See also Case C-150/05 *Van Straaten* [2006] ECLI:EU:C:2006:614, para 59; Case C-467/04 *Gasparini* [2006] ECLI:EU:C:2006:610, para 27; Case C-486/14 *Kossowski* [2016] ECLI:EU:C:2016:483, para 44.

[50] Joined Cases C-187/01 & C-385/01 *Hüseyin Gözütok & Klaus Brügge* [2003] ECLI:EU:C:2003:87, paras 38, 40. See also Case C-436/04 *Van Esbroeck* [2006] ECLI:EU:C:2006:165, paras 33–34; Case C-150/05 *Van Straaten* [2006] ECLI:EU:C:2006:614, paras 57, 59; Case C-467/04 *Gasparini* [2006] ECLI:EU:C:2006:610, para 27.

[51] Case C-486/14 *Kossowski* [2015] ECLI:EU:C:2015:812, Opinion of AG Bot, para 38; Case C-129/14 *Spasic* [2014] ECLI:EU:C:2014:739, Opinion of AG Jääskinen, para 45; Joined Cases C-187/01 & C-385/01 *Hüseyin Gözütok & Klaus Brügge* [2002] ECLI:EU:C:2002:516, Opinion of AG Ruiz-Jarabo Colomer, para 49. See also Van Bockel (2016), pp. 13–14.

[52] Some states had argued that the Schengen Contracting parties intended to limit the scope of the *bis* element to final decisions delivered by a criminal court after a full trial. The CJEU set this argument aside. Joined Cases C-187/01 & C-385/01 *Hüseyin Gözütok & Klaus Brügge* [2003] ECLI:EU:C:2003:87, para 41. *A contrario* see Joined Cases C-187/01 & C-385/01 *Hüseyin Gözütok & Klaus Brügge* [2002] ECLI:EU:C:2002:516, Opinion of AG Ruiz-Jarabo Colomer, paras 108–110.

[53] Joined Cases C-187/01 & C-385/01 *Hüseyin Gözütok & Klaus Brügge* [2003] ECLI:EU:C:2003:87, para 40.

[54] Case C-150/05 *Van Straaten* [2006] ECLI:EU:C:2006:614, paras 57–59; Case C-467/04 *Gasparini* [2006] ECLI:EU:C:2006:610, paras 27–28.

that the legal classification of an act in national law and the legal interests protected should not be the guiding criteria in deciding whether acts are in fact 'the same', since this is liable to impose as many barriers to free movement as there are legal systems.[55] The court, therefore, adopted a factual approach, meaning that for acts to be classified as the same, they need to be 'inextricably linked together in time, in space and by their subject-matter'.[56]

The case law on *ne bis in idem* described above does not only show that the CJEU has adapted its scope of protection in conformity with the unique peculiarities of the AFSJ. It also reveals that the constituent elements of the *ne bis in idem* principle have to a large extent been harmonised due to a multitude of preliminary references to the CJEU.[57] This constitutes an important difference between Article 54 CISA applicable in the AFSJ and *ne bis in idem* provisions in human rights treaties, such as Article 14(7) International Covenant on Civil and Political Rights (ICCPR) and Article 4 of Protocol 7 to the ECHR. Protocol 7 to the ECHR has, for instance, been poorly ratified by the Member States and is subjected to several declarations and reservations.[58] This means that the ECtHR case law regarding *ne bis in idem* in Article 4 of this Protocol does not have a similar harmonising effect as the CJEU case law. Similarly, Member States have issued reservations regarding the application of the *ne bis in idem* principle as codified in Article 14(7) ICCPR and the decisions of the Human Rights Committee have so far not had a harmonising effect, either.[59]

10.4.2.4 *Pupino:* The Duty of Conform Interpretation

The duty of conform interpretation entails that the national authorities of Member States, including national courts and members of the executive, such as Ministers interpret national law to the greatest extent possible in light of the text and purpose of the applicable EU instrument in order to achieve the result pursued by this instrument. With regard to national courts, the duty of conform interpretation ensures that these authorities ensure the full effectiveness of EU law, within the boundaries of

[55] By declining the interpretation of 'the same acts' as the same 'legal interests' the CJEU deviated from its case law on the *ne bis in idem* principle in competition law cases. Those cases show a threefold condition covering the identity of the facts, unity of the offender and unity of the legal interest protected. Joined Cases C-204/00, C-205/00, C-211/00, C-213/00, C-217/00 & C-219/00 *Aalborg Portland and Others v Commission* [2004] ECLI:EU:C:2004:6, para 338.

[56] See e.g. Case C-436/04 *Van Esbroeck* [2006] ECLI:EU:C:2006:165, paras 29–35; Case C-150/05 *Van Straaten* [2006] ECLI:EU:C:2006:614, paras 41–47; Case C-288/05 *Kretzinger* [2007] ECLI:EU:C:2007:441, para 33.

[57] Vervaele (2013), p. 221.

[58] See Reservations and Declarations for Treaty No.117 – Protocol No. 7 to the Convention for the Protection of Human Rights and Fundamental Freedoms <https://www.coe.int/en/web/conventions/full-list/-/conventions/treaty/117/declarations?p_auth=AvvZ1o8p> accessed 20 September 2021.

[59] Vervaele (2013), pp. 213–215.

their jurisdiction and powers, when deciding on the concrete case before them.[60] In *Pupino*, this duty of conform interpretation which characterised the communitarian dimension of the first pillar under the Treaty of Maastricht was transferred to the more intergovernmental third pillar, which covered judicial cooperation in criminal matters.[61] The CJEU based this transfer on the position that it would be complicated for the Union to achieve the objective of creating an ever closer Union among the peoples of Europe if the duty of loyal cooperation and duty of conform interpretation does not apply in relation to framework decisions regulating judicial cooperation in criminal matters.[62] This decision shows how the CJEU uses the preliminary ruling procedure to influence the tasks and responsibilities of national courts and other national authorities in relation to the establishment of the EU legal order as laid down in the treaties.[63] The decision to apply the duty of conform interpretation to third pillar instruments ensures that national authorities, including those in EAW procedures, contribute to the development of the EU legal order as an Area of Freedom, Security and Justice. Hence, the tasks of national authorities have received a European dimension which is absent in cooperation procedures in the intergovernmental context, which also does not focus on the establishment of common judicial areas.

[60] Case C-84/12 *Koushkaki* [2013] ECLI:EU:C:2013:862, paras 75–76; Case C-573/17 *Poplawski II* [2019] ECLI:EU:C:2019:530, paras 55, 94. In *Poplawski II* the CJEU clarified that when the national courts are incapable of explaining the national law in full compatibility with EU law, because this would for instance constitute a *contra legem* interpretation, they should at least interpret the national law in such a way that it fulfills the objective of the EU instrument. More specifically, it stated that when the Amsterdam District Court is not in a position to interpret the mandatory refusal ground for the surrender of Dutch nationals and those with an equivalent position in Article 6 SA in a way in which it would provide itself as the executing judicial authority with a certain margin of discretion in deciding whether or not to apply the refusal ground, it should at least adopt an interpretation of Article 6 SA which guarantees that impunity is avoided. Case C-573/17 *Poplawski II* [2019] ECLI:EU:C:2019:530, paras 104–107.

[61] Case C-105/03 *Pupino* [2005] ECLI:EU:C:2005:386, para 43. See also Case C-554/14 *Ognyanov* [2016] ECLI:EU:C:2016:835, para 59; Case C-573/17 *Poplawski II* [2019] ECLI:EU:C:2019:530, para 73.

[62] Case C-105/03 *Pupino* [2005] ECLI:EU:C:2005:386, paras 41–42.

[63] In addition, the duty of conform interpretation extends to other non-judicial public authorities, such as the Dutch Minister of Justice and Security as well. Case C-573/17 *Poplawski II* [2019] ECLI:EU:C:2019:530, para 94.

10.5 Development of Judicial Cooperation in the AFSJ: Post-Lisbon

10.5.1 Changes Brought About by the Treaty of Lisbon

10.5.1.1 The EU Legislative Procedure: The Role of the EU Citizen

The explicit connection between EU citizenship and the establishment of an AFSJ was introduced by the Treaty of Lisbon and is absent in its predecessors. Article 3(2) TEU appoints the EU citizen as the primary beneficiary of the AFSJ, since it states that the EU will offer its citizens an AFSJ in which free movement and security are ensured.[64] In addition, the Preamble of the EU Charter of Fundamental Rights states that the EU citizen should be at the heart of the EU project and its activities. This increased focus on the EU citizenship dimension of the AFSJ is more concretely reflected in another change brought about by the Treaty of Lisbon, which is the introduction of the ordinary legislative procedure for criminal justice measures.

The Treaty of Lisbon abandoned the three-pillar system of the Treaty of Maastricht, and with that the predominantly intergovernmental legislative procedure of the third pillar, prescribed for the adoption of criminal law measures for the purpose of establishing an AFSJ. Third-pillar law required a unanimous vote in the Council of Ministers, which represents the states and indirectly EU citizens, while the European Parliament, which direct represents the EU citizen, only had an advisory role.[65] In the ordinary legislative procedure which replaced this legislative procedure, the Council of Ministers and European Parliament share legislative authority, and both institutions need to consent to the adoption of a proposed legislative instrument.[66] The vote by unanimity in the Council was replaced by qualified majority voting and where each Member State previously had the right of initiative, this right can now only be exercised by the European Commission and a quarter of the Member States.[67] Hence, before the Treaty of Lisbon, the Member States were most strongly represented in the EU legislative procedure, and the European Parliament only had a marginal role. The Treaty of Lisbon changed this by strengthening the representation of the EU citizen in the EU legislative process for criminal justice

---

[64] Schönberger (2015), p. 620.

[65] The Treaty of Lisbon is the first treaty which dedicates a specific and explicit title to Democratic Principles. Article 10(2) TEU states that the Council of Ministers and the European Council are democratically responsible to their national parliaments or their citizens. TEU, arts 34(2) and 39(1) (old).

[66] TFEU, art 294. This legislative procedure is the standard one in the field of criminal justice as follows from Chap. 4 TFEU on judicial cooperation in criminal matters. Some exceptions exist, as illustrated by Article 86(1) TFEU which prescribes the special legislative procedure for the establishment of a European Public Prosecutor's Office.

[67] TFEU, art 76.

measures. Consequently, both stakeholders and their interests are now represented in the institutions which constitute the EU legislator.[68]

10.5.1.2 Extending the Scope of the Preliminary Procedure and Infringement Procedure

Before the Treaty of Lisbon entered into force, the jurisdiction of the CJEU to issue preliminary rulings had to be explicitly acknowledged by the Member States in a declaration in which they could also specify which national courts were competent to issue a preliminary question.[69] After a transition period of 5 years which expired on the first of December 2014, the CJEU received full jurisdiction over former third pillar instruments regulating judicial cooperation in criminal matters.[70] All last-instance courts are now obliged to refer preliminary questions on EU criminal justice instruments when their interpretation is relevant to decide the case before them and all other national courts are competent to do so.[71] The expansion of the scope of the preliminary procedure increases the chance of the establishment of a common framework for the operation of the EAW. We will see in the next sections that, especially after the expiration of the transition period, many preliminary questions have been referred to the CJEU, which both show the development of a common framework and reveal the European dimension of the tasks of the national judicial authorities.[72]

Besides the preliminary procedure, the infringement procedure in Article 258 TFEU has also become fully applicable after the expiration of the transition period. Hence, the European Commission is now competent to monitor whether Member States act in conformity with EU law, including the EAW. These procedures may result in a referral to the CJEU with a request to impose monetary sanctions.[73]

---

[68] Furthermore, the role of the national parliaments was strengthened by the Treaty of Lisbon. They can issue reasoned opinions on the subsidiarity of proposed legislation. See Protocol (No 1) on the role of national parliaments in the European Union [2004] OJ C310/204; Protocol (No 2) on the application of the principles of subsidiarity and proportionality [2008] OJ C115/206, art 7(2).

[69] TEU, art 35 (old). However, national courts still had to obey the duty of conform interpretation when their governments had not accepted the possibility to submit preliminary questions. Borgers (2010), p. 105.

[70] Protocol (No 36) on transitional provisions [2008] OJ C115/322, art 10(1)(3).

[71] TFEU, art 267.

[72] Borgers (2010), p. 103. See also Lenaerts (2019), pp. 3–4.

[73] TFEU, art 260(3).

10.5.1.3 Fundamental Rights

The Treaty of Lisbon designates an important position to fundamental rights. Article 2 TEU states that the rule of law and fundamental rights constitute the foundation of the EU.[74] In addition, the EU has its own Charter of Fundamental Rights, which has become primary law and part of the constitutional framework of the EU.[75] It binds the (legislative) actions of bodies, offices and agencies of the Union, but only addresses the Member States when they are implementing Union law.[76]

10.5.2 Post-Lisbon 5-Year Programmes

The post-Lisbon 5-year programmes of the European Council and their progress reports, as well as the legal literature, reflect a stronger emphasis on the EU citizen and his or her different interests when it comes to decisions on how to further develop the AFSJ.[77] The 5-year programmes or guidelines adopted by the European Council have called upon the Union to ensure that EU citizens are capable of exercising their specific rights, including free movement rights, to the fullest extent.[78] Similar to the pre-Lisbon Tampere Programme and The Hague Programme, the post-Lisbon programmes have predominantly linked the protection of free movement to the need for crime-fighting measures.[79] In this light, the 2009 Stockholm Programme states that 'Member States should further safeguard and protect the right to free movement by working together, and with the Commission to combat actions of a criminal nature with forceful and proportionate measures'.[80] Hence, contrary to the Roadmap on Procedural Safeguards, adopted just before the Treaty of

---

[74] See also TEU, art. 6.

[75] TEU, art 6(1). The Treaty of Lisbon also imposes the obligation to accede to the ECHR in Article 6(2) TEU.

[76] CFR, art 51(1).

[77] Stockholm Programme 2009; European Council, 'Strategic guidelines for the legislative and operational planning in the Area of Freedom, Security and Justice' (Strategic Guidelines) EUCO (2014) 79/14; European Commission, 'Towards an EU Criminal Policy: Ensuring the effective implementation of EU policies through criminal law' (Communication) COM (2011) 573 final, p. 12; European Parliament resolution of 2 April 2014 on the mid-term review of the Stockholm Programme [2017] OJ C408/8; Reding (2014), pp. 81–82; Meyer (2011), pp. 189–191; Blackstock (2012), p. 23; Meyer and Böse (2011), p. 341. See also Nettesheim (2009), pp. 28–29.

[78] Stockholm Programme 2009, p. 4; Strategic Guidelines 2014, p. 6. Free movement is less present in European Council, *A new strategic agenda for the EU 2019–2024* <https://www.consilium.europa.eu/en/eu-strategic-agenda-2019-2024/> accessed 20 September 2021.

[79] Stockholm Programme 2009, pp. 8–10; European Commission, 'Delivering an area of freedom, security and justice for Europe's citizens – Action Plan Implementing the Stockholm Programme' (Communication) COM (2010) 171 final, p. 5; Strategic Guidelines 2014, 9; European Commission, 'The European Agenda on Security' (Communication) COM (2015) 185 final, p. 2.

[80] Stockholm Programme 2009, p. 9.

Lisbon entered into force, the post-Lisbon 5-year programmes do not explicitly link the protection and facilitation of free movement to fundamental rights protection.[81] As explained in Sect. 9.4.2, the same is true for the Directives harmonising different procedural safeguards adopted in light of the Roadmap.

However, even though fundamental rights protection is not explicitly connected to free movement, it has been linked to EU citizenship, in particular in the 2009 Stockholm Programme.[82] This Programme states that, in order to meet the interests and needs of the EU citizen, 'It is of paramount importance that law enforcement measures and measures to safeguard individual rights, the rule of law, international protection rules go hand in hand in the same direction and are mutually reinforced.' Hence, turning European citizenship into a tangible reality requires adequate protection of fundamental rights.[83] This focus on the need for a balance between crime-fighting measures and measures protecting fundamental rights constitutes an important difference between the context of the AFSJ and the outer-EU context. In this light, it is also important to note that the adoption of the Directives harmonising procedural safeguards, even though they are not predominantly based on free movement and EU citizenship, is in itself unique for the context of the AFSJ, since such measures usually do not exist in the outer-EU context.

10.5.3 *The Case Law of the CJEU*

10.5.3.1 Article 4(6) FDEAW Further Explained: *Da Silva Jorge* and *Poplawski*

Da Silva Jorge is the third preliminary ruling on Article 4(6) FDEAW. In this case, the CJEU decided that the French implementation of Article 4(6) FDEAW, which only protected French nationals, was incompatible with EU law, more specifically the prohibition of discrimination on the basis of nationality in Article 18 TFEU.[84] This case further illustrates the development of the right to free movement into a so-called *Abwehrrecht*, in the sense that the CJEU prohibits national measures and actions which hamper free movement or even discriminate on the basis of nationality.[85]

[81] It was, however, included in the Stockholm Programme.

[82] The 2014 Strategic Guidelines also refer back to the aims established in the Stockholm Programme to ensure a balance between fundamental rights protection and security measures. Strategic Guidelines 2014, para 4; European Commission, 'An open and secure Europe: making it happen' (Communication) COM (2014) 154 final, pp. 3, 13; European Commission, 'The EU Justice Agenda for 2020 – Strengthening Trust, Mobility and Growth within the Union' (Communication) COM (2014) 144 final, pp. 5–7.

[83] Stockholm Programme 2009, p. 4.

[84] Case C-42/11 *Da Silva Jorge* [2012] ECLI:EU:C:2012:517, para 59.

[85] See also Sect. 10.4.2.2.

In *Poplawski I*, the CJEU decided that the executing judicial authority may only refuse the execution of the EAW when it commits to enforcing the foreign sanction itself.[86] Therefore, a mere declaration of willingness to do so is insufficient. This ruling of the CJEU is based on the position that even though the purpose of Article 4(6) FDEAW is reintegration, this should not result in impunity, because the executing state is in the end not capable of actually enforcing the sanction imposed.[87] This explanation of Article 4(6) FDEAW further sharpens the contrast between this refusal ground and the nationality exception in, for instance, Article 6 of the Council of Europe Convention on Extradition whose application is not subject to a similar *aut dedere aut punire* rule.[88] It also shows that national authorities, both judicial authorities and non-judicial authorities, do not only or even primarily protect the interests of the state. It follows from *Poplawski* that they need to act and apply the EAW in a way that protects common interests, including the combatting of cross-border crime in the AFSJ.[89] Hence, where in the context of intergovernmental cooperation procedures, states primarily protect national interest, including their own nationals, and conduct international diplomacy, national judicial authorities are in the context of cooperation in the AFSJ jointly responsible for the achievement of common goals and the combatting of common problems.[90]

Secondly, as already mentioned in Sect. 9.4.3, in *Poplawski I* the CJEU reconsidered its decision in *Wolzenburg* in which it accepted the Dutch implementation of Article 4(6) FDEAW, which offered automatic protection to Dutch nationals. Such an interpretation of Article 4(6) FDEAW allows the Member States to provide strong protection to their national citizens which is a sign of the intergovernmental perspective. In *Poplawski I*, the CJEU prohibits the implementation of Article 4(6) FDEAW as a mandatory refusal ground on the basis of which nationals of the executing state are automatically not surrendered. It states that the national executing authorities should have a certain degree of discretion to decide whether the refusal ground should be applied.[91] This marks a more definite goodbye to the nationality exception in the EAW procedure.

10.5.3.2 EU Citizenship and Free Movement: *Petruhhin* and *Pisciotti*

In addition to the rulings on Article 4(6) FDEAW discussed in the previous paragraph, the CJEU had developed another string of case law in which the EAW protects EU citizens against interferences with their free movement rights and

[86] Case C-579/15 *Poplawski* [2017] ECLI:EU:C:2017:503.

[87] Case C-579/15 *Poplawski* [2017] ECLI:EU:C:2017:503, paras 22–23.

[88] Bargis (2018), pp. 301, 310.

[89] See also Case C-573/17 *Poplawski II* [2019] ECLI:EU:C:2019:530, paras 82, 85, 102–103.

[90] See also Luchtman (2017), pp. 17, 20–21.

[91] Case C-579/15 *Poplawski* [2017] ECLI:EU:C:2017:503, para 21.

violations of the non-discrimination principle. As explained in Sect. 9.4.3, both in *Petruhhin* and *Pisciotti* the CJEU was confronted with the question whether the protection against extradition to third states offered by an EU Member State to its own nationals should also be offered to other EU citizens who are nationals of another Member State.[92] The CJEU decided that such national rules on extradition which exclusively protect nationals and not other EU citizens who used their free movement rights constitute a violation of the EU non-discrimination principle and hamper the exercise of free movement rights. Such a violation is only justified when the state of nationality of the requested person has been informed and been offered the chance to issue an EAW.

In principle, I agree with the point discussed in Sect. 9.4.3 in relation to the *Petruhhin* string of case law, that in light of EU citizenship, the CJEU could have gone further than an obligation to ask the Member State of nationality to issue an EAW.[93] However, I also think that this case law solidifies the argument that judicial cooperation on the basis of the EAW takes place in an entirely different context than extradition procedures. The cases in question show how the CJEU uses the EAW to enforce the prohibition of non-discrimination and protect free movement rights of EU citizens by giving priority to prosecution by the state of nationality over extradition to a third state.[94] In the *Petruhhin* string of case law the EAW is, therefore, an instrument with a protective dimension.[95] The focus on keeping EU citizens on the territory of the EU where they enjoy specific EU citizenship rights implies that the EU and outer-EU context are not viewed as 'the same'.[96]

In this light, the *Petruhhin* string of jurisprudence could in fact be viewed as the *Zambrano*[97] version of the AFSJ, since extradition to a third state would deny an EU citizen the genuine enjoyment of the substance of his citizenship rights, in particular the right to free movement.[98] So, the protection offered by the *Zambrano* and *Petruhhin* jurisprudence entails being allowed to stay in the EU in which the unique

[92] Case C-182/15 *Petruhhin* [2016] ECLI:EU:C:2016:630, paras 47–49; Case C-191/16 *Pisciotti* [2018] ECLI:EU:C:2018:222, paras 51–54.

[93] The CJEU could also have picked or added the EU state of residence.

[94] Case C-182/15 *Petruhhin* [2016] ECLI:EU:C:2016:630, para 33; Case C-191/16 *Pisciotti* [2018] ECLI:EU:C:2018:222, paras 44–45. See also Strumia (2020), pp. 518–519. This legal scholar uses the two cases to illustrate that the home state of the EU citizen is an important guarantor of equal treatment and free movement.

[95] João Costa (2017), p. 214; Nic Shuibhne (2019), p. 299.

[96] See Nic Shuibhne (2019), pp. 291–305.

[97] However, the ruling in *Petruhhin* was based on Article 21 TFEU. Case C-34/09 *Ruiz Zambrano* [2011] ECLI:EU:C:2011:124. The *Zambrano* case is explained in Sect. 2.2.1. See also Glerum (2020), p. 699.

[98] Böse (2017), p. 1787. National case law also shows that part of the significance of the Petruhhin case is that EU citizens should be protection against *de facto* expulsion from the territory of the EU. Rb. Amsterdam 13 December 2016, ECLI:NL:RBAMS:2016:8435 (Amsterdam District Court). See also Case C-398/19 *BY* [2020] ECLI:EU:C:2020:1032, para 31. However, Coutts has argued that *Pisciotti* dimishes the importance of *Petruhhin* for EU citizenship. In Petrhuhhin the CJEU connected the protection offered to the status of EU citizenship and the EU's role in

free movement rights granted to EU citizens can be exercised.[99] A similar message is sent in the case *Raugevicius*. The CJEU concluded that when a Member State protects its own nationals against extradition for the purpose of the execution of a sanction and has provisions in place that allow for the sentence pronounced abroad to be served on its territory, in light of the right to free movement, the same protection should be offered to EU citizens who are permanent residents in the requested state.[100] Contrary to *Petruhhin* and *Pisciotti*, the CJEU also limits its ruling to the tasks and duties of the host state and does not impose an obligation to contact the Member State of nationality.[101]

In addition, the importance of free movement also follows from the fact that the CJEU seems to prioritise the protection of this right over the need for security. The court has decided that when the execution of an EAW issued by the EU Member State of nationality is possible, it should in all cases be given priority, even when the requesting third state is the *locus delicti*, which is often also the state where most of the evidence is available. In light of the right to free movement, surrender to the state of nationality is still preferred, despite the fact that in such situations, criminal proceedings may in the end not succeed, because the third state is unable or unwilling to aid the prosecution in the state of nationality. In other words, the CJEU seemed to accept that the protection of free movement EU may result in impunity.[102]

10.5.3.3 The Establishment of a Common Framework for the Issuing of an EAW

In the post-Lisbon era, the CJEU has issued multiple preliminary rulings which contribute to the establishment of a common framework for the operation of the FDEAW. Many of the cases that were already discussed in Chap. 4 are examples of this process. Important ones are the cases *Bob-Dogi*, *Kovalkovas*, *Poltorak* and *Özçelik*, which were the beginning of a string of case law clarifying the issuing procedure and limiting the discretion of the national Member States in setting the requirements for the issuing of an EAW.[103] In this relatively long line of rulings, the

protecting its citizens. Coutts argues that in *Pisciotti* the CJEU, among other things, focuses on the right of the Member State of nationality to exercise jurisdiction. Coutts (2019).

[99] Case C-182/15 *Petruhhin* [2016] ECLI:EU:C:2016:630, para 47; Glerum (2017), p. 173. See also Klip (2017), p. 202.

[100] Case C-247/17 *Raugevicius* [2018] ECLI:EU:C:2018:898.

[101] This case could therefore even less be viewed as a reiteration of national citizenship at the expense of a more supranational EU citizenship which recognises the specific rights EU citizens are provided with. See also Sect. 10.8.

[102] Glerum (2017), p. 173; Böse (2017), p. 1791. See also Klip (2017), p. 200.

[103] Case C-241/15 *Bob-Dogi* [2016] ECLI:EU:C:2016:385; Case C-477/16 *Kovalkovas* [2016] ECLI:EU:C:2016:861; C-452/16 *Poltorak* [2016] ECLI:EU:C:2016:858; Case C-453/16 *Özçelik* [2017] ECLI:EU:C:2016:860. See also Joined Cases C-508/18 & C-82/19 *OG & PI*

CJEU has provided an autonomous interpretation of the term 'issuing judicial authority' in Article 6(1) FDEAW.[104] In short, the issuing judicial authority needs to be a national authority which participates in the administration of justice and can exercise its responsibilities objectively and independent from the executive power of the state.[105] Moreover, in the recent case *AZ*, the CJEU decided that the executing judicial authority should meet similar requirements, including the requirement of independence.[106]

Besides the requirements regarding the appointment of the issuing judicial authority, the CJEU has also set more specific conditions for the procedure for the issuing of an EAW.[107] For instance, in the case *PI and OG*, the CJEU changed the previously non-mandatory proportionality assessment conducted by the issuing judicial authority into an obligation, even though a proportionality test is not included in the text of the FDEAW.[108] Furthermore, in *Bob-Dogi*, the CJEU decided that an EAW needs to be based on a national judicial decision, such as a national arrest warrant to ensure that fundamental rights protection is offered both at the national level and at the level of the EAW.[109] In subsequent case law, the court ruled that at least at one of these two levels the decision has to meet the conditions of effective judicial protection.[110] On top of that, in cases in which the decision to issue an EAW is not made by a court or judge, the requested person must be offered the possibility to challenge the decision to issue an EAW before a court in the issuing Member State.[111]

[2019] ECLI:EU:C:2019:456; Case C-509/18 *PF* [2019] ECLI:EU:C:2019:457; Case C-489/19 *NJ* [2019] ECLI:EU:C:2019:849; Joined Cases C-566/19 & C-626/19 *JR & YC* [2019] ECLI:EU:C:2019:1077; Case C-627/19 *ZB* [2019] ECLI:EU:C:2019:1079; Case C-625/19 *XD* [2019] ECLI:EU:C:2019:1078.

[104] *Özçelik* concerned Article 8(1)(c) FDEAW. In this case the CJEU decided that the national judicial decision underlying the FDEAW needs to be issued or confirmed by a national authority which participates in the administration of justice of the state. Case C-453/16 *Özçelik* [2017] ECLI:EU:C:2016:860, para 33.

[105] Case C-477/16 *Kovalkovas* [2016] ECLI:EU:C:2016:861, para 34; Joined Cases C-508/18 & C-82/19 *OG & PI* [2019] ECLI:EU:C:2019:456, paras 50–51, 73; Case C-625/19 *XD* [2019] ECLI:EU:C:2019:1078, para 31. See also Mitsilegas (2020), pp. 63–70, 76.

[106] Case C-510/19 *AZ* [2020] ECLI:EU:C:2020:953, para 54.

[107] These conditions do not determine whether the requirement of an issuing judicial authority is met, but concern the procedure for the issuing of an EAW. Case C-625/19 *XD* [2019] ECLI:EU:C:2019:1078, para 30.

[108] Handbook on how to issue and execute a European arrest warrant (European Commission Notice) [2017] OJ C335/1, pp. 14–15; Joined Cases C-508/18 & C-82/19 *OG & PI* [2019] ECLI:EU:C:2019:456, para 71.

[109] Case C-241/15 *Bob-Dogi* [2016] ECLI:EU:C:2016:385, para 48.

[110] Joined Cases C-508/18 & C-82/19 *OG & PI* [2019] ECLI:EU:C:2019:456, para 68; Case C-648/20 *PI* [2021] ECLI:EU:C:2021:187, paras 48, 60. See also Case C-206/20 *VA* [2021] ECLI:EU:C:2021:509.

[111] These court proceedings also need to meet the requirements of effective judicial protection. Joined Cases C-508/18 & C-82/19 *OG & PI* [2019] ECLI:EU:C:2019:456, para 75; Joined Cases C-566/19 & C-626/19 *JR & YC* [2019] ECLI:EU:C:2019:1077, paras 62–63.

This line of case law on the issuing procedure once again shows the continuing development of a common framework for the operation of the EAW. The cases *JZ* and *Mantello* are other examples of this process. In *JZ*, the CJEU provided an autonomous interpretation of 'detention' in Article 26 FDEAW.[112] In *Mantello*, the court linked the interpretation of the *ne bis in idem* principle in Article 3(2) FDEAW to Article 54 CISA.[113]

10.5.3.4 The Position of Fundamental Rights Protection in and Outside the Context of the EAW

In Chap. 9, I explained why I think that the *Aranyosi and Căldăraru* and *LM* string of case law reflect the intergovernmental perspective on fundamental rights.[114] However, in other ways the role of fundamental rights in the EAW procedure differs from the role they have in extradition procedures. Firstly, in the *Bob-Dogi* and *Kovalkovas* string of case law discussed in the previous section, the protection of fundamental rights of the requested person is an important consideration in the decisions which the court makes.[115] For instance, the CJEU states in *Bob-Dogi* that compliance with the requirements in Article 8(1)(c) FDEAW is important, because the requested person needs to receive fundamental rights protection at two levels, including at the stage of issuing the national judicial decision on which the EAW is based and at the stage of the issuing of the EAW.[116] Furthermore, at least at one of these two levels, the decision has to meet the conditions of effective judicial protection, and when the EAW is not issued by a court or judge, the requested person should always have the possibility to challenge the decision to issue an EAW before a court in the issuing Member State.[117] This integration of and focus on fundamental

[112] Case C-294/16 *JZ* [2016] ECLI:EU:C:2016:610. However, with regard to this case see Mitsilegas (2020).

[113] Case C-261/09 *Gaetano Mantello* [2010] ECLI:EU:C:2010:683, para 40.

[114] Joined Cases C-404/15 & C-659/15 *Aranyosi & Căldăraru* [2016] ECLI:EU:C:2016:198; Case C-216/18 *LM* [2018] ECLI:EU:C:2018:586.

[115] Rosanò has argued that the cases *Poltorak*, *Özçelik,* and *Kovalkovas* represent the need to establish a balance between the need for swift surrender procedures and the need to guarantee effective judicial protection. In this light, the author states, 'Only genuine judicial authority can ensure that this balance is achieved and preserved from any form of political – meaning, non-legal – influence. As such, driven by a sort of Montesquieuian spirit, the Court has confirmed the fundamental principle of separation of powers for the purposes of the EAW and this should lead to a reinforcement of the mechanism resulting from Framework Decision 2002/584/JHA.' Rosanò (2017), pp. 97–98. For a critical assessment of the case law on the independence of public prosecutors, see Böse (2020).

[116] Case C-241/15 *Bob-Dogi* [2016] ECLI:EU:C:2016:385, paras 54–56.

[117] Joined Cases C-508/18 & C-82/19 *OG & PI* [2019] ECLI:EU:C:2019:456, paras 68, 75; Joined Cases C-566/19 & C-626/19 *JR & YC* [2019] ECLI:EU:C:2019:1077, paras 60, 62; Case C-625/19 *XD* [2019] ECLI:EU:C:2019:1078, paras 39, 41. See also Case C-510/19 *AZ* [2020] ECLI:EU:C:2020:953, para 54.

rights protection in the surrender procedure is often absent in extradition agreements, such as the Council of Europe Convention on Extradition. The explanatory memorandum of this Convention only states that the national arrest warrants or orders underlying the extradition request should be issued by judicial authorities, including the judiciary and the public prosecutor, but not the police.[118] The memorandum does not explicitly base this decision on the protection of fundamental rights of the requested person, nor does it set the same requirements regarding effective judicial protection.

Secondly, the post-Lisbon case law on Article 54 CISA and Article 50 CFR, which classifies the *ne bis in idem* principle as a fundamental right, shows how the CJEU continues with the establishment of a common framework for the application of the *ne bis in idem* principle and interprets its conditions in light of Article 3(2) TEU. An important example is the case *Spasic*, in which the CJEU was presented with the question whether the enforcement clause of Article 54 CISA—binding the application of the *ne bis in idem* principle to the condition that the sentence in question has been executed, is executed or can no longer be executed—is compatible with Article 50 CFR, which does not contain such a condition.[119] The court decided that the enforcement clause constitutes a justified restriction of Article 50 CFR, since it contributes to the prevention of impunity which is important in light of the general objective of combatting crime referred to in Article 3(2) TEU, and this prevention of impunity cannot be achieved by less interfering measures.[120] Hence, the CJEU viewed the security dimension of the AFSJ as a legitimate reason to allow for a limitation of the scope of protection of the *ne bis in idem* principle.[121]

Contrary to *Spasic*, which focuses on the security dimension of Article 3(2) TEU, the CJEU searches in the *Kossowski* case for a balance between free movement and security within the scope of application of the *ne bis in idem* principle.[122] The CJEU states that Article 54 CISA should be interpreted in light of Article 3(2) TEU,

---

[118] Explanatory Report to the European Convention on Extradition [1957] ETS No 24, 4, 9.

[119] Case C-129/14 *Spasic* [2014] ECLI:EU:C:2014:586.

[120] Case C-129/14 *Spasic* [2014] ECLI:EU:C:2014:586, paras 60–72. In paragraph 77, the CJEU even states that the prevention of impunity is one of the rationales of the *ne bis in idem* principle. I agree with Wasmeijer that this is probably a drafting error, especially considering the preceding case law in which legal certainty and free movement are presented as the rationale. The prevention of impunity, which is part of the second goal of the AFSJ to combat and prevent crime, is in that case law presented as a possible justification for a restriction to the application of the *ne bis in idem* principle. Wasmeijer (2014), pp. 541, 545–546. See Case C-469/03 *Miraglia* [2005] ECLI:EU:C:2005:156, paras 33–34. See also Case C-491/07 *Vladimir Turanský* [2008] ECLI:EU:C:2008:768, paras 42–43; Case C-486/14 *Kossowski* [2016] ECLI:EU:C:2016:483, paras 45–49; Case C-268/17 *AY* [2018] ECLI:EU:C:2018:602, paras 56–58; Vervaele (2015), pp. 1355–1356.

[121] See also Case C-469/03 *Miraglia* [2005] ECLI:EU:C:2005:156, paras 32–35. In *Miraglia,* which is one of the earlier cases, the CJEU already explicitly determined that the free movement ratio of Article 54 CISA can be limited by the second goal of Article 3(2) TEU which is the prevention of impunity.

[122] C-486/14 *Kossowski* [2016] ECLI:EU:C:2016:483. See also Case C-665/20 *X* [2021] ECLI:EU:C:2021:339, paras 96–104.

covering both the need to ensure free movement and the need to combat crime. In this light, the decision of the prosecuting authority to terminate criminal proceedings without carrying out a detailed investigation cannot be classified as a 'final decision' in light of Article 54 CISA. Extending the scope of the *bis* element to these type of decisions would increase the risk of impunity and therefore threaten security.[123]

Hence, the *Spasic* and *Kossowski* case are two clear examples in which the CJEU has considered the application and scope of protection of the *ne bis in idem* principle in light of the normative setting of the AFSJ, as laid down in Article 3(2) TEU. Both objectives of the AFSJ play a role in the determination of the scope of protection of the *ne bis in idem* principle and in the context of determining whether an exception to this fundamental right and principle is allowed. This interpretation of *ne bis in idem* in light of the common objectives in Article 3(2) TEU and in particular in case of *Kossowski* the search for a balance between free movement and security illustrate the adaption of this fundamental right and principle in such a way that it fits the unique normative setting of the AFSJ.

10.6 The National Legal Orders

The previous chapter concluded that the intergovernmental perspective seems relatively strongly embedded in the national legal orders, mainly in Germany, which greatly values the bond between the state and the German national.[124] However, the examination of the implementation and application of the EAW in the national legal orders, in particular the English and Dutch legal order, also show subtle indications which contradict the intergovernmental perspective.

Firstly, in the Netherlands, the Dutch legislator has adopted the terminology of the FDEAW and implemented this instrument in a separate Act.[125] The latter was considered necessary, because even though the Dutch Extradition Act could be the model for the Surrender Act, the scope of the surrender procedure was too broad to include it in the Extradition Act. In other words, an adequate implementation of the FDEAW could not be realised with a simple adjustment of the Extradition Act.[126] This decision implicitly recognises that extradition and surrender are in fact two different systems and, therefore, clashes with the statement of the Dutch legislator that the EAW constitutes another form of cooperation under international law.

Secondly, in the Netherlands and in the English legal order, the role of the government has been restricted in conformity with the FDEAW. In the Netherlands, the Minister of Justice and Security is only competent to make a decision in case of competing EAWs and extradition requests for the same offence, and to decide

[123] Case C-486/14 *Kossowski* [2016] ECLI:EU:C:2016:483, paras 46–48.

[124] Section 9.5.

[125] Section 5.3.1.

[126] *Kamerstukken II* 2002/03, 29,042, nr. 3, p. 7.

whether or not to suspend domestic prosecutions which compete with an EAW.[127] In the UK, the role of the Home Secretary has also been restricted. He or she may now decide between competing Part 1 and Part 2 requests for extradition and may prevent extradition in case of national security matters.[128] In addition, the English courts have taken up the responsibility of ensuring protection against exorbitant jurisdiction, since this can no longer be provided by governmental organs in the EAW procedure. In other words, the courts try to act in conformity with the spirit of the FDEAW to restrict the role of the government in surrender proceedings without limiting the protection of the individual against exorbitant jurisdiction claims.

Thirdly, the Amsterdam District Court has in the past years increasingly embraced the European dimension of its task and accepted the jurisdiction of the CJEU. The national case law shows that it has a long history of faithfully obeying the duty of conform interpretation in case of clashes between EU and national law and it has issued a relatively large amount of preliminary questions to the CJEU since 2016. Furthermore, rulings of the CJEU are usually applied in national cases only days after they have been issued and the Amsterdam District Court often tries to follow them to the letter. For instance, in *Aranyosi* and *Câldâraru*, the CJEU states that when the two-step test is met, a possible violation of Article 4 CFR in the issuing state can trigger the obligation for the executing judicial authority to 'end' the surrender procedure.[129] The CJEU did not present this fundamental rights exception as an additional refusal ground, though. In this light, the Amsterdam District Court also refrained from referring to the decision not to surrender the requested person as a refusal. Instead, the formal decision in these cases was to not accept the request of the public prosecutor to consider the EAW.[130]

Lastly, similar to the Amsterdam District Court, the English courts also seem very aware of the European dimension of their task, including the duty to act in conformity with EU law. It follows from the jurisprudence that the courts acknowledge that discrepancies between the FDEAW and the Extradition Act exist.[131] In these situations, they often try to find a compromise between the ratio of the refusal ground of domestic origin and the FDEAW. The interpretation of Section 12A EA, which prohibits the surrender when the issuing state has not yet 'charged' the requested person, constitutes a concrete example of this search for the middle way. This section was introduced to protect the right to liberty of the requested person, but it was argued that the section imposed UK rules and standards regarding the protection of the right to liberty on the issuing state and forced the District Judge

[127] Sections 5.3.5 and 5.3.7.

[128] Section 7.3.1. In addition, the Home Secretary is responsible for designating states as Category 1 or 2 states and may nominate the authority through which incoming EAWs are received. The former power fits with the intergovernmental perspective, as explained in Sect. 9.5.

[129] Joined Cases C-404/15 & C-659/15 *Aranyosi and Căldăraru* [2016] ECLI:EU:C:2016:198, para 104.

[130] Rb. Amsterdam 26 January 2017, ECLI:NL:RBAMS:2017:414 (Amsterdam District Court).

[131] *Officer of the King's Prosecutor (Brussels) v Armas* [2005] UKHL 67, [2006] 2 AC 1, 10.

to investigate its law, which conflicts with mutual trust.[132] Hence, the English courts adopted a cosmopolitan interpretation of the requirements 'decision to charge' and 'decision to try' which accepts and respects the differences in the criminal procedures of the Member States.[133] As a result, Section 12A was brought more in compliance with the principle of mutual trust and mutual recognition.

10.7 Does the Intergovernmental Shoe Still Fit?

The previous sections have set out the different arguments against the intergovernmental perspective on the EU and national level. The first string of argumentation focused on the substantive and procedural differences between the surrender and extradition procedure, including the appointment of the competent authorities, the amount and scope of refusal grounds, the time limits etc. In my opinion, however, this line of argumentation is in itself not sufficient to conclude that the FDEAW is not just a modern form of extradition.[134] When viewing the FDEAW in isolation, meaning separate from the normative context of the AFSJ within which it operates, I do not find its classification as a more efficient and expedient form of intergovernmental cooperation without merit. I agree with legal scholars adhering to the intergovernmental perspective that looking solely at the text of the FDEAW and comparing its provisions with those in international extradition treaties leads to the conclusion that, in addition to important differences, there are also many important remaining similarities between the surrender procedure and extradition procedure.[135] Hence, in this light, the differences do not, in my opinion, unambiguously lead to the conclusion that the EAW is a fundamentally different procedure.

[132] Spencer has stated 'In crude terms, the traditional British view is that the United Kingdom, as part of its "common law heritage", enjoys a type of criminal procedure called "the accusatorial system" (alias the "adversarial" system), which is righteous, fair and morally sound, whereas the citizens of continental Europe suffer under something called "the inquisitorial system", alias "the Napoleonic system", which is evil, unjust and morally corrupt.' Spencer (2009), p. 535; Davidson et al. (2016), pp. 750–751.

[133] In *Puceviciene* a decision to charge was defined as 'the decision which is made when there is sufficient evidence under the relevant procedural system to make an allegation that the defendant has committed the crime alleged'. A decision to try was defined as 'a decision where the relevant decision maker (who may be a police authority, prosecutor or judge under the relevant procedural system) has decided to go ahead with the process of taking to trial the defendant against whom the allegation is made'. *Puceviciene* [2016] EWHC 1862, [2016] 1 WLR 4937 [55]–[56]. See also *Kandola*[2015] EWHC 619, [2015] 1 WLR 5097; Explanatory Notes to the Anti-Social Behaviour, Crime and Policing Act 2014, para 463.

[134] Also AG Colomer and AG Sharpston have combined the two strings of arguments. See Case C-303/05 *Advocaten voor de Wereld* [2006] ECLI:EU:C:2006:552, Opinion of AG Ruiz-Jarabo Colomer, paras 40–41, 46; Case C-551/18 *IK* [2018] ECLI:EU:C:2018:890, Opinion of AG Sharpston, paras 37–47.

[135] Section 9.4.1.

However, the combination of the first and second string of argumentation, of which the latter takes a broader perspective and focuses on the operation of the EAW in the normative context of the AFSJ, in my opinion leads to the conclusion that the intergovernmental perspective is no longer the only perspective on the surrender procedure or the most appropriate one. The development of judicial cooperation in the AFSJ, especially after the Treaty of Lisbon entered into force, reveals fundamental differences between the setting within which the EAW operates and the setting within which extradition procedures operate. As explained in Sect. 10.3, these differences and their development can roughly be divided into four interrelated categories. The first category covers the EU institutional framework in which the EU citizen has a role, as well. The second category concerns the free movement dimension of the AFSJ, as well as the actions and initiatives aiming for a correct balance between its two objectives—security and free movement. The third category covers the position of fundamental rights in the AFSJ in general and more specifically in relation to judicial cooperation mechanism which enhance security. The fourth category is the European dimension of the tasks of the national authorities, including national courts.

With regard to the first category, it follows from the previous sections that the EAW operates within a different institutional framework than extradition procedures, especially since the expiration of the transition period after the entering into force of the Treaty of Lisbon. Since that date, the CJEU has full jurisdiction over the EAW and the European Commission may start an infringement procedure when Member States do not act in conformity with EU criminal justice measures.

Furthermore, within this institutional framework, the CJEU has in many preliminary rulings further harmonised the surrender procedure and is in the process of establishing a common framework for the operation of the EAW. Such a framework is largely absent in extradition procedures. In addition, in cases such as *Kozlowski, Da Silva Jorge* and *Poplawski I*, the CJEU has limited the discretion of the Member States to return to classical extradition concepts and rules, in particular the nationality exception. In light of the free movement and security dimension of the AFSJ, the court has decided in these cases that states may not solely protect their own nationals against surrender and in some situations they also are obliged to execute the foreign sanction themselves when they refuse the EAW.

Another important difference with the intergovernmental context is the representation of the EU citizen in the EU institutional framework and EU legislative procedure for most criminal justice measures. In the ordinary legislative procedure, the EU citizen is directly represented by the European Parliament and indirectly by the Council of Ministers. Contrary to the post-Lisbon era, these two institutions now have a more equal position in the EU legislative process.

With regard to the second category the EU policy and legislative level, but in particular the CJEU case law, show a stronger focus on the free movement aspect of the AFSJ and the establishment of a common judicial area in which both security and free movement are ensured. The 2009 Roadmap on Procedural Safeguards stated that a minimum level of procedural safeguards had to be ensured in all the Member States, since this would increase the trust of EU citizens and facilitate free movement. However, this focus on the protection of free movement has not been repeated in most of the directives harmonising procedural safeguards that were subsequently adopted. Still, in the CJEU case law, the right to free movement has been developed into an *Abwehrrecht*, since the court has prohibited multiple national measures and actions which hamper free movement or even discriminate on the basis of nationality. At the same time, in the *Petruhhin* string of case law, the CJEU protects free movement by imposing the obligation on the requested state to first contact the state of nationality of the requested person in case of an extradition request and execute an EAW issued by that state when the requirements for surrender are met.

Thirdly, the position of fundamental rights in the intergovernmental context differs to some extent from the EU context. Contrary to the intergovernmental setting, the EU has its own Charter of Fundamental Rights, which binds both the EU institutions and the Member States when implementing EU law. The EU legislator has also adopted instruments harmonising certain procedural safeguards that bind the EU Member States. Furthermore, as follows from cases like *Bob-Dogi* and *Kovalkovas*, fundamental rights are more strongly integrated in the issuing procedure than in the requesting procedure. In its jurisprudence, the CJEU allocates an important role to fundamental rights protection in its interpretation of the different conditions of the issuing procedure. In addition, the *ne bis in idem* case law, in particular the *Kossowski* case, shows that the CJEU is interpreting the *ne bis in idem* principle in light of the normative context of the AFSJ as laid down in Article 3(2) TEU.

Lastly, in cases like *Pupino* and *Poplawski*, the CJEU has emphasised the European dimension of the tasks of the national courts and other national authorities, which marks an important difference between the extradition and surrender procedure. In the AFSJ, national authorities are subjected to the duty of conform interpretation. National courts are also obliged to refer preliminary questions on the interpretation of EU law, when they are the court of last instance in a concrete case. After the entering into force of the Treaty of Lisbon, and even more so after the passing of the transition period the national courts have taken this obligation and possibility more to heart which has resulted in an increasing amount of preliminary questions. Furthermore, as follows from *Poplawski,* national authorities share the responsibility of pursuing common interests, such as the establishment of an AFSJ. Hence, national authorities no longer primarily protect the interests of their own states, but need to apply the EAW in a way in which they protect common interests, including the combatting of cross-border crime in the AFSJ.[136]

On the basis of the above, I come to the conclusion that the intergovernmental perspective is not the only or most suitable way to view judicial cooperation in criminal matters in the AFSJ. Consequently, it cannot serve as a valid justification for the conclusion drawn in Chap. 8 that currently the EAW is not viewed as a mechanism that could enforce jurisdiction claims which may be incompatible with

[136] See eg Taupiac-Nouvel (2012), p. 250.

Articles 49 and 47 CFR, because they are unforeseeable or not based on a transparent EU or international legal framework for forum choices. In my view, the arguments against the intergovernmental perspective reveal a second transnational perspective on the EAW which does not justify, but question the conclusions in Chap. 8. This transnational perspective is discussed in the next section.

10.8 A New Perspective on the EAW: Transnational Cooperation in the Normative Context of a Shared AFSJ

As explained in Chap. 9, the intergovernmental perspective views the EAW as an intergovernmental extradition procedure which operates in a context in which states are the main actors. The arguments against the intergovernmental perspective set out in the previous sections, however, draft a picture of the EAW as a form of transnational cooperation which occurs in a shared legal order consisting of both states and EU citizens. In this shared legal order, which is based on the rule of law and fundamental rights, both free movement and security are guaranteed, while fundamental rights are respected.[137] The different aspects of this perspective and the indications for its existence are discussed in the next paragraphs.

The legal literature shows many different interpretations and definitions of the concept of transnational law enforcement.[138] Luchtman has argued that the EAW as a form of transnational cooperation is based on the direct cooperation between national judicial authorities, which can be prosecution bodies as well as judges and courts.[139] As the role of the state or the government was intentionally restricted in the surrender procedure, the EAW is better viewed as a form of transnational cooperation.[140] On a similar note, the classification of the EAW as cross-border cooperation is less suitable. The EAW aims to set up a system of direct cooperation between national judicial authorities for the purpose of the prosecution and trial of persons who are situated abroad without the need for foreign authorities to enter the territory of the state in which these individuals are present.[141]

Besides the fact that the elements which make cooperation predominantly 'international' or 'cross-border' cooperation are largely eliminated in the EAW procedure, the context in which this transnational form of cooperation occurs is also different

---

[137] TEU arts 2 and 3(2); TFEU, art 67(1).

[138] For an overview and a discussion, see Gleß (2015).

[139] Luchtman (2017), p. 19. See also Spencer (2013), p. 63.

[140] See FDEAW, recital 5. See also Case C-477/16 *Kovalkovas* [2016] ECLI:EU:C:2016:861, para 42.

[141] Luchtman (2017), p. 19.

from the intergovernmental setting.[142] The EAW operates in a shared legal order, consisting of both states and EU citizens. The roots of the EU as a shared legal order date back to the *Van Gend and Loos* case, in which the CJEU described the EU as a legal order consisting of both states and their nationals, who are nowadays designated as EU citizens.[143] In this shared legal order, EU citizens and their interests have at least an equal position to that of the state. In addition, the Treaty of Lisbon introduced Article 3(2) TEU, which explicitly designates the EU citizen as the main stakeholder of the AFSJ, which is in itself multi-dimensional. The latter entails that according to the treaties, the AFSJ should guarantee both free movement and security while respecting fundamental rights and the national legal systems of the Member States.[144] In particular, the post-Lisbon era reveals a slow but visible trend towards the realisation of this shared legal order and the fulfilment of the objectives and obligations laid down in Articles 3(2) TEU and 67(1) TFEU in practice.

Firstly, the position of the EU citizen in the EU legislative process for criminal justice measures has been strengthened.[145] As explained before in the ordinary legislative procedure, the EU citizen is directly represented in the European Parliament and indirectly, via national elections, in the Council. Both institutions can introduce amendments and both need to consent to EU legislation concerning judicial cooperation in the AFSJ.[146]

Secondly, EU citizens are not just nationals of an EU Member State, but are provided with specific free movement rights inherently connected to this status, which are protected in practice. The European Council's Roadmap on Procedural Safeguards of 2009, for instance, encouraged fundamental rights protection for the purpose of free movement. However, the main protection of the EU citizen exercising free movement rights is provided by the CJEU. The court has been developing the right to free movement into an *Abwehrrecht*, as follows from cases such as *Da Silva Jorge* and *Bickel and Franz*. In addition, the main message in the *Petruhhin* line of case law is that in light of the right to free movement, prosecution by the EU Member State of nationality is preferred over prosecution by a third state.[147] In my view, while accepting the fact that nationality is and remains the gateway to EU citizenship,[148] this development of the moving EU citizen seems to takes the content of EU citizenship beyond 'mere' membership of the state of nationality. In that light, I also agree with Strumia, who argues that a 'return to national citizenship' following

[142] See also Wouter van Ballegooij, 'European Arrest Warrant, European Implementation Assessment', European Parliamentary Research Service (2020) available at <https://www.europarl.europa.eu/RegData/etudes/STUD/2020/642839/EPRS_STU(2020)642839_EN.pdf> accessed 20 September 2021, para 3.6.

[143] Case C-26/62 *Van Gend & Loos* [1963] ECLI:EU:C:1963:1.

[144] TEU, art 3(2) and TFEU, art 67(1).

[145] See eg TFEU, arts 82–83.

[146] See Sect. 10.5.1.

[147] Sections 10.4 and 10.5.

[148] TFEU, art. 20.

from the CJEU's recuperation of the role of the Member State of nationality in cases like *Petruhhin* is not equal to a suppression of EU citizenship. She argues that while EU citizenship is dependent on national citizenship, it also constitutes an upgrade of national citizenship and changes its prospects. Being an EU citizen changes the benefits EU citizens can derive from their national citizenship, in particular the right to free movement. This upgrade also changes the duties of both the host state and the state of nationality which need to facilitate and protect this right to cross borders. According to Strumia the right to free movement 'raises the voice of national citizens beyond national borders, it brings their economic and social claims to the borders of other Member States, it projects their interests into the territorial space of other nationals, and it blends the values on which national citizenship rests with those of other national citizenships'.[149] So, in my view, the exercise of free movement rights for a particular purpose and its protection by the CJEU clashes with the idea that EU citizenship exclusively means being the legal subject of the state of nationality.[150] Instead, it suggests that EU citizenship unites multiple memberships to different entities and legal orders. Free movement rights are an important tool in shaping and developing these memberships according to the EU citizen's own preferences and wishes.[151] As stated by Thorhauer, 'Everyone's freedom of choice as to where he wants to move or reside in the Union territory is an essential part of self-determination and concerns the very substance of the right to free movement.'[152] Free movement as an essential part of the EU citizen's personal autonomy and the possibility to live a self-determined life is the starting point of the moving EU citizen.

Thirdly, besides the development of the position of the EU citizen and free movement in the AFSJ, the evolution of the EU legal order, and more specifically the AFSJ, is also characterised by its fundamental rights dimension.[153] Article 2 TEU states that the EU legal order is founded on the rule of law and fundamental

---

[149] Strumia (2020), pp. 522, 525. See also Eleftheriadis (2014), p. 778; Beck and Grande (2007), pp. 5, 97–99. Beck and Grande also made a similar point in relation to the role of the nation state in Europe. These legal scholars stated 'However, when we speak of *cosmopolitan* Europe we do not mean to imply the dissolution and replacement of the nation but its reinterpretation in light of the ideals and principles for which Europe in essence always stood and stands, that is, in light of a new conception of political comspolitanism'.

[150] Benhabib (2004), pp. 148–149. See also Delanty (2005), p. 417. Delanty states 'It is possible to conceive of European identity as a cosmopolitan identity embodied in the pluralized cultural models of a societal identity rather than as a supranational identity or an official EU identity that is in a relation of tension with national identities. As a cosmopolitan identity, European identity is a form of post-national self-understanding that expresses itself within, as much as beyond, national identities.'

[151] Luchtman (2013).

[152] Thorhauer (2015), p. 97.

[153] AG Bot referred in his Opinion for the *Bob-Dogi* case to the need for an essential balance between the requirements of an effective criminal justice system and the need to safeguard fundamental rights, which forms an integral part of the creation of a European judicial area. Case C-241/15 *Bob-Dogi* [2016] Opinion of AG Bot, ECLI:EU:C:2016:131, para 55.

rights and Article 67(1) TFEU states that fundamental rights need to be respected in the AFSJ. Furthermore, the EU has its own Fundamental Rights Charter and mechanisms for the monitoring and, if necessary, the punishment of fundamental rights violations by the Member States.[154] In addition, the *ne bis in idem* case law discussed in Sects. 10.4.2 and 10.5.3 shows how the CJEU has picked up the task of adjusting the scope of protection of this principle and fundamental right to the normative context of the AFSJ which aims to guarantee both free movement and security. This development is however limited to the *ne bis in idem* principle, which I discuss further in the next chapter.

10.9 Conclusion

This chapter has presented two strings of arguments which contradict the intergovernmental perspective and constitute the basis of an alternative perspective that views the EAW as a form of transnational cooperation, which does not occur in an intergovernmental context consisting of states, but in a shared legal order comprising both states and EU citizens. The prominent position of EU citizens in the shared legal order is illustrated by their direct representation by the European Parliament and their indirect representation by the Council in the EU legislative procedure from criminal justice measures as well as the protection of their right to free movement by the CJEU. Free movement is also not only a specific EU citizenship right, but one of the two core objectives of the AFSJ—which is in itself connected to EU citizenship as the area needs to be offered to EU citizens—according to Article 3(2) TEU. Furthermore, the establishment of the two-dimensional AFSJ needs to be realised while respecting fundamental rights. The next chapter discusses the possible consequences of this transnational perspective on the EAW for the acceptability of the conclusions in Chap. 8 and the position of fundamental right in the AFSJ.

References

Bargis M (2018) Personal freedom and surrender. In: Kostoris R (ed) Handbook of European criminal procedure. Springer

Beck U, Grande E (2007) Cosmpolitan Europe. Polity Press

Benhabib S (2004) The rights of others - aliens, residents and citizens. Cambridge University Press

Blackstock J (2012) Procedural safeguards in the European Union: a road well travelled? Eur Crim Law Rev 2:20

[154] Section 10.5.1.3; European Commission, 'A new EU Framework to strengthen the Rule of Law'(Communication) COM (2014) 158 final; TEU, art 7; TFEU, art 258; Case C-619/18 *Commission v Poland* [2019] ECLI:EU:C:2019:531.

Borgers M (2010) Mutual recognition and the European court of justice: the meaning of consistent interpretation and autonomous and uniform interpretation of union law for the development of the principle of mutual recognition in criminal matters. Eur J Crime Crim Law Crim Just 18:99
Böse M (2017) Mutual recognition, extradition to third countries and union citizenship: *Petruhhin*. Common Mark Law Rev 54:1781
Böse M (2020) The European arrest warrant and the independence of public prosecutors: OG & PI, PF, JR & YC. Common Mark Law Rev 57:1259
Coutts S (2019) From union citizens to national subjects: Pisciotti. Common Mark Law Rev 56:521
Davidson R, Lloyd B, Payter A (2016) Extradition law – recent developments and the potential impact of Brexit. Crim Law Rev:743
Delanty G (2005) The idea of a cosmopolitan Europe: on the cultural significance of Europeanization. Int Rev Sociol 15:405
den Brink V, Marguery T (2018) Hogere Evenwichtskunst in het Europees Aanhoudingsbevel. Meer rechtsbescherming en ook meer Europa? SEW:46
Eleftheriadis P (2014) The content of European citizenship. German Law J 15:777
Fichera M (2011) The implementation of the European arrest warrant in the European Union: law, policy and practice. Intersentia
Glerum V (2013) De weigeringsgronden bij uitlevering en overlevering – Een vergelijking en kritische evaluatie in het licht van het beginsel van wederzijdse erkenning. Wolf Legal Publishers
Glerum V (2017) Bescherming van een onderdaan van een andere lidstaat tegen uitlevering aan een derde land. SEW:172
Glerum V (2020) Case note Het Hof van Justitie breidt de bescherming tegen ongelijke behandeling bij uitlevering uit: Petruhhin is naar analogie van toepassing op EVA–/EER-onderdanen. SEW:697
Gleß S (2015) Bird's-eye view and worm's-eye view: towards a defendant-based approach in transnational criminal law. Transnatl Legal Theory 6:117
João Costa M (2017) The emerging EU extradition law. Petruhhin and beyond. New J Eur Crim Law 8:192
Klip A (2007) Case note HR 28 November 2006. NJ:489
Klip A (2017) Europeans First! Petruhhin, an unexpected revolution in extradition law. Eur J Crime Crim Law Crim Just 25:195
Kraniotis T (2016) Het vertrouwensbeginsel bij de interstatelijke samenwerking in strafzaken. Kluwer
Lenaerts K (2019) Upholding the rule of law through judicial dialogue. Yearb Eur Law 38:3
Luchtman M (2013) Choice of forum and the prosecution of cross-border crime in the European Union – what role for the legality principle? In: Luchtman M (ed) Choice of forum in cooperation against EU financial crime. Freedom, security and justice and the protection of specific EU-interests. Eleven International Publishing
Luchtman M (2017) Transnationale rechtshandhaving: Over fundamentele rechten in de Europese strafrechtelijke samenwerking. Boom
Merkel R, Scheinfeld J (2012) Ne *bis* in idem in der Europäischen Union – zum Streit um das Vollstreckungselement. ZIS:206
Meyer F (2011) Das Strafrecht im Raum der Freiheit, der Sicherheit und des Rechts. EuR 46:169
Meyer F, Böse M (2011) Die Beschränkung nationaler Strafgewalten als Möglichkeit zur Vermeidung von Jurisdiktionskonflikten in der Europäischen Union. ZIS 6:336
Mitsilegas V (2016) EU criminal law after Lisbon: rights, trust and the transformation of justice in Europe. Hart Publishing
Mitsilegas V (2020) Autonomous concepts, diversity management and mutual trust in Europe's area of criminal justice. Common Mark Law Rev 57:45
Nettesheim M (2009) Grundrechtskonzeptionen des EuGH im Raum der Freiheit, der Sicherheit und des Rechts. EuR 44:24

Nic Shuibhne N (2019) The 'territory of the union' in EU citizenship law: charting a route from parallel to integrated narratives. Yearb Eur Law 38:267
Ouwerkerk J (2011) Case C-261/09 criminal proceedings against Gaetano Mantello, judgment of the court of justice (grand chamber) of 16 November 2010. Common Mark Law Rev 48:1687
Reding V (2014) Believing in people – balancing the scales in European criminal law. Eur Crim Law Rev 4:79
Rosanò A (2017) If You Are a Judicial Authority and You Know It, Raise Your Hands – Case Note on C-452/16 PPU, Poltorak, C-453/16 PPU, Özçelik, C-477/16 PPU, Kovalkovas. Eur Crim Law Rev 7:89
Satzger H (2018) International and European criminal law. CH Beck/Hart/Nomos
Schönberger C (2015) Positive transnationale Jurisdiktionskonflikte – Causae, rechtliche Lösungsnotwendigkeit und -konzepte. Schulthess Verlag
Spencer J (2009) Mutual recognition of decisions in criminal justice and the United Kingdom. In: Vernimmen-Van Tiggelen G et al. (eds) The future of mutual recognition in criminal matters in the European Union. University of Brussel
Spencer J (2013) Mutual recognition and choice of forum. In: Luchtman M (ed) Choice of forum in cooperation against EU financial crime. Freedom, security and justice and the protection of specific EU-interests. Eleven International Publishing
Strumia F (2020, 507) Supranational citizenship enablers. Free movement from the perspective of home member states. Eur Law Rev 45
Taupiac-Nouvel G (2012) The Prinicple of mutual recognition in criminal matters: a new model of judicial cooperation within the European Union. Eur Crim Law Rev 2:236
Thorhauer N (2015) Conflicts of jurisdiction in cross-border criminal cases in the area of freedom, security, and justice. Risks and opportunities from an individual rights-oriented perspective. New J Eur Crim Law 6:78
Van Bockel B (2016) The 'European' Ne Bis in Idem principle: substance, sources and scope. In: van Bockel B (ed) Ne bis in idem in EU law. Cambridge University Press
Van Sliedregt E (2007) The European arrest warrant: between trust, democracy and the rule of law: introduction. The European arrest warrant: extradition in transition. Eur Const Law Rev 3:244
Vervaele J (2013) Ne Bis in idem: towards a transnational constitutional principle in the EU? Utrecht Law Rev 9:211
Vervaele J (2015) Schengen and charter-related Ne Bis in idem protection in the area of freedom, security and justice: M and Zoran Spasic. Common Mark Law Rev 52:1339
Wasmeijer M (2014) Ne bis in idem and the enforcement condition: balancing freedom, security and justice? New J Eur Crim Law 5:534

Chapter 11
A Transnational Legality Principle and Its Possible Effect on the EAW

11.1 Introduction

This chapter discusses the potential consequences of the transnational perspective on the surrender procedure for the scope and position of the substantive legality principle in Article 49 CFR and the right to a tribunal established by law in Article 47 CFR. In this light, Sect. 11.2 explains that the acceptability of the conclusions drawn in Chap. 8 is questionable in view of the characteristics of the transnational perspective. In short, these conclusions covered the current state-focused interpretation of fundamental rights in the AFSJ and the fact that currently no strong indications exist on the EU and national level that the EAW is viewed as a mechanism which can contribute to or enforce violations of the legality principle by surrendering EU citizens while they are in the underlying criminal cases confronted with unforeseeable jurisdiction claims or arbitrary forum decisions. In addition, Sect. 11.2 argues that the transnational perspective set out in Chap. 10 can trigger the need for a deviation from the state-focused interpretation of fundamental rights. It can require the adoption of a transnational fundamental rights framework, including a transnational legality principle, as an adequate counterbalance to transnational cooperation mechanisms, such as the FDEAW.

Section 11.3 then analyses what a transnational *nullum crimen sine lege* principle and tribunal established by law should look like to fit in the normative context of the AFSJ. It will discuss the content and scope of the transnational legality principle when taking the perspective of the EAW as a transnational cooperation instrument which operates in a shared legal order. Section 11.4 elaborates on the possible consequences for the EAW of the adoption of a transnational legality principle as proposed in Sect. 11.3. In this light, the section first explains that a transnational interpretation of the legality principle could turn the surrender procedure into an enforcement mechanism for violations of Articles 47 and 49 CFR by surrendering the requested person while the jurisdiction claim of the issuing state is incompatible with these fundamental rights. Afterwards, the section explains that the current EU

J. Graat, *The European Arrest Warrant and EU Citizenship*,
https://doi.org/10.1007/978-3-031-07590-2_11

legal framework for the surrender procedure, consisting of the FDEAW and complementary CJEU case law, does not provide national legislators or competent authorities the possibility to prevent this effect from occurring in concrete cases. The section therefore concludes that the adoption of a transnational interpretation of Articles 49 and 47 CFR requires additional action on the EU level to avoid the EAW from becoming an enforcement mechanism for violations of this transnational legality principle. Recommendations for such actions are later on provided in Chap. 13. This chapter ends with a conclusion in Sect. 11.5.

11.2 Transnational Cooperation Requires a Transnational Legality Principle

Chapter 9 introduced the intergovernmental perspective as an explanation for the lack of attention for problems which EU citizens may encounter that arise at the interface of national legal orders as well as the current state-focused interpretation of the legality principle. In this perspective, the state is the main actor and fundamental rights primarily aim to establish the necessary trust between states to cooperate with one another. With regard to the potential role of EU citizenship in judicial cooperation procedures, Chap. 9 explains that the main focus is on national citizenship.[1] The transnational perspective on the EAW as set out in Chap. 10 opens the door to a different view with regard to the problems with which EU citizens can be confronted, since it places EU citizenship and EU citizenship rights in the centre. It presents EU citizenship as a concept which, in particular in light of the right to free movement, unites multiple memberships to different national legal orders and, therefore, goes beyond being a national of one of the Member States. Free movement is considered a crucial element of the personal autonomy of the EU citizen and his or her self-determination.[2] In this light, I would argue that it follows from the transnational perspective that in an EU legal order which is explicitly based on the rule of law and which facilitates free movement for a selected group of individuals which are designated as EU citizens, the negative effects of crime-fighting efforts, such as the FDEAW cannot simply be swept under the carpet with the argument that it is important to prevent safe havens for criminals.[3] Nor can the state-focused interpretation of fundamental rights and the lack of a solution for the possible complications for EU citizens arising at the interface of national legal orders be justified on the basis of the argument that cooperation is a matter in which sovereign states act from hermetically separated positions, assisting each other on a reciprocal basis in

[1] Section 9.3.

[2] Section 10.8.

[3] See also European Council, Presidency Conclusions 1999 (Tampere Programme) <https://www.europarl.europa.eu/summits/tam_en.htm> accessed 20 September 2021, para 5.

protecting national security interests.[4] On top of that, the *culpa in causa* (fault in the cause) argument that the transnational consequences of the exercise of free movement rights are at the EU citizen's own risk neglects the fact that EU citizens are not merely provided with the possibility of free movement, but with a right to free movement. Hence, the position that the EU citizen can avoid complications arising at the interface of national legal orders by staying at home does not do justice to the position of EU citizens in the AFSJ and the rights granted to them because of this status.[5]

On the basis of the above, I am of the opinion that the transnational perspective suggests that taking the central position of EU citizens in the shared legal order and their right to free movement seriously, requires not only transnational crime-fighting efforts to ensure a safe AFSJ, but a suitable transnational rule of law framework as well which ensures a balance between crime-fighting efforts and the effect which they can have on the legal position of the EU citizen with free movement rights.[6] More generally, the transnational perspective in my opinion opens the door to the view that all fundamental aspects of criminal justice, most importantly protection against crime and protection of individual rights and safeguards against arbitrary interferences by public authorities, should be re-evaluated and adapted in conformity with the peculiarities of the AFSJ to do justice to its unique features, in particular EU citizenship and free movement rights.[7] In other words, as argued by many legal scholars, the fundamental rights and principles in the Charter should be adapted and interpreted in conformity with Article 3(2) TEU, which refers to an AFSJ in which EU citizens have free movement rights—not just free movement possibilities—and receive protection against cross-border criminality.[8] Article 52(3) CFR also allows for a change in the interpretation of fundamental rights to address new challenges in

[4]Luchtman (2017), pp. 35, 37; Case C-303/05 *Advocaten voor de Wereld* [2006] ECLI:EU:C:2006:552, Opinion of AG Ruiz-Jarabo Colomer, paras 42, 44–45. See also Glerum who states that states conclude extradition treaties, because they themselves may need the help of another state for the purpose of extradition one day. Glerum (2013), p. 13

[5]See Schönberger (2015), pp. 370–372.

[6]Schönberger (2015), pp. 292, 302; Luchtman (2017), pp. 9, 35, 37; Luchtman (2020). See also Thorhauer (2015), p. 101.

[7]Meyer (2014), p. 186; Ouwerkerk (2015), p. 23. See also Mancano (2019a); Mancano (2019b), p. 125ff; Sicurella (2018), p. 325. Sicurella stated 'the recent developments in European law, especially after the entry into force of the Lisbon Treaty establishing a criminal law competence of the EU and also furthering in general EU integration in criminal matters going much beyond the traditional paradigm of interstate cooperation, had a significant impact on the traditional understanding of the general principles of criminal law and they logically require that a common understanding of these principles is developed'.

[8]Not all authors refer to the need for a 'transnational' fundamental rights framework specifically, but they make the same general argument that the scope of fundamental rights needs to be adapted in conformity with the current normative context of the AFSJ. Schönberger (2015), pp. 292, 302; Meyer (2014), pp. 206–207; Thorhauer (2019), pp. 574–575; Luchtman (2017), pp. 9, 33–34, 36–37. See also Böse (2014), p. 152; Gleß (2015), pp. 130–131; Sinn (2013), p. 1; Mancano (2019); Franken (2013), p. 111.

the EU, as long as the changes do not reduce the standard of protection below the minimum.[9]

In light of the above, a transnational interpretation of fundamental rights, and in particular the legality principle, requires in my opinion that their scope and meaning are in conformity with the normative setting of the AFSJ set out in Article 3(2) TEU. The CJEU case law on *ne bis in idem* laid down in Articles 54 CISA and 50 CFR is one of the rare examples, which in fact illustrates the exercise of adapting fundamental rights and principles in conformity with the normative setting of the AFSJ which places EU citizens at the heart of its activities and provides them with free movement rights.[10] This jurisprudence shows how the CJEU searches for a balance between the protection of free movement, which is the main ratio of *ne bis in idem*, and the need for protection against cross-border criminality.[11] This is most clearly illustrated by the case *Kossowski* in which the CJEU considered both objectives of Article 3(2) TEU and in light thereof decided that despite the free movement ratio the decision of the prosecuting authority to terminate criminal proceedings without carrying out a detailed investigation could not be classified as a 'final decision'. According to the court, extending the scope of the *bis* element to these kinds of decisions would increase the risk of impunity and therefore threaten security.[12] Other examples are the cases *Miraglia* and *Spasic*, in which the CJEU viewed the security dimension of the AFSJ as a legitimate reason to restrict the scope of protection of the *ne bis in idem* principle. In the former, the CJEU decided that the national decision in question did not constitute a 'final decision' and therefore did not trigger the application of the *ne bis in idem* principle. This decision was based on the argument that accepting the national decision as a final decision would run counter to the objective of security and the prevention of crime in the AFSJ.[13] In *Spasic*, the CJEU determined that the enforcement clause in Article 54 CISA—binding the application of *ne bis in idem* to the condition that the sentence in question has been executed, is executed or can no longer be executed—constitutes a justified restriction to *ne bis in idem* in Article 50 CFR, which does not set the same condition. The court based this decision on the argument that this enforcement clause contributes to the establishment of a safe AFSJ.[14]

So, the *ne bis in idem* case law constitutes an important example of the adjustment of a fundamental right and principle to the normative setting in which it applies,

[9] In fact, one of the aims of the Charter was to guarantee a standard of fundamental rights protection which is risk sensitive and can adequately address new challenges resulting from new forms of EU cooperation and governance. Meyer (2014), pp. 193, 207.

[10] Schönberger (2015), p. 302. See also Sinn (2013), p. 1.

[11] As will be further explained in Chap. 12, the *ne bis in idem* jurisprudence shows the importance of EU rules on the subject-matter concerned when it comes to adapting fundamental rights in conformity with the normative context of the AFSJ. See also Sect. 10.5.3.4.

[12] Case C-486/14 *Kossowski* [2016] ECLI:EU:C:2016:483, paras 46–48. See also Case C-665/20 *X* [2021] ECLI:EU:C:2021:339, paras 96–104.

[13] Case C-469/03 *Miraglia* [2005] ECLI:EU:C:2005:156, paras 32–35.

[14] Case C-129/14 *Spasic* [2014] ECLI:EU:C:2014:586, paras 60–72. See also Sect. 10.5.3.4.

defined by Article 3(2) TEU. In that light, it can be viewed as a significant first step in the establishment of a transnational fundamental rights framework in the AFSJ. The next sections explore in light of Article 3(2) TEU the transnational interpretation of the accessibility and foreseeability requirement for criminal offences and sanctions in Article 49 CFR and the right to a tribunal established by law in Article 47 CFR. Also discussed is the extent to which a transnational legality principle could be integrated in the current legal framework of the surrender procedure.

11.3 A Transnational Interpretation of Articles 49 and 47 CFR

11.3.1 The Scope of Application of the Charter of Fundamental Rights

Before elaborating on the exact content and scope of a transnational *nullum crimen sine lege* principle and a transnational right to a tribunal established by law, it is important to note that these interpretations can only be adopted and subsequently applied when the CFR is in fact applicable to the situation at hand.[15] They are, therefore, dependent on the application of the CFR. As already explained in Chap. 3, the surrender procedure does not necessarily provide a clear opportunity to raise the matter regarding the link between jurisdiction and forum choices and the legality principle, since the FDEAW does not regulate the Member States' jurisdiction to prescribe and discretion to prosecute a case. However, the legislation route and free movement route could in the context of the national criminal procedure provide the opportunity to raise the matter regarding the interpretation of the legality principle in Article 47 and 49 CFR, more specifically the foreseeability of criminal offences, sanctions and tribunals, and its link to jurisdiction and forum decisions.[16]

With regard to the legislation route which covers national measures implementing specific obligations imposed by EU law, raising the matter of the interpretation of the legality principle is possible in cases in which the applicable national jurisdiction rule has been influenced by EU harmonisation measures for specific criminal offences and sanctions. In such situations, the judge in the national criminal case could, for instance, ask preliminary questions concerning the link between jurisdiction and the legality principle in Article 49 CFR. With regard to forum choices on the transnational level, the application of national measures implementing Framework Decision 2009/948 on conflicts of jurisdiction or other EU rules on forum decisions in the national criminal procedure can bring the case within the scope of the CFR and offer the possibility to link transnational forum decisions to Article 47 CFR.[17]

[15] CFR, art 51(1).

[16] Section 3.2.

[17] Section 3.2.2.3.

The free movement route towards a transnational interpretation of the legality principle is, for instance, available to a judge in a national criminal case in which the problem of unforeseeable jurisdiction claims or forum choices without a transparent legal framework occurs. The national judge could, for example, ask the CJEU the preliminary question whether the applicable national jurisdiction rules interfere with the right to free movement. If this is the case, the national measures need to be based on a justification ground offered by EU law.[18] These justifications need to be interpreted in conformity with fundamental rights and in that light, the national measures need to be assessed in light of the CFR. However, as explained in Chap. 3, the case law of the CJEU does not provide a straightforward answer to the question whether jurisdiction rules and rules regarding the decision to prosecute can be classified as obstacles to free movement, because they cause serious inconveniences in the professional or personal life of EU citizens. In my view, the uncertainty resulting from the possible exposure to different national substantive criminal laws and the absence of a clear system for forum choices could cause serious inconveniences for EU citizens, such as the unexpected criminality of certain conduct and parallel proceedings in multiple Member States.[19] These inconveniences, in my opinion, interfere with the right to free movement as the risk of their occurrence often also increases when free movement rights are used. In case the CJEU would reach the same or a similar conclusion, the fundamental rights check which needs to be conducted when relying on justification grounds in EU law offers the possibility to adopt a transnational interpretation of Articles 49 and 47 CFR.

It follows from the above that different routes are available to bring the questions regarding the link between the right to foreseeable criminal offences, sanctions and tribunals and jurisdiction claims and forum choices within the scope of the Charter and in that light, to address the interpretation of the legality principle. However, as also explained in Chap. 3, the possibilities described above are not always completely straightforward. For instance, it remains uncertain whether the CJEU would in fact classify jurisdiction rules and rules regarding the decision to prosecute as possible barriers to free movement. In addition, in relation to Article 49 CFR the legislation route may be limited to cases concerning criminal offences which have been subjected to EU harmonisation measures which also cover rules of jurisdiction.

11.3.2 A Transnational Interpretation of Article 49

Before elaborating on the transnational interpretation of the *nullum crimen sine lege* principle, this section first briefly reiterates the most important conclusions drawn in Chap. 3 with regard to the current scope of Article 7 ECHR and 49 CFR, which is

[18] Case C-390/12 *Pfleger* [2014] ECLI:EU:C:2014:281, para 36. See also Case C-390/12 *Pfleger* [2013] ECLI:EU:C:2013:747, Opinion of AG Sharpston, para 46.

[19] See Sects. 3.2.3 and 3.2.4.

restricted to criminal offences and sanctions. It follows from Chap. 3 that the substantive legality principle demands that the law codifying criminal offences and sanctions is accessible and foreseeable. The accessibility requirement entails that an individual must be provided with an adequate indication of the applicable rules in a given case.[20] The foreseeability requirement demands that individuals are able to understand from the wording of the law, if necessary with the help of the court's interpretation, for what behaviour they can be held criminally liable and what penalty can be imposed.[21]

According to the case law of the ECtHR and CJEU, the EAW does not fall within the scope of the *nullum crimen sine lege* principle as it does not constitute a penalty or criminal offence.[22] In addition, neither court has explicitly and clearly discussed the existence of a link between the requirement of accessible and foreseeable criminal offences and sanctions, and national jurisdiction. Only limited case law exists on the influence which jurisdiction could have on the accessibility and foreseeability of criminal offences and sanctions, and these cases exclusively concern situations on the national level.[23] Consequently, in light of the current scope of Article 49 CFR as demarcated in the case law, the EAW is currently not classified as a mechanism which facilitates the surrender of an EU citizen while the jurisdiction claim of the issuing state is incompatible with Article 49 CFR, since it was not foreseeable at the time of the offence.

Furthermore, in the legal literature, the view that the substantive legality principle requires that the application of a particular national criminal law is foreseeable at the time of the offence is a minority opinion. The most commonly taken positions are either that jurisdiction is not related to the criminality of behaviour and sanctions at all or that the *nullum crimen sine lege* principle does influence criminal jurisdiction, but only to the extent that that the individual should have been able to know that his or her conduct was criminal somewhere.

In my opinion, there are in principle two ways to reach a transnational interpretation of the current scope and meaning of Article 49 CFR, in particular the accessibility and foreseeability requirements. The first is to link the accessibility and foreseeability of criminal offences and sanctions to the foreseeability of a jurisdiction claim, and transfer the rulings of the ECtHR in the cases *Camilleri* and *Seychell*, in which several penalty brackets were applicable to the same situation, to the transnational level.[24] The second one is to bring the surrender procedure within

[20]ECtHR 26 April 1979, 6538/74 (*Sunday Times/UK*) para 49.

[21]ECtHR 11 November 1996, 17862/91 (*Cantoni/France*) para 29; ECtHR 19 March 2006, 67335/01 (*Achour/France*) para 41. See also Case C-42/17 *M.A.S., M.B* [2017] ECLI:EU:C:2017:936 (*Taricco II*), para 56; Case C-72/15 *Rosneft* [2017] ECLI:EU:C:2017:236, para 162.

[22]EcHR 6 July 1976, 7512/76 (*X/ the Netherlands*) paras 185–186; ECtHR 7 October 2008, 41138/05 (*Monedero Angora/Spain*); ECtHR 23 October 2012, 1997/11 (*Giza/Poland*) paras 30–31.

[23]ECtHR 22 January 2013, 42931/10 (*Camilleri/Malta*); ECtHR 28 August 2018, 43328/14 (*Seychell/Malta*).

[24]ECtHR 22 January 2013, 42931/10 (*Camilleri/Malta*); ECtHR 28 August 2018, 43328/14 (*Seychell/Malta*).

the scope of Article 49 CFR. However, this is, in my opinion, an unsuitable option and will only be discussed briefly.

11.3.2.1 Option 1: The Foreseeability of a Particular National Criminal Law

To ensure that both objectives in Article 3(2) TEU are taken into account and that the ratio of the substantive legality principle—protection against arbitrary prosecution, conviction and punishment—is not eroded,[25] I propose that the transnational legality principle requires that criminal offences and sanctions codified in a particular national criminal law are not accessible and foreseeable when citizens could at the time of the offence not have foreseen that that particular national criminal law was applicable to them.[26] In light of the free movement objective of the AFSJ and EU citizens' right to free movement this should mean that EU citizens should only have to know and abide by the law of the state to which they choose to move and/or decided to stay.[27] In other words, EU citizens have the right not to be 'bothered' by the criminal laws of other states than the one of their host state which they can choose by (not) exercising their free movement rights.[28] However, whereas this interpretation of the legality principle increases the foreseeability of the applicable national criminal law at the time of the offence—and, therefore, the legal certainty of EU citizens who want to exercise their free movement rights—it is also liable to endanger the security objective of the AFSJ. Situations in which only one law, the law of the state to which the EU citizen decided to move or remain in, is applicable, could result in impunity when this state is for a particular reason not in a position or not willing to prosecute.[29] In addition, restricting the overlap of applicable national criminal laws allows for forum shopping by the EU citizen who could move to the state with the most lenient legal system. Besides the threat to the security objective of the AFSJ, another—interlinked—argument against the proposed transnational interpretation of Article 49 CFR is that it could neglect the legitimate interests of other states than the host state to prosecute the case.[30] In an EU which is viewed as a shared legal order consisting of both Member States and EU citizens, these legitimate interests should, in my view, be taken into account when considering the protection offered by transnational fundamental rights. Consequently, for the

[25] ECtHR 17 September 2009, 10249/03 (*Scoppola/Italy No. 2*) para 92.

[26] As mentioned before, this transnational interpretation of Article 49 CFR is dependent on the application of the CFR. See Sect. 11.3.1.

[27] For a discussion on the right 'not' to move see Luchtman (2013), pp. 16–17.

[28] See also Luchtman (2013), pp. 16, 22–24.

[29] By extension, the free movement dimension of the AFSJ could also be negatively affected, since EU citizens are less likely to exercise free movement rights in an AFSJ which is unsafe. Thorhauer (2015), pp. 90, 93. See also Thorhauer (2019), p. 579.

[30] Luchtman (2013), pp. 23–24.

purpose of protecting the security angle of Article 3(2) TEU and the interests of the Member States, other states than the host state should also be allowed to establish criminal jurisdiction.[31] However, these exceptions or limitations to the transnational right to foreseeable and accessible criminal offences and sanctions should themselves be sufficiently demarcated to avoid arbitrary prosecutions, convictions and punishments. In that light, I propose a transnational interpretation of the ECtHR's ruling in the case *Camilleri* and *Seychell*.[32] This would mean that more than one law may be applicable as long as the law ensures that the discretion to appoint the applicable national criminal law in a concrete case is sufficiently restricted to avoid arbitrariness.

To sum up, criminal offences and sanctions are accessible and foreseeable when the application of a particular national criminal law, which should be the law of the host state, was foreseeable at the time of the offence. Exceptions to this 'default right' are only allowed when the law ensures that in case more national criminal laws are applicable, the discretion of the authority deciding which particular national criminal law is applied in the concrete case is sufficiently delineated to avoid arbitrary decisions. In my view, this transnational interpretation of the right to an accessible and foreseeable law for criminal offences and sanctions fits with the twofold objective of the AFSJ as well as the ratio of the substantive legality principle, which is protection against arbitrary prosecution, conviction and punishment.

11.3.2.2 Option 2: The EAW Falls Within the Scope of Article 49 CFR

Another way to transform Article 49 CFR into a transnational fundamental right is by pulling the EAW within the scope of application of the substantive legality principle. This would mean that the law on surrender also needs to meet the accessibility and foreseeability requirement. The reasoning could then be that these requirements are not met when the applicability of the national criminal law of the state issuing the EAW is not foreseeable at the time of the offence. In other words, the law should inform citizens when they can be subjected to an EAW, which it does not do in an adequate manner when the applicability of the national criminal offences and sanctions of the issuing state are not foreseeable at the time of the offence. Such an interpretation of the legality principle would also facilitate free movement as it increases the foreseeability of EAWs. However, in my opinion this is not a suitable transnational interpretation of Article 49 CFR and should, therefore, not be explored in further detail. As explained in Sect. 11.2, the need and possibility for a transnational legality principle are founded on the many fundamental differences between the surrender and extradition procedure set out in Chap. 10. Yet, one

[31] See also Luchtman (2013), pp. 16, 22–24.

[32] ECtHR 22 January 2013, 42931/10 (*Camilleri/Malta*); ECtHR 28 August 2018, 43328/14 (*Seychell/Malta*).

of the remaining similarities between the EAW and extradition instruments is that they are measures which facilitate the determination of a criminal charge or the execution of a sanction.[33] The development of the surrender procedure over the course of time has not changed this 'facilitating' role of the EAW, meaning that the surrender procedure has not become part of the underlying criminal case. This is also confirmed by the fact that some of the main characteristics of the EAW are its high level of automaticity and the formal nature of the procedure in which the merits of the case hardly play a role.[34] Hence, realising a transnational interpretation of Article 49 CFR by extending its scope to include the EAW contradicts the facilitating role which this instrument still has in relation to national prosecutions and the execution of sanctions.

11.3.3 A Transnational Interpretation of Article 47 CFR

Similar to the previous section, this one first briefly repeats the current scope of the right to a tribunal established by law as it follows from the case law of the CJEU and ECtHR before elaborating on the transnational interpretation of Article 47 CFR. As follows from Chap. 3, the right to a tribunal established by law reflects both the principle of the rule of law and the separation of powers doctrine.[35] In that light, it entails that the organisation of the judicial system in a democratic state should not be dependent on the discretion of the executive or the judicial power.[36] Instead, it should be regulated by laws emanating from Parliament.[37] Forum choices fall within the scope of the right to a tribunal established by law, but it does not grant citizens the right to choose their court nor does it prohibit conflicts of jurisdiction as such.[38] In other words, Article 47(2) CFR does not require that the law ensures that only one court is in fact competent to prosecute and try the case. What it does require is that, once a system for case allocations is laid down by law, these laws ensure that forum

[33]Case C-303/05 *Advocaten voor de Wereld* [2006] ECLI:EU:C:2006:552, Opinion of AG Ruiz-Jarabo Colomer, para 41. See also EcHR 6 July 1976, 7512/76 (*X/the Netherlands*) paras 185–186; ECtHR 7 October 2008, 41138/05 (*Monedero Angora/Spain*).

[34]These were also part of the argumentation of the ECtHR when determining that the EAW does not determine a criminal charge as a result of which Article 6 ECHR does not apply to the surrender procedure. ECtHR 7 October 2008, 41138/05 (*Monedero Angora/Spain*).

[35]ECtHR 5 October 2010, 19334/03 (*DMD Group/Slovakia*) para 58; ECtHR 22 June 2000, 32492/96, 32547/96, 32548/96, 33209/96, 33210/96 (*Coëme and others/Belgium*) para 98.

[36]ECtHR 22 June 2000, 32492/96, 32547/96, 32548/96, 33209/96, 33210/96 (*Coëme and others/Belgium*) para 98; Panzavolta (2013), p. 151.

[37]EcHR 12 October 1978, 7360/76 (*Leo Zand/Austria*) para 69; ECtHR 22 June 2000, 32492/96, 32547/96, 32548/96, 33209/96, 33210/96 (*Coëme and others/Belgium*) para 98; Luchtman (2011), p. 86.

[38]ECtHR 9 June 2005, 26384/02 (*Vokhmina/Russia*); ECtHR 12 July 2007, 74613/01 (*Jorgic/Germany*) para 65; ECtHR 22 January 2013, 42931/10 (*Camilleri/Malta*); Panzavolta (2013), p. 154.

decisions are based on reasonable grounds.[39] This also entails that when public prosecutors or judicial authorities are competent to make the forum decision, the law needs to sufficiently restrict their discretion to avoid arbitrariness.[40] Still, the current case law on the matter of forum choices in light of the right to a tribunal established by law only concerns situations that occur on the national level and does not answer the question whether the requirement of a reasonable forum decision also applies in case of conflicts of national jurisdictions.[41]

With regard to the transnational interpretation of the right to a tribunal established by law in light of the twofold goal of the AFSJ set out in Article 3(2) TEU, the existing jurisprudence on forum choices set out in the previous paragraph provides, in my opinion, a good starting point. Translating the existing requirements for forum choices on the national level following from the case law on Article 47 CFR and Article 6 ECHR to the transnational context would in my view mean that the law does not need to avoid conflicts of national jurisdiction all together. Instead, a transnational interpretation of Article 47 CFR should entail that a national court or tribunal is not established by law when the national jurisdiction to which it belongs has not been appointed on the basis of a clear or transparent law aiming for reasonable forum decisions in light of the good administration of justice. In light of this definition, a clear law does not mean a stringent set of rules which prevents conflicts of jurisdiction altogether and ensures that citizens are able to know at the time of the offence in which specific national jurisdiction the case will be tried. Instead, similar to forum choices on the national level, in the transnational setting the law should ensure that any discretion allocated to the executive or judiciary is sufficiently restricted to avoid arbitrary and unreasonable forum decisions.[42]

In my view, the transnational interpretation of Article 47 CFR proposed above fits better in an AFSJ with a twofold objective and consisting of states and EU citizens than a more strict interpretation. This is because the proposed interpretation could facilitate free movement as increases the legal certainty of the moving EU citizen with regard to the potential consequences of exercising the right to free movement. This transnational interpretation ensures protection against arbitrary forum decisions by national or EU authorities. In addition, this transnational legality principle also allows for a degree of discretion and flexibility when it comes to forum choices which ensures that other important interests, such as security can be taken into account as well. Some legal scholars have, however, argued in favour of a stricter transnational interpretation of Article 47 CFR, more specifically one which ensures a high degree of foreseeability regarding the national jurisdiction for prosecution and

[39] EcHR 10 October 1990, 16875/90 (*G/Switzerland*). Other cases in which the Commission considered whether reasonable grounds existed for the authorities to establish jurisdiction are ECtHR 2 December 1992, 17495/90 (*Kübli/ Switzerland)*; EcHR 25 November 1996, 28899/95 (*Stieringer/Germany*).

[40] Panzavolta (2013), p. 154. For the explanation why forum decisions by public prosecutors most likely also fall within the scope of Article 47 CFR, see Sect. 3.4.2.2.

[41] Meyer (2014), p. 206.

[42] See also Thorhauer (2015), p. 95.

trial at the time of the offence. For instance, Gropp has stated that encouraging individuals to act in conformity with the law requires both that they are able to know at the time of the offence which particular national substantive criminal law applies and in which national jurisdiction the case will be prosecuted and tried.[43] Consequently, the law should as clearly as possible appoint the national jurisdiction which will try the case and by extension the discretion of the executive or judiciary in relation to the forum decision should be restricted as much as possible.[44]

In comparison to my proposal, this strict transnational interpretation of the right to a tribunal established by law could ensure a higher level of legal certainty for the moving EU citizen, but it could also have certain drawbacks. Firstly, this strict interpretation which is best served with a law that either prevents conflicts of jurisdiction from occurring or establishes a strict and hierarchical system for case allocations facilitates the abuse of free movement rights, in the sense that EU citizens can more easily choose the state with the most lenient sanctioning system to commit the offence.[45] Secondly, a more strict interpretation of the transnational right to a tribunal established by law also limits the possibility of a system for forum choices on the basis of the concrete circumstances of the case and in light of the good administration of justice. A more flexible approach to forum decisions may be less advantageous in light of legal certainty and foreseeability, but it also provides the possibility to appoint the most appropriate forum for prosecution and trial in each concrete case. The discretion offered to the decision-making authorities by a more flexible system could ensure that in light of the good administration of justice, the relevant interests of the different parties affected by a forum decision, including fundamental rights protection and security, can be considered and weighed. This approach also fits with an AFSJ that has a twofold objective, including free movement and security and consists of both states and EU citizens.

Besides the fact that a less stringent transnational interpretation of the right to a tribunal established by law can both ensure legal certainty for the EU citizen who wants to exercise free movement rights and meet the practical need for flexibility in forum choices,[46] it also provides the opportunity to make a forum decision at a later stage in the procedure when more information is available to determine the most appropriate forum.[47] In this light, several legal scholars have argued that individuals should know in which national jurisdiction they will have to defend themselves before the commencement of the criminal case.[48] This could, for instance, mean at the time the decision to prosecute is made or before the case is officially brought to

[43] Gropp (2012), pp. 53–54. See also Fuchs (2006), p. 364.

[44] Gropp (2012), pp. 53–54.

[45] Eser (2012), p. 567; Thorhauer (2015), p. 95; Luchtman (2013), p. 24.

[46] Böse (2013), p. 81.

[47] Eser (2012), p. 567.

[48] Böse (2013), p. 80.

trial.[49] This point is further discussed in Chap. 13, which sets out recommendations for a system for forum choices on the EU level.

To sum up, in my view, the right to a tribunal established by law should come to mean that a national court or tribunal is only established by law when the national jurisdiction of which the court or tribunal is part has been appointed on the basis of a transparent system for forum choices in light of the good administration of justice. More concretely, the law should ensure that reasonable forum decisions are made in concrete cases and in that light, it should sufficiently limit the power of the decision-making authority to avoid arbitrary decisions. This transnational interpretation of Article 47 CFR allows for more flexible systems for forum choices in light of the good administration of justice in which all interests can be taken into account, including those of the competent states as well as the suspect and perhaps even the victim.

11.4 The Consequences of a Transnational Legality Principle for the EAW and Their Implementation in the Surrender Procedure

11.4.1 The EAW as an Enforcement Measure for Fundamental Rights Violations

This section answers the twofold question what the possible effect of the transnational interpretation of Article 49 and 47 CFR could be on the surrender procedure and whether the FDEAW and complementing CJEU case law offer the opportunity to implement this effect in an adequate manner in the issuing or executing procedure. With regard to the first question the conclusion is that a transnational legality principle can turn the EAW into an enforcement mechanism for violations of Articles 49 and 47 CFR in the issuing state. In other words, the surrender of the requested person while the jurisdiction claim of the issuing state is not in conformity with the transnational interpretation of Articles 49 or 47 CFR could contribute to the violation of these fundamental rights by the issuing state. In the next sections, I argue that the current EU legal framework for the EAW does not offer the national legislators and courts an adequate possibility to prevent the EAW from functioning as an enforcement mechanism for violations of the transnational legality principle in concrete cases.[50] These sections enumerate the few opportunities provided in the

---

[49] See also Panzavolta (2013), pp. 160–161.

[50] In this light, Chap. 4 already explained that the conditions of the issuing and execution procedure laid down in the FDEAW were not installed with the intent to offer protection against unforeseeable jurisdiction claims and the risk of arbitrary forum decisions. The same goes for the CJEU case law which has further clarified the issuing and executing procedure. However, contrary to Chap. 4, the relevant question in this section is not what protection the EAW currently offers against problems

issuing and executing procedure to 'integrate', so to speak, the transnational legality principle in the surrender procedure—meaning avoiding the EAW from functioning as an enforcement mechanism for violations of the transnational legality principle in the requested person's national criminal case—and explain why none of these possibilities are in my opinion suitable.

11.4.2 The Issuing Procedure: Articles 6 and 8(1)(c) FDEAW

As explained before, the issuing procedure is scarcely regulated in the FDEAW. This section focuses on the conditions for the issuing of an EAW laid down in Articles 6 and 8(1)(c) FDEAW. Whereas the texts of these legal provisions do not show a clear opening to integrate the transnational legality principle in the surrender procedure, the interpretation of the conditions laid down in these provisions by the CJEU may provide such opportunities in the surrender procedure on the national level.[51]

Firstly, as explained in Chap. 4, the preliminary rulings on Article 6(1) FDEAW also establish other requirements for the issuing of an EAW which are not linked to the appointment of the issuing judicial authority.[52] In these rulings, the CJEU has determined in relation to prosecution EAWs that when the issuing judicial authority is not a court or judge, the requested person must be offered the possibility to challenge the decision to issue an EAW before a court in the issuing Member State.[53] These court proceedings in the issuing state need to meet the requirements of effective judicial protection.[54] As also explained in Chap. 4, this possibility to challenge the issuing decision is most likely not intended as an opportunity to address the underlying jurisdiction claim of the criminal case or the decision to prosecute. This follows, for instance, from the fact that the CJEU case law restricts the possibility of a review to the issuing decision.[55] However, in my view, the proportionality assessment, which is part of the issuing procedure, does offer a

occurring at the interface of national legal orders, but whether the legal framework provides the opportunity to prevent the EAW from becoming an enforcement mechanism for violations of the transnational legality principle in concrete cases.

[51] Articles 6 and 8 FDEAW do not set any requirements touching upon the jurisdiction to prescribe and adjudicate. In light of the principle of mutual trust, the executing state should also trust that the criminal offenses fall within the scope of application of the national criminal law of the issuing state and that this state is competent to prosecute. Glerum (2013), p. 572. See also Rb. Amsterdam 15 October 2004, ECLI:NL:RBAMS:2004:AR4237 (Amsterdam District Court).

[52] Joined Cases C-566/19 & C-626/19 *JR & YC* [2019] ECLI:EU:C:2019:1077, paras 48–49; Case C-509/18 *PF* [2019] ECLI:EU:C:2019:457, para 56.

[53] Joined Cases C-508/18 & C-82/19 *OG & PI* [2019] ECLI:EU:C:2019:456, para 75; Joined Cases C-566/19 & C-626/19 *JR & YC* [2019] ECLI:EU:C:2019:1077, paras 62–63; Case C-627/19 *ZB* [2019] ECLI:EU:C:2019:1079.

[54] Joined Cases C-566/19 & C-626/19 *JR & YC* [2019] ECLI:EU:C:2019:1077, paras 61–63.

[55] Joined Cases C-566/19 & C-626/19 *JR & YC* [2019] ECLI:EU:C:2019:1077, paras 63.

possibility to address the jurisdiction claim and decision to prosecute of the issuing state. For instance, during the review procedure in the issuing state the question could be raised to what extent the issuing of an EAW is proportional when it enforces a jurisdiction claim or forum decision which is incompatible with Articles 47 and 49 CFR?[56] A disadvantage of the use of this possibility to integrate the transnational legality principle in the surrender procedure is, however, that it would only be available in case of prosecution EAWs, even though questions regarding the jurisdiction claim and forum decision of the issuing state could also arise in case of EAWs issued for the execution of a judgement in a criminal case.[57]

Secondly, with regard to Article 8(1)(c) FDEAW the CJEU decided in the case *Bob-Dogi* that an EAW is invalid when it is not based on an enforceable national judicial decision, such as a national arrest warrant or another judicial decision which has the equivalent legal effects of an arrest warrant.[58] In these cases, an EAW may not be issued and, if it is, the executing judicial authority should refuse to give effect to it. In my opinion, *Bob-Dogi* offers an opportunity to avoid surrender in situations in which it would enforce a violation of the transnational interpretation of Articles 49 and 47 CFR. This opportunity follows from the generally assumed connection between national arrest warrants, which are part of criminal procedural law, and a state's jurisdiction to prescribe, which covers the scope of applicability of a national substantive criminal law. For instance, the purpose of the Dutch Code of Criminal Procedure is to realise or enforce Dutch substantive criminal law. In that light, investigatory powers may also only be exercised when the case falls within the ambit of Dutch substantive criminal law or in case of a valid request for international assistance.[59] In relation to the transnational substantive legality principle, the argument would become that, since Dutch offences and sanctions are not compliant with Article 49 CFR, the national criminal provisions in question are in principle not applicable to the behaviour of the citizen.[60] Consequently, the Dutch authorities would not be allowed to exercise investigative and prosecutorial powers, which would mean that any national arrest warrant or equivalent order would not be a valid basis for the EAW.[61] Hence, the requirement of an enforceable national judicial decision in Article 8(1)(c) FDEAW could be used to avoid the EAW from becoming an enforcement mechanism for violations of the transnational legality principle by the issuing state. This requirement can block the power of the issuing judicial authority to issue an EAW and, if an EAW is issued anyway, the requested person

[56] The national court could also request a preliminary ruling on this question.

[57] Case C-627/19 *ZB* [2019] ECLI:EU:C:2019:1079. See also Case C-627/19 *ZB* [2019] ECLI:EU:C:2019:1014, Opinion of AG Campos Sánchez-Bordona, paras 19–34.

[58] Case C-241/16 *Bob-Dogi* [2016] ECLI:EU:C:2016:385, para 48; Case C-414/20 *MM* [2021] ECLI:EU:C:2021:4, para 53.

[59] HR 24 January 1984, ECLI:NL:HR:1984:AD5669 (Supreme Court); Corstens et al. (2018), p. 198.

[60] Altena (2016), p. 184.

[61] Wolswijk (2013), p. 353.

could argue in the executing state that the EAW should not be executed due to the absence of an enforceable national judicial decision. However, raising the question of the existence of an enforceable national judicial decision in light of the compliance of the issuing state with the transnational legality principle in the executing procedure clashes with the principle of mutual recognition. In order to assess the existence of an enforceable national arrest warrant, the executing judicial authority would, for instance, have to examine whether in the national criminal case in the issuing state the transnational legality principle is complied with. In addition, the use of this *Bob-Dogi* backdoor to integrate the transnational legality principle in the surrender procedure also has other important drawbacks that are discussed in the next paragraph.

It follows from the above that the possibility to challenge the issuing decision in the issuing state and Article 8(1)(c) FDEAW as interpreted by the CJEU in *Bob-Dogi* could be used for the integration of the transnational legality principle in the issuing procedure. However, the use of these opportunities also comes with risks, in particular security threats. In the current AFSJ in which Member States have broad extraterritorial jurisdiction and the EU has not adopted legislation which generally regulates jurisdiction and forum choices, there is a relatively high chance that the EAW will in many future cases enforce violations of the transnational legality principle. Consequently, the use of one of the two options is accompanied by a considerable risk that the power to issue an EAW is severely restricted. Integrating the transnational legality principle in the issuing procedure could therefore derail the effective operation of the EAW, which clashes with the security dimension of the AFSJ and the fact that the EU is a shared legal order. Security is an important interest for both the Member States and EU citizens, who are not only suspects, but victims and witnesses as well.[62] Hence, in light of their disadvantages and possible drawbacks neither of the two options constitutes, in my view, a suitable tool to prevent the EAW from becoming an enforcement mechanism for violations of the transnational legality principle in the requested person's national criminal case.

11.4.3 The Execution Procedure: The Fundamental Rights Route

It follows from the CJEU case law that Articles 3, 4 and 4A FDEAW provide an exhaustive list of refusal grounds, which does not include a general fundamental rights exception.[63] However, as explained in Chap. 4, Opinion 2/13 opened the door to the integration of a fundamental rights exception in the surrender procedure, since it states that the presumption of mutual trust can be rebutted in exceptional

[62] Van der Beken et al. (2002), p. 628; Eicker (2005), p. 634; Eser (2012), p. 563.

[63] Case C-123/08 *Wolzenburg* [2009] ECLI:EU:C:2009:616, para 57.

circumstances.[64] In these situations, Member States are allowed to deviate from the prohibition not to verify the fundamental rights situation of another state in a concrete case.[65] In the context of the EAW, the CJEU has so far accepted fundamental rights exceptions in case of potential violations of the prohibition of torture and inhuman and degrading treatment in Article 4 CFR and the right to an independent tribunal in Article 47 CFR.[66] In relation to both fundamental rights, it has adopted a rather similar two-step test which needs to be met before the executing judicial authority is allowed to end the surrender procedure. In short, the first step is to establish systemic or general deficiencies concerning the detention conditions of the issuing state or concerning the judiciary of this state relating to the guarantee that courts and tribunals are independent.[67] These systemic or general deficiencies should be based on objective, reliable, specific and properly updated information.[68] When this step is met, the executing judicial authority needs to determine specifically and precisely, whether there are substantial grounds to believe that the surrender of the requested person will expose him or her to a real risk of such a violation.[69]

In theory, the possibility offered by Opinion 2/13 to conduct a fundamental rights check in the surrender procedure could also be used to integrate a transnational interpretation of Article 49 and the right to a tribunal established by law in the executing procedure.[70] The CJEU would then have to classify the risk of a violation of Article 49 CFR and the right to a tribunal established by law in Article 47 CFR as exceptional circumstances, as well. Most likely, it would then also set the same twofold test for these violations, meaning that systemic and general deficiencies need to exist concerning the judiciary of the issuing Member State relating to the requirement to bring the case before a tribunal established by law or concerning the foreseeability and accessibility of criminal offences and sanctions. When this is the case, the executing judicial authority should determine whether there is a real risk

---

[64] Section 4.2.6.

[65] Opinion 2/13 [2014] ECLI:EU:C:2014:2454, paras 191–192.

[66] See Joined Cases C-404/15 & C-659/15 *Aranyosi and Căldăraru* [2016] ECLI:EU:C:2016:198; Case C-216/18 *LM* [2018] ECLI:EU:C:2018:586.

[67] Joined Cases C-404/15 & C-659/15 *Aranyosi and Căldăraru* [2016] ECLI:EU:C:2016:198, para 89; Case C-216/18 *LM* [2018] ECLI:EU:C:2018:586, paras 60–61.

[68] Joined Cases C-404/15 & C-659/15 *Aranyosi & Căldăraru* [2016] ECLI:EU:C:2016:198, para 89.

[69] With regard to Article 47 CFR, the second step is also twofold. The executing judicial authority first needs to establish to what extent the general deficiencies regarding the independence of the courts and tribunals could impact the level of courts with jurisdiction over the proceedings for which the surrender is requested in the issuing state. The next step is to determine in light of the specific concerns expressed by the requested person whether substantial grounds exist to assume that he or she will be exposed to the risk of a violation of the right to an independent tribunal after his or her surrender. Case C-216/18 *LM* [2018] ECLI:EU:C:2018:586, paras 68, 74–75; Joined Cases C-404/15 & C-659/15 *Aranyosi & Căldăraru* [2016] ECLI:EU:C:2016:198, para 94.

[70] On the discussion of extending the fundamental rights exception to other fundamental rights than Article 4 and 47 CFR see Šubic (2020).

that in the concrete situation the requested person will be subjected to violations of Articles 49 and 47 CFR after being surrendered to the issuing state.

However, as already explained in Chap. 4, it is questionable whether the risks of a violation of Article 49 CFR and the right to a tribunal established by law in Article 47 CFR could qualify as exceptional circumstances.[71] The CJEU has so far only accepted the application of a fundamental rights exception in relation to Article 4 CFR and the right to an independent tribunal in Article 47 CFR, and it has based this acceptance on very specific reasons. With regard to Article 4 CFR, one of the main reasons for allowing the exception to mutual trust was that it constitutes an absolute fundamental right.[72] In relation to Article 47 CFR, the fact that judicial independence is an essential element of the right to a fair trial which is in turn an important aspect of the rule of law on which the EU is founded played an important role.[73] Even though it can be argued that both Article 49 CFR and the right to a tribunal established by law in Article 47 CFR also contribute to the rule of law, whether the CJEU would allocate the same essential role to these fundamental rights as to the right to an independent judge remains yet unclear and undecided.

Besides the doubts as to whether the CJEU would consider possible violations of the transnational legality principle as exceptional circumstances justifying a deviation from mutual trust, this fundamental rights route for the integration of the transnational legality principle in the surrender procedure is, in my view, an unsuitable one in light of the following important drawbacks it can have. Firstly, it may be difficult to find the necessary objective and updated information to pass the first test regarding general and systemic deficiencies. Most of the sources of information and evidence referred to by the CJEU are external sources, such as relatively recent ECHR judgements, CPT reports on detention conditions or reasoned proposals addressed by the Commission to the Council on the basis of Article 7(1) TEU.[74] Such information may not exist or be available on the right to a tribunal established by law or the *nullum crimen sine lege* principle.

Secondly, the CJEU considers the two possibilities to end a surrender procedure because of fundamental rights concerns as exceptional ones and in each particular case the twofold test needs to be met.[75] The national case law shows that in legal practice the twofold step, in particular the one for Article 47 CFR, is not easily met.[76] For instance, in Ireland the flagrant denial of justice test applies in the context of the

---

[71] Section 4.2.6.

[72] Joined Cases C-404/15 & C-659/15 *Aranyosi and Căldăraru* [2016] EU:C:2016:198, paras 83–87.

[73] Case C-216/18 *LM* [2018] ECLI:EU:C:2018:586, paras 48–54.

[74] Case C-216/18 *LM* [2018] ECLI:EU:C:2018:586, para 61; Joined Cases C-404/15 & C-659/15 *Aranyosi & Căldăraru* [2016] ECLI:EU:C:2016:198, para 89; Konstadinides (2019), p. 752.

[75] An automatic refusal of the execution of an EAW issued by a particular Member State is only allowed in the context of the Article 7(2) TEU procedure. Case C-216/18 *LM* [2018] ECLI:EU: C:2018:586, paras 43, 69, 73. See also Konstadinides (2019), p. 751.

[76] Konstadinides (2019), p. 753. On the implementation of the *LM* ruling in national case law see Wahl (2020), pp. 323–327.

second step, which is a standard that is often difficult to meet.[77] In addition, the case law of the Amsterdam District Court reveals that despite the amount of times that Article 47 CFR concerns are raised in the procedure, the court is reluctant to deny the surrender of the requested person on the basis of these arguments.[78] Furthermore, national courts could have different opinions as to the question when the twofold test is met, which could result in different standards of fundamental rights protection.[79] Hence, it is very well possible that due to the difficulty to meet the twofold test as implemented in the national surrender procedures and the possible differences in the application of this test, the surrender procedure will only in a small amount of cases be ended because of the risk of violations of the transnational legality principle in the issuing state.

Thirdly, it is in theory possible that the executing judicial authorities of the Member States adopt a more lenient approach towards the fulfilment of the twofold test in relation to the transnational legality principle. However, such an approach has its own drawbacks, since it can result in a high amount of refusals, which threatens the security of the AFSJ.[80] In other words, a fierce protection of the fundamental rights in Articles 47 and 49 CFR in the context of the surrender procedure could severely affect the security of the AFSJ and the safety of EU citizens.

Lastly, extending the fundamental rights exception offered by Opinion 2/13 is in conflict with the objective of the FDEAW which is to offer a simple and efficient surrender procedure on the basis of mutual recognition. Applying refusal grounds or other bars to surrender which are not explicitly included in Articles 3-4A FDEAW collides with the principle of mutual recognition which in its purest form means automatic recognition and enforcement of judicial decisions. In addition, to be able to judge whether the requested person runs the risk of being subjected to a violation of Articles 49 and 47 CFR in the issuing state, the executing judicial authority may have to acquire knowledge on the general criminal justice system of the issuing state and its compliance with fundamental rights obligations.[81] This may be a time-consuming process which could delay the execution of EAWs and contradicts the idea of a high level of confidence in relation to fundamental rights compliance that is deemed to exist among the EU Member States.

---

[77] *The Minister for Justice and Equality v Celmer No.5* [201] IEHC 639, paras 6, 70. See also *Lis v Poland* [2018] EWHC 2848, [2018] 10 WLUK 450 and the discussion of this case in Simonelli (2019), pp. 329–341. See also Case C-396/11 *Radu* [2013] ECLI:EU:C:2013:39, Opinion of AG Sharpston, para 83.

[78] An exception is the case Rb. Amsterdam 10 February 2021, ECLI:NL:RBAMS:2021:420 (Amsterdam District Court). In this decision the Amsterdam District Court determined that the twofold test was met. Consequently, the EAW, issued by Poland, was not executed.

[79] See Simonelli (2019), pp. 329–341. The author compares the interpretation of the twofold test by an English and an Irish court. See also Bárd and Van Ballegooij (2016), p. 460.

[80] See also Konstadinides (2019), p. 753.

[81] See also Joined Cases C-566/19 & C-626/19 *JR &YC* [2019] ECLI:EU:C:2019:1012, Opinion of AG Campos Sánchez-Bordona, para 100.

11.5 Conclusions and Observations

This chapter has explained that the transnational perspective on the EAW questions the current state-focused interpretation of the legality principle. It can be argued that in an AFSJ in which a specific group of individuals is designated as EU citizens who are provided with free movement rights, transnational crime-fighting instruments need to be counterbalanced by a transnational fundamental rights framework. In this light, the *nullum crimen sine lege* principle and the right to a tribunal established by law should be adapted in conformity with the normative context of the AFSJ described in Article 3(2) TEU as has been done before for the *ne bis in idem* principle. With regard to the transnational interpretation of Article 49 CFR, Sect. 11.3 proposed that criminal offences and sanctions are not sufficiently accessible and foreseeable when the application of the national criminal law of which they are part was not foreseeable at the time of the offence. In light of the free movement dimension of the AFSJ, EU citizens should in principle only have to know and abide by the law of the host state, which is the state they choose by (not) exercising their free movement rights. However, in light of the security objective of the AFSJ and the legitimate interests of other Member States than the host state, exceptions to the transnational interpretation of Article 49 CFR are allowed if the law ensures that the discretion to decide on a particular national criminal law in a concrete case is sufficiently demarcated to avoid arbitrary prosecutions, convictions and sanctions. Furthermore, a transnational interpretation of the right to a tribunal established by law in Article 47 CFR would mean that a tribunal is only established by law when the national jurisdiction of which it is part is appointed on the basis of a set of rules that ensures reasonable forum decisions in light of the good administration of justice. More specifically, the law should adequately restrict the power granted to the competent decision-making authorities to avoid arbitrary forum choices.

Section 11.4 explained that the transnational interpretation of Articles 49 and 47 CFR could turn the surrender procedure into an enforcement mechanism for violations of these fundamental rights in practice. The EAW can ensure the surrender of the requested person to a state whose jurisdiction claim is incompatible with the transnational legality principle. In addition, it follows from Sect. 11.4 that the current EU legal framework for the surrender procedure does not offer national legislators and competent authorities the necessary tools to avoid this possible effect from occurring in concrete cases. The possible options for integrating the transnational legality principle in the EAW procedure that can be derived from the FDEAW as interpreted in the CJEU case law come with significant drawbacks, including for other valid interests, such as security and safety. Hence, in my opinion, additional EU legislative action is required to avoid the EAW from becoming an enforcement mechanism for violations of the transnational legality principle. Such legislative action could be the amendment of the FDEAW which ensures that the issuing or execution of EAWs is prevented when the surrender of the requested person would result in a violation of Articles 49 and 47 CFR. Another possibility is to adopt EU measures preventing or solving conflicts of jurisdiction on the basis of Article 82(1)

(b) TFEU and then adapt the FDEAW in conformity with this legislation. The latter option could transform the surrender procedure into a mechanism facilitating prosecution by the most appropriate state. These two options are further elaborated on in Chap. 13, which provides concrete recommendations for EU legislative actions. The next chapter first discusses the possibility of EU citizenship as a vehicle towards the transnational legality principle as discussed in Sect. 11.3. For this purpose, Chap. 12 introduces two EU citizenship narratives on the basis of the development of EU citizenship as described in the previous chapters. We will see that one of these narratives of EU citizenship closely aligns with the previous conclusion regarding the necessity of EU legislative action.

References

Altena J (2016) Het legaliteitsbeginsel en de doorwerking van Europees recht. Meijers-reeks

Bárd P, Van Ballegooij W (2016) Mutual recognition and individual rights. Did the court get it right? New J Eur Crim Law 7:439

Böse M (2013) Choice of forum and jurisdiction. In: Luchtman M (ed) Choice of forum in cooperation against EU financial crime. Freedom, security and justice and the protection of specific EU-interests. Eleven International Publishing

Böse M (2014) Fundamental rights of the EU-charter. In: Böse M, Meyer F, Schneider A (eds) Conflicts of jurisdiction in criminal matters in the European Union. Volume II: rights, principles and model rules. Nomos

Corstens G, Borgers M, Kooijmans T (eds) (2018) Het Nederlands Strafprocesrecht. Kluwer

Eicker A (2005) Zur Vermeidung simultaner Strafverfahren im zwischenstaatlichen Kontext: Modell einer (über)individuell-konkreten Kriterien Gewichtung. StV:631

Eser A (2012) Kritische Würdigung der Modellentwürfe eines Regelungsmechanismus zur Vermeidung von Jurisdiktionskonflikten. In: Sinn A (ed) Jurisdiktionskonflikte bei grenzüberschreitender Kriminalität. Ein Rechtsvergleich zum Internationalen Strafrecht. V&R Unipress

Franken S (2013) The perspective of the Defence lawyer. In: Luchtman M (ed) Choice of forum in cooperation against EU financial crime. Freedom, security and justice and the protection of specific EU-interests. Eleven International Publishing

Fuchs H (2006) Regulation of jurisdiction and substnative criminal law. In: Schünemann B (ed) Ein Gesamtkonzept für die europäische Strafrechtspflege. Heymanns

Glerum V (2013) De weigeringsgronden bij uitlevering en overlevering – Een vergelijking en kritische evaluatie in het licht van het beginsel van wederzijdse erkenning. Wolf Legal Publishers

Gleß S (2015) Bird's-eye view and worm's-eye view: towards a defendant-based approach in transnational criminal law. Transnatl Legal Theory 6:117

Gropp W (2012) Kollision nationaler Strafgewalten – nulla prosecutio transnationalis sine lege. In: Sinn A (ed) Jurisdiktionskonflikte bei grenzüberschreitender Kriminalität. Ein Rechtsvergleich zum Internationalen Strafrecht. V&R Unipress

Konstadinides T (2019) Judicial independence and the rule of law in the context of non-execution of a European arrest warrant: *LM*. Common Mark Law Rev 56:743

Luchtman M (2011) Choice of forum in an area of freedom, security and justice. Utrecht Law Rev 7:74

Luchtman M (2013) Choice of forum and the prosecution of cross-border crime in the European Union – what role for the legality principle? In: Luchtman M (ed) Choice of forum in cooperation against EU financial crime. Freedom, security and justice and the protection of specific EU-interests. Eleven International Publishing

Luchtman M (2017) Transnationale rechtshandhaving: Over fundamentele rechten in de Europese strafrechtelijke samenwerking. Boom

Luchtman M (2020) Transnational law enforcement cooperation – fundamental rights in European cooperation in criminal matters. Eur J Crime Crim Law Crim Just 28:14

Mancano L (2019a) Storming the bastille: detention conditions, the right to liberty and the case for approximation in EU law. Common Mark Law Rev 56:61

Mancano L (2019b) The European Union and deprivation of liberty. A legislative and judicial analysis from the perspective of the individual. Hart

Meyer F (2014) An area of freedom, security and justice. In: Böse M, Meyer F, Schneider A (eds) Conflicts of jurisdiction in criminal matters in the European Union. Volume II: rights, principles and model rules. Nomos

Ouwerkerk J (2015) Criminal justice beyond national sovereignty. An alternative perspective on the Europeanisation of criminal law. Eur J Crime Crim Law Crim Just 23:11

Panzavolta M (2013) Choice of forum and the lawful judge concept. In: Luchtman M (ed) Choice of forum in cooperation against EU financial crime. Freedom, security and justice and the protection of specific EU-interests. Eleven International Publishing

Schönberger C (2015) Positive transnationale Jurisdiktionskonflikte – Causae, rechtliche Lösungsnotwendigkeit und -konzepte. Schulthess Verlag

Sicurella R (2018) Fostering a European criminal law culture: in trust we trust. New J Eur Crim Law 9:308

Simonelli M (2019) "...And justice for all?" the right to an independent tribunal after the ruling of the court of justice in *LM*. New J Eur Crim Law 10:329

Sinn A (2013) Die Vermeidung von strafrechtlichen Jurisdiktionskonflikten in der Europäischen Union – Gegenwart und Zukunft. ZIS 1:1

Šubic N (2020) Resisting a European arrest warrant: a social perspective. New J Eur Crim Law 11: 299

Thorhauer N (2015) Conflicts of jurisdiction in cross-border criminal cases in the area of freedom, security, and justice. Risks and opportunities from an individual rights-oriented perspective. New J Eur Crim Law 6:78

Thorhauer N (2019) Jurisdiktionskonflikte im Rahmen transnationaler Kriminalität. Zur Koordination der Strafgewalten über natürliche Personen und Unternehmen in der Europäischen Union. Dike Verlag and Nomos

Van der Beken T, Lagodny O, Vermeulen G (2002) Kriterien für die jeweils Strafgewalt in Europa – Zur Lösung von Strafgewaltskonflikten jenseits eines transnationalen Ne-bis-in-idem. NStZ:624

Wahl T (2020) Refusal of European arrest warrants due to fair trial infringements. review of the CJEU's Judgment in "LM" by National Courts in Europe. EUcrim 4:321

Wolswijk H (2013) Country report the Netherlands. In: Böse M, Meyer F, Schneider A (eds) Conflicts of jurisdiction in criminal matters in the European Union. Volume I: national reports and comparative analysis. Nomos

Chapter 12
EU Citizenship as a Vehicle Towards a Transnational Legality Principle: Two Possible Narratives

12.1 Introduction

The previous chapters have elaborated on the development of EU citizenship as such and more specifically its position in the AFSJ. They have shown two interlinked ways in which EU citizenship could be a vehicle towards fundamental rights protection, which is as an essential argument against the intergovernmental perspective on the EAW and as a crucial building block of the transnational perspective. The latter clashes with the current state-focused interpretation of fundamental rights and constitutes the foundation of a transnational legality principle. This chapter adds to these observations regarding the role of EU citizenship by examining how two specific EU citizenship narratives, which can be derived from the development of EU citizenship over time, could contribute to the realisation of the application of the transnational legality principle in the AFSJ. For this purpose, Sect. 12.2 will first elaborate on the two main narratives of EU citizenship, which are free-movement-based EU citizenship (FMB EU citizenship) and representative-democracy-based EU citizenship (RDB EU citizenship). Section 12.3 then takes a conceptual approach, discussing to what extent it is possible to capture these narratives in an existing EU citizenship concept as conceptualisation also affects questions regarding the future role, rights and duties of EU citizens. This is followed by Sects. 12.4 and 12.5, which explain how each of the two EU citizenship narratives could be a vehicle for transnational fundamental rights protection. These sections also describe the drawbacks of each narrative and that they should be viewed as complementing one another. Section 12.6 contains the conclusion.

J. Graat, *The European Arrest Warrant and EU Citizenship*,
https://doi.org/10.1007/978-3-031-07590-2_12

12.2 Two Narratives of EU Citizenship

One of the main conclusions that can be drawn from the analysis of the development of EU citizenship within and outside the context of the AFSJ as described in the previous chapters is that it is quite difficult to determine exactly what EU citizenship entails.[1] In other words, the content of EU citizenship seems quite thin.[2] Article 20 TFEU provides a basic and pragmatic definition, which states that EU citizenship is granted to all nationals of the Member States as an addition to—not a replacement of—national citizenship.[3] Those who fall within this definition are provided with certain rights, but these rights are the consequence of the status of EU citizenship and not part of the definition itself. In addition, the CJEU has in its case law often referred to EU citizenship as the future 'fundamental status' of the nationals of the Member States but has not clarified what this fundamental status encompasses exactly.[4] Hence, the definition provided in the Treaty and the classification of EU citizenship as a 'fundamental status' in the CJEU case law do not tell us much about the actual content or meaning of EU citizenship.

However, what does follow from the previous chapters, in particular Sects. 2.2 and 10.8, is the development of an EU citizenship which goes beyond national citiziensship by providing EU citizens with the right to cross borders. The strong and clear link between EU citizenship and free movement constitutes the foundation of the first narrative, which I call FMB EU citizenship.[5] This narrative is, for instance, based on the introduction of a so-called fifth fundamental right to free movement by the Treaty of Maastricht which is not linked to the general objective to establish an internal market.[6] This free movement right for EU citizens has also been strongly protected in the CJEU case law, including in cases dealing with criminal justice issues in the AFSJ. In relation to the latter, the evolution of FMB EU citizenship is

[1] Luchtman (2020), p. 15. See also Coutts (2019); Eleftheriadis (2014), pp. 777–778; Neuvonen (2017).

[2] De Witte views EU citizenship as procedural citizenship, which relates to communitarian solidarity. The author states, 'Communitarian solidarity in the EU does not see to the production of a catalogue of substantive rights for all EU citizens, nor does it seek to mirror the role of national citizenship in reflecting the normative quality of a polity. Rather, it seeks to reassess national conceptions of belonging, and asks Member States to rethink who the members of their 'community of care' are—not based on lazy ideas of nationality, ancestral lineage, or ethnic belonging, but on conceptually more sophisticated ideas such as reciprocity deriving from the social relationship between a migrant citizen and the host state polity.' In this light, procedural EU citizenship constitutes the entitlement to communitarian solidarity arrangements in the different Member States, which also depend on the link between the EU citizen and the Member State in question. De Witte (2015), pp. 123–139. See also Seubert (2019), pp. 55–56.

[3] Douglas-Scott (1998), p. 34.

[4] Case C-184/99 *Grzelczyk* [2001] ECLI:EU:C:2001:458, para 31; Case C-224/98 *D'Hoop* [2002] ECLI:EU:C:2002:432, para 28; Case C-148/02 *Garcia Avello* [2003] ECLI:EU:C:2003:539, paras 22-23; Case C-224/02 *Pusa* [2004] ECLI:EU:C:2004:273, para 16.

[5] See Strumia (2020), pp. 509–512.

[6] TFEU, art 21.

confirmed and strengthened in two particular strings of post-Lisbon case law. The first string prohibits national measures and actions in the field of criminal justice which hamper the exercise of free movement on the basis of Article 21 TFEU or which violate the non-discrimination clause in Article 18 TFEU. In these judgements the right to free movement is developed into an *Abwehrrecht*, setting the parameters within which the Member States may act.[7] The second string of case law consists of the *Petruhhin* and post-*Petruhhin* rulings in which the CJEU offers protection to EU citizens exercising their right to free movement from being removed from the territory of the EU as a result of an extradition request.[8]

EU citizenship has also evolved outside the context of free movement. This is illustrated by the *Rottman*, *Zambrano* and post-*Zambrano* case law, in which the CJEU, very carefully and on a more *ad hoc* basis, puts more flesh on the bones of EU citizenship. It follows from this case law that EU citizens who have not exercised their free movement rights can still be protected against certain national measures when the application of these measures would result in the removal of the EU citizen from the territory of the EU. As explained in Chap. 2, the *Zambrano* string of case law still has a link to free movement, but from a different perspective, since it focuses on the potential future exercise of free movement rights. In essence, the case law constitutes a small step towards 'self-standing' rights derived from Article 20 TFEU for 'static EU citizens' who have not exercised their free movement right.[9]

In addition, the development of EU citizenship outside the free movement context is reflected in the replacement of the intergovernmental legislative procedure for criminal justice measures with the ordinary legislative procedure.[10] The latter allocates the right of initiative to the European Commission who proposes a legislative measure to the Council and the European Parliament, which both need to consent.[11] As a result of this equal position of the Council and the European Parliament—pre-Lisbon the European Parliament only had to be consulted on proposed criminal justice measures—EU citizens are both directly and indirectly represented at the EU legislative level. Firstly, they are directly represented by the European Parliament, which they elect by direct universal suffrage.[12] In this light, it also is interesting to note that the CJEU already stated in van *Gend en Loos* that 'it must be noted that the nationals of the states brought together in the Community are called upon to cooperate in the functioning of this Community through the

[7] See also Sects. 10.4.2.2 and 10.5.3.1.

[8] See Sect. 10.5.3.2.

[9] See Sect. 2.2.1.

[10] See eg TFEU, art 82(1). See also Sects. 2.2.2 and 10.5.1.1.

[11] The right of initiative can also be exercised by a quarter of the Member States. Furthermore, despite the role of the European Commission in the legislative process, the treaties state that only the European Parliament and the Council have legislative functions. In this book, any reference to the legislative procedure or legislative process will, however, include the stage in which the Commission uses the right of initiative and provides the official EU legislator with a legislative proposal. TFEU, arts 76 and 294; TEU, art 17(1-2).

[12] TEU, arts 10(2) and 14(2-3). De Wilde (2014), p. 127.

intermediary of the European Parliament'.[13] Secondly, EU citizens are represented in the European Council which consists of the heads of state and government, and in the Council of Ministers which consists of the national Ministers responsible for the subject matter in question.[14] Article 10(2) TEU states that these two institutions represent the Member States, and that its members are accountable to their national parliaments and therefore to their citizens. Hence, through national elections for national parliaments, who task is generally to supervise the actions of the executive power, the nationals of the Member States, which are also EU citizens, are in this case indirectly represented in both the European Council and the Council of Ministers.[15]

Hence, it can be concluded that with the replacement of the more intergovernmental legislation procedure for the ordinary legislative procedure, EU citizenship has become more integrated in the EU as a representative democracy in which the politicians who have the power to make decisions are elected by the people and exercise these powers in the name of the people.[16] In the specific context of the EU, the representative democracy entails that the two main stakeholders, including both the EU citizens and the Member States, are represented at the Union level.[17] Hence, besides the narrative of FMB EU citizenship, the development of EU citizenship over time also shows a narrative of EU citizenship as a cornerstone of the EU's representative democracy, which I refer to as RDB EU citizenship.

---

[13] Case C-26/62 *Van Gend & Loos* [1963] ECLI:EU:C:1963:1. In addition, in *Roquette Frères* the CJEU stated that the consultation role of the EP in the legislative process 'reflects at Community level the fundamental democratic principle that the peoples should take part in the exercise of power through the intermediary of a representative assembly'. Case C-138/79 *Roquette Frères* [1980] ECLI:EU:C:1980:249, para 33.

[14] TEU, art 10(2). In relation to the composition of the Council see TEU, art 16(2).

[15] Lock (2019), pp. 109–110; De Wilde (2014), p. 127. However, in the legal literature, the sidenote is sometimes made that the European Council and the Council do not represent EU citizens as such, but the nationals of the Member States. The responsibility of each Head of State and each Minister is in principle to their electorate, meaning the nationals of the state, either directly or via the national parliaments. See eg Schütze (2017), p. 84; Lock (2019), p.110 and the sources referred to in footnote 15 and 16.

[16] The EU as a representative democracy is part of the EU's Democratic Principles laid down in title II TEU.The Treaty of Lisbon is the first treaty which allocates a specific title to the Democratic Principles of the EU. TEU, art 10; Peers (2017), pp. 37–38; Schütze (2017), p. 81; Lock (2019a), p. 110.

[17] TEU, art 10(1-2). However, there is still a lot of discussion on the existence of democratic deficits in the EU legislative process and the need to enhance the EU as a representative democracy. On this discussion, see eg Lock (2019b), p. 102; Alemanno (2020).

12.3 How to Conceptualise EU Citizenship: What's in a Name?

The development of EU citizenship as described above has in the academic literature been approached from a conceptual perspective in light of the question how EU citizenship is and should be viewed as well as which role it could have in the advancement of the AFSJ and the rights and obligations of the EU citizen. Over time, many different possible concepts of EU citizenship have been presented which provide different answers to these questions. However, no consensus seems to exist on the best conceptual model to describe the status quo of all that EU citizenship entails or a conceptual model that constitutes the foundation for future developments.[18] In this light, the next paragraphs will briefly reflect on market citizenship, cosmopolitan citizenship, republican citizenship and composite citizenship which all seem to fit in some way with the development of EU citizenship discussed above and in the previous chapters.

Firstly, the academic literature shows a discussion on the classification of EU citizenship as market citizenship in light of its strong link with free movement. The concept of market EU citizenship does not include the capacity of EU citizens to engage in public life for the purpose of creating and ordering civil society. Instead, as market citizens, EU citizens are primarily viewed as economic actors who contribute to the establishment of the internal market in light of which they are provided with fundamental free movement rights.[19] The concept of market citizenship also constitutes an exclusionary form of EU citizenship, since those who do not offer an economic contribution to the internal market, in principle do not enjoy EU citizenship rights, including free movement and protection against discrimination on the basis of nationality.[20] However, as a result of the changes brought about by the Treaty of Lisbon which directly connects EU citizenship to the AFSJ and the development of EU citizenship beyond free movement for economic purposes, this exclusionary character of the concept of market citizenship questions its remaining relevance. It has been argued that the free movement right codified in Article 21 TFEU which is granted to all EU citizens is of another character than the internal market free movement rights. This so-called fifth free movement right is not intended as a functional freedom for the establishment of the internal market, but as a goal in itself. It is in fact intended to be an inherent part of being an EU citizen.[21]

Secondly, those who do not believe in the remaining dominance of market citizenship have approached the development of EU citizenship from the perspective of, for instance, cosmopolitan citizenship, republican citizenship and composite

[18] Douglas-Scott (1998), p. 29.

[19] See O'Brien (2017), p. 33; Van Eijken (2014), p. 11. See also Everson (2012).

[20] Douglas-Scott (1998), pp. 36-37; Strumia (2020), p. 512.

[21] C-378/97 *Wijsenbeek* [1999] ECLI:EU:C:1999:144, Opinion of AG Cosmas, paras 84-86; Van Eijken (2014), pp. 11-12. See also Case C-158/07 *Förster* [2008] ECLI:EU:C:2008:399, Opinion of AG Mazák, para 54.

citizenship. Cosmopolitan citizenship constitutes a very inclusive form of citizenship and in that sense it represents the opposite site of the spectra in comparison to market citizenship. It recognises the EU citizen as an individual independent of his or her membership to a particular social, cultural or political community.[22] Rights can be claimed solely on the basis of common humanity.[23] In this light, the idea of the EU citizen as a cosmopolitan citizen goes well with the view that human rights are universal and granted to all human beings.[24] It would also fit well with the idea that a solution to the problems caused by unforeseeable jurisdiction claims and the lack of an EU system for forum choices as well as the EAW as a mechanism for the transfer of citizens in these situations should be offered to all individuals and not just the nationals of the Member States.

Thirdly, as a result of the changes made by the EU—for the AFSJ primarily in the Treaty of Lisbon—to repair the democratic deficits in its legislation process, EU citizenship could also have a link to republican citizenship. This concept of citizenship has a legal and ethical dimension, of which the former covers the right to participate in public and political affairs, and the latter the expectation that the citizen exercises this right actively and in a well-informed manner, placing community interests over personal interests.[25] Because of the civic virtue included in this concept, which nowadays means active participation in public affairs and commitment to the common good, the republican citizen is also referred to as the 'good citizen'.[26]

Lastly, another possibly fitting concept of EU citizenship is composite EU citizenship, which links EU citizens to different layers of the multi-layered European legal order. The latter includes the local legal order, the national legal order, the EU legal order and sometimes the international legal order.[27] The institutions at the different levels have within their own field of competences their own responsibilities towards citizens. In this setting, EU citizenship itself is composed of different statuses, rights and duties which are derived from the different government layers in the EU multi-layered legal order.[28] A concrete example of this form of citizenship can be found in the area of fundamental rights protection, since the EU citizen is protected by different fundamental rights mechanisms, such as the ECHR, the CFR and national (constitutional) laws, which can both complement or

[22] Seubert (2018), p. 198.

[23] Seubert (2018), p. 198. See also Benhabib (2004), p. 21.

[24] Hloušek and Koska (2018), p. 167. See also Benhabib (2011), pp. 1–20.

[25] Under the Greek and Roman concept of republican citizenship, those without the right to participate in political affairs were not citizens, even though they were subjects of the law and may even have had some rights. Dagger (2002), pp. 149–150.

[26] Dagger (2002), p. 149; Van Gunsteren (1998), p. 21; Douglas-Scott (1998), p. 43.

[27] See Case C-300/04 *Eman* [2006] ECLI:EU:C:2006:545; Van Eijken (2014), p. 156.

[28] Van Eijken (2014), pp. 233–234, 237; Hanneke van Eijken and others, 'Exploring Obstacles in Exercising Core EU Citizenship Rights' <http://beucitizen.eu/wp-content/uploads/D7.3-FINAL.pdf> accessed 20 September 2021, 4.

contradict each other.[29] In relation to the problems EU citizens may face that are discussed in this book, we have seen that currently neither the CFR nor the ECHR offers clear protection. Only some national legal orders solve this lack of protection to a certain extent, like Germany where the national Constitution protects German nationals against surrender when they did not have to expect the application of foreign criminal laws. Hence, this also shows that there may still be gaps in the protection of EU citizens' fundamental rights in the multi-layered legal order.

So, it is quite difficult to capture EU citizenship, more specifically the two narratives on EU citizenship discussed in the previous section, within one existing concept. However, the academic debate set out above does reflect two distinguishable mainstreams on the conceptualisation of EU citizenship. The first one believes that market citizenship is still dominant, while the second one believes that EU citizenship goes beyond market citizenship.[30] The narratives of the EU citizen as a moving citizen and the EU citizen as part of the EU's representative democracy fall within the second category as follows from the fact that the Treaty of Lisbon ensures a stronger integration of the EU citizen in the EU legislative process for the adoption of most criminal justice measures, including mutual recognition instruments. Furthermore, the CJEU has fiercely protected the right to free movement both in and outside the context of the AFSJ. In this light, I am of the opinion that it is difficult to hold on to the view that the EU citizen is exclusively a factor of production contributing to the establishment of the internal market. I would argue that even though we do not know where the departure from market citizenship will take us exactly with regard to the meaning of EU citizenship, the development seems to come with a certain promise of a more inclusive EU citizenship. In light of this conclusion the next sections discuss to what extent the two narratives of EU citizenship, which show the promise of a more inclusive EU citizenship, could constitute vehicles towards a transnational legality principle in the AFSJ.

12.4 The Narrative of FMB EU Citizenship

12.4.1 FMB EU Citizenship as a Vehicle Towards a Transnational Legality Principle

As a vehicle towards a transnational legality principle, the narrative of FMB EU citizenship has, in my opinion, a twofold role which is closely linked to the role which the right to free movement can have in bringing a case within the scope of application of the CFR explained in Sects. 3.2 and 11.3.1. Firstly, the exercise of free movement by the EU citizen contributes to exposing the issues concerning the

---

[29] Another example presented by the author are electoral rights. Van Eijken et al. (2015), p. 253; Van Eijken (2016), p. 257; Van Eijken (2014), p. 235.

[30] See also Strumia (2020), pp. 511–512.

foreseeability of jurisdiction claims and forum decisions without a transparent legal framework which can arise as a result of this decision. As explained before the exercise of free movement rights increases the risk of the occurrence of these possible complications. In that light, it has also been argued in Sect. 11.2 that the current lack of a solution or even unambiguous recognition of these possible issues on the EU and national level is difficult to understand. It clashes with the fact that EU citizens are provided with free movement rights and not merely free movement possibilities.

Closely connected to the observation that FMB EU citizenship lays bare the possible complications in question, is the second observation that the exercise of the right to free movement could also open the door to the adoption of a transnational legality principle by the CJEU. In concrete cases in which EU citizens have exercised the right to free movement and are confronted with one of the two complications, national courts may or must refer preliminary questions to the CJEU asking whether such complications in fact mean that national jurisdiction rules or national rules regarding the decision to prosecute restrict the right to free movement.[31] In case the national measures in fact constitute barriers to the right to free movement, which as explained in Sect. 3.2.3 is not a certainty, Member States have to rely on justification grounds provided by the treaties or accepted under the rule of reason. As described in Sect. 11.3.1, this brings the national measures within the scope of the CFR as these justifications grounds need to be interpreted in light of EU fundamental rights. This is clearly illustrated by the *Carpenter* case, in which the CJEU first decided that the national measure in question violated the right to family life and then balanced respect for this fundamental right against the justification ground for the national measure to determine whether it was a justified restriction of free movement.[32] Hence, when assessing whether national jurisdiction rules constitute a justified interference with free movement, the CJEU could consider the compliance of these national rules with Articles 49 and 47 CFR and in that context adopt a transnational interpretation of these fundamental rights.

In case the CJEU uses this possibility, it also needs to determine whether the national jurisdiction rule in the concrete case constitutes a violation of the transnational legality principle which outbalances the submitted justification for its existence, for instance, the prevention of impunity. If this is the case, the national rule constitutes an unjustified restriction of the right to free movement and may in light of the supremacy of EU law not be applied.[33] Consequently, the EU citizen could not be subjected to the criminal jurisdiction of that particular state whose power to issue an EAW is also blocked, unless it can exercise jurisdiction on the basis of another principle. In case the EU citizen has not yet been surrendered to this state, the ruling of the CJEU could, therefore, protect him or her against the EAW functioning as an

[31] TFEU, art 267.

[32] In that specific case, the CJEU conducted the balancing exercise in the context of the proportionality assessment. See Sect. 3.2.3.1.

[33] Case C-6/64 *Costa* [1964] ECLI:EU:C:1964:66.

enforcement mechanism for violations of the transnational legality principle.[34] However, it may be the case that the EU citizen has already been surrendered to the prosecuting state whose jurisdiction claim is then invalidated by its classification as an unjustified interference with free movement. In these situations, the EU citizen has in fact been subjected to the EAW as an enforcement mechanism for violations of the transnational legality principle, as he or she has been surrendered to a state whose jurisdiction claim was not in compliance with this principle.

It follows from the above that FMB EU citizenship could potentially open the door to the adoption of a transnational legality principle. In case the CJEU uses this door and concludes that the national jurisdiction rule in question constitutes an unjustified interference with the right to free movement, the application of the national jurisdiction rule in the concrete case is prohibited and with that the surrender of the requested person could be prevented. However, the next sections explain why, in my opinion, this narrative is on its own not a suitable vehicle towards a transnational legality principle and why it should only be followed in combination with the narrative of RDB EU citizenship.

12.4.2 The Drawbacks of This Narrative and its (Un)suitability

The narrative of FMB EU citizenship as a vehicle towards a transnational legality principle has several disadvantages. The first three to be discussed show that the narrative of FMB EU citizenship comes with an ample amount of more practical hurdles for realising a transnational interpretation of the legality principle and preventing the EAW from functioning as an enforcement mechanism for violations of this principle. In this light, the first disadvantage of the narrative of FMB EU citizenship is that the adoption of a transnational legality principle and the conclusion that its violation outweighs other interests is dependent on a lot of different steps in the legal framework for assessing national measures in light of the right to free movement. As follows from the above, national courts first have to issue preliminary questions, which they are only obliged to do when they are the court of last instance in the concrete case. The CJEU then has to classify the national jurisdiction rule as a barrier to free movement. If this condition is met the CJEU needs to adopt a new interpretation of Articles 49 and 47 CFR, assess whether these rights are violated and conduct a proportionality assessment.

Besides this substantial amount of conditions that needs to be satisfied, it is also in no way certain that the CJEU would reach the required conclusions in every step of the process in each concrete case. As already explained before, the case law of the CJEU does, for instance, not provide a conclusive answer to the question whether national jurisdiction rules, more specifically unforeseeable jurisdiction

[34] Section 11.4.

claims constitute barriers to free movement, because they cause serious inconveniences in the private and professional life of the EU citizen.[35] The decision of the CJEU with regard to this question in possible future cases will most likely also depend on the specific circumstances of the situation and the content of the national jurisdiction rule. The court could, for instance, reach a different conclusion in relation to jurisdiction on the basis of the effects doctrine than in relation to jurisdiction on the basis of the active nationality principle. Furthermore, if this first condition is met and the CJEU is willing to go as far as to adopt a transnational legality principle, it is in no way guaranteed that in each case the respect for this principle will also outweigh the interests which the national jurisdiction rule aims to protect.[36]

In addition, the CJEU could decide that a national jurisdiction rule constitutes a justified barrier to free movement. This conclusion could provide an incentive for the EU legislator to adopt EU legislation resolving such barriers, for instance on the basis of Article 82(1)(b) TFEU, but this is not achieved overnight. Furthermore, in the concrete case, the conclusion that the national measure is not an unjustified interference with free movement entails that the national court is not obliged to disapply it in light of the right to free movement. The follow-up question, then, is how the issuing and execution of an EAW can be prohibited when the national measure violates the transnational legality principle, but is not an unjustified interference with the right to free movement. As already explained in Chap. 10, the current legal framework for the surrender procedure itself does not provide adequate tools to prevent the EAW from functioning as an enforcement mechanism for violations of the transnational legality principle in future cases.

Besides the more practical disadvantages of the narrative of FMB, EU citizenship as a vehicle towards a transnational legality principle, it is also dubious for other reasons. Firstly, the narrative of FMB EU citizenship exclusively focuses on the free movement aspect of EU citizenship while Sects. 12.2 and 12.3 have explained that EU citizenship goes beyond free movement. The treaties provide EU citizens with political rights, and they are represented in the EU legislative procedure.[37] This more inclusive concept of EU citizenship does not fit with the development of a transnational legality principle in the specific context of the right to free movement. In relation to this, it is important to remember that not only the moving EU citizen can be confronted with a EAW while jurisdiction claims are not compliant with the

[35] See Sect. 3.2.3.

[36] See e.g. Böse (2014), p. 77. The author argues that the CJEU accepted jurisdiction on the basis of the effects doctrine in the case *Liga Portuguesa de Futebol Profissional*. In this case the free movement of services was hampered by a Portuguese rule on the basis of which a company in Gibraltar was penalized for offering games of chance in Portugal via the internet. The CJEU decided that the national rule prohibiting foreign operators from offering games of chance via the internet in Portugal was a justified interference with the right to free movement in light of its purpose to protect consumers against fraud and crime. Case C-42/07 *Liga Portuguesa de Futebol Profissional* [2009] ECLI:EU:C:2009:519.

[37] For the political rights, see eg TFEU, art 20(2)(b).

transnational legality principle, but non-moving EU citizens and third county nationals, as well.[38] Article 49 and 47 CFR are also not EU citizenship rights, but human rights. Secondly, in my view, this narrative creates undesirable expectations of the CJEU. The court would have the task of adopting a transnational interpretation of fundamental rights and assessing in concrete cases whether the violation of these fundamental rights entails that national jurisdiction rules constitute unjustified interferences with free movement, even though the jurisdiction to prescribe and adjudicate is only to a limited extend regulated by EU law. In my opinion, without such EU legislation the adoption of a transnational legality principle which links jurisdiction and forum decisions to the foreseeability of criminal offences, sanctions and tribunals, has a more undemocratic character. Hence, in my view, the CJEU should not go down the path of adopting a transnational legality principle, which could also profoundly interfere with the sovereignty of the Member States, until the EU legislator has adopted clear and general legislation addressing jurisdiction and forum decisions.

In relation to the last disadvantage, the case law of the CJEU shows that the court also considers the existence of EU legislation when interpreting fundamental rights in the CFR. The next paragraphs illustrate this by discussing the decision of the CJEU in *Taricco II*, *Menci, Melloni* and the *ne bis in idem* case law on Article 54 CISA.[39] *Taricco II* is an example of a case in which the CJEU answers a preliminary question concerning a (potential) clash between fundamental rights and other EU principles and obligations, in particular the obligation to enforce EU law, and in which it emphasises the need for EU legislation. In this case, the CJEU was confronted with the question whether the Italian rules on limitation in criminal proceedings had to be disapplied in cases concerning VAT fraud when they barred the application of effective and deterrent sanctions countering crimes affecting the financial interests of the EU, even though this would violate the national substantive legality principle.[40] Contrary to Article 49 CFR, the Italian *nullum crimen sine lege* principle also covers rules on limitation. The CJEU decided that in the absence of EU legislation on rules on limitation at the material time it was in fact for the national court to decide whether the national legality principle blocked the duty to disapply national rules which hamper the effective enforcement of EU law.[41] Hence, the

---

[38] See also Iglesias Sánchez (2017), pp. 389–391; Van Eijken and Marguery (2017), pp. 567–569; Strumia (2020), p. 512.

[39] See Luchtman (2018), pp. 2687–2689.

[40] Case C-42/17 *M.A.S., M.B* [2017] ECLI:EU:C:2017:936 (*Taricco II*).

[41] See also Case C-378/97 *Wijsenbeek* [1999] ECLI:EU:C:1999:439. *Wijsenbeek* concerned the question of whether criminal penalties for refusing to show your passport when entering the Netherlands violate the right to free movement. The CJEU stated that in the absence of common or harmonised rules on external border controls Member States are allowed to restrict the free movement of citizens, but the criminal penalties may not constitute disproportionate obstacles to free movement. Hence, in the absence of rules on external border control which influence free movement within the EU, the CJEU did not consider the passport control and the criminal penalties a violation of free movement as long as the penalty was not disproportionate. The latter was,

absence of secondary EU legislation on limitation meant that the CJEU did not conduct its own balancing exercise between the two competing interests—foreseeability and effective enforcement of EU law—but left this to the national courts. In this case, the discretion allocated to the national courts favoured fundamental rights protection, but was liable to hamper the effective enforcement of EU law.

In the case *Menci*[42] the CJEU sent the same message as in *Taricco II,* but contrary to the latter, the considerations at the national level favoured the effective enforcement of EU law over the protection offered by the *ne bis in idem* principle. The case concerned the decision of the Italian authorities to start criminal proceedings for not paying VAT within the established time limits while an administrative penalty had already been imposed in the case in question. The CJEU decided that the duplication of procedures and sanctions in case of allegations of VAT offences affecting the financial interest of the Union are allowed as an exception to the *ne bis in idem* principle in Article 50 CFR when the requirements of Article 52(1) CFR are met, including a proportionality test. However, in light of the fact that EU law did not harmonise the applicable penalties for VAT offences, the CJEU established the proportionality test which needed to be applied, but it left the actual application of this test to the national courts. Hence, the CJEU did not decide whether the rules which allowed for a duplication of procedures were in fact justified interferences with Article 50 CFR and did not conduct its own assessment in relation to the balance between the protection of the financial interests of the Union and the protection of the individual against interferences with the *ne bis in idem* principle, which protects free movement. Hence, *Taricco II* and *Menci* show that in the absence of secondary EU legislation on the matter at hand, the CJEU refrains from conducting its own balancing exercise between two competing interests of which fundamental rights protection was one as well as from developing a transnational interpretation of the fundamental rights in question.

The opposite, namely the adaption of fundamental rights in conformity with the normative context of the AFSJ when the matter in question is regulated by EU law, is illustrated by the *ne bis in idem* jurisprudence regarding Article 54 CISA.[43] When confronted with preliminary questions on this fundamental right, the CJEU could rely on the rules in Articles 54–58 CISA. In its case law, the CJEU has also stated that neither the treaty provisions on judicial cooperation nor the Schengen agreement and CISA make the application of the *ne bis in idem* principle conditional upon EU harmonisation or approximation of the criminal laws of the Member States.[44] Consequently, the court has interpreted the *ne bis in idem* principle in light of Article

however, for the national courts to determine. See also Case C-310/16 *Dzivev* [2019] ECLI:EU:C:2019:30.

[42] Case C-524/15 *Menci* [2018] ECLI:EU:C:2018:197.

[43] Here, I am referring exclusively to the jurisprudence concerning the duplication of criminal prosecutions. See also Sects. 10.4.2.3, 10.5.3.4, and 11.2.

[44] Joined Cases C-187/01 & C-385/01 *Hüseyin Gözütok & Klaus Brügge* [2003] ECLI:EU:C:2003:87, paras 32-33.

3(2) TEU as explained in Chapters 10 and 11. In this light, the CJEU has, for instance, broadened its scope to out-of-court settlements, which is in contrast with the initial intent of the Schengen contracting states not to include such decisions under the protection of *ne bis in idem*.[45] The interpretation of *ne bis in idem* in light of Article 3(2) TEU also follows clearly from the case *Kossowski*. In this case, the CJEU conducted its own assessment and reached its own conclusion with regard to the question whether a national prosecutor's decision to terminate criminal proceedings without carrying out a detailed investigation could be considered as a final decision in light of both objectives of the AFSJ referred to in Article 3(2) TEU.[46]

The *Melloni* case sends a similar message as the *ne bis in idem* jurisprudence. In this case, the Spanish court which had to rule on the execution of an EAW for an *in absentia* judgement applied a constitutional fair trail standard which was higher than the one in the CFR.[47] The national court argued that as a result of its national constitutional standard, the execution of the EAW was dependent on the possibility of a retrial in the issuing state, even though the case fell under the exceptions to the application of the refusal ground covering *in absentia* judgements enumerated in Article 4a FDEAW. The CJEU then ruled that the application of a higher national constitutional fair trial standard is not allowed when it threatens the primacy, unity and effectiveness of EU law. As Article 4a(1) FDEAW in fact harmonises the rules on the recognition on *in absentia* judgements, the CJEU decided that the application of the national fundamental rights standard would compromise the efficiency of the FDEAW.[48] Hence, in this case EU rules existed with regard to the recognition of *in absentia* rulings, as a result of which the CJEU did not open the door to a subsidiarity consideration on the national level and simply concluded that the higher national constitutional fair trial standards had to be set aside in light of the efficiency, primacy and unity of EU law.

On the basis of the case law discussed above, it can be concluded that the CJEU takes the existence of EU legislation into account when interpreting fundamental rights in the CFR.[49] It does not seem willing to act like a constitutional or fundamental rights court, interpreting—and adapting—fundamental rights in conformity with the normative context of the EU when the matter in question has not been regulated by EU law. To put it differently, the CJEU may be less hesitant to formulate its own view on the scope of application of fundamental rights and the balance between fundamental rights and other EU principles when EU rules on the topic exist. Hence, this case law, therefore, also indirectly indicates that the chances are limited that the CJEU will consider or even adopt a transnational legality principle in the context of the free movement route when the national jurisdiction

45 Joined Cases C-187/01 & C-385/01 *Hüseyin Gözütok & Klaus Brügge* [2003] ECLI:EU:C:2003:87, para 40.

46 Case C-486/14 *Kossowski* [2016] ECLI:EU:C:2016:483.

47 Case C-399/11 *Melloni* [2013] ECLI:EU:C:2013:107.

48 Case C-399/11 *Melloni* [2013] ECLI:EU:C:2013:107, paras 55–64.

49 See Luchtman (2018), pp. 2687–2689; Luchtman (2020), pp. 33–35, 42.

measures in the concrete case are not subject to EU rules regulating jurisdiction and/or forum choices.

12.4.3 *Interim Conclusion: The Need for EU Legislative Action*

In my view, it can be concluded that the narrative of FMB EU citizenship is on its own not an ideal vehicle towards a transnational legality principle, especially in light of the fragmented regulation of jurisdiction and forum choices by EU law. Without general rules addressing these matters which have been adopted in a legislative process in which EU citizens and Member States are represented, a transnational interpretation of Articles 49 and 47 CFR affecting the Member States' jurisdiction to prescribe and adjudicate is not appropriate. The same conclusion follows from the CJEU case law, which emphasises the need for EU legislation on a particular topic for the court to conduct its own assessment in case of a clash between fundamental rights and other interests and in order to interpret fundamental rights in light of the normative context of the AFSJ.

Hence, similar to Chap. 11, the conclusion is that EU legislative action is required in the field of jurisdiction and forum decisions. The adoption of EU rules addressing these topics in which the protection of the transnational legality principle is already integrated as well as other important interests in the EU shared legal order—elaborated on in Chap. 13—would provide the CJEU with a set of rules on the basis of which it can interpret Articles 49 and 47 CFR in light of the normative context of the AFSJ. In addition, as is further explained in Chap. 13, the adoption of such EU rules could also solve the risk of the EAW turning into an enforcement mechanism for violations of the transnational legality principle discussed in Sect. 11.4. In light of these conclusions the next section discusses the narrative of RDB EU citizenship, which fits with this need for EU legislation and therefore complements the narrative of FMB EU citizenship.

12.5 The Narrative of RDB EU Citizenship

EU Citizenship: a Cornerstone of the EU's Representative Democracy

A legislative perspective on EU citizenship directs the attention to how citizenship as a cornerstone of the EU's representative democracy may function as a vehicle to create legislation that serves the objectives of the AFSJ as laid down in Article 3(2) TEU and 82(1)(b) TFEU. As stated before, since the Treaty of Lisbon, the European Parliament which directly represents the EU citizen has to approve the adoption of most criminal justice measures. EU citizenship is equally key to the Council, by which EU citizens are indirectly represented, and which has an equal say in the legislative process for criminal justice measures. In other words, EU citizenship is the cornerstone of the EU legislature composed of the European Parliament and Council. Together with the other EU institutions, these institutions have the collective mission to advance EU objectives and serve the interests of the two main stakeholders, including EU citizens and Member States.[50] The powers of the EU legislature are both limited and guided by the EU objectives as well as by the specific obligations for their attainment laid down in the treaties. One of these objectives, which is also formulated as an obligation, is the establishment of an AFSJ in which free movement and protection against cross-border crime are guaranteed, while fundamental rights and the different national legal systems are respected.[51] With regard to the realization of this objective, the treaties both provide the legal bases for appropriate legislative actions and obligations to regulate certain topics, such as conflicts of jurisdiction.[52] Hence, the narrative of RDB EU citizenship emphasises EU citizens' right to the legislative action prescribed by the treaties. In other words, the direct and indirect representation of EU citizens in the EU legislature entails that it needs to ensure that EU citizens are provided with what is promised to them by the treaties.

In relation to the previous paragraph it should be noted that the European Commission, which is responsible for promoting the general interests of the EU and taking appropriate initiatives to that end, also plays an important role in the EU legislative process.[53] The European Parliament and Council, which officially comprise the EU legislature,[54] have the power of amendment and the power to consent and veto, but the right of initiative is granted to the Commission.[55] However, the Commission does not directly or indirectly represent the EU citizen in a manner similar to the European Parliament and the Council of Ministers.[56] A commissioner is not directly elected by EU citizens or appointed by the European Parliament, nor is he or she democratically accountable to national parliaments.[57] This means that the Commission does not have a direct democratic mandate to exercise its power of initiative.

Still, the Commission is also bound by the same collective mission as the EU legislature to advance EU objectives, such as the establishment of an AFSJ and to serve the interests of EU citizens and Member States. In that light, the treaties also impose the obligation to sincerely cooperate on all EU institutions.[58] Hence, the Commission's power of initiative is also demarcated and guided by the common

---

[50] TEU, art 13(1-2).

[51] TEU, art 3(2) and TFEU art 67(1).

[52] TFEU, art 82(1)(b; Luchtman (2020), p. 23.

[53] TEU, art 17(1).

[54] TEU, art 10.

[55] TFEU, art 76. The right of initiative can also be exercised by a quarter of the Member States.

[56] Lock (2019), p. 110.

[57] TEU, art 17(5). This provision states 'The members of the Commission shall be chosen from among the nationals of the Member States on the basis of a system of strictly equal rotation between the Member States, reflecting the demographic and geographical range of all the Member States.'

[58] TEU, art 13(2).

objective to establish an AFSJ and the legislative obligation to prevent and solve conflicts of jurisdiction. Furthermore, the treaties construct a more indirect democratic foundation for the actions of the Commission by establishing a set of checks and balances. The Commission is, for instance, accountable to the European Parliament which can vote on a motion of censure forcing the Commission to resign.[59] The European Parliament also has a strong say in the composition of the Commission as well as the election of its president.[60] On top of that, the Commission's power of initiative does not mean much without cooperation with the European Parliament and the Council of Ministers, which can veto any legislative proposal.[61]

The Need for EU Legislation

The emphasis which the narrative of RDB EU citizenship puts on satisfying the objectives and complementary legislative obligations in the treaties fits with the need for EU legislation on jurisdiction and forum choices referred to in Sect. 12.4.3. The adoption of such EU legislation could enable the adoption and application of a transnational legality principle, especially when the conditions in the EU rules already comply with its requirements.[62] In addition, EU legislation on jurisdiction and forum choices could contribute to preventing the EAW from turning into an enforcement mechanism for violations of this transnational legality principle once adopted and applicable. As explained in Sect. 11.4, the current legal framework for the EAW does not provide adequate tools to integrate a transnational legality principle in the surrender procedure. Furthermore, the narrative of RDB EU citizenship also seems to be favoured by the CJEU, which, as described in Sect. 12.4, has placed a strong emphasis on the existence of EU legislation when interpreting fundamental rights in light of the normative setting of the AFSJ.[63]

However, it should be noted that this narrative does not necessarily guarantee the required EU legislation. The EU institutions representing the EU citizen could, for

---

[59] See TEU, art 17(8).

[60] TEU, arts 14(1) and 17(7). The EP does not have the official power to veto the appointment of an individual Commissioner, but informally it can influence the appointment of individual nominees by threatening to reject the Commission as a body. It should also be remembered that the EU citizen is indirectly represented in the European Council. Even though this institution is not part of the ordinary legislative procedure, it does direct the actions of the Commission. TEU, art 15(1); TFEU, art 68; Peers (2017), pp. 42 68; Craig and De Búrca (2015), p. 49. See eg European Commission, 'A Union that strives for more' (Communication) COM (2020) 37 final, p. 1.

[61] Chalmers et al. (2014), pp. 60, 122. In this light, the practice of trilogues has developed, which entails that representatives of the European Parliament, European Commission and Council negotiate a Commission proposal behind closed doors.

[62] Chapter 13 provides recommendations for such EU rules.

[63] EU legislation on jurisdiction and forum choices could also bring national measures or actions more easily within the scope of EU law and therefore within the scope of application of the CFR. As explained in Sect. 3.2 one way for national measures, like jurisdiction rules to fall within the scope of application of the CFR, which is the first step towards the interpretation of the fundamental rights in the CFR, is when the matter at hand has been regulated by EU law.

instance, neglect to pick up the tasks laid down in the treaties or they could fail in meeting their obligations. They could also make the argument that the obligation in Article 82(1)(b) TFEU has been met with the adoption of Framework Decision 2009/948/JHA on conflicts of jurisdiction. In my view, such an argument could, however, be countered with the fact that this legal framework does not suffice in a shared legal order in which EU citizens are granted free movement rights and not just free movement possibilities. This right to free movement has a prominent position in the AFSJ as also follows from the narrative of FMB EU citizenship, which is built on the relatively strong protection of the right to free movement offered primarily by the CJEU. As explained before, the exercise of the free movement rights often increases the risk of being confronted with problems which occur at the interface of national legal orders and are the result of a lack of adequate EU rules for conflicts of jurisdiction, such as EAWs issued by states whose jurisdiction claim was not foreseeable. In this light, the argument that with the current legal framework for solving conflicts of jurisdiction the obligation in Article 82(1)(b) TFEU is satisfied, does not fit with the view that the AFSJ is a shared legal order in which EU citizens are provided with free movement rights.

For a long time, the chances of new legislative initiatives regulating jurisdiction and forum choices in order to adequately prevent or solve conflicts of jurisdiction appeared limited. Even though in the pre-Lisbon era conflicts of jurisdiction seemed to be on the radar of the EU institutions, this did not result in a solid legal instrument to prevent or solve such conflicts.[64] Legislative initiatives concerning conflicts of jurisdiction either failed or were severely dressed-down during the legislative process leading to their adoption.[65] One of the primary reasons for this was the Member States urge to protect state sovereignty.[66] Potential solutions to conflicts of jurisdiction, such as the harmonisation of jurisdiction grounds or a binding system for forum choices could require fundamental changes to the national legal systems.[67] In the post-Lisbon era, which is also important for the development of the narrative of RDB EU citizenship, the issue of conflicts of jurisdiction and forum choices has not been

[64] European Commission, 'Green paper on Conflicts of Jurisdiction and the Principle of *ne bis in idem* in Criminal Proceedings' COM (2005) 696 final; European Council, The Hague Programme: strengthening freedom, security and justice in the European Union (The Hague Programme) [2005] OJ C53/1, p. 12. See also European Commission, 'Mutual Recognition of Final Decisions in Criminal Matters' (Communication) COM (2000) 495 final, pp. 18–19.

[65] Initiative of the Hellenic Republic with a view to adopting a Council Framework Decision concerning the application of the "*ne bis in idem*" principle [2003] OJ C100/24; Draft Council Framework Decision on the transfer of proceedings in criminal matters' [2009] OJ C219/7; Council Framework Decision 2009/948/JHA of 30 November 2009 on prevention and settlement of conflicts of exercise of jurisdiction in criminal proceedings [2009] OJ L328/42.

[66] Suominen (2011), p. 4. See also BVerfG 30 June 2009, 2 BvE 2/08 [253]; Erbežnik (2012), p. 15; Council, 'Proposal for a Council Framework Decision on prevention and settlement of conflicts of jurisdiction in criminal proceedings' (General approach/Outstanding issues) [2009] 7683/09, p. 2.

[67] Mitsilegas (2015), pp. 460, 465. See also European Commission, 'Mutual Recognition of Final Decisions in Criminal Matters' (Communication) COM (2000) 495 final, pp. 17–20.

marked as a vital priority in the five-year programmes of the European Council or the political guidelines of the European Commission.[68]

Still, in the past years, the discussion on conflicts of jurisdiction and their effect on judicial cooperation on the basis of mutual recognition has stirred up again.[69] In a report from the Romanian Presidency, the need to reassess Framework Decision 2009/948/JHA on conflicts of jurisdiction and to issue a legislative proposal on the transfer of criminal proceedings was emphasised.[70] In a subsequent report from the Council, the European Commission was requested to consider such a legislative proposal.[71] The European Commission is currently in the process of developing a proposal on the transfer of criminal proceedings between EU Member States. This initiative focuses on the establishment of common conditions for the transfer of criminal proceedings. The new rules should improve the efficiency of criminal proceedings and the administration of justice.[72] However, focusing solely on the transfer of criminal proceedings, rasises a few important questions. For instance, to what extent will the decision to request and/or accept the transfer of criminal

---

[68]European Council, *A new strategic agenda for the EU 2019-2024* <https://www.consilium.europa.eu/en/eu-strategic-agenda-2019-2024/> accessed 20 September 2021; Ursula von der Leyen, *A Union that strives for more – My agenda for Europe* (Political Guidelines 2019–2024) <https://ec.europa.eu/info/sites/info/files/political-guidelines-next-commission_en_0.pdf> accessed 20 September 2021; European Commission, 'Commission Work Programme 2020. A Union that strives for more' (Communication) COM (2020) 37 final; European Council, 'Strategic guidelines for the legislative and operational planning in the Area of Freedom, Security and Justice' EUCO (2014) 79/14; José Manuel Barosso, *Political guidelines for the next Commission 2009-2014* <ec.europa.eu/archives/commission_2010-2014/president/about/political/> accessed 20 September 2021; European Council, 'The Stockholm Programme – An Open and Secure Europe Serving and Protecting Citizens' [2009] OJ C115/1; European Commission, 'Delivering an area of freedom, security and justice for Europe's citizens. Action Plan Implementing the Stockholm Programme' (Communication) COM (2010) 171 final.

[69]See Committee on Civil Liberties, Justice and Home Affairs, 'Report on the implementation of the European Arrest Warrant and the surrender procedures between Member States' (rapporteur Javier Zarzalejos) A9-0248/2020, p. 21. Wouter van Ballegooij, 'European Arrest Warrant, European Implementation Assessment', European Parliamentary Research Service (2020) available at <https://www.europarl.europa.eu/RegData/etudes/STUD/2020/642839/EPRS_STU(2020)642839_EN.pdf> accessed 20 September 2021, paras 2.2.4, 4.1, 4.4; De Jong (2020); Eurojust, Report of strategic seminar, Conflicts of jurisdiction, transfer of proceedings and *ne bis in idem*: successes, shortcomings and solutions (2015, Council doc. No. 14172/15); Eurojust, Report on Eurojust's casework in the field of prevention and resolution of conflicts of jurisdiction (2018) <www.eurojust.europa.eu> accessed 20 September 2021.

[70]Romanian Presidency, 'The way forward in the field of mutual recognition in criminal matters' [2019] 9728/19, p. 18.

[71]Council, 'The European arrest warrant and extradition procedures – current challenges and the way forward' (Council conclusions) [2020] 13214/20, para 38. See also Csonka (2019).

[72]European Commission, 'Commission work programme 2022 (Commission Communication) COM 2021 (645) final, p. 10; European Commission, 'Effective justice – common conditions for transferring criminal proceedings between EU countries' https://ec.europa.eu/info/law/better-regulation/have-your-say/initiatives/13097-Effective-justice-common-conditions-for-transferring-criminal-proceedings-between-EU-countries_en, last visited 28 January 2022.

proceedings remain within the discretion of the competent authorities? Discretion in deciding whether to use the procedure would not guarantee a solution to all conflicts of jurisdiction or the appointment of the best forum in each concrete case. Another question is how and by whom the decision on the best forum in light of the good administration of justice will be made? Will, for instance, all competent states as well as the suspect and/or victim have a say in the decision to which state the prcoeedings should be transferred? As will be futher explained in Chap. 13, I am of the opinion that the Commission should propose legislation which specifically focuses on preventing and solving conflicts of jurisdiction. The rules should ensure that in light of the proper administration of justice, one state is appointed as the competent state. Rules on the transfer of criminal proceedings and the surrender procedure could and should, in my opinion, primarily have the purpose of facilitating the prosecution and adjudication of the case in the appointed competent state.

In case the initiative of the Commission fails or does not sufficiently guarantee an adequate legal framework for solving conflicts of jurisdiction, it is difficult to imagine a way for EU citizens to force the EU institutions to take action on the basis of Article 82(1)(b) TFEU and in light of Article 3(2) TEU in order to ensure that the promises made to them are realised.[73] The treaties do provide some mechanisms with which EU citizens could, for instance, try to influence the EU legislative agenda and the actions of the EU institutions involved in the legislative process. An example is the EU citizen's initiative, but even if the requirements of this procedure are met and the Commission agrees that EU action is required in relation to the topic at hand, it is not obliged to propose legislation.[74] Hence, it can be concluded that the narrative of EU citizenship does not necessarily guarantee the desired outcome, which is EU legislation on jurisdiction and forum choices.

12.6 Conclusion

This chapter has explained how the narrative of FMB EU citizenship and the narrative of RDB EU citizenship could be vehicles towards a transnational legality principle. It can be concluded that both narratives have a different connection to the transnational interpretation of fundamental rights. The narrative of FMB EU citizenship strongly relies on the adoption of a transnational interpretation of Articles 49 and 47 CFR by the CJEU, which can be achieved in the context of the legal

[73] Article 265 TFEU provides the possibility of judicial action in case certain EU institutions, including the Commission, European Parliament and Council, in infringement of the treaties fail to act. However, a national person may only complain to the CJEU when EU institutions have 'failed to address to that person any act other than a recommendation or an opinion'. Hence, this option is only available when individuals are directly concerned, or sometimes directly and individually concerned, by the act that should have been adopted. See eg Case T-167/04 *Asklepios Kliniken v Commission* [2007] ECLI:EU:T:2007:215; Chalmers et al. (2014), p. 465.

[74] TEU, art 11(4).

framework for assessing interferences with the right to free movement. However, this legal framework contains a lot of different conditions and it is not guaranteed that all of them will be met. In addition, it does not clearly reflect the fact that EU citizenship goes beyond free movement and that Articles 47 and 49 CR are not EU citizenship rights, but human rights. On top of that, I am of the opinion that this narrative is on its own an unsuitable vehicle towards the adoption of a transnational legality principle in light of the absence of clear and general EU rules on jurisdiction and forum choices adopted in a legislative process in which both EU citizens and Member States are represented. In the absence of such legislation, the adoption of a transnational legality principle by the CJEU, which could affect the Member States' discretion in regulating criminal jurisdiction, could, in my view, have a somewhat undemocratic character. Furthermore, in its case law the CJEU often takes the existence of EU legislation on the matter at hand into account when interpreting EU fundamental rights. This limits the chances of success of the narrative of FMB EU citizenship as a vehicle towards a transnational legality principle.

The need for EU legislation addressing jurisdiction and forum choices, however, fits well with the second narrative of EU citizenship. This narrative emphasises the representation of EU citizens in the EU legislature, which is bound by the obligations laid down in the treaties. Two important obligations are the establishment of an AFSJ in which both free movement and security are guaranteed and in that light, the adoption of EU legislation preventing or solving conflicts of jurisdiction. The narrative of RDB EU citizenship, therefore, entails that the institutions representing EU citizens in the legislative process need to ensure that the promises which the treaties make to EU citizens are realised.

Hence, even though both narratives clearly have a different connection to the transnational interpretation of fundamental rights, they are complementary. The legislative perspective taken by the second narrative could answer the need for legislation in the first narratives which emphasises the role of the judiciary in adopting a transnational legality principle in the context of EU citizens' right to free movement. In addition, in light of the conclusion that EU legislation regarding jurisdiction and forum decisions is required for the purpose of a transnational legality principle in the AFSJ, the next chapter provides specific recommendations as to the form and content of such legislation. It also recommends that the proposed measures already integrate the protection offered by a transnational legality principle as laid down in Chap. 11. This could facilitate the adoption of a transnational legality principle by the CJEU later on.[75]

[75]EU legislation on jurisdiction and forum choices could also bring national measures or actions more easily within the scope of EU law and, therefore, within the scope of application of the CFR. Hence, such EU rules could also be the stepping stone for preliminary questions to the CJEU regarding Articles 49 and 47 CFR.

References

Alemanno A (2020) Europe's democracy challenge: citizen participation in and beyond elections 20 challenges in the EU in 2020. German Law J 21:35
Benhabib S (2004) The rights of others - aliens, residents and citizens. Cambridge University Press
Benhabib S (2011) Dignity in adversity: human rights in troubled times. Cambridge Polity Press
Böse M (2014) Fundamental freedoms of the union. In: Böse M, Meyer F, Schneider A (eds) Conflicts of jurisdiction in criminal matters in the European Union. Volume II: rights, principles and model rules. Nomos
Chalmers C, Davies G, Monti G (2014) European Union law. Cambridge University Press
Coutts S (2019) Citizenship, crime and community in the European Union. Hart
Craig P, De Búrca G (2015) EU law text, cases, and materials. Oxford University Press
Csonka P (2019) Guest editorial. Eucrim 77
Dagger R (2002) Republican citizenship. In: Isin E, Turner B (eds) Handbook of citizenship studies. Sage
De Jong B (2020) Transfer of criminal proceedings: from stumbling block to cornerstone of cooperation in criminal matters in the EU. ERA Forum 21:449
De Wilde P (2014) Representative claims analysis: theory meets method. In: Kröger S, Friedrich D (eds) The representative turn in EU studies. Routledge
De Witte F (2015) Justice in the EU: the emergence of transnational solidarity. Oxford University Press
Douglas-Scott S (1998) In search of union citizenship. Yearb Eur Law 18:29
Eijken V, Marguery T (2017) The federal entrenchment of citizens in the European Union member states' criminal laws: or how EU citizenship is shaping criminal law. In: Kochenov D (ed) EU citizenship and federalism. Cambridge University Press
Eleftheriadis P (2014) The content of European citizenship. German Law J 15:777
Erbežnik A (2012) The principle of mutual recognition as a utilitarian solution, and the way forward. Eur Crim Law Rev 2:3
Everson M (2012) A very cosmopolitan citizenship: but who pays the Price? In: Dougan M, Shuibne NN, Spaventa E (eds) Empowerment and disempowerment of the European citizen. Hart Publishing
Hloušek V, Koska V (2018) Shifting borders and contested identities: the quest for republican EU citizenship and polity. In: Seubert S, Eberl O, van Waarden F (eds) Reconsidering EU citizenship: contradictions and constraints. Edward Elgar
Iglesias Sánchez S (2017) A citizenship right to stay? The right not to move in a union based on free movement. In: Kochenov D (ed) EU citizenship and federalism: the role of rights. Cambridge University Press
Lock T (2019a) Article 10 TEU. In: Kellerbauer M, Klamert M, Tomkin J (eds) The EU treaties and the charter of fundamental rights: a commentary. Oxford University Press
Lock T (2019b) Provisions on democratic principles. In: Kellerbauer M, Klamert M, Tomkin J (eds) The EU treaties and the charter of fundamental rights: a commentary. Oxford University Press
Luchtman M (2018) Kroniek van het Europees strafrecht. 2684
Luchtman M (2020) Transnational law enforcement cooperation – fundamental rights in European cooperation in criminal matters. Eur J Crime Crim Law Crim Just 28:14
Mitsilegas V (2015) The symbiotic relationship between mutual trust and fundamental rights in Europe's area of criminal justice. New J Eur Crim Law 6:457
Neuvonen P (2017) EU citizenship and its "very specific" essence: Rendón Marin and CS. Common Mark Law Rev 54:1201
O'Brien C (2017) Unity in adversity: EU citizenship, social justice and the cautionary tale of the UK. Bloomsbury Publishing
Peers S (2017) The EU's political institutions. In: Barnard C, Peers S (eds) European Union law. Oxford University Press

Schütze R (2017) Constitutionalism and the European Union. In: Barnard C, Peers S (eds) European Union law. Oxford University Press

Seubert S (2018) EU citizenship and prospects for cosmopolitanism. In: Seubert S, Eberl O, van Waarden F (eds) Reconsidering EU citizenship: contradictions and constraints. Edward Elgar

Seubert S (2019) Shifting boundaries of membership: the politicisation of free movement as a challenge for EU citizenship. Eur Law J 16:48

Strumia F (2020) Supranational citizenship enablers. Free movement from the perspective of home member states. Eur Law Rev 45:507

Suominen A (2011) The principle of mutual recognition in cooperation in criminal matters. A study of the principle in four framework decisions and in the implementation legislation in the Nordic Member States. Intersentia

Van Eijken H (2014) European citizenship and the Constitutionalisation of the European Union. Europa Law Publishing

Van Eijken H (2016) De Europese burger en het Handvest voor de Grondrechten: nieuwe sporen naar een Europese rechtsstaat? In: Gerbrandy A, Rampersad R (eds) De sociale markteconomie van de EU en de kansen voor Nederland: Gedachten over de toekomst van niet-positivistische driesporenbenadering van Bart Hessel. Boom

Van Eijken H et al (2015) The European citizen as bearer of fundamental rights in a multi-layered legal order. In: van den Brink T, Luchtman M, Scholten M (eds) Sovereignty in the shared legal order of the EU: Core values of regulation and enforcement. Intersentia

Van Gunsteren H (1998) A theory of citizenship: organizing plurality in contemporary democracies. Westview Press

Chapter 13
Conclusions and Recommendations

13.1 Introduction

This chapter has a twofold purpose. It first provides the answer to the main research question of this book in Sect. 13.2. Secondly, it sets out specific recommendations for EU rules addressing the Member States jurisdiction to prescribe and adjudicate. As explained in Chaps. 11 and 12 such EU measures are important for the adoption of a transnational interpretation of Articles 49 and 47 CFR and to avoid the EAW from turning into an enforcement mechanism for violations of these transnational fundamental rights. In relation to the former, it follows from Sects. 12.5 and 12.6 that EU rules on jurisdiction and forum decisions in which the content of the transnational legality principle is already integrated could facilitate the adoption and application of a transnational interpretation of Articles 49 and 47 CFR in the AFSJ. In relation to the latter Sect. 11.4 has explained that the current FDEAW does not contain adequate tools to prevent the surrender of EU citizens when they would be subjected to violations of the transnational legality principle in their criminal cases.

The recommendations set out in Sects. 13.3–13.5 are based on these conclusions. In that light, the proposed EU rules regulating jurisdiction and forum decisions aim to reflect the transnational legality principle as described in Sect. 11.3 and to enable the transformation of the EAW from a mechanism which could potentially enforce fundamental rights violations into a mechanism which enforces prosecution by the *forum conveniens*. More specifically, Sect. 13.3 will discuss the legal bases in the treaties for the adoption of EU measures on jurisdiction and forum choices. Sections 13.4 and 13.5 then provide specific recommendations regarding the content of such measures, including the different interests—those of the state and the EU citizen—which should be taken into account, how to balance these interests, the competent decision-making authorities, the type of measure—directive or a regulation—and the point in time at which a forum decision should be made. These recommendations are

J. Graat, *The European Arrest Warrant and EU Citizenship*,
https://doi.org/10.1007/978-3-031-07590-2_13

based on the multitude of studies proposing possible regulatory approaches, blueprints and models for preventing and settling conflicts of jurisdiction.

It is important to note beforehand that I recommend to include the proposed rules in new EU instruments instead of integrating them in the FDEAW. As explained before, the EAW was never intended to be a mechanism for forum decisions and the surrender procedure does not necessarily play a role in all cases in which conflicts of jurisdiction occur. In that light, Sect. 13.6 provides additional recommendations regarding the amendment of the FDEAW which should follow the adoption of the proposed EU rules on jurisdiction and forum decisions. They explain that the proposed rules allow for a significant reduction of the conditions for the issuing and execution of an EAW. Section 13.7 then contains the conclusion which also reflects on the impact which the amendments to the EAW could have on its functioning in practice and its classification as a mutual recognition instrument.

13.2 Conclusions

13.2.1 The Context of the Research Question

It follows from the previous chapters that EU citizenship has since its introduction by the Treaty of Maastricht undergone important developments, including in the context of the criminal justice angle of the AFSJ. As explained in Chaps. 1 and 2, Article 3(2) TEU designates EU citizens as the main stakeholders of the AFSJ which should guarantee both free movement and security while respecting fundamental rights. The promise of such an AFSJ is also emphasised in the policy guidelines and objectives of the EU institutions and has resulted in the adoption of new measures for judicial cooperation in criminal matters, such as the EAW. These cooperation mechanisms often contribute to its security objective. However, the combination of these judicial cooperation mechanisms and the broad extraterritorial scope of application of many national criminal laws could also cause a set of foreseeability complications for EU citizens, in particular for those who exercise their free movement rights. The first complication that has been discussed comprises the difficulties for EU citizens to foresee which particular national substantive criminal law is applicable to them. In the absence of a uniform EU criminal code which fully harmonises criminal offences and sanctions, this foreseeability issue could be disadvantageous to the EU citizen. The second foreseeability complication relates to the lack of an adequate EU mechanism which ensures the prevention or settlement of conflicts of jurisdiction. The absence of such a system comes with the risk that forum choices are made by chance or in a so-called 'black box' in which the competent national authorities have broad discretion to decide which state should handle the case. This situation could be harmful to EU citizens in the AFSJ, since national criminal procedures, including rules on pre-trial detention and admissibility of evidence still differ to a large extent. Within this picture, the EAW does not constitute either the core or the cause of these two possible foreseeability complications. They can also arise when no EAW is issued or executed. However, the EAW constitutes an additional dimension as it can ensure the surrender of EU citizens, even though the two foreseeability complications have arisen in their underlying national criminal cases.

The first complication raises questions in light of the substantive legality principle in Article 49 CFR, which demands that criminal offences and sanctions are accessible and foreseeable. More concretely, the question is whether criminal offences and sanctions meet these requirements when the applicability of the national criminal law of which they are part was not foreseeable at the time of the offence. The second complication raises questions in light of the right to a tribunal established by law, which demands that the judicial organisation of a state is regulated by a law emanating from Parliament and is not dependent on the unfettered discretion of the executive or judiciary. The question which follows from this fundamental right is whether a national court or tribunal is established by law when the national jurisdiction to which it belongs was not appointed as the competent forum on the basis of a set of rules which sufficiently limit the power of the decision-making authorities, which can be public prosecutors or courts. With regard to the EAW, the main question is whether the surrender procedure could potentially be a mechanism which enforces fundamental rights violations by transferring EU citizens to states whose jurisdiction claim may not be compatible with Article 49 or 47 CFR.

These possible complications and their relationship to the EAW as well as the legality questions which they raise are not unique to the AFSJ as they can also occur in the outer-EU setting in which extradition agreements can have the same possible effect as the EAW. In the outer-EU setting these complications have so far not been solved or occupied a prominent role, which could be explained in light of the central position of the state and state sovereignty in extradition procedures. However, the AFSJ has an EU citizenship dimension and these EU citizens are provided with free movement rights. The development of a more prominent position of EU citizenship over time and the emphasis which is put on the promises made to these EU citizens both justifies and requires a critical reflection of the current level of fundamental rights protection offered to EU citizens when they are confronted with complications arising at the interface of national legal orders. In addition, it allows for an examination of the influence which EU citizenship itself could have on the interpretation of fundamental rights. For this purpose, the following research question was formulated: What are the foreseeability problems of jurisdiction claims and forum choices that citizens may be faced with in the context of the EAW, and to what extent could EU citizenship help to address these problems?

The next two subsections answer this research question. Subsection 13.2.2 addresses the first part regarding the existence of foreseeability problems of jurisdiction claims and forum choices and the extent to which they are currently recognised as legality problems. Subsection 13.2.3 covers the question to what extent EU citizenship can help to address the foreseeability problems.

13.2.2 The Current Level of Fundamental Rights Protection

The current type and level of protection against arbitrary interferences with fundamental rights granted to EU citizens has been described and analysed in Chaps. 3–7. On the basis of those analyses the answer to this first part of the research question—also provided in Chap. 8—is that the scope of protection of the legality principle on both the EU and the national level is quite state-focused. With regard to the EU level this follows from the limited case law on the existence of a link between jurisdiction and the right to an accessible and foreseeable law for criminal offences and sanctions, and the limited case law on forum choices and the right to a tribunal established by law. The rulings which have been issued by the CJEU and ECtHR on these matters cover situations which occur within the borders of one particular state. In this light, the ECtHR has decided in relation to the substantive legality principle that overlapping penalty brackets are not prohibited as long as the law avoids arbitrariness by sufficiently restricting the power to pick a certain penalty bracket. On the topic of forum choices and the right to a tribunal established by law the case law shows that when a state has established a system for forum decisions the law needs to ensure its reasonableness. However, as said, these rules follow from cases concerning national situations, meaning that it remains unclear to what extent they also apply in case of overlapping national substantive criminal laws and conflicts of national jurisdictions. Hence, unforeseeable jurisdiction claims and the lack of a clear EU system for forum decisions can on the basis of the CJEU and ECtHR case law currently not be classified as legality problems.

In Chap. 8, a similar conclusion has been drawn in relation to the national level. The German, Dutch and English legal order have not clearly and unambiguously linked the national equivalents of the right to accessible and foreseeable criminal offences and sanctions and the right to a tribunal stablished by law to the foreseeability of jurisdiction claims and forum choices on the cross-border level. Germany recognises the potential problem of being confronted with unforeseeable jurisdiction claims, but this recognition is founded on the constitutional prohibition of the extradition of German nationals and not on the basis of the German substantive legality principle. The protection, therefore, has a strong state and sovereignty connotation, instead of a free movement and EU citizenship one.

As illustrated by the above, both the EU legality principle and the national legality principle currently have a state-focused interpretation and do not touch upon the two problems, which occur at the interface of national legal orders or on a cross-border level. In addition to this, the surrender procedure on the EU and national level does not contain ample safeguards against the surrender of EU citizens when these complications arise in their underlying criminal cases. The fact that the EAW could ensure the surrender of an EU citizen while the jurisdiction claim of the issuing state was not foreseeable or its decision to prosecute was not based on a set of clear rules ensuring the proper administration of justice was not considered during the drafting of the FDEAW and has not (yet) been recognised in the CJEU case law on the issuing and executing procedure. With regard to the national level protection against both problems is hardly integrated in the conditions of the surrender procedure. The German legislator has on the basis of the constitutional safeguard in Article 16(2) GG adopted refusal grounds which aim to prevent surrender in case of unforeseeable jurisdiction claims, but this protection is primarily granted to German nationals. Another rare example of safeguards against the two problems can be found in the English legal order where the problems arising as a result of the lack of a clear system for case allocations in cross-border cases have been acknowledged. This has resulted in a set of rules addressing the forum decision in some of these cross-border cases, which used to apply in the context of the issuing procedure as well. On top of that, the English executing procedure contained refusal grounds, like the forum bar which were introduced to increase the transparency of forum decisions.

So, it can be concluded that the protection offered by the legality principle on both the EU and the national level is 'state-focused' and currently does not extend to problems arising from unforeseeable jurisdiction claims or forum decisions on the cross-border level. Aligned with this conclusion is the conclusion that the surrender procedure on the EU and national level does not contain conditions which reflect the view that the EAW could function as a mechanism enforcing violations of the legality principle by surrendering EU citizens who are confronted with one of the two complications in their criminal case.

This answer to the first part of the research question is understandable and acceptable, when the EAW is viewed from an intergovernmental perspective. This perspective classifies the EAW as an extradition procedure and allocates a central position to the state and state interests. As explained in Chap. 9, the main role of fundamental rights in the intergovernmental perspective is to establish and verify the necessary trust between states to cooperate with each other. This could explain and justify the state-centric interpretation of fundamental rights, since the required mutual trust to enter into a cooperation agreement demands that each state guarantees fundamental rights protection within its own borders. In addition, the intergovernmental perspective is characterised by national citizenship as the protection of one's nationals is often closely related to state sovereignty and classified as a state interest. This could clarify why the current limited protection against the complications at hand is also primarily provided to national citizens as illustrated by Chap. 6 on the German legal order.

The intergovernmental perspective is still represented on the EU and the national level, but its validity can be questioned on the basis of the development of the AFSJ as the normative context in which the EAW operates. EU citizenship has also had an important role in this development. The next section further elaborates on this point and answers the second part of the research question.

13.2.3 *The Role of EU Citizenship in Addressing the Foreseeability Problems*

The answer to the question to what extent EU citizenship could help to address the foreseeability problems has three layers. The first two layers relate to the acceptability of the answer to the first part of the research question and the validity of the intergovernmental perspective as an explanation and justification for this answer. As explained in Chap. 10, the answer to the first part of the research question is, in my view, difficult to accept, because the EAW does not primarily operate in an intergovernmental setting, but in a transnational context. In this light, EU citizenship constitutes both an important argument against the intergovernmental perspective as well as a fundamental aspect of the transnational perspective which opens the door to a transnational legality principle. The next paragraphs elaborate on this point.

As explained in Chap. 10, besides the more formal differences between the substantive and procedural conditions in the extradition and surrender procedure, the normative context in which the EAW operates strongly differs from the intergovernmental setting. This is illustrated by the EU institutional framework, in particular the role of the CJEU. As a result of a large amount of preliminary questions, the CJEU is in the process of developing a common framework for the surrender procedure. Such a common framework is largely absent in extradition procedures. In addition, another significant difference between the intergovernmental context and the AFSJ is the latter's EU citizenship and interrelated free movement dimension. The Treaty of Lisbon officially and explicitly connected the establishment of a twofold AFSJ to EU citizenship and designated EU citizens as the beneficiaries of this common EU objective. These EU citizens are also provided with free movement rights which the CJEU has often defended and protected in its case law. Furthermore, EU citizens are represented in the EU legislative process for most criminal justice measures by the European Parliament and the Council.

This unique EU citizenship dimension and its development over time also constitutes a fundamental building block of the transnational perspective on the EAW. This perspective emphasises the direct cooperation between national judicial authorities in the AFSJ, which is viewed as a shared legal order consisting of both EU citizens and the Member States. Contrary to the intergovernmental perspective, the transnational perspective does not just view EU citizens as nationals of Member States—so more in their capacity of national citizens—but as the main stakeholders of the AFSJ, who are provided with unique free movement rights. In my opinion, this transnational perspective on the EAW fits a lot better with the current position EU citizens have in the AFSJ as described above and the promise of an AFSJ in which both free movement and security are guaranteed. In that light, I am also of the opinion that this transnational perspective could clash with the current state-focused interpretation of the legality principle and the lack of safeguards which protect EU citizens against surrender in case of unforeseeable jurisdiction claims and possible arbitrary forum decisions. Taking EU citizenship and EU citizenship rights—as well as the promise in Article 3(2) TEU—seriously requires that the problems with which

EU citizens can be confronted in the AFSJ as a result of transnational crime-fighting efforts like the EAW are not ignored. The characteristics of the transnational perspective, therefore, seem to both allow and argue in favour of a transnational fundamental rights framework which establishes a balance between transnational cooperation instruments like the EAW and the effect which they can have on the legal position of EU citizens.

With regard to the content of a transnational legality principle, Chap. 11 suggests that Articles 49 and 47 CFR follow in the footsteps of the *ne bis in idem* principle, which the CJEU has adapted in conformity with Article 3(2) TEU. In that light, the substantive legality principle in Article 49 CFR should come to mean that criminal offences and sanctions are accessible and foreseeable when the application of the national criminal law of which they are part was foreseeable at the time of the offence. In light of the free movement dimension of the AFSJ, the default right should be that EU citizens only have to know and abide by the law of the host state. However, exceptions to this default right are allowed in light of the security objective of the AFSJ and the need to consider in a shared legal order the legitimate interests in prosecution of other Member States. With regard to these exceptions the law should at least ensure that the discretion of the authority deciding which national criminal law is applied in the concrete case is sufficiently delineated to avoid arbitrary decisions. The transnational right to a tribunal established by law in Article 47 CFR should entail that a national court or tribunal is not established by law when the national jurisdiction to which it belongs has not been appointed as the competent forum on the basis of a clear law aiming for reasonable and non-arbitrary forum decisions in light of the good administration of justice. This transnational interpretation could facilitate free movement, as it increases the foreseeability of the legal consequences of one's actions, but it also provides the possibility to take other interests, such as security into account when making a forum decision.

On the basis of the above, it can be concluded that EU citizenship constitutes a vehicle towards more fundamental rights protection as it undermines the intergovernmental perspective as a viable explanation for the current state-focused interpretation of the legality principle. In line therewith, EU citizenship constitutes an important building block of the alternative transnational perspective which opens the door to a transnational interpretation of the legality principle, which captures jurisdiction and forum decisions on the cross-border level.

The third layer of the answer to the question to what extent EU citizenship could help to address the foreseeability problems has been presented in Chap. 12. This chapter has set out two specific narratives on EU citizenship and explained how they could be linked to the transnational legality principle in order to realise its application in the AFSJ. This third layer is further discussed in the following paragraphs.

As vehicles towards a transnational legality principle the narrative of FMB EU citizenship and the narrative of RDB EU citizenship are complementary and not mutually exclusive. The first narrative opens the door to a transnational legality principle via the framework which the CJEU has established for assessing national measures in light of the right to free movement. In case national jurisdiction rules constitute barriers to the right to free movement, they need to be justified on the basis of one of the grounds provided by the treaty or the rule of reason. These justifications grounds derived from EU law must be interpreted in light of EU fundamental rights, which brings the national measures within the scope of application of the CFR. This would provide the CJEU the opportunity to adopt a transnational legality principle. However, in my opinion, this is an opportunity the court should not take in the absence of EU legislation generally addressing jurisdiction and forum decisions. The adoption and application of a transnational legality principle while these matters are only to a limited extent regulated by EU rules—adopted in a legislative process in which both EU citizens and Member States are represented—has an undemocratic flavour. A transnational legality principle could deeply interfere with the sovereignty and criminal justice systems of the Member States and should in that light have a foundation in EU rules adopted in a democratic legislative process.

This is where the second narrative of RDB EU citizenship could complement the first narrative as a vehicle towards a transnational legality principle. This second narrative is based on the direct and indirect representation of the EU citizen by the European Parliament and the Council in the EU legislative process for the adoption of criminal justice measures. The EU legislature and the Commission which has the right of initiative have the joint mission and obligation to advance the establishment of an AFJS as laid down in Article 3(2) TEU and in that light, to adopt EU legislation preventing and solving conflicts of jurisdiction on the basis of Article 82(1)(b) TFEU. In case such EU legislation would already comply with and reflect the protection which the proposed transnational legality principle offers, the CJEU would also be facilitated in adopting and applying a transnational interpretation of Articles 49 and 47 CFR. In addition, such EU legislation could contribute to preventing the EAW from turning into an enforcement mechanism for violations of the transnational legality principle once it is adopted. Together with certain amendments to the FDEAW, it could in fact allow the EAW to be transformed into a mechanism which contributes to prosecution by the most appropriate state—the *forum conveniens*.[1] This is further elaborated on in the next sections. However, as also explained in Chap. 12, even though the treaties impose the obligation to establish an AFSJ in which free movement and security are guaranteed and to adopt EU legislation on the basis of Article 82(1)(b) TFEU, the Commission and EU legislature could neglect these obligations or fail to meet them. In these situations, the EU citizen is not presented with strong tools to, for instance, challenge the failure to take adequate actions before the CJEU.

To sum up, EU citizenship could help to address the two foreseeability problems discussed in three interlinked ways. The first and second one concern EU citizenship as an argument against the intergovernmental perspective and a building block of the transnational perspective. The latter opens the door to and, in my opinion, demands the adoption of a transnational legality principle, which captures jurisdiction and forum decisions on the cross-border level. In addition, the two narratives of EU citizenship that can be derived from its development could contribute to the

[1] Ouwerkerk (2012), p. 464. See also Swart (1983).

realisation of the application of the transnational legality principle in the AFSJ. However, it also follows from the above that, even though both narratives on EU citizenship could be vehicles towards a transnational legality principle, the second one has a more democratic character. Hence, the narrative of FMB EU citizenship is not a suitable one without the narrative of RDB EU citizenship focusing on the adoption of EU legislation solving or preventing conflicts of jurisdiction. The next sections provide recommendations for such EU legislation.

13.3 The Legal Bases for the Proposed EU Rules on Jurisdiction and Forum Decisions

The next sections propose EU measures on jurisdiction and forum decisions which also approximate national criminal laws to some extent, in particular rules of jurisdiction, and allocate a role to Eurojust. The legal bases for the proposed EU instruments are Article 82(1)(b) TFEU and Article 85(1)(c) TFEU. The former states that judicial cooperation in criminal matters shall be based on the principle of mutual recognition and enumerates a set of issues which need to be regulated. This list includes preventing or solving conflicts of jurisdiction. In light of the EU objective of establishing an AFSJ in which judicial cooperation is based on mutual recognition, Wasmeijer has argued that Article 82(1)(b) TFEU allows for the adoption of measures which to some extent approximate national rules. He states that EU measures addressing the exercise of the jurisdiction to prescribe or adjudicate can be viewed as a prerequisite for an AFSJ on the basis of mutual recognition.[2] This link between cooperation on the basis of mutual recognition and the regulation of the Member States' jurisdiction to prescribe and adjudicate has also been more generally recognised and promoted on the EU level.[3] In its Communication of 2000, the Commission stated, 'Where it is clear according to commonly established rules that the authorities of (only) one Member State are competent to pronounce on a certain case, it will be much easier for the other Member States to recognise and thus accept such a decision than in a situation where it might as well have been their own authorities who would have been competent to decide.'[4] In The Hague Programme, the European Council also recognised the need for rules on jurisdiction for the purpose of cooperation on the basis of mutual recognition and the Council's and

---

[2] Wasmeier (2018), pp. 90–93. The legal literature shows discussion with regard to the question of whether this legal basis allows for rules which approximate national rules. An argument against the adoption of approximation measures is that Article 82(1) TFEU states that judicial cooperation in criminal matters 'shall include the approximation of the laws and regulations of the Member States in the areas referred to in paragraph 2 and in Article 83.' Hence, the power to approximate national laws seems limited to these specific areas. See also Böse (2014), pp. 368–370.

[3] See also TEU, art 31(1)(d) (old) as included by the Treaty of Amsterdam.

[4] European Commission, 'Mutual Recognition of Final Decisions in Criminal Matters' (Communication) COM (2000) 495 final, p. 19.

Commission's Action Plan Implementing this Programme categorised conflicts of jurisdiction under 'Approximation'.[5]

In addition, the measures proposed below also allocate a role to Eurojust which should be competent to reach a binding forum decision when the Member States cannot reach an agreement. Article 85(1)(c) TFEU provides a legal basis for this power, since it states that by means of a regulation the task of strengthening judicial cooperation, including the resolution of conflicts of jurisdiction, may be imposed upon Eurojust.[6] Hence, in case this task is allocated to Eurojust, this would also require amendment of the Eurojust Regulation on the basis of Article 85(1)(c) TFEU.[7]

13.4 Three Categories of Regulatory Approaches to Address Positive Conflicts of Jurisdiction

The legal literature roughly shows three different regulatory approaches to prevent and solve positive conflicts of jurisdiction: the *Restriktionsmodell* (restrictions model) *Zustandigkeitsmodelle* (competence/jurisdiction model) and one which separates the decision on the applicable national substantive criminal law from the decision on the competent forum. Rules which fall under the *Restriktionsmodell* address positive conflicts of jurisdiction at the level of the Member States' jurisdiction to prescribe. They aim to prevent positive conflicts of jurisdiction by delineating the Member States' sovereign powers to determine the scope of application of their national criminal laws.[8] Examples are rules which exclude certain extraterritorial jurisdiction grounds, such as the passive personality principle or limit the scope of an extraterritorial jurisdiction ground to certain serious offences.[9] Hence, these mechanisms focus on preventing instead of solving conflicts of jurisdiction.[10]

[5]European Council, The Hague Programme: strengthening freedom, security and justice in the European Union (The Hague Programme) [2005] OJ C53/1, p. 12; Council and European Commission, Action Plan implementing the Hague Programme on strengthening freedom, security and justice in the European Union [2005] OJ C198/18–19. In the area of judicial cooperation in civil matters, rules on 'conflicts of laws and jurisdiction' have been developed. See Regulation (EU) No 1215/2012 of the European Parliament and of the Council of 12 December 2012 on jurisdiction and the recognition and enforcement of judgments in civil and commercial matters [2012] OJ L351/1. See also Ortolani (2018), pp. 204–231.

[6]Herrnfeld (2013), p. 201. See also Hecker (2011), p. 62; Wasmeier (2018), pp. 112–115; Deboyser (2013), pp. 107–108.

[7]Regulation (EU) 2018/1727 of the European Parliament and of the Council of 14 November 2018 on the European Union Agency for Criminal Justice Cooperation (Eurojust), and replacing and repealing Council Decision 2002/187/JHA [2018] OJ L295/138.

[8]See eg Böse (2014), p. 369.

[9]Klip (2011), p. 119.

[10]Schönberger (2015), pp. 321–322; Böse (2014), p. 369.

Contrary to the *Restriktionsmodell*, rules which fall under the *Zustandigkeitsmodelle* often regulate and restrict the Member States' jurisdiction to adjudicate. These rules focus on solving positive conflicts of jurisdiction when they arise. Hence, these instruments do not regulate whether and to what extent a state may establish extraterritorial criminal jurisdiction, but whether it may prosecute and try a particular case when it has jurisdiction.[11] In this light, it is important to note that in criminal cases, choosing the forum in principle normally also means choosing the applicable substantive and procedural criminal laws.[12] Furthermore, within the category of *Zustandigkeitsmodelle*, a division is made between *ex ante* and *ex post* models. The former covers systems on the basis of which the forum for prosecution and trial is already predetermined at the time of the criminal act—*ex ante*—whereas the latter covers rules which determine the forum after the criminal act—*ex post*.

The *ex ante* mechanisms are generally more rigid and guarantee legal certainty and foreseeability by providing clarity at the time of the offence with regard to the national criminal laws that should be obeyed.[13] This is illustrated by the statutory determination model proposed by Sinn which appoints the state in which the conduct occurs as the competent forum. Only when the criminal act is committed on the territory of multiple Member States is the case allocated to the state where the consequences of the criminal act occurred. An exception to this rule is then again solely possible when the criminal consequences occurred in a state in which none of the criminal conduct was committed. In that case, the suspect's state of residence is competent.[14] This model allows citizens to predict the forum and applicable national substantive criminal law to a large extent at the time of the offence. The risk of such a system is, however, that it appoints a forum which in light of the concrete circumstances of the case is not the most appropriate one.

The *ex post* mechanisms have a case-by-case approach and aim to appoint the 'best' or 'most qualified' forum for prosecution and trial in each concrete case.[15] Examples are mechanisms which set an overall criterion for appointing the best place for prosecution, such as the good administration of justice or the *Qualitätsprinzip* (quality principle) and provide a non-exhaustive and non-hierarchical list of factors on the basis of which this criterion should be assessed.[16] These models grant the competent executive or judicial authorities more discretion in considering the

[11] Schönberger (2015), p. 321.

[12] Schönberger (2015), p. 335; Panzavolta (2013), p. 160.

[13] Schönberger (2015), pp. 480–482; 'Draft models of a regulatory mechanism for the avoidance of jurisdictional conflicts' in Arndt Sinn (ed), *Jurisdiktionskonflikte bei grenzüberschreitender Kriminalität. Ein Rechtsvergleich zum Internationalen Strafrecht* (V&R Unipress 2012) p. 608.

[14] 'Draft models of a regulatory mechanism for the avoidance of jurisdictional conflicts' in Arndt Sinn (ed), *Jurisdiktionskonflikte bei grenzüberschreitender Kriminalität. Ein Rechtsvergleich zum Internationalen Strafrecht* (V&R Unipress 2012) pp. 609–611.

[15] Schönberger (2015), p. 335.

[16] See e.g. Biehler et al. (2003), p. 13; Lagodny (2001), p. 104ff.

different factors on the basis of the specific circumstances of the case.[17] However, this flexibility also comes with certain risks. Where the *ex ante* models increase legal certainty but often restrict flexibility, this is exactly the other way around with many *ex post* models. The latter can interfere with the foreseeability of national applicable laws at the time of the offence and can increase the risk of arbitrary forum choices depending on the extent to which the law restricts the discretion of the competent decision-making authority.[18]

The third regulatory approach is twofold and separates the decision on the applicable national substantive criminal law from the decision on the competent forum. Legislative acts in this category, therefore, require national courts to apply foreign criminal laws.[19] The use of this regulatory approach, which occurs in international private law, would be quite the step, since in the area of criminal justice the substantive criminal law and the forum for prosecution and trial are viewed as a unity.[20] In other words, to choose a forum also means to choose the applicable substantive criminal law.[21]

13.5 A Proposal for EU Rules on Jurisdiction and Forum Choices

13.5.1 Balancing the Relevant Different Interests

When deciding on the most suitable regulatory approach or regulatory approaches it is key to remember that any action taken on the basis of Article 82(1)(b) TFEU should not only guarantee compliance with the transnational legality principle explained in Chap. 11, but should fit in the normative context of the AFSJ in general.[22] In this light, it is important to recall that the AFSJ has a twofold objective, namely security and free movement, which is demarcated by the twofold obligation to respect fundamental rights and the national legal systems of the Member States. The AFSJ is also a shared legal order consisting of states and EU citizens, which means that the interests of both stakeholders should be reflected in EU rules regarding conflicts of jurisdiction.[23] After all, positive conflicts of jurisdiction do

[17] See e.g. Van der Beken et al. (2002a), p. 51; Biehler et al. (2003), p. 13; Van der Beken et al. (2002b), pp. 626–627.

[18] Thorhauer (2019), p. 638; Böse (2013), pp. 74–75.

[19] Schönberger (2015), pp. 322–323.

[20] Böse (2013), p. 87.

[21] Schönberger (2015), p. 335; Panzavolta (2013), p. 160.

[22] See also Gbandi who states that a solution to conflicts of jurisdiction should be based on the understanding that 'the Union is a supranational organization aligned to its constitutional treaties (TEU and TFEU) and to its Charter of Fundamental Rights.' Kaiafa-Gbandi (2020), p. 210.

[23] Van der Beken et al. (2002b), p. 625; Van der Beken et al. (2002a), p. 46.

not only affect EU citizens, but can also have an impact on the interests of the Member States. The *ne bis in idem* principle as the single forum rule could, for instance, trigger a race between the national jurisdictions towards a final decision with the risk that some Member States will in the end have wasted time and resources on the investigation and prosecution.[24] Furthermore, states may view the decision of the 'winning' state as an injustice, for instance, when this state has classified the conduct as a minor offence.[25]

With regard to the interests of the EU citizen it is first important to note that positive conflicts of jurisdiction do not only affect EU citizens in their capacity of suspects, but in their capacity of victims or witnesses as well.[26] However, when viewing positive conflicts of jurisdiction from the perspective of the EU citizen as a (potential) suspect, the protection of fundamental rights, including the transnational legality principle, exists next to other valid and sometimes contradictory interests, such as the need for security, the possibility of resocialisation[27] and free movement. These different interests may point in the direction of different forums as the most appropriate ones.

To sum up, in my opinion the EU legislator should choose the regulatory approaches which ensure that the different interests of both the Member States and the EU citizen are represented in the legislative measures preventing or solving conflicts of jurisdiction. These measures should fit with the context of the AFSJ, demanding protection of security and free movement as well as respect for fundamental rights and national legal systems and traditions. Considering these parameters set by the normative setting of the AFSJ, the most appropriate solution to conflicts of jurisdiction requires, in my opinion, a combination of a *Restriktionsmodel* and *Zustandigkeitsmodelle.*[28]

13.5.2 Rules Addressing the Jurisdiction to Prescribe: Double Criminality Requirement

In my opinion, all grounds for extraterritorial jurisdiction, including the effects doctrine, should be subjected to the double criminality requirement. Tying the jurisdiction to prescribe to the requirement that the conduct also constitutes a criminal act according to the law of the state where either the act or omission occurred does not completely prevent conflicts of jurisdiction, but could contribute

[24] Lagodny (2001), p. 61; Van der Beken et al. (2002b), p. 625; Schomburg (2020), p. 320. See also Kaiafa-Gbandi (2020), p. 210.

[25] Lagodny (2001), p. 62; Hecker (2012), p. 90; Van der Beken et al. (2002a), p. 625.

[26] Van der Beken et al. (2002a), pp. 628; 634; Eser (2012), p. 563.

[27] Eicker (2005), p. 634.

[28] See also Giuffrida (2017), pp. 152–153. He discusses the balance between the legality principle and the space for flexibility reflected in the rules on forum decisions in the EPPO Regulation.

to it. Furthermore, in light of the *nullum crimen sine lege* principle, it contributes to the foreseeability of criminal offences and sanctions as it often guarantees that the citizen could have known that his behaviour was criminal somewhere in the EU.[29] It is true that the double criminality requirement does not necessarily make the applicability of a particular criminal law, such as the national criminal law of the state of nationality of the victim foreseeable but the criminality of the conduct as such can in principle no longer come as a surprise. The application of the double criminality requirement is also a logical step in light of free movement in the sense that the EU citizen should not have to worry that he can be prosecuted for conduct which was legal according to the law of the state to which he or she choose to move.[30]

In my opinion, this approach should be preferred over the restriction of the jurisdiction to prescribe by excluding one or more jurisdiction grounds.[31] In light of the transnational substantive legality principle as introduced in Sect. 11.3.2, the latter would provide more legal certainty and increase the foreseeability of the applicable national criminal law. However, as also stipulated in Chap. 11 exceptions to the transnational legality principle should in certain situations be allowed to protect other valid interests of EU citizens and the Member States.[32] Prohibiting certain or all but one jurisdiction ground could result in negative conflicts of jurisdiction or impunity, because the one or few competent states may not be in a position or willing to prosecute due to, for instance, mistakes made by police officers during the investigation or because most of the evidence is located abroad.[33] These risks constitute a threat to safety and security which are commonly shared interests.[34] In addition, as explained before overlapping jurisdiction claims have been viewed as an important tool in fighting cross-border criminality.[35]

[29] The double criminality requirement does not necessarily facilitate foreseeability in case the EU citizen is prosecuted for criminal offenses which do not focus on the conduct, but on the consequences of conduct. Section 13.5.3 discusses this further.

[30] Meyer and Böse (2011), p. 340. See also Luchtman (2013), p. 29. See also Fuchs (2006), pp. 364–365. Fuchs states that appointing the home state as the sole competent state would fit best with the EU citizen's freedom of movement.

[31] See in relation to restricting the jurisdiction to prescribe Schönberger (2015), p. 550.

[32] Schönberger (2015), p. 553; Luchtman (2012).

[33] Schönberger (2015), pp. 550–551; Eser (2012), p. 569. According to Eser another reason for a state not to prosecute is the fear that such a prosecution will trigger terrorist acts on its territory. See also Thorhauer who recognises that limiting the jurisdiction to prescribe demands even close judicial cooperation, including a review of existing refusal grounds in mutual recognition instruments, to reduce the risk of impunity. Thorhauer (2015), p. 100.

[34] Schönberger (2015), pp. 550–551. Furthermore, it could have practical difficulties when the victim starts a civil law suit against the suspect in one state, but the prosecution takes place in another state. Eicker (2005), p. 633; Eser (2012), p. 569; Panzavolta (2013), p. 163.

[35] See Sect. 2.4; Schönberger (2015), p. 552; Eckstein (2012), pp. 491492. Excluding jurisdiction grounds would also severely limit the power of the EU to fight cross-border crime on the basis of Article 83(1) TFEU. The harmonisation measures for criminal offenses adopted on the basis of this

13.5.3 *An EU System for Forum Choices:* Ex Ante *and* Ex Post

The above should be combined with a *Zustandigkeitsmodelle* merging the *ex ante* and *ex post* approach, which in my view offers the best chance of striking a balance between the different interests of EU citizens and Member States.[36] However, several legal scholars have argued that a predominantly *ex post* EU instrument of which the primary objective is to appoint the best state in each concrete case on the basis of a set of criteria which represent both the interests of the citizen and the Member States does justice to the EU as a shared legal order.[37] In addition, the old EU initiatives to solve conflicts of jurisdiction often seemed to favour a predominantly *ex post* system over a predominantly *ex ante* system.[38] As explained before, the adoption of an *ex ante* system for forum choices establishing a pecking order of competent states limits uncertainty in relation to the applicable substantive national criminal law, but it can also result in prosecution by a state which is not the most suitable forum when taking all circumstances into account.[39] For instance, a system which appoints the state on whose territory the crime was committed as the first competent state neglects the fact that the interests of the suspect may be better served by appointing his or her state of residence as the forum.[40] However, more flexible *ex post* systems for forum choices could threaten the foreseeability of the applicable national criminal law of a particular state and could increase the risk of arbitrary forum choices when the rules do not sufficiently limit the discretion of the competent decision-making authorities.

In light of the above, I am in agreement with the legal scholars who favour and propose mechanisms which combine the *ex ante* and *ex post* approach. Eckstein has, for instance, argued that the territoriality principle should have precedence, but that exceptions are allowed in light of other interests and in the context of the specific circumstances of the case.[41] On a similar note, Herrnfeld has stated that deviating from the territoriality principle is allowed when other interests provide reasonable

---

legal basis often contain the obligation to establish extraterritorial jurisdiction. Panzavolta (2013), p. 163.

[36] As mentioned before, it is important to note that in criminal cases choosing the forum in principle normally also means choosing the applicable substantive and procedural criminal laws.

[37] See eg Van der Beken et al. (2002a), pp. 625–626.

[38] See eg Green paper on Conflicts of Jurisdiction and the Principle of *ne bis in idem* in Criminal Proceedings, COM (2005) 696 final, pp. 7–8; Council, 'Proposal for a Council Framework Decision on prevention and settlement of conflicts of jurisdiction in criminal proceedings' [2009] 5208/09.

[39] See eg the statutory determination model proposed by Sinn. 'Draft models of a regulatory mechanism for the avoidance of jurisdictional conflicts' in Arndt Sinn (ed), *Jurisdiktionskonflikte bei grenzüberschreitender Kriminalität. Ein Rechtsvergleich zum Internationalen Strafrecht* (V&R Unipress 2012) pp. 609–611

[40] Linke (1970), p. 88.

[41] Eckstein (2012), p. 507.

grounds to do so.[42] Such a combination of the *ex ante* and *ex post* approach can be found in systems based on a presumption that the state on whose territory the act occurred is the competent state for prosecution and trial. In light of the transnational substantive legality principle, such a presumption or main rule contributes to the foreseeability of the application of a particular national substantive criminal law at the time of the offence. This presumption is also in compliance with the rule that EU citizens should in principle only have to know and abide by the law of the host state which they can choose by (not) exercising their free movement rights. However, exceptions to the presumption should be allowed when other important factors or more generally the proper administration of justice designate another state as the most appropriate forum. A more concrete example of a mixed *ex ante* and *ex post* mechanism is the regulatory model proposed by Sinn, which is based on the presumption that the *locus delicti* is competent unless other important factors, such as citizenship, the residence of the suspect and the location of evidence appoint another state as the most appropriate forum.[43] Another example is the third mechanism of the Draft Legislative Proposals for the prevention and resolution of conflicts of jurisdiction in criminal matters in the European Union, proposed by the ELI working group. The gist of this mechanism is that Member States only exercise jurisdiction over offences committed on their own territory, unless another state is more suitable in light of other interests of the good administration of justice represented by factors such as the ordinary residence of the suspect, location of evidence etc. If this is the case, the state where the crime occurred should transfer the criminal proceedings.[44]

The decision to use a general criterion like the proper administration of justice to decide on the forum, requires a catalogue of factors which represent the different interests of the EU citizen and the Member States. In this light, I would argue in favour of a non-hierarchical, but exhaustive list.[45] In light of the transnational legality principle, a hierarchy would contribute to the avoidance of arbitrary decisions when determining the applicable national criminal law and forum, but it can also hamper the appointment of the most appropriate forum.[46] To compensate for the

---

[42] Herrnfeld (2013), p. 193.

[43] 'Draft models of a regulatory mechanism for the avoidance of jurisdictional conflicts' in Arndt Sinn (ed), *Jurisdiktionskonflikte bei grenzüberschreitender Kriminalität. Ein Rechtsvergleich zum Internationalen Strafrecht* (V&R Unipress 2012) 605. See also Hecker (2011), p. 62.

[44] *Draft Legislative Proposals for the prevention and resolution of conflicts of jurisdiction in criminal matters in the European Union* (2017) <https://www.europeanlawinstitute.eu/projects-publications/publications/> accessed 20 September 2021, 55, pp. 58–59.

[45] An alternative general criterion is, for instance, 'sufficiently justified grounds'. Council Regulation (EU) 2017/1939 of 12 October 2017 implementing enhanced cooperation on the establishment of the European Public Prosecutor's Office [2017] OJ L283/1, art 36(3).

[46] Sections 11.3.2;11.3.3; Panzavolta (2013), p. 164; Van der Beken et al. (2002b), p. 45; Hecker (2012), p. 99; Herrnfeld (2013), p. 193. *A contrario* see Council Regulation (EU) 2017/1939 of 12 October 2017 implementing enhanced cooperation on the establishment of the European Public Prosecutor's Office [2017] OJ L283/1, arts 36(3) and 26(4).

absence of a hierarchy, the EU instrument should provide an exhaustive list of factors, which sufficiently restricts the discretion of the decision-making authority in deciding on the forum and in that light, the applicable national substantive criminal law.[47] Without such a list, the forum decision could be exposed to a high risk of arbitrariness and forum shopping by the prosecuting authorities, which contradicts the transnational legality principle.[48]

With regard to the content of the factors, inspiration can be drawn from the previously mentioned ELI proposals which provide a positive and a negative list.[49] The negative list excludes factors which could be used with the intent to disadvantage the accused, such as the sentencing powers of the competent states and differences between the national rules on the admissibility of evidence. Hence, the competent authorities may not appoint a state, because its national criminal law provides the most severe sentence or the lowest burden of proof.[50] The factors on the positive list include territoriality, trial-readiness, interests of the suspect and the victim, the need for judicial cooperation and the need to concentrate the proceedings. In my opinion, state sovereignty should be added to this list in order to ensure that the interests of the competent states are sufficiently guaranteed as well. In addition, adding this criterion makes it possible to eliminate several refusal grounds in the FDEAW which aim to protect state sovereignty. The protection of this interest will already have been covered at the stage of the forum decision, which can increase the speed and efficiency of the surrender procedure.[51] Furthermore, the 'interests of the suspect' should include an assessment of the foreseeability of the applicability of the national substantive criminal laws of all competent states at the time of the offence. The reason for this is that the restriction of the Member States' jurisdiction to prescribe proposed in Sect. 13.5.2 does not necessarily facilitate foreseeability in case the EU citizen is prosecuted for criminal offences which do not focus on the

---

[47] Schönberger (2015), p. 348; Van der Beken et al. (2002b), p. 30; Biehler et al. (2003), p. 14. See also Hecker (2011); Monar (2013), p. 197. See also the vertical mechanism in ELI, *Draft Legislative Proposals for the prevention and resolution of conflicts of jurisdiction in criminal matters in the European Union* (2017) <https://www.europeanlawinstitute.eu/projects-publications/publications/> accessed 20 September 2021, p. 26.

[48] 'Draft models of a regulatory mechanism for the avoidance of jurisdictional conflicts' in Arndt Sinn (ed), *Jurisdiktionskonflikte bei grenzüberschreitender Kriminalität. Ein Rechtsvergleich zum Internationalen Strafrecht* (V&R Unipress 2012) p. 604. See also also Hecker (2011), p. 62.

[49] ELI, *Draft Legislative Proposals for the prevention and resolution of conflicts of jurisdiction in criminal matters in the European Union* (2017) <https://www.europeanlawinstitute.eu/projects-publications/publications/> accessed 20 September 2021.

[50] ELI, *Draft Legislative Proposals for the prevention and resolution of conflicts of jurisdiction in criminal matters in the European Union* (2017) <https://www.europeanlawinstitute.eu/projects-publications/publications/> accessed 20 September 2021, p. 21; Van der Beken et al. (2002a), p. 626; 'Draft models of a regulatory mechanism for the avoidance of jurisdictional conflicts' in Arndt Sinn (ed), *Jurisdiktionskonflikte bei grenzüberschreitender Kriminalität. Ein Rechtsvergleich zum Internationalen Strafrecht* (V&R Unipress 2012) p. 605. See also also Hecker (2011), p. 62.

[51] This is discussed in Sect. 13.6.

conduct, but on the consequences of conduct.[52] The double criminality requirement is less effective in ensuring foreseeability in case an EU citizen is prosecuted for such offences, especially since it may at the time of the offence not be foreseeable where the consequences will occur.[53]

It follows from the above that even when the list of factors is exhaustive, the factors themselves can still be relatively broad. For instance, factors generally referring to the interests of the suspect and the victim are quite broad, which could be problematic in light of the transnational legality principle as it could increase the risk of arbitrary decisions on the forum and applicable substantive criminal law. Such broad factors could be used to hide the real unfair reason for choosing a certain forum.[54] Still, such factors also extend the opportunity to choose the best forum in a particular case on the basis of the concrete circumstances. Considering the large amount of different interest which may be in play in cross-border cases and the need for an appropriate choice in the concrete case, it is in my opinion best to allow this 'unclarity' or 'vagueness' of the meaning and scope of the different factors. These disadvantages relating to the transnational legality principle should in my view be solved by other means, such as the possibility of a (judicial) review of the forum decision.[55]

13.5.4 Forum Decision: At What Point in Time?

An important question is at what point in time a definite forum decision should be made in a cross-border case. In other words, from what point in time onwards should parallel prosecutions be prohibited and should investigations in different states exclusively serve the prosecution by the appointed forum. When answering this question it is important to remember that the transnational right to a tribunal established by law does not require that the individual is able to predict the forum for prosecution and trial at the time of the offence.[56] Its main purpose is to protect the suspect against arbitrariness and abuse of power by the executive and judiciary.[57]

[52] Article 307 DCC constitutes an example. It states that individuals who can be blamed for the death of another can be held criminally liable. Criminal liability arises from the consequences of the conduct and is less related to the conduct itself.

[53] See also Wolswijk (1998), p. 86.

[54] Swart (1983), p. 10; Swart (1982), p. 216.

[55] See also Sect. 13.5.6.

[56] ECtHR 9 June 2005, 26,384/02 (*Vokhmina/Russia*); ECtHR 12 July 2007, 74,613/01 (*Jorgic/Germany*) para 65. In addition, procedural law follows the principle *tempus regit actum* and is, therefore, in principle not subject to the prohibition of the retroactive application of the law correlating from art 7(1) ECHR. ECtHR 17 September 2009, 10,249/03 (*Scoppola/Italy No. 2*) para 110. See also ECtHR 12 February 2004, 7856/02 (*Mione/Italy*).

[57] Böse (2013), p. 80.

Hence, the forum for prosecution and trial does not need to be foreseeable at the time of the offence.[58]

In general, two positions exist in relation to the question at what point in time a forum decision should be made.[59] The first one is to allocate the case as early as possible, meaning already during the pre-trial stage.[60] In this case, the earliest point in time to make the forum decision is during the investigatory proceedings.[61] A forum decision at this point in time means that other states may from then on only continue investigations on the request of or for the purpose of prosecution and trial in the appointed state. On the one hand, the advantage of this first position is that it largely avoids the risk of parallel investigations in which suspects are subjected to the same investigatory acts in different Member States. In addition, early forum decisions allow the non-competent states to take the *lex fori* into consideration when contributing to the collection of evidence.[62] On the other hand, one disadvantage of the first position is that the point in time at which a prosecution decision is made differs in the Member States and sometimes even within one Member State depending on the procedure.[63] In some legal systems, the prosecution phase only starts when the case is brought before the competent judge, while in other states the investigation into a particular offence cannot even start before the prosecutor has officially initiated a prosecution by indicting the suspect.[64] Furthermore, parallel investigations can be essential for effective prosecutions as they contribute to the collection of evidence.[65] Moreover, when the decision to prosecute occurs at an early stage of the preliminary proceedings, it could obstruct the possibility to appoint the *forum conveniens*. At the time of the decision, not all relevant evidence and information may have been collected to ensure that the most appropriate forum can be appointed on the basis of a fair weighing of all the interests of the parties involved.[66] Hence, allowing parallel prosecutions for some time could be

[58] The point in time at which the forum decision should be made in turn influences the amendments that need to be made to the FDEAW to transform it into a mechanism which facilitates prosecution and trial by the most appropriate forum. The amendments are discussed in the next sections.

[59] Schönberger (2015), p. 336.

[60] Schönberger (2015), p. 336; Eicker (2005), p. 636; Lagodny (2001), p. 129.

[61] German criminal procedural law, for instance, makes a distinction between the suspect and the accused. Generally speaking, a suspect becomes an accused when he or she is subjected to an act of prosecution. A suspect is, therefore, generally not considered to be directly subjected to a criminal prosecution. Schönberger (2015), pp. 336–338; Eicker (2005), p. 636.

[62] Panzavolta (2013), p. 159. Dickson (2014), p. 64.

[63] 'Draft models of a regulatory mechanism for the avoidance of jurisdictional conflicts' in Arndt Sinn (ed), Jurisdiktionskonflikte bei grenzüberschreitender Kriminalität. Ein Rechtsvergleich zum Internationalen Strafrecht (V&R Unipress 2012) pp. 604–605.

[64] See Lelieur (2013), p. 206.

[65] Lelieur (2013), p. 206; Herrnfeld (2013), p. 209; Eurojust, Report on Eurojust's casework in the field of prevention and resolution of conflicts of jurisdiction (2018) < www.eurojust.europa.eu> accessed 20 September 2021, p. 5. *A contrario* see Kaiafa-Gbandi (2020), p. 211.

[66] Eser (2013), p. 683; Heger (2013), p. 685; Luchtman (2013), p. 30; Green paper on Conflicts of Jurisdiction and the Principle of *ne bis in idem* in Criminal Proceedings, COM (2005) 696 final, p. 7.

advantageous for the purpose of finding the most appropriate forum and for effective investigations.[67]

The second position is to make a definite forum decision before the start of the trial on the merits of the case or before another decision disposing of the case is made.[68] On the one hand, the start of court proceedings usually suggests that most or at least sufficient essential information and evidence has been collected to decide on the case, which also increases the chance of appointing the best qualified state for prosecution on the basis of a fair balance between the different interests.[69] In addition, this point in time is also compatible with the transnational right to a tribunal established by law as the national jurisdiction and court for the case do not have to be established at the time of the offence.[70] On the other hand, a forum decision just before the start of the trial increases the risk that the suspect is subjected to parallel procedures and the same investigatory measures interfering which his or her fundamental rights for quite a long period of time. However, this disadvantage can, for instance, be resolved by EU legislation which obliges or encourages the national investigation and prosecution authorities to coordinate their criminal investigations.[71] In fact, the EU legal framework already provides a range of possibilities for increased coordination among which the establishment of a joint investigation team.

In my opinion, the EU legislator should adopt an instrument requesting the competent authority or authorities to make the forum decision as early as possible, but definitely before the start of the main proceedings.[72] Once a particular Member State has been appointed as the forum in a concrete case, the other competent Member States should discontinue their own national criminal proceedings or refrain from starting any.[73] However, the national authorities in the competent states are not prohibited from deciding to bring a case to trial before a forum decision has been reached.[74] Setting such an obligation would interfere with state sovereignty, especially for states according to whose criminal procedure cases need to be brought to trial in an early phase. In addition, the situation in which one of the states brings the

[67] Herrnfeld (2013), pp. 193, 209.

[68] Herrnfeld (2013), p. 205; Luchtman (2013), pp. 28, 30.

[69] Green paper on Conflicts of Jurisdiction and the Principle of *ne bis in idem* in Criminal Proceedings, COM (2005) 696 final, p. 7. See also Luchtman (2013), pp. 28, 30.

[70] Böse, has stated that the fact that the tribunal needs to be 'previously' established by law does not mean that it has to be established at the time of the offense, but before the commencement of the trial before the court. Böse (2013), footnote 47.

[71] Schönberger (2015), pp. 340–341.

[72] See also Herrnfeld (2013), p. 205.

[73] This obligation may be particularly troublesome for states who apply the legality principe, meaning that each case which on the basis of the facts and available evidence could be prosecuted should be prosecuted.

[74] See also ELI, *Draft Legislative Proposals for the prevention and resolution of conflicts of jurisdiction in criminal matters in the European Union* (2017) <https://www.europeanlawinstitute.eu/projects-publications/publications/> accessed 20 September 2021, p. 35.

case to trial before a forum decision is made and the situation in which the cross-border dimension of the criminal case surfaces after the case has already been brought before a particular national judge are tricky ones, since some Member States adhere to the general principle that when the examination in court has started, the suspect has in principle a right to a continuation of the procedure until a final ruling is provided.[75] In this light, I would argue that after the case has been brought to court in a particular state, a forum decision on the basis of the proposed instrument should only be made and enforced when *ne bis in idem* does not yet apply and the suspect consents to a change of forum.

13.5.5 The Choice for an Instrument: A Directive or a Regulation?

As explained before, Article 82(1)(b) TFEU provides the main legal basis for new EU rules on preventing and solving conflicts of jurisdiction. It allows the EU legislator to choose between a directive which needs to be transposed into national law and a regulation which is directly applicable.[76] As a directive is binding on the result and leaves Member States the competence to choose the form and methods of its transposition, it may be more suitable for the approximation rules restricting the Member States' jurisdiction to prescribe proposed in Sect. 13.5.2.[77] However, with regard to the proposed EU rules regarding the Member States' jurisdiction to adjudicate a directly applicable regulation which provides a uniform set of clear and precise rules seems to be a more appropriate instrument, since the proposal contains binding rules on settling conflicts of jurisdiction, aims to increase protection against arbitrariness and the legal certainty of the EU citizen, and allocates the task of taking binding forum decisions to both states and an EU agency.[78] Furthermore, the tasks allocated to Eurojust also require an amendment of the Eurojust Regulation on the basis of Article 85(1)(c) TFEU.[79]

[75] HR 28 February 1984, ECLI:NL:HR:1984:AC8323 (Dutch Supreme Court).

[76] TFEU, arts 288(2–3).

[77] See also ELI, *Draft Legislative Proposals for the prevention and resolution of conflicts of jurisdiction in criminal matters in the European Union* (2017) <https://www.europeanlawinstitute.eu/projects-publications/publications/> accessed 20 September 2021, p. 26.

[78] Zimmerman (2015), p. 369ff; Böse (2014), p. 376; ELI, *Draft Legislative Proposals for the prevention and resolution of conflicts of jurisdiction in criminal matters in the European Union* (2017) <https://www.europeanlawinstitute.eu/projects-publications/publications/> accessed 20 September 2021, p. 26. For a different opinion see Herrnfeld (2013), pp. 200–202.

[79] Regulation (EU) 2018/1727 of the European Parliament and of the Council of 14 November 2018 on the European Union Agency for Criminal Justice Cooperation (Eurojust), and replacing and repealing Council Decision 2002/187/JHA [2018] L295/138.

13.5.6 Appointing Competent Authorities

With regard to the question who or which authority should be competent to take the forum decision in case multiple states have jurisdiction to adjudicate, it is in my view best to adopt a multifold system as described by Hecker and the ELI project in which horizontal cooperation between authorities of the Member States which have a jurisdictional link to the offence in question is the starting point.[80] This horizontal mechanism should be complemented with the possibility of a binding decision by Eurojust, which should in turn be open to judicial review. On the first level of horizontal cooperation, all states who have or had a jurisdictional link to the case should be allowed to participate. This includes states who can at the time of the forum decision not exercise their jurisdiction to adjudicate, because of national rules on amnesty or because the statute of limitations has run out. Including these states in the negotiations and weighing their interests in the considerations could allow for the abolition of several refusal grounds in the FDEAW, increasing its speed and efficiency. The abolition of these refusal grounds is further elaborated on in the next sections. Furthermore, the Member States can appoint judges, tribunals or courts as well as public prosecutors as the competent authorities to participate in the forum negotiations. The latter are often the most familiar with the criminal case, which makes them suitable authorities for deciding on the best forum, even more so since their discretion is also restricted by the exhaustive list of factors in the proposed set of rules, which reduces the risk of arbitrary case allocations.[81]

The proposed horizontal mechanism would also preserve the existing legal framework for the exchange of information and obligatory consultations laid down in Framework Decision 2009 on conflicts of jurisdiction, but with some important additions.[82] Firstly, the suspects as well as the victims should in principle be provided with the opportunity to express their views on the most appropriate forum.[83] Secondly, Framework Decision 2009/948 on conflicts of jurisdiction requires that national competent authorities contact and consult each other when reasonable grounds exist to believe that parallel proceedings are being conducted. In the new horizontal mechanism, this obligation should be triggered at an earlier point

[80] The horizontal and vertical mechanism of the ELI, *Draft Legislative Proposals for the prevention and resolution of conflicts of jurisdiction in criminal matters in the European Union* (2017) <https://www.europeanlawinstitute.eu/projects-publications/publications/> accessed 20 September 2021, pp. 29–52. See also Hecker (2011), pp. 62–63.

[81] See also Panzavolta (2013), p. 164.

[82] See the horizontal mechanism proposed by the ELI working group. ELI, *Draft Legislative Proposals for the prevention and resolution of conflicts of jurisdiction in criminal matters in the European Union* (2017) <https://www.europeanlawinstitute.eu/projects-publications/publications/ > accessed 20 September 2021, pp. 29–38.

[83] See the horizontal mechanism proposed by the ELI working group. ELI, *Draft Legislative Proposals for the prevention and resolution of conflicts of jurisdiction in criminal matters in the European Union* (2017) <https://www.europeanlawinstitute.eu/projects-publications/publications/ > accessed 20 September 2021, art 8(3).

in time, namely when 'indications' arise that parallel proceedings are conducted or are about to be conducted in different Member States.[84] The regulation should also mention that the receipt of an EAW by definition constitutes such an indication of parallel proceedings.[85] Thirdly, as follows from the previous sections, contrary to the current horizontal mechanism, the proposed instrument contains an exhaustive list of factors on the basis of which the forum decision should be made.

In case the appointed national authorities of the competent Member States fail to reach an agreement or when the suspect disagrees with the forum decision, there should be a possibility to refer the case to an EU body for which Eurojust seems well suited.[86] This EU agency already has the task as well as the experience of assisting the Member States in case of conflicts of jurisdiction.[87] As mentioned before, Article 85(1)(c) TFEU states that Eurojust may be provided with the task to resolve conflicts of jurisdiction. An advantage of granting Eurojust the power to issue binding forum decisions is that it could compensate for the absence of a pecking order for the factors which the national competent authorities should consider and the fact that many factors, such as the interests of the suspect are relatively broad and undefined. National competent authorities are encouraged to refrain from arbitrary decisions and forced to carefully consider all interests involved as their decision can be checked and overruled by Eurojust.

For the same reason, it is recommended to install the possibility for national authorities and the suspect the challenge Eurojust's decision before a court which would be competent to assess its reasonableness.[88] The follow-up question, of course, is which courts or tribunals should be appointed. On the one hand, some legal scholars have suggested to allocate the power of judicial review to the CJEU. The annulment procedure in Article 263 TFEU could be used for this purpose.[89] The

[84] See horizontal mechanism proposed by the ELI working group. ELI, *Draft Legislative Proposals for the prevention and resolution of conflicts of jurisdiction in criminal matters in the European Union* (2017) <https://www.europeanlawinstitute.eu/projects-publications/publications/> accessed 20 September 2021, art 5.

[85] See also *Draft Legislative Proposals for the prevention and resolution of conflicts of jurisdiction in criminal matters in the European Union* (2017) <https://www.europeanlawinstitute.eu/projects-publications/publications/> accessed 20 September 2021, p. 32.

[86] Van der Beken et al. (2002a), p. 627; 'Draft models of a regulatory mechanism for the avoidance of jurisdictional conflicts' in Arndt Sinn (ed), *Jurisdiktionskonflikte bei grenzüberschreitender Kriminalität. Ein Rechtsvergleich zum Internationalen Strafrecht* (V&R Unipress 2012) pp. 604–605.

[87] Regulation 2018/1727 of the European Parliament and of the Council of 14 November 2018 on the European Union Agency for Criminal Justice Cooperation (Eurojust), and replacing and repealing Council Decision 2002/187/JHA [2018] OJ L295/138, art 5(2)(i); FD on conflicts of jurisdiction [2009] OJ L328/42, art 12(2).

[88] *Draft Legislative Proposals for the prevention and resolution of conflicts of jurisdiction in criminal matters in the European Union* (2017) <https://www.europeanlawinstitute.eu/projects-publications/publications/> accessed 20 September 2021, pp. 22, 24–25; Van der Beken et al. (2002a), p. 627. See also Hecker (2012), pp. 100–101. See also Franken (2013), p. 111.

[89] See also Kaiafa-Gbandi (2020), pp. 211–212.

legality of the Eurojust decision could, for instance, be questioned on the basis of an alleged infringement of EU secondary legislation, more specifically the application of the criteria and factors in the instrument proposed, or perhaps even on the basis of misuse of power.[90] If the CJEU rules that the forum decision is void, the case should return to Eurojust as the CJEU is in principle not competent to issue a forum decision itself.[91] A disadvantage of the infringement procedure is, however, that it is not certain whether the suspect would have standing, since he or she needs to fulfil the difficult criteria in Article 263(4) TFEU.[92] On the other hand, the task of judicial review could also become the responsibility of the national courts, in particular the national court of the Member State appointed as the forum. The possible risk that this national court takes a national perspective instead of a European one is reduced by the obligation and competence to request the CJEU for preliminary rulings on the applicable EU rules. In addition, the duty of applying or considering EU law exists for quite some time now, meaning that national courts are getting more and more accustomed to it.[93]

13.5.7 Interim Conclusion

To sum up, when viewing the AFSJ as a shared legal order in which EU citizens and states have an equal position, I recommend the EU legislator to adopt a directive addressing the Member States' jurisdiction to prescribe and a regulation addressing the Member States' jurisdiction to adjudicate. The former should restrict extraterritorial jurisdiction grounds with the double criminality requirement and the latter should set up a system for solving conflicts of jurisdiction by combining the *ex ante* and *ex post* approach of the *Zustandigkeitsmodelle*. Together, these proposals can achieve an appropriate balance between the different interests involved in a forum decisions. The double criminality requirement in the directive and *ex ante* elements in the regulation, such as the presumption that the state where the crime occurred is the competent one would protect the transnational substantive legality principle. The *ex post* elements which allow for a deviation from the main presumption ensure the necessary flexibility to guarantee that in each case the most appropriate national jurisdiction is chosen in light of the proper administration of justice. With regard to

[90] Herrnfeld (2013), p. 204.

[91] TFEU, art 264; Lenaerts et al. (2014), p. 411ff.

[92] The ELI group proposes an instrument which in fact states that the suspect meets the criteria for standing in Article 263 TFEU. In addition, some have argued that the treaties may have to be adapted to ensure that the suspect has standing before the CEJU in relation to forum decisions made by Eurojust. Herrnfeld (2013), pp. 203–204; *Draft Legislative Proposals for the prevention and resolution of conflicts of jurisdiction in criminal matters in the European Union* (2017) <https://www.europeanlawinstitute.eu/projects-publications/publications/> accessed 20 September 2021, pp. 25–26, 50. See also Wasmeier (2018), p. 114; Hecker (2011), p. 63.

[93] Herrnfeld (2013), pp. 205–206.

this general criterion, the factors which the competent authorities need to consider when deciding on the forum and applicable national criminal law should be exhaustively laid down to restrict the risk of arbitrary decisions. Furthermore, the regulation should state that the forum decision should in principle be made by national competent authorities. Only when they fail to do this or the suspect disagrees with the decision is Eurojust competent to issue a binding decision, which itself should be open to judicial review on the EU or national level. Lastly, the decision on the forum should be made as early as possible, but at the latest before the commencement of the trial before a court.

13.6 Recommendations as to How to Amend the FDEAW

13.6.1 Introduction

The adoption of the proposed directive and regulation requires, in my view, certain changes to the preamble and provisions of the FDEAW. The former should, for instance, state that one of the goals of the EAW is also to facilitate prosecution and trial by the most appropriate forum in each concrete case.[94] With regard to the operative provisions, the next sections set out the recommended changes to the provisions regulating the executing and issuing procedure. In my view, two sets of rules should apply; one set for the situation in which no forum decision is made and one set for the situation in which a forum decision is made. We will see that only the second situation triggers fundamental amendments to the executing and issuing procedure. The discussion of these amendments is, however, limited to the provisions on prosecution EAWs, since the proposed EU instruments preventing and solving conflicts of jurisdiction solely focus on the stage of prosecution and not on the enforcement of a sanction. In other words, conditions and criteria in the FDEAW regarding execution EAWs, such as Article 4(6) FDEAW, are not considered.

13.6.2 The Operation of the EAW in the Absence of an Official Forum Decision

This category covers different types of situations. An example is a case in which the national prosecuting authorities or Eurojust have not yet decided upon a forum on the basis of the EU rules. Another one is the situation in which the cross-border dimension of the case only surfaces after the case has been brought to trial in one of the competent states and the suspect does not consent to a change of forum. In these scenarios, the EAW can in principle continue to function as it does now, but I would

[94] This could be added to recital 5 of the Preamble of the FDEAW.

propose some minor changes to Articles 4(2), 4(7)(a) and 16 FDEAW. Firstly, I recommend to repeat in Article 4(2) FDEAW, the refusal ground based on domestic proceedings, that the receipt of an EAW constitutes an indication of parallel proceedings which triggers the obligation to initiate direct consultations with the issuing state on the basis of the proposed regulation. Secondly, the same statement should be added to Article 4(7)(a) FDEAW for cases in which the executing state refuses the EAW, because the offence was partly committed on its territory and decides to initiate a prosecution itself. Thirdly, when the executing judicial authority has received multiple EAWs for the same person and the same offence it should first notify the issuing authorities of the situation. In case the proposed regulation is applicable, Article 16 FDEAW should oblige the executing judicial authority to postpone its decision until the conditions in the proposed regulation have been complied with.[95]

13.6.3 The Operation of the EAW After an Official Forum Decision

13.6.3.1 Introduction

This section describes the proposed amendments to the FDEAW for both the executing and issuing procedure. In relation to the former, I recommend that most of the mandatory and optional refusal grounds in Articles 3–4A FDEAW are abolished and that some of the guarantees in Article 5 FDEAW are adapted.[96] In addition, a situation in which multiple EAWs are issued for the same offence and the same person should in principle no longer occur, which has consequences for Article 16 FDEAW. In relation to the issuing procedure, the most important changes are the eradication of the proportionality check in Article 2(1) FDEAW and the restriction of the power to issue an EAW which should be exclusively granted to the issuing judicial authority of the competent forum.

13.6.3.2 The Execution Procedure: The Double Criminality Check (Arts 2 and 4(1) FDEAW)

In my opinion, the adoption of the proposed EU directive and regulation justify a complete abolition of the double criminality requirement in the surrender procedure,

[95] When the case has been brought before a national court in one of the issuing states, the decision on the execution of an EAW should only be postponed when the requested person consents to an assessment on the basis of the proposed regulation as to which state is the most appropriate forum.

[96] See also Green paper on Conflicts of Jurisdiction and the Principle of *ne bis in idem* in Criminal Proceedings, COM (2005) 696 final, p. 9; European Commission, 'Mutual Recognition of Final Decisions in Criminal Matters' (Communication) COM (2000) 495 final, p. 18.

since the interests which this requirement aims to protect would to a large extent also be covered by these proposed instruments, in particular the directive. As explained in Chap. 4, the primary ratio of the double requirement in the surrender procedure is to protect the sovereignty of the executing state which should not be forced to assist foreign prosecutions of acts and omissions it does not classify as criminal conduct in its own national law. In addition, it has been argued in the legal literature that the double criminality requirement also protects the legal certainty of citizens. The loss of this protection as a result of the complete elimination of the double criminality requirement in the surrender procedure could to a large extent be compensated by the proposed EU directive which obliges Member States to restrict their extraterritorial jurisdiction with the double criminality requirement. In this context, the double criminality requirement entails that extraterritorial jurisdiction is only established when the conduct also constitutes a criminal offence according to the law of the state where it occurred.[97] The compensation which it can offer is best illustrated with the example in which an EU citizen, who has been living in another Member State than his state of nationality for a few years, refuses to pay child alimony. This constitutes a criminal act according to the law of his state of nationality, but not according to the law of his state of residence which is also the state where the conduct occurs. In the current surrender procedure, his state of residence could refuse an EAW issued by his state of nationality on the basis of the double criminality requirement.[98] However, the proposed directive could achieve a similar result, since its effect is that the state of nationality does not have extraterritorial jurisdiction to prosecute the case and can, therefore, not issue an EAW. Hence, the double criminality requirement imposed by the proposed directive could in this example both protect the sovereignty of the Member State of residence, which does not have to aid another state in the prosecution of conduct it has not criminalised itself, and the legal certainty of the EU citizen who can be sure that, as long as he abides by the law of the state of residence, there is no need to fear prosecution and trial in his state of nationality.

However, the loss of protection currently offered by the double criminality requirement in the surrender procedure will not be compensated in all cases. Imagine the situation in which the Netherlands receives a French EAW for an act which is a criminal offence according to the law of the *locus delicti*, which is Germany, but not according to Dutch law. Even though the French prosecution clashes with the Dutch views on criminal behaviour, the Netherlands is obliged to aid the French authorities if France is appointed as the most appropriate forum. However, in my view, the fact that the sovereignty of the Netherlands as the executing state is not protected in this situation is acceptable, since the need for prosecution by a state which is appointed on the basis of a system in which the interests of all the parties with an actual link to

[97] In that sense, it differs from the double criminality requirement in the surrender procedure which demands that the act in question is a criminal offense according to the law of the executing state, which is not necessarily the state where the conduct occurred.

[98] Assuming the state of residence has implemented Article 4(1) FDEAW which constitutes an optional refusal ground.

the underlying criminal case are taken into account should prevail over the need to protect the national sovereignty of a state which has no link to the criminal act at all, except for the fact that it has received an EAW. In addition, the abolition of the double criminality requirement in the surrender procedure serves judicial cooperation on the basis of mutual recognition which is based on the idea that the differences between the national criminal systems of the Member States are accepted and do not stand in the way of cooperation. To conclude, the adoption of the proposed instruments on conflicts of jurisdiction justifies the abolition of the double criminality requirement in the surrender procedure.

13.6.3.3 The Execution Procedure: Mandatory Refusal Grounds (Art 3)

With regard to the mandatory refusal grounds, it could in my view be justified to abolish both Articles 3(1) and 3(3) FDEAW. Article 3(1) FDEAW obliges the executing state to refuse the execution of the EAW when the offence is covered by amnesty and the executing Member State was in fact competent to prosecute this offence itself. Similar to the double criminality requirement, this refusal ground aims to protect state sovereignty as states should not be forced to aid foreign prosecutions when these prosecutions clash with their own views on crime and crime-fighting efforts.[99] In light of the fact that this refusal ground only applies when the executing state itself had jurisdiction to prosecute the offence, it is in my view preferable that its sovereignty interests are raised at the stage of the forum decision in which the executing state will have taken part as well.[100] The matter of amnesty could, for instance, be brought forward by the national authority representing the executing state at the time of the forum negotiations.[101] Hence, in my view, the discussion on the protection of state sovereignty should preferably occur at the stage of the forum decision as a result of which it no longer needs to be considered in the surrender procedure facilitating prosecution by the forum appointed as the most appropriate one.

A similar reasoning applies in relation to Article 3(3) FDEAW, which states that the executing state has to refuse the EAW when the requested person may not, due to his or her age, be held criminally responsible for the acts in question under the law of the executing state. It has been argued that the ratio of this refusal ground is to protect state sovereignty in the sense that states should not have to assist foreign prosecutions and investigations when these clash with their own ideas on the criminality of certain acts and/or what kind of response is appropriate in a particular criminal case.[102] However, in my opinion, it is better to consider these sovereignty interests at

[99] Glerum (2013), p. 587.

[100] Section 13.5.6 explained that all states which in principle have or had jurisdiction to adjudicate should be involved in the forum negotiations.

[101] For a discussion whether amnesty constitutes a barrier to prosecution or affects the criminality of the conduct, see Glerum (2013), pp. 586–589.

[102] Glerum (2013), p. 372.

the time of the forum decision in which the executing state will be allowed to participate if it has jurisdiction to adjudicate. These interests should then no longer be able to hamper prosecution by the most appropriate forum via the subsequent surrender procedure. Nevertheless, contrary to Article 3(1) FDEAW the application of this refusal ground is not dependent on the competence of the executing state to exercise jurisdiction over the case itself. Consequently, similar to the situation in which the double criminality requirement is completely abolished, the executing state may have to surrender citizens who would have been too young to be held criminally responsible on the basis of its own law, while this fact has not been considered at the time of the forum negotiations in which the executing state as a non-competent state was not included. Still, in my view, this loss of protection of state sovereignty seems like an acceptable consequence of the establishment of a system of forum choices in light of the good administration of justice, especially since in this situation the executing state itself has no jurisdictional link to the criminal act in question. Hence, it would in my view be incorrect to give precedence to the sovereignty interests of this state over the interests of another state appointed as the most appropriate forum and whose national legal order has been violated.

Article 3(2) FDEAW contains the *ne bis in idem* principle which prohibits the executing judicial authority from executing an EAW when the case has already been finally disposed of in one of the Member States and any imposed sentence has been served, is currently being served or may no longer be executed under the law of the sentencing Member State. In principle, this refusal ground should no longer be necessary, because a final decision on the case would have surfaced at the time of the forum negotiations. However, it could happen that after the forum decision is made and an EAW is issued, it is discovered that the case was already finally decided on by a Member State whose link to the criminal act was unknown at the time of the forum decision. In such situations, the requested person should be protected against *ne bis in idem* violations and, therefore, Article 3(2) FDEAW should not be abolished.

In addition to the preservation of Article 3(2) FDEAW and the possible abolishment of Articles 3(1) and 3(3) FDEAW, I would also recommend to include a new mandatory refusal ground prohibiting the execution of an EAW which is issued by a state which is not the forum appointed on the basis of the proposed EU regulation. Hence, when a Member State ignores the forum decision which is made and issues an EAW, the executing state should be obliged to refuse its execution, unless the forum state has explicitly indicated that it is no longer willing or capable to prosecute the case. Then the situation becomes one in which no forum decision has been made (yet), as discussed in Sect. 13.6.2.

13.6.3.4 The Execution Procedure: Optional Refusal Grounds (Arts 4 and 4A)

The adoption of the proposed directive and regulation would, in my opinion, allow for the abolishment of all optional refusal grounds applicable to prosecution EAWs with the exception of Article 4(5) FDEAW.[103] The latter prohibits the execution of the EAW when a final decision on the case has already been reached in a third state. The existence of such a final decision could fall under the interests of the suspect which should be discussed at the stage of the forum decision, but it may occur that it only surfaces after a forum decision has been made. In this light, it is in my view in the interest of the requested person to preserve this refusal ground which offers the executing state the discretion to protect the requested person against surrender in *ne bis in idem* situations.

With regard to the other optional refusal grounds, Article 4(1) FDEAW on double criminality has already been discussed in the previous sections. The refusal ground in Article 4(2) FDEAW allows the executing judicial authority to refuse the execution of an EAW when the requested person is already being prosecuted in the executing state for the same offence. The adoption of the proposed EU instruments would leave this refusal ground without purpose, because all states except for the appointed state are obliged to discontinue their criminal proceedings.[104] Hence, this refusal ground is no longer necessary.

Article 4(3) FDEAW in fact comprises three separate refusal grounds. One of them prohibits the execution of an EAW when a final judgement has been passed on the act in question in another Member State which prevents further proceedings in the executing state. The exact scope of this refusal ground is not very clearly established, but it was most likely introduced to allow Member States to refuse the execution of an EAW when the case has been dealt with in out-of-court proceedings in another Member State.[105] However, as a result of the case law of the CJEU, such final judgements nowadays fall under the scope of the *ne bis in idem* principle in Articles 54 CISA and 50 CFR and are, therefore, prohibited by Article 3(2) FDEAW.[106] Hence, if it turns out that Article 4(3) FDEAW has exactly the same scope as Article 3(2) FDEAW, it no longer seems necessary and can be taken out. In addition, the other two refusal grounds in Article 4(3) FDEAW cover situations in which the judicial authorities of the executing Member State have decided not to prosecute the conduct for which the EAW is issued or have decided to halt criminal proceedings.[107] In the legal literature, it has been argued that these refusal grounds were installed because states have an interest in enforcing their own prosecution decisions and should not have to set them aside in favour of the interests of the issuing state.[108] In other words, these two refusal grounds aim to protect state

[103] As mentioned before, Article 4(6) FDEAW is not discussed, since it applies in case of execution EAWs.

[104] Section 13.5.4.

[105] Glerum (2013), pp. 527, 529. See also Suominen (2011), p. 247.

[106] See eg Joined Cases C-187/01 & C-385/01 *Hüseyin Gözütok & Klaus Brügge* [2003] ECLI:EU:C:2003:87.

[107] It should be noted that when these decisions classify as final decisions on the basis of the case law on the *ne bis in idem* principle in Articles 54 CISA and 50 CFR, Article 3(2) FDEAW is applicable.

[108] Glerum (2013), p. 528.

sovereignty. As this refusal ground covers situations in which the executing state most likely has a jurisdictional link to the criminal offence, this state will also be allowed to participate in the forum negotiations if the proposed EU regulation on conflicts of jurisdiction is adopted.[109] As follows from Sect. 13.5.3 its sovereignty interests are a relevant factor to be considered in these negotiations. Hence, it is in my view not necessary to allow Member States to hamper the prosecution by the appointed forum on the basis of these sovereignty interests in the context of the surrender procedure which follows the forum decision.

Article 4(4) FDEAW covers situations in which criminal prosecution is statute barred according to the law of the executing state and the acts fall within the jurisdiction of that Member State under its own criminal law. In light of the fact that this refusal ground requires that the national criminal law of the executing state is applicable to the act in question it can be assumed that the executing state officially also has jurisdiction to adjudicate, but would not be able to exercise it in the concrete case due to the statute of limitations. As explained in Sect. 13.5.6, these states will also be allowed to participate in the forum negotiations if the proposed EU instruments on conflicts of jurisdiction are adopted. Furthermore, these rules on forum choices include state sovereignty as a factor which needs to be assessed in the forum negotiations. Hence, as the sovereignty interests of the executing state which Article 4(4) FDEAW protects should be taken into account in the procedure establishing the forum, this refusal ground no longer seems necessary.[110]

Article 4(7)(a) FDEAW allows the executing state to refuse the EAW when the act was wholly or partly committed on its territory. As explained in Chap. 4, under the current operation of the FDEAW this territoriality exception also compensates for the partial abolition of the double criminality requirement. It provides the executing state with the possibility to refuse the EAW when the act is not a criminal offence under its own national criminal law, even when this offence falls under the scope of Article 2(2) FDEAW. The ratio of the territoriality exception as a compensation mechanism is to protect the sovereignty of the executing state and the legal certainty of the citizen. On the one hand, in case Article 4(7)(a) FDEAW would be abolished, the protection of these interests could be ensured by the proposed directive, which obliges the Member States to restrict all grounds for extraterritorial jurisdiction with the double criminality requirement. In that setting the double criminality requirement demands that the act constitutes a criminal offence in the prosecuting state and the state where the conduct occurred. As a result of this requirement, a state would not be confronted with extraterritorial jurisdiction claims and EAWs from other states when the act wholly occurred on its territory and does not constitute a criminal act under is national law. On the other hand, the territoriality exception also applies when the conduct constitutes a criminal offence according to the law of the executing state. In this situation, it allows the executing state to give precedence to its own convictions on how the case should be dealt with. The

---

[109] See Section 13.5.6.

[110] Glerum (2013), pp. 603, 607.

proposed directive addressing the Member States' jurisdiction to prescribe would not replace this protection of state sovereignty when the territoriality exception is abolished. However, in my opinion, the adoption of the proposed regulation addressing the Member States' jurisdiction to adjudicate should ensure that the territorial link of a state to the offence and the interlinked sovereignty interests are already considered during the procedure for a forum decision. When it turns out that the territoriality argument has in this procedure been overruled by other important interests, such as the interest of the suspect in being prosecuted in his or her state of residence then Article 4(7)(a) FDEAW should in the subsequent surrender procedure not stand in the way of prosecution by this more appropriate forum. Hence, it would in my view be possible to abolish the territoriality exception as well.

As explained in Chap. 4, Article 4(7)(b) FDEAW comprises the extraterritoriality exception, which provides Member States with the option to refuse the EAW when the issuing state is exercising extraterritorial jurisdiction and the national law of the executing state would not allow prosecution in a similar case. This refusal ground aims to protect the sovereignty of the executing state and it is often linked to the principle of reciprocity.[111] As argued before, I am of the opinion that when the executing state is also a state which has jurisdiction to adjudicate its sovereignty interests should be considered at the stage of the forum decision. For this purpose, the proposed regulation on conflicts of jurisdiction also includes sovereignty interests as a relevant factor which the decision-making authority has to take into account. However, if the executing state does not have any jurisdictional link to the case in question, its interests should in my view not take precedence over prosecution by a state which is appointed as the most appropriate forum on the basis of a procedure in which the relevant interests of the suspect and competent states are carefully balanced against each other. Hence, the state to whose national legal order the criminal act has no link should not be in a position to bar prosecution and trial by the most appropriate forum. Hence, Article 4(7)(b) FDEAW could also be abolished.

Article 4A FDEAW prohibits the execution of an EAW issued for the enforcement of a custodial sanction that was imposed following a trial *in absentia,* unless one of the enumerated exceptions applies. In principle, execution EAWs fall outside the scope of this chapter, but one of the exceptions refers to the possibility of a retrial or appeal in the issuing state in which the requested person may participate and in which the merits of the case, including fresh evidence, are re-examined.[112] In light of this exception, the EAW issued for the enforcement of a sentence has a strong resemblance to an EAW issued for the purpose of prosecution and, therefore, the exception in subsection 1 (d) should be discussed. As this exception covers situations in which the *ne bis in idem* principle does not yet apply, I recommend to add the statement that the issuing state will comply with the conditions in the proposed regulation on conflicts of jurisdiction. Hence, in situations in which more Member States are competent to prosecute the case

---

[111] Glerum (2013), pp. 340–341; Suominen (2011), p. 289. See also Keijzer (2009), p. 96; Blekxtoon (2005), p. 238.

[112] FDEAW, art 4A(1)(d).

and no forum negotiations have occurred before the issuing state tried the requested person *in absentia*, the procedure for the appointment of the most appropriate forum should in principle be followed. However, as requested persons have in this situation already been tried once, even though it was in their absence, I am of the opinion that they should be allowed to veto the initiation of forum negotiations in compliance with the proposed regulation, since this could, for instance, result in a substantial delay of a decision on the merits of their criminal cases.

13.6.3.5 The Execution Procedure: The Fundamental Rights Exception

The adoption of the proposed EU directive and regulation also raises the question whether the fundamental rights exception in the surrender procedure provided by Opinion 2/13 should remain intact. As explained in Chap. 4, the CJEU has allowed the use of this exception in cases in which the requested person would in the issuing state be subjected to a real risk of inhuman and degrading treatment prohibited by Article 4 CFR or a violation of the right to an independent court in Article 47 CFR. In my opinion, the matter of compliance with fundamental rights should be taken up at the stage of the forum decision where the different competent states can discuss it with each other. As explained in Sect. 13.5.3, the list of factors which the Member States and/or Eurojust should take into account when making a forum decision includes the 'interests of the suspect' which also comprises fundamental rights protection. In my view, the fact that one of the states is allegedly not in compliance with certain fundamental rights standards which could be detrimental to the suspect, should already be considered in the decision whether that state could be appointed as the best forum for prosecution.

13.6.3.6 The Execution Procedure: The Return Guarantee (Art 5(3))

Article 5(3) FDEAW allows the executing state to request a return guarantee for its nationals and residents for the execution of a custodial sanction imposed in the issuing state. One of the main objectives of this return guarantee is to increase the requested person's chance of reintegration. However, the power to ask for a return guarantee could in case the proposed regulation on conflicts of jurisdiction is adopted block the surrender to the appointed state when this state is not willing to issue such a guarantee. In my view, this dilemma could best be solved by complementing the proposed EU regulation regarding the forum for prosecution and trial with a complementary set of EU rules appointing he best forum for the execution of a sanction in relation to which reintegration can be designated as an important consideration.[113] Article 5(3) FDEAW could then, for instance, be

[113] The best forum for prosecution and the best forum for the execution of a sanction are not necessarily the same. In addition, EU rules on the latter could possibly be adopted on the basis of Article 82(1)(b) TFEU. See also European Commission, 'Proposal for a Council Framework

reformulated in such a way that it grants the executing state the power to request for its nationals and residents the guarantee that when the issuing state imposes a custodial sentence it automatically starts the procedure for appointing the best forum for the execution of this sanction.[114]

13.6.3.7 The Execution Procedure: Multiple EAWs (Art 16)

Article 16(1) and (2) FDEAW currently regulate both the situation in which multiple EAWs are issued for the same person, but for different offences, and the situation in which multiple EAWs are issued for the same person and the same offence. The rules regulating the former situation remain relevant and should stay intact.[115] However, the rules regulating the second situation can be taken out, since a forum decision on the basis of the proposed regulation will prohibit all but one Member State to prosecute the case. As a result, only one state will also be competent to issue an EAW, which means that the rules on multiple EAWs for the same person and the same offence are no longer required.

13.6.3.8 Changes to the Issuing Procedure (Arts 2(1), 6, 8)

Article 2(1) FDEAW sets the requirement that a prosecution EAW may only be issued for acts for which a custodial sentence or detention order of at least 12 months may be imposed in the issuing state. This requirement in fact constitutes a proportionality assessment as it aims to avoid that citizens are subjected to arrests, detention and surrender for minor offences.[116] Besides this more general proportionality criterion the CJEU has imposed the obligation on issuing judicial authorities to conduct a more *in concreto* proportionality assessment. In this light, the issuing judicial authority should on the basis of the specific circumstances of a concrete case decide whether it is proportionate to issue an EAW.[117]

In my opinion, both proportionality assessments should in principle no longer be necessary if the proposed regulation on conflicts of jurisdiction is adopted and it includes the need for judicial cooperation between the competent states and the interests of the suspect as relevant factors in the decision-making process.[118] At the stage of this forum

---

Decision on the European arrest warrant and the surrender procedures between the Member States' COM (2001) 522 final, recital 12.

[114] Another possibility is to change Article 5(3) FDEAW into a guarantee which the issuing state must provide in all cases.

[115] Article 16(3) FDEAW, which concerns the situation in which an EAW and an extradition request are issued for the same person and the same offense, should remain intact as well. The same goes for Article 16(4) FDEAW.

[116] Glerum (2013), p. 795.

[117] Joined Cases C-508/18 & C-82/19 *OG & PI* [2019] ECLI:EU:C:2019:456, para 71.

[118] See Section 13.5.3.

decision, the decision-making authorities can already take into account that it could be in the interest of the suspect to appoint the state in which he or she is already present to avoid the need of an EAW, especially when the case concerns a minor offence and the surrender procedure would gravely interfere with the daily life of the suspect.

In addition, it would be my recommendation to reformulate Article 6(1) FDEAW in such a way that it solely designates the power to issue an EAW to the issuing judicial authority of the state appointed as the most appropriate forum on the basis of the proposed regulation. In addition, the requirements with regard to the content of a EAW laid down in Article 8(1) FDEAW should not be abolished as they can still serve their purpose. This includes subsection (d) and (e), which require that the EAW describes the nature and legal classification of the offence and the circumstances within which the crime was committed. This information could, for instance, be important to be able to assess whether one of the remaining refusal grounds is applicable and in light of the speciality principle in Articles 27 and 28 FDEAW. In addition, the EU legislator should, in my view, add a provision to Article 8 FDEAW demanding that the EAW includes a transcript of the forum decision made on the basis of the proposed regulation.

13.7 Conclusion and Reflections

This chapter has laid down the answer to the main research question and provided several recommendations for the EU legislator concerning the adoption of EU rules preventing or solving conflicts of jurisdiction. In this light, it has proposed the adoption of a directive demarcating the Member States' jurisdiction to prescribe and a regulation addressing the Member States' jurisdiction to adjudicate. The combination of these proposed instruments would both protect the transnational legality principle and establish a system for forum choices which fits in the normative context of the AFSJ laid down in Article 3(2) TEU. In addition, the adoption of the proposed directive and regulation would allow the current surrender procedure to be amended for situations in which the forum decision has been made on the basis of the proposed EU rules. In this light, Sect. 13.6 has recommended the abolishment of most of the refusal grounds applicable in case of prosecution EAWs and to grant the power to issue an EAW exclusively to the appointed forum.

These amendments to the surrender procedure could, in my view, also have a significant positive effect on its classification as a mutual recognition instrument and its functioning in practice. With regard to the former, the amendments could increase the speed and efficiency of the surrender procedure and, therefore, strengthen its foundation on the basis of the principle of mutual recognition.[119] As explained in

[119]FDEAW, art 1(2). See also European Commission, 'Mutual Recognition of Final Decisions in Criminal Matters' (Communication) COM (2000) 495 final, p. 19; The Hague Programme: strengthening freedom, security and justice in the European Union (The Hague Programme) [2005] OJ C53/1, p. 12.

Chaps. 1 and 2, mutual recognition in its most absolute form means that the executing judicial authority should promptly and automatically or at least with a minimum of formality recognise and execute an EAW.[120] In this light, the proposed changes, in particular the abolition of most of the refusal grounds, would support the characterisation of the surrender procedure as a mutual recognition procedure. Secondly, the combination of the proposed EU rules on conflicts of jurisdiction and the proposed amendments to the FDEAW could prevent the EAW from turning into a mechanism enforcing violations of the transnational legality principle as explained in Chap. 10. In fact, this combination could turn the EAW into a mechanism which facilitates prosecution by the *forum conveniens*, which is appointed on the basis of an EU system for forum decisions in light of the good administration of justice. Hence, the EAW could become a means to an end in the sense that it constitutes a swift surrender mechanism for the purpose of facilitating prosecution by a Member State appointed on the basis of a system which fits in the shared legal order of the AFSJ and complies with the transnational legality principle.

References

Biehler A et al (eds) (2003) Freiburg proposal on concurrent jurisdictions and the prohibition of multiple prosecutions in the European Union. Max Planck Institute for Foreign and International Criminal Law

Blekxtoon R (2005) Commentary on an article by article basis. In: Blekxtoon R, van Ballegooij W (eds) Handbook on the European arrest warrant. Asser

Böse M (2013) Choice of forum and jurisdiction. In: Luchtman M (ed) Choice of forum in cooperation against EU financial crime. Freedom, security and justice and the protection of specific EU-interests. Eleven International Publishing

Böse M (2014) The legal basis (Art. 82 TFEU). In: Böse M, Meyer F, Schneider A (eds) Conflicts of jurisdiction in criminal matters in the European Union. Volume II: rights, principles and model rules. Nomos

Deboyser C (2013) Eurojust's role in the matter of choice of forum. In: Luchtman M (ed) Choice of forum in cooperation against EU financial crime. Freedom, security and justice and the protection of specific EU-interests. Eleven International Publishing

Dickson D (2014) Cross border investigation and prosecution of bribery and corruption offences. ERA Forum 15:51

Eckstein K (2012) Grund und Grenzen transnationalen Schutzes vor mehrfacher Strafverfolgung in Europa. ZStW 124:490

Eicker A (2005) Zur Vermeidung simultaner Strafverfahren im zwischenstaatlichen Kontext: Modell einer (über)individuell-konkreten Kriterien Gewichtung. StV 631

Eser A (2012) Kritische Würdigung der Modellentwürfe eines Regelungsmechanismus zur Vermeidung von Jurisdiktionskonflikten. In: Sinn A (ed) Jurisdiktionskonflikte bei grenzüberschreitender Kriminalität. Ein Rechtsvergleich zum Internationalen Strafrecht. V&R Unipress

Eser A in Omar Abo Youssef und Gunhild Godenzi (2013) Diskussionsbeiträge der Strafrechtslehrertagung 2013 in Zürich. ZStW 125:659

[120] Mitsilegas (2016), p. 126–127.

Franken S (2013) The perspective of the defence lawyer. In: Luchtman M (ed) Choice of forum in cooperation against EU financial crime. Freedom, security and justice and the protection of specific EU-interests. Eleven International Publishing
Fuchs H (2006) Regulation of jurisdiction and Substnative criminal law. In: Schünemann B (ed) Ein Gesamtkonzept für die europäische Strafrechtspflege. Heymanns
Giuffrida F (2017) Cross-border crimes and the European public Prosecutor's office. EUcrim 149
Glerum V (2013) De weigeringsgronden bij uitlevering en overlevering – Een vergelijking en kritische evaluatie in het licht van het beginsel van wederzijdse erkenning. Wolf Legal Publishers
Hecker B (2011) Statement: Jurisdiktionskonflikte in der EU. ZIS 6:60
Hecker B (2012) Die rechtlichen Möglichkeiten der Europäischen Union zur Lösung von Kompetenzkonflikten. In: Sinn A (ed) Jurisdiktionskonflikte bei grenzüberschreitender Kriminalität. Ein Rechtsvergleich zum Internationalen Strafrecht. V&R Unipress
Heger M in Omar Abo Youssef und Gunhild Godenzi (2013) Diskussionsbeiträge der Strafrechtslehrertagung 2013 in Zürich. ZStW 125:659
Herrnfeld H-H (2013) Mechanisms for settling conflicts of jurisdiction. In: Luchtman M (ed) Choice of forum in cooperation against EU financial crime. Freedom, security and justice and the protection of specific EU-interests. Eleven International Publishing
Kaiafa-Gbandi M (2020) Addressing the problems of jurisdictional conflicts in criminal matters within the EU. EUcrim 209
Keijzer N (2009) *Locus delicti* Exceptions. In: Keizer N, van Sliedregt E (eds) The European arrest warrant in practice. Asser
Klip A (2011) Substantive criminal law of the EU. Maklu
Lagodny O (2001) Empfiehlt es sich, eine europäische Gerichtskompetenz für Strafgewaltskonflikte vorzusehen? Gutachten im Auftrag des Bundesministeriums der Justiz
Lelieur J (2013) 'Transnationalising' ne bis in idem: how the rule of ne bis in idem reveals the principle of personal legal certainty. Utrecht Law Rev 9:198
Lenaerts K, Maselis I, Gutman K (2014) EU procedural law. Oxford University Press
Linke R (1970) Zwischenstaatliche Kompetenzkonflikte auf dem Gebiet des Strafrechts. In: Oehler D, Pötz P (eds) Beiträge zur Gestaltung des internationalen und supranationalen Strafrechts. Heinrich Grützner zum 65. Geburtstag. Decker
Luchtman M (2012) Principles of European criminal law: jurisdiction, choice of forum, and the legality principle in the area of freedom, security, and justice. ERPL 20:347
Luchtman M (2013) Towards a transnational application of the legality principle in the EU's area of freedom, security and justice? Utrecht Law Rev 9:11
Meyer F, Böse M (2011) Die Beschränkung nationaler Strafgewalten als Möglichkeit zur Vermeidung von Jurisdiktionskonflikten in der Europäischen Union. ZIS 6:336
Mitsilegas V (2016) EU criminal law after Lisbon: rights, trust and the transformation of justice in Europe. Hart Publishing
Monar J (2013) Eurojust's present and future role at the frontline of European Union criminal justice cooperation. ERA Forum 14:187
Ortolani P (2018) Conflicts of jurisdiction in criminal law. Lessons from European civil procedure. In: Ligeti K, Robinson G (eds) Preventing and resolving conflicts of jurisdiction in EU criminal law. Oxford University Press
Ouwerkerk J (2012) Goede rechtsbedeling en internationale rechtshulp in strafzaken. De oratie van A.H.J. Swart. Strafblad 10(461)
Panzavolta M (2013) Choice of forum and the lawful judge concept. In: Luchtman M (ed) Choice of forum in cooperation against EU financial crime. Freedom, security and justice and the protection of specific EU-interests. Eleven International Publishing
Schomburg W (2020) Criminal matters: transnational *ne bis in idem* in Europe-conflict of jurisdictions-transfer of proceedings. ERA Forum 13:311
Schönberger C (2015) Positive transnationale Jurisdiktionskonflikte – Causae, rechtliche Lösungsnotwendigkeit und -konzepte. Schulthess Verlag

Suominen A (2011) The principle of mutual recognition in cooperation in criminal matters. A study of the principle in four framework decisions and in the implementation legislation in the Nordic member states. Intersentia

Swart B (1982) De overdracht van strafvervolgingen. NJB 210

Swart B (1983) Goede Rechtsbedeling en Internationale Rechtshulp in Strafzaken. Kluwer

Thorhauer N (2015) Conflicts of jurisdiction in cross-border criminal cases in the area of freedom, security, and justice. Risks and opportunities from an individual rights-oriented perspective. New J Eur Crim Law 6:78

Thorhauer N (2019) Jurisdiktionskonflikte im Rahmen transnationaler Kriminalität. Zur Koordination der Strafgewalten über natürliche. Personen und Unternehmen in der Europäischen Union. Dike Verlag and Nomos

Van der Beken T et al (2002a) Finding the best place for prosecution: European study on jurisdiction criteria. Maklu

Van der Beken T, Lagodny O, Vermeulen G (2002b) Kriterien für die jeweils Strafgewalt in Europa – Zur Lösung von Strafgewaltskonflikten jenseits eines transnationalen Ne-bis-in-idem. NStZ 624

Wasmeier M (2018) The legal basis for preventing and resolving conflicts of criminal jurisdiction in the TFEU. In: Ligeti K, Robinson G (eds) Preventing and resolving conflicts of jurisdiction in EU criminal law. Oxford University Press

Wolswijk H (1998) Locus delicti en rechtsmacht. Gouda Quint

Zimmerman F (2015) Strafgewaltkonflikte in der Europäischen Union. Ein Regelungsvorschlag zur Wahrung materieller und prozessualer strafrechtlicher Garantien sowie staatlicher Strafinteressen. Nomos